EARLY MODERN RUSSIAN LETTERS:
Texts and Contexts

Studies in Russian and Slavic Literatures,
Cultures and History

Series Editor: *Lazar Fleishman*

EARLY MODERN RUSSIAN LETTERS:
Texts and Contexts

Selected Essays by
Marcus C. Levitt

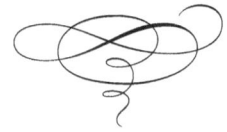

BOSTON
2009

Library of Congress Cataloging-in-Publication Data

Levitt, Marcus C., 1954-
  Early modern Russian letters : texts and contexts : selected essays / by Marcus C. Levitt.
    p. cm. — (Studies in Russian and Slavic literatures, cultures and history)
  ISBN 978-1-934843-68-0
  1. Russian literature — 18th century — History and criticism. 2. Sumarokov, Aleksandr Petrovich, 1717-1777 — Criticism and interpretation. I. Title.
  PG3007.L48 2009
  891.709'002—dc22
              2009038955

Copyright © 2009 Academic Studies Press
All rights reserved

ISBN 978-1-61811-808-0

Book design by Ivan Grave

Published by Academic Studies Press in 2009
28 Montfern Avenue
Brighton, MA 02135, USA
press@academicstudiespress.com
www.academicstudiespress.com

Table of Contents

Foreword vii

Part One
SUMAROKOV AND THE LITERARY PROCESS OF HIS TIME

Preface 3
1. Sumarokov: Life and Works 6
2. Sumarokov's Reading at the Academy of Sciences Library 22
3. Censorship and Provocation: The Publishing History of Sumarokov's "Two Epistles" 44
4. Slander, Polemic, Criticism: Trediakovskii's "Letter… from a Friend to a Friend" of 1750 and the Problem of Creating Russian Literary Criticism 64
5. Sumarokov's Russianized "Hamlet": Texts and Contexts 76
6. Sumarokov's Drama "The Hermit": On the Generic and Intellectual Sources of Russian Classicism 103
7. "The First Russian Ballet": Sumarokov's "Sanctuary of Virtue" (1759) Defining a New Dance 119
8. Was Sumarokov a Lockean Sensualist? On Locke's Reception in Eighteenth-Century Russia 158
9. *Barkoviana* and Russian Classicism 173
10. The Illegal Staging of Sumarokov's *Sinav and Truvor* in 1770 and the Problem of Authorial Status in Eighteenth-Century Russia 190
11. Sumarokov and the Unified Poetry Book: His *Triumphal Odes* and *Love Elegies* Through the Prism of Tradition 218
12. The Barbarians Among Us, or Sumarokov's Views on Orthography 248

Part Two
VISUALITY AND ORTHODOXY IN EIGHTEENTH-CENTURY RUSSIAN CULTURE

Preface 267
13. The Rapprochement Between "Secular" and "Religious" in Mid to Late Eighteenth-Century Russian Culture 269
14. The "Obviousness" of the Truth in Eighteenth-Century Russian Thought .. 294
15. The Theological Context of Lomonosov's "Evening" and "Morning Meditations on God's Majesty" 305
16. The Ode as Revelation: On the Orthodox Theological Context of Lomonosov's Odes 320
17. An Antidote to Nervous Juice: Catherine the Great's Debate with Chappe d'Auteroche over Russian Culture 339
18. The Polemic with Rousseau over Gender and Sociability in E. S. Urusova's *Polion* (1774) 358
19. Virtue Must Advertise: Self Presentation in Dashkova's Memoirs 379
20. The Dialectic of Vision in Radishchev's *Journey from Petersburg to Moscow* 398

Sources 413

Index 415

Foreword

This book contains a collection of my writings on eighteenth-century Russian literature and culture from over the last fifteen years. Some are from American journals; some are translated from Russian publications; one is from an encyclopedia; and one is based on a conference presentation. The writings thus represent several genres and were addressed to various audiences, but center on a fairly limited period of time and cast of characters and so may profit from being grouped together. There have been some minor changes and editing (especially in the case of translations) as well as some updating of footnotes, although in each case the documentation style of first publication has been maintained. I have also corrected a few errors of my own as well as misprints.

The many friends and colleagues who have provided advice, encouragement, criticism, and stimulating dialogue over the years are too many to name, but I will try and make a start. Thanks, first of all, to my colleagues and collaborators at the Institute of Russian Literature (Pushkin House) of the Russian Academy of Sciences, especially Natal'ia Dmitievna Kochetkova, Nadezhda Iurev'na Alekseeva, Sergei Nikolaev, and V. P. Stepanov, as well as the late A. M. Panchenko. G. A. Moiseeva, E. B. Mozgovaia and Iu. V. Stennik. I also owe innumerable intellectual debts to: Victor Zhivov (whose works have helped shape my overall conception of eighteenth-century Russia), as well as to Irina Reyfman, Alexander Levitsky, Gitta Hammarberg, Gary Marker, Lev Berdnikov, Ronald Vroon, Joachim Klein, Roger Bartlett, W. Garreth Jones, Petr Bukharkin, Lidiia Sazonova, William Todd, Amanda Ewington, Elise Wirtschafter, Olga Tsapina, Tatiana Smoliarova, Hilde Hoggenboom, Anna Lisa Crone, Luba Golbert, Kelly Herold, Mariia Shcherbakova, and the late Stephen Baehr and Lindsay Hughes. All have provided encouragement, ideas, and helpful criticism at various stages of my work. My gratitude also goes to my colleagues at the University of Southern California, Sally Pratt, Thomas Seifrid, John Bowlt, Lada Panova, Alik Zholkovsky and Susan Kechekian for their continued advice and support.

Foreword

I would also like to acknowledge the organizations that over the years have provided material support for the research represented in this volume. These include: the National Endowment for the Humanities; the Kennan Institute for Advanced Studies, Woodrow Wilson Center, Washington D.C; the Davis Center for Russian and Eurasian Studies of Harvard University; the Summer Research Laboratory, University of Illinois at Champaign-Urbana; the International Research and Exchanges Board; and University of Southern California.

Finally, thanks to the following publishers for permission (or confirmation of my right) to republish my work: La Fenice Libri for "Was Sumarokov a Lockean Sensualist? On Locke's Reception in Eighteenth-Century Russia," *A Window on Russia: Proceedings of the V International Conference of the Study Group on Eighteenth-Century Russia, Gargano, 1994*, ed. Maria Di Salvo and Lindsey Hughes (Rome: La Fenice Edizioni, 1996), pages 219–227; "Alexander Petrovich Sumarokov," from Levitt, Marcus C. (Editor), *Dictionary of Literary Biography*, © Gale, a part of Cenage Learning, Inc, reproduced by permission, www.cenage.com; the Johns Hopkins University Press (copyright © 1998) for "An Antidote to Nervous Juice: Catherine the Great's Debate with Chappe d'Auteroche over Russian Culture," which first appeared in *Eighteenth-Century Studies*, Volume 32, Issue 1, 1998, pages 49–63; the American Association of Teachers of Slavic and East European Languages for "The Illegal Staging of Sumarokov's *Sinav i Truvor* in 1770 and the Problem of Authorial Status in Eighteenth-Century Russia," *The Slavic and East European Journal*, Volume 43, Number 2 (Summer 1999), pages 299–323; Elsevier Inc. for "Sumarokov and the Unified Poetry Book: *Ody toržestvennyia* and *Elegii ljiubovnyja* Through the Prism of Tradition," *Russian Literature* (North Holland). Special Issue: Eighteenth Century Russian Literature, vol. LI no. I/II/III (1 July — 15 August — 1 October 2002), pages 111–139; John Bowlt and *Experiment / Эксперимент* for: "Sumarokov's *Sanctuary of Virtue* (1759) as 'the First Russian Ballet'," *Experiment / Эксперимент*, Volume 10 (2004), pages 51–84; the American Philosophical Society for: "Virtue Must Advertise: Dashkova's 'Mon histoire' and the Problem of Self-Representation," in *The Princess and the Patriot: Ekaterina Dashkova, Benjamin Franklin, and the Age of Enlightenment*, edited by Sue Ann Prince (*Transactions of the American Philosophical Society*, Volume 96, Part 1) (Philadelphia: American Philosophical Society, 2006), pages 39–56; @ 2007 the Board of Trustees for the *Russian Review*, for "The Polemic with Rousseau over Gender and Sociability in E. S. Urusova's *Polion* (1774)," *Russian Review*, Volume 66 (October 2007), pages 586–601; LIT-Verlag for "The Barbarians Among Us, or Sumarokov's Views on Orthography," in *Eighteenth-Century Russia: Society, Culture, Economy, Papers from the VII. International Conference of the Study Group on Eighteenth-Century Russia, Wittenberg 2004*, edited by Roger Bartlett and Gabriela Lehmann-Carli (Münster: LIT-Verlag, 2007), pages 53–67.

*Dedicated to my wife and helpmate Alice —
for her love and forbearance
as well as her intellectual help and support*

Part One

SUMAROKOV
and
THE LITERARY PROCESS
OF HIS TIME

Preface

For many people, the name Alexander Sumarokov conjures up some of the worst stereotypes that have become associated with the alleged "pseudo-Classicism" (lozhno-klassitsizm) of eighteenth-century Russia — fatally linked with the all too memorable lines from the young Pushkin's poem "To Zhukovskii": *ditia chuzhikh urokov, / Zavistlivyi gordets, kholodnyi Sumarokov...* (child of foreign lessons, / Envious and arrogant, cold Sumarokov). Yet as my undergraduate professor of Russian literature Gary Browning used to say, there are two types of "great writer" — one who is acknowledged to write for the ages, and endures among readers; and the one who is acclaimed in his or her own generation but forgotten or rejected by posterity.[1] From a historical perspective, the fact of their celebrity itself suggests a unique contribution and vital connection to the literary life of their day.

---

[1] Some of the bestsellers that come to mind who were at the center of literary life of their day but whose works have mostly faded from cultural consciousness include Leonid Andreev, Maxim Gorky, Boris Pil'niak and Fedor Gladkov. In a discussion of Russian professors on the SEELANGS list-serv (March 12, 2009) other names that were suggested for the category of "forgotten superstars" included (in no strict order): Vladislav Ozerov, Vladimir Benediktov, Nestor Kukol'nik, Mikhail Zagoskin, Alexander Druzhinin, Vsevolod Garshin, Gleb Uspenskii, Konstantin Fofanov, Anastasiia Verbitskaia, Mikhail Artsybashev, Pavel Mel'nikov-Pecherskii, Semen Nadson, Petr Boborykin, Nikolai Pomialovskii, Pavel Zasodimskii, Fedor Reshetnikov, Aleksandr Amfiteatrov, Sergei Gorodetskii, Vladimir Nemerovich-Danchenko, Dmitrii Tsenzor, Lidiia Charskaia, Apollon Maikov, Lev Mei, Aleksei Apukhtin, Konstantin Sluchevskii, Demian Bednyi, Viacheslav Shishkov, Mirra Lokhvitskaia, Petr Pavlenko, Igor' Serverianin, Aleksandr Sheller-Mikhailov, Semen Babaevskii, Ivan Shevtsov, Panteleimon Romanov, Marietta Shaginian, Lidia Seifullina, Boris Polevoi, Eduard Asadov, Anatolii Gladilin, Vladimir Orlov, Leonid Dobychin, Sergei Zaiaitskii, and Sergei Malashkin. Thanks to my colleagues who contributed to this list.

Part One. Sumarokov and the Literary Process of His Time

Moreover, Sumarokov's position differs from that of the standard "forgotten 'great writer'" in that in many respects he saw himself (and could arguably be seen) as the "father of modern Russian Literature" (rodonachal'nik novoi russkoi literatury) — the title ultimately bestowed on Alexander Pushkin. Of course, even in the eighteenth century Sumarokov had serious rivals for primacy (Trediakovskii, Lomonosov, and later, Derzhavin and Karamzin), and various arguments may always be made for rivals and predecessors; ultimately, the decision on who is to play the role of "national poet" depends on a complex of social, cultural, and political factors (not to mention of course the role of talent).[2] Like Pushkin, Sumarokov attended a special school for noblemen, intended for future leaders of the country. Like Pushkin, he was very conscious of his place as a "professional Russian writer," and in his career attempted to establish models for practically all of the major modern poetic and dramatic genres, many of which began their development in Russia thanks to him. Like Pushkin, Sumarokov felt restricted by a court-centered patronage system and was torn between allegiance to the reigning monarch and his own creative (and financial) independence. And also like Pushkin, he saw his reputation decline at the end of his career and expressed serious misgivings about the viability of modern Europeanized culture in Russia.

Unlike Pushkin, however, Sumarokov's reputation never experienced a posthumous rehabilitation (although there was an unsuccessful attempt by a few supporters at the start of the nineteenth century). Yet in recent years, scholars have begun to reevaluate and appreciate Sumarokov's pioneering role in eighteenth-century letters. Notable, in particular, are Victor Zhivov's analysis of his contributions to the literary language; Amanda Ewington's analysis of Sumarokov's adaptation of Voltairean literary and cultural models to Russia; Joachim Klein's work on his pastoral poetry and drama; Ronald Vroon's studies of Sumarokov's poetic collections; Sergei Nikolaev's reconsideration of the problem of "plagiarism" and "translation"; Kirill Ospovat's work on Sumarokov in the context of court culture; Oleg Proskurin's examination of his connections to obscene verse; Vladimir

---

[2] In the case of Pushkin, see: Marcus C. Levitt, *Russian Literary Politics and the Pushkin Celebration of 1880*. Studies of the Harriman Institute (Ithaca: Cornell UP, 1989); Paul Debreczeny, *Social Functions of Literature: Alexander Pushkin and Russian Culture*. (Stanford, Calif: Stanford UP, 1997); Stephanie Sandler, *Commemorating Pushkin: Russia's Myth of a National Poet* (Stanford: Stanford UP, 2004), and her "'Pushkin' and Identity," chap. 11 in *National Identity in Russian Culture: An Introduction*, ed. Simon Franklin and Emma Widdis (New York: Cambridge UP, 2004).

Stepanov's work on his fables and Alexander Levitsky's and Liudmilla Lutsevich's analysis of his religious verse.[3]

My own explorations in the articles that follow take up various aspects of Sumarokov's activity and the literary life of his era. These include: the problem of Sumarokov's status as a writer, both his legal position and self-image; analyses of several of his key works (epistles, works for the theater, ballet, poetic collections); censorship and publishing history; the problem of literary critical discourse; Sumarokov's reading; his philosophical writing; and his views on the literary language and orthography. Several of these studies make use of new archival material; others are based on close textual and comparative textological analysis; still others focus on problems of genre and interpretation. Most center on phenomena that were new to Russian literature and culture and that played unique roles in the formation of the "new Russian literature." Among these is an article on "Barkoviana" (obscene poetry), in which Sumarokov was involved both as author and target. I have chosen to begin with an overview of Sumarokov's life and works written for the *Dictionary of Literary Biography*.

---

[3] See the "Selected Bibliography" that follows chap. 1, "Sumarokov: Life and Works."

1

SUMAROKOV:
Life and Works

The Russian Boileau, the Russian Racine, the Russian Molière, the Russian Lafontaine, the Russian Voltaire — these are some of the titles contemporaries accorded Alexander Petrovich Sumarokov. The foremost representative of Russian Classicism, Sumarokov aspired to be the founder of a new, modern European literature in Russia. He founded and directed the Russian national theater (for which he supplied most of its early repertory), published the first private literary journal in Russia, helped establish the norms of the new literary language, and provided models of virtually every current European poetic and dramatic genre, including fable, song, sonnet, elegy, satire, eclogue, idyll, epigram, ballad, madrigal, rondeau, folktale, and a wide variety of odes — panegyric, spiritual, philosophical, Anacreontic, Horatian, and Sapphic — as well as the first Russian tragedies, comedies, operas, and ballets. While his reputation declined in the early nineteenth century when a new Romantic generation repudiated the tradition Sumarokov had tried to establish, Sumarokov was arguably the first professional writer in Russia, in that (at least after 1756) he was the first to dedicate himself to literary pursuits full-time. He was also arguably the first to fashion of his career a modern literary biography.

Sumarokov was born on November 14, 1717, the second of three brothers. According to one of his poems he was born near the town of Vil'mandstrand (Lappeenranta) in present-day Finland, where his father, Peter Pankrat'evich Sumarokov, was probably serving against the Swedes in the Great Northern War. Sumarokov took great pride in his noble lineage and his family's loyal service to the state. His grandfather Pankratii Bogdanovich Sumarokov had served Tsar Fedor and was rewarded for faithful service by Peter the Great, who reportedly became godfather to his son, Sumarokov's father. In the unfinished "The Second Streletskii Uprising" Sumarokov told the story of his great-uncle Ivan Bogdanov. Nicknamed "the Eagle" for saving Tsar Aleksei Mikhailovich from a bear while on a hunt, he later refused, despite prolonged torture, to bear false witness against Tsarina Sofia's enemies. The story is indicative of Sumarokov's moral and political convictions and also reflects his self-image as a writer and truthsayer.

Almost nothing is known of Sumarokov's early years. He ascribed his "first groundings in the Russian language" to his father, who had been educated by the Serb I. A. Zeikan, a man whom the tsar had appointed as tutor to the Naryshkin family and who later tutored Peter II. On May 30, 1732, Sumarokov entered the newly opened Sukhoputnyi Shlakhetskii Kadetskii Korpus (Noble Infantry Cadet Corps), established by Empress Anna to prepare noblemen for service as officers in the army. At the so-called "chivalric academy" (rytsarskaia akademiia) courses on military science took second place to a secular and humanistic curriculum—unique for Russian schools of that day—which included history, geography, jurisprudence, Latin, modern languages (German, French, Italian), as well as fencing, drawing, horsemanship, music, and dancing, which helped cadets develop the special skills and new Europeanized manners needed to participate in aristocratic court life. Literature was clearly a major pursuit at the corps, which produced many eighteenth-century literary figures (including Ivan Elagin, Mikhail Kheraskov, Andrei Nartov, Sergei Poroshin) and which in the late 1750's opened its own press; according to some accounts there was even a literary society among the cadets in Sumarokov's day. Sumarokov's first published work was an ode to Empress Anna in the name of the corps in 1740, written in accord with Vasilii Trediakovskii's verse reform of 1735; he later disclaimed this ode and advised young poets to burn their immature works, as he said he had done to his first nine years' production.

Sumarokov graduated from the corps on April 14, 1740. He was made an adjutant to Count M. G. Golovkin, who was arrested and sent into exile soon after Empress Anna's death in the fall of that year. Sumarokov was then appointed to the suite of Count A. G. Razumovskii, Empress Elizabeth's morganatic husband and brother of K. G. Razumovskii, president of the Academy of Sciences. Sumarokov was appointed Razumovskii's adjutant on June 7, 1743; from late in 1745 he was put in charge of the administration of the *leib-kompaniia*, a military body created by Elizabeth as a reward to the troops that had supported her ascension to the throne. Sumarokov found in Razumovskii a patron as well as entry into high court circles. Sumarokov's presence at court led to his marriage on November 10, 1746, to Johanna Khristiforovna Balk (or perhaps Balior), lady-in-waiting to Princess Sofia of Anhalt-Zerbst, the future Catherine the Great, with whom Sumarokov's literary fortunes were to be intimately linked. Sumarokov's first marriage, which ended in divorce in 1766, produced two daughters, Ekaterina and Praskov'ia. Ekaterina, long thought to be a poet because of some verses Sumarokov signed with her name, married Sumarokov's protégé, the tragedian Iakov Kniazhnin, some time before 1769.

Sumarokov first attracted general attention by writing fashionable songs that became the rage at court. In contrast to Trediakovskii's syllabic songs, Sumarokov created the first examples of the modern Russian (syllabo-tonic) romance, in his day often put to the music of minuets or other fashionable European dances and accompanied by a lute; some were put to music by the court musician Timofei Belogradskii and others by Grigorii Teplov who pirated them for his popular collection *After Work, Idleness, or a Collection of Various Songs* (*Mezhdu delom bezdel'e ili sobranie raznykh pesen*, circa 1745–1751). In the latter case, Sumarokov complained about the "audacity of publishing someone else's works without the authors' permission… spoiling that which others have composed with care and imposing indecent titles on others' works, something which is nowhere practiced, and nowhere permitted." Actually, in an era before copyright Sumarokov had no legal recourse and his only alternative was to republish the songs himself in their correct versions.

The love song, a relatively insignificant genre for European Classicists, became an important vehicle through which Sumarokov developed the language and rhythms of his new lyric poetry. As opposed to Trediakovskii's songs, which reflected the flirtatious affectation of Parisian salons, Sumarokov's songs are closer in theme to the more serious songs of the Russian folk tradition. As the scholar Il'ia Z. Serman has noted, Sumarokov's songs pointed the way to his later tragedies, in which the psychological torments his protagonists undergo may be seen as an extension of those experienced by the lyric personae of his songs. Furthermore, as Sumarokov asserts in his "Epistle on Poetry" (1748): "Слог песен должен быть приятен, прост и ясен, / Витийств не надобно; он сам собой прекрасен" (A song's style should be pleasant, simple and clear, / Orations are not needed; it's beautiful all by itself). This couplet expresses a central plank of Sumarokov's Classicism, which stressed precision, simplicity, and clarity of expression — as opposed both to Trediakovskii's clumsy and convoluted style and to the ornate, quasi-baroque poetics of Mikhail Lomonosov's odes.

Sumarokov's notorious and often bitter rivalry with Trediakovskii and Lomonosov may be counted as one of the major literary facts of the

Chapter 1. Sumarokov: Life and Works

middle of the century, as all three strove for preeminence in establishing the rules and norms for the fledgling literature. Their competition dates to the early 1740's; in 1744 they jointly published three verse paraphrases of Psalm 143 (Psalm 144 in English Psalters) for public judgment. Various perspectives on their rivalry have been asserted. Some scholars have stressed Sumarokov's extraordinarily cantankerous and argumentative personality, although in this respect Lomonosov was surely a close second; their rude behavior should be seen within the context of the blunt and often coarse manners of the day, when the polite society of salons existed more in theoretical pronouncements than in actuality. Various polemics reveal such minutia as that Sumarokov was a redhead and may have had a nervous tic and stutter.

Unlike Trediakovskii, who was primarily a literary scholar, and Lomonosov, who was first and foremost a scientist and who viewed poetry as a sideline, Sumarokov dedicated himself to Russian letters, and what has appeared to many readers to be unseemly self-promotion was due at least in part to the great resistance he met in trying to establish the profession of writer in Russia as something worthy of respect. Further, the view of the time that equated public glory with virtue made an overriding concern with public image natural and even expected (Catherine the Great, who was a champion self-promoter, is a case in point). Others have argued that deeper class antagonisms were at work — that Sumarokov represented the interests of the hereditary nobility, as opposed to Trediakovskii, son of a priest, and Lomonosov, son of a peasant fisherman who was patronized by newly risen grandees close to Elizabeth's throne. In the later 1750's the hostility of antagonistic court factions, each of which adopted its own poet and egged him on against the others, also clearly played a role in Sumarokov's feud with Lomonosov. Finally, not the least significant factor in this hostility was the legacy of medieval Russian patterns of thinking, which assumed that there was only one right and immutable way to do things. This was eminently amenable to Classicism, which assumed the existence of perfect, fixed, impersonal laws of nature, one consequence of which was to elevate minor personal disagreements into battles over absolute truths.

While Sumarokov was clearly indebted to Trediakovskii's and Lomonosov's reforms of Russian versification, he arguably did far more than they in putting it into practice and creating a modern poetic system of genres and a tradition of actual poetic practice. Disclaiming apprenticeship from his rivals, Sumarokov asserted in his "To Senseless Rhymsters" (K nesmyslennym rifmotvortsam, 1759) that at the time when he made his literary debut

There were no poets in Russia yet, and no one to learn from. It was as if I was going without a guide through a dark forest which screened the dwelling of the Muses from my eyes. Although I am much indebted to Racine, I only espied him once I was out of the woods, when Mount Parnassus had already presented itself to my gaze. But Racine is a Frenchman and could not instruct me in Russian. For the Russian language and purity of style I am indebted to no one but myself, both in poetry and prose.

In 1747–1748 Sumarokov published his first major works, at his own cost, at the Academy of Sciences typography. These included the tragedies *Khorev* (1747) and *Gamlet* (Hamlet, 1748) and *Dve epistoly* (Two Epistles, 1748), one epistle on the Russian language and the other on the art of poetry. They established Sumarokov as a major figure in Russian letters and helped to galvanize support of other young poets, mostly graduates of the corps, around him. The epistles, a "manifesto of Russian classicism," were based on Boileau's *L'Art poétique* (1674) — which was in turn based on Horace — and set forth Sumarokov's Russianized version of the classicist hierarchy of genres. The author triumphantly concluded:

Всё хвально: драма ли, эклога или ода —
Слагай, к чему тебя влечет твоя природа;
Лишь просвещение писатель дай уму:
Прекрасный наш язык способен ко всему.

(All are laudable: the drama, eclogue, or ode — / Compose that to which your nature draws you; / Only, writer, let your mind be enlightened: / Our beautiful tongue is capable of anything!)

Sumarokov's tragedies, written in the Russian equivalent of French Alexandrine verse (iambic hexameter with caesura after the third foot, with paired rhymes), employed a minimum of means — few characters, little action or plot, abstract settings (mostly labeled as ancient Russia), and no props except a dagger (traditional symbol of tragic theater) — to maximum emotional and emotive effect. All share a classical (mostly five-act) structure and observe the three unities of space, time, and action. The crisis usually involves two lovers' struggle between love and duty on the one hand and their conflict with the throne (a jealous, evil, or badly advised monarch) on the other. Sumarokov's tragedies have been called "a school of civic virtue," embodying an enlightened ideal of the Russian nobility's new corporate sense of honor and admonitions to the autocracy to rule justly under law.

Chapter 1. Sumarokov: Life and Works

Perhaps in response to Trediakovskii's criticism that tragedy should be "an imitation of God's actions on earth," with evil defeated and good triumphant, Sumarokov gave *Hamlet* and most of his later tragedies happy endings (hence Hamlet lives to marry Ophelia and ascend the Danish throne). For his basic acquaintance with William Shakespeare's play Sumarokov was indebted to Pierre Antoine de La Place's 1745 French translation, although records in the Academy of Sciences library indicate that Sumarokov, who did not know English, borrowed the fourth folio version of Shakespeare's plays from the Academy of Sciences library. However, apart from the famous "To be, or not to be" monologue — for which Sumarokov consulted (and borrowed from) Voltaire's version in the *Lettres philosophiques* (1734) — Sumarokov himself noted that his version "hardly resembles" Shakespeare's tragedy. While the later tradition tended to see Sumarokov's play as a travesty of Shakespeare, several modern critics have been more charitable toward Sumarokov's attempt to create a unique play.

Sumarokov's tragedies, staged by cadets at the corps with all-male casts, were brought to Elizabeth's attention by Razumovskii. The empress invited the cadets to perform at court in early 1750 and took a personal hand in dressing up the handsome young cadets in lavish regalia and even lent the leading "lady" her crown diamonds. The performances were a great success, and in 1750–1751 Sumarokov added *Sinav i Truvor* (Sinav and Truvor, 1751), *Artistona* (1751), and *Semira* (1768) to his tragic repertoire; Sumarokov was doubtless pleased when the tragedies commissioned from his rivals Trediakovskii and Lomonosov proved unworthy of the stage. Sumarokov also wrote the first Russian comedies, in prose, the one-act *Tresotinius* (1786) and *Chudovishchi* (Monsters, 1786), which Sumarokov later renamed "Treteinoi sud" (Court of Arbitration); posthumous editions of the play mistakenly retained the discarded title. These were transparently satiric burlesques, closer to the old *intermedia* — brief comical interludes that came in between acts of the often interminably long school dramas — or to Russian *igrishchi* (folk farces) which Sumarokov theoretically repudiated, rather than to classical comedy.

On August 30, 1756, Elizabeth brought a national Russian theater into being by official proclamation. The kernel of the troupe was formed by actors from Fedor Volkov's private Yaroslavl troupe, which had been brought to the capital to perform at court in 1750; several actors had been subsequently sent to the corps for further training. Sumarokov was named director and assigned a yearly salary of one thousand rubles beyond what he received according to his rank of brigadier, although from that date Sumarokov was freed from his other official responsibilities.

During the later 1750's Sumarokov also regularly contributed poetry to the Academy of Sciences miscellany *Ezhemesiachnye sochineniia* (Monthly Compositions), actively experimenting in a variety of verse forms and genres. In 1759 he published his own journal, *Trudoliubivaia pchela* (The Industrious Bee), the first private literary journal in Russia, although precedence is sometimes accorded to *Prazdnoe vremia, v pol'zu upotreblennoe* (Idle Time Used Well), begun the same year by former cadets and to which Sumarokov also contributed. Sumarokov dedicated *Trudoliubivaia pchela* to Catherine, an act of considerable boldness considering that the Grand Princess was in disgrace following a failed court intrigue in 1758. The episode had resulted in Aleksei Bestuzhev-Riumin's arrest; according to one source Sumarokov himself was subjected to interrogation during the investigation.

Trudoliubivaia pchela included essays on history, philosophy, and literature, as well as original poetry (mostly Sumarokov's) and translations from classical and modern authors (including Voltaire and Jonathan Swift). Particularly notable were Sumarokov's satiric essays, which served as prototypes for the later Russian satiric journals. Among his targets were the abuse of serfs by landowners, bribe-taking, favoritism, and other bureaucratic and social ills—themes that informed many of Sumarokov's works (especially his fables) throughout his later career. Increasing difficulties with censors at the academy typography, some of them instigated by his archenemy Lomonosov, forced Sumarokov to cease publication of the journal after a year. The final issue included the poem "Farewell to the Muses" (Rasstavanie s muzami) in which Sumarokov vowed never to write again, a vow the author was to make and break repeatedly in future years.

Sumarokov met with even greater frustrations organizing the new Russian theater. Although it became an official "court" (rather than "free") theater in 1759 and hence presumably eligible for greater state support, Sumarokov was burdened by constant financial hardships—his salary withheld; no money to pay the actors or his own rent; lack of costumes, which forced cancellation of performances; no stagehands or other assistants; and at times not even enough to eat. On top of this there were endless bureaucratic obstacles put in his way by the officials on whom he had to rely, especially K. I. Sivers (Sumarokov had his revenge by ridiculing him in a memorable article in *Trudoliubivaia pchela*). Among other problems with which Sumarokov was forced to contend were the lack of a fixed venue for the theater, competition with French and Italian troupes (which were far better paid) and other court activities, performances canceled due to a prematurely thawed Neva River (preventing its crossing by travelers), and his own illnesses. Sumarokov struggled heroically to improve conditions for his troupe; for instance, he fought to get them decent medical care and the privilege for his male actors to wear swords (a sign of noble prerogative). After repeated threats to resign from the theater, Sumarokov was finally taken at his word and forced out of the directorship in 1761. Apart from his writing, Sumarokov laid the institutional groundwork for the later Imperial Russian Theater and helped establish a tradition of distinguished Russian acting that lasted well into the nineteenth century.

Sumarokov complained of having little time to write, but in the later 1750's he managed to compose a sixth tragedy, *Dimiza* (1758), later revised as *Iaropolk i Dimiza* (1768); a "drama," *Pustynnik* (The Hermit, 1769), written in 1757; the first Russian operas, *Tsefal i Prokris* (Cephalus and Procris, 1755) and *Al'tsesta* (Alceste, 1759), with music by Francesco Araia and Hermann Friedrich Raupach, respectively; the ballet *Pribezhishche dobrodeteli* (Sanctuary for Virtue, 1759), choreographed by Franz Anton Christophe Hilferding; and an allegorical prologue, *Novye lavry* (New Laurels, 1759), to celebrate the Russian army's victory over the Prussians near Frankfurt. In the early 1760's he also contributed to the new Moscow journals *Poleznoe uveselenie* (Useful Amusement, 1760–1762) and *Svobodnye chasy* (Free Hours, 1763), around which a new generation of young poets had arisen, including Mikhail Kheraskov, A. A. Rzhevskii, and Vasilii Maikov, commonly referred to (after Gukovskii) as the "Sumarokov school."

Catherine the Great's coup of June 28, 1762, which put an end to her husband Peter III's brief reign, promised Sumarokov good fortune. He was promoted in rank, and his debts to the academy typography (which had vexed him since 1748) were annulled, although he spent many years trying to collect money that he felt had been wrongly withheld during his tenure at the theater. Catherine also granted Sumarokov the unique lifetime privilege of having all of his works printed at her cost, which may help explain Sumarokov's prodigious list of publications. Their popularity, given the nebulous nature of the Russian reading public in the eighteenth century, is hard to gauge, although many of his contemporaries unquestionably considered Sumarokov's work to be classic. Catherine's ascension must have seemed to Sumarokov like a triumph for his own political ideals, and he celebrated the empress in a series of laudatory odes (notably, in the later 1750's he had largely disdained writing such works to Elizabeth). The longest of these, an ode printed on July 8, 1762, and reissued three weeks later, has been called a poeticized version of the famous manifesto that Catherine had published on coming to the throne, in which she echoed Montesquieu's condemnation of despotism and praise of monarchy based on law.

Part One. Sumarokov and the Literary Process of His Time

At the same time Sumarokov found himself in a somewhat unusual position professionally, since he continued to receive a salary but had no official position or duties; in 1764 he even proposed that Catherine finance a trip to France and Italy so that he could write travel notes for the edification of his countrymen. Committed both to the political program of enlightened monarchy which Catherine espoused and to the prestige and independence of Russian letters, Sumarokov increasingly found himself in a quandary, as his personal and political impertinences often threatened to alienate the empress, on whose goodwill he relied both as writer and ideologue. The first indications of a problem may have been that Sumarokov did not publish his outspoken coronation speech of September 22, 1762, and that a portion of his "Chorus to a Perverted World" (Khor ko prevratnomu svetu) was cut from the published verses he had written for the elaborate three-day celebration titled "Minerva Triumphant" (Torzhestvuiushchaia Minerva), which he helped organize together with Volkov and Kheraskov and which was held in Moscow in early 1763 to honor Catherine's coronation; both works were first published in the posthumous complete works. Other, more certain grounds for Catherine's discontent were an ode Sumarokov dedicated to her former lover, the Polish king Stanislav Augustus, in 1765 (she ordered the Academy to burn the work, and no copies have survived) and the satiric fable "Two Cooks" (Dva povara), published the same year, which she had confiscated. Sumarokov's letters to Catherine with which he often "bombarded" her (as she put it) are remarkable for their frank and outspoken tone and as expressions of Sumarokov's marked self-regard as a poet.

Sumarokov's father died in 1766, and a scandal ensued when Sumarokov went to Moscow to claim his inheritance; Catherine intervened on his mother's behalf after she appealed to the empress for protection against her son, who had terrified her household and threatened her with physical violence. Sumarokov was enraged at the thought that his mother was taking sides against him with his hated brother-in-law A. I. Buturlin (whom the poet lampooned in several of his comedies). The situation was probably complicated by the fact that by this time Sumarokov's wife had left him and he had taken up with a serf woman, Vera Prokhorovna, whom he officially married in 1774; some have speculated that this relationship may have brought the poet some measure of social ostracism. Prokhorovna bore Sumarokov two more children, Anastasiia and Pavel, who received gentry status at the time of their parents' marriage.

In his response to the essay contest Catherine suggested to the Free Economic Society in 1766 concerning the desirability of granting property rights to peasants and in his notes on the draft of the empress's *Nakaz* (Instruction, 1767), Sumarokov staunchly defended the institution of serfdom. Catherine was apparently not pleased with what he wrote and commented that "Mr. Sumarokov is a good poet but…he does not have sufficient clarity of mind to be a good lawgiver." Be that as it may, Sumarokov was an outspoken defender of serfs' human and legal rights and sharply attacked such practices as selling serfs "like cattle," that is, apart from their land. While asserting fundamental human equality according to nature, Sumarokov also defended the necessity of social hierarchy. The essential point was that each social order fulfill its duty appropriately. Some of his most memorable attacks were against *pod'iachie* (clerks or bureaucrats), in which category he sometimes included those granted noble status by appointment, and against *otkupshchiki* (concessionaires), notorious in the eighteenth century for extorting high prices for vodka after obtaining the right to sell it under the state liquor monopoly. But the main target as well as audience for Sumarokov's admonitions was his own class, the hereditary Russian nobility. As he wrote in his programmatic satire "On Nobility" (O blagorodstve, 1774);

> Дворяне без меня свой долг довольно знают,
> Но многие одно дворянство вспоминают,
> Не помня, что от баб рожденным и от дам
> Без исключения всем праотец Адам.
> На то ль дворяне мы, чтоб люди работали,
> А мы бы их труды по знатности глотали?…
> Не в титле — в действии быть должен дворянином…

(The nobles know their duty quite well without me, / But many only recall their nobility, / Forgetting that all people, born of country gals or ladies / Without exception have Adam as progenitor. / Are we nobles so that people should work, / So that we exalted ones swallow up their labor?… / One must be noble not in title but in action…)

The failure to keep to one's proper station is repeatedly ridiculed in Sumarokov's fables, published in three volumes between 1762 and 1769 (three more books of fables were published in his collected works, bringing the total number of fables to about 380). Among Sumarokov's most popular works during his lifetime, the fables were full of coarse humor and sharp, mocking invective and were often directed at contemporary political targets or literary enemies. They were also among his most innovative works, written mostly in iambic lines of varied length and capturing the dynamic intonations of popular and folk speech. While such things were permissible in a "low" genre such as the fable, Sumarokov resolutely rejected those new bourgeois literary phenomena that he felt threatened the classical hierarchy. He was disdainful of the flood of translated novels that hit Russia in the 1760's (and scornful of their Russian imitations by writers like Fedor Emin) and resolutely opposed the new dramas that combined comic and tragic elements. In the preface to *Dimitrii Samozvanets* (Dimitrii the Pretender, 1771) Sumarokov triumphantly published a letter written to him by Voltaire dated February 26, 1769 (new style), in which Voltaire praised Sumarokov and approved his rejection of "comédies larmoyantes" (tearful comedies).

On January 26, 1767, Catherine awarded Sumarokov the Order of Anna, possibly in part for several more odes he had written to her. He was in Moscow during the summer of that year while Catherine was organizing the Commission for a New Law Code. He spent 1768 and early 1769 in St. Petersburg, where he published a prodigious number of old, new, and revised works, including the comedies *Likhoimets* (The Extortioner, 1768), *Iadovityi* (The Poisonous One, 1768), *Tri brata sovmestniki* (Three Brother Rivals, 1768), *Nartsiss* (Narcissus, 1769), and *Pridannoe obmanom* (Dowry by Deceit, 1769); the popular but heretofore unpublished tragedy *Semira*, written in 1751; revised versions of *Khorev*, *Sinav i Truvor*, *Iaropolk i Dimiza*, and *Pustynnik*; and his seventh tragedy, *Vysheslav* (1768). In addition he published his historical essay *Pervyi i glavnyi streletskii bunt* (The First and Main Streltsy Uprising, 1768) and the collection *Raznyia stikhotvoreniia* (Various Poems, 1769), as well as the third volume of his fables.

In March 1769 Sumarokov moved to Moscow, where he became involved in complicated negotiations to establish a permanent theater there. He managed to quarrel with many people in the theatrical world, which led to a conspiracy to embarrass the extraordinarily vain author publicly. At the center was Moscow's commander in chief Count P. S. Saltykov. Saltykov forced Belmonti's troupe to stage *Sinav and Truvor* on January 31, 1770, despite the fact that the actors were not ready or willing and violating Sumarokov's contract with Belmonti that explicitly forbade him to put on any of Sumarokov's plays without the author's permission. Two days before the performance Sumarokov took to his bed in grief and from there wrote a series of desperate letters to Catherine imploring her help. In one he included an autobiographical elegy — "Now my vexation has exceeded all bounds" (Vse mery prevoshla teper' moia dosada), and in another he appealed to her, citing lines adapted from his recent tragedy *Vysheslav*: "Не емлю сил вельмож вокруг стоящих трона, / И от предписанна рукой твоей закона" (I have neither the power of grandees who surround the throne, / Nor that of the law prescribed by your hand). Catherine responded caustically that "it will always be more pleasant for me to see presentations of

Chapter 1. Sumarokov: Life and Works

passion in your plays than to read them in your letters." It was a remarkable exchange over the proper limits of literature between the Classicist poet and the enlightened despot. On the accompanying letter Sumarokov had written to her secretary, Catherine noted to herself with a pun, "Sumarokov bez uma est' i budet" (Sumarokov is and will be brainless). The scandal continued as Saltykov circulated copies of Catherine's letter to the poet, and mocking epigrams proliferated, including one against Sumarokov by the young Derzhavin.

Catherine's refusal to intervene dramatically demonstrated the limits of her patronage and possibly also her impatience with Russian writers in general (although it should be noted that her intervention would have been against a trusted senior official). This was the period (1769–1774) of the short-lived satiric journals that Catherine's *Vsiakaia vsiachina* (All Sorts and Sundries) had initiated. Sumarokov contributed little to them, but his works were held up as the prime example of "satira na litso" (personal satire), which Novikov in particular advocated, as opposed to the generalized "satira na porok" (satire of vices), which the empress tried to promote. Catherine's political liberalism was wearing thin, and she tried increasingly to regulate Russian letters, either through her own efforts or by turning to such truly subservient court poets as Vasilii Petrov. Characteristically, two years earlier Catherine had again played the role of Sumarokov's personal censor and, despite Sumarokov's protests, had supported theater director Ivan Elagin's excision of several lines from the comedy *Likhoimets* that referred to religion and to the Commission on the New Law Code in a flippant manner.

Despite the debacle in Moscow, Sumarokov completed his next and by general consensus his greatest tragedy, *Dimitrii the Pretender*, which opened in St. Petersburg on February 1, 1771. In the foreword to the play Sumarokov lambasted Pierre-Augustin Beaumarchais's tearful drama *Eugénie* (1767) and the Moscow audiences that had recently applauded a Russian version of it; he appended Voltaire's letter, which had become a kind of talisman for the beleaguered author. *Dimitrii the Pretender*, set during the time of troubles of the early seventeenth century, was the most contemporary, most truly historical, and most patriotic of Sumarokov's tragedies, which the author said would "show Russia Shakespeare." Dimitrii was Sumarokov's most shocking anti-utopian tyrant, and the play balances between a staunch defense of the hierarchical and autocratic principle, on the one hand, and legitimacy based on merit rather than birth, on the other — "Коль он достоин царь, достоин царска сана" (He is a worthy tsar if he is worthy of the tsar's station). At the end of the play nobles and people alike rise up to oust Dimitrii, to the chiming of Kremlin bells. *Dimitrii the Pretender* remained in the repertory through 1812 and was the prototype for many later plays on the theme, most notably Alexander Pushkin's *Boris Godunov* (1831). Scholars have tried, not too successfully, to see this and other of Sumarokov's tragedies as covert commentaries on specific contemporary issues (that is, as criticisms of Elizabeth's or Catherine's despotism), but their fundamental political message — a defense of lawful monarchy and an attack on the abuses of despotism — is clear. Nevertheless, Sumarokov's eloquent denunciations of tyranny were a starting point for the republican trend in later Russian literature, most notably Iakov Kniazhnin's *Vadim Novgorodskii* (Vadim of Novgorod, 1793), which Catherine had burned and which was in turn a link to the Decembrists.

Dimitrii the Pretender also presented a defense of Russian Orthodoxy, which was juxtaposed to Catholicism's "false doctrine" that demanded blind obedience. Characteristically, Sumarokov advocated a rationalistic view of Orthodoxy that did not see any necessary or apparent contradiction between reason and divine revelation. Sumarokov's religious thought was in the quasi-Protestant tradition of Feofan Prokopovich, main architect of Peter I's church reform, a stance characteristic of eighteenth-century Russian religious thought. The harmonizing of faith and reason also corresponded to the mid-century attempt to create a new literary language based on both Church Slavonic and vulgar Russian, so-called "Slavenorossiiskii" (Slaveno-Russian), and to the blurring of boundaries between religious and secular literature (secular poets writing psalm paraphrases, as well as clerics writing sermons and catechisms in the vernacular). While Sumarokov was an advocate of such a literary, linguistic, and philosophical rapprochement between secular and religious traditions, in subsequent literary consciousness he was largely associated with Karamzin's reforms, which were oriented on the secular spoken language of the salon; this association occurred partially by negative analogy with Trediakovskii, who was identified with the camp of the politically and religiously conservative *arkhaisty* (archaists).

On March 29, 1771, Sumarokov renewed his agreement with Belmonti, paving the way to present his works on the Moscow stage, but all plans were postponed when the black plague began to ravage the city. Sumarokov left Moscow on account of the epidemic and did not return until April 1772, to find Belmonti dead and most of the actors scattered. Again Sumarokov involved himself in the politics of theatrical plans and proposals. Despite chronic medical problems, he also continued to write. On Metropolitan Platon's advice he finished his poetic paraphrase of the Psalter, which he published in 1774. The same year saw publication of collections of his *Eklogi* (Eclogues); *Elegii liubovnyia* (Love Elegies); *Ody torzhestvennyia* (Triumphal

Odes); *Satiry* (Satires); his last tragedy, *Mstislav*; and several shorter works, including poems decrying the Pugachev rebellion. He also continued to write comedies; his last three — *Rogonosets po voobrazheniiu* (The Imaginary Cuckold, 1786), *Mat' sovmestnitsa docheri* (Mother-Daughter Rivalry, 1786), *Vzdorshchitsa* (The Argumentative One, 1786) — manifest the influence of Denis Fonvizin's *Brigadir* (wtn. 1769) in their depiction of Russian types and their earthy language. Many readers consider *Rogonosets* a minor masterpiece.

While he continued to publish through 1775, Sumarokov was afflicted in his final years by sickness, poverty, and probably alcoholism. He spent part of 1773 and 1774 in St. Petersburg, where with the help of his new patron, Grigorii Potemkin, he arranged for his son Pavel's entry into the Preobrazhenskii Regiment and attended the presentation of *Mstislav*. In Moscow accumulated unpaid debts threatened to deprive the poet and his family of their home, and he was further insulted when refused the customary free entrance to performances of his own work. He published his last ode to Catherine in July 1775, celebrating the peace of Kuchuk-Kainardji, but financial relief was not forthcoming from the empress. A final crisis occurred after the death of Sumarokov's wife Vera in May 1777, as Sumarokov's mother unsuccessfully attempted to prevent her son's third marriage to another serf, his second wife's niece Elena Gavrilova. The details are obscure, but Sumarokov may have desired the marriage to protect his daughter or perhaps simply to have someone to take care of him. He died on October 1, 1777, approximately four months after this marriage and just a few days after his Moscow home had been sold at auction for debts.

Legend has it that almost no one attended the funeral of the destitute poet, apart from several Moscow actors who had carried his coffin to the Donskoi Monastery, where he was buried in an unmarked grave. A lasting monument to the writer was the exemplary ten-volume *Polnoe sobranie vsekh sochinenii, v stikhakh i proze* (Complete Works in Verse and Prose) published by Novikov in 1781–1782 and revised in 1787. Unfortunately, the poet's papers, which Novikov rescued after Sumarokov's death and used for the complete works, were lost after the editor's arrest in 1792. Although in the nineteenth century Sumarokov's name became synonymous with Russian "pseudo-classicism," a term that denied to most eighteenth-century writing the right to be considered as literature, in 1772 Novikov expressed the prevailing view of Sumarokov's contemporaries when he wrote that the poet had "achieved great and immortal fame for himself via works in a variety of poetic and prose genres, not only from Russians but from foreign Academies and from the most famous European writers."

Part One. Sumarokov and the Literary Process of His Time

Selected Bibliography[1]

Berkov, P. N. *Aleksandr Petrovich Sumarokov, 1717–1777*. Russkie dramaturgi, nauchnopopuliarnye ocherki. Moscow, Leningrad: Iskusstvo, 1949.

Berkov, P. N. *Lomonosov i literaturnaia polemika ego vremeni, 1750–1765*. Moscow, Leningrad: Akademiia nauk, 1936.

Berkov, P. N. "Neskol'ko spravok dlia biografii A. P. Sumarokova," *XVIII vek*, 5 (1962): 364–375.

Berkov, P. N. Berkov, "Zhiznennyi i literaturnyi put' A. P. Sumarokova," in Sumarokov, *Izbrannye proizvedeniia*, edited by Berkov, Biblioteka poeta, Bol'shaia seriia (Leningrad: Sovetskii pisatel', 1957), pp. 5–46.

Bulich, N. N. *Sumarokov i sovremennaia emu kritiki*. St. Petersburg: Eduarda Pratsa, 1854.

Ewington, Amanda. *A Voltaire for Russia? Alexander Petrovich Sumarokov's Journey from Poet-Critic to Russian Philosophe*. Diss. University of Chicago, 2001.

Grinberg, M. S. and B. A. Uspenskii, *Literaturnaia bor'ba Trediakovskogo i Sumarokova v 1740-kh — nachale 1750-kh godov*, special issue on Sumarokov, *Russian Literature*, 31: 2 (1992): 133–272.

Gukovskii, G. A. *Ocherki po istorii russkoi literatury XVIII veka: Dvorianskaia fronda v literature 1750-kh — 1760-kh godov*. Moscow, Leningrad: Akademiia nauk, 1936.

Gukovskii, G. A. *Rannie raboty po istorii russkoi poezii XVIII veka*. Moscow: Iazyki russkoi kul'tury, 2001.

Klein, Joachim. *Puti kul'turnogo importa: Trudy po russkoi literature XVIII veka*. Moscow: Iazyki slavianskoi kul'tury, 2005.

Lang, David M. "Boileau and Sumarokov. The Manifesto of Russian Classicism," *Modern Language Review*, 43 (October 1948): 500–506.

Lang, David M. "Sumarokov's 'Hamlet': A Misjudged Russian Tragedy of the Eighteenth Century," *Modern Language Review*, 43 (January 1948): 67–72.

Levitsky, Alexander. *The Sacred Ode in Eighteenth Century Russian Literary Culture*. Diss. University of Michigan, 1977.

Livanova, Tamara. *Russkaia muzykal'naia kul'tura XVIII veka, v sviazi s literaturoi, teatrom i bytom*, vol. 1. Moscow: Muzgiz, 1952, pp. 65–92.

Longinov, M. V. "Poslednie gody zhizni Alexander Petrovicha Sumarokova (1766–1777)." *Russkii arkhiv* (1871): cols. 1637–1717, 1955–1960.

Lutsevich. L. F. *Psaltyr' v russkoi poezii*. St. Petersburg: D. Bulanin, 2002.

Mstislavskaia, E. P., and E. V. Ivanova. *Aleksandr Petrovich Sumarokov 1717–1777: zhizn' i tvorchestvo: Sbornik statei i materialov*. Moscow: Pashkov dom, 2002.

---

[1] I have updated the bibliography that originally appeared with this essay. See also my own articles elsewhere in this volume which I have not listed here.

Nikolaev, S. I. "Original'nost', podrazhanie i plagiat v predstavleniiakh russkikh pisatelei XVIII veka: Ocherk problematiki." *XVIII vek*, 23 (2004): 3–19.

Nikolaev, S. I. "A. P. Sumarokov — perevodchik s russkogo iazyka na russkii." *Russian Literature* 52: 1–3 (2002): 141–49.

Ospovat, K. A. "Literaturnyi spor Lomonosova i Sumarokova." Diss. na soiskanie uchenoi stepeni kandaidate filosofskikh nauk. Moscow, 2005.

Ospovat, K. A. "Sumarokov — literator v sotsial'nom kontekste 1740 — nachala 1760-h gg." *Eighteenth-Century Russia: Society, Culture, Economy*, ed. Roger P. Bartlett and Gabriela Lehmann-Carli. Berlin: Lit, 2007, 35–52.

Ospovat, K. A. "Tragediia Sumarokova Khorev: K semanticheskoi strukture pridvornoi dramaturgii." *Russian Literature and the West: A Tribute for David M. Bethea*, ed. Alexander Dolinin, Lazar Fleishman, and Leonid Livak. Stanford Slavic Studies, 35–36. Stanford, Calif: Dept. of Slavic Languages and Literatures, Stanford University, 2008, 13–40.

Osterwald, Birgit. *Das Demetrius-Thema in der russischen und deutschen Literatur: dargestellt an A. P. Sumarokovs "Dimitrij Samozvanec," A. S. Puškins "Boris Godunov" und F. Schillers "Demetrius."* Studia Slavica et Baltica, Bd. 5. Munich: Aschendorff, 1982.

Serman, Il'ia Z. *Russkii klassitsizm: Poeziia, drama, satira*. Leningrad: Nauka, 1973.

Stennik, Iu. V. *Zhanr tragedii v russkoi literature: epokha klassitsiz*ma. Leningrad: Nauka, 1981.

Stoiunin, Vladimīr. *Aleksandr Petrovich Sumarokov*. St. Petersburg, 1856.

Sumarokov, Aleksandr. *Ody torzhestvennyia, Elegii liubovnyia: Reprintnoe vosproizvedenie sbornikov 1774 goda. Prilozhenie: Redaktsii i varianty. Dopolneniia. Kommentarii. Stat'i*, ed. Ronald Vroon. Moscow: OGI, 2009.

Vindt, L. "Basnia sumarokovskoi shkoly," *Poetika*, 1 (1926): 81–92.

Vroon, Ronald. "Aleksandr Sumarokov's *Elegii liubovnye* and the Development of Verse Narrative in the Eighteenth Century: Toward a History of the Russian Lyric Sequence." *Slavic Review*, 59: 3 (Fall 2000): 521–46.

Vroon, Ronald. "Aleksandr Sumarokov's *Ody torzhestvennye* (Toward a History of the Russian Lyric Sequence in the Eighteenth Century)." *Zeitschrift fur Slavische Philogie*, 55: 2 (1995–96): 223–263.

Zhivov, V. M. *Language and Culture in Eighteenth Century Russia*. Boston: Academic Studies Press, 2009.

Zhivov, V. M. "Pervye russkie literaturnye biografii kak sotsial'noe iavlenie: Trediakovskii, Lomonosov, Sumarokov." *Novoe literaturnoe obozrenie*, 25 (1997): 24–83 (also in his *Razyskaniia v oblasti istorii i predystorii russkoi kul'tury. Iazyk, semiotika, kul'tura*. [Moscow: Iazyki slavianskoi kul'tury, 2002]).

2

SUMAROKOV'S READING AT THE ACADEMY OF SCIENCES LIBRARY

Although Alexander Sumarokov played a central role in establishing eighteenth-century Russian literature, we have at our disposal relatively little information concerning his biography and the creative history of his works. The remnants of his personal archive that Nikolai Novikov used in preparing the posthumous *Full Collected Works in Verse and Prose* (*Polnoe sobranie vsekh sochinenii, v stikhakh i proze*) of 1781–82 (second edition, 1787) were lost after the arrest and exile of the publisher-editor. For this reason, almost any new information on Sumarokov, particularly concerning his early career before his appointment as director of the first Russian national theater in 1756, are particularly valuable. This article consists of an annotated list of books that Sumarokov borrowed from the Library of the Academy of Sciences in the late 1740's and in 1755. The list is of interest not only as a source of information about Sumarokov and his literary activities but also as evidence of Russian interest in various classical and modern European writers. Of special note is the fact that Sumarokov borrowed Shakespeare in the fourth folio edition, the earliest evidence of Russian acquaintance with the bard in English.

The accompanying list is based on materials from the St. Petersburg branch of the Academy of Sciences Archive. It documents twenty-two works that Sumarokov borrowed from the Academy Library. The list is divided into two parts. The second is based on discharges recorded in the Library's "record of books issued" (zhurnal vydachi knig), which indicates not only the year (1755) but also the precise day on which Sumarokov borrowed particular books (f. 158, op. 1, no. 410, l. 15). It is more difficult to determine the purpose and dating of the document on which the first part of the list is based (f. 158, op. 1, d. 407, l. 9). Academicians frequently complained about the disorder (neporiadki) and neglect of books in the library when it was under the control of the Academy secretary and librarian Johann-Daniel

Chapter 2. Sumarokov's Reading at the Academy of Sciences Library

Schumacher (I.-D. Shumakher, 1690–1761). After Elizabeth's ascension to the throne in 1741 an investigating commission was appointed, and for a time Schumacher was even held under arrest. However, he was subsequently fully rehabilitated with the help of influential friends at court.[1]

One of the repeated complaints about Schumacher was that the Library did not keep systematic records of the books it lent out. According to the report of the assembly of professors (professorskoe sobranie) of September, 1745, which was signed among others by Lomonosov and Trediakovskii, "the books that are given out to anyone are not recorded in a notebook, to [keep track of] whom they are lent to and when they are to be returned. In lending books from the library, records of borrowing (rospiski) are [made on] separate pages or on scraps [of paper], most of which get lost, so that when the books are returned one can't get them back.[2] And it is possible that many books were given out without records of borrowing, so it is not surprising that many library books have been lost."[3] It was only in the early 1750's that yearly alphabetical journals began to be kept to keep track of borrowed books, but of these only a few have survived (those from 1753–1755 and 1761–1762).[4]

The first document that provides evidence of the books Sumarokov borrowed in the late 1740's is located in a folder with miscellaneous lists of books and borrowing receipts from various years. The document lists books "that are missing from the library" (headings on ll. 12–13). The list is organized by section of the library (by "kamora" or "kamera," that is, by hall), which corresponds to the so-called "kamernyi katalog" of 1741–1742.[5] All but one

---

[1] On the Academy Library under Schumacher's direction, see: P. P. Pekarskii, *Istoriia Imperatorskoi akademii nauk v Peterburge*, 2 vols. (1870–73; rpt. Leipzig: Zentralantiquariat der Deutschen Demokratischen Republik, 1977), 2: iv-xix, and via index; *Istoricheskii ocherk i obzor fondov rukopisnogo otdela Biblioteki Akademii Nauk. Vyp. 1: XVIII vek* (Moscow: Akademiia nauk SSSR, 1956), 171–176; S. P. Luppov and M. S. Filippov, et al., *Istoriia Biblioteki Akademii nauk SSSR, 1714–1964* (Leningrad: Nauka, 1964), 39–43 and via the index.

[2] That is, borrowers were not given receipts for returned books.

[3] M. I. Sukhomlinov, *Materialy dlia istorii Imperatorskoi Akademii nauk*, vol. 7: 1744–1745 (St. Petersburg, 1895), 640.

[4] I came across several of these "rospiski" among the pages of various volumes of the handwritten catalogue of 1751–1753 (f. 158, op. 1, № 154, 158, 163, 164). This suggests that the new procedures for borrowing were not instituted until after 1753. The receipts and other records of books borrowed from the Academy Library represent a very rich and practically untapped source of information about academicians, writers and translators in the mid-eighteenth century, and await systematic investigation.

[5] *Bibliothecae Imperialis Petropolitanae*, 4 vols. (St. Petersburg, 1741–42).

of Sumarokov's books are under the rubric "Poetae" (Poets) and marked with numbers from that section of the catalogue (no. 14, Olearius' travel memoir, is catalogued under "Exotica"). It is possible that this document is connected with the audit (reviziia) in the Library of 1744–1746 whose conduct Schumacher stubbornly resisted and the results of which have not survived.[6]

Because of this and the "disorders" in the Library it is difficult to determine the precise dates of borrowing. The preceding separate pages in the folder are lists of books borrowed through the end of 1745, ordered by surname of the borrowers (ll. 6–7).[7] There is also a separate record for books lent to G. N. Teplov on June 29, 1747 (l. 8), that is probably the terminus post quem for Sumarokov's borrowing. The terminus ante quem is difficult to determine for the simple reason that books may have been kept for a long time, or not even been returned. Nevertheless we may suggest that they were borrowed from the Library no later than 1746–1748 for the following reasons. First of all, among the borrowers listed together with Sumarokov is the Academy librarian and adjunct in history Johann Friedrich Brehm (Brem) who was fired from his Academy responsibilities on August 1, 1747.[8] Secondly, it seems very likely that Sumarokov borrowed these books in connection with his work on the tragedy "Hamlet" (Gamlet)

---

[6] According to M. N. Murzanova, "a fire in the Library in 1747 which followed put a definitive end to the further course of the audit" (*Istoricheskii ocherk i obzor*, 176). See also *Istoriia Biblioteki*, 42 and 80. It is possible that no audit took place at all; see Pekarskii, *Istoriia Imperatorskoi akademii nauk*, 2: xix.

[7] The latest date indicated on these pages is December 30, 1745 (l. 6). It is clearly for this reason that E. B. Ryss and G. M. Korovin ascribed them to this year. See their "M. V. Lomonosov — chitatel' Biblioteki Peterburgskoi akademii nauk," *Trudy BAN SSSR i FBON AN SSSR*, vol. 3 (Moscow, Leningrad: Akademiia nauk, 1958), 283 and 290.

[8] Pekarskii, *Istoriia*, I: 586. The documents also contain the names of: Christian Gottfried Crusius, professor of antiquities and the history of literature, who was released from service August 20, 1749 (he left Russia forever at the end of the month); and the professor of astronomy Christian Nicolaus von Winsheim (Vinzgeim) who died on March 4, 1751. On Crusius see Pekarskii, *Istoriia*, I: 696, and on Winsheim, see Akademiia Nauk SSSR, *Personal'nyi sostav 1724–1974*, vol. 1 (Moscow: Nauka, 1974), 8.

Many books on this list were marked with the initials "G. H." and were from among the books belonging to Pushkin's great-grandfather Gibrahim Hannibal (Ibragim Gannibal). They had been confiscated in 1726 after the death of Peter I in connection with Hannibal's exile and only returned to him in the 1740's when he came back into favor. Unfortunately, a comparison of this document with the list of books returned to Hannibal and with the list of books that perished in the fire of December 5, 1747, did not shed any light on the date our list was compiled (SPb.O AAN, f. 158, op. 1, № 466, l. 7 ob.–9 ob. and l. 1–6 ob.). On Hannibal's books and the fire, see *Istoriia Biblioteki*, 48–50.

Chapter 2. Sumarokov's Reading at the Academy of Sciences Library

and the "Two Epistles," which the writer submitted for publication in early October, 1748.⁹ (More on this below.)

The record of books issued (zhurnal vydachi knig) for 1755, from which the second part of our list was compiled, is alphabetical. In it books that have been returned are crossed out. Some of the records only list the books by number, without title or author. A comparison of these numbers with the catalogues preserved in the Academy Archive reveals that they correspond to the large handwritten catalogue of books and manuscripts in foreign languages in 26 volumes, compiled in 1751–1753.¹⁰ A detailed examination of this catalogue, lacking an index, permitted us to determine the identity of all of the books except one (no. 12). In the appended list below, I have included both a modern bibliographical description of the given edition together with the notation from the 1751–1753 catalogue on whose basis the identification of the books was made.

We now turn to the question of the possible importance of these books for Sumarokov. The two parts of the list relate to different periods of his literary activity. The first, from the late 1740's, connects with Sumarokov's earliest published works, the first two Russian-language tragedies "Khorev" (St. Petersburg, 1747) and "Hamlet" (St. Petersburg, 1748), and his "manifesto of Russian Classicism" the "Two Epistles" (St. Petersburg, 1748).¹¹ The second part relates to the period of his participation in the new journal *Ezhemesiachnyia sochineniia* (Monthly Compositions).

All of the books in the first group — the works of Shakespeare, Vondel, Scarron, and French translations of Lucan and Virgil — are directly relevant to Sumarokov's work on the "Two Epistles." The epistles, which included "Notes," a short annotated list of writers, as an appendix, served as a kind of Cliff Notes designed for "the reader lacking in elementary knowledge of literary history."¹² All of the authors of the first part of our list are named

---

9   See chap. 3 "Censorship and Provocation: The Publication History of Sumarokov's 'Two Epistles.'"
10 *Catalogi Generalioris Bibliothecae Imperialis Petropolitanae*, SPb.O AAN, f. 158, op. 1 № 142–143 (1751), 144–152 (1752), 153–167 (1753). On this catalogue, see *Istoriia Biblioteki*, 115–117.
11 This does not include his ode to Anna Ioanovna published in 1740, written in the name of the Cadet Corps, and the anonymous brochure *Tri ody parafrasticheskie Psalma 143, sochinennyia chrez trekh stikhotvortsev* (St. Petersburg, 1744).
12 I. [Joachim] Klein, "Russkii Boalo?: Epistola Sumarokova 'O stikhotvorstve' v vospriiatii sovrremennikov," *XVIII vek*, 18 (St. Petersburg: Nauka, 1993), 44.
    See also P. N. Berkov, *Vvedenie v izuchenie istorii russkoi literatury XVIII veka* (Leningrad: Universitet, 1964), 22.

in the "Two Epistles" except for Scarron, who is clearly referred to in the section on mock heroic (iroi-komicheskie) poems in the second epistle (II: 285–310).[13] (We would note that Sumarokov's validation of the genre contradicted Boileau, who excluded "coarse" burlesque, and it is probably for this reason that Scarron's name was not mentioned.[14])

As is well known, in the epistles Sumarokov followed Voltaire in his description of Shakespeare as a writer who deserves a place on Helicon "although [he was] unenlightened" (II: 38), a writer "in whom there is much that is bad and very much that is extraordinarily good" (from the "Notes" to the epistles). That Sumarokov was acquainted with Shakespeare's texts in English represents an unexpected discovery both for scholars of Sumarokov and of Shakespeare's influence in Russia, although it should be recalled that the bare fact of borrowing a book from the library in and of itself proves little, especially in the given case when there is no evidence that Sumarokov knew any English. The same goes for his acquaintance with the tragedies of the Dutch playwright Joost van den Vondel (1587–1679), whom he could hardly read in the original. In his response to Trediakovskii's criticism of his "Hamlet" in 1750, Sumarokov wrote: "My Hamlet, he [Trediakovskii] says,... is translated from the French prose [version] of the English tragedy by Shakespeare, but he is very mistaken. My Hamlet, except for the monologue at the end of the third act and Claudius' falling down onto his knees hardly, hardly resembles Shakespeare's tragedy" (PSVS X: 117).

Perhaps intentionally, Sumarokov does not specify what Trediakovskii's precise error is, and which version—the original or P.-A. LaPlace's translation—he consulted in writing his play. A comparison of texts indicates that his adaptation of the passages in question was indeed based on LaPlace's version (from the second volume of *Le theatre anglois* of 1746) with the notable influence of Voltaire's earlier verse translation of the famous "To be or not to be" monologue. Still, the relationship between English, French and Russian texts of "Hamlet," as well as the influence of Shakespeare on

---

[13] In citing the "Two Epistles" the Roman numeral I refers to first and II to second. Line numbering accords to the *Polnoe sobranie vsekh sochinenii, v stikhakh i proze*, 10 vols., ed. N. I. Novikov (Moscow: Universitetskaia tipografiia, 1781–1782), I: 329–356. References to this edition in the text will refer to it as PSVS plus volume and page.

[14] See A. P. Sumarokov, *Stikhotvoreniia*, ed. A. S. Orlov. Biblioteka poeta, bol'shaia seriia (Moscow: Sovetskii pisatel', 1935), 438. On the development of the mock epic in Russia, see *Iroi-komicheskaia poema*, ed. B. Tomashevskii. Biblioteka poeta, bol'shaia seriia (Leningrad: Izd-vo pisatelei v Leningrade, 1933), 77–85 and 706–7; and Angelina Vacheva, *Poema-burlesk v russkoi poezii XVIII veka* (Sofia: M. Drinov, 1999).

Sumarokov's later plays, still awaits detailed investigation.[15] Nevertheless, whatever our conclusions, the list published below is the earliest evidence of acquaintance with in Shakespeare's original texts in Russia.

In the "Two Epistles" among the writers reigning on Mount Helicon Sumarokov names "the incomparable Virgil" and Lucan (II: 44 and 46). In his notes on these writers Sumarokov mentions the "Pharsalia" by Lucan (Marcus Annaeus Lucanus) and Virgil's "Eclogues." Sumarokov borrowed both of these works in French translation (no. 2 and 4). He remarked on Lucan in his "Notes" that "He was in great favor with Nero, but later was murdered by this torturer by opening his veins. He wrote a poem about the Battle of Pharsalia between Caesar and Pompey." Characteristically, Sumarokov is interested in both the writer's literary achievement (his unfinished epic poem in ten books) as well as his fate as court poet.[16] The same may be said of his note on Virgil, where most attention is paid to the *Aeneid*. Among other things, Sumarokov writes (echoing the commonplace from Pliny and Suetonius): "In his 'Eclogues' he imitated Theocritus, in the 'Georgics' Hesiod, in the 'Aeneid' Homer." In the epistle on poetry, the pastoral genres of eclogue and idyll occupy a central place (II: 65–86 and 365–376). Sumarokov only began to try his own hand at eclogues in the second half of the 1750's (excluding a translation of Fontenelle's fifth eclogue — see note 29), but by 1774 had written a sufficient number for a separate edition.[17] Four other classical writers from among the books Sumarokov borrowed in 1755 — Horace, Tibullus, Propertius and Pindar (nos. 6, 7, 16, 17) — are also described in the "Notes" to the epistles.

The books Sumarokov took out between March 21 and August 24, 1755, relate to the period of his active participation in the new journal *Ezhemesiachnyia sochineniia k pol'ze i uveseleniiu sluzhashchie* (Monthly

---

[15] See my subsequent examination of the textual issue in "Sumarokov's Russianized 'Hamlet': Texts and Contexts," chap. 5 below.

[16] Cf. Sumarokov's references to Roman poets in his later letters to Catherine the Great. For example, on January 28, 1770, he complained of his enemies that "they treat a well-known poet more autocratically and more cruelly than Nero. He was a Roman emperor; but even he supported all poets except Lucan" (*Pis'ma russkikh pisatelei XVIII veka* [Leningrad: Nauka, 1980], 127–28).

[17] *Eklogi Aleksandra Sumarokova* (St. Petersburg, 1774). On Sumarokov's pastoral verse, see Joachim Klein, *Die Schäferdichtung des russischen Klassizismus*. Veröffentlichungen der Abteilung für Slavische Sprachen und Literaturen des Osteuropa-Instituts [Slavisches Seminar] an der Freien Universität Berlin, Bd. 67 (Wiesbaden: O. Harrassowitz, 1988), in Russian in his *Puti kul'turnogo importa: Trudy po russkoi literature XVIII veka* (Moscow: Iazyki slavianskoi kul'tury, 2005).

Compositions Providing Utility and Enjoyment, 1755–1764) published by the Academy of Sciences.[18] This was Russia's first popular literary and scientific journal. A. N. Neustroev noted that "During the entire course of its ten-year publication *Monthly Compositions* was read greedily by the Russian public despite the fact that belles letters occupied a lesser place than other types of literature."[19] Prior to the creation of his own literary journal *Trudoliubivaia pchela* (The Industrious Bee) in 1759 and of *Prazdnoe vremia v pol'zu upotreblennoe* (Idle Time Spent Usefully) (1759–60) this was Sumarokov's only outlet for publishing his shorter (non-dramatic) works, and he made ample use of it. As the Academician Jakob von Staehlin (Ia. Ia. Shtelin) recalled, "brigadier Sumarokov even made it a rule for himself that not a single issue of the Monthly booklet would come out without him sending a poem to it, and therefore every month for several years running one could find one or more of his works in it."[20] This is no exaggeration; during the period of his collaboration with the journal, he published 98 original poems and 11 verse translations in it, and in 1755–56 his works appeared in 19 of 24 issues. At this time Sumarokov was intensively experimenting with new genres and types of versification. In the unpublished article "On Meter" (O stoposlozhenii) he later wrote that during his years of friendship with Lomonosov (i.e., the late 1740's) he still "did not understand the nuances of versification; but after long term practice I gained a true understanding of it for myself" (PSVS X: 56). These words probably relate to the period of his writing for *Monthly Compositions*, a time when he was involved in an open dispute with Trediakovskii over questions of versification and tried his hand at many types of classical, folk, and contemporary European meters and strophic forms. The extent of Sumarokov's experimentation with genres is remarkable: he wrote triumphant and spiritual odes, sonnets, fables, songs, ballads, madrigals, idylls, stanzas, inscriptions, imitations of classical stanzas (Sapphic, Anacreontic, Horatian), translations from German (sonnets by Paul Fleming) and French (works by Racine,

---

[18] The name of the journal subsequently changed twice: from *Ezhemesiachnyia sochineniia k pol'ze i uveseleniiu sluzhashchie* (1755–1757) it became *Sochineniia i perevody k pol'ze i uveseleniiu sluzhashchie* (1758–1762) and then *Ezhemesiachnyia sochineniia i izvestiia o uchenykh delakh* (1763–1764). See A. N. Neustroev, *Istoricheskoe rozyskanie o russkikh povremennykh izdaniiakh i sbornikakh za 1703–1802 gg.* (St. Petersburg: Obshchaia pol'za, 1875), 46–50; P. N. Berkov, *Istoriia russkoi zhurnalistiki XVIII veka* (Moscow: Akademiia nauk SSSR, 1952), 77–107.
[19] Neustroev, *Istoricheskoe rozyskanie*, 47.
[20] Cited from Pekarskii, *Istoriia*, 2: 651.

Fontenelle, Des Barreaux). If in the late 1740's Sumarokov wanted to become Russia's first tragedian and literary lawgiver, he now wanted to prove his right to the title (in Trediakovskii's words) of "father of Russian poetry."

Our goal here is not to provide a detailed comparison of the works in our list with Sumarokov's publications in *Monthly Compositions,* but we may point to several major coincidences and problems for further investigation. It is clear that Sumarokov borrowed the three editions of Paul Fleming at the end of March, 1755 (nos. 9. 10. 11) in connection with his translations of the German poet's three "Moscow sonnets" published in the April issue of the journal. In connection with this project Sumarokov mostly likely also borrowed the travel memoir of Adam Olearius, Fleming's colleague and companion in the diplomatic service; the memoir quotes Fleming's sonnets.[21] It was Sumarokov's historical interest in seventeenth-century Moscow rather than questions of genre or versification that apparently inspired his interest in these works of this early Baroque German poet, although he soon became involved in a dispute with Trediakovskii over these issues.[22]

In his "Letter in Which is Contained A Discussion of the Poetry Published Up to Now by the Author of Two Odes, Two Tragedies and Two Epistles, Written from a Friend to a Friend" of 1750, Trediakovskii charged Sumarokov with ignorance of the classical tongues and called this one of his major weaknesses as a poet. "He does not have the slightest knowledge of the so-called scholarly languages, while it is at least necessary for him to know Latin... he doesn't even know a brass farthing's worth (ni pula) of Greek."[23] It is hard to know to what extent Trediakovskii's criticism is justified. In the Cadet Corps Sumarokov had learned French and German, and studied Italian, but not Latin or Greek, and we have no evidence he studied them on

---

[21] See no. 14 on the list below. Olearius' work appeared in many editions and was widely translated. A French version was published by Abraham de Wicquefort (*Voyages en Moscovie, Tartarie et Perse, par Adam Olearius,* Paris, 1656), an English version was made by John Davies of Kidwelly (*Travels of the Ambassadors sent by Frederic, Duke of Holstein, to the Great Duke of Muscovy and the King of Persia,* London, 1662 and 1669); a Dutch translation was prepared by Dieterius van Wageningen (*Beschrijvingh van de nieuwe Parciaensche ofte Orientaelsche Reyse,* Utrecht, 1651); and Italian translation of the sections on Russia also appeared (*Viaggi di Moscovia,* Viterbo and Rome, 1658).

[22] See L. B. Modzalevslkii, *Lomonosov i ego literaturnye otnosheniia v Akademii nauk (Iz istorii russkoi literatury i Prosveshcheniia serediny XVIII veka),* Diss. Leningrad, 1947, 122, cited by L. I. Berdnikov, *Schastlivyi feniks: Ocherki o russkom sonete i knizhnoi kul'ture XVIII — nachala XIX veka* (St. Petersburg: Akademicheskii proekt, 1997), 51.

[23] A. Kunik, ed., *Sbornik materialov dlia istorii Imperatorskoi Akademii nauk v XVIII veke,* vol. 2 (St. Petersburg, 1865), 496 and 486.

his own.²⁴ Nevertheless, our list of books that includes nine editions in Latin or in Greek with Latin translation, and one each in English and Dutch may serve as circumstantial evidence of Sumarokov's familiarity with (or at least interest in) the original texts.

Many of Sumarokov's borrowed works themselves might well be connected in one way or another with his disputes with Trediakovskii. They had long been quarrelling over metrics and versification. Their disagreements concerned both Trediakovskii's *New and Short Method for Writing Russian Verse* (Novyi i kratkii sposob k slozheniiu rossiiskii stikhov) of 1735 and the revised *Method for Writing Verse* (Sposob k slozheniiu stikhov) that had appeared in the first volume of his *Works and Translations* of 1752. Polemics were renewed after the appearance of Trediakovskii's article "On Ancient, Modern and Intermediate Russian Poetry" in the June, 1755, issue of *Monthly Compositions*. The article posed a challenge to Sumarokov both on the question of emulating classical meters and on the issue of whose opinions were to have priority for Russian verse. For the July issue of the journal Sumarokov submitted his own examples of Sapphic and Anacreontic odes together with a "Letter on Sapphic and Horatian Stanzas" written specifically as a refutation of Trediakovskii's views.²⁵ The Academy's Assembly that had oversight over the contents of the journal offered Trediakovskii the opportunity to publicly respond to Sumarokov's criticisms.²⁶ Trediakovskii took them up on the offer and read his rejoinder at an Assembly meeting of June 19. Although the Assembly had already approved publication of Sumarokov's article on June 12, it now decided not to allow the publication either of Sumarokov's letter or Trediakovskii's response.²⁷

---

24   Documentary material on Sumarokov's education in the Cadet Corps is contained in the Tsentral'nyi gos. Voenno-istoricheskii Arkhiv (Moscow), f. 314, op. 1, d. 1629, l. 19 ob., 22, 49, 62 etc. (1738); f. 314, № 1850, l. 22 ob. (1739).

25   Of course, we need to beware of mechanically associating time of publication with time of publication; as P. N. Berkov notes of Sumarokov's "Oda Goratsianskaia," it was not written in 1758, when it appeared in *Monthly Compositions*, but in the fall of 1754 (Sumarokov, *Izbrannye proizvedeniia*, 525).

26   *Protokoly zasedanii konterentsii imperatorskoi Akademii nauk s 1725 po 1803 god*, vol. 2 (1744–1770) (St. Petersburg, 1899), 333.

27   *Protokoly zasedanii*, 333. It seems to us that the discussion whether or not to allow Sumarokov's "epistle" to be published relates not to the poem "Epistola (Zhelai, chtob na bregakh sikh muzy obitaly)" that appeared in the August issue of *Monthly Compositions*, as Pekarskii seems to assume (*Istoriia*, 2: 184), but to the "Letter on Sapphic and Horatian Stanzas." The confusion stems from the fact that the Latin "epistola" is used for both words, epistle and letter. L. B. Modzalevskii apparently thought that the discussion concerned a different verse epistle — see his "Lomonosov

Chapter 2. Sumarokov's Reading at the Academy of Sciences Library

It seems no accident that all of the Latin authors from the second part of our list were discussed in the seventh chapter of Tredikovskii's 1752 *Method*, including Catullus, Statius and Claudius Claudian, references to whom we have not been able to find anywhere in Sumarokov's works. Most likely, Sumarokov borrowed these works in order to verify or challenge the views of his opponent.[28] In general, his interest in the classical poets he borrowed (Horace, Catullus, Tibullus, Propertius, Statius, and Claudius Claudian in Latin, and Pindar and eight lyric poets in Greek) could be explained by his desire to reproduce classical meters and stanzas in Russian, stimulated by his disputes with Trediakovskii. His choice of poems to translate and publish in *Monthly Compositions* seems to have mostly been dictated by his desire to outdo his rival.[29] Possibly, his borrowing of the four-volume French edition of Horace (no. 6) was also connected with this effort. The first volume contains a discussion of the problems of translating Horace by the well-known French Latinist André Dacier (1651–1722) which Trediakovskii later cited in his defense against Sumarokov's criticisms.[30] The fact that Sumarokov borrowed an Academy Library catalogue of classical and European poets (no. 8) might also be associated with these issues.

The remaining two works on the list of books Sumarokov borrowed (nos. 13 and 15) are two well-known contemporary reference works for

---

i 'O kachestvakh stikhotvortsa rassuzhdenie' (Iz istorii russkoi zhurnalistiki 1755 g.)" in *Literaturnoe tvorchestvo M. V. Lomonosov: Issledovaniia i materialy* (Moscow, Leningrad: Akademiia nauk SSSR, 1962), 159. Sumarokov's treatise has only been partially preserved in the quotations cited by Trediakovskii in his letter of refutation, first published by Pekarskii in *Istoriia*, 2: 250–257.

[28] In his "Letter" of 1750 Trediakovskii had mocked Sumarokov saying that "clearly... he himself has never heard of the Theban war because Statius hasn't been translated from Latin into French" (Kunik, *Sbornik materialov*, 2: 461).

[29] For example, Sumarokov translated the sonnet by Jacques Des Barreaux (1599–1673), "Dieu, tes jugements sont remplis d'équité" (*Monthly Compositions*, February, 1756, 146) that Trediakovskii had translated earlier for his *New and Short Method* of 1735 (*Sbornik materialov*, 1: 40; cf. Berdnikov, *Schaslivyi feniks*, 74–78). In the same work (1: 72) Trediakovskii had praised Bernard Fontenelle (1657–1757) as "reformer (ispravitel') of the eclogue" and as model for bucolic verse, and Sumarokov's first published eclogue was a translation of Fontenelle's fifth eclogue; it appeared in that same year's *Monthly Compositions* (March, 1756, 268–70).

[30] Pekarskii, *Istoriia*, 254. In 1752 Trediakovskii mentioned Dacier and his wife, the well known translator of Homer and Plutarch Anne Lefevre (d. 1720), as well as "the Jesuit Sanadon" (Noël Etienne Sanadon, 1676–1733), who took part in the 1735 edition of Horace on our list (no. 6). V. K. Trediakovskii, *Sochineniia i perevody*, vol. 2 (St. Petersburg: Akademiia nauk, 1752), viii–ix.

Classicist writers. The first is *L'histoire poëtique, pour l'intelligence des poëtes & des auteurs anciens* by Father Pierre Gautruche (1602–1681), entitled by its English translator as *The Poetical History: Being a Complete Collection of all of the Histories that are Necessary for a Perfect Understanding of Greek and Latin Poets and Other Ancient Authors* (London, 1701) (that is, a collection of mythological plots). It had undergone 17 editions by 1714 and been translated into practically all European languages. The second is the multi-volume collection by Pierre Brumoy (168–1741) entitled *Le theatre des grecs* which contains: the complete Greek tragedies and comedies in French prose translations; excerpts on similar themes from Seneca and modern European Classicists (Corneille, Racine, Jean Rotrou, and the Italians Orsato Giustiniano and Ludovico Dolce, also translated into French); and a series of discussions of Greek theater and its relation to modern dramaturgy. Voltaire remarked that this publication was "one of the best and most useful that we have," and it was also valued by Russian writers.[31] Further exploration of the importance of these books for Sumarokov's oeuvre is the subject for future research.

LIST OF BOOKS THAT SUMAROKOV BORROWED FROM THE ACADEMY OF SCIENCES LIBRARY

Note that in some cases the format of the book given in the list and in eighteenth-century Russian catalogues does not correspond to that given in later bibliographies. Eighteenth-century Russian catalogues were commonly divided into three formats (folio, quarto, and octavo; books of smaller format were grouped with the books in octavo), and the same edition was often published in multiple formats. These formats were not uniform and may

---

[31] Michel Prévost, and Roman d'Amat, ed., *Dictionnaire de biographie française*, fasc. 38 (Paris: Letouzey et Ané, 1954), 506. In his "Letter" criticizing Sumarokov Trediakovskii imagined how he would go about writing a tragedy about Oedipus. "Our author would not take Sophocles in the original, or did not [i.e., if he had already written such a play], because he doesn't know a brass farthing's worth of Greek; but he would get hold of the translation made by either Dacier or the one done by the Jesuit Brumoy (Briumoá)" (Kunik, *Sbornik materialov*, 2: 486). Tredikovskii himself also made used of Brumoy's book (no. 15 on our list). In the last part of his "Treatise on Comedy" (Rassuzhdenie o komedii) of 1752, in a section left out of the printed version he referred to the "original" comedies of Aristophanes which he contrasted to "French copies... all of which I have in the Greek theater [i.e., *Le Théâtre des Grecs*] of the Jesuit Brumoy" (Pekarskii, *Istoriia*, 2: 168–169).

be very close in size, thus easily leading to errors. We also need to keep in mind that (in the words of the report of the Assembly of Professors in 1745) "the printed and compiled catalogues are so defective that they could not be worse."[32]

I. Books Which Sumarokov Borrowed in 1746–1748

The bold face writing following the number reproduces the notations from SPb.O AAN f. 158, op. 1, d. 407, l. 9.[33] There follows a full description of the identified book with bibliographical references.

1. **Sumorokoff. Shakespear's [William] Comedies, histories and Tragedies, Lond. 1685. Fol. — 34.**
   Mr. William Shakespear's comedies, histories, and tragedies. Published according to the true original copies; Unto which is added, seven plays, never before printed in folio: viz. Pericles Prince of Tyre. The London Prodigal. The History of Thomas Lord Cromwel. Sir John Oldcastle Lord Cobham. The Puritan Widow. A Yorkshire Tragedy. The Tragedy of Locrine. 4th ed. London, Printed for H. Herringman, E. Brewster, and R. Bentley... 1685.

   Kam. kat. 34; Brit. Lib. 299:208; Bib. Nat. 171: 818; Nat. Un. Cat. 540: 576; Trésor 6_1: 381; OCLC 213833504. This is the fourth folio edition of Shakespeare. There exist several facsimile editions, including: Dover, NH: D. S. Brewer, 1985 (in RGB) and London: Routledge/Thoemmes Press, 1997.

2. **Sumorocoff. La pharsale de Lucain ou les guerres civiles de César et de Pompée en Vers François p. Mr. de Brebeuf. Paris 1682. 8^0 — 47.**
   [Lucanus, Marcus Annaeus]. La Pharsale de Lucain, ou les Guerres civiles de César et de Pompée. En vers françois. Par mr [Georges] de Brébeuf. A Paris, Chez Jean Cochart, 1682. In 12^0.

   Kam. kat. 47; Brit. Lib. 202: 26; Bib. Nat. 101: 183; Nat. Un. Cat. 344: 111; Trésor 4: 275; OCLC 165673736.

---

[32] *Materialy dlia istorii*, 7: 640.
[33] In reproducing Cyrillic from handwritten and printed documents I have preserved punctuation, spelling, and capitalization, but not orthography, that is, I have replaced ѣ by e, i by и, and eliminated hard signs at the end of words; in Latin script (English and German) I have replaced the old f and ff (ß) by s and ss.

This is French translation of the historical poem "Pharsalia" by Marcus Annaeus Lucanus (Lucan). The first edition came out in 1654. RGB owns the following editions: Leiden, 1658; Paris, 1670; Le Haye, 1683 (all in 12⁰).

3. Sumarocoff. Vondels Treuerspeelen. Amst. 1682. 8⁰ — 105.

Vondels, J. V. [Vondel, Joost Van de(n)]. Treuerspeelen. Begreepen in Twee Deelen. Amsterdam: Kornelis de Bruyn [also: Bruin], 1662 [1661–1665]. 2 vols. in 8⁰.

Kam. kat. 105; Brit. Nat. 200: 764–765; Brit. Lib. 342: 77; Nat. Un. Cat. 642: 276; OCLC 64474906.

Apparently, the reference is to the first volume that contains twelve tragedies by the Dutch dramatist J. V. Vondel: "Palamedes," "Hecuba," "Hippolytus," "Elektra," "Edipus," "Gysbreght van Aemstel," "Maria Stuart," "Leeuwendaelers," "Maeghden," "Peter en Pauweis," "Lucifer," and "Salmoneus." The second volume contains plays based on Old Testament subjects. In Dutch.

BAN has a copy of this first volume that came from the collection of A. Vinius which was incorporated into the Academy Library after his death in 1718 by order of Peter I.[34] Most likely this was the very book that Sumarokov used. The second volume was apparently not in the Academy Library, as the Kam. kat. (as well as later eighteenth century catalogues of the Library) only assign one number to the edition.

4. Sumarocoff. Traduction des Eclogues de Virgile avec des notes critiques. Paris 1708. 8⁰ — 261.

[Virgil (Publius Vergilius Maro)]. Traduction des Églogues de Virgile, aves des notes critiques et historiques, par le P[ere François] Catrou. Paris: Jacques Estienne. 1708. In 12⁰.

Kam. kat. 261; Bib. Nat. 212: 202; Trésor 62: 358; OCLC 83624355.

This French translation and commentary of Virgil's eclogues includes the Latin text as well as the biography of the poet by the Roman grammarian Aelius Donatus, also in Latin.

---

[34] *Slovar' russkikh pisatelei XVIII veka*. Vyp. 1 (Leningrad: Nauka, 1988), 153; *Istoriia biblioteki Akademii nauk SSSR*, 18.

5. Sumarocoff. Virgile Travesty en vers burlesques de M. Scarron. Paris 1651. 8⁰ — 509.

This notation refers either to:
1) the first edition of the sixth book of Paul Scarron's Le Virgile travesty en vers burlesques, de Monsieur Scarron. Livre sixiesme. Paris : Toussaint Quinet, 1651. In 4⁰. [Kam. kat. 509; Scar. 33; Bib. Nat. 164: 483–484; Trésor 62: 366 and 61: 291], or to:
2) the reprint of the first five books (same title) "suivant la copie imprimée à Paris" [Leiden: Elzevier], 1651. In 12⁰ [Scar. 36; Brit. Lib. 291: 326; Nat. Un. Cat. 523: 318; RGB]. The fact that in the "Two Epistles" Sumarokov refers to the famous caricature of Dido from the fourth book might speak in favor of the second, Elzevier, edition.

II. Books Which Sumarokov Borrowed in 1755

Key: **a.** — Notation in boldface type reproduces the notation from the journal for issuing books (zhurnal vydachi knig) from the Academy of Sciences Library in 1755 (SPb.O AAN, f. 158, op. 1, no. 410, l.15–15 ob.).

b. — Reproduction of the entry from the manuscript catalogue of 1751–1753 (SPb.O AAN, f. 158, op. 1, no. 147–167) whose numbers correspond to those in the journal for issuing books. Also in boldface.

c. — Reconstructed modern bibliographical data (where possible), plus annotations and references.

6–8. a. 1755 году марта 21 дня из Библиотеки о<т>пущены гд-ну Сумарокову пять книг in 8ᵛᵒ п<о>д титул ᵒᵐ OEUVRES D. HORACE 4. тома. п<о>д № 295–298, еще п<о>д титул ᵒᵐ Catull. Tibull. propert. scal. № 273. Еще каталог стихотворцам гд-ну Сумарокову [On the margin of the page is written «Poet.,» a reference to the catalogue section «Poetae» in which were included all of the books on this list save no. 14.]

6. a. OEUVRES D. HORACE 4. тома. п<о>д № 295–298.

b. Horatii Flacii. [Opéra.] Amst. 1735. Vol. 1–8. 8⁰ 295 bis 302 [f. 158. on. 1, № 149, l. 109 ob.]

c. [Horace (Horatius Flaccus, Quintus)]. Oeuvres d'Horace en latin, traduites en françois par M. [André] Dacier, et le P[ere Noël Etienne] Sanadon. Avec les remarques critiques, historiques, et géographiques, de l'un et de l'autre. Amsterdam: J. Wetstein et G. Smith. 1735. 8 vols. In 8⁰.

Trésor 3: 354; Nat. Un. Cat. 254: 542; Bib. Nat. 73: 666–667 and Brit. Lib. 152: 361 indicate in 12°; OCLC 221521722. Sumarokov evidently borrowed the first four volumes that contain: Suetonius' life of Horace and André Dacier's essay on translation and commentaries, both in French (vol. 1); and Horace's odes and epodes (Latin text with French prose translation on facing pages, vols. 2–4).

7. a. Еще п<о>д титул^{ом} Catull. Tibull. propert. scal. № 273.

   b. **Catulli, Tibulli & Propertii. Opéra recens. Jos. Scaligero Antw. 1582. 8⁰. 273** [f. 158. on. 1, № 144, l. 14].

   c. [Catullus, Gaius Valerius; Tibullus, Albius; Propertius, Sextus.] Catulli. Tibulli, Propertii, nova editio. Iosephus Scaliger Iul. Caesaris f. recensuit. Eiusdem in eosdem castigationum liber. Ad. Cl. Puteanum Consiliarum Regium in suprema Curia Parisiensi. Antuerpiae, Apud. Aegidium Radaeum. 1582. in 8⁰.

Kam. kat. 272; Trésor 2: 86; Brit. Lib. 56: 343; Bib. Nat. 24: 1245; Nat. Un. Cat. 100: 209; BAH; RGB. This book, all in Latin, includes the poetry of Catullus, four books of Tibullus' elegies,[35] and four books of Propertius' elegies, plus commentaries.

8. a. Еще каталог стихотворцам.

   This most likely refers to an offprint of the section "Poetae, Latini. Germ. Gall. Graeci, &c. Camera N. Repositoria 26. 27. 28," pages 361–414 from the *Bibliothecae Imperialis Petropolitanae*, vol. 1 (St. Petersburg, 1742), the so-called "kamernyi katalog," that was printed in 32 separate sections.[36]

9–13. a. марта 24. Ему же гд-ну Суморокову из поетов шесть книг о<т>пущено in 8vo п<о>д № 291, 345, 530, 509–510, 785, по приложению здесь записок.[37]

9. a. № 291.

   b. **Flemmingii [:Pauli]. Deutsche Poëmata. Mersebl. [sic] 1685. 8⁰. 291** [f. 158. on. 1, № 148, l. 50]

---

[35] Subsequent scholarship has determined that the second pair of these books were ascribed to Tibullus erroneously.
[36] See V. A. Filov, et al., *Svodnyi catalog knig na inostrannykh iazykakh, izdannykh v Rossii v XVIII veka, 1701–1800*, vol. 1 (Leningrad: Nauka, 1984), 130.
[37] These "zapiski" (receipts or notations) have not been preserved.

c. [Fleming (or Flemming), Paul]. Teutsche Poëmata. In Verl[ag] Chr. Kolbens, Buchh. zu Naumberg. Merseburg, druckts Chr. Gottschick F. S. Hosbuchh, Im J[ahr] 1685. in 8⁰.

Kam. kat. 450; Brit. Lib. 110: 137; Trésor 2: 594–595; OCLC 186817964. Collected poetry of the seventeenth-century German poet Paul Flemming. There exists a facimile edition of the first edition of this collection: *Teutsche Poemata* (Lübeck: L. Jauchen, 1642), published by Georg Olms, Hildesheim, 1969 (OCLC 297449883).

10. a. № 345.

b. Flemmingii [:Pauli]. Geistl[iche] u[nd] weltl[iche] Poemata. Jen[a], 1651. 8⁰. 345 [f. 158, on. 1, № 148, l. 50]

c. [Fleming (or Flemming), Paul]. Geist-, und Weltliche Poëmata, Paull Flemmings, Med. D. & Poet. Laur. Caes. Jetzo Auffs neue wieder mit Churf. Sächs. Privilegio aussgefertiget in Verlegung Christian Forbergers seel. Wittibe in Naumberg. Jena Gedruckt bey Georg Sengenwalden, 1651. In 8⁰.

Kam. kat. 65; Bib. Hand. 1: 624; Brit. Lib. 110: 137 ; OCLC 51431188. GBL owns a 1660 edition of this book (OCLC 16914480).

11. a. № 530

b. Flemmingii [:Pauli]. Poëtische Wälder. 8⁰. 530 [f. 158. on. 1, № 148, l. 50; cf. Kam. kat. 258]

c. I have not succeeded in finding a book by Fleming with the title "Poëtische Wälder" in any reference work. In RGB there is a volume of Flemming missing its title page (A 130 / 75), and its first preserved page — the beginning of the first section of the book — bears the title "Erstes Buch Poëtischer Wälder" ("poetic trees" refers to occasional verse, after Statius' "Silvae" — see no. 19). The content of this book matches that of the previous volume (no. 10), so it seems as if the section title may simply have been taken as the title of the book as a whole.

12. a. № 509–510.

b. I have been unable to find the books that correspond to these numbers in the catalogue of 1751–1753 (on which basis the identities of nos. 6–11 and 13–23 were determined).

13. a. № 785.

b. Autruche [O. D.] [sic] L'histoire Poëtique pour Intelligence des Poëtes & auteurs anciens. 8⁰. à Paris 1691. 785 [f. 158, on. 1, № 142, l. 114 06.; № 149, l. 76; cm. Kam. kat. 100 and 385]

c. [Gautruche (or Gaultruche), (Le Pere) Pierre]. L'histoire poétique pour Intelligence des poètes et auteurs anciens. Par le P. P. Gautruche de la Compagnie de Jesus. Paris: Nicolas le Gras, 1691.

Bib de Comp. 3: 1287–1288. This is apparently the twelfth edition of this popular corpus of classical mythology. I have not found this edition listed in other major bibliographies (e.g., Bib. Nat. 58: 397 or Nat. Un. Cat. 193: 20; cf. the eleventh edition of 1683, OCLC 15268679).

14. a. Ему же гд-ну Сумарокову о<т>пущена книга п<о>д титул^{ом} Adami Olearius. Путешествие в Россию и Персию на немецком языке in fol. 1755 марта 29. exotici 55.

c. Olearius, Adam. Offt begehrte Beschreibung Der Newen-Orientalishchen Reise, So durch Gelegenheit einer Holsteinischen Legation an den König in Persien geschehen. Worinnen Derer Orter und Länder durch welche die Reise gangen, als fürnemblich Russland, Tartarien und Persien, sampt ihrer Einwohner Natur, Leben, und Wesen fleissig beschreiben, und mit vielen, Kupfferstücken, so nach dem Leben gestellet gezieret... Schlesswig. Bey Jacob zur Glocken. Im Jahr 1647. in 2⁰ (in fol).

Kam. kat. 55 (Section "Exotica"); Bib. Nat. 126: 897; Nat. Un. Cat. 429: 334; PGB; RGADA; OCLC 220762719. This is the first edition in German of Adam Olearius' travel notes.

15–17. a. 1755: года 2: авgycra, 2 дня о<т>пущено из Библиотеки в дом гд-на полковника Александра Сумаро<ко>ва следующия книги, а именно — п<о>д №
1. Le Theatre des Grecs. № 360–365.
2. Pindari olympia pythia Nemea isthmia № 156.
3. Pindari olympia pythia Nemea isthmia caeterorum octo. № 745.

Оные книги принял Сержант лейб-компании копеист Алексей Дьяконов.

D'iakonov served as copyist in the Leib-kompaniia which Sumarokov had supervised since 1745 as general-adjutant (general's-ad'iutant) to A. G. Razumovskii. The order of August 30, 1756, that established the Russian theater with Sumarokov as its director appointed D'iakonov superintendant of the Golovin House, the residence of the new theater.[38]

15. a. 1. Le Theatre des Grecs. № 360–365.

b. Theatre des Grecs par R. P. Brumoy. Amst. 1732. Vol. 1–6. 8⁰. 360–364 [f. 158, on. 1, № 161, l. 35; apparently, this last number is in error, and should be 365; it is corrected on f.158, on. 1, № 410, l. 15, cited above].

c. [Brumoy, Le Pere Pierre]. Le Théatre des Grecs, Par Le R. P. Brumoy, de la Compagnie de Jesus. A Amsterdam, Aux dépens de la Compagnie. 1732. 6 Vols. In 16⁰.

Bib. de Comp. 2: 246 (as 12⁰); Trésor 1: 552; Nat. Un. Cat. 80: 490; RGB; OCLC 13872450. BAN owns the 3-volume edition of 1730 (in 4⁰). This work contains all of the surviving tragedies of Aeschylus, Sophocles and Euripides; excerpts from plays on similar subjects by Seneca, Corneille, Racine, Jean Rottrou, Orsatto Gustiniano, Lodovico Dolce; the comedies of Aristophanes; and a series of treatises on the Greek theater and its differences from the modern. All of the Greek and Italian plays and excerpts are given in French prose translation.

16. a. 2. Pindari olympia pythia Nemea isthmia № 156.

b. Pindari, Olympia Nemea Pythia, Isthmia, gr. & lat. 1598. 8⁰. 156 [f. 158, on. 1. № 156, l. 79 ob.].

c. [Pindarus.] Pindari Olympia, Pythia, Nemea, Isthmia. Craece & Latine. Latinam interpretationem M. Aemilius P[ortus] Francisci] Porti C[retensis] F[ilius] Linguae Graecae Professor, novissime recognouit, accurate repurgauit, & passim illustrauit. Lyrica Carminum poetarum nouem, lyricae poesews principum, fragmenta: Alcaei, Sapphus, Stesichori, Ibyci, Anacreontis, Bacchylidis, Symonidis, Alcmanis, Pindari, nonulla etiam aliorum, cum Latina interpretatione, partim soluta oratione, partium carmine. Apud

---

[38] V. P. Pogozhev, et al., *Arkhiv Direktsii imperatorskikh teatrov*, vyp. 1 (1746–1801gg.) (St. Petersburg: Direktsiia imperatorskikh teatrov, 1892), otd. II, 54.

Hieronymum Commelinum, elect. palat. typographum, 1598. [Heidelbergae], 1598. In 8⁰.

Kam. kat. 237; Trésor 5: 294; Bib. Nat. 137: 833–834; Brit. Lib. 259: 162; Nat. Un. Cat. 458: 637; BAH; RGB; OCLC65411527. The book contains two parts which contain the four books of Pindar's odes and the poetry of eight other Greek poets (Alcaeus, Sappho, Stesichorus, Ibycus, Anacreon, Bacchylides, Simonides, Alcman); in Greek with Latin commentary.

17. a. 3. pindari olympia pythia Nemea isthmia caeterorum octo. № 745.

b. [Same as 16 b.] **1600. 8⁰. 745** [f. 158. on. 1, № 156, l. 79 ob.]

c. [Pindarus.] Pindari Olympia, Pythia, Nemea, Isthmia. Caeterorum octo lyricorum carmina, Alcaei, Sapphus, Stesichori, Ibyci, Anacreontis, Bacchylidis. Symonidis, Alcmanis, nonulla etiam aliorum. Editio IIII. Graecolatina, H. Steph[ani] recognitione quorundam interpretationis locorum, & accessione lyricorum carmina locupletata. Excudebat Paulus Stephanus. [Geneva]. 1600. In 16⁰.

Kam. kat. 560; Bib. Nat. 137: 831–832; Brit. Lib. 259: 163; Nat. Un. Cat. 458: 637; BAH; PGB; OCLC 8543077. Same contents as 16.

18–23. a. 1755 году августа 24 дня из Библиотеки отпущены Г. Сумарокову следующия книги, а именно
    1. Cl. Claudiani. № 27.
    2. Publii papinii Statii. № 92 NB.³⁹
    3. Statii papinii neapolitani. № 811:
    4. Cl. Claudianus. Theod. pulmani. № 762.   } Poetae in 8ᵛᵒ
    5. P. Papini Statii opera. № 823 NB.
    6. Cl. Claudiani... № 828.

18. a. 1. Cl. Claudiani. № 27.

b. Claudiani Cl. quae extant [sic] cum notis variorum. Amst. **1665. 8⁰. 27** (f. 158, on. 1. № 144, l. 88]

c. [Claudianus, Claudius.] Cl. Claudiani quae exstant. Nic[olaas] Heinsius Dan. Fil. Recensuit ac notas addidit, post primam editionem altera fere parte nunc auctiores. Accedunt selecta Variorum Com-

---

[39] There is no indication what the "nota bene"s refer to.

Chapter 2. Sumarokov's Reading at the Academy of Sciences Library

mentaria, accurante C[ornelisJ S[chrevelio] M. D. Amstelodami. Ex officina Elzeviriana. 1665. In 8^0.

Kam. kat. 133; Bib. Nat. 29: 778–780; Brit. Lib. 63: 449; Nat. Un. Cat. 111: 522; Trésor 2: 194; RGB ; LCCN: 34040605. All of Claudius Claudianus' surviving works with commentaries and biography; in Latin.

19. a. 2. Publii papinii Statii. № 92 NB.

b. Statii [:Papinii] Sylvarum libri 5. Thebaidos libri 12. Achilleidos libri 2 cum notis Variori ex Officina Hackiana Lugd. B. 1671. 8^0'. 92 [f. 158, on. 1, № 160, 1. 61]

c. [Statius. Publius Papinius, et al.] Publii Papinii Statii Sylvarum lib. V. Thebaidos lib. XII. Achilleidos lib. II. Notis selectissimis in Sylvarum libros Dimitii. Morelli, Bernartii, Gevartii, Crucei, Barthii, Joh. Frid. Gronovii Diatribe. In Thebaidos praeterea Placidi Lactantii, Bernartii, &c. quibus in Achilleidos accedunt Maturantii, Britannici, acuratissime illustrati a Johanne Veenhusen. Ex Officina Hackiana: Lugd[uni] Batav[orum] [Leiden], 1671. In 8^0.

Kam. kat. 146; Trésor 14: 481; Brit. Lib. 311: 463; Bib. Nat. 176: 1105; Nat. Un. Cat. 565: 438 ; OCLC13595643. The collected works of the Roman poet Publius Papinius Statius (ca. 45–96), containing: five books of "silvae" (occasional poems); the epic poem "Thebaid" in 12 books and two books of the only partially preserved epic "Achilleid"; commentaries by various authors; and two biographies of Statius. In Latin.

20. a. 3. Statii papinii neapolitani № 811:

b. [The same as no. 18 b.]. **Lugd. 1547. 8^0. 811** [f. 158. on. 1, № 160, l. 61]

c. [Statius. Publius Papinius.] Statii Papinii Neapolitani Sylvarum libr V. Thebaidos lib. XII. Achileeidos lib. II. Apud Seb[astien] Gryphium: Lugduni. 1547. In 16^0.

Kam. kat. 564; Trésor 61: 480 (as 12^0); Brit. Lib. 311: 463; Nat. Un. Cat. 565: 438 ; OCLC 257701358. Same contents as no. 19.

21. a. 4. Cl. Claudianus. Theod. pulmani. № 762.

b. [The same as no. 18 b.]. **Antw. 1596. 8^0. 762** [f. 158. on. 1, № 144, l. 88]

c. [Claudianus, Claudius]. Cl. Claudianus Theod. Pulmanni diligentia. & fide summa. e vetustis codicibus restitutus, una cum M[artiniJ Ant[onii] Del-Rio notis. Ex officina Plantiniana, apud viduam & I[oannem] Moretum: Antuerpiae, 1596. 2 vols. In 16^0.

Kam. kat. 558; Brit. Lib. 63: 448; Nat. Un. Cat. 111: 520; RGB has the edition of 1585 in 16^0. The poetry of the Roman poet Claudian (Claudius Claudianus, d. c. 404) with commentaries. In Latin.

22. a. 5. P. Papini Statii opera. № 823 NB.

b. [The same as no. 20 b.] **Lugd. 1665. 8^0. 823** [f. 160. on. 1, № 160, l. 61]

c. [Statius. Publius Papinius.] P. Papinii Statii Opera. Lugduni, Apud vid. Iacobi Carteron, 1665.

Kam. kat. 414; Nat. Un. Cat. 565 : 431; OCLC 55295141 and 136700690. Same contents as no. 19.

23. a. 6. Cl. Claudiani... № 828.

b. [The same as no. 18 b.] **ex emendatione Heinsii. Amsterd[am]. 1688. 8^0. 828** [f. 158. on. 1, № 144, l. 88]

c. [Claudianus, Claudius]. Cl. Claudianus quae exstant: ex emendatione Nicolai Heinsy Dan. I. Amstelodami. sumptibus Societatis, 1688.

Kam. kat. 426; Nat. Un. Cat. 111:522. OCLC 257672608. All of Claudian's surviving poetry with commentaries. In Latin.

Abbreviations

BAH	—	Biblioteka Rossiiskoi akademii nauk, Otdel redkikh knig, St. Petersburg
Bib. de Comp.	—	Backer, Augustin de. *Bibliothèque de la Compagnie de Jésus*. 1. ptie. *Bibliographie*. 10 vols. Paris, 1890–1900; Bruxelles: Gregg Associates, 1960. (OCLC 40466860)
Bib. Hand.	—	Dünnhaupt, Gerhard. *Bibliographisches Handbuch der Barockliteratur: hundert Personalbibliographien deutscher Autoren des*

Chapter 2. Sumarokov's Reading at the Academy of Sciences Library

	siebzehnten Jahrhunderts. Stuttgart: Hiersemann, 1980. (OCLC 7511780)
Bib. Nat.	— Bibliothèque nationale (France). *Catalogue général des livres imprimés de la Bibliothèque nationale: Auteurs.* Paris: Impr. nationale, 1897–1981. (OCLC 15132380)
Brit. Lib.	— British Library. *The British Library General Catalogue of Printed Books to 1975.* London: C. Bingley; London, New York: K. G. Saur, 1979–1987. (OCLC 5688739)
d.	— archival unit (delo)
f.	— archival fund (fond)
Kam. kat.	— *Bibliothecae Imperialis Petropolitanae.* Pars. 1–4. St. Petersburg, 1741–1742. All catalogue numbers on the list refer to the section "Poetae. Latini. Germ. Gall. Graeci. &c.," pp. 316–414, except for no. 14, which refers to the section "Exotica." The so-called "Kamernyi katalog."
l.	— archival page, folio (list)
LCCN	— Library of Congress Control Number
Nat. Un. Cat.	— *The National Union Catalog, Pre-1956 Imprints.* 754 vols. London : Mansell, 1968–1981. (LCCN 67030001)
OCLC	— Online Computer Library Center (book number)
ob.	— reverse side of archival page, verso (oborotnaia storona)
op.	— archival inventory (opis')
RGADA	— Arkhivokhranilishche staropechatnykh i redkikh izdanii, Rossiiskii gosudarstvennyi Arkhiv drevnikh aktov, Moscow.
RGB	— Muzei redkikh knig, Rossiiskaia gosudarstvennaia biblioteka, Moscow.
Scar.	— Magne, Émile. *Bibliographie générale des œuvres de Scarron, documents inédits.* Paris: L. Giraud-Badin, 1924. (LCCN 25010851)
SPb.O AAN	— Sankt Peterburgskoe otdelenie Arkhiva Rossiiskoi Akademii nauk
Trésor	— Graesse, Johann Georg Theodor. *Trésor de livres rares et précieux ou nouveau dictionnaire bibliographique...* 7 vols. Dresden, Kuntze, 1859–1869. (OCLC179946578)

3

CENSORSHIP AND PROVOCATION:
The Publishing History of Sumarokov's "Two Epistles"

Critics have long recognized the importance of Sumarokov's "Two Epistles"[1] on the Russian language and on poetry not only as "the manifesto of Russian Classicism" but as a programmatic work that in many respects mapped out the writer's own further career.[2] However, there still exists no critical edition of this work.[3] Analysis of the manuscript of the "Two Epistles" preserved in the Petersburg branch of the Academy of Sciences Archive (Razriad II,

---

[1] *Dve epistoly: V pervoi predlagaetsia o ruskom iazyke, a vo vtoroi o stikhotvorstve* (St. Petersburg: Akademiia nauk, 1748).

[2] N. Bulich, *Sumarokov i sovremennaia emu kritika* (St. Petersburg, 1854), 116, 132, 414–42; P. N. Berkov, "Zhiznennyi i literaturnyi put' A. P. Sumarokova," in A. P. Sumarokov, *Izbrannye proizvedeniia*, ed. P. N. Berkov. Biblioteka poeta, Bol'shaia seriia (Leningrad: Sovetskii pisatel', 1957), 23–36; G. N. Pospelov, "Sumarokov i problema russkogo klassitsizma," *Uchenye zapiski MGU*, vyp. 120, Trudy kafedry russkoi literatury, 3 (1948), 221–223; D. M. Lang, "Boileau and Sumarokov: The Manifesto of Russian Classicism," *Modern Language Review*, 43 (October 1948): 500–506; O. V. Orlov and V. I. Fedorov, *Russkaia literatura XVIII veka* (Moscow, 1973), 128–130; A. M. Peskov, *Bualo v russkoi literature XVIII — pervoi treti XIX veka* (Moscow, 1989), 23–30. Joachim Klein challenges the notion of the work as a "manifesto of Russian Classicism" in "Russkii Bualo? (Epistola Sumarokova "O stikhotvorstve" v vospriiatii sovremennikov)," *XVIII vek*, 18 (1993), 40–58.

[3] Following Novikov's editions of Sumarokov (1781–2 and 1787) the "Two Epistles" weren't published again in full, including the "Notes," until Berkov's edition of 1957 cited in note 2 (pp. 112–129). In this edition, as in the earlier *Stikhotvoreniia* (Biblioteka poeta, malaia seriia, Leningrad, 1953), Berkov took note of the first attempt give a critical description of the manuscript of "Two Epistles" by V. I. Rezanov in "Rukopisnye teksty sochinenii A. P. Sumarokova," *Izvestiia Otdeleniia russkogo iazyka i slovesnosti*, 3 (St. Petersburg, 1904), 37–40 (and separate edition, St. Petersburg, 1904). G. P. Blok gives a short history of the censoring of the work in his notes to M. V. Lomonosov, *Polnoe sobranioe sochinenii*, 11 vols. (Moscow: AN SSSR, 1950–835), 9: 938–939 (hereafter cited as *PSS* plus volume and page number).

Chapter 3. Censorship and Provocation: History of Sumarokov's "Two Epistles"

op. 1, № 132) reveals significant new information both about the materials that were not included into the final published text and also concerning the work's complex censorship history. The manuscript includes all of the changes Sumarokov made in the text from his first submission for publication to the Academy of Sciences' typography until the time it was finally typeset. The goal of this article is to piece together the history of the "Two Epistles"' editing on the basis of this manuscript, analyzing all of the added and omitted material as well as the other changes in the text, trying to put them into context of the literary practices of the time.

The changes Sumarokov made in the epistles were directly connected to the process of having them published by the Academy typography. At the start of his career this was "practically the sole institution in the whole of Russia that published books of secular content," that possessed not only printing presses but also the single existing commercial network for bookselling.⁴ After the adoption of the Academy's new regulations (reglament) in 1747, given the absence of a special article on censorship the right to approve works for publication fell to the Academy's administration, that is, directly to the Academy president, Count K. G. Razumovskii, or, as was more often the case, to the Academy Chancellery that was subordinate to him. When Sumarokov wanted to publish his first tragedy "Khorev" on October 28, 1747, he addressed himself directly to Razumovskii, who was also brother of Sumarokov's superior and the morganatic husband of Empress Elizabeth, A. G. Razumovskii. Permission to publish was given quickly, apparently without any review of the text.⁵ However, after a year, when Sumarokov submitted his second tragedy, "Gamlet" (Hamlet), the Academy Chancellery turned it over for review to Academy members "to determine...whether or not there is anything blameworthy in it," adding that "as far as the style, it may remain as it is written."⁶ The Chancellery demanded the review in twenty-four hours,

---

4   D. V. Tiulichev, "Tsenzura izdanii Akademii nauk v XVIII v.," *Sbornik statei i materialov po knigovedeniiu*, vol. 2 (Leningrad, 1970), 72.

5   *Materialy dlia istorii imperatorskoi Akademii nauk*, vol. 8 (1746–1747) (St. Petersburg, 1895), 581, 585. In connection with the publication of Sumarokov's "Slovo pokhval'noe o gosudare imperatore Petre Velikom" (1759) Razumovskii "was so good as to order that the aforementioned 'Pokhval'noe slovo' be printed due to the persistent demand of mister author [i.e., Sumarokov], reasoning that even before...many of his works were printed without Academy censorship" (Arkhiv Rossiiskoi Akademii nauk, no. 239, ll.50–51, quoted from D. S. Shamrai and P. N. Berkov, "K tsenzurnoi istorii 'Trudoliubivoi pchely' A. P. Sumarokova," *XVIII vek*, 5 [1965], 405).

6   *Materialy dlia istorii imperatorskoi Akademii nauk*, vol. 9 (1748–1749) (St. Petersburg, 1897), 457.

"a condition unprecedented in Academy practice."[7] But the most surprising, even potentially fatal circumstance was that the Chancellery turned the job of reviewing Sumarokov's works over to his two most prominent literary rivals, Trediakovskii and Lomonosov, who, unlike Sumarokov, were professors and Academy members. The fact that Trediakovskii and Lomonosov were made Sumarokov's censors, and in particular of the "Two Epistles," which contained criticism of them, greatly problematized the process of censoring.

In his report on "Hamlet" of October 10, 1748, Trediakovskii approved the play, and even praised it somewhat, calling it better than "Khorev" and "quite good" (dovol'no izriadnaia), although he added that "as in the author's first tragedy, as in this new one, there is an uneven style throughout, that is, in some places it is overly Slavonic for the theater and in others much too low, in street [style], and there are also many grammatical defects." Despite his instructions, he proposed a series of stylistic, semantic, and grammatical corrections and revisions, which he wrote in pencil on the back side of the manuscript pages.[8] Lomonosov gave his approval without any comment.[9] Then, as G. P. Blok has written, "after having familiarized himself with the reviews, in three days Sumarokov returned the manuscript to the Chancellery, having made some corrections but also having assiduously erased Trediakovskii's penciled suggestions, leaving only the underlining [that corresponded to them]," which he instructed the typesetters to ignore.[10] On October 14, the same day Sumarokov resubmitted the manuscript and requested an official order to have it published, the Chancellery granted permission. The document mentioned Lomonosov's approval and K. G. Razumovskii's "approbation," but said nothing about Trediakovskii's review.[11] The play came out on December 1.

Two days after finishing his review of "Hamlet," Trediakovskii received a new assignment from the Chancellery: to review the "Two Epistles" and to get Lomonosov's opinion of them. In his report of October 12 he wrote:

---

[7] Lomonosov, *PSS*, 9, 937. Blok suggests that this was due to "Sumarokov's prominent position in the service."

[8] Lomonosov, *PSS*, 9, 937. "If the author sees fit," Trediakovskii wrote, "let them serve for his use, but if they do not please him, I beg pardon for my well intentioned audacity; because I have not blackened out his own verses or harmed them [i.e., made them illegible]." *Materialy*, 9, 461.

[9] Lomonosov, *PSS*, 9, 620; *Materialy*, 9, 461

[10] Lomonosov, *PSS*, 9, 937. The manuscript of "Gamlet" is located in the Petersburgskoe otdelenie Arkhiva Rossiiskoi Akademii nauk, Razriad II, op. 1, no. 62.

[11] *Materialy*, 9, 479–80.

Chapter 3. Censorship and Provocation: History of Sumarokov's "Two Epistles"

> I am of the following opinion of them, namely, that however good they are, and however worthy of publication, they could have been even better and more worthy if there was less satire in them, especially in the first, and if it were more like an epistle. In it there is such great acrimoniousness that it is not so much writers' vices that are stigmatized as writers themselves, so that the vocative case is used for [addressing] one, and practically [by] his own name, according to the example of the so-called ancient Aristophanic comedies, which by the way were also strictly forbidden by the authorities in Athens at the time, as we see from history. But perhaps the privilege of poetic license will be cited against this, my opinion, however there is a danger that this license will grow into obduracy (svoevol'nost'); for as Cicero says in his Letter to Servius Sulpicius [Rufus] (Servii Sul'[p]itsii) bk. 4, that which is done as a trial people think has been done by right; so they try little by little to go even further and do as much as they can themselves.[12]

Trediakovskii's objection is two-fold: on the one hand, he charges Sumarokov with violating the boundaries of the genre, turning an epistle into a satire; and secondly, he asserts that his satirical manner is impermissible insofar as it is directed at personalities (in this case, at Trediakovskii himself!).

What exactly did Trediakovskii take so personally? It is hard to say with full certainty, and scholars have been of varying opinions. There are several places in the epistles where Sumarokov polemicizes with Trediakovskii's literary and theoretical positions (for example, the criticism of his songs in the second epistle[13]). But Trediakovskii had written that the epistles "could have been even better and more worthy if in them, *especially in the first*, there was less satire." He was apparently referring to the following passage:[14]

> Один, последуя несвойственному складу,
> Влечет в Германию Российскую Палладу
> И, мня, что тем он ей приятства придает,
> Природну красоту с лица ея берет.

---

[12] P. Pekarskii, *Istoriia imperatorskoi Akademii nauk v Peterburge*, vol. 2 (St. Petersburg, 1873), 131–32. Apparently Trediakovskii was referring to Cicero's Letter to Servius Sulpicius Rufus (In Achaia), no. 18, from the fourth book of his Letters, but I find no such idea expressed there.

[13] See I. Z. Serman, *Russkii klassitsizm: Poeziia, Drama, Satira* (Leningrad, 1973), 118–119.

[14] P. N. Berkov thought that Trediakovskii's complaint was due to the four lines concerning "Shtivelius" cited below (*Literaturnaia polemika*, 95), which Sumarokov apparently only added after the first review of the manuscript. But in any case Trediakovskii's objection was to the first and not to the second epistle.

> Другой, не выучась так грамоте, как должно,
> По-русски, думает, всего сказать не можно,
> И, взяв пригоршни слов чужих, сплетает речь
> Языком собственным, достойну только сжечь.
> Иль слово в слово он в слог русский переводит,
> Которо на себя в обнове не походит. (I, 21–30)[15]

According to P. N. Berkov, the first four lines refer to Academy translators, although the opinion of earlier commentators that they were about Lomonosov, who had started to write poetry in Germany, and under the influence of German verse, seems more convincing.[16] However this may be, as Berkov noted, Lomonosov evidently did not take the lines personally. In the lines that follow it is easier to recognize Trediakovskii. As a response to Trediakovskii's championing of the principle of maximally accurate translation (see, for example, the preface to his *Sochineniia i perevody* of 1752), in the first epistle Sumarokov expressed a strong affirmation of "free translation" (see also I, 75–80).[17]

After the lines cited above, Sumarokov revised lines 31 and 32:[18]

> тот прозой скаредной стремится
> [иной витийствуя возшедши / или: «стихами» /] к небесам,
> и хитрости своей
> [читая что писал] не понимает сам.

In the first version (that is, before the crossing out) the criticism was addressed at a different writer from that described in the previous lines ("*inoi*

---

[15] In citing the epistles, "I" indicates the "Epistle on the Russian Language," "II" — the "Epistle on Poetry," followed by an Arabic numeral indicating the line(s). Citations are from A. P. Sumarokov, *Polnoe sobranie vsekh sochinenii*, ed. N. I. Novikov, 10 vols. (Moscow, 1781–82), 1, 329–356 (hereafter *PSVS*).

[16] Sumarokov, *Izbrannye sochineniia*, 527. Cf. Bulich, *Sumarokov*, 57; Pekarskii, *Istoriia*, 2, 133–134; A. P. Sumarokov, *Stikhotvoreniia*, ed. A. S. Orlov. Biblioteka poeta, Bol'shaia seriiia (Leningrad, 1935), 432.

[17] M. H. Berman, "Trediakovskij, Sumarokov and Lomonosov as Translators of Western European Literature," Diss., Harvard University, 1971, 110.

[18] In quoting the manuscript of the "Two Epistles," we preserve the punctuation, stress marks, and capitalization, but not the orthography, which differs significantly even from the published text. When we cite lines from the published text, we cite that text and not the manuscript. Here and below material in square brackets indicates that it has been crossed out in the manuscript.

Chapter 3. Censorship and Provocation: History of Sumarokov's "Two Epistles"

vitiistvuia vozshedshii k nebesam"); this might even have been Lomonosov, especially if we read *stikhami* in place of *vozshedshii*. But in the revised text these lines are a continuation of the criticism of the bad translator-writer and serve as bridge to the following added segment (ll. 33–34; in the manuscript on l. 2 rev.), where the hints at Trediakovskii are quite transparent:

> Тот прозой скаредной стремится к небесам
> И хитрости своей не понимает сам.
> Тот прозой и стихом ползет, и письма оны,
> Ругаючи себя, дает писцам в законы.
> Хоть знает, что ему во мзду смеется всяк,
> Однако он своих не хочет видеть врак.
> Пускай, он думает, меня никто не хвалит.
> То сердца моего нимало не печалит:
> Я сам себя хвалю, на что мне похвала?
> И знаю то, что я искусен до зела.
> Зело, зело, зело, дружок мой, ты искусен,
> Я спорить не хочу, да только склад твой гнусен.
> Когда не веришь мне, спроси хотя у всех:
> Всяк скажет, что тебе пером владети, грех.

Sumarokov could have taken the image of a vain and talentless poet from Boileau, but his barbs, directed here at Trediakovskii and at his *Conversation Between a Foreigner and a Russian About Orthography* (*Razgovor mezhdu chuzhestrannym chelovekom i Rossiiskim ob ortografii*) (St. Petersburg, 1748), in which he defended the use of the letter "zelo" (Ѕ) in place of "zemlia" (З or Ꙁ) were so effective that subsequently, in the words of B. A. Uspenskii, the phrase "zeló zeló" (meaning, "very very") became a "mark of identification signaling a polemical attack on Trediakovskii."[19]

While it is possible that Sumarokov added these lines after Trediakovskii's negative review of October 12,[20] it seems more probable that Trediakovskii's angry words referred to these already added lines, in which the references to him were very clear and he was labeled "practically by his own name." That is, Sumarokov added them before the review, most probably, during those two days after he received Trediakovskii's "corrected" version of "Hamlet" (October 10), but before he submitted the "Two Epistles" for

---

[19] B. A. Uspenskii, "K istorii odnoi epigrammy Trediakovsogo (Epizod iazykovoi polemiki serediny XVIII veka)," *Russian Linguistics*, 8:2 (1984), 113.
[20] As G. N. Blok suggests, Lomonosov, *PSS*, 9, 938–939.

review, apparently on October 11 or 12.[21] That the added lines concern Trediakovskii's inability to understand questions of style support the hypothesis that Sumarokov was getting back at Trediakovskii for his unsolicited criticism of "Hamlet."

On the same October 12, Lomonosov wrote his response to Trediakovskii's letter that included the "Two Epistles," that has not survived. He wrote that "one could advise the writer of these epistles in a friendly way not to rush them into print, and that he himself should find some way that he could somewhat alter (otmenit' neskol'ko) his argumentation concerning certain persons."[22] Although Lomonosov warned Trediakovskii that in absence of an official request from the Chancellery he was responding "only to your letter," Trediakovskii nevertheless submitted Lomonosov's answer to the Chancellery on the same day, together with his own negative recommendation.

The matter ended here for now, but a month later, on November 9, Sumarokov again renewed his request to publish the epistles, as in the analogous letter of October 14 concerning "Hamlet," referring only to the approval of Academy president K. G. Razumovskii. By this time, he had made some other changes in the work. In a resolution dated the same November 9, the Chancellery ordered the publication, "following certification (svidetel'stvo) by professors Trediakovskii and Lomonosov."[23] However, in his second review, Trediakovskii stated that "although they have been somewhat corrected, the acrimoniousness in them has not only not been eliminated but has even been increased. Therefore, in view [of the fact] that they are indeed malicious satires and only epistles in name, and [hence] defaming that kind of work, in all impartial conscience I cannot approve them...However, there is nothing in these epistles against the law or the state."[24] Trediakovskii passed the epistles on to Lomonosov for

---

[21] Blok argues (Lomonosov, *PSS*, 9, 938) that the epistles must have been submitted for publication to the Chancellery "by an unofficial route," since there is no record of this in the official chancellery records. Because of this, we also don't know exactly when they were submitted, but this was clearly before October 12, when Trediakovskii wrote his review.

[22] P. S. Biliarskii, *Materialy dlia biografii Lomonosova* (St. Petersburg, 1865), 115–116; Pekarskii, *Istoriia*, 2, 132; Lomonosov, *PSS*, 10, 460–461.

[23] *Materialy*, 9, 598–99.

[24] *Materialy*, 9, 535. In his "Letter...Written from a Friend to a Friend" of 1750 Trediakovskii repeated that Sumarokov, "after the insults and barbs...employed in his epistles not only not considered it proper not to get rid of them, but increased them and to some extent [made them] worse and even more intolerable" (*Sbornik materialov dlia*

Chapter 3. Censorship and Provocation: History of Sumarokov's "Two Epistles"

a second review, and after a week, on November 17, Lomonosov attested that "they contain many wonderful verses providing just rules about poetry. The satirical verses which are included in them do not concern anything important, but only contain criticism of some bad writers without their names. And since this kind of poetry touching the improvement of the verbal arts, aside from the satire that all civilized peoples allow, and among the Russian people the Satires of Prince Antiokh Dmitrievich Kantemir were received with general approbation...I reason that the above mentioned epistles may be published according to the author's wishes."[25] Apparently, in force of this one positive review, the "Two Epistles" were sent to be typeset on December 5 and printed by December 14. This may have been one of the only instances in history when the number of objectionable places was increased due to censorship rather than the reverse.

The question of Sumarokov's relationship to his censor-rivals is closely tied up with the other changes he made in the "Two Epistles" after the first review.[26] In the first place, in the concluding lines of the second epistle appeared a strongly-worded evaluation of his two colleagues (II. 389–392; l. 22 rev.):

> ... Возьми гремящу лиру
> И с пышным Пиндаром взлетай до небеси,
> Иль с Ломоносовым глас громкий вознеси:
> Он наших стран Мальгерб: он Пиндару подобен:
> А ты, Штивелиус, лишь только врать способен.

Some scholars consider the compliment to Lomonosov back-handed, insofar as in Boileau's scheme Malherbe occupies a mostly historical, outmoded place, and L. B. Pumpianskii even suggested that "from this [passage] one

---

   istorii imp. Akademii nauk v XVIII veke, ed. A. A. Kunik., vol. 2 [St. Petersburg, 1865], 621). On this, see: "Slander, Polemic, Criticism: Trediakovskii's "Letter...Written from a Friend to a Friend" of 1750 and the Problem of Creating Russian Literary Criticism," chap. 4 below.
25 *Materialy*, 9, 554–55; Lomonosov, *PSS*, 9, 621.
26 Most of the changes were apparently made between the first and second reviews, but it is also possible that Sumarokov made some of them even later; he probably also made some minor changes on the galley proofs (that have not been preserved). Among the latter were probably some orthographic changes, typographical errors and minor stylistic editing. See Rezanov, "Rukopisnye teksty," 37–40. In his article "Otvet na kritiku" Sumarokov himself noted two misprints in the second epistle (II,7: "tokmo" instead of "tamo," and II, 89: the word "sklad" was left out) (*PSVS*, 10, 119).

could derive an accusation of plagiarism."[27] This does not seem correct. Elsewhere Sumarokov refers to Malherbe with respect, as in the revised version of the "Two Epistles," "Nastavlenie khotiashchim byti pisateliami" (Instructions for Would-Be Writers) of 1774, in which he stands together with Racine and Molière ("Стихосложение не зная прямо мер, / Не мог бы быть Малгерб, Расин и Молиер" [Without knowing versification properly / One can't become a Malherbe, Racine or Molière]), and in the "Notes" to the epistles themselves Sumarokov changed the description of Malherbe as "a very good (ves'ma khoroshii) lyric" to the more positive "renowned (slavnyi) lyric" (l.9) — this last addition probably in connection with the comparison to Lomonosov that he had added.

Lomonosov is the single Russian writer named in the "Two Epistles," and the reference to him is even more emphasized by its placement in the work's concluding lines. He is contrasted as "the great Russian poet" to the pitiable, comic Trediakovskii — "Shtivelius."[28] This is also underscored by another addition to the manuscript "Notes" (l. 10). Sumarokov here replaced the phrase "very good" with the word "great" and also added a sentence about his academic position ("Member and professor of chemistry of the Petersburg Academy of Sciences and historical assembly"); in the final published version, however, Lomonosov is labeled as only a "good lyric [poet]." While one may seek grounds for future disagreements between Sumarokov and Lomonosov in the "Two Epistles," for example in Sumarokov's criticism of "rhetoric" and defense of "simplicity," in other places one may see further approval for Lomonosov as a poet, e.g. the possible reference to his epic poem on Peter the Great (II, 112) or in his own "purely Lomonosovian evaluation of the ode."[29] Hence apart from the questionable indirect criticism of Lomonosov in the first epistle ("Odin...vlechet v Gemaniiu Rossiiskuiu Palladu"), which

---

[27] L. V. Pumpianskii, "Ocherki po literature pervoi poloviny XVIII veka," XVIII vek, [1] (Leningrad, Moscow, 1935), 111–12; cf. P. N. Berkov, *Vvedenie v izuchenie istorii russkoi literatury XVIII veka* (Leningrad, 1964), 22–3; Berkov cites an unpublished paper by G. A. Gukovskii. On the equivocal place of Pindar and Malherbe in Russian Classicism and in debates over the Russian literary language, see V. M. Zhivov, *Iazyk i kul'tura v Rossii XVIII veka* (Moscow: Iazyki russkoi kul'tury, 1996), via the index.

[28] On the parodic name "Shtivelius" and its sources see M. I. Sukhomlinov's notes in M. V. Lomonosov, *Sochineniia*, vol. 2 (St. Petersburg, 1893), 391–99. B. A. Uspenskii suggests that Sumarokov may have borrowed the name from Lomonosov — see "K istorii," 113n. On the mythological opposition between "great poet" and "pitiful fool" as applied to Lomonosov and Trediakovskii, see Irina Reyfman, *Vasilii Trediakovsky: The Fool of the New Russian Literature* (Stanford: Stanford UP, 1990).

[29] Berkov, *Lomonosov i literaturnaia polemika*, 71.

Chapter 3. Censorship and Provocation: History of Sumarokov's "Two Epistles"

Lomonosov could easily pass over, Lomonosov occupied a very positive position in the epistles. As we suggest below, it seems likely that Sumarokov made some alterations in the epistles on the advice of Lomonosov, with whom Sumarokov was at the time in friendly relations, to the point that Trediakovskii could even suspect that (in Berkov's words) "the instigator of the satirical attacks against him in the epistles was Lomonosov" himself.[30]

The last barb against Trediakosvkii is connected to ten lines on the Russian language and its connection to Church Slavonic which Sumarokov eliminated from the first epistle. As Boris Uspenskii has shown, Sumarokov was polemicizing with Trediakovskii's linguistic position as expressed especially in the *Conversation…About Orthography*. Sumarokov made several changes to that part of the first epistle that describes the relationship of the literary and conversational languages. Firstly, he crossed out the following four lines after I, 60 ("S otsutstvuiushchimi obychnu rech' vedet"):

Она составлена быть должно без витеек;
Нет хуже ни чево ненадобных затеек,
Нам можно всяко их писать как мы хотим;
Однако должно так, как просто говорим. (l. 3)

He replaced these with the following:

быть должно без затей и [ясно непременно.]
  [кратко сочиненно] кратко сочиненно
        ясно
[Какое бы мнение в ней] [точно положенно]
        изъясненно
Как просто говорим, так просто [непременно].
Но кто ненаучен исправно говорить,
Тому не без труда и грамотку сложить. (l. 2 rev.)

(That is, in the final published version:

Быть должно без затей и кратко сочиненно,
Как просто говорим, так просто изъясненно.
Но кто не научен исправно говорить,
Тому не без труда и грамотку сложить.)

---

[30] Berkov, *Lomonosov i literaturnaia polemika*, 95–6; on the good relations between Sumarokov and Lomonosov during this period, see 68–71.

Sumarokov is making two points here: first, that correct speech should not be weighted down with excess ornament, and second, that good oral speech should serve as the basis for the literary language. In editing this passage he replaced the idea that "each of us may write as we wish" ("simply as we speak") with the stricter demand that a writer have the necessary education. As V. M. Zhivov has shown, reference to the conversational tongue as basis for the literary language was a tribute to the reigning French purist theory but in the Russian context (in which there was no conversational norm) essentially a fiction.[31] The notion of writing "simply as we speak" is progressively undercut by references to book learning, and especially to the vital educational function of Church Slavonic:

Перенимай у тех, хоть много их, хоть мало,
Которых тщание искусству ревновало,
И показало им, коль мысль сия дика,
Что не имеем мы богатства языка.
Сердись, что мало книг у нас, и делай пени:
Когда книг русских нет, за кем идти в степени?
Однако больше ты сердися на себя
Иль на отца, что он не выучил тебя.
А если б юность ты не прожил своевольно;
Ты б мог в писании искусен быть довольно.
Трудолюбивая пчела себе берет,
Отвсюду, то, что ей потребно в сладкий мед,
И посещающа благоуханну розу,
Берет в свои соты частицы и с навозу.
Имеем сверх того духовных много книг:
Кто винен в том, что ты Псалтыри не постиг,
И бегучи по ней, как в быстром море судно,
С конца в конец раз сто промчался безрассудно. (I, 113–30)

Sumarokov later entitled his literary journal *Trudoliubivaia pchela* (The Industrious Bee), emphasizing perhaps the eclecticism of his literary and linguistic position which would combine elements of the bookish Church Slavonic language with Russian vernacular speech. The bee metaphor, of course, is quite ancient, and widespread in the classical and Orthodox literary

---

31 *Iazyk i kul'tura*, 177–79, 291f, 327, 440, and via the index. Zhivov (292) rejects Uspenskii's view that in the epistles Sumarokov "appears...as true follower of that linguistic program that was formulated by Trediakovskii (together with Adodurov) in the 1730's, and which Trediakovskii renounced in the second half of the 1740's" (B. A. Uspenskii, "K istorii," 102). The program of the 1730's was based on that very nonexistent conversational usage and on rejecting Church Slavonic.

Chapter 3. Censorship and Provocation: History of Sumarokov's "Two Epistles"

traditions. After the passage above come ten lines that are crossed out in which Sumarokov continues to defend the Church Slavonic literary tradition as source for modern Russian:

> На нашем языке, хоть нечто темно в ней;
> Познать /или: «Но знать»?/ согласие и красота речей
> Как писана она в творении преславно.
> Есть нечто, что совсем преведено изправно,
> Из Греческих нам книг в приятии их веры.
> Довольны ли тебе толь к ученье те примеры?
> Ты скажешь: что там чту, я не пойму таво,
> И что там писана, не знаю ничево,
>   Ты скажешь: я книжну
> [(Я?)книжну] языку и сроду не учился.
> Начто ево учить, коль Русским ты роди́лся? (ll. 5-6)

Significantly, Sumarokov defends the "harmony and beauty" of the Church Slavonic language despite its "something obscure" (nechto temno) (which Trediakovskii had condemned in the foreword to the *Voyage to the Island of Love*[32]) and points to books written in this tongue as example of correct translation and model for emulation. While Sumarokov orients himself (at least in theory) on the vernacular speech of enlightened society, he rejects the young Trediakovskii's view that Russian and Church Slavonic are two separate languages. In the epistles Sumarokov refers to Church Slavonic as "Russian" and as "our language," that is, he sees both as part of a larger "Slaveno-Russian" (Slavenorossiiskii) unity.[33] See in the final version I, 135–139:

> Не мни, что наш язык, не тот, что в книгах чтем,
> Которы мы с тобой не Русскими зовем.
> Он тот же, а когда б он был иной, как мыслишь
> Лишь только оттого, что ты его не смыслишь,
> Так чтож осталось бы при Русском языке?

That Sumarokov had Trediakovskii in mind when he eliminated these lines is shown by two other lines which were to replace the fifth and sixth lines of the passage cited earlier on this page:

---

32 See Uspenskii, "K istorii," 75, 105, 124. Uspenskii suggests that Trediakovskii's use of the epithet "temnyi" refers back to Feofan Prokopovich.
33 On "Slavenosossiiskii," see Zhivov, *Iazyk i kul'tura*, chap. 3.

Из греческих нам книг, для чтения в церквах;
Но то арабския слова́ в твоих [глаза́х] уша́х. (l. 5 rev.)

The second line is a clear swipe at Trediakovskii and foreshadows Sumarokov's comedy *Tresotinius* of 1750 in which Trediakovskii is pilloried as a conceited pedant who boasts of his knowledge of esoteric languages, including Arabic. As in this passage, Sumarokov makes fun of his rival's claim that serious knowledge of foreign languages is a basic requirement for any literary activity. And as in the play, the debate over language and literature is reduced to an *ad hominem* attack.

It seems likely that Sumarokov added these lines after Trediakovskii's first review, and then, when he cut the ten lines about language cited earlier, he decided to eliminate these two as well. It is also possible that he cut the lines only after the second review. This, together with the line about Shtivelius at the end, would explain Trediakovskii's complaint that the "insults and barbs" had been increased and turned the epistles into "malicious satires."

The cited passages that were cut from the "Two Epistles" emphasize the importance of the "old" religious literary tradition as source for the literary language and for education—an unusual position, it may seem, for a European enlightener. That may even be the reason he cut them. The impropriety of discussing the religious literary tradition may also have been a factor in another major excision from the "Two Epistles"—the eight lines that come after I, 74, concerning religious oratory (on ll. 3–4). In this passage Sumarokov gives a short history of rhetoric:

В том древний
[Лет древних] Демосфе́н в пример быть может дан,
Лет   [посл после]
[Из] средних, Златоу́ст, [из новых Феофан] последних, Феофа́н,
Последователь сей пресладка Цицерона,
И красноречия российского корона.
Хоть в чистом слоге он и часто погрешал;
Но красноречия премного показал.
Он ри́тор из числа во всей Евро́пе главных,
Как Мо́сгейм, Бурдалу́, между мужей пресдавных.[34]

---

[34] Part of this passage is cited by Blok and Makeeva in Lomonosov, *PSS*, 7, 821. For Sumarokov's corresponding notes on the figures named here, that were also cut, see below.

Chapter 3. Censorship and Provocation: History of Sumarokov's "Two Epistles"

Why did Sumarokov eliminate this passage from the "Two Epistles"? Several explanations are possible. In the first place, this is the single place in the epistles where Sumarokov describes a literary tradition in such historical detail; here he cites classical, medieval and modern orators, and indeed these are the only writers he cites by name in the first epistle at all. For these formal reasons he might have found the passage inappropriate. But this does not explain why he decided to exclude oratory in the epistles altogether. This might have been to emulate Boileau more closely, as the French author had not only not touched on oratory in *L'Art poétique* (understandably as oratory is not poetry) but also made denigrating reference to Christian literature; arguably, discussion of oratory is also out of place in an epistle on language. G. N. Blok and V. N. Makeeva suggest that Sumarokov made the cut on the advice of Lomonosov, who had recently eliminated reference to Feofan Prokopovich from his *Short Guide to Oratory*. In their words, "both of them evidently found it out of place to praise the talent of an orator in print who 'in purity of style often sinned.'"[35] If this is the case, it also explains why Sumarokov cut another twelve lines from the second epistle concerning Prokopovich and Kantemir that Berkov decided to reinstate in his editions of Sumarokov of 1953 and 1957.[36] In this passage both writers receive low ratings as poets: Kantemir "Стремился на Парнас, но не было успеха… / Однако был Пегас всегда под ним ленив" (strove to Parnassus but without success… / Pegasus was always lazy beneath him); and Prokopovich, although "красой словенского народа, / Что в красноречии касалось до него, / Достойного в стихах не сделал ничего" (ornament of the Slavic people, / As far as it concerns oratory… / [But] he created nothing worthy in verse).[37] Indeed, why name these, the single native writers in the epistles (apart from Lomonosov, whose name he added at the end) in order to render them such very mixed praise? On the other hand, Sumarokov greatly valued Prokopovich as a preacher, which is clear from the note on him (cited below) that he originally planned to include at the end of the epistles. If we are to believe some commentators, Lomonosov was more critical of modern church orators and possibly of the Orthodox Church as a whole than Sumarokov, and it is possible that he advised Sumarokov to eliminate the names of Prokopovich and the other church orators from the epistles. In that case, his words from the letter to Trediakovskii in which he suggests that "the writer of these epistles… should

---

35   Lomonosov, *PSS*, 7, 821.
36   See Sumarokov *Izbrannye proizvedeniia*, 116 and 527.
37   Berkov's editions mistakenly have "ne sozdal nichego" instead of "ne sdelal nichego."

find some way that he could somewhat alter (otmenit' neskol'ko) his argumentation concerning certain persons (nekotorykh person)" might refer not to Trediakovskii (or not only to Trediakovskii) but to Kantemir, Prokopovich and the other "persony" named in the passage on oratory.

The following are Sumarokov's biographical notes that were crossed out on the manuscript [ll. 24–25]) after these figures were cut from the text of the epistles. All but the last correspond to the figures named in the passage on oratory discussed above. The notes on Nicolas Pradon (1632–1698) and Jean Chapelain (1595–1674), named at the start of the second epistle as "bad French poets" were also crossed out; their names had come to stand for untalented and envious writers largely due to Boileau's *L'Art poétique*, which was the principle model for Sumarokov's epistles. It seems logical that mention of them was rendered redundant by the satirical portrait of Trediakovskii-Shtivelius.

ДЕМОСФЕ́Н, Преславный афинский ритор. Роди́лся за 379: лет до рождества Христо́ва. Умер за 320: лет.
ЗЛАТОУСТ, Патриарх цар-града. Златоустом назван он от красноречия своего. Родился в 354: год по рождестве Христовом, в (Λ - - гирлии?).[38] Представился в 407: году сентября 14 дня.
ФЕОФАН, Архиепископ нова́-града, преславный ри́тор (- -?) из числа знатнейших самых лучших ри́торов во всей Евро́пе. Некоторые ево слова́, а особливо из тех которыя теперь пришли на память: слово о полтавской победе; слово на рождение (цесаревича?) Петра́ Петро́вича на смерть Государя императора Петра Великого и на смерть Государыни императрицы Екатерины Алексеевны, так хороши, что едва может ли больше человеческий разум показать изкуства в красноречии.[39]
ЦИЦЕРОН, Преславный латинский Ритор. Роди́лся в Риме, в 684: году от создания города, января 3: дня. Умер на 64: годы века своево; в 43: по рождестве христовым. Почитется единогласно превеликим Ритором.

---

[38] Ioann Zlatoust (John Chrysostom) was born in Antioch in Syria.
[39] Sumarokov is referring to the following of Feofan's sermons: 1) "Slovo o Polstavskoi pobede" (1717), or possibly the "Slovo pokhval'noe o proslavnoi nad voiskami shveiskimi pobede" (1709); 2) "Slovo pokhval'noe v den' rozhdestva blagorodneishego gosudaria tsarevicha i velikogo kniazia Petra Petrovicha" (1716; pub. 1717); 3) "Slovo na pogrebenie Petra Velikogo" (1725), "Slovo na pokhvalu blazhennyia i vechno dostoinyia pamiati Petra Velikogo" (1725); 4) "Slovo na pogrebenie…imperatritsy Ekateriny Alekseevny" (1727). See Feofan Prokopovich, *Sochineniia*, ed. I. P. Eremin (Moscow, Leningrad: AN SSSR, 1961). The titles of these works is taken from *Katalog russkoi knigi kirillovskoi pechati peterburgskikh tipografii XVIII veka (1715–1800)* (Leningrad: Gosudarstvennaia publichnaia biblioteka imeni M. E. Saltykova-Shchedrina, 1972), 74–5.

Chapter 3. Censorship and Provocation: History of Sumarokov's "Two Epistles"

МОСГЕ́ЙМ, немчи́н, знатный проповедник закона своево. Еще жив.[40]
БУРДАЛУ́, францу́з, славный проповедник закона своево. Родился в Лио́не, 20: дня, а́густа в 1632: году́. Умер в пари́же 13: ма́йя, в 1704: году́, на 72: жизни свое́й.[41]
ПРАДО́Н, и
ШАПЕЛЕ́Н, худыя францу́зския стихотворцы.[42]

This material significantly adds to Sumarokov's "Notes" accompanying the "Two Epistles," that have been referred to as "the first Russian dictionary of writers,"[43] and demonstrates his broad interest not only in classical and contemporary European oratory but also with the native Orthodox tradition, and especially with Feofan Prokopovich's sermons. Sumarokov's high praise for Prokopovich (as "a most renowned orator," "among the most distinguished [and] very best orators in all of Europe," and that "human reason could hardly demonstrate greater art in rhetoric") and his great familiarity with his works, allowing him to name the most important ones by memory, are noteworthy.[44]

The decision to eliminate these lines led to the reorganization of the "Notes," which at first had been listed in order of their appearance in the epistles. After the cut Sumarokov numbered the names in the "Notes" so that the typesetters could set them in alphabetical order, which is the way they appear in the final published version. He also slightly altered the title of the "Notes on the Orators and Poets Named in These Epistles" (Primechaniia na upotreblennye v sikh epistolakh ritorov, stikhotvortsev imena), crossing out the word "Orators" but preserving the "in These Epistles," even though after the excision no names remained in the first epistle to be annotated. Thus this title was a remnant of the initial version of the work. It also indicates that the "Two Epistles" is and was conceived

---

[40] Johann Lorenz von Mosheim (c. 1694–1755), German Lutheran preacher and church historian.
[41] Louis Bourdaloue (1632–1704), French Jesuit preacher.
[42] Nicolas Pradon (1632–1698), French playwright, and Jean Chapelain (1595–1674), French poet and a founder of the Académie française.
[43] Berkov, *Vvedenie v izuchenie*, 22.
[44] In his posthumously published article "O Rossiiskom Dukhovnom Krasnorechii," written after 1770, Sumarokov appraised Prokopovich as a "great orator" (ritor) and "the Russian Cicero" (*PSVS*, 6, 295–602). The question of Prokopovich's importance for Sumarokov still awaits study. Cf. N. D. Kochetkova, "Oratorskaia proza Feofana Prokopovicha i puti formirovaniia literatury klassitsizma," *XVIII vek*, 9 (1974), 65–6 and 76–80; and my comments in "Sumarokov's Drama 'The Hermit': On the Generic and Intellectual Sources of Russian Classicism," chap. 6 in this volume.

as one single composition, as two parts composing a larger "Art of Poetry," despite the fact that some scholars may want to treat the two parts as separate poems.

APPENDIX
Changes made to the manuscript of the "Two Epistles" that were not discussed in the article

I. Эпистола о русском языке

1) I, 6 (l. 2): This line was changed several times and then crossed out:

   мысль свою на нем (де?) на нем
   понятие мое делим в малч(а)йши части и мысли голосом делим

   The final version ("и мысли голосом делим на мелки части") is written on l. 1 rev.

2) I, 53 (l. 3): A line is crossed out:

   Нет тайны ни какой без разума пис

   Apparently, Sumarokov began to write line 55 ("Нет тайны никакой безумственно писать") but caught his error and stopped.

3) I, 96 (l. 4): This line underwent several changes:

   скупо   [на нем] вносим мы в него
   Но [редко (он? мы?) еще видал] хороший склад;

   The first version of these lines was apparently: "Но редко он еще видал хороший слад"; other possible readings are: "Но редко мы на нем видал/и/ хороший склад" or "Но редко мы еще видал/и/ хороший склад." The final printed version is: "Но скупо вносим мы в него хороший склад."

II. Эпистола о стихотворстве

1) The changes to the lines on Kantemir and Feofan Prokopovich are cited in A. P. Sumarokov, *Izbrannye proizvedeniia*, ed. P. N. Berkov, 116; V. I. Rezanov, "Rukopisnye teksty," 39. They come after II, 18 (l. 7): "разумный" is changed to "(великий?)" and "славенского" to "Российского." The last line is: "Достойного в стихах не сделал ничево." See note 34.
2) II, 29 (l. 7): "мало" was changed to "тщетно."
3) II, 39 (l. 11): "взоидем и у́зри/м/" was changed to "взоидем, увидим."
4) II, 47 (l. 11): The word order in the phrase "французов хор реченный" was changed several times; the final version is on l. 7 rev.

Chapter 3. Censorship and Provocation: History of Sumarokov's "Two Epistles"

5) II, 48 (l. 11): The following line (with changes) was crossed out:

> мильтон и   в п/ьес?/ах не очень хоть ученный,
> там (мильтон?) шекеспир хотя непросвещенныи

On l. 7 rev. it was replaced by: "Мильтон и Шекеспир, хотя не просвещенный."

6) II, 50 (l. 11): "Гинтер там и остроумный Поп" is replaced by "Гинтер там, там остроумный Поп."

7) Two crossed out lines following II, 50 (l. 11) are illegible.

8) II, 52 (l. 11): "А ты" was replaced by "Пускай."

9) Two lines after II, 52 were crossed out. The first is: "Пусть время, когда ему себе он ставит то за честь." The second is illegible.

10) The following two lines after II, 80 (l. 12) were crossed out:

> В идилии не пой ни ад ни небеса
> вспевай в них чистый луг потоки древеса

It is possible that Sumarokov eliminated these lines because they were too similar to II, 114 ("Взлетает к небесам, свергается во ад"). They were replaced by the passage on l. 11 rev., whose first two lines were crossed out:

> [оставь другим стихам воински чудеса:]
> [в идилии пой луг, потоки, древеса]
> вспевай в идилии мне ясны небеса,
> кустарники, леса,
> зеленыя луга́, [потоки, древеса]

11) II, 87 (l. 12): "тогда" was replaced by the word "стихом" in the line "И позабыть стихом мирскую суету." In the published text this line is: "И позабыть, стих читая, суету." See Rezanov, "Rukopisnye teksty," 38.

12) II, 103 (l. 13): "Гремящий (в мире?) звук" was replaced by "Гремящий в оде звук."

13) II, 104 (l. 13): This line was changed many times:

> [хреб] хребет   гор [далёк]   превышает
> [(И?) воды вышних гор] рифейских [воздымает] далёко [оставляет]

The final version is: "Хребет рифейских гор далеко превышает."

14) II, 105 (l. 13): "та молния" was replaced by "в ней молния."

15) II, 115 (l. 13): This line with many changes was crossed out:

> и дерзостно во все края всея летящ в последний край вселенны

It was replaced by "и мчался в быстроте во все края вселенны" on l. 12 rev.

16) II, 130 (l. 13):

> то [куп] купидо́н
> Любовь, [венерин сын,] венéра красота.

The final version is: "Любовь, то купидон, венера красота."

17) After II, 172, the following four lines were crossed out (l. 15):

> Явлениями множ смотрителю желанье,
> Познать, какое ты положишь окончанье.
> веди как лесницей меня зреть пышный дом,
> Что
> (- -) б действо тучей шло,
> (как?) туча (- - - -) и вдруг ударил гром.

The last line possibly reads: "Что б действо тучей шло, и вдруг ударил гром." See Rezanov, "Rukopisnye teksty," 40. These lines were replaced by the following (on l. 14 rev.):

> [смотретилево (sic) множ желание прит притом;]
> [смотрителево (или: «смотрителю»)]
> явлениями множ желание творец,
> познать, как действию положишь ты конец.

These last two lines became the final published version (II, 173–174).

18) II, 178 (l. 15): The first version of this line was crossed out (l. 15)

> Трезе́нский князь живущ с младенчества в лесах

There are several illegible words in the manuscript here. The above line was replaced by the following on l. 14 rev.:

> Трезенский князь забыл о рыцарских играх

This line also has several crossed out words, including "лишь в рыцарских играх."

19) II, 198 (l. 16): The manuscript does not have "И Клитемнестрин плод" as in the published text, but "и клитемне́стры дочь." Apparently Sumarokov made this change in the proofs.

20) II, 262 (l. 18): "Печется" was replaced by "Пекутся."

21) II, 281 (l. 19): "так кажется" was replaced by "быть кажется."

22) II, 314 (l. 21):

> Что б был   в них
> [Что когда] порядок [чист,] и в слоге чистота.

(That is, in the final version: "Что б был порядок в них и в слоге чистота.")

23) II, 319 (l. 21): "Пускай" was replaced by "Но пусть."

24) II, 320 (l. 21): The line "И есть меж дел ево, часы ему свободны" was replaced by: "Хороши вымыслы и тамо благородны."

25) II, 333 (l. 21):

>   б   нем
> Что [раз]ум в [них] был сокрыт...

(That is, in the final version: "Чтоб ум в нем был сокрыт.")

Chapter 3. Censorship and Provocation: History of Sumarokov's "Two Epistles"

26) II, 341 (l. 22): "мне" was replaced by "их" and II. 342–343 added (on l. 21 rev.).
27) II, 374 (l. 23): "вскинет" is replaced by "кинет."
28) II, 376 (l. 23):

> вот мысли там тебе по склонности
> [Вот мысли многия тебе уже] готовы.

III. Примечания к эпистолам

1) The description of Voltaire underwent editing (ll. 25 and 56):

> ВОЛЬТЕ́Р, великий стихотворец, и преславный французский тра́гик. [(- - - -) в Париже]. Лу́чшия ево траге́дии суть: АЛЬЗИ́РА, МЕРО́ПА, БРУТ, и МАРИА́МНА. ГЕНРИА́ДА [сочиненная им] геро́ическая ево поэ́ма, есть [прекрасная поема (- - - -) (- - - -)] некое сокровище стихотворства. Как Генриа́да, так и трагедии ево [суть наполнены] важностью, сладостью, остротой и великолепием / сверху: "наполнены" / <...> все то показывает в нем [и великого человека и] великого стихотворца. [Ныне он (много?) (известен?) (- - -) в Пари́ж/е/.]

2) Sumarokov somewhat reworked the description of Günter (Ginter) (l. 10). The changes are illegible, but apparently not substantive.
3) Camoens (Kamoens): the epithet "славный" was added (l. 9).
4) Lope (de Vega) (Lop): the epithet "славный" was added (l. 9).
5) Menander (Menandr): the first word "славнейший" was changed to "лучший" (l. 27).
6) (Alexander) Pope (Pop): the word "писатель" was added (l. 10).
7) Propertius (Propertsii): the phrase "по взятии города перу́гии" is crossed out after the words "казнен по повелению августа, отсечением головы, за то он" (ll. 8–9).
8) Tasso (Tass): added on l. 8 rev.: "Родился в королевстве неаполита́нском."
9) Terentius (Terentii): the word "лучший" is added (l. 8).
10) Shakespeare (Shekespir): the words "очень" (худова) and "чрезвычайно" (хорошева) were added (l. 12).
11) Vondel (Fondel'): the epithet "славный" was added (l. 9).

— 4 —

SLANDER, POLEMIC, CRITICISM:
Trediakovskii's "Letter...from a Friend to a Friend" of 1750 and the Problem of Creating Russian Literary Criticism

Among P. N. Berkov's many scholarly achievements, he was first to pose the problem of "the appearance of literary criticism as an independent phenomenon of [Russian] social life," and he also was one of the first to describe the problem of its development in the eighteenth century.[1] It is quite difficult to frame this issue, as in any era the notion of "criticism" is closely tied to the level of development of the given literary system, and the literary system in eighteenth-century Russia was in a very rapid state of flux. Two methodological extremes need to be avoided: on the one hand, presuming literary criticism to be a permanent, unchanging ontological category (for example, to describe Andrei Kurbskii or Archpriest Avvakum as literary critics); and on the other, to assume a teleological approach, e.g., seeing all roads leading to Belinskii and the nineteenth-century canon of criticism, that is, raising criticism of one particular type into the ideal. The challenge is not only defining criticism as opposed to other types of writing and opinion, but also understanding its place in the dynamics of the literary process, a role that Hugh Duncan has described as the key factor in any modern literary system.[2]

As an example, this article will analyze the "Letter in Which is Contained A Discussion of the Poetry Published Up to Now by the Author of Two

---

[1] P. N. Berkov, "Razvitie russkoi kritiki v XVIII veke," in *Istoriia russkoi kritiki*, ed. B. P. Gorodetskii. Vol. 1 (Leningrad: Akademiia nauk SSSR, 1958), 46.
This article was given as a lecture on December 18, 1996, at the conference "Berkovskie chteniia" (Readings of Berkov) at the Institute of Russian Literature (Pushkin House) of the Russian Academy of Sciences, St. Petersburg. I have reinstated several sentences that were eliminated in the published text.

[2] Hugh Dalziel Duncan, *Language and Literature in Society: A Sociological Essay on Theory and Method in the Interpretation of Linguistic Symbols* (Chicago: University of Chicago Press, 1953), 60.

Odes, Two Tragedies and Two Epistles, Written from a Friend to a Friend" (Pis'mo, v kotorom soderzihtsia rassuzhdenie o stikhotvorenii, ponyne na svet izdannom ot avtora dvukh od, dvukh tragedii i dvukh epistol, pisannoe ot priiatelia k priiateliu) written by V. K. Trediakovskii in 1750. On its basis Berkov called Trediakovskii "chronologically the first Russian critic, [and one] who consistently applied the theory of French Classicism in his criticism." A series of other scholars followed his lead, and have referred to the "Letter" as "the first Russian critical article."[3] The "Letter" is well known to specialists of the eighteenth century and is a rich source of information about language, genres and other important issues of mid-century Russian language and literature. In contrast to other texts such as rhetorical manuals, epigrams, forewords, personal correspondence, and so on, that contain "critical materials," Trediakovskii's "Letter" is arguably the century's single example of close analysis of literary texts. The "Letter" is also important as the first conscious attempt (even if unsuccessful) to establish a literary-critical etiquette. In his first book, Berkov discussed the problem nature of this work, and argued that it should not be classified not only as "criticism" but even as a "polemic." He wrote:

> It is very characteristic as an example of Trediakovskii's critical judgments but does not constitute an organic link in the literary polemic of the time; official in its origin and instigated practically by the deceit of G. N. Teplov, who was then on good terms with Sumarokov, the "Letter to a Friend" lay untouched for more than a century in the Academy of Sciences archive and did not evoke any response in contemporary literature. True, it became known to Sumarokov, who wrote a special article, "Answer to Criticism," in response, but this article also too, one presumes, only became known when published by Novikov in the first edition of Sumarokov's works in 1781. It is possible that both of these works were known to a very narrow circle of the era's very small number of readers... However, one must emphasize that while polemical in content, Trediakovskii's "Letter" and Sumarokov's "Answer" did not turn out

---

[3] Berkov, "Razvitie russkoi kritiki," 58. On the French Classicist influence on Russian critical thought, see Gerda Achinger, *Der französische Anteil an der russischen Literaturkritik des 18. Jahrhunderts unter besonderer Berücksichtigung der Zeitschriften (1730–1780). Osteuropastudien der Hochschulen des Landes Hessen. Reihe 3: Frankfurter Abhandlungen zur Slavistik*, Bd. 15. (Bad Homburg v.d.H.: Gehlen, 1970). Achinger calls Tredikovskii's "Letter" "the first critical writing in Russian literature" (p. 49). The first publisher of the "Letter," A. A. Kunik, referred to it as "the first attempt at Russian literary criticism"; see *Sbornik materialov dlia istorii imp. Akademii nauk v XVIII veke,* ed. A. A. Kunik. Vol. 2 (St. Petersburg, 1865), 436.

to be polemical in function (po funksii svoei ne okazalis' polemicheskim). This causes us to pass over them in silence in examining to genuine facts of the public polemics of their epoch.[4]

The passage is remarkable for a number of questions it raises, including the notion of "genuine...public polemics" and the suggestion of a certain requisite function of criticism. Unfortunately, Berkov does not clarify these ideas, and the very term "polemic" remains somewhat vague. It clearly involves an element of belonging to the public sphere and of authorial independence, although to what extent remains unspecified. The point here is not to cavil at Berkov's formulation (especially considering the era in which he wrote) but to consider the basic underlying issue that he was raising: what was the state of literary criticism in the eighteenth century, and if "genuine" criticism did not exist, but only something in between "polemics" and "literary warfare,"[5] why was this the case, and why and how did the existing forms of critical writing fail to fulfill this function?

Trediakovskii's "Letter" highlights the difficult status of criticism at a time when it had "not become...a specific branch of literature" and an "independent phenomenon of social life,"[6] and in a situation in which its forms and even its very right to exist had not been established. For the writer this was a first step, and one filled with risk. Let us recall the circumstances of the "Letter." In the first place, Trediakovskii was criticizing his open literary opponent and rival, as both men claimed the tight to the title of "father of Russian poetry" (Trediakovskii's words). Even though their literary programs were essentially similar, each sought to establish the role of his works as the sole correct and permissible ones. Furthermore, all of the three leading poets of the period, Sumarokov, Trediakovskii and Lomonosov, unfortunately found themselves in a situation in which they had the opportunity of

---

[4] P. N. Berkov, *Lomonosov i literaturnaia polemika ego vremeni, 1750–1765* (Leningrad: Akademiia nauk SSSR, 1936), 95.

[5] Cf. M. S. Grinberg and B. A. Uspenskii, "Literaturnaia voina Trediakovskogo i Sumarokova v 1740-kh — nachale 1750-kh godov," *Russian Literature* [North Holland], 31 (1992), 133–272, also as: *Literaturnaia voina Trediakovskogo i Sumarokova v 1740-kh — nachale 1750-kh godov. Chteniia po istorii i teorii kul'tury*, vyp. 29. (Moscow: Rossiiskii gos. gumanitarnyi universitet, 2001).

[6] N. I. Mordovchenko, *Russkaia kritika pervoi chetverti deviatnadtsatogo veka* (Moscow: Akademiia nauk SSSR, 1959), 17. See also: Berkov, "Razvitie russkoi kritiki," 46; G. A. Gukovskii, "Russkaia literaturno-kriticheskaia mysl' v 1730–1750 gody," *XVIII vek*, 5 (Moscow, Leningrad, 1962), 98–128; *Ocherki istorii russkoi literaturnoi kritiki*, ed. V. A. Kotel'nikov and A. M. Panchenko. Vol. 1: *XVIII — pervaia chetvert' XIX v.* (St. Petersburg: Nauka, 1999), 37–94.

Chapter 4. Slander, Polemic, Criticism

thwarting publication of each others' works. Trediakovskii and Lomonosov's clash over who was first to introduce syllabotonic verse is well known, and Sumarokov joined their public competition in 1744 when the three poets published their three anonymous versions of the 143rd Psalm.[7] The rivalry became sharper when Sumarokov submitted his second tragedy "Hamlet" (Gamlet) and the "Two Epistles" for publication by the Academy typography and they were passed on to Trediakovskii and Lomonosov for censorship.[8] Lomonosov gave his approval (Uspenskii and Grinberg hypothesize that he had concluded a tactical alliance with Sumarokov against Trediakovskii[9]), while Trediakovskii had objections to "Hamlet" and wanted to stall publication of the "Two Epistles" because of the satirical barbs directed at Trediakovskii himself. To his great displeasure, Sumarokov not only succeeded in having his works published, but included even more ridicule of him in the published version of the epistles. As I have commented elsewhere, "This may have been one of the only instances in history when the number of objectionable places was increased due to censorship rather than the reverse."[10] Furthermore, Sumarokov publicly mocked Trediakovskii on the stage, depicting him as the pathetic pedant Tresotinius (from the French "très sot," "very stupid") in his first comedy of the same name. At the start of his letter, Trediakovskii noted with irritation that the author of the comedy "had not only not considered it proper not to get rid of [the insults and barbs of his previous works] but to some extent increased them and [made them] worse and even more intolerable (eshche onyia i otchasu bol'she i nesnosneishe nyne umnozhil)" (437).[11] He declared that the comedy had been "composed

---

[7] On versification, see most recently: I. Klein (Joachim Klein), "Trediakovskii: Reforma russkogo stikha v kul'turno-istoricheskom kontekste," *XVIII vek*, 19 (St. Petersburg, 1995), 15–42. On the competition, see: G. A. Gukovskii, "K voprosu o russkom klassitsizme (Sostiazanie i perevody)," *Poetika*, 4 (Leningrad, 1928), 126–48; K. B. Jensen and P. U. Møller, "Paraphrase and Style: A Stylistic Analysis of Trediakovskij's, Lomonosov's and Sumarokov's Paraphrases of the 143rd Psalm," *Scando-Slavica*, 16 (1970), 57–63; A. B. Shishkin, "Poeticheskoe sostiazanie Trediakovskogo, Lomonosova i Sumarokova," *XVIII vek*, 14 (Leningrad, 1983), 232–46.

[8] See P. Pekarskii, *Istoriia imperatorskoi Akademii nauk v Peterburge*, vol. 2 (St. Petersburg, 1873), 129–33, 151–54; and my articles "Censorship and Provocation: The Publishing History of Sumarokov's 'Two Epistles'" and "Sumarokov's Russianized 'Hamlet': Texts and Contexts," chaps. 3 and 5 in this volume.

[9] Grinberg and Uspenskii, "Literaturnaia voina," 147.

[10] See "Censorship and Provocation," 51.

[11] Page references in parentheses refer to Kunik, ed., *Sbornik materialov*, vol. 2. The "Letter" has been reprinted in A. M. Ranchin and V. L. Korovin, eds., *Kritika XVIII veka*. Biblioteka russkoi kritiki (Moscow: Olimp, AST, 2002), 29–109.

only so that it would be not only be harsh but what one may consider a satire aimed at destroying honor (pochitai ubistvennoiu chesti satiroiu), or rather, a new but precisely a libel, of the kind, moreover, that are not presented at theaters anywhere in the world; because comedies are created to correct the mores of an entire society and not to destroy the honor of a particular person" (437–8). Thus the first motive for writing the "Letter" was to publicly respond to this libel against a "particular (private) person" before the "reading public" (obshchestvo chitatelei) (437). The problem was that this private person was Trediakovskii himself.

Trediakovskii fully realized his personal interest in the "Letter" that in the very first sentence he described as "apologetical and critical." Its authorial pose that the "Letter" was written anonymously "from a friend to a friend" as a defense a third "common friend" fooled no one. In a report to Academy of Sciences President K. G. Razumovskii of March 8, 1751, Trediakovskii asserted that he had written the letter "on the order of the former Academy assessor Grigorii Teplov" (436), but there is no grounds for considering it motivated by official reasons. Teplov's role and motivations here were questionable. He himself took part in literary quarrels of the time and soon became Trediakovskii's outspoken foe.[12] Furthermore, there are no indications in the "Letter" itself of being an official document, and apart perhaps from censors' reports no kind of official literary criticism existed (nor for that matter did any other kind). Trediakovskii's claim that he had been ordered to write the letter thus represented another attempt at self protection. What is curious here in considering the creation of a new literary-critical discourse is not so much the device of the anonymous letter, common enough in the European as well as the later Russian tradition, but the fact that Trediakovskii was unable to maintain the illusion of anonymity. Apologetics continually gets in the way of the objective "critical" voice of the "Letter," revealing the author's hurt pride, undermining the conceit, and frustrating the main aim of the work.

The problem of Trediakovskii's "personal interest" highlights both the specific situation of mid-century Russia in which he was writing and the more general issue of the assertion of the rights of the individual voice in the public sphere.[13] This moment is of major theoretical interest from

---

[12] Pekarskii, *Istoriia*, 188–97. Pekarskii suggests that Teplov ordered Treiakovskii to write the letter "of course [!] to egg on the two literary adversaries and by this to amuse people who knew them" (p. 152). Cf. Trediakovskii's warning to Sumarokov that something similar was happening to him (see below).

[13] The terms of Habermas' well known theory of the "public sphere" come into play here, along with the attendant questions about to what extent they may be applied

Chapter 4. Slander, Polemic, Criticism

a political, psychological and broad cultural perspective. The unresolved conflict between apologetics and objective criticism also defines the generic dualism of Trediakovskii's letter. Here is a case of a traumatic violation of the perceived boundary between public discussion of the arts and sciences (a relatively new innovation in Russia) and the "individual" discourse of literary criticism, criticism in the name of "a particular person" rather than a state institution or the court. This act of criticism, as Terry Eagleton has emphasized, is first of all a political one.[14] Entrance into the public arena presumed a political right to speak and marked the opening of a discursive space that on some level implicitly challenged state hegemony. In absolutist Russia, however, literature was still conceived of in terms of state service and largely reflected state policies and ideals. Trediakovskii found himself in a somewhat ill-defined, at times contradictory position. At the same time as he himself was opening up public space with his letter he was trying to limit Sumarokov's access to it by characterizing Sumarokov's comedy as an impermissible libel. He argued for denying Sumarokov the right to speak at the same time as he asserted his own. The issue boiled down to defining the permissible limits of public speech. When Trediakovskii criticized the right of comedy (and to a lesser extent, epistles) to function as satire he was also objecting to the blurring of boundaries between the public and private spheres and so some extent demanding restriction on free speech. Insofar as Trediakovskii hoped to alert the authorities to Sumarokov's abuses, practically charging him with subversion, his letter might be seen to have a semi-official character. This episode was the first round in what was a political conflict over the permissibility of personal satire,

---

to old regime and non-bourgeois societies. In Habermas' theory, literary criticism plays an important role in the transition to full-fledged public (politically recognized) discourse. See Jürgen Habermas *The Structural Transformation of the Public Sphere: An Inquiry into a Category of Bourgeois Society*. Studies in Contemporary German Social Thought (Cambridge, Mass: MIT Press, 1989). See also Terry Eagleton, *The Function of Criticism: From the Spectator to Post-Structuralism* (London: Verso, 1984), which sees "the function of criticism" as explicity political.

In the years since this article was written, there have been some provocative attempts to define the nature of eighteenth-century Russian civil society and political discourse. See, for example: Douglas Smith, *Working the Rough Stone: Freemasonry and Society in Eighteenth-Century Russia* (DeKalb, IL: Northern Illinois UP, 1999); Cynthia H. Whittaker, *Russian Monarchy: Eighteenth-Century Rulers and Writers in Political Dialogue* (DeKalb, IL: Northern Illinois UP, 2003); and Elise Kimerling Wirtschafter, *The Play of Ideas in Russian Enlightenment Theater* (DeKalb, IL: Northern Illinois UP, 2003).

14 Eagleton, *The Function of Criticism*.

a conflict that continued to play out in the second half of the century, most famously in the debates of the so called satirical journals of 1769–1774.[15]

Trediakovskii's attacks on Sumarokov exhibit not only the anxiety of self-defense but also the fear of making a claim on the still unfamiliar public sphere. In view of the almost complete absence of critical discourse in Russia of the period, this thinly-veiled "anonymous" assault on Sumarokov could be perceived as a kind of political denunciation; in essence, Trediakovskii was denying Sumarokov's qualifications, and right, to be a writer. As K. Papmehl wrote, "during practically the whole first half of the century both the letter of the law and administrative practice were directly inimical to any form of independent expression."[16]

The notorious "word and deed" (slovo i delo), officially established by the Law Code of 1649 and reinforced by Peter I, made any statement, oral or written, that could be interpreted as an offense against the person or policies of the tsar punishable by torture, exile, and even death. Under Empress Elizabeth the threat of "word and deed" significantly lessened, in part as a reaction against the period of "bironovshchina" under Empress Anna, although the law itself was not officially abrogated until Peter III's manifesto of Feb. 21, 1762. Public speech was to some extent sanctioned by such institutions as the Academy of Sciences, with its publications and typography, and by the patronage of such grandees who ran them (such as Teplov and Razumovskii). Within a few years, as Trediakovskii's enmity toward Sumarokov escalated and he felt himself even more isolated, he resorted to such measures as a denunciation (izvet) on Sumarokov to the Holy Synod and an anonymous condemnation (podmetnoe pis'mo), that is, an old-style political denunciation. However, these attempts to utilize authoritarian methods to silence his critics merely served to further undermine Trediakovskii's position.

In general terms, G. A. Gukovskii noted that for Russian Classicism both criticism and literature functioned as "the aesthetic embodiment of the idea of state discipline," that is, no difference was yet perceived between personal and state interests. According to contemporary notions, literature, like the state which it served, was governed by ideal, obligatory, normative laws. As

---

[15] See Jones, W. Gareth, "The Polemics of the 1769 Journals: A Reappraisal," *Canadian-American Slavic Studies*, 16: 3–4 (Fall-Winter 1982): 432–43.

[16] K. A. Papmehl, *Freedom of Expression in Eighteenth Century Russia* (The Hague: Nijhoff, 1971), 6. On political crimes in the eighteenth century, see E. V. Anisimov, *Dyba i knut: politicheskii sysk i russkoe obshchestvo v XVIII v. Historia Rossica.* (Moscow: Novoe literaturnoe obozrenie, 1999).

Chapter 4. Slander, Polemic, Criticism

Gukovskii wrote, "At no other time did criticism so resemble a court trial in which the judge pronounced a strict, final and categorical verdict, dictated by a codex created not by him but considered binding and even holy."[17] Faith in such an objective set of aesthetic laws turned even minor disagreements into unavoidable clashes over unconditional truths. The incursion of private or personal elements into literature (in Trediakovskii's words, Sumarokov's "low passions") thus appeared almost as state crimes. For the same reason, the personal element was impermissible in criticism, insofar as the Classicist writer wrote not in his own name but that of eternal norms and truths. Hence Trediakovskii found himself in a paradoxical position, forced to defend his personal interests in the name of the absolute and supra-personal. In his opinion, Sumarokov's satire violated the boundary between the private and public spheres, claiming authority for his personal (false) opinions. According to this normative logic, there was no such thing as an honest disagreement: if a writer violated the rules, it meant that he was tainted by passion — insane, drunk, or simply a bad person. On the one hand, Trediakovskii insisted on his objectivity but almost simultaneously resorted to ad hominem attacks hardly different from those libels he denounces in Sumarokov (for example, he refers to Sumarokov's red hair, his nervous tick, and so on). Sumarokov cleverly parodied Trediakovskii's method in his "Answer to Critcism":

> I am not surprised, he writes, that our author's actions completely accord with the color of his hair, the movement of his eyes, the use of his tongue and the beating of his heart. What heart beats he is referring to I have no idea; but how wonderful is this newfangled kind of criticism![18]

Authoritarian discourse with its binary axiology had a major influence on Trediakovskii's language, replete with political and juridical terms like "court," "verdict," and "imposture" (samozvantsvo). The influence of older Orthodox polemical models is also evident, offering a graphic example of the projection of old "medieval" type polemics onto the "modern" European-style model. Deviations from the aesthetic norm of classicism are described in corresponding moral terms, like "sins" (grekhi), "errors" (pogreshnosti), "faults" (poroki), "passions," "heresy" (nepravoverie), etc. Sumarokov is compared to a schismatic, and his personal failings — "unbearable vanity" and "self-promotion" (samokhval'stvo) — are declared to be the definitive

---

[17] Gukovskii, "Russkaia literaturno-kriticheskaia mysl'," 126.
[18] A. P. Sumarokov, *Polnoe sobranit vsekh sochinenii*, ed. N.I.Novikov. Vol. 10 (Moscow, 1787), 105.

indicators of his literary worth. "Low usage" is equated to evil usage, and theatrical "buffoonery" (skomoroshestvo)—blasphemy. Trediakovskii charges that Sumarokov's major flaw is his ignorance, his lack of knowledge, first of all, of church books and Slavonic, but also of classical languages and of the many spheres of knowledge necessary to a poet (450). As V. M. Zhivov has noted, Trediakovskii attacks Sumarokov from the position of rationalist purism; his stance is in many ways identical to that of Sumarokov, but more strict.[19] If Sumarokov considered himself the "Russian Boileau," a literary lawgiver, Trediakovskii presents himself as a superior guardian of correct usage. Sumarokov's innovations, based on modern French models and on French translation-adaptations of the classics, are contrasted to the "authentic" classics of the Greek, Roman and Orthodox traditions.

The equation of Church Slavonic books and Greek and Roman classics was a fundamental plank of the new conception of the "Slaveno-Russian" (slavenorossiiskii) literary language of the mid-eighteenth century, although these traditions did not always completely harmonize.[20] Thus in the "Letter" Trediakovskii at times questions the combination of classical mythology with Orthodox values. As opposed to Sumarokov, who was of aristocratic origins and graduate of the First Noble Cadet Corpus, Trediakovskii was son of a clergyman and graduate of the Moscow Slavic-Greek-Latin Academy, and in the "Letter" this general cultural opposition is rather clearly evident. In his *New and Short Method for Composing Russian Verse* (1735) Trediakovskii himself had defended the use of mythological figures in poetry, but when in the "Letter" he attacks Sumarokov for such usage in his panegyric odes, trying to cast doubt on the poet's political reliability, his orientation on what we may call "archaism" (political, philosophical, aesthetic) is striking.

That Trediakovskii's main criticism of Sumarokov is of his ignorance (and his lack of understanding of his limitations) somewhat mitigates the

---

[19] On linguistic purism, see B.A. Uspenskii, *Iz istorii russkogo literaturnogo iazyka XVIII— nachalo XIX veka: iazykovaia programma Karamzina i ee istoricheskie korni* (Moscow: Moskovskii universitet, 1985), 166; V. M. Zhivov, *Kul'turnye konflikty v istorii russkogo literaturnogo iazyka XVIII — nachala XIX veka* (Moscow: Institut russkogo iazyka, 1990), chap. 2 (later revised as: *Iazyk i kul'tura v Rossii XVIII veka* [Moscow: Iazyki russkoi kul'tury, 1996] and in English as *Language and Culture in Eighteenth-Century Century Russia* [Boston: Academic Studies Press, 2009]); on the closeness of Trediakovskii and Sumarokov's positions, see also my comments in "Sumarokov's Russianized 'Hamlet'" , chap. 5 in this volume and Grinberg and Uspenskii, "Literaturnaia voina," 198–201 and 214–16.

[20] On the Slaveno-rossisskii linguistic and cultural synthesis, see Zhivov, *Iazyk i kul'tura*, chap. 2.

inquisitorial pathos of the "Letter." But at the same time Trediakovskii also puts forward quite a different type of "Orthodox" discourse. On the one hand, as noted, the binary "medieval" model is projected onto Classicism in order to demonstrate the "faults" of his opponent. On the other hand, Trediakovskii appeals to the Gospels as an alternative non-critical paradigm based on the principle "Judge not, that ye be not judged" (Mathew 7: 1). A detailed critical examination of Sumarokov's works indicates, in Trediakovskii's words, that "in justice, no one has less right than the author to mock others, not to say to abuse and insult them. The words of Christ our Savior are very appropriate for him: Physician, heal thyself [Luke 4:23], And why beholdest thou the mote that is in thy brother's eye, but considerest not the beam that is in thine own eye? [Matthew 7:3; Luke 6:41]" (452). Condemning Sumarokov for allegedly blasphemous quoting from the Gospels in "Tresotinius," Trediakovskii adds: "here where there is not the least blasphemy, may I not dare to do the same thing, but with reverence, and cite for my consolation a passage from the same salvific Gospel, namely, 'he that endureth to the end shall be saved [Matthew 10:22]'" (440). This is both a self-defense and a negation of criticism per se; Trediakovskii appeals to a higher judgment. Here and in the later tradition citations of the Gospel play opposite roles, on the one hand to suggest absolute moral authority and on the other as an ideal of non-judgmental criticism (i.e., essentially the negation of criticism).

In the given case, Trediakovskii sacrifices all pretense of such "uncritical" criticism, as the "Letter" is permeated with tedious captiousness and relentless fault-finding. His obvious partiality and one-sided representations put even his most effective and judicious criticisms of Sumarokov's works in doubt. Trediakovskii the apologist overwhelms Trediakovskii the critic. In his concluding tirade, Trediakovskii writes:

> We have seen, dear Sir, that this ode by the author is faulty in composition, empty of sense, obscure and ambiguous in choice of words, poor in select phrases, false in the narration of past actions, without order, filled with unnecessary repetition of the same words, faulty in versification, illogical in the use of legend, and finally — and this is worse than anything else —, also partly heretical (otchasti i nepravoverna) (471)

This is but one of a host of similar harangues.

Trediakovskii's "Letter…Written from a Friend to a Friend" offers a striking example of the problems connected to the emergence of the new Russian literature, burdened by the lack of "genuine," independent literary criticism. Trediakovskii was unable to escape from the confines of his own personal interests. Classicism as a system of normative rules found ready soil in Russia's tradition of religious and political absolutism, and time and new institutions were needed to create a new literary space and new means for the exchange of opinions and ideas. These new institutions were to include the theater, journalism, book publishing, a reading public, and literary criticism. As Berkov noted, neither Trediakovskii's "Letter" nor Sumarokov's response were published during their authors' lives. This was because, first of all, of the Academy's policy of disallowing the publication of "indecorous" (neblagopristoinyi) debate. Still, there is evidence that both texts were familiar to contemporaries (if only, to use Berkov's phrase, "to a very narrow circle of the relatively small number of readers of the time"). The "Letter" was sufficiently well known so that theater-goers could undertstand the hints and parodic references to it in Sumarokov's following comedy "Chudovishchi" (later renamed "Treteinyi sud") in which Trediakovskii was again satirized on stage as the pedant "Krititsiondiusa"; the very name referred to the "Letter," and M. S. Grinberg and B. A. Uspenskii have directly characterized the play as "an anti-critical composition."

Trediakovskii felt the full weight of Sumarokov's satire and all of the fragility of a writer's position in Russian society. He attributed his problems in part to the absence of mediating criticism, a lack he himself tried to remedy with his "Letter." He saw the danger not only of what he saw as Sumarokov's unrestrained self-esteem but also of his dependence on what Trediakovskii suggested were overly worshipful admirers who could not help asserting a negative influence on his writing. He wrote that "He would be very fortunate if he could at least understand by whom and in what spirit he is praised. For there are, most probably, those who themselves don't know what they praise in his works. There are perhaps also those who flatter him on purpose, to lure him out further in order to make him the object of derision. Finally, there are those who praise him even while they hate him in order to encourage him by praise so as to rouse him to the most obvious unwise acts so as to destroy him, or at least, to bring him to misfortune and poverty" (453). These words could be taken as an epitaph for both Trediakovskii and Sumarokov. Their own reputations that they tried so hard to bolster fell victim to their constant feuding. The failure to establish "genuine criticism" that could regulate literary practice and social consciousness thus directly affected their fates as writers; both died out of favor and in poverty, victims in part of their own images as frustrated men of false pride. Their inability to work out a discursive space that could accommodate the exchange of opinions also helped determine the further course of criticism's development, if only as a negative example. Trediakovskii's and Sumarokov's polemics became a model of what criticism should not be.

In 1792, V. S. Podshivalov published a generally positive review in Karamzin's *Moskovskii zhurnal* of F. I. Tumanskii's translation of a book by the classical Greek writer Palaephatus. In a letter to the editor Tumanskii disputed his right to publish literary criticism of this kind. His objections to it suggest an inventory of the things that stood in the way of developing literary criticism:

> There are two kinds of judge: those appointed by the authorities and those elected. Those who do not belong to these groups are imposters (samozvantsy). "Judge not, that ye be not judged…" The judgments of private persons communicated in newspapers, magazines, etc., have never been respected by intelligent people; everyone knows that for gifts they run out of good words; out of bias, self-love, personal quarrel or envy they seek all means possible to denigrate someone else's labor. Mr. Sumarokov made himself judge over Mr. Lomonosov; Mr. Trediakovskii wrote criticism of his creations; posterity, learning that their judgments were based on envy, condemned both of them.[21]

In the first place, Tumanskii does not admit a private person's *political right* to critical activity; the right to such activity must come directly from the state or be delegated by means of election; otherwise criticism remains imposture. In the second place, the Gospel also rejects the right to personal judgment (that belongs to God, not the individual), thus equating criticism to a *moral evil*. In the third place, Tumanskii rejects periodical criticism and its capacity for evenhandedness insofar as it is corrupted either by patronage (gifts) or *personal interest*. Lastly, Tumanskii describes the problem in *historical* terms, taking the conflict between Trediakovskii, Sumarokov and Lomonosov as a warning to later generations about the harmfulness of criticism. A consequence of Karamzin's notion that "a bad person cannot be a good writer" was the idea that criticism of Classicism on ethical grounds (its writers' excessive and prideful polemics) signaled its aesthetic bankruptcy. The negative model of eighteenth-century literary disputes led to the attempt by Karamzin and his followers to create a different kind of openly subjective, sympathetic, "non-critical" type of criticism (that was in turn rejected as too mild by the Decembrist critics). But by that time the necessity of criticism as an integral component of the literary and cultural process had achieved general recognition, even though the character of that criticism continued to be a subject of intense debate.

---

[21] Cited in B. F. Egorov, *O masterstve literaturnoi kritiki: zhanry, kompozitsiia, stil'* (Leningrad: Sovetskii pisatel', 1980), 48.

—5—

SUMAROKOV'S RUSSIANIZED "HAMLET":
Texts and Contexts

The truism about the eighteenth century's rejection of Shakespeare as a "barbarian" who was lacking in "good taste" upon closer examination reveals a much more complex and nuanced picture of cultural reception. The question to consider is not how eighteenth-century writers misunderstood or corrupted Shakespeare but how they adapted him to meet specific needs of their own. This perspective is especially pertinent as regards Alexander Sumarokov's "Hamlet" ("Gamlet," pub. 1748) not only because this was the first appearance of Shakespeare in Russia, often viewed as an outrageous travesty of the bard (Hamlet and Ophelia survive to presumably live happily ever after on the throne of Denmark), but also because the play stands at the virtual beginning of modern Russian dramaturgy. However, as with many texts of eighteenth-century Russian literature, from which the modern reader is divided by a great chronological and cultural chasm, the text alone—isolated from the larger cultural (con)text of the time—can yield only partial results; many of the cultural codes and maps needed to navigate it have become invisible. For most of Sumarokov's plays, including "Hamlet," we have precious little cultural context in which to place them—specific information (for example) about their staging, performance, reception, or other indications about their literary or intellectual significance to their time. In this paper, I aim to begin to reconstruct the context and meaning of Sumarokov's adaption of "Hamlet" in two ways. The first is to examine Sumarokov's actual use of Shakespeare's text and the French translations he consulted as intermediaries. The recent discovery that Sumarokov borrowed the fourth folio edition of Shakespeare of 1685, in English, from the library of the Academy of Sciences just at the time when he was writing his own "Hamlet" makes such a reexamination especially pertinent (Levitt, "Sumarokov's Reading"). Secondly, I will analyze Sumarokov's play in light of the one extended contemporary discussion of Sumarokov's early

Chapter 5. Sumarokov's Russianized "Hamlet"

writings that we do have, V. K. Trediakovskii's "Letter...from a Friend to a Friend (Pis'mo...ot priiatelia k prijateliu)" of 1750. In this way I hope to better define the central dramatic and philosophical concerns of Sumarokov's play and to consider the basic presuppositions of Russian Neoclassical tragedy.

Although nowhere in the published version of his play did Sumarokov explicitly acknowledge a connection with Shakespeare, the problem of Sumarokov's borrowing was raised in extreme form already in 1750, the year after the play was first staged, by Sumarokov's then arch-enemy Trediakovskii. Trediakovskii had reviewed "Hamlet" for publication as a "censor" for the Academy of Sciences two years earlier. Trediakovskii's criticism and suggested stylistic corrections at that time evidently angered Sumarokov, who soon after attacked Trediakovskii in the famous closing lines of the second of his "Two Epistles" and lampooned him as the eponymous anti-hero of his comedy "Tresotinius" (Levitt, ""Censorship and Provocation "; Grinberg and Uspenskii, 142–44 and 160–70). In his response to "Tresotinius," Trediakovskii charged that all of Sumarokov's works were bad imitations of foreign models, or rather, bad imitations of *imitations* of foreign models, and included "Hamlet" in this latter group:

> Гамлет, как очевидныи сказывают свидетели, перведен был прозою с Англинския Шекеспировы, а с прозы уже зделал ея почтенный Автор нашими стихами. (Trediakovskii, 441)[1]
>
> (As eyewitnesses report, Hamlet was translated from Shakespeare's English into [French] prose, and from prose our respected Author then made his own in our [Russian] verses.)

To this Sumarokov answered (in his posthumously published "Answer to Criticism"):

> Гамлет мой, говорит он, Не знаю от кого услышав, переведен с Французской прозы Аглинской Шекеспировой Трагедии, в чем он очень ошибся. Гамлет мой кроме Монолога в окончании третьяго действия и Клавдиева на колени падения, на Шекеспирову Трагедию едва, едва походит. (Sumarokov, PSVS, X, 117)
>
> (My Hamlet, he says, and I do not know from whom he heard it, was translated from a French prose [version] of Shakespeare's tragedy—in this he is very

---

[1] Quotes from Russian (and from Shakespeare's English) have been given in modern orthography in accord with accepted practice; minor errors of punctuation in Sumarokov, PSVS, have been corrected.

mistaken. My Hamlet, apart from the Monologue at the end of the third act and Claudius' falling down on his knees hardly resembles Shakespeare's tragedy whatsoever.)

While repudiating Trediakovskii's statement that "Hamlet" was based on the French prose version (from the second volume of La Place's well-known *Le theatre anglois* of 1745, which combined direct translation of the original prose and verse with a good deal of prose paraphrase), on closer scrutiny Sumarokov's statement about the character of his borrowing is rather ambiguous. In the two passages in which Sumarokov explicitly does acknowledge resemblance, he leaves it unclear whether this refers to a resemblance to the French version or to the original play. His larger point, however, is unequivocal: "My Hamlet...hardly resembles Shakespeare's tragedy whatsoever." Indeed, were it not for the characters' names, and the two plays' basic point of departure, one might hardly connect them. In contrast to Shakespeare, as well as to Corneille and Voltaire, Sumarokov's tragic dramaturgy was based (as Gukovskii noted) "on the principles of an extreme economy of means, simplification, so to speak restraint and 'naturalness'" (69). First of all, Sumarokov has greatly streamlined the cast of characters: there are eight named players to Shakespeare's seventeen, and of these eight, only five are from Shakespeare. Gone are Horatio, Laertes, Rozencrantz and Guildenstern, among others; added are confidants to Hamlet and Ophelia, making a neat tetrad of the four leading players (Hamlet, Gertrude, Claudius, Ophelia) and confidants, if we include among them Polonius (confidant to Claudius) and Ratuda (Ophelia's "mamka" [nurse]). The plot, too, is greatly simplified, with all those things considered improper from the point of view of Neoclassisist dramaturgy expunged, including the visit of the ghost (here reduced to an appearance in a dream, and not the herald of the murder). Also gone are Hamlet's feigned insanity, Ophelia's madness and suicide, the graveyard scene, the duel, and the famous play within the play. Polonius, in Sumarokov's version, is co-conspirator with Claudius (in this version not Hamlet's uncle) and the actual murderer of the old king. The killing is committed by sword, rather than by poison in the ear, and Hamlet learns of the crime from the servants (after a year's hesitation, Ophelia's "mamka" tells Hamlet's confidant Armans). Needless to say, Ophelia's struggle against Claudius' plan to dump Gertrude and marry her—which according to Karlinsky mechanically turned Shakespeare's plot into one from Corneille, and "Hamlet" into "Le Cid" (Karlinsky, 68)—is absent in the original. Most egregiously departing from Shakespeare, as we have noted, Sumarokov gave his play a happy ending.

By choosing to call his play "Hamlet" Sumarokov was following common eighteenth-century practice of adopting well-known titles and character names but informing them with new content. He was not "copying" the works of other authors so much as announcing his appropriation of those works for his own uses, thus often signaling a competition with them. In Shakespeare's case, "Hamlet" was a prime candidate for being "improved upon" because it was a play leading European classicists (especially Voltaire) had criticized, and was by a writer, as Sumarokov himself wrote (in the notes to his "Epistle on Poetry" of the same year), "in whom there is a lot that is very bad and very much that is extraordinarily good" (Sumarokov, PSVS, I, 355; on the possible sources for this opinion, see Alekseev, Shekspir, 19–22). Furthermore, Shakespeare probably held an added attraction for Sumarokov insofar as even Shakespeare's detractors acknowledged his position as founder of the English theater, a role to which Sumarokov aspired in Russia. Voltaire pointed the way, by the example of his own dramas, by the famous discussion of Shakespeare's defects in his *Lettres philosophiques,* and by his own attempt in that work to render the uncouth Englishman's rough blank verse into acceptable French alexandrines. Sumarokov, probably Voltaire's greatest Russian admirer and disciple (see Zaborov, 14–25), took the next logical step.

While the dependence of parts of Sumarokov's play (particularly, the "To be, or not to be" monologue) upon Voltaire's free translation — included together with a discussion of Shakespeare and English tragedy in letter eighteen of the *Lettres philosophiques, ou Lettres anglaises* first published in 1734 — and upon La Place's prose and verse translation of the play, has long been noted, there has been no systematic attempt to evaluate the nature of Sumarokov's borrowings or to put them into the context of his play (as Alekseev remarked, *Shekspir,* 24; cf. Lang). The tentative reevaluations that Alekseev suggests (e.g., downplaying Voltaire's role) and new attempts at textual analysis that have been made (esp. Toomre), however, in our view significantly miss the mark.

A close comparison of the text of "Hamlet" with the three earlier versions of the "To be, or not to be" monologue[2] — Shakespeare's text (accord-

---

[2] I am only dealing here with these obvious candidates for discussion as sources for Sumarokov, and do not pretend to be exhaustive. Other potential sources include several French versions of the monologue that appeared as responses to Voltaire's admittedly free reworking. Among these are Abbé Prévost's in his one-man journal *Pour et Contre,* no. 12 (1733), and the one in the *Bibliothèque Britannique* cited by Lirondelle (17n). On alleged German influence, see the literature cited in Alekseev, *Shekspir,* 28–29.

ing to the fourth folio version), Voltaire's 1734 version from the *Lettres philosophiques,* and La Place's prose translation of 1745 — reveals, first of all, that Sumarokov made repeated and very specific use of Voltaire's version (*pace* Alekseev, *Shekspir,* 24–5, and Toomre, 8, who asserts that "whereas La Place's influence was specific, Voltaire's was diffused"; texts are appended to this article). Sumarokov borrowed specific phrases and images from Voltaire — phrases and images that do not occur either in the original or in La Place — from almost every other line of Voltaire's 24-line text (see Appendix Two). At the same time, however, it would be equally wrong to conclude that Sumarokov "blindly followed in Voltaire's footsteps" (e.g., Bulgakov, 52, who does note elsewhere that Sumarokov created "a completely new play" in comparison to Shakespeare's [49]). Sumarokov did not utilize any of Voltaire's explicitly anti-clerical additions to the speech, in particular what Voltaire had substituted for Shakespeare's catalogue of earthly woes ("the whips and scorns of time, / The oppressor's wrong... / The pangs of dispriz'd Love" etc.). Here Voltaire inserted his own list (headed off by "nos Prêtres menteurs benir l'hipocrisie" [line 16]; on Voltaire's "misuse" of Shakespeare, see Serrurier).[3] In general, one may say that while Sumarokov may have borrowed liberally from Voltaire, in the monologue as a whole he is closer to the spirit of the original and to La Place's more faithful paraphrase, even while echoes of La Place's prose text are more distant and less easily pinned down.

The discovery that Sumarokov borrowed the fourth folio English original while working on "Hamlet" may be significant, insofar as Sumarokov might have gotten a colleague to help him interpret the English, few though English speakers were in eighteenth-century Russia (see Alekseev, "Angliiskii iazyk"). There is no evidence that Sumarokov himself knew English, although as I have shown elsewhere ("Sumarokov's Reading") Sumarokov also borrowed other books from the Academy library in languages that he didn't know or know well (Dutch, Latin, Greek) in connection with various projects he was working on. Turning to Sumarokov's monologue, there are a few individual words that might indicate direct borrowing from Shakespeare, that is, words which appear in Shakespeare but not in Voltaire or La Place. These are the references to: "country" (*strana*), rather than "world" in the French (*monde*); to "flesh" (*plot'*); and to poverty (*nishcheta*) — both absent in the French versions.

---

[3] Voltaire's discussion of the need for free translation which accompanies his version of the monologue seems a possible likely source for the disputed passage criticizing "word for word" translation at the beginning of Sumarokov's "Epistle on the Russian Language," which is sometimes (but not undisputedly) taken as a criticism of Trediakovskii.

Chapter 5. Sumarokov's Russianized "Hamlet"

Note that in the last instance other editions of Shakespeare's monologue have "proud man's contumely" where the fourth folio version, the text Sumarokov had at his disposal, has "*poor* man's Contumely." More compelling are two lines absent from the French versions which clearly recall Shakespeare's text: "For in that sleep of death, what dreams may come ..." (No chto za sny siia noch' budet predstavliat'!) and "the thousand natural shocks / That flesh is heir to" (Kakim ty estestvo surovstvam podchinenno!). Further, Sumarokov's rendition of the refrain "To dye [sic], to sleep ..." (1. 69), and "To die to sleep / To sleep, perchance to dream" (11. 72–73), captures the syntactic cadence of the original verses far more effectively than the French versions. In his text Sumarokov accentuates the rhythm by the use of dashes, something which, notably, later editors of Shakespeare used to punctuate these and other lines from the monologue. In general, as Toomre notes of the central part of Sumarokov's text, "the intensification of poetic devices" (which was contrary to Sumarokov's usual striving for simplicity) "plus the clear echoes of the original syntax help give this passage a flavor at least reminiscent of Shakespeare" (14). In sum, however, and despite the distinctly Shakespearean spirit we may at times feel in the monologue, the evidence for direct borrowing, while suggestive, remains weak. In contrast, Sumarokov's specific borrowing of poetic images from Voltaire is far more compelling and convincing. There does not seem to be sufficient reason to overturn the traditional wisdom that for his basic acquaintance with the play and monologue Sumarokov was indebted to La Place.

As an example of Sumarokov's transformation of Shakespeare's monologue, let us look at the concluding section. First, Shakespeare's text from the fourth folio, followed by the prose translation from La Place:

> Who would these Fardles bear
> To grunt and sweat under a weary life,
> But that the dread of something after death,
> The undiscovered Country, from whose Born
> No Traveller returns, puzzles the will,
> And makes us rather bear those ills we have,
> Than fly to others that we know not of.
> Thus Conscience does make Cowards of us all,
> And thus the Native hue of Resolution
> Is sicklied o'er, with the pale cast of thought,
> And enterprizes of great pith and moment,
> With this regard their Currents turn away,
> And lose the name of action.
>
> (Shakespeare, 71, sep. pag.; cf. III: i: 76–88 in Farnham)

Ne vaudroit-il pas mieux, s'affranchir d'un fardeau dont le poids nous accable?...Mais la terreur qu'inspire l'idée d'un autre monde, du monde inconnu, dont nul mortel n'est jamais retourné, ralentit ce désir, & glace nos pensées. Nous connoissons nos maux, & nous les supportons, dans la crainte d'en affronter d'autres que nous ne conoissons pas! La conscience nous parle, nous l'écoutons, elle nous arrête; elle calme l'impétuosité de nos transports; & la réfléxion, détruit par dégrés, les projets enfantés par le désespoir... (La Place, 334)

Voltaire compresses this fifteen-line concluding section of Shakespeare's monologue into four lines, eliminating both of the extended discussions—about the afterlife ("the undiscovered Country") and about that "pale cast of thought" which erodes human resolution. The lines become, instead, a logical reaction to the catalogue of evils which had preceded:

La mort serait trop douce en ces extrémités;
Mais le scruple parle & nous crie, Arrêtez;
Il défend à nos mains cet heureux homicide,
Et d'un Héros guerrier, fait un chrétien timide, &c.
(Voltaire, II, 82)

Consistent with the anti-clerical slant Voltaire gives to Hamlet's monologue, he transforms the conflict here into a simplistic clash between Christian cowardice (note how "le scruple" replaces Shakespeare's more positive "conscience," which La Place reinstates) and heroic bravery, which has a distinctly rationalist tinge (cf. Voltaire's earlier addition of the line "Dieux cruels! s'il en est..." and "De nos Prêtres menteurs benir l'hipocrisie" cited above). Sumarokov's version is significantly different:

Когдаб мы жили в век, и скорбь жила б в век с нами.
Во обстоятельствах таких нам смерть нужна;
Но ах! во всех бедах еще страшна она.
Каким ты естество суровствам подчиненно!
Страшна — но весь страх прейдет — прейдет мгновенно.
Умри! — но что потом в несчастной сей стране,
Под тяжким бременем народ речет о мне?
Он скажет, что любовь геройство победила,
И мужество мое тщетою учинила:
Что я мне данну жизнь безславно окончал,
И малодушием ток крови проливал,
Котору за него пролить мне должно было.
Успокоение! почто ты духу льстило?

Chapter 5. Sumarokov's Russianized "Hamlet"

Не льзя мне умереть исполнить надлежит,
Что совести моей днесь истина гласит.
          (Sumarokov, PSVS, III, 95–6)

(If we lived forever we would live forever in sorrow. In such circumstances we need death. But oh! For all our sorrows it is still dreaded. To what severities are you subject, nature! Dreaded — but all dread will pass — pass in an instant. Die! — but what then will the people in this unfortunate country, under heavy burden, say of me? They will say that love conquered heroism, and made my courage futile, that I finished the life given me without glory, and because of my cowardice caused blood to flow that I should have spilled for them. Tranquility! Why did you flatter my spirit? I cannot die, I must fulfill [my duty] that the truth now discloses to my conscience.)

While Sumarokov obviously borrowed the second line from Voltaire ("Vo obstoiatel'stvakh takikh nam smert' nuzhna" = "La mort serait trop douce en ces extrémités"), he has restored much of the content of the original monologue and made it much closer to Shakespeare's in length. However, at the same time Sumarokov has significantly modified its basic emphasis. Where Shakespeare (and La Place) focus on "the dread of something after death," Sumarokov's Hamlet is terrified at the idea of dying itself and, what really disturbs him, the consequences of his death for this world. Sumarokov's hero, like Shakespeare's in the opening lines of the monologue, meditates upon life's sea of troubles, but Sumarokov fundamentally changes the import of the discussion of "the undiscovered country":

Умри! — но что потом в несчастной сей стране,
Под тяжким бременем народ речет о мне?

(Die! — but what then will the people in this unfortunate country, under heavy burden, say of me?)

"That unhappy country"—absent from Voltaire's version and described as "l'autre monde, du monde inconnu" in La Place—here signifies not the terrifyingly mysterious afterlife but Russia herself, and the sufferer "pod tiazkim bremenem" not Hamlet but the Russian people. This transformation of Shakespeare's "country" is emblematic of Sumarokov's changes both in Shakespeare's and Voltaire's texts. Sumarokov's hero struggles with the problem of his country's fate, and his conflict is neither with a Voltairean anticlerical "scruple" nor with the abstract metaphysical ratiocination about the other world of Shakespeare's hero, but rather a concrete choice between love or duty, here described as the opposition between heroism and cowardice (*geroistvo* versus *malodushie*). While this opposition may also have been suggested by Voltaire's text, its context again has been fundamentally altered: Sumarokov's protagonist worries about his honor and posthumous national reputation rather than the limits of his reason. Sumarokov slavishly follows neither Shakespeare nor Voltaire. His hero resolves (at least for the moment) on doing his duty, which is unequivocally presented as the voice of truth and conscience (*sovest'* here may also suggest "reason"):

Не льзя мне умереть исполнить надлежит,
Что совести моей днесь истина гласит.

(I cannot die, I must fulfill [my duty] that the truth now discloses to my conscience.)

Sumarokov's appropriation of Shakespeare's text for his own purposes and basic shift of emphasis is even more evident in the second passage he admitted borrowing — Claudius' "falling down on his knees" at the start of his second act (III: xvii in La Place's version; III: iii in modern editions of "Hamlet"). Sumarokov's borrowing in this case is limited primarily to the basic *gesture of* Claudius' kneeling; the 37-line monologue, which was one of the few passages in the play La Place rendered in verse, in standard rhymed alexandrine couplets, is reduced in Sumarokov's version to 14 lines, but its resemblance to La Place or the original monologue hardly goes farther than dealing with the similar situation of a king's attempt at repentance. Both the content of the speech and its dramatic context and emphasis have been changed beyond what may be called "borrowing." The divergences from the original, as with Hamlet's monologue, are characteristic. Whereas Hamlet's play within a play has "caught the conscience of the king" and moved Claudius to prayer, which he attempts as Hamlet secretly watches (indeed the fact of his praying induces Hamlet to put off his revenge), Sumarokov's Klavdii attempts to pray in front of his evil advisor Polonii, but then decides that he can't. In this, his first, appearance in the play Klavdii asks God to

Принудь меня, принудь прощения просить!
Всели желание искать мне благодати;
Я не могу в себе сей ревности сыскати!
Противных божеству исполнен всех страстей.
Ни искры добраго нет в совести моей.
При покаянии ж мне что зачати должно?
Мне царствия никак оставить невозможно.

Chapter 5. Sumarokov's Russianized "Hamlet"

На что мне каяться и извергати яд;
Коль мысли от тебя далеко отстоят.
(Sumarokov, PSVS, III, 74)

(Compel me, compel me to ask forgiveness! Sow in me the desire to seek grace; I cannot find this fervor in myself! I am filled with all kinds of passions that God detests. There is no spark of good in my conscience. If I repent what could I undertake? There is no way I can abandon the kingdom. Why should I repent and disgorge poison when my thoughts are so far from you.)

He then arises to continue his evil plotting (to kill Hamlet, get rid of the repentant Gertrude, and marry Ophelia). Once again, Sumarokov does not concern himself with the problematic metaphysical status of the afterlife with which the characters of Shakespeare's play are preoccupied, from the question of the status of ghosts in purgatory to the question of the confessional state of the soul at the moment of death, as in Claudius' case. Sumarokov's Klavdii, rather, recognizes that he is essentially evil and doomed to damnation:

Когда природа в свет меня производила!
Она свирепствы все мне в сердце положила.
Во мне изкоренить природное мне зло,
О воспитание, и ты не возмогло!
(Sumarokov, PSVS, III, 73)

(When nature brought me forth into the world it put only cruelty in my heart. O education, even you were unable to root out the natural evil in me!)

One of the crucial issues that emerges from Sumarokov's versions of the Shakespearean monologues hence becomes: can anyone or anything (i.e., a rational education, and clear knowledge of the truth) overcome "nature" and "eradicate natural evil"? As opposed to Shakespeare, Sumarokov's play centers on the problem of good and evil in *this* world; when Sumarokov's characters invoke the afterlife, it is as the place where evil is unequivocally punished or good rewarded, and hence an eloquent argument for proper behavior in the here and now. For Sumarokov, the issue becomes: To what extent can an individual overcome evil in him or herself? Can evil be overcome? And by extension, how should one act toward evil in others?

Such a preliminary reconstruction of the play's philosophical crux is supported by the single detailed contemporary critique of Sumarokov's dramaturgy, Trediakovskii's "Letter in Which is Contained A Discussion of the Poetry Published Up to Now by the Author of Two Odes, Two

Tragedies and Two Epistles, Written from a Friend to a Friend" (Pis'mo, v kotorom soderzihtsia rassuzhdenie o stikhotvorenii, ponyne na svet izdannom ot avtora dvukh od, dvukh tragedii i dvukh epistol, pisannoe ot priiatelia k priiateliu) of 1750. Although intended to destroy Sumarokov's reputation as a writer, Trediakovskii's letter provides unique evidence to help us to understand the precise terms in which the issues are framed in Sumarokov's play and to reconstruct the way this important contemporary conceived of Russian Neoclassical drama. Trediakovskii attacks Sumarokov from a position of rationalist or classicizing linguistic purism (Uspenskii, 166; Zhivov, chap. 2, esp. 81–95), but his literary and philosophical program is in essential respects identical to Sumarokov's. He attacks the man who set himself up as the "Russian Boileau" and literary lawgiver by taking the high ground of an even more stringent application of the classicist "rules." The terms in which Trediakovskii criticizes Sumarokov and the philosophical issues posed in his plays reflect positions he and Sumarokov held in common.

One of the many places where Trediakovskii took issue with Sumarokov was precisely his depiction of Claudius' failed repentance. Among his numerous criticisms of Sumarokov's language (in particular, his use of the word *pobornik* in the meaning "enemy" [Trediakovskii, 480; see Uspenskii, 160]), he also found fault with the idea of Claudius asking God to "compel" him to ask for forgiveness (as if this were Sumarokov speaking rather than his evil character). Trediakovskii found this notion

> somewhat suspicious; but I will leave it to theologians to argue about the logic of Orthodoxy (o razume pravoslaviia); they know that God's assistance (sodeistvie) to human will never occurs by compulsion, but only by forewarning (po predvareniiu), by inclination, and by arousal to good, or by keeping us back from, or [making us feel] repulsion to evil: otherwise our free will would perish, that which we all feel within our conscience. (480)

The question here is how to understand *God's action in the world*, which Trediakovskii elsewhere in the letter defines as the fundamental substance of tragedy:

> According to its most important and primary statute (ustanovlenie), tragedy is produced in order to inculcate the audience (vlozhit' v smotritelei) with love for virtue and an extreme hatred for evil... Hence... one must always give priority to good deeds, and evildoing, however many successes it may have [in the play], must always end up in retreat (v popranii), *in this way imitating the very actions of God.* (494–5, italics added)

Chapter 5. Sumarokov's Russianized "Hamlet"

This criticism, aimed at Sumarokov's first tragedy "Khorev," may serve as a working description of "Hamlet," in which the hero lives to marry Ophelia and reign in Denmark, while the villain Claudius is killed and his evil genius Polonius commits suicide.

However, as the previous passage from Trediakovskii's letter suggests, the existence of evil (for example, in Claudius) and its intractability present a fundamental philosophical problem: how and to what extent are human passions to be overcome? What role does the divine agency play in men's affairs, and in Neoclassical tragedy? Despite his objection to the idea of divine compulsion, Trediakovskii at the same time acknowledges, indeed welcomes, God's interventions (forewarning, inclination, arousal, restraint, repulsion). Perhaps as a rebuff to Trediakovskii's criticism, in a poem of 1755 Sumarokov specifically described the action of the tragic poet in terms of compulsion:

> В героях кроючи стихов своих творца,
> Пусть тот трагедией вселяется в сердца:
> Принудит чувствовать чужие нам напасти
> И к добродетели направить наши страсти.
> (Sumarokov, *Izbr. proizv.*, 130)

(Speaking in verse through his heroes, the creator should sow [his audience's] hearts. He compels us to feel alien misfortunes and direct our passions toward virtue.)

The tragedian, like the divine Creator, actively "sows" emotions into the hearts of the audience and compels them toward virtue "by means of tragedy," thus "imitating the very actions of God."[4] Far from being an abstract rationalist principle, the Russian classicist God emerges as a living, active force in the world, an ideal working within the world. Reason and divinity are identified with one another; yet they are living, interactive forces, and all of creation is seen as informed with divine goodness. Reacting against a line in one of Sumarokov's early odes, Trediakovskii declared (in a Russified Leibnitzian strain): "God in his great wisdom provided for, in his goodness

---

[4] Compare from the "Epistle on the Russian Language" on the miracle of language:
> Прияв драгой сей дар от щедрого творца,
> Изображением вселяемся в сердца.

(Having accepted this valuable gift from the generous Creator we sow [become rooted or implanted in] each other's hearts by means of images.)

forechose, and in his omnipotence created the fairest (samyi preizriadnyi) and greatest world" (470).

How then to explain the existence of evil and "God's action in the world" and in human nature? For both Trediakovskii and Sumarokov, nature has two hypostases. One is divine and rational, often designated as *estestvo*, which Nebel denotes as "essential nature" (Nebel, 4 and 6); Sumarokov characteristically often rhymes it with *bozhestvo*, "divinity." The other is physical and passionate: Claudius' *prirodnoe zlo* or more neutrally, simply *priroda*.[5] Reacting against what he saw as Sumarokov's defense of nature in its second aspect, Trediakovskii charged (with characteristic hyperbole) that

Все сие ложь! все сие нечестие! все сие вред добронравию! Сие есть точное учение Спинозино и Гоббезиево; а сии люди давно уже оглашены справедливо Атеистами. Не *обычай* Во свете сем устав всему; Но есть *право естественное, от Создателя естества вкорененное в естество*...Не безумие правила жития установляет; Но *разумная любовь к добру естественному*. Не *лехкомыслие* [sic] те права утверждает; Но *благоразумное и зрелое рассуждение, смотря на сходство с естественным порядком,* оныя одобряет...
Внутренняя совесть запрещает заключить, чтоб то неправедно и худо было, *когда кто сам себе чего не желает, того и другим не делает.* Сие принадлежит до естественныя правды. Но естественная честность в том, чтоб жить по *разумной любви к добродетели, то есть, искренно, благоразумно, и постоянно действия наши внутренним и внешним располагать так, чтоб получить крайнее и внутреннее блаженство.* Ибо благотворительнейший Зиждитель, сотворяя человека, не мог его не такова сотворить, чтоб ему не быть блаженну, и следовательно естественно одолжил весь человеческий род, имеющий произойти от Адама, к тому, чтоб им стараться о *взаимном себе благополучии,* а больше о получении *каждому крайняго блаженства.* Нет иного конца, чегоб ради был человек сотворен: ибо *славословие Творцу,* есть точно соединено с человеческим блаженством.
Но для получении блаженства, надобны *действия человеческия.* И понеже могли сии быть *пристойныя и неприличныя* к тому; того ради, Не мог того оставить всеблагий Бог, чтоб не различать их *естественными знаками.* Следовательно, всеял в разумы человеческий такое знание, что они рассуждают себе получить от иных *внутренния совести хвалу или стыд,* а от других следующую *приятность или болезнь,* то есть, всеял в них знание правды и лжи,

---

[5] Note however that these two terms are not always used in these senses. See Nebel, 6–7 and Chernaia's remarks (in Robinson, 220–232) on this dualistic view of nature and on the split between faith and reason as a philosophical problem inherited from the late seventeenth century.

Chapter 5. Sumarokov's Russianized "Hamlet"

добра и зла; сиеж для того, дабы, что хвальное с природы, тоб они делали, а от бесчеснаго с природыж, убегали…инако, человеческий разум мог бы то приятным или болезненным почитать, что ему токмо по одной природе приятно или болезненно…словом, был бы человек токмо скот бессловесный, *то есть, был бы он скот* с желанием без рассуждения*…одной токмо природе, но природе повреждённой по падении, должно последовать.* (490–491, italics in original)

(This is all false, all dishonest, all harmful to proper behavior! This is precisely the teaching of Spinoza and Hobbes; and those people have long been rightly proclaimed Atheists. It is not *habit* that is the rule (ustav) for people in this world, but *natural law, inculcated into nature* by nature's Creator…It is not *madness* that establishes rules for living but *rational love for natural good*. It is not *thoughtlessness* that confirms those rights but *sensible and mature reasoning, which is based on resemblance to the natural order* which approves them…
Our inner conscience forbids us to conclude that it is bad and unjust if we *do unto others as we would have others do unto us*. This belongs to [the order of] natural truth. But natural honesty [means] living according to *rational love for virtue, that is, sincerely and sensibly, constantly arranging our inner and outer actions so as to receive maximum inner bliss.* Because our most beneficent Creator, in creating man, could not create him so as not to be blissful, he consequently naturally favored mankind, which descended from Adam, with the desire for *mutual well-being for itself,* and even more with the desire for *maximum bliss for everyone.* There is no other end for which man would have been made; for human bliss is always combined with *glorifying the Creator.*
But to achieve bliss *human actions* are needed. And because these may be *appropriate or inappropriate* [to that end], because of that God, who is all good, could not leave us without *natural signs* with which to distinguish them. Consequently he *sowed* such *knowledge* into human minds (razumy) that they could reason with themselves and receive from some [actions] *the praise or shame of inner conscience* and from others the consequent *pleasure or pain,* that is, he *sowed* in them *the knowledge of truth and falsehood, good and evil;* this in order that man do what is praiseworthy in nature, and avoid what is dishonest in it…otherwise human reason would consider pleasure or pain only according to what nature alone [i.e., empirical, physical nature] dictated was pleasurable or painful…in a word, man would be only a dumb animal (skot besslovesnyi), that is, an animal *with desire but without rationality…,* having to follow only nature alone, a nature tainted by the fall. (490–91)[6]

---

[6] This passage comments on a speech by Astrada from Sumarokov's first tragedy "Khorev." Trediakovskii italicizes several of Astrada's phrases and contrasts them to his own (also italicized) "correct" interpretations. Sumarokov left the offending passage out of the play when he revised it in 1768.

The terms and terminology of Trediakovskii's analysis (for all their repetitive clumsiness of exposition) are virtually identical to those Sumarokov uses in his tragedies, which explore the consequences of this dualistic view of human nature. For convenience sake we may call the two conflicting imperatives the "tragic" (in the traditional sense of "man on his own,"[7] and not to be confused with the genre appellation) and the "Christian." The world of the tragic is the anti-utopian world of man after the fall and without God (hence Trediakovskii's charge of atheism), man desirous of individual bliss and understanding pleasure and pain, but in whom the voice of passion and the flesh deafens inner conscience. Claudius clearly personifies this evil aspect of nature in extreme form, which Polonius rationalizes into a self-serving political theory of might makes right.

Readings of Sumarokov's tragedy often see the problem of good and evil — and the structure of Sumarokov's plots — as a more or less mechanical clash between love and duty. In Harder's and Stennik's descriptions of the play's structure, for example, it is described as the combination of two interrelated conflicts between love and duty: Hamlet's struggle to avenge his father's murder, which conflicts with his love for Ophelia, and Ophelia's struggle against her father's plan to unite her with the evil Claudius (Harder, 14; Stennik, 37).[8] This reading, while true as far as it goes, leaves out the parallel conflicts facing Gertrude and Claudius, and misses the way in which each of the four major characters confronts the problem of evil in him or herself. It also obscures the way in which the very opposition between love and duty breaks down or transcends itself during the course of the play.

Gertrude, as opposed to both Claudius and, to a lesser extent, to Hamlet,[9] is able to overcome her passionate — in this case, adulterous and

---

[7] As in George Steiner's working definition: "the dramatic representation or, more precisely, the dramatic testing of a view of reality in which man is taken to be an unwelcome guest in the world" (xi).

[8] Karlinsky sees "the formal structure of French seventeenth-century tragedy...copied...almost photographically" (68), a combination of Corneille's "Le Cid" and Racine's "Brittanicus." For a discussion of the formal differences between Sumarokov and French Neoclassical dramaturgy, see Gukovskii, "0 sumarokovskoi tragedii."

[9] Despite the obvious differences in their situations, Gertrude's and Hamlet's respective crises are described in much the same terms. Gertrude's reference to her "bludiashchikh dum" (Sumarokov, PSVS, III, 70), for example, recalls Hamlet's "bludiashchii um" in the "To be, or not to be" speech (95). More fundamentally, both suffer from love that destroys honor (chest'). As Trediakovskii's commentary indicates, "ches(t)nost' " (honor, honesty) is a fundamental divine imperative reflecting the conscience

Chapter 5. Sumarokov's Russianized "Hamlet"

murderous — self. It is Gertrude who in Sumarokov's play truly engages the issue of whether or not she is in a condition to pray, and who most directly confronts the horrible prospect of eternal punishment in the afterlife. With the encouragement of Hamlet and his confidant Armans, she is able finally to reconcile divine commandment and the voice of heaven with her own inner voice of repentant conscience (see Sumarokov, PSVS, III, 77 and 82). Gertrude embodies traditional Russian Orthodox values of kenotic humility toward herself and forgiveness toward others, explaining for example to Claudius that "Vragov svoikh proshchat' est' dolzhnost' nashei very" (77) (cf. Kasatkina). She challenges Claudius and Polonius:

> Свидетельствуйте вы, что я слагаю грех,
> Всещедрый Бог мне дал в сей день к сему успех.
> Не тщетно многи дни мысль ум мой угрызала,
> И человечество в зло серце возвращала...
> Доколе во грехах сих будешь утопать?
> И долголи Царя к мученыо поощрять?
> Иль ты [Клавдий] терпение господне презираешь...?
> Брегись, чтоб вскоре он тебя не поразил,
> Он терпит; но терпеть когда нибудь престанет,
> И в час, когда не ждешь, в твою погибель грянет.
> (Sumarokov, PSVS, III, 76 and 78)

(Bear witness that I am renouncing my sin, as this day all-merciful God has shown me the way. It was not in vain that for many days my mind felt pangs and was reclaiming the humanity in my evil heart... How long will you wallow in these sins? And will you encourage the Tsar to suffer for long? Or do you [Claudius] disdain the Lord's forbearance...? Beware that He doesn't surprise you soon; He is patient, but at some moment this will cease, and when you don't expect it your ruin will strike.)

Gertrude is able to overcome her passionate self both through her own efforts at prayer and, more essentially, via divine agency ("Bog mne dal v sei den' k semu uspekh"). Like the hero of Sumarokov's religious drama "The Hermit," Gertrude rejects her tainted, evil, "tragic" self, including her crown and

---

that God placed in all men. Contrast this with other interpretations which see "honor" in Sumarokov's tragedies in distinctly un-Christian terms. Gukovskii connects the concept with the new corporate aristocratic consciousness imported from France (*Ocherki*, 48f). Serman relates the problem of honor in Sumarokov's tragedies to the notion of honor in Montesquieu and that in early medieval Russia (122–27).

spouse, in order to cleanse herself in the wilderness (Levitt, "Sumarokov's Drama").[10]

Ophelia, on the other hand, personifies the ideal "Christian," utopian model of behavior. It is she who "constantly arranges her inner and outer actions so as to receive maximum inner bliss." Ophelia clearly states the theological point Trediakovskii seemed to be hedging on—the mystical and miraculous aspect of divine nature that reason alone cannot achieve. Ophelia explains her position to her father Polonius, who demands her blind obedience and who denigrates the inner voice of conscience—the main instrument of divine truth within us—as superstition. She responds:

Я суеверия с законом не мешаю,
И Бога чистою душею почитаю,

---

[10] Sumarokov's tragedies, at least his early ones, were paired with his "small comedies" (malye komedii) in prose, which Trediakovskii defined in his "Rassuzhdenie o komedii voobshche i v ososblivosti" of 1752 as "a kind of maidservant (nekotorym rodom sluzhanki)" or "natural sister (rodnaia sestra)" to the tragedies with which they seem to have been matched in performance (Pekarskii, 168–69; Grinberg and Uspenskii, 183, 228 and 246–47). The small comedies functioned first of all as a change of pace, like the old intermedia, or the German "nachspiel" or "nachkomedie." More than that, Sumarokov's early comedies commented upon the tragedies with which they were performed; "Tresotinius" follows (and cites) "Khorev," "Chudovishchi"—"Sinav i Truvor" (see the list of performances in *F. G. Volkov*, 212–18). Records show that "Semira" paired (at least once) with Teplov's translation of Molière's "Le marriage forcé" (Prinuzdennaia zhenit'ba). By process of elimination, this suggests that Sumarokov's generically anomalous one-act verse "drama" "The Hermit (Pustynnik)" of 1757—which was listed together with Sumarokov's "small comedies" in a surviving register of the existing Russian repertory from the early 60's (Rezanov, 31–33)—may have been paired with the only other of Sumarokov's tragedies performed in 1757, "Hamlet." (It is recorded that in early 1758 "Hamlet" paired with "Reka zabveniia," translated from LeGrand, and with "Prinuzhdennaia zhenit'ba" two years later.) "Pustynnik" explicitly dramatizes the philosophical and dramatic problem of "going to the wilderness" (pustynia) which Gertrude faces in "Hamlet." Furthermore, the conclusions that I reach in this article reinforce the "religious" reading of Sumarokov's Neoclassicist dramaturgy which my analysis of "Pustynnik" suggests (Levitt, "Sumarokov's Drama ").

The first to assert the Christian message of Sumarokov's early plays and their connection to the old Russian tradition was E. A. Kasatkina (1955), although she did not attempt to systematize her insights or provide a coherent picture of Sumarokov's literary or intellectual indebtedness. More recently, scholars like A. S. Demin and L. I. Safronova have drawn specific philosophical and literary connections between the late seventeenth and early eighteenth centuries. See Demin, 198–208, Robinson, 68, and note 4 above.

Chapter 5. Sumarokov's Russianized "Hamlet"

Который в естестве мне добродетель влил,
И откровением меня в ней утвердил.
(Sumarokov, PSVS, III, 87)

(I do not confuse superstition and the law and with a pure soul revere God who in nature has sown virtue in me and by revelation has confirmed me in this.)

In Ophelia natural and divine natures meet; she recognizes those "natural signs" (the voice of conscience) which God "pours" or "sows" into human beings and which is analogous to divine Revelation. Reason or true knowledge, like the traditional Russian Orthodox view of the Holy Spirit, both informs creation (its ontology) and is the instrument of its knowability (its epistemology). It is this divine gift Claudius asks God to "sow" into him as well, although it is prevented by his "evil nature." Ophelia privileges "estestvo" over "priroda" and "love" for Hamlet over her "duty" to her father, thus significantly changing the terms of the dramatic conflict, or shifting it to another level.

Like many of Sumarokov's "tragic" lovers, Hamlet is unable — until the very end, I would argue — to resolve the conflict between love and duty, a conflict he has grappled with from his very first lines in the play. Up until its final moments, Hamlet's basic dilemma whether or not to kill Polonius remains unresolved.[11] Like Claudius, Hamlet seems habitually unable to transcend his passionate self. Despite repeated resolves (as in the reworked "To be, or not to be" monologue) to deny his love for Ophelia in order to wreak vengeance on her father, as duty to his dead father demands, he cannot do so. As Ophelia's confidant remarks, despite the fact that Hamlet

Противиться во всем сей нежной страсти чает,
И хочет быти раб разсудка своего;
Но тщетны мысли те, любовь сильняй всево.
(Sumarokov, PSVS, III, 98)

(Hopes to resist this tender passion in all he does and to be a slave to his reason, these ideas are in vain — love is stronger than anything!)

At the end, however, Hamlet is forced to act. He saves himself and Gertrude from Polonius' band of hired assassins, kills Claudius and rescues Ophelia

---

11   Cf. Gukovskii's comments on the endings to Sumarokov's tragedies: "The initial situation, also simplified to an extreme, continues practically throughout the entire tragedy and at the end is [merely] removed, cancelled; one can hardly call the ending of such a play a denouement, insofar as there are no events from which it could have flowed" ("O sumarokovskoi tragedii," 69).

from imminent death at her father's hands. However, these are still somewhat passive actions taken under compulsion; the intervention of the people, roused by Armans, has a lot to do with saving Hamlet and his mother,[12] and Claudius' death is described in terms that almost suggest suicide: Hamlet relates that he "fell under this sword (pal pod sim mechem)." However, as far as Hamlet's positive duty to take revenge for his father's murder, the play has still essentially not moved beyond the situation at its opening. Though Hamlet once again resolves to kill Polonius, now a prisoner, Ophelia's frantic appeals to their love (strast') — which had blunted Hamlet's resolve before — and her dramatic challenge that he use his sword on her first finally achieve their goal. Hamlet proclaims:

> Владычествуй, любовь, когда твоя днесь сила,
> И рассуждение и дух мой покорила!
> Восстань, Офелия! ты власть свою нашла.
> Отри свои глаза! напасть твоя прешла.

(Have your sway, love, as you've shown your power today and defeated my reasoning and my spirit! Arise, Ophelia, you've found your power. Wipe your eyes, misfortune is over.)

Ophelia's power of love here, however, is not or not merely the "vlast' " of "strast' " (power of passion) that she appeals to a few lines earlier, but — I would argue — the power of divine mercy that has been lauded throughout the play. "Passion" is not only victorious here but assumes the axiological weight of "reason," that is, duty is downgraded to a position of "rassuzhdenie" (reasoning) or "low nature," while "love" achieves the status of "divine reason." The terms of the love-duty conflict are reversed, and because of this Hamlet becomes the play's true hero. Hamlet here "imitates divine action," proclaiming as it were the reign of God on earth ("Vladichestvui, liubov',...Vosstan', Ofeliia!") and thereby resurrecting the fallen true believer as reward for her faith.

The earthly crisis — what to do with Polonius — is resolved when the prisoner conveniently does away with himself, declaring (as reported by a guard):

---

[12] Even in this early play we may say that the "narod" is the hero, not merely as a passive object of the players' political concern, but even as the main, active, positive force in history. Such a view should cause us to rethink the changing role of "confidants" in Sumarokov's plays (discussed by Gukovskii, "O sumarokovskoi tragedii," 70–71, in reference to French practice), who here serve not merely as dramatic foils but as plot catalysts and as carriers of important ideological weight.

Chapter 5. Sumarokov's Russianized "Hamlet"

…когда ваш Князь уже остался жив,
Напрасно дочь моя, там просит и стонает.
Прощением вину свою усугубляет;
Я не хочу от них щедроты никакой,
И их владетельми не ставлю над собой.
Скажите им, что я о том лишь сожалею,
Что больше погубить их силы не имею.
(Sumarokov, PSVS, III, 118)

(…when your Prince was out of danger my daughter begged and pleaded in vain. Begging for forgiveness deepens one's guilt. I want no generosity from them and I won't accept their power over myself. Tell them that I only regret that I have no power left to destroy them.)

He then stabs himself. This is not merely a neat solution to Hamlet's intractable dilemma and, as it might seem at first, a cheap way for the dramatist to tie up a difficult loose end and avoid confronting a serious issue. Ophelia and Hamlet's very generosity and willingness to offer divine mercy are the very things that move this antiutopian villain to self-destruction; he is destroyed not by earthly "tragic" means (i.e., Hamlet claiming an eye for an eye, as duty demands) but by the working out of divine reason. In behavioral and theological terms, non-resistance to evil triumphs. Evil — theologically speaking, the embodiment of non-being — is left to take its own course, i.e. self-destruct, after being exposed for what it is. In the closing lines of the play, Ophelia herself underscores the message of divine justice divinely enacted:

Ты само небо здесь Полонья покарало!
Ты, Боже мой, был долготерпелив!
Я чту судьбы твои! Твой гнев есть справедлив!
(Sumarokov PSVS, III, 119)

(You, heaven itself, has here punished Polonius! You, My God, were long suffering! I trust your providence! Your anger is just!)

This is not a "deus ex machina" ending which would signal real divine "compulsion" in human affairs and which would, because of its lack of (human) motivation, paradoxically demonstrate God's distance from men's affairs or deny their free will. Rather, Sumarokov depicts human psychology as God's will working though men — a "sodeistvie" — either to the good, or, as in Polonius' case, to the evil.

Sumarokov's "Hamlet," then, centers on the working out of divine theodicy on earth, and in that sense is fundamentally inimical to traditional notions of the tragic. George Steiner, in his book *The Death of Tragedy* has argued that it was the eighteenth century's

> triumph of rationalism and secular metaphysics which mark the point of no return [for tragedy]. Shakespeare is closer to Sophocles than he is to Pope and Voltaire. To say this is to set aside the realness of time. But it is true, nevertheless. The modes of the imagination implicit in Athenian tragedy continued to shape the life of the mind until the age of Descartes and Newton. It is only then that the ancient habits of feeling and the classical orderings of material and psychological experience were abandoned. With the *Discours de la methode* and the *Principia* the things undreamt of in Horatio's philosophy seem to pass from the world. (193)

Russia had never known the spirit of ancient tragedy, and its ethos was alien to both the Orthodox and Neoclassicist worldviews. Perhaps no clearer proof of this is Sumarokov's "Hamlet" itself, from which the things undreamt of in Horatio's philosophy have been systematically deleted. In the terms we have presented it is specifically the "tragic" aspect of nature (priroda) — associated with man's fallen state — that is overcome in the play by the action of divine mercy and justice.

A common Russian view of Sumarokov's tragedies stresses their political message, and sees the plays as allegories on good and bad monarchs. In "Hamlet," for example, Gertrude and Polonius debate the question whether or not tsars are above the law, the evils of bad advisors are exposed, enlightenment rhetoric is used to justify blatantly evil actions, and so on. Going still further in this vein, some commentators have seen in the play an allegorical defense of Empress Elizabeth's ascension to the throne; other critics ascribe the play's absence from the stage after 1762 to disturbing parallels contemporaries may have seen between the "Hamlet" plot and Catherine II's manner of coming to power; by the end of her reign Pavel Petrovich (the future Paul I) was often associated with the unhappy Danish prince (on both issues see Alekseev's review of the literature, *Shekspir*, 730). The obvious anachronism of this reading suggests the larger problem of applying all such allegorical interpretations to Sumarokov's tragedies. Gukovskii was much nearer the mark when he noted that Sumarokov's tragedies have the "character of a panegyric to individual virtues," and are "meant to inspire ecstasy in the viewer in the face of virtue, to act on his emotional receptivity,... to correct the viewers' souls and not their minds, and also not the state apparatus" (Gukovskii, "O sumarokovskoi tragedii," 73–74). Scholars have noted passing similarities between the language and message of Sumarokov's tragedies and Russian triumphal odes, whose goals were to glorify, and indirectly edify, the tsar; Sumarokovian "tragedy," in the non-tragic terms we have described it, perhaps approaches even more closely the spiritual ode, which is addressed not to tsar but to God, and whose ultimate goal — as Trediakovskii put it — duplicates man's proper function on earth of "glorifying the Creator." This notion has deep affinities to traditions of Russian Orthodoxy, the very word for which denotes the primary Russian cultural imperative of "correct glorying" (pravoslavie). From this perspective, the "tragic" in Russian eighteenth century tragedy is but the fallen, human, transient element which Sumarokov's protagonists must struggle to overcome in their quest "to imitate God's actions on earth" (and on stage) in order to assert the reality of a divinely rational utopia.

Works Cited

Alekseev, M. P. "Angliiskii iazyk v Rossii i russkii iazyk v Anglii." *Uchenye zapiski Leningradskogo universiteta*, 72, Seriia filologicheskikh nauk, 9 (1944): 77–137.
Alekseev, M. P., ed. *Shekspir i russkaia kul'tura*. Moscow, Leningrad: Nauka, 1965.
Bulgakov, A. S. "Ranee znakomstvo s Shekspirom v Rossii." *Teatral'noe nasledie*, I. Leningrad, 1934. Pp. 47–117.
Demin, A. S. *Russkaia literatura vtoroi poloviny XVII — nachala XVIII veka: Novye khudozhestvennye predstavleniia o mire, prirode, cheloveke*. Moscow: Nauka, 1977.
F. G. Volkov i russkii teatr ego vremeni: sbornik materialov. Moscow: AN SSSR, 1953.
Farnham, Willard, ed. William Shakespeare, *Hamlet Prince of Denmark*. The Pelican Shakespeare. Baltimore: Penguin Books, 1974.
Grinberg, M. S. and B. A. Uspenskii. *Literaturnaia bor'ba Trediakovskogo i Sumarokova v 1740-kh — nachale 1750-kh godov. Russian Literature*, 31: 2 (1992): 133–272.
Gukovskii, G. A. *Ocherki po istorii russkoi literatury XVIII veka: Dvorianskaia fronda v literature 1750-kh — 1760-kh godov*. Moscow, Leningrad: AN SSSR, 1936.
Gukovskii, G. A. "O sumarokovskoi tragedii." *Poetika*, I. Leningrad, 1926; rpt. Munich: Wilhelm Fink Verlag, 1970. Pp. 67–80.
Jusserand, J. J. *Shakespeare en France sous l'ancien regime*. Paris: Armand Colin, 1898.
Harder, Has-Bernd. *Studien zur Geschichte der russischen klassizistischen Tragödie 1747–1769*. Wiesbaden: Otto Harrassowitz, 1962.
Karlinsky, Simon, *Russian Drama from Its Beginnings to the Age of Pushkin*. Berkeley: University of California Press, 1986.
Kasatkina, E. A. "Sumarokovskaia tragediia 40-kh i nachala 50-kh godov XVIII veka." *Uchenye zapiski Tomskogo ped. Institute*, 13 (1955): 213–261.
Lang, D. M. "Sumarokov's `Hamlet': A Misjudged Russian Tragedy of the Eighteenth Century." *Modern Language Review*, 43: 1 (January 1948): 67–72.

La Place, Pierre Antoine de. "Hamlet, Prince de Danemarc, Tragedie, traduite de l'anglois de Shakespeare." In *Le theatre anglois*. Vol. 2. Paris, 1745. Pp. 275–416.

Levitt, Marcus C. "Sumarokov's Drama 'The Hermit': On the Generic and Intellectual Sources of Russian Classicism" (1993), translated in this volume.

Levitt, Marcus C. "Censorship and Provocation: The Publishing History of Sumarokov's 'Two Epistles'" (1994), translated in this volume.

Levitt, Marcus C. "Sumarokov's Reading at the Academy of Sciences Library" (1995), translated in this volume.

Lirondelle, Andre. *Shakespeare en Russie, 1748–1840*. Paris: Hachette, 1912.

Pekarskii, P. *Istoriia Imperatorskoi Akademii Nauk v Peterburge*. Vol. 2. St. Petersburg, 1873.

PSVS, I–X — A. P. Sumarokov, *Polnoe sobranie vsekh sochinenii v stixakh i v proze*. 10 vols. Moscow, 1781–2.

Rezanov, V. I. "Parizhskie rukopisnye teksty sochinenii A. P. Sumarokova." *Izvestiia otdeleniia russkogo iazyka i slovesnosti*, 12:2 (1907): 135–69.

Robinson, A. N., ed. *Razvitie barokko i zarozhdenie klassitsizma v Rossii XVII — nachala XVIII v*. Moscow: Nauka, 1989.

Serman, I. Z. *Russkii klassitsizm: Poëziia, drama, satira*. Leningrad: Nauka, 1973.

Serrurier, C. "Voltaire et Shakespeare: À propos du monologue d'Hamlet." *Neophilologus*, 5 (rept. N.Y., 1963): 205–209.

[Shakespeare, William.] *Mr. William Shakespear's Comedies, Histories, and Tragedies: The Fourth Folio [of 1685] reproduced in facsimile*. Cambridge: D. S. Brewer, 1985.

Steiner, George. *The Death of Tragedy*. New York: Oxford University Press, 1961.

Stennik, Iu. V *Zhanr tragedii i russkoi literature: epokha klassitsizma*. Leningrad: Nauka, 1981.

Sumarokov, A. P. *Izbrannye proizvedeniia*. Leningrad: Sovetskii pisatel', 1957.

Toomre, Joyce S. "Sumarokov's Adaption of *Hamlet* and the 'To Be or Not To Be' Soliloquy." *Study Group on Eighteenth Century Russia Newsletter*, 9 (1981): 6–20.

Trediakovskii, V. K. "Pis'mo v kotorom soderzhitsia rassuzhdenie o stikhotvorenii, ponyne na svet izdannom ot avtora dvukh od, dvukh tragedii, i dvukh epistol pisannoe ot priiatelia k priiateliu. 1750." In: A. A. Kunik, *Sbornik materialov dlia istorii imperatorskoi Akademii Nauk v XVIII veke*. Vol. 2. St. Petersburg, 1865. Pp. 435–96.

Uspenskii, B. A. *Iz istorii russkogo literaturnogo iazyka XVIII — nachala XIX veka*. Moscow: Izd. Mosk. gos. universiteta, 1985.

Voltaire. *Lettres philosophiques*. Edition critique avec une introduction et un commentaire par Gustave Lanson. 2 vols. Paris, 1909.

Zaborov, P. R. *Russkaia literatura i Vol'ter: XVIII — pervaia tret' XIX veka*. Leningrad: Nauka, 1978.

Zhivov. V. M. *Kul'turnye konflikty v istoriii russkogo literaturnogo iazyka XVIII — nachala XIX veka*. Moscow: Institut russkogo iazyka, 1990.

Chapter 5. Sumarokov's Russianized "Hamlet"

APPENDIX ONE
Shakespeare's "To be, or not to be" Monologue from the Fourth Folio (1685)

To be, or not to be, that is the Question:
Whether 'tis nobler in the mind to suffer
The Slings and Arrows of outragious Fortune,
Or to take Arms against a Sea of troubles,
And by opposing end them: to dye, to sleep
No more: and by a sleep, to say we end
The heart-ache, and the thousand natural shocks
That flesh is heir to. 'Tis a consummation
Devoutly to be wish'd. To die to sleep,
To sleep, perchance to dream; I, there's the rub,
For in that sleep of death, what dreams may come,
When he hath shuffled off this mortal Coyle,
Must give us pawse. There's the respect
That makes Calamity of so long life:
For who would bear the whips and scorns of time,
The oppressors wrong, the poor mans Contumely,
The pangs of dispriz'd Love, the Laws delay,
The insolence of office, and the spurns
That patient merit of the unworthy takes,
When he himself might his *Quietus* make
With a bare Bodkin? Who would these Fardles bear
To grunt and sweat under a weary life,
But that the dread of something after death,
The undiscovered Country, from whose Born
No Traveller returns, puzzles the will,
And makes us rather bear those ills we have,
Than fly to others that we know not of.
Thus Conscience does make Cowards of us all,
And thus the Native hue of Resolution
Is sicklied o're, with the pale cast of thought,
And enterprizes of great pith and moment,
With this regard their Currents turn away,
And lose the name of action. Soft you now,
The fair *Ophelia*? Nymph, in thy Horizons
Be all my sins remembred.
(Shakespeare, 71, sep. pag.)

APPENDIX TWO
Voltaire's Version of the "To be, or not to be" Monologue from *Lettres Philosophiques*, Dix-huitième lettre (1734)

(Words and phrases unique to Voltaire which have parallels in Sumarokov's text are underlined, with the Russian equivalents given underneath bracketed in italics.)

Demeure; il faut choisir, & passer <u>à l'instant</u>
                                [*мое сей тело час*]
De a vie à la mort, ou de l'être au néant:
Dieux cruels! s'il en est, éclairez mon <u>courage.</u>
                                [*мужество*]
Faut-il vieillir courbé sous la main qui m'outrage,
<u>Suporter ou finir mon malheur</u> et mon sort?
[*бедствы окончати...или претерпевати*]
Qui suis-je? qui m'arrête? & qu'est-ce que la mort?
C'est la fin de nos maux, c'est mon unique <u>asile;</u>
                                [*пристанище*]
Après de longs transports c'est un <u>sommeil tranquille;</u>
                                [*покойна сна;* cf. *спокойствие, сон*]
On s'endort & tout meurt; mais un affreux réveil,
Doit <u>succeder</u> peut-être aux <u>douceurs du sommeil.</u>
   [*последует*]   [*сну сладку*]
On nous menace, on dit que cette courte vie,
De <u>tourments éternels</u> est aussi-tôt suivie.
   [*мучительное; вечна*]
<u>O mort! moment fatal!</u> affreuse eternité,
[*О смерть! противный час!*]
Tout <u>coeur à ton seul nom</u> se glace épouvanté.
   [*сердцам...единым именем твоим*]
Eh qui pourroit sans toi suporter cette vie,
De nos Prêtres menteurs benir l'hipocrisie;
D'une indigne maitresse encenser les erreurs,
Ramper sous un Ministre, adorer ses hauteurs,
Et montrer les langueurs de son âme abatue,
A des <u>amis ingrats</u> qui détournent la vue?
   [*неверности друзей*]
<u>La mort serait trop douce en ces extrémités;</u>
[*Во обстоятельствах таких нам смерть (нужна)*]
Mais le scruple parle & nous crie, Arrêtez;
Il defenda nos mains cet heureux homicide,
Et d'un <u>Héros</u> guerrier, fait un chrétien <u>timide,</u> &c.
    [*мужество*]   [*малодушие*]
                                     (Voltaire, II, 82)

Chapter 5. Sumarokov's Russianized "Hamlet"

APPENDIX THREE
La Place's Prose Translation of the "To be, or not to be" Monologue from *Le theatre anglois* (1745)

Etre, ou n'être plus? arrête, it faut choisir!...Est-il plus digne d'une grande âme, de supporter l'inconstance, & les outrages de la fortune, que de se révolter contre ses coups?...Mourir...Dormir...Voilà tout. Et si ce sommeil met fin aux miséres de l'humanité, ne peut-on pas du moins le désirer sans crime?... Mourir...Dormir...rêver pent-être!...fatale incertitude!...Qu'espere-t'on gagner, en se délivrant des maux de ce monde, si l'on ignore quel fera son sort dans l'autre? Cette réfléxion seule ne mérite-t'elle pas toute notre attention?...Oui, sans doute, puisque c'est elle qui soumet l'âme la plus altiere, aux longues calamités de la vie!...Eh, qui pourroit souffrir la perversité du siècle, l'injustice des hommes, l'arrogance des ambitieux, les tourmens de l'amour dédaigné, les lenteurs de la Justice, l'insolence des Grands, & les indignes préférences que la faveur obtient sur le mérite? Ne seroit-il pas plus court, de se procurer, tout d'un coup, le repos? Ne vaudroit-il pas mieux, s'affranchir d'un fardeau dont le poids nous accable?...Mais la terreur qu'inspire l'idée d'un autre monde, du monde inconnu, dont nul mortel n'est jamais retourné, ralentit ce désir, & glace nos pensées. Nous connoissons nos maux, & nous les supportons, dans la crainte d'en affronter d'autres que nous ne conoissons pas! La conscience nous parle, nous l'écoutons, elle nous arrête; elle calme l'impétuosité de nos transports; & la réfléxion, détruit par dégrés, les projets enfantés par le désespoir...Mais j'apperçois Ophelia!...(La Place, 333–34)

APPENDIX FOUR
Sumarokov's Version of the "To be, or not to be" Monologue from "Gamlet" (1748)

Что делать мне теперь? Не знаю что зачать.
Легколь Офелию на веки потерять!
Отец! любовница! о имена драгия!
Вы были щастьем мне во времена другия!
Днесь вы мучительны, днесь вы несносны мне;
Пред кем нибудь из вас мне должно быть в вине.
Пред кем я преступлю? вы мне равно любезны:
Здержитеся в очах моих потоки слезны!
Не зрюсь способен быть я к долгу моему,
И нет пристаница блудящему уму.
(Хватается за шпагу.)
В тебе едином меч надежду ощущаю,
А праведную месть я небо поручаю.

Постой, — великое днесь дело предлежит:
Мое сей тело час с душею разделить.
Отвереть ли гроба дверь, и бедствы окончати?
Или во свете сем еще претерпевати?
Когда умру; засну, — засну и буду спать;
Но что за сны сия ночь будет представлять!
Умереть — и внити в гроб — спокойствие прелестно;
Но что последует сну сладку? — неизвестно.
Мы знаем, что сулит нам щедро божество:
Надежда есть, дух бодр; но слабо естество.
О смерть! противный час! минута вселютейша!
Последняя напасть, но всех напастей злейша!
Воображение мучительное нам!
Неизреченный страх, отважнейшим серцам!
Единым именем твоим, вся плоть трепешет,
И от пристанища опять в валы отмещет.
Но есть ли бы в бедах здесь жизнь была вечна;
Ктоб не хотел иметь сего покойна сна?
И кто бы мог снести зла щастия гоненье,
Болезни, нищету, и сильных нападенье,
Неправосудие безсовестных судей,
Грабеж, обиды, гнев, неверности друзей,
Влиянный яд в серца великих льсти устами?
Когдаб мы жили в век, и скорбь жилаб в век с нами.
Во обстоятельствах таких нам смерть нужна;
Но ах! во всех бедах еще страшна она.
Каким ты естество суровствам подчиненно!
Страшна — но весь сей страх прейдет — прейдет мгновенно.
Умри! — но что потом в несчастной сей стране,
Под тяжким бременем народ речет о мне?
Он скажет, что любовь геройство победила,
И мужество мое тщетою учинила:
Что я мне данну жизнь безславно окончал,
И малодушием ток крови проливал,
Котору за него пролить мне должно было.
Успокоение! почто ты духу льстило?
Не льзя мне умереть исполнить надлежит,
Что совести моей днесь истина гласит.
А ты отчаянну Гертруда в мысль не впала,
Жестокость Клавдия и на тебя возстала.
Пойдем, и скажем ей, чтоб Клавдия береглась;
Чтоб только кровь одних тиранов пролилась.

(Sumarokov, PSVS, III, 94–96)

6

SUMAROKOV'S DRAMA "THE HERMIT":
On the Generic and Intellectual Sources of Russian Classicism

Among Sumarokov's twenty-six works for the stage his single drama, "The Hermit" (Pustynnik, 1759), occupies a somewhat enigmatic place, raising questions about both the author's conception of the genre and the play's status as a work of Russian Classicism. As is well known, the notion of genre played a leading role in Classicist poetics, and with Sumarokov in particular. While he often used the word "drama" (Russian, *drama*) in the general sense (as synonym for "play" or "dramatic work" and in such phrases as "drama and music"), nowhere in his works is there a definition of drama as a special genre. In the "Epistle on Poetry," following Boileau, he includes under "drama" comedy and tragedy — the only theatrical genres recognized by Classicism. Furthermore, none of the scholars who have considered Sumarokov's dramaturgy (G. A. Gukovskii, P. N. Berkov, V. N. Vsevolodskii-Gerngross, H.-B. Harder, I. Z. Serman, G. N. Moiseeva, Iu. V. Stennik) have paid attention to the "drama" for the same reason: it did not belong to the standard genres of Classicism and even to some extent conflicted with them.[1] The French scholar Jean Patouillet, who noted this seeming anomaly in passing, expressed surprise that Sumarokov, a violent "foe of the drama" himself had tried his hand at "a genre which he struggled

---

[1] G. A. Gukovskii, "O sumarokovskoi tragedii," *Poetika*, 1 (Leningrad, 1926), 67–80; P. N. Berkov, *Aleksandr Petrovich Sumarokov, 1717–1777*. Leningrad: Iskusstvo, 1949.; V. N. Vsevolodskii-Gerngross, *Russkii teatr ot istokov do serediny XVIII veka* (Moscow: Akademiia nauk, 1957); Hans Bernd Harder, *Studien zur Geschichte der russischen klassizistischen Tragödie, 1747–1769* (Wiesbaden: O. Harrassowitz, 1962); G. N. Moiseeva, *Drevnerusskaia literatura v khudozhestvennom soznanii i istoricheskoi mysli Rossii v XVIII veke* (Leningrad: Nauka, 1980); Iu. V. Stennik, *Zhanr tragedii v russkoi literature: epokha klassitsizma* (Leningrad: Nauka, 1981).

against."² A solution to the riddle of "The Hermit"'s genre and its unexpected defense of its hero's ascetic withdrawal from life require a new consideration of Sumarokovian Classicism.

"The Hermit" does not correspond to usual notions of Sumarokov's dramaturgy either in its form or content. How did it come to be written?

By the middle of the eighteenth century when Sumarokov founded the new national theater, Classicist theater in the West was already experiencing a period of crisis and decadence. In England as a result of Puritan attacks on the theater a new "bourgeois drama" arose; its early prototype, George Lillo's "The London Merchant, or the History of George Barnwell" (1743), achieved popularity across Europe. In France a new mixed dramatic genre appeared, called at times "serious" or "tearful" tragedy, and at times "tearful comedy" or simply "drama" (le drame).³ Forerunners and founders of this trend are considered Nivelle de La Chaussée, Philippe Néricault Destouches and Denis Diderot. As early as 1741 the French critic and translator Pierre Defontaine suggested the term "drama" for this new phenomenon but it took a long time to catch on and did not figure in the repertoire of plays at the Comédie Française until 1769.⁴ By this time there was a large theoretical literature on the subject, in particular well-known treatises by Diderot and Beaumarchais. One hundred years after Defontaine's suggestion Belinskii defined "drama" as "a special type of dramatic poetry that occupies a middle place between tragedy and comedy."⁵ This definition basically coincided with that of eighteenth-century French critics, but for those raised on the classical hierarchy of genres the new phenomenon was far more problematic than for Romantic critics. The terminological lack of clarity continued for a long time. It was hard to decide whether the new plays were closer to comedy or tragedy (there was no other choice) and furthermore they were disparate in form (some in prose and some in verse) and in content (there were "bourgeois," "domestic," and "serious" dramas). In the register of plays

---

[2] Jean Patouillet, "Une episode de l'histoire de la Russie: La Lettre de Voltaire à Sumarokov (26 Février 1769)," *Revue de littérature comparée*, 7 (1927), 448–49.

[3] On the French definition, see: Eleanor F. Jourdain, *Dramatic Theory and Practice in France 1690–1808* (New York: B. Blom, 1968); Félix A. Gaiffe, *Le drame en France au XVIIIᵉ siècle* (Paris: A Colin, 1971); Barrett H. Clark, *European Theories of the Drama...An Anthology of Dramatic Theory and Criticism* (New York: Crown Publishers, 1965).

[4] Gaiffe, *Le drame*, 93, 167; Patouillet, "Une episode," 444–48.

[5] V. G. Belinskii, "Razdelenie poezii na rody i vidy" (1841), *Polnoe sopbranie sochinenii*, vol. 5 (Moscow: Akademiia nauk, 1954), 62.

Chapter 6. Sumarokov's Drama "The Hermit"

of the early Russian theater published by V. I. Rezanov that P. N. Berkov dated to the first half of the 1760's "The Hermit" is listed with Sumarokov's "small" (i.e. one-act) comedies.[6] Kheraskov's first theatrical attempt "The Venetian Nun" (Venetsianskaia monakhina) of 1758 may be considered the first Russian "bourgeois" or "tearful" drama, although the author himself labeled it a tragedy. In contrast to "The Hermit," in this play (which was never staged) monastic vows frustrate the union of the lover — protagonists, which was a fairly common theatrical plot complication.[7] By the mid 1760's many of the new dramas were translated into Russian and in 1770, the year in which Beaumarchais' "tearful drama" *Eugénie* which Sumarokov attacked was staged in Russia, the anonymous one-act drama (*dramma*) "Good Deeds Win Hearts" (Blagodeianiia priobretaiut serdtsa), possibly a translation from French, also appeared.[8] In the mid 1770's Kheraskov wrote two plays subtitled "tearful dramas."[9] As Berkov has demonstrated, the new trend developed mostly as a rejection of Sumarokov's comedic practice. In France these domestic and bourgeois dramas posed provocative social issues and served a new, middle class audience, but in Russia the question of the new form was connected to the creation of a national repertory and the challenge of adapting plays "to Russian mores" (sklonenie na russkie nravy). However, this debate only arose after the creation and staging of "The Hermit."

In regard to its content, there is no clear connection between "The Hermit" and contemporary French dramaturgy. True, there did exist the tradition of "Christian tragedy" (Corneille's "Polyeucte" of 1640, Racine's "Esther" and "Athalie" and of 1689 and 1691, plays that were well known to Sumarokov), but their plots, concerning the martyrdom of early Christian

---

[6] V. I. Rezanov, "Parizhskie rukopisnye teksty A. P. Sumarokova," *Izvestiia Otdeleniia russkogo iazyka i slovesnosti*, 2 (St. Petersburg, 1907), 135–69; P. N. Berkov, *Istoriia russkoi komedii XVIII veka* (Leningrad: Nauka, 1977), 50–2. Apparently in terms of the repertoire, "The Hermit" filled the same role as one-act comedies that were presented along with tragedies, and meant to provide relief to audiences after the presentation of the longer, more serious works.

[7] Michael Green, "Italian Scandal as Russian Tragedy: Kheraskov's *Venetsiasnaia Monakhina*," *Russia and the World of the Eighteenth Century: Proceedings of the Third International Conference*, ed. Roger P. Bartlett, Anthony Glenn Cross, and Karen Rasmussen (Columbus, Ohio: Slavica Publishers, 1988), 388–99.

[8] See *Svodnyi catalog russkoi knigi grazhdanskoi pechati XVIII veka: 1725–1800*, vol. 1 (Moscow: Gos. biblioteki SSSR imeni V. I. Lenina, 1962), 106 (no. 591). Of course, many translations remained in manuscript; see Berkov, *Istoriia*, 84–5.

[9] P. N. Berkov, "Iz istorii russkoi teatral'noi terminologii XVII–XVIII vekov," *Trudy otdeleniia drevnerusskoi literatury*, 11 (Moscow, Leningrad, 1965), 299.

believers, are far from "The Hermit."[10] Sumarokov highly valued Voltaire's Christian tragedy "Alzire" (1736), referring to it as "Voltaire's crown" in the "Epistle on Poetry."[11] While critics have disagreed about whether he wrote genuinely Christian tragedies or masked attacks on religion, it is significant that in his article "Opinion About French Tragedies in a Dream" Sumarokov not only defended Voltaire as a Christian writer but insisted that true writers are always religious.[12] Be that as it may, Voltaire was a fundamental foe of monasticism, and his well-known argument with Pascal, begun in the twenty-fifth of the *Lettres anglaises* known as "Anti-Pascal" (1734), continued throughout his creative life.[13] However, the complex of theological issues that formed the general background for French Classicism on the whole had little direct relevance for Russia.

The most probable source of the new genre for Sumarokov was indigenous "school drama." Transplanted from Poland and Ukraine in the second half of the seventeenth century by Simeon Polotskii and others, by the time that the new secular theatre was established it was already on the wane. For its debut in St. Petersburg in 1752 Fedor Volkov's Yaroslavl troupe that was to become the nucleus of Sumarokov's theater presented both Sumarokov's first tragedy "Khorev" and Dimitri Rostovskii's school drama "On a Repentent Sinner" (O kaiushchemsia greshnike). Three other plays by Rostovskii were also labeled "dramas" ("Uspenskaia," "Rozhdestvenskaia" and "Dmitrievskaia"; all also carried the subtitle "comedy") as was Isaakii Khmarnoi's "Drama of Ezikiel, King of Israel" (Drama o Ezekii, tsare Izrail'skom) of 1728. The importance of school drama for the new secular theater has long been suggested, and E. A. Kasatkina strongly asserted its importance for Sumarokov, although direct borrowings are difficult to demonstrate.[14] The closest direct prototype for "The Hermit" is the drama

---

[10] Nevertheless, Iu. V. Stennik suggests that N. Khrushchev's translation of "Polyeucte" of the late 1750's that was produced in the court theater had an influence on Sumarokov's play. See A. P. Sumarokov, *Dramaticheskie sochineniia*, ed. Iu. V. Stennik (Leningrad: Iskusstvo, 1990), 29–30, 475.

[11] A. P. Sumarokov, *Izbrannye proizvedeniia*, 2nd ed. P. N. Berkov, ed. Biblioteka poeta, Bol'shaia seriia (Leningrad: Sovetskii pisatel', 1957), 121; see also: Michael Green, "Kheraskov and the Christian Tragedy," *California Slavic Studies*, 9 (1976), 1–25.

[12] A. P. Sumarokov, *Polnoe sobranie vsekh sochinenii*, ed. N. I. Novikov. 2nd ed. Vol. 5 (Moscow, 1787), 351–55 (hereafter PSVS).

[13] Mina Waterman, *Voltaire, Pascal and Human Destiny* (New York: Octagon Books, 1971); M. Sina, *L'anti-Pascal di Voltaire*. (Milan: Vita e pensiero, 1970).

[14] E. A. Kasatkina, "Sumarokovskaia tragediia 40-kh i nachala 50-kh godov XVIII veka," *Uchenye zapiski Tomskogo ped. universiteta*, 13 (1955), 213–61.

"Aleksei, Man of God" (Aleksei, Bozhii chelovek) whose plot similarity to Sumarokov's play was suggested by V. N. Vsevolodskii-Gerngross.[15] The Life of Aleksei, Man of God, was one of the most popular and widespread saints lives in Russia, and as V. P. Adrianova-Peretts demonstrated, its story was echoed in many other works, both high church genres (including sermons) and in folk genres (spiritual verse, songs).[16] The play "Aleksei, Man of God" is dated to 1672 or 1673, and is one of the oldest school dramas. In it are combined elements of medieval mystery play and those of newer, Baroque dramaturgy. There are almost forty characters in the play, including angels, allegorical figures, and a variety of "low" types — beggars, peasants, servants. The supernatural plays a major role; angels converse with men, a voice from heaven summons Aleksei, and at the play's end the spirit of the beatified Aleksei gives a speech. All this is far from Sumarokov's dramaturgy, of course. The similarity with Sumarokov's play is in the central subject matter concerning the retreat from worldly goods. This theme, as in "The Hermit," is developed in a series of discussions and complaints concerning the protagonist's voluntary ascetic withdrawal. In particular, the laments by Aleksei's betrothed that she has been "shamed" and "abandoned" by him, and that he has broken his promise to her, generally recall those of Parfeniia in the last act of "The Hermit."[17]

The key problem for Aleksei is that of marriage. Like Sumarokov's protagonist Evmenii, he wants "to serve God," although otherwise there is little similarity. The young Aleksei, single son of a Roman senator, runs away from his wedding and returns home later, incognito, to live the impoverished life of a servant in his father's house; his family only learns of his identity after his death. Evmenii stubbornly defends his retreat from worldly affairs, while Aleksei of the drama (as opposed to the hero of the saint's life) constantly wavers under the influence of various characters (angels, the goddess Juno, his parents, etc.). In Sofronova's words, "Aleksei constantly serves as field of action for higher forces," as opposed to Evmenii who is the independent arbiter of his own fate.[18] Aleksei is thus kin to such other "pathetic heroes" of seventeenth-century literature as the *dobryi*

---

15 Vsevolodskii-Gerngross, *Russkii teatr*, 195.
16 V. P. Adrianova-Peretts, *Zhitie Alekseia cheloveka Bozhiia v drevnei russkoi literature i narodnoi slovesnosti* (Petrograd: Ia. Bashmakov, 1917).
17 "Aleksei, Bozhii chelovek," *Russkie dramaticheskie proizvedeniia 1672–1725 godov*, ed. N. S. Tikhonravov. Vol. 2 (St. Petersburg: D. E. Kozhanchikov, 1874), 55–6.
18 L. A. Sofronova, *Poetika slavianskogo teatra: XVII — pervaia polovina XVIII v.: Pol'sha, Ukraina, Rossiia* (Moscow: Nauka, 1981), 175.

molodets from the "Povest' o Gore-Zochastii" and Savva from the "Povest' o Savve Grudtsyne."[19] Notably, both of these figures end their wanderings in a monastery, although as William Harkins noted, this monastic retreat can hardly be considered a positive resolution.[20] In seventeenth-century literature, the motif of taking refuge in a monastery often had negative connotations (as a place of political imprisonment, escape from something evil, or as a place of worldly rather than spiritual profit). All of this again emphasizes the distance separating "The Hermit" and school drama, but it seems entirely probable that this association was what Sumarokov had in mind in using the generic label "drama." As P. N. Berkov noted, "the new Russian culture and theater of the eighteenth century did not reject the terminology that had arisen in the seventeenth, but filled it with new content."[21]

Before considering this new content, we should note "The Hermit"'s unusual form. Many formal aspects of the play suggest that it broadens the poetics of Sumarokovean tragedy. The main difference is that "The Hermit" is in one act. The play's meter may be considered variable iambic, although more than 86% of the lines (348 of 408) are alexandrines (iambic hexameter) with caesura after the third foot — the standard metrical form for Russian tragedy introduced by Sumarokov. If we add to this the three-foot iambic lines that may be perceived as half-lines or as a continuation of the alexandrine rhythm, the figure rises to almost 95%. The other lines of variable length (one, two, four and five foot lines) taken together comprise less than 5.5% of all lines (.25, 2.7, .75 and 1.4% respectively). This variability of line length is far less than, for example, in Sumarokov's fables. Sumarokov also uses mostly standard paired rhymes, with a small number of ring and one alternating rhyme. In the entire fourth scene (Evmenii's monologue) the tragic norm is preserved.

As in seven of Sumarokov's tragedies, the action takes place in ancient Russia, "in the wilderness near Kiev," and as in them "the world of objects" is largely absent. The single prop, as in most of the tragedies, is a dagger (kinzhal), which plays the same role in the denouement of the play as in the tragedies.[22] The dagger itself, of course, is the symbol of tragic theater. The number of players is seven, the average number for Sumarokov's tragedies,

---

[19] See William E. Harkins, "The Pathetic Hero in Russian Seventeenth-Century Literature," *American Slavic and East European Review*, 14: 4 (1955), 512–27.
[20] Harkins, "The Pathetic Hero," 523.
[21] Berkov, "Iz istorii," 299.
[22] Gukovskii, "O sumarokovskoi tragedii," 70.

Chapter 6. Sumarokov's Drama "The Hermit"

and as in them, the protagonists are close to the throne, although here unlike the tragedies kings and queens play no part. All have traditional ancient Russian names, but even though they are not made up (as may be the case in the tragedies), none has an historical prototype. The high station of the characters that is requisite for tragedy (in sharp contrast to bourgeois and domestic drama) is also crucial in "The Hermit," in which the elevation, seriousness and purity of the passions depicted are equally important.

"The Hermit" is structured according to the system of Sumarokov's tragedies as described by G. A. Gukovskii and Iu. V. Stennik, and even to a greater degree than the tragedies themselves.[23] For example, the drama observes the three unities even more strictly than the tragedies insofar as the play consists of one continuous segment of time and action. All of the elements defined as Sumarokov's system — the striving for clarity, simplicity, unity, and the corresponding economy of dramatic means — here are subject to even greater simplification. As in the tragedies, the drama "is made up in significant measure by disclosing the content of the basic situation as it relates to [each] single pair of heroes separately."[24] This is even more accurate a description of "The Hermit" than the tragedies, insofar as its basic structure is a series of dialogues between Evmenii, who wants to reject the "vanity of life," and the other characters who try to talk him out of it. Gukovskii spoke astutely of the "device of repetition-gradation of the very same situation."[25] The one-act drama that replaces the five-act tragedy has a mirror structure, hinging on the fourth act:

    Act 1 — Evmenii's monlolgue
        Act 2 — Evmenii and Afinogen, Izidor
           Act 3 — Evmenii and Visarion
               Act 4 — Evmenii's monlolgue
           Act 5 — Evmenii and Visarion
       Act 6 — Evmenii and Dometiian, Minodora
    Act 7 — Everyone plus Parfeniia; Evmenii's concluding monologue.

This scheme easily divides into a classical five-part structure and may be considered a microcosm of Sumarokov's tragic structure.

---

[23] Gukovskii, "O sumarokovskoi tragedii," 70; Stennik, *Zhanr tragedii* and "O khudozhestvennoi structure tragedii A. P. Sumarokova," *XVIII vek*, 5 (Moscow, Leningrad, 1962), 273–94.
[24] Gukovskii, "O sumarokovskoi tragedii," 69.
[25] Gukovskii, "O sumarokovskoi tragedii," 75.

All of these features that link Sumarokov's drama with his tragedies suggest that he understood "drama" as a broadening (or narrowing) of tragic practice. It is clear that the notion of drama as a mixed genre — what he later sharply denounced — was not part of his conception.

To turn to the plot of the play, the question of "withdrawing from life" is posed at the very start of the play in Evmenii's first monologue. He reasons:

> Забавы здешние утоплены в слезах,
> И светлостию тьма мечтуется в глазах:
> Век краток здесь, а смерть ужасна;
> Прелестна жизнь; однако и несчастна.
> Для нас, не ради бед земля сотворена;
> Но нашим промыслом бедам покорена.
> Повергли идолов в стране мы сей прехвально;
> Однако и поднесь еще живем печально.
>   Нам чистый дан закон,
> Но мы не делаем, что предписует он.
>   Грехами поражены,
> Мы в тину прежнюю глубоко погружены. (PSVS, 4, 283–284)[26]

> Worldly amusements are soaked in tears
> And darkness seems like light to the eyes.
> Our span is short and death horrible;
> Life has charms but is also wretched.
> The earth was created for us, not for misfortunes,
> And misfortunes are overcome by our action.
> Most laudably we have toppled the idols in this land;
> However, to this day we still live in sadness.
>   A perfect law was given us,
> But we do not do what it prescribes.
>   Struck by sins,
> We are deeply mired in former slime.

The posing of the problem clearly describes the limits of Sumarokov's rationalism. On the one hand, Evmenii is a typical enlightener, asserting humanism, logic, and belief that the world may be improved. On the other, the ancient religious perception of the sinfulness and vanity of life predominates. Both the lexicon (utopleny v slezakh, prelestna zhizn', tina prezhniaia) and tropes (the oxymoron "svetlostiiu t'ma," the aphoristic juxtapositions "prelestna" — "neschastna," "prekhval'no" — "pechal'no")

---

[26] The text has been republished in Sumarokov, *Dramaticheskie sochineniia*, 434–50.

underscore this Biblical (and common Baroque) theme, whose presence in Sumarokov's works A. A. Morozov argued contradicted the basic postulates of classicism.[27] The theme of *vanitas vanitatum* reoccurs in Sumarokov's works, and should not be ascribed merely to literary fashion or Masonic caprice.[28]

In Sumarokov's philosophical writings the problem of the world's vanity revolves around the issue of theodicy — that sin often goes unpunished on earth and evil keeps increasing. He believed that education (uchenie) is "medicine for our spoiled hearts" but also admitted "that this medicine is little used for the common happiness and sometimes even turns into poison" (PSVS, 6, 231; cf. PSVS, 6, 295–97). This rather pessimistic position lead Sumarokov to the conclusion that history and human activity in general may be justified ethically only by reference to life after death. This is what he writes in his history of the first strel'tsy uprising: "Who from these tyrannical actions that almost transcend human nature [in their evil], who from this alone does not see that there is life after our death; when there is no compensating punishment for these evildoers on earth, and when ferocious thunder and terrible lightning did not fall on the heads of these creatures unworthy of their Creator!" (PSVS, 6, 199–200). This is a typical example of Sumarokov's philosophical reasoning, juxtaposing earthly reality with the divine ideal. God, justice, and the afterlife are necessary and inseparable notions for Sumarokov. To contradict Pushkin's Salieri, if there is no justice on earth, in must be sought above.

Sumarokov consistently asserts the harmony of reason and religion, science and revelation. Like many enlighteners of his day he had a distaste for metaphysics (as he understood it). "Almost all Cartesian philosophy," he wrote, "is a naked novel (roman). All metaphysicians without exception were delirious"; only "the wisdom of the Deity is inexhaustible" (PSVS, 9, 290). Sumarokov thus substituted traditional religious idealistic metaphysics for the modern rationalist type. Elsewhere he asks: "What

---

[27] A. A. Morozov, "Sud'by russkogo klassitsizma," *Russkaia literatura*, 1 (1974), 19–20, 25–7.

[28] See for example the poems: "Na suetu cheloveka (Sueten budesh', ty chelovek)" (1759); "Oda na suetu mira (Sredi igry, sredi zabavy)" (1763), in Sumarokov, *Izbrannye proizvedeniia*, 83 and 89–90; and "Iz Siraha. Glava V. (Begi o smertnyi, suety)," PSVS, 1, 252–53. The "Oda na suetu mira" was originally published as "Oda k M. M. Kheraskovu," and the theme is central to Kheraskov's religious poetry; it deserves serious independent study from the theological point of view as an important anti-rationalist strain in Russian Classicism.

then will be after our demise? To the good, good; to the evil, evil. Might someone think that by this I am asserting [the existence of] heaven and hell? No, heaven and hell do not belong to natural philosophy (*estestvennoe mudrovanie*); but I am writing not about revelation, but practice natural metaphysics (*metafizichestvuiu estestvenno*), while that is a matter for religious [thinkers]..." (PSVS, 6, 268). "*Ia metafizichestvuiu estestvenno*" (*I metaphysicize naturally*) — this in lapidary form expresses the basis of Sumarokov's theology and ethics.

The philosophical question posed in the monologue cited above also evidently has a historical aspect, as the parallel between Peter the Great and Grand Prince Vladimir was a topos of the tradition. For all of the praise of the conversion to Christianity ("Most laudably we have toppled the idols in this land...A perfect law was given us"), analogous to the Petrine reforms, Sumarokov's protagonist, like the author, was not so much pessimistic as fatalistic concerning their ultimate success. As with the tragedies, having the action of the plays take place in ancient Rus' may have even bolstered their topicality, both because of the Petrine parallel and as offering images of modern Russian identity as grounded in a legendary past. "The Hermit" may also have an autobiographical subtext, insofar as it was staged in the first year of Sumarokov's fledgling Russian theater, and as we know from Sumarokov's correspondence he threatened to quit his post as its director due to the many difficulties involved with it (in 1761 he was fired from his duties, as the authorities took advantage of one of his requests to be released).

This is a secondary issue. What is most important in our view is that the problematic of "The Hermit" suggests that the philosophical premises of Sumarokov's classicist dramaturgy are less based on French (or German) rationalism, as is often stated, but on the tradition of Russian Enlightenment religious thought. This tradition has been ignored or denigrated not only by nineteenth and twentieth-century positivists, who in general did not acknowledge the religious component of culture, but also by nineteenth-century defenders of the Orthodox tradition who rejected the Enlightenment traditions of the eighteenth-century church. Understanding this aspect of eighteenth-century culture and its profound influence on the new Russian literature is a very important challenge that scholars have yet to fully recognize.

The Enlightenment religious tradition, whose outstanding early representative was Feofan Prokopovich, had a fundamental influence on Sumarokov's works and world-view. Like many of his cohort, Sumarokov idolized Peter the Great (see, for example, PSVS, 9, 302–303), but at the same time he insisted that the roots of the Petrine transformation extended back to

Chapter 6. Sumarokov's Drama "The Hermit"

the previous century, in particular to the early Enlightenment Latinizing tradition of which Prokopovich was the culmination. Sumarokov wrote, for example, that Petr Mogila (Petro Mohyla), founder of the Kiev Mogilianskaia Academy (1632) "was first to open the path to learning for the Russian people" (PSVS, 6, 320), and often noted the progressive enlightening role of church figures in modern Russian history. In his article "On Russian Religious Oratory" (written after 1770) Sumarokov demonstrated his wide familiarity not only with Prokopovich's sermons (he refers to him as "the Russian Cicero") but also with the works of his followers, the leading preachers and church figures of the second half of the eighteenth century. This familiarity, personal and literary, is evidenced by many of Sumarokov's poetic and prose works as well as by his correspondence.

Sumarokov himself wrote in many "religious" genres. Alexander Levitsky has rightly noted the important place of the "spiritual ode" in eighteenth-century Russian literature, including Sumarokov's oeuvre, although the role of the Orthodox tradition in Russian Classicism remains largely terra incognita.[29] It is precisely here that "The Hermit" seems to offer a point of convergence between secular and religious traditions, and also highlights the religious metaphysics that underlies Sumarokov's philosophical and literary position.

In contrast to the tragedies, "The Hermit" does not seem to pursue direct publicistic goals. As in the tragedies, the drama forefronts the conflict of reason and passion. Its peculiarity, however, is that the hero's withdrawal from public life in the play is characterized as rational while passion is equated to the duty of serving the fatherland. In this sense the usual evaluation of thematic categories as seen in the tragedies is reversed. The philosophical justification of such withdrawal occupies a central place in the play. Its political consequences do not turn out to be decisive, as one might have expected. It is suggestive that the arguments against Evmenii's withdrawal are sufficiently convincing that an American historian recently came to the erroneous conclusion that in "The Hermit" Sumarokov rejected the protagonist's position, suggesting that the playwright meant the play as an object lesson to Russian aristocrats who neglect their social responsibilities. But as Evmenii explains:

---

[29] Alexander Levitsky, "The Sacred Ode In Eighteenth-Century Russian Literary Culture," Diss., University of Michigan, 1977; L. F. Lutsevich, "Svoeobrazie zhanra prelozheniia psalmov A. P. Sumarokov," *Problemy izucheniia russkoi literatury XVIII veka*, vyp. 4 (Leningrad, 1980), 10–19.

> Я свету отдал долг, и оставляю свет;
> Бегу мирских сует. (PSVS, 4, 287)
>
> (I have done my duty to the world, and I abandon it;
> I run from worldly vanities.)

He further says to his father:

> Для вас я в свете жил,
> И обществу служил:
> А ныне к вечности открыв себе дорогу,
> Служу я Богу. (PSVS, 4, 296)
>
> (For you I lived in the world
> And served society.
> But now, having discovered the path to eternity for myself,
> I serve God.)

The main obstacle to this service is not the thirst for wealth and power (his father offers him "the first place … in the entire people"), but the passionate love for his wife. As in the tragedies, the social and amorous themes run in parallel or merge. Evmenii's argument that he has already paid his social debt does not encounter any substantial challenge and the problem of choosing either love for his wife or love for God takes center stage.

The arguments pro and con withdrawal from public life focus on the issue how the Creator relates to His creation. The protagonist's brother Visarion and father Dometiian put forward a series of propositions that one may call deist: in their view, Evmenii demands from himself something that is beyond human nature, and therefore unreasonable. The demands of nature, argues Dometiian, represent those of God. In withdrawing from life Evmenii "counters nature" and the universally accepted norm of civilization:

> Внимая неба глас, внемли ты глас природы;
> Сам хочет Бог того и всей земли народы.
> Я знаю то и сам, что наше естество
> Во основание имеет Божество.
> Но что и сам Создатель,
> В сердца посеял нам святую добродетель;
> Котора к должности безвременной зовет;
> Противу строгости на небо вопиет… (PSVS, 4, 294–95)

(Heeding the voice of heaven you are heeding the voice of nature;
God himself wants this, as well as all the earth's peoples.
I also know myself that our nature
At its base has the Divinity.
 But also that the Creator Himself
Sowed in our hearts holy virtue
That calls us to unchanging duty,
That cries out to heaven against extremes...)

Virtue, love for parents and spouse — all these have been "sown" into people by God as a legitimate part of His being. The desire to withdraw from life is characterized as brutishness (zverstvo) and tyranny against the family. Furthermore, the fact that people are mortal and God is merciful also speaks against Evmenii's "extreme" stance. Evmenii's wife Parfeniia voices the ultimate expression of this argument when she insists that the denial of matrimony and marriage vows represents "a most immeasurable falsehood" (nepravda prebezmerna) that God will not tolerate; she even threatens her husband with lightning bolts from heaven. (This, by the way, is how Kheraskov's "Christian tragedy" "Iulian the Apostate" ends, but Sumarokov did not approve of such supernatural resolutions.[30]) Evmenii holds to a different "divine law," the law of higher reason, and when Parfeniia, after an episode threatening herself with the dagger, finally gives in to her husband, she declares: "The voice of the All-High has sown its law in me as well" (Glas Vyshniago i mne ustav uzhe vseliaet).

The main point is not that Sumarokov rejects the "deist," "natural" argument as such, and certainly not that he is denying the logic of this world. While Sumarokov always recognized logical truth, he just as strongly rejected a naïve faith in the all-conquering power of human reason. "With healthy reasoning we may approach the center of understanding," he wrote, but "mortals can never touch" that point (PSVS, 4, 317). Divine law is the prerequisite and highest "pure source" for earthly human reason. God acts, and the drama is resolved, not by supernatural means (as in Kheraskov's play) but through people themselves. The theological issues in "The Hermit" go beyond any raised in Sumarokov's tragedies, in which the action mostly remains within the earthly sphere of inevitable passions. The play may be taken as a demonstration of the metaphysical basis of Sumarokov's tragic world-view, as a glimpse of that ideal "center of understanding"

---

[30] See Green, "Kheraskov and the Christian Tragedy," 21.

that "mortals can never touch" but which is conditioned by "common sense." In the same passage in which Sumarokov speaks of the potential harmfulness of learning, he continues: "However, be that as it may, our conscience, that spark of the Divine that has been given to us, demands that in all we strive for we keep virtue in sight; and that we remember in particular that there is a God in the world and that the life given to us by God will return to its pure source; thus it must be, that it is pure. Let us follow our duty; it consists in virtue. And if there is a God, then there will be retribution; and God surely exists" (PSVS, 6, 231–32). In his prose works Sumarokov often makes similar types of argument "proving" God's existence, because for him God represents the center of understanding, the source of reason, the basis for virtue and justice as well as the single possible perfection. That some sort of divine perfection is possible on earth is the theme of "The Hermit."

In our view, one must contextualize this drama on the background of that Enlightenment theological tradition spoken of earlier. In conclusion I will mention several points of intersection of "The Hermit" with this tradition. I will limit my observations to the comparison of several of Sumarokov's ideas with those of Metropolitan Platon (Levshin) (1737–1812).[31] One of the leading clergymen of his age, Platon was a well known orator who in the first half of the 1760's occupied the place of court preacher, a reformer of religious education and author of the first systematic theological system in Russia. Sumarokov was personally acquainted with him (it was he who suggested that Sumarokov create a transposition of the entire psalter[32]) and greatly valued him as a speaker. Platon took his vows in 1758, so could hardly have had any influence on "The Hermit," but many of his theological ideas were common to those developed in Sumarokov's drama.

---

[31] On Platon, see: I. M. Snegirev, *Zhizn' moskovskogo Mitropolita Platona* (Moscow, 1856); S. K. Smirnov, *Istoriia Moskovskoi Slaviano-greko-latinskoi akademii* (Moscow: V. Got'e, 1855); A. A. Beliaev, *Mitropolit Platon kak stroitel' natsional'noi dukhovnoi shkoly* (Sergiev posad, 1913); K. A. Papmehl, *Metropolitan Platon of Moscow (Petr Levshin 1737–1812): The Enlightened Prelate, Scholar and Educator* (Newtonville, Mass.: Oriental Research Partners, 1983); K. A. Papmehl, "Platon," in *Dictionary of Literary Biography*, vol. 150: *Early Modern Russian Writers, Late Seventeenth and Eighteenth Centuries*, ed. Marcus C. Levitt (Detroit: The Gale Group, 1995), 285–290. See also Platon's autobiographical writings in *Moskvitianin*, ch. 1, otd. III (1849), 27–40; ch. 4, otd. III, 1–24; *Chteniia v imp. Obshchestve istorii i drevnostei rossiiskikh pri Mosk. Universitete*, 4 (1881), 55–84.

[32] M. N. Longinov, "Poslednie gody zhizni Aleksandra Petrovicha Sumarokova," *Russkii arkhiv*, 10 (1871), col. 1694.

Chapter 6. Sumarokov's Drama "The Hermit"

The first possible correlation concerns the "Enlightenment" view of monasticism and "withdrawal from life." Platon explained to Catherine II that he had taken vows "out of special love for enlightenment." According to Platon, the primary reason for becoming a monk was "the state of not having a wife" (bezzhennoe prebyvanie) — hardly a traditional reason in Russia — but (according to G. Florovskii) "even more it was love of seclusion, not only for prayer as much as for scholarly pursuits and friendship" (in which Florovskii sees "features of an unusual Rousseauism").[33] Evmenii also seeks peace and seclusion, and one may find in other of Sumarokov's works an analogous defense of "Rousseauian" isolation and a retreat from the clamor of city life (see, for example, his "Letter on the Beauty of Nature," 1759).[34] An examination of attitudes toward monasticism in mid-eighteenth century Russia would probably shed new light on the issues "The Hermit" raises.[35]

Another, even more important area of coincidence is Sumarokov's drama and Platon's Enlightenment version of Orthodoxy theology. Platon, like other high clergymen of his cohort, was in Joseph II's words "plus philosophe que prêtre."[36] Grand Prince Pavel Petrovich (the future Paul I) for whom Platon served as tutor in 1763–65 explained the essence of Platon's theology in this way: "You assert it as a rule to always demonstrate the conformity (soglasovanie) of the rules and facts (bytii) contained in Holy Writ with natural reason, and to affirm them by means of the conclusions of healthy human reasoning."[37] The "natural" philosophical arguments that Sumarokov puts forward to prove God's existence are strikingly similar to those Platon puts forward in the first part of his widely known *Catechesis*. This section is dedicated to "Natural Knowledge of God" (Bogopoznanie

---

[33] Georgii Florovskii, *Puti russkogo bogosloviia* (Paris: YMCA Press, 1937), 110. On the other hand, the roots of such a view may also go back to the seventeenth century; see, for example, A. M. Panchenko, *Russkaia stikhotvornaia kul'tura XVII veka* (Leningrad: Nauka, 1973), 150–61.

[34] Thomas Newlin suggests that the given theme in "The Hermit" as analyzed in this article may be related to the emancipation of the nobility of 1762; see his *The Voice in the Garden: Andrei Bolotov and the Anxieties of Russian Pastoral, 1738–1833* (Evanston, IL: Northwestern UP, 2001), 81.

[35] On the one hand, during Catherine's reign the Orthodox Church's property was nationalized and the number of monasteries was cut by almost seventy percent. On the other hand, Platon and his cohort strove to preserve and support traditional monastic (and ascetic) traditions.

[36] Florovskii, *Puti russkogo bogosloviia*, 109.

[37] Platon (P. E. Levshin), *Raznye sochineniia*. [2nd ed.] vol. 7 (Moscow, 1780), 274. The first edition was in 1764.

estestvennoe) (the second and last parts are "About the Gospel Faith" and "About God's Law"), and it is indicative that Platon begins his instruction in religion with natural law (i.e., the conclusions of reason), and not with dogma. This type of theology is in the tradition of "Protestant Latin scholastics" of Prokopovich and other church reformers-enlighteners of the late seventeenth and early eighteenth century.

Platon was strongly influenced by his reading of Paul's epistles and the works of St. Augustine in a Lutheran spirit, with emphasis on the struggle between mind and will. This approach was alien to the older Russian religious tradition but became widespread among eighteenth century Russian church enlighteners. Its basic similarity to Classicist emphasis on the conflict of reason and passion is obvious. It is precisely such a coincidence of "neo-Protestant" ideas and Sumarokovian Classicism may be seen in Evmenii's monologue in the fourth scene when he asks God to

> Наполни разум мой любовию святою,
> Чтоб только пленен был я сею красотою:
> Желанием мое ты сердце согласи,
> И мысли к одному направи небеси... (PSVS, 4, 291)

(Fill my reason with holy love
So that I be captivated by that beauty.
Bring my heart into agreement with my desire
And direct my thoughts to heaven alone...)

Evmenii, like Sts. Paul and Augustine, understands that he can only escape the bondage of earthly attachments with God's help. Reason alone, however much applied, is incomplete, insufficient, and without the help of higher forces a person cannot overcome the passions.[38] This is the cause of the failure of many characters in Sumarokov's tragedies, and arguably, is at the center of the author's notion of the tragic. The correction of society or of man is ultimately possible only by means of inexplicable workings of God. This does not mean, however, that Sumarokov's final conclusion is to reject this world. On the contrary, the "extreme" action taken by the hero of "The Hermit" demonstrates the rational and moral structure of the world and reaffirms the notion of enlightenment that is central to Russian Classicism.

---

[38] Cf. Romans 7: 21-5; Galatians 6: 17; St. Augustine, *Confessions*, Bk. 8, chap. 5.

— 7 —

"THE FIRST RUSSIAN BALLET":
Sumarokov's "Sanctuary of Virtue" (1759), Defining a New Dance

If in the 1920's Russian pioneers of modern dance strove to liberate it from representationalism and from the narrow conventions of classical ballet, in the second half of the eighteenth century, the theoretical and practical challenge was essentially the opposite: champions of ballet asserted its independence as a new and independent art form by rejecting the notion of dance as abstract motion.[1] It was the assertion of dance's mimetic content that they felt elevated it to the status of an autonomous "sister art," on a level with painting or drama, and distanced it from older Baroque practices of festive court dance that to the later tradition seemed merely decorative and empty of emotional content. This paper will explore the theoretical and practical problems in creating and defining the "new" kind of dance in eighteenth-century Russia, drawing a parallel to the assertion of a "new" Russian literature. The two issues come together in the career of Alexander Sumarokov (1717–1777), one of the founders of the new, European-style vernacular literature in Russia.[2] Among his other many firsts, Sumarokov is often credited with having written the libretto for what is often referred to as "the first Russian ballet," "The Sanctuary of Virtue" (Pribezhishche dobrodetelei), that debuted in 1759. In what sense was this an actual first?

The 1750's was a key period in the formation of modern Russian culture. In literature as in dance, by the time of "The Sanctuary of Virtue," some of the theoretical and institutional groundwork had been laid, and it

---

[1] This article originally appeared in *Experiment / Эксперимент*, 10 (2004): 51–84, a special issue devoted to "Performing Arts and the Avant-Garde."
[2] For an outline of Sumarokov's career, see "Sumarokov: Life and Works" elsewhere in this volume.

was now a time of creative experimentation, and attempts to establish new model works in practice. Sumarokov had been appointed director of the first national Russian theater upon its creation in 1756; three years later, at his request, this became an official "court" theater, which gave it more institutional viability and better funding.[3] Together with writing and producing Russia's first tragedies and comedies, Sumarokov also branched out into other new areas — with librettos for the first operas in Russian ("Tsefal i Prokris" [Cephalus and Procris], 1755, and *"Al'tsesta"* [Alceste], 1759), a "prologue" ("Novye lavry" [New Laurels], 1759), a *sui generis* "drama" ("Pustynnik" [The Hermit], 1769), as well as "The Sanctuary of Virtue."[4]

To say that literature or ballet was a "new" phenomenon is of course a judgment call, and depends on how we define our terms. It is more than

---

[3] The overwhelming majority of private theaters only lasted a few years. Sumarokov's court theater, on the other hand, went on to form the basis for the Imperial Theaters later in the century.

[4] On Sumarokov's operas and ballets, see the passing references in: Cyril W. Beaumont, *A History of Ballet in Russia (1613–1881)*, preface by André Levinson (London, C. W. Beaumont, 1930); N. Findeizen, *Ocherki po istorii muzyki v Rossii s drevneishikh vremen do kontsa XVIII veka*, vol. 2 (Moscow, Leningrad; Gos. Izdat. Muzsektor, 1929); A. Gozenpud, *Muzykal'nyi teatr v Rossii, Ot istokov do Glinki: Ocherk* (Leningrad: Gos. Muz. Izdat., 1959); V. Krasovskaia, *Russkii baletnyi teatr: ot vozniknoveniia do serediny XIX veka* (Leningrad, Moscow: Iskusstvo, 1958); Serge Lifar, *A History of Russian Ballet from its Origins to the Present Day*, trans. Arnold Haskell (London: Hutchinson, [1954]); T. N. Livanova, *Russkaia muzykalnaia kultura XVIII veka v ee sviaziakh s literaturoi teatrom i bytom; issledovaniia i materialy*, vol. 1 (Moscow: Gos. muzykalnoe izd-vo, 1952); R. Aloys Mooser, *Annales de la musique et des musiciens en Russie au XVIIIme siècle*. Vol. 1 ([Geneva] Mont-Blanc, [1948–51]); Iakob Shtelin, *Muzyka i balet v Rossii XVIII veka*, trans. B. I. Zasurskii (Leningrad: Triton, 1935); V. N. Vsevolodskii-Gerngross, *Istoriia russkogo teatra*, intro. and ed. A. V. Lunacharskii. 2 vols. (Leningrad: Tea-kino-pechat, 1929); and especially the works of and edited by L. M. Starikova: *Teatr v Rossii XVIII veka: opyt dokumental'nogo issledovaniia* (Moscow: Ministerstvo kul'tury Rossiĭskoĭ Federatsii, Gos. Institut iskusstvovedeniia, 1996); *Teatral'naia zhizn' Rossii v epokhu Anny Ioannovny: dokumental'naia khronika, 1730–1740* (Moskva: Radiks, 1995); *Teatral'naia zhizn' Rossii v epokhu Elizavety Petrovny: Dokumental'naia khronika, 1741–1750*, vyp. 2, ch. 1 (Moscow: Nauka, 2003). See also the other works cited below. Livanova's complaint that "the entire musical aspect of Sumarokov's theatrical activity is the least examined in the literature on him. We can never find more than a few lines written on Sumarokov's ballets and operas" (73) remains valid. The single article on the subject I have found (Ol'ga Vsevolodskaia-Golushkevich, "Balety Aleksandra Sumarokova," *Sovetskii balet*, 4 [1986], 37–40) does not offer any new material. On the unusual character of "Pustynnik," see "Sumarokov's Drama 'The Hermit'," chap. 6 in this volume.

Chapter 7. "The First Russian Ballet"

the simple fact that Sumarokov wrote the libretto for "The Sanctuary of Virtue" in Russian, or that it was performed by Russians; and it also involves more than the fact that Sumarokov *called* this work a ballet ("The Sanctuary of Virtue" actually combines song, declamation, and dance, and Mooser — despite Sumarokov's own designation — assigns it to the older genre of "opera-ballet"[5]). The argument was being put forward by dance reformers of Sumarokov's day — and I am going to include Sumarokov in their cohort — that the new type of dance performance was a qualitatively new phenomenon. From this point of view the newness consisted not in creating a certain *kind* of literature or a particular type of dance — but in establishing a *new language* with which a whole range of works could be expressed. The idea of ballet as a language (rather than a canon of figures, steps, works, styles, or techniques of movement) is central in some of the theoretical writings about ballet reform of the period, to which I will return.

We may observe in Sumarokov's ballet, as in his literary works, the transition from a "Baroque" aesthetic to a more "Classicist" one. Much ink has been spilled over the precise meaning of these terms, and, as in dance and theater, the change is one of relative degree and emphasis, at times more evident on paper than in practice. In theater (especially opera and ballet, which were institutionally resistant to change) it might be more accurate to describe a process of "classicizing" or "rationalizing" of what existed as a fundamentally Baroque art form. The vulgar literary language too, despite theoretical adherence to Vaugelas' linguistic purist doctrine, remained grounded in the Slavonic literary tradition, as most clearly demonstrated by the central place of the triumphal ode.[6] While the lines separating the Slavonic syllabic tradition from Russian syllabo-tonic versification might seem at first glance clearly

---

[5] R.-Aloys Mooser, *Opéras, intermezzos, ballets, cantates, oratorios joués en Russie durant le XVIIIe siècle*. 3rd rev. ed. (Bale: Barenreiter, [1964]), 113; also in his *Annales de la musique*, 315 and 325. This was probably also the source for the same designation elsewhere in the literature, e.g., Marian Hannah Winter, *The Pre-Romantic Ballet* (London: Pitman, 1974), 97.

[6] On the application of Vaugelas' linguistic ideas to Russian, see Victor Zhivov, *Language and Culture in Eighteenth Century Russia*, trans. Marcus C. Levitt (Boston: Academic Studies Press, 2009); on the importance of the ode in this connection, see chap. 2, section 2. The new Russian literary consciousness saw itself as in a basic sense opposed to the older Church Slavonic language (perceived as "Baroque" and "impure") — like the opposition between French and Latin in France. However, in practice (especially in panegyric genres like odes) the developing literary tongue was deeply indebted to the Slavonic Baroque tradition as providing the only available model.

evident, in practice the situation was far more complex, as Victor Zhivov has demonstrated.

In institutional terms, there are also many striking parallels between the creation of new literature and reform ballet in Russia. This was time when the place and function of literature and of dance in society were beginning to change. This involved a gradual transition from an exclusively court-centered cultural system to the beginnings of a public sphere — based on such institutions as schools, academies, and universities; book publishing and journalism; independent associations (like freemasonry) — as well as the theater.[7] The new kind of European dancing (ballroom or social dancing) — had been introduced into Russian high society by Peter the Great, who had also posed the demand for a new literary language in the vulgar tongue and devised the print-friendly "civil" script.[8] The modern word for "dance" (tanets) itself entered Russian under Peter (from German- -this as opposed to the word for Russian folk dance or "pliaska").[9] By mid century dance had become part of an aristocrat's expected skills. It was still closely connected with the court and court culture, but dance and the theater may arguably also be seen as having some role in the formation of what has been referred to as an eighteenth-century intelligentsia, or, to use a less loaded term, a new educated aristocratic public, or even a public sphere. In the first half of the century a central function of theatrical dance was to serve the court and to contribute panegyric works to court celebrations; literature in Russian also served the court; it was commissioned from the Academy of Sciences, whose (mostly German) professors (like Juncker and Staehlin) supplied odes, orations, allegorical programs for fireworks, dedicatory verse (nadpisi) and translated librettos; both Trediakovskii and Lomonosov were professors at the Academy, and among their other duties they took part in this production of translated and original works "on order."

---

[7] See, variously, M. M. Shtrange, *Demokraticheskaia intelligentsiia Rossii v XVIII veke* (Moscow: Nauka, 1965); Gary Marker, *Publishing, Printing, and the Origins of Intellectual Life in Russia, 1700–1800* (Princeton, N.J.: Princeton UP, 1985); Douglas Smith, *Working the Rough Stone: Freemasonry and Society in Eighteenth-Century Russia* (DeKalb, IL: Northern Illinois UP, 1999); and Elise Wirtschafter, *The Play of Ideas in Russian Enlightenment Theater* (DeKalb, IL: Northern Illinois UP, 2003).

[8] Elizabeth Clara Sander, *Social Dancing in Peter the Great's Russia: Observations by Holstein Nobleman Friedrich Wilhelm von Bergholz, 1721 to 1725*. Terpsichore, Bd. 6 (Hildesheim: G. Olms, 2007), chap. 1.

[9] Natalia P. Roslavleva, *Era of the Russian Ballet* (London: Gollancz, 1966), 17.

Chapter 7. "The First Russian Ballet"

Because of the international nature of court culture and especially of dance — the unceasing circulation from court to court of first-rank artists, architects, musicians, singers, actors, dancers, ballet masters and composers — Germans, Austrians, French, Italians, Englishmen, etc. — it took a relatively short time for the eighteenth-century Russian court to become a full fledged stop on the larger European court circuit. The preparatory period was about twenty years, roughly the end of Anna's reign (1730–40) and the start of Elizabeth's (1741–62).[10] In dance, by mid-century, Russia had become one of the cultural front lines in the larger European reform movement. As Serge Lifar put it, by 1759 Russia had become a "battleground for the vast armies of great European ballet reformers," "the place for the diffusion of reformist tendencies and new ideas."[11] It would be wrong to think of this as some have as a provincial backwater. Internationally recognized ballet masters like "Hilferding and Angiolini...turned St. Petersburg into a centre of dancing that could rival Paris, Stuttgart and Vienna."[12]

Historians of ballet usually date the formal introduction of ballet into Russia to 1735 or 1736, when Empress Anna hired a permanent Italian dance troupe at court and when the Russian pupils of the dancer and ballet-master Jean-Baptiste Landé presented their first court performance.[13] Notably, this is about the same time that literary historians often take as the start of the new Russian literature, as it saw the assertion of the new syllabo-tonic versification, heralded by Trediakovskii's *New and Short Method to Composing Russian Verse* (*Novyi i kratkii sposob k slozheniiu rossiiskikh stikhov*, 1735) which proffered models for new Russian poetry. Furthermore, Sumarokov's theater and the Russian corps de ballet had their institutional roots in the famous Cadet Corps (Pervyi sukhoputnyi shkhlatkhetskii kadetskii korpus, literally the First Infantry Noble Cadet Corps), founded in 1732. Despite its name, the Cadet Corps offered a humanistic curriculum unique in Russia of

---

10   See especially Starikova's works cited in note 2. E. V. Anisimov gives a lively description of Elizabeth's court in *Rossiia v seredine XVIII v.: bor'ba za nasledie Petra* (Moscow: Mysl', 1986), in English as *Empress Elizabeth: Her Reign and Her Russia, 1741–1761*, ed., trans. and preface by John T. Alexander (Gulf Breeze, FL: Academic International Press, 1995).
11   The first quote is from Serge Lifar, *A History*, 33 and the second from his *Ballet, Traditional to Modern*, trans. Cyril W. Beaumont (London: Putnam, 1938), 124.
12   Lifar, *A History*, 36; this was also certainly the self-consciousness of the time, as evidenced e.g. by Staehlin's testimony (Shtelin, *Muzyka i balet v Rossii*, 161).
13   Most recently and most authoritatively, Starikova's *Teatral'naia zhizn' Rossii v epokhu Elizavety Petrovny* gives their court debut as March, 1736 (21 and 42).

the day and was designed to produce military, administrative and cultural leaders; it put its main stress on the upbringing of noblemen. Together with military and academic subjects, students learned foreign languages as well as such subjects as fencing, horseback riding, drawing, and dance. The cadets took part in various court spectacles, and their staging of Sumarokov's first tragedies in the late 1740's (together with Fedor Volkov's Yaroslavl troupe, whose members were sent to the Corps for training) led to the establishment of the national theater. The Cadet Corps was also the incubator, so to speak, for Russian ballet. Landé taught dance here and students from the Corps formed the first Russian court corps de ballet. Landé founded the first Russian ballet school (in 1738) which formed the basis for the illustrious Russian Imperial dance school.[14] It was this troupe begun by Landé that took part in "The Sanctuary of Virtue."

THE "REVOLUTION" IN DANCE

Before we turn to "The Sanctuary of Virtue" itself it is useful to consider the larger changes taking place in dance and the reformist definition of ballet. The choreographer of Sumarokov's ballet was Franz Anton Christophe Hilferding (Hilverding) (1717–1768), the renowned ballet-master whom Maria Theresa had released from his duties at the Austrian court to visit Russia for a few years at the request of Elizaveta Petrovna. In the words of Jakob von Staehlin (Ia. Ia. Shtelin), Hilferding was invited "to perfect ballet in Russia and to introduce new elements."[15] He took the place of Landé, who had recently passed away. "The Sanctuary of Virtue" was Hilferding's first work in Russia.

Hilferding is one of the major figures in eighteenth-century ballet, together with such innovators as the Englishman John Weaver (1673–1760); Marie Sallé (1707–1756), French dancer and tragic actress, known

---

[14] See V. N. Vsevolodskii-Gerngross, *Istoriia teatral'nogo obrazovaniia v Rossii* (St. Petersburg: Izd. Direktsii Imp. teatrov, 1913); and M Borisoglebskii, *Proshloe Baletnogo otdeleniia Peterburgskogo teatralnogo uchilishcha nyne Leningradskogo gosudarstvennogo khoreograficheskogo uchilishcha: Materialy po istorii russkogo baleta*, vol. 1 ([Leningrad]: Izd. Leningradskogo gos. khoreograficheskogo uchilishcha, 1938). On the composition of the troupe, see L. M. Starikova, "Pervaia russkaia baletnaia truppa," in *Pamiatniki kul'tury: Novye otkrytiia. 1985* (Moscow: Nauka, 1987), 102–107.

[15] Lifar, *A History of Russian Ballet*, 33; see also Peter Brinson, *Background to European Ballet* (New York: Books for Libraries, 1980), 84.

for having discarded masks and cumbersome costumes; Hilverding's disciple Gasparo Angiolini (1731–1803), also from Austria, who assumed the position of Russian court *balletmeistr* in 1764;[16] and — last and perhaps most famous — Jean-Georges Noverre (1727–1810), renowned for his influential *Letters on Dancing and Ballets,* first published in 1760, which was the main and most comprehensive statement of the reform. Noverre was the teacher of two very important ballet masters who worked in Russia, Charles Le Picq (during the last decades of the century) and Charles-Louis Didelot (in the first decades of the next). Didelot we might say took Noverre's ideas to their logical conclusion, going much farther than Noverre in implementing them. Notably, the last and most complete version of the *Letters on Dancing and Ballets* was published in four volumes in Russia in 1803, while Didelot was working there; this French edition was the basis for Cyril Beaumont's English translation of 1930, which he dedicated to Fokine.[17] The new ideas about ballet and theatrical reform were also shared by Diderot, Voltaire, and Grimm, and reflected in the *Encyclopédie* (which had begun publishing in 1751).[18] Perhaps the most eloquent illustration of the connection between Enlightenment ideas and the new ballet was Angiolini's allegorical "Prejudice Defeated" (Pobezhdennyi predrassudok) which was staged in 1768 to celebrate Catherine the Great's having vaccinated the imperial family against small pox.[19]

To turn to the definition of the new art, which I take from Noverre,[20] the French choreographer drew a dividing line between dance performed for court festivals, that were part of a larger complex of entertainments, and ballet as a separate art form, which he variously terms *action dances, action ballet,*

---

[16] Angiolini is known especially for his collaborations with Gluck in Vienna; together they carried the new reform ideas into opera.

[17] Jean Georges Noverre, *Letters on Dancing and Ballets,* trans. Cyril W. Beaumont from the revised and enlarged edition published at St. Petersburg, 1803 (London: C. W. Beaumont, 1930). This is the edition from which I will be quoting. References to it will be given in parentheses in the text.

[18] See Gozenpud, *Muzykal'nyi teatr v Rossii,* 200, and Ivor Forbes Guest, *The Ballet of the Enlightenment: The Establishment of the ballet d'action in France, 1770–1793* (London: Dance Books, 1996), which mostly concerns Noverre's work in Paris.

[19] Its program is reproduced in Shtelin, *Muzyka i balet,* 164–68.

[20] Angiolini, by the way, vehemently disputed Noverre's claims about instituting the reforms, claiming priority for Hilverding. See the *Lettere di Gasparo Angiolini a Monsieur Noverre sopra i balli pantomini* (Milan: Apresso G. B. Bianchi, 1773). The consensus among scholars, though, is that the substance of their positions was the same.

and *ballet-pantomimes* — ballet that tells a story and effectively communicates emotion. Noverre writes:

> I am of the opinion, then, that the name of ballet has been wrongly applied to such sumptuous entertainments, such splendid festivals which combine magnificent scenery, wonderful machinery, rich and pompous costumes, charming poetry, music and declamation, seductive voices, brilliant artificial illumination, pleasing dances and *divertissements*, thrilling and perilous jumps, and feats of strength: all of which parts when separated form as many different spectacles, but when united form one complete entertainment worthy of the most powerful monarch.
>
> These festivals were the more pleasing according as they were the more varied, so that each spectator could find something to his own taste and fancy, but even in all this I discover nothing of what I seek to find in a ballet. Setting aside all enthusiasm and professional prejudice, I consider this complicated entertainment as one of variety and magnificence, or as an intimate union of the pleasing arts wherein each holds an equal rank which they should similarly occupy in the production as a whole. Nevertheless, I do not see how the title of ballet can be accorded to those *divertissements* which are not *danses d'action,* which express nothing and are superior in no way to the other arts, each of which contributes to the elegance and wonder of these representations. (52)

Noverre sketches out a series of oppositions here that describe what the new dance is not. It is defined against court dance, which is characterized as entertainment, celebratory in function, and marked by sumptuousness, variety, and magnificence. Court festivals are complicated, combining many different kinds of spectacle. They are multi-media, including poetry, music and declamation, as well as dancing, with all of these arts of more or less equal importance. Dance is incorporated into other "spectacles" or events — as part of a ball, a masquerade (which were often held in theaters), or as a *divertissement* (Italian *intemezzi*), that is, an entertainment presented between the acts of an opera or a tragedy or as an occasional component within an opera.

Indeed, ballet as a genre of dance performance developed directly out of opera. On the one hand, there was the *opera-bouffe* (Italian comic opera), which was renowned for its "low style," folk-style and acrobatic dancing. Just at the time "The Sanctuary of Virtue" was first staged, Locatelli's theatrical enterprise (that is, private theater) had a brief but meteoric success in Russia staging *opera-bouffe* (as well as more serious works and masquerades). Vsevolodskii-Gerngross goes so far as to suggest

Chapter 7. "The First Russian Ballet"

"The Sanctuary of Virtue" was meant to "do battle" with Locatelli's theater.[21] Noverre's criticism of allegedly old style court theatrical dancing just cited includes pointed criticism of *opera-bouffe* ("thrilling and perilous jumps, and feats of strength") and so does suggest the dual targets of the reform. The other branch of opera dancing that offered a model for ballet, and that was likewise opposed to *opera-bouffe*, was the *opera-seria*, "serious opera," which was classical ballet's most direct progenitor, indeed this genre was often referred to in the eighteenth-century as "opera-ballet." Even in operatic ballet, however, dance did not serve to advance the plot, but usually marked a celebration within the opera (for example, a wedding, feast, or some other similar set scene) and often came into play in the final apotheosis — that is, dance retained a basically panegyric, narrowly "decorative" function even *within* the plot of the opera.[22]

Vsevolodskii-Gerngross rightly emphasizes that ballet emerged from court culture and from the spectrum of other courtly arts:

> Triumphal court dinners, *kurtagi* [i.e., "court days"], masquerades, the reception of ambassadors, the imperial hunt, promenades, coronation, marriage, funeral, carousels (knightly tournaments), court and chamber music concerts (*gof-i kamer-muzyki*), cantatas and serenades, divertissements, prologues, fireworks, operas, ballets, tragedies — these were all part of one phenomenon, simply with the emphasis on different components. The aphorism that court life of the era was thoroughly theatrical, and theater thoroughly imbued by court etiquette is profoundly true.[23]

According to Noverre's opposition, court dance is opposed to genuine "ballet": ballet is a mimetic art, it *represents* something, i.e., the passions, and is not merely eye candy. It does not function as *divertissement* (as mere

---

21 *Istoriia russkogo teatra*, I: 416.
22 In the plot of "Cephalus and Procris" there were "special 'lacunae' [left in the libretto] allowing the balletmaster Antonio Rinaldi or Fusano ... to give rein to his imagination" (Mariia Shcherbakova, "From the Archives of the Marinsky Theatre; Francesco Araia, *Tsefal and Procris*, Domenico Cimarosa, *La Cleopatra*, June 14, 2001" [Theatrical Program, St. Petersburg: Marinsky Theater, 2001], 3 [p. 19 in Russian]). Shcherbakova adds, however, that the final balletic insert did "philosophically develop" the final tragic action, as Cephalus' loss of Procris is paralleled to Orpheus' death at the hands of a group of bacchae. She cites the description of this scene included in the first publication of the libretto (*Tsefal i Prokris* [St. Petersburg, 1755], 36).
23 *Istoriia russkogo teatra*, I: 384.

diversion, amusement, or time filler, to occupy the audience between acts) but should have content, represent an action. Its purpose is thus no longer narrowly panegyric or entertaining but expressive and communicative; its complexity, variety, magnificence must all be subordinated to a larger artistic goal. Dance should not have to compete for attention within a work offering many different attractions (song, dance, declamation, poetry), but should take the central place, telling one unified story through pantomime. Dance — ballet — then is an independent art form with its own special claim to greatness, and, correspondingly, the ballet-master assumes the primary role as *auteur* of the new dramatic spectacle.

There is still some fairly strong blurring of categories in Noverre's definition. Even as he criticizes dancing at court entertainments as not worthy of the title "ballet," insofar as they "express nothing" in themselves and their dances "are superior in no way to [i.e., do not distinguish themselves from among] the other arts," Noverre is clearly cognizant of its positive theatrical qualities. "Sumptuous, splendid, magnificent, wonderful, rich, pompous, charming, seductive, brilliant, pleasing, thrilling, varied" are qualities that he at times also claims for ballet. Indeed, at many moments in his treatise, Noverre seems to be arguing simply for a better quality, rather than a different kind, of dance. On a more fundamental level, however, Noverre's "revolution" (as he himself refers to it) also seems partial and incomplete, especially in hindsight. It was not until the age of Didelot that the old-style opera-ballet and operas with *divertissements* between the acts disappeared, as Noverre's reforms (e.g., of costume) were taken much further. Even though from mid century ballets began to be written and performed as separate works of art, for many decades ballet continued to manifest its roots in *opera-seria*, and indeed the tradition of grand opera continues to incorporate balletic interludes to this day.

Ballet and opera were still culturally, institutionally, and financially primarily supported by the court, and this helps explain their relatively slow pace of change (slower, for example, than the dramatic theater, in which Sumarokov could be more radically "classicist"-minimalist). While the larger contours of the dance reform suggest a transition from a "Baroque" to a "Classicist" aesthetic, from a stress on visual ornament to one on reason and transparency, there remained a significant and understandable inertia, starting with the design of theaters themselves. The roots of ballet in opera-ballet and court panegyric theater are certainly very evident in "The Sanctuary of Virtue."

Chapter 7. "The First Russian Ballet"

SUMAROKOV AS REFORMER: THE MADRIGALS

Nevertheless, I base Sumarokov's connection to the reform both on his collaboration with Hilferding and on several poetic statements in which he allies himself to the new reform art. These are a series of three short poems — madrigals — Sumarokov wrote and published in 1756, connected with the opening of "Cephalus and Procris," which we may take as direct statements on theatrical reform. While the poems concern opera and not ballet, they nevertheless help characterize Sumarokov's position, which I would argue, is in line with that of Hilferding, Noverre, and new Enlightenment ideas about the theater.

Sumarokov's three madrigals were published together and offer variations on a central theme. All assert the unity of the drama (of the action) and the music. The focus is on the effective communication of passions. In the first two, Sumarokov addresses Araia and Belogradskaia, composer and diva of "Cephalus and Procris," and in the third, the famous castrati Giovanni Carestini (1705-1760), on tour at the Russian court at the time. The poems describe the issue of unity from the point of view of the composer; the performers; the author-librettist (Sumarokov himself); and the audience.

In the first madrigal, addressed to Francesco Araia (Araja) (1700-1770), the prolific court musician and composer who had composed the music for "Cephalus and Procris," Sumarokov asserts the central place of passion and drama in opera, and claims that Araia's music is so well matched to Sumarokov's words that the language barrier disappeared:

Арая изъяснил любовны в драме страсти
И общи с Прокрисой Цефаловы напасти
Так сильно, будто бы язык он русский знал,
Иль паче, будто сам их горестью стенал.[24]

(Araia clarified love's passions in the drama / And the shared misfortunes of Cephalus and Procris / So strongly that it was as if he knew Russian, / Or rather, as if he himself was groaning with their sorrow.)

---

[24] *Ezhemesiachnye sochineniia*, mart, 1756, 273; A. P. Sumarokov, *Polnoe sobranie vsekh sochinenii, v stikhakh i proze*, 10 vols., edited by N. I. Novikov (Moscow: Universitetskaia tipografiia, 1781–1782), IX: 154–55. I will refer to this edition henceforth as "PSVS."

(According to Staehlin, Araia and Sumarokov had worked very closely together, as Sumarokov had supplied the composer with a line-by-line translation of the opera.[25]) Sumarokov comments on both the dramatic function of the music, its unity with the libretto, and on the opera's subject matter. Suffering in love was a main plot for serious operas (as it was for reform ballet), and Sumarokov had purposefully chosen a "most tender" plot from Ovid's *Metamorphoses*.[26] The function of the music was to "clarify (or explain) love's passions."

The second madrigal describes Elizaveta Belogradskaia's performance. Belogradskaia was a child prodigy and had debuted with the court's Italian opera troupe; at the opening of "Cephalus and Procris," she was 16 years old (although the newspapers reported her age as not yet 14);[27] but she was still among the oldest in the company, which was making its debut.[28] The poem stresses that the center of dramatic art is "to touch the heart with passion" — here by a combination of song and movement:

Со страстью ты, поя, тронула все сердца
И действом превзошла желаемые меры,...

(You, singing with passion, touched all hearts / And with your acting surpassed the desired standards...)

The poem compares Belogradskaia to Adrienne Lecouvreur (1692–1730), one of the most famous names of the eighteenth century tragic stage. A French star of the 1720's, she was also known for her highly dramatic life story and the scandal at her death, when the church denied her a Christian burial, which inspired a bitter poem by Voltaire. Sumarokov's madrigal

---

[25] Shcherbakova writes that in the "*secco* scenes and recitatives (accompanied by harpsichord alone)" the music aimed to convey the prosody of Sumarokov's text, with lines of mixed length as in his fables, while in the arias the "basic dramaturgic task was to convey the emotional and psychological depth of the heroes' feelings rather than to render the melodically flexible intonation of their speech." "From the Archives," 3 (in Russian on 17–18).

[26] See Shtelin, *Muzyka i balet*, 91. Sumarokov gave the plot a serious, tragic interpretation. Among other reasons, *Metamorphoses* was a popular choice for librettos because it offered rich opportunities for stage machinery to be employed; Ovid was also a popular source for palace decoration, as in the work of Valeriani, discussed below. See M. S. Konopleva, *Teatral'nyi zhivopisets Dzhiuseppe Valeriani: Materialy k biografii i istorii tvorchestva* (Leningrad: Gos. Ermitazh, 1948), 26.

[27] Repeated in Shtelin, *Muzyka i balet*, 91; see Mooser, *Annales de la musique*, I: 256.

[28] Mooser, *Annales de la musique*, I: 258.

thus connects tragic acting with the opera, emphasizing drama as a crucial component.[29]

The last madrigal in this group offers the most explicit authorial statement on the necessary unity of action and singing. It begins:

> Я в драме пения не отделяю
> > От действа никогда;
> Согласоваться им потребно завсегда.

(In drama I never separate the singing / From the action; / They must always be harmonized.)

The poem goes on to compare action to the body and vocal music to the soul of a successful performance. Despite the fact that this and the other poems refer to music, the notion of dramatic unity based on action was a central plank of Hilferding and the reform movement in ballet. "To touch the heart with passion" as Belogradskaia did defined the goal of both Sumarokov's tragedies and operas, and this aim extended to serious opera as well as the new ballet. There were many works that existed in (or rather, circulated among) the three genres. Many reform *ballets d'action* were produced by adapting tragedies; for example, Angiolini later staged Sumarokov's tragedies *Sinav and Truvor* and *Semira* as ballets. And there were many ballet — opera doubles (e.g., the many versions of the *Alceste* and *Dido* theme), a tradition which continued into the nineteenth century.[30]

"THE SANCTUARY OF VIRTUE": THE PRODUCTION

"The Sanctuary of Virtue" was a quadruple (or quintuple) collaboration, with libretto by Sumarokov, music by Raupach, choreography by Hilferding,

---

[29] Apart from this, the reference to Lecouvreur probably serves more as a great reputation to emulate rather than a specific stylistic model. Here, if anything it might suggest a canonized past ideal rather than a radical reformism. In the realm of stage costume, Lecouvreur confirmed the tendency toward lavish court dress on stage, as opposed to the movement towards simplicity on the part of the reformers. On this and on Noverre's reform of ballet costume, see V. N. Vsevolodskii-Gerngross, "Teatral'nyi kostium XVIII veka i khudozhnik Boke," *Starye gody*, 1–2 (1915), 35; Boquet was Noverre's costume designer. See also the discussion below.

[30] Gozenpud, *Muzykal'nyi teatr*, 99. In the eighteenth century it was also common to have multiple scores by different composers based on the same libretto.

and theatrical design by Peresinotti; there was also additional dance music provided by Starzer. The composer, the German Hermann Friedrich Raupach (1728–1778), had recently replaced Araia, and also wrote the music for Sumarokov's "Alceste" and "New Laurels." The music for "Sanctuary" — like most of Raupach's music — has not survived; according to Staehlin, the great success of "Alceste" in 1758 had shown Raupach to be very proficient in the "Italian manner."[31] Raupach later collaborated with Angiolini in the 1760's. The libretto for "The Sanctuary of Virtue" credits Hilferding with the ballet's "dances and basis for the drama" (Tantsy i osnovanie dramy); this somewhat curious formulation may suggest his artistic mission, to inform this, his first work in Russia, with "new elements" — probably, a greater sense of dramatic unity. The libretto also credits Joseph Starzer (Shtartser) (1726?–1787, Austrian), who had come to Russia with Hilferding, with having supplied dance music. Having two composers — one for vocal performance and one for dance — might seem to emphasize the work's segmentation, typical of the court spectacles Noverre criticized; yet it must also be significant that Hilferding brought along his own composer for the dance. A composer who specialized in dance music (a "ballet composer") was a new phenomenon,[32] and clearly it was precisely in these dances that Hilferding's "new elements" would presumably be most clearly manifested.

The "theatrical painter" Antonio Peresinotti (Perizinotti) of Bologna (1707–1778) did the ballet's set design. Brought to Russia by Francesco Araia, whom Elizabeth Petrovna had sent to Italy at the start of her reign to hire artists, dancers, musicians and other court performers, Peresinotti specialized in architectural "perspective" painting. He came to Russia as assistant to Giuseppe (Iosif) Valeriani, with whom he collaborated on painting ceiling panels (*plafony*) for many of the great eighteenth-century palaces built by Rastrelli and others. Valeriani had died on April 7, 1762, and a surviving drafthandbill for a performance of September, 1762, gives the two men joint credit for the decorations of "Cephalus and Procris" (Fig. 1).[33] In cases of some other works for Sumarokov, Peresinotti is listed as having "corrected the colors" of the decorations ("pri ispravlenii

---

[31] Shtelin, *Muzyka i balet*, 93; Mooser, *Annales de la musique* I: 324.
[32] A. L. Porfireva, "Shtartser," *Muzykalnyi Peterburg: Entsiklopedicheskii slovar*, ed. A. L. Porfireva et al. (St. Petersburg: "Kompozitor," 2000), vol. 1, bk. 3 279.
[33] Shcherbakova has identified four of Valeriani's sketches for "Cepalus and Procris," that are reproduced in "From the Archives," 16. The originals are in the State Hermitage. The handbill (Fig. 1), whose location and precise nature I have unfortunately been unable to ascertain, is reproduced in Borisoglebskii, *Proshloe Baletnogo otdeleniia*, 29.

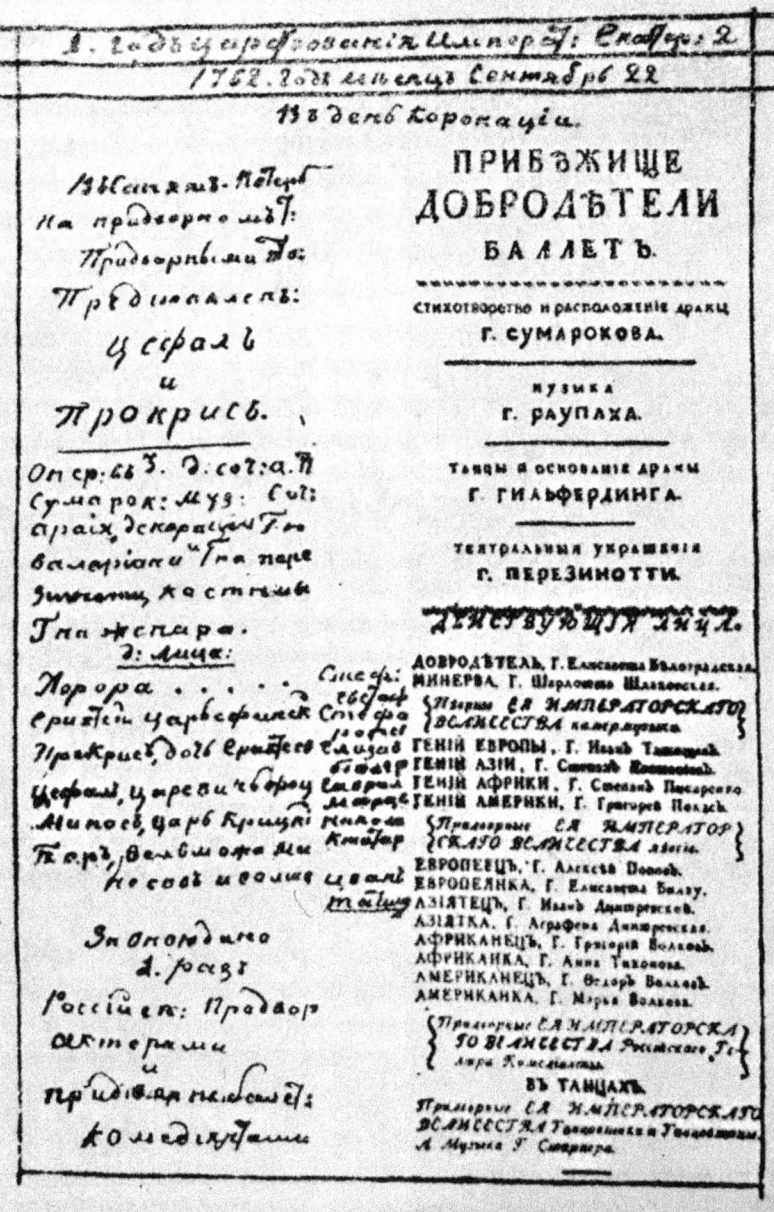

Fig. 1. Draft of a program announcement or playbill for "Cephalus and Procris" and "Sanctuary of Virtue." Reproduced in M. Borisoglebskii, *Proshloe Baletnogo otdeleniia Peterburgskogo teatralnogo uchilishcha nyne Leningradskogo gosudarstvennogo khoreograficheskogo uchilishcha: Materialy po istorii russkogo baleta*, vol. 1 ([Leningrad]: Izd. Leningradskogo gos. khoreograficheskogo uchilishcha, 1938), 29.

kraskami Zhivopisets"), i.e. he refreshed already existing scenery. This was a fairly usual practice since creating theatrical scenery and machinery was a major project, and new operatic productions were only undertaken about once a year. They were staged either for some special event (like a coronation, marriage, or treaty) or on the empress' birthday or anniversary of her coronation.[34] The fact that the handbill advertises a performance held on the actual coronation day (the coronation itself took place in Moscow), recalls the fact that "The Sanctuary of Virtue" (like the "prologue" "New Laurels") was explicitly a panegyric spectacle, written with the express purpose of praising the empress.

---

[34] Shtelin, *Muzyka i balet*, 88–9. Konopleva has been able to identify seven (named) operas that Valeriani designed; twenty-eight more of his plans for decorations have survived, but it is not always clear what works they illustrated or if they were turned into actual theatrical sets (*Teatral'nyi zhivopisets*, 8–9).

As Peter Brinson has noted, from the seventeenth century, "all of the great courts of Europe, seeking to emulate what the Venetians had developed, tried to attract from Italy its best designers and machinists" (*Background to European Ballet*, 80). "Perspective art" was a unique Italian specialty embracing painting, engraving, and the theatrical arts (especially set design, but also theatrical architecture and machinery). Valeriani and Persinotti were part of a renaissance of the Venetian school of art, which included Luca Carlevaris (c. 1665–1731) and Giovanni Tiepolo (1696–1770) and such dynasties of artists and designers as the Bibiena family, members of which worked at courts across Europe; Carlo Galli Bibiena (1728–1787) was one of them who worked in Russia. According to Staehlin, during his time in Rome, Valeriani had taught Giovanni Battista Piranesi (1720–1778) (*Muzyka i balet*, 87). Konopleva, who wrote a valuable short monograph on Valeriani, ranks him as a "outstandingly gifted" master artist, on the level with the illustrious Francesco Bartolomeo Rastrelli, with whom he worked. Valeriani was hired as an "historical and perspective artist (istoricheskim i perspektivnym khudozhnikom)" (*Teatral'nyi zhivopisets* 4), and this curious position came to embrace many disparate areas of creativity, that underscore the many connections between theatrical design (including sets, decorations, architecture and machinery) and architecture. Many of his designs for set decorations seem interchangeable with his designs for palace halls; and Valeriani's ceiling paintings could be used to decorate theaters, or as part of theatrical sets; in palace halls; and also in churches (Fig. 2). Among the palaces Valeriani and Peresinotti helped decorate for Rastrelli included the Hermitage, Peterhof, and the Anchikov and Stroganov palaces. On imperial order Valeriani also supervised a famous album of St. Petersburg cityscapes (the so called "Makhaevskii al'bom" of 1753, for which he designed and built a *camera obscura*); he was also designer and architect of a large stone opera house, built in 1750 after its wooden predecessor burned down (*Teatral'nyi zhivopisets*, 12). His role in designing theatricals included not only painting (or supervising) the huge backdrop scenery for productions, but also the theatrical machinery. He also taught the theatrical arts at the Academy of Sciences and then at the fledgling Academy of Arts (*Teatral'nyi zhivopisets*, section 4).

Chapter 7. "The First Russian Ballet"

Fig. 2. Giuseppe (Iosif) Valeriani, "Projet d'un plafond allégorique." From the album of G. de Leuchtenberg (G. N. Leikhtenbergskii). *Starye gody*, mai, 1912, after p. 8.

"The Sanctuary of Virtue" was put on by members of four court artistic organizations: a singer of the court-chamber music group (Sharlotta Shlakovskaia); members of the court church chorus; actors from the Russian Theater; and court dancers ("Pridvornye...pevchiia, Pridvornye... Rossiiskogo Teatra Komedianty; Pridvornye...Tantsovshchiki i Tantsovshchitsy").[35] There are fourteen named roles in the ballet plus additional dancers. Choristers played the four "geniuses" (Europe, Asia, Africa, America), and members of Sumarokov's theatrical troupe played the paired Europeans, Asiatics, Africans and Americans. Russian operas had begun to be produced thanks to the efforts of court church *pevchie* or choristers, who had been regularly brought in to perform at secular court functions. From the start of Elizabeth's reign, Staehlin had been giving them instruction in the art of Italian singing, and he tells the story that one of them, Gavriila Martsenkevich (or Martsinkovich), had shown himself so adept at Italian

---

35 Sumarokov, PSVS, 4, 190.

arias that the empress had the idea of commissioning an opera in Russian, for which she turned to Sumarokov. The fruit of this was Sumarokov's first opera, "Cephalus and Procris," in which Martsenkevich sang the role of Procris.[36] Three of the six-person cast of "Cephalus and Procris," which according to the handbill preceded the ballet as part of one evening's program, also played in it (Elizaveta Belogradskaia and two choristers), reminding us of the close connection between this "first ballet" and opera.

"THE SANCTUARY OF VIRTUE": THE LIBRETTO

As noted, "The Sanctuary of Virtue" seems in many ways close to the older Baroque "opera-ballet" model, although judging from the libretto alone is perilous. Without the music and a record of the dances that were performed, it is impossible to make very firm judgments. This was a panegyric spectacle, and is clearly addressed to the empress.[37] The story is that of Virtue seeking a haven. She is unable to find it in Europe, Asia, Africa or America, but finally does — as one might expect — in Russia under the benevolent rule of Elizabeth. Virtue's visit to each continent makes up a short dramatic scene in verse, apparently accompanied by "national dances" (not indicated in the libretto — more on this in a moment).[38]

Clearly this is a multi-media spectacle of the kind Noverre described, with more or less segmented dances, pantomimes, choruses, arias, dramatic monologues, and dialogues, both in song and declamation.[39] The ratio of

---

[36] Shtelin, *Muzyka i balet*, 91.

[37] According to the handbill mentioned above (Fig. 1), the ballet was also presented on Sept. 22, 1762, Catherine II's coronation day. The text published later (PSVS, 4, 214) twice refers to Elizabeth in the last act, but we may speculate that in the 1762 production the name was changed to Catherine.

[38] The image of the four continents (or "ends of the earth," i.e., directions of the compass) was very common in Russian panegyrical literature and allegorical festival, and also a staple in eighteenth century ballet, where, as in "The Sanctuary of Virtue," it allowed for a spectrum of "national dances." For a characteristic example of festival imagery, see Lomonosov's "Inscription (nadpis') for the Illumination... [of] April 25, 1751" (*Polnoe sobranie sochinenii* [Moscow, Leningrad, 1950–83], 8, 393): "The rays from your wreath, Monarch, / Have poured out onto the four corners of the Universe. / Europe Africa, America, Asia / Are amazed at the brilliance shining / From Russia, enlightening all parts of the earth."

[39] As noted above, R.-Aloys Mooser, one of the best scholars on this period, actually mistakes "The Sanctuary of Virtue" for an "opera-ballet" (see note 2). He refers to

song to declamation (poetry) is 116 lines to 262[40] or about 1 to 2.25 (44%); the percentage of singing rises through Acts 3–4 until in the final act (the apotheosis) there is more singing than declaiming.

Act 1	12:66 = 1:5.5	18% song
Act 2	20:56 = 1:2.8	40%
Act 3	32:58 = 1:1.8	55%
Act 4	28:66 = 1:2.3	42%
Act 5	24:16 = 1:0.6 (1.5:1)	67%

The dancing was also episodic in "The Sanctuary of Virtue," and is only indicated in the libretto in the last act; as noted, there was music by different composers for the vocals and for the dances.

What seems most unusual about the plot of "The Sanctuary of Virtue," and what sets it apart from the similarly segmented, but exclusively panegyric "prologue," "New Laurels," is the combination of the panegyric and the tragic.[41] Here the serious, tragic element enters directly into the ballet. Each of Virtue's first four dramatic encounters ends in failure, in what amount to four tragic playlets. These mini-tragedies, written in paired Russian alexandrines (iambic hexameter) that Sumarokov had made standard for tragic verse, were declaimed by the well-known actors of Sumarokov's theater group — including Ivan Dmitrevskoi and his wife Agrafena, Fedor and Grigorii Volkov, and Fedor's wife Mariia Volkov. Just as "Cephalus and Procris" had transferred high tragedy into opera, "The Sanctuary of Virtue" made a similar claim for the high seriousness of the new balletic art form by highlighting a series of tragic, highly dramatic peripeties.

The ballet consists of five short acts (chasti), each taking place on a different continent — Europe, Asia, Africa, America, and finally, Russia. Each continent is represented by a genius, who enters into dialogue and

---

it as "un spectacle à la fois dramatique, lyrique et chorégraphique" (*Annales de la musique*, 313). Cf. V. Krasovskaia, *Russkii baletnyi teatr: ot vozniknoveniia do serediny XIX veka* (Leningrad, Moscow: Iskusstvo, 1958), 48.

40 Lines of song are italicized in the libretto, at least that is what I presume the italics signify. I have counted lines of poetry split between two or more characters as single lines.

41 Of course, the eighteenth-century notion of the "tragic" means something more like "highly serious and noble" rather than the ancient Greek or Shakespearean notion. See my discussion in "Sumarokov's Russianized 'Hamlet': Texts and Contexts," chap. 5 in this volume.

duet with Virtue, who is dismayed by her inability to influence the unhappy encounters. A chorus also occasionally takes part in the dialogues between the geniuses and Virtue, and returns at the end of the ballet.

In the first tragic vignette, Virtue is unable to change the mind of the *Evropeianka*'s father, who plans to have her married against her will, for money, and despite her love for the *Evropeets*. In disgust Virtue decides to abandon Europe forever:

> Когда пряла здесь неправда полну власть,
> Пойду в иную я подсолнечныя часть.
> Прости страна, где я сидела на престоле,
> И где народ моей повиновался воле:
> Простите области, где жервенник науке;
> Отколе проницал вселенну славы звук,
> Прости позорище труда умов толиких.
> Простите гробы все и прах мужей великих. [...]
> Не буду зреть тебя, Европа! я во веки.⁴²

(Since injustice has attained full sway here / I will depart for some other domain under the sun. / Farewell, country, where I sat on the throne, / And where the people were subservient to my will. / Farewell, regions where the altar of the arts [once stood]; / From where the sound of glory permeated the universe. / Farewell, spectacle of such minds' labor. / Farewell, all the graves and dust of great men... / I will not see you, Europe!, ever more.)

This recalls the common eighteenth century theme of "translatio studii" — the circulation of learning that was held to travel from ancient Greece and Rome to Western Europe, and from there to Russia.⁴³

In the second act, the innocent *Aziatka* is stabbed by her jealous husband the *Aziatets* — played by Ivan Dmitrevskoi — who undergoes a horrific realization and faints when he learns that he has mistaken her brother for her lover. In act three, the impoverished *Afrikanets* decides to sell his wife for money, and coldly rejects her pleas for mercy. Virtue then rejects the old world (vselenna drevniaia) for the new, and goes to America. However, European corruption and tyranny have reached even here, as a pair of

---

42 Sumarokov, PSVS, 4, 196.
43 See Stephen Lessing Baehr, *The Paradise Myth in Eighteenth-Century Russia: Utopian Patterns In Early Secular Russian Literature And Culture* (Stanford, CA: Stanford UP, 1991), 56. This moment may be juxtaposed to Ivan Karamazov's famous lines of more than a hundred years later about Europe as a "precious graveyard" in *The Brothers Karamazov* 2, 5, 3.

Chapter 7. "The First Russian Ballet"

American (i.e., native American) lovers are forcibly separated. The blameless *Amerikanets*, played by Fedor Volkov, has been condemned to death by the king whom he had served faithfully because this tyrant, a European, wants the woman for himself. The *Amerikanets* and *Amerikanka* proceed to stab themselves to death on stage with a dagger, itself symbol of the tragic Muse.

At this point, Virtue is ready to quit the earth because

> Я правды на земле ни где не нахожу!
> (I cannot find truth anywhere on earth!)

But then Minerva "in the guise of a Russian (v obraze Rossianki)" appears and takes her to the "third world (tretiiago sveta)" — neither west nor east, but to the "northern world (polnochnyi svet)" where Elizabeth rules[44] and

> Где смертныя не знают бед,
> Нестрашен тамо вечный лед.
> (Where mortals know no evils / And where eternal ice is not to be feared.)

The last act — an apotheosis in song and dance — begins with a dramatic shift in scenery.[45] I quote the libretto:

> While the following tercet of choral music is playing uninterruptedly, and before the singing begins, the theater is transformed, presenting a great expanse of sea. Virtue approaches the shores of Russia. Suddenly the sea turns into a pleasant habitation (prevrashchaetsia v priiatnoe zhilishche). A magnificent building appears on seven columns that signify the seven liberal arts that are practiced in this realm. The Russian eagle appears, protected by a crowd of geniuses in bright clouds, and with outspread wings it depicts how the sciences are protected in its domain. Joy and amazement reign in the hearts of the inhabitants, who, taken up with zealous enthusiasm and gratitude, strive to celebrate this happy day, and to express their joy and complete happiness that their dwelling is the "The Sanctuary of Virtue."[46]

---

44 On the image of Russia as northern ("midnight land") see Otto Boele, *The North in Russian Romantic Literature*. Studies in Slavic Literature and Poetics, v. 26 (Amsterdam: Rodopi, 1996).

45 The first two acts had taken place in rooms (chertogi); in a desert (pustynia, a place of sand, rocky mountains, and dry forest) (Africa); and in a pastoral "pleasant locale with a grove, meadow and spring (priiatnoe mestopolozhenie roshchi, luga i istochniki)" (i.e., America).

46 Sumarokov, PSVS, 4, 213. Fig. 3 is a sketch for such an apotheosis, and possibly even for this one.

Fig. 3. Giuseppe (Iosif) Valeriani (?), sketch for an apotheosis.
From the album of G. de Leuchtenberg (G. N. Leikhtenbergskii).
Starye gody, mai, 1912, after p. 8.

Chapter 7. "The First Russian Ballet"

Like the motif of the "four continents" representing the world, the basic scenario depicted here, a temple with a central emblem — an eagle, monogram or portrait — highlighted as the focal point of an ecstatic apotheosis, is characteristic of much panegyric court art, for example, fireworks and illuminations. The use of elaborate stage machinery was a fundamental part of grand court opera, and was one reason experts like Valeriani and Persinotti were brought in from Italy (stage design and machinery continued to be a particularly Italian specialty).[47]

Miraculous transformations such as these took place in full view of the audience. Mariia Shcherbakova, archivist at the Mariinsky Theater in St. Petersburg, has recently described the machinery employed in "Cephalus and Procris," which was undoubtedly the same used for "The Sanctuary of Virtue":

> the well-orchestrated movement of decorative screens from two sides of the stage was made possible by unique mechanisms of eighteenth-century stage machinery, including "frames of the German type with little wheels." These "frames" (pial'tsy) — i.e., big wooden scaffolds on wheels — allowed the instantaneous change of decorative screens, which were connected to it my numerous "steel wires"... For the "flights," various "disappearances" or sudden "appearances" of the heroes, special "belts sowed into sleeveless jackets (poiasy nitianye na kamzoly) for flying on ropes" were employed, attached to "iron rings and clasps." The actual "lifting" and "lowering" of actors was usually accomplished by "workmen in the upper curtains (sluzhiteli u verkhnikh shirm)" (for example, a team of "twelve men who [stood] by the screens during the opera"), who wore special "elk-skin gloves for working the ropes."[48]

During the course of the performance of "Cephalus and Procris," a prophesy of Minerva was accompanied by thunder and lightning (real fire was used, shot out of special tin pipes); Cephalus was carried off by a whirlwind; a "beautiful valley" was instantaneously turned into a "most horrid desert" before the eyes of the audience; and at the end Aurora appeared from the sky (a genuine *deus ex machina*). Notably, the new dance reform did not reject this kind of extravagant operatic stage spectacle. Noverre defends the use of stage machinery arguing that "there are few themes taken from Ovid which can be represented without changes of scenery, flights, transformations, etc. Hence a *maître de ballet* cannot make use of subjects of

---

[47] See, note 34.
[48] Shcherbakova, "From the Archives," 18–9.

this kind unless he himself be a machinist" (33). The reasoning here seems a bit backward — plots from the *Metamorphoses* and similar works were chosen for theatricalization precisely because they involved spectacular transformations.

The libretto of "The Sanctuary of Virtue" does not indicate at which points the dancing takes place, except at the very end of the end of the last act, where, framing the final twelve lines sung by the chorus, the directions indicate the "beginning" and "end of the dances." Scholars assume that each of the acts that take place on different continents feature "national dances" associated with the locale,[49] a natural assumption because it was common practice for operas and ballets throughout the century to include similar dance "world tours."

NATIONAL DANCE AND COSTUME

The nature of these presupposed "national dances," and in general, of elements of "Russianness" in opera and ballet, is an extremely complex one, made even more so by much of the scholarship, which often reflects anachronism or bias (either patriotically Russian or condescendingly Europocentric). One naturally asks: "What makes this a *Russian* ballet?" After all, "The Sanctuary of Virtue" had music composed by a German in Italian style, was danced in the primarily French manner, was choreographed with additional dance music by an Austrian, and featured set designs by an Italian. However, this is arguably the wrong question, because the eighteenth-century notion of "Russianness" was far different than today's, indeed, the goal of high art of the age, including ballet, was to *avoid* the kind of national peculiarity that the next century explicitly sought after. Its goal, rather, was to imitate "la belle nature" — conceived as a universal and universally comprehensible ideal that transcended individual and national particularities. To demonstrate Russianness in this context meant to assert the nation's place among enlightened nations, that is, emphasizing its fundamental pan-European *likeness* and rejecting the notion of national difference. The very thing that the later tradition was to prize, i.e, the mysterious distinctiveness of peasant culture, was deemed "low" and shameful, reflecting ignorance and superstition. Ballets based on "national dances" excluded actual peasant dances, as strange as that may now

---

[49] E.g., Krasovskaia, *Russkii baletnyi teatr*, 48 and Winter, *The Pre-Romantic Ballet*, 97.

Chapter 7. "The First Russian Ballet"

seem.[50] Despite the unmistakable influence of folk, carnival and burlesque dancing on ballet, the "Classicist" position on dance — whatever actual practices may have been — was to seek theoretical justification and precedents not in popular culture but in the classics, especially Augustan Rome.[51]

Even so, "national dance" was considered one of the three basic genres of "serious" ballet (together with those on historical and mythological subjects). According to Staehlin, Hilferding's second ballet in Russia, the one that followed "Sanctuary," consisted of "all kinds of village scenes (derevenskikh kartin)" including "peasants" and their (Tyrolean) "country dances."[52] The "national" element in this ballet, which ends with a marriage celebration, is manifested in the idealized "pastoral" mode, which seems to be characteristic of eighteenth-century ballet's overall conception of the national. Staehlin's articles, one of the most valuable contemporary sources on music and dance in eighteenth century Russia, also testify to the consistent intense interest in things "Russian." For example, Staehlin describes "an unusual ballet composed [by Angiolini in 1767] from old-time (stariinykh) Russian dances...for which he composed the music from Russian songs then in use."[53] The last phrase clues us in to the fact that these "folk songs" were probably those (or like those) from G. N. Teplov's popular songbook *After Work, Idleness, or a Collection of Various Songs* (*Mezhdu delom bezdel'e iii sobranie raznykh pesen*, c. 1745–1751), which Staehlin elsewhere praises,[54] and which features songs and arias by contemporary Russian poets like Sumarokov,[55] with music by

---

50 See, for example, Noverre, *Letters on Dancing*, 42. A basic irony is that most social and ballet dances were rooted in regional folk dances, as indicated by their names (e.g., rigaudon, musette, loure, tambourin, chaconne, etc.).

51 This issue is also obviously relevant to many genres of Sumarokov's oeuvre. One example is his comedies, which, despite Sumarokov's explicit rejection of folk *igrishchi*, owes much to such farces. Another example is Sumarokov's carnivalesque choruses written for "Minerva Triumphant," the public masquerade for Catherine's coronation festivities in Moscow. Several of these choruses seem to have points in common with those in "The Sanctuary of Virtue." Both center on the problem of the "prevratnyi mir" (prevratnyi — inconstant, fickle, inverted), although in "The Sanctuary of Virtue" this is an evil, archly serious dystopian world devoid of virtue, while in Sumarokov's festival choruses (e.g., the "Khory prevratnomu svetu") this may be seen as the topsy-turvy satirical world of carnival.

52 Shtelin, *Muzyka i balet*, 157.

53 Shtelin, *Muzyka i balet*, 162; see also Krasovskaia, *Russkii baletnyi teatr*, 54.

54 Shtelin, *Muzyka i balet*, 89–90.

55 Sumarokov's songs were pirated; see "The Illegal Staging of Sumarokov's *Sinav and Truvor* in 1770 and the Problem of Authorial Status in Eighteenth-Century Russia," chap. 10 below.

Teplov and Belogradskaia's father, the court musician T. Belogradskii. Hence Sumarokov's own Classicist folk song stylizations could themselves be taken as sources of the "Russian style."

As another example of the problem of defining the national element, we may consider eighteenth-century ballet costume. Among the more visible marks of reform with which Noverre was associated was changes in ballet dress. He was known for having finally rid French ballet of masks in about 1772 (although they had already long been discarded on most other stages by that time; Hilferding, for example, had eliminated masks in Vienna in 1752).[56] Noverre also made dance costume less stiff and more user-friendly. He did away with the obligatory *tonnelet* (something like a tutu on a frame) for men and huge *panniers* (hoop dresses) for women, allowing a bit more female ankle to be exposed. (In eighteenth-century ballet, women still wore shoes with heels; the *pointe* system was not introduced until the next century.) Until the end of the era, no one attempted ethnographic verisimilitude, and the basic form of (especially female) ballet costume was French court dress, whatever national tradition was being represented. As in the costumes for Noverre's ballet designed by Louis-René Boquet (1717–1814), a viewer of today, uninitiated into the slight, often allegorical modifications would be hard pressed to distinguish what countries these costumes were meant to signify.[57] (See Figs. 4–6; it is unclear why one is "Greek," one "Roman," and one "Bollo(g)nese" for example, and even whether the costumes are meant to depict ancient or modern characters.)

Turning to the dancing itself, this is the hardest (perhaps impossible) thing to reconstruct with any specificity; Chernova and Bowlt note the methodological dilemma in studying the history of dance given the "absence of the object [of study] itself, i.e., of the actual movements in three-dimensional space" — and in their case concerning a period more than 150 years after Sumarokov's ballet.[58] Because of the lack of information concerning the production of "The Sanctuary of Virtue," about which virtually only the libretto remains, in the following sections of this article I will try and situate its choreography by considering the shift from older style court dancing to new reformed ballet. I will sketch out some brief historical

---

[56] Roslavleva, *Era of the Russian Ballet*, 24.
[57] See Vsevolodskii-Gerngross, "Teatral'nyi kostium."
[58] Natalia Chernova and John Bowlt, "Introduction," *Experiment / Эксперимент*, 2. Special issue on "MOTO-BIO — The Russian Art of Movement: Dance, Gesture, and Gymnastics, 1919–1930" (1996), 5.

Fig. 4

Fig. 5

Fig. 6

Figs. 4–5. Louis-René Boquet, two designs ("Greque" and "Romaine") from the collection "Costumes différents." *Starye gody*, ianvar'-fevral', 1915, after p. 40.

Fig. 6. Theatrical costume labeled "Bollonese," evidently also by Boquet, "from the period of Catherine II." K. A. Somov collection. *Starye gody*, iiul'-sentiabr', 1911, after p. 130.

and institutional background of the reform; use Noverre's *Letters on Dance* to describe some of the basic theoretical issues defining reform choreography; draw parallels to Sumarokov's literary program; and, lastly, consider the new dance's aesthetics of performance.

BALLROOM AND STAGE

Ballet was rooted in court dancing, and through the later eighteenth century there was a blurring of boundaries between court and stage, ballroom and theater. Noverre, like Sumarokov, was asserting the independence of his art from the court, and struggling for recognition of its practitioners as professionals.[59] In both cases, however, the court remained both the historical and principal institutional locus for their activity. To start with the theaters where ballets were staged: while there were several separate opera houses and theater buildings in Petersburg (of which only Quarenghi's Hermitage Theater [c. 1783] has survived), in the eighteenth century Russian palaces themselves commonly had two theaters (a *bolshoi* and *malyi*), although the "small" theater in some cases consisted in portable sets and equipment that could be assembled as needed in one of the palace's larger halls. Masquerades were held in palace ballrooms and gardens as well as in theaters; independent theaters (like Locatelli's in 1759) sold tickets for masquerades to the aristocratic and rich merchant public, with attendees dancing on stage as well as in the aisles and other parts of the theater. Masquerades, as segments of larger celebratory events, often followed court theatricals, and on those occasions, the audience might even wear their masks during the performance![60] Furthermore, court dancing, since at least the time of Louis XIV, was patronized and also personally practiced by monarchs, who not only danced at court but occasionally even on stage. Marie Antoinette was known for performing on stage, and the ten-year-old Pavel Petrovich, son of Catherine the Great, played the role of the god Hymen (Hymenaeus) at the end of Starzer's

---

[59] For a discussion of Sumarokov's tribulations, see my "The Illegal Staging of Sumarokov's *Sinav and Truvor*," chap. 10 below.

[60] Vsevolodskii-Gerngross, *Istoriia russkogo teatra*, I: 407 and 462–3. Vsevolodskii-Gerngross also cites an instance in 1723 when during a celebration for the Treaty of Nystad masqueraders attended a church service in masks and makeup (only slightly covering their heads with their capes, we are told) (I: 364).

Chapter 7. "The First Russian Ballet"

"Acis et Galatée," staged by Hilferding in 1764.[61] It was also very common at court for high-ranking noblemen to join the orchestra or to step onto the stage (as in "Acis et Galatée") and there were also special performances at court by what Staehlin refers to as "highly-placed dilettantes" (vysoko-postavlennye diletanti).[62]

In terms of choreography, "court" or "ballroom dancing" also represented a particular style and repertoire of dances. One court dance which played a key historical role in the development of ballet was the minuet. The minuet was one of the sources (and popular reflections) of the "serious style," reflecting and shaping a basic trend in ballet aesthetics, and it also represented an important choreographical link between ballroom and stage. The court dance par excellence at Versailles, the minuet had marked "the high point of the festivities."[63] The minuet took its name from "pas menu" (small step), and derived from a French folk dance from Poitou, but it became "the unrivalled king of the social dances" in the highest society. It continued to be extremely popular throughout Europe — especially Russia — at least through the French Revolution. Significantly, Sumarokov had earned his initial popularity in the later 1740's as a writer of songs (unpublished until Teplov's anthology), songs that were danced as minuets. With its "small steps" and slow to moderate 3/4 march-waltz tempo, the minuet emphasized grace, ease, elegance, stately simplicity and polished manners, all of which were staples of opera-ballet dancing. The terms used to teach the minuet were also those used in ballet, and in general, the minuet was considered equivalent to "the serious style" in dancing.[64]

Minuets especially stressed the importance of making a good entrance, and this as well as the moderate tempo and small steps were basic components of the opera-ballet style, which has been described (in somewhat oversimplified terms) as an elaborate sequence of "entrées," a codified type of dance formation. According to Charles Compan's *Dictionnaire de dance* (1787),

---

61　*Russkii balet: entsiklopediia* (Moscow: Soglasie, 1997), 128; Shtelin, *Muzyka i balet*, 160.
62　Shtelin, *Muzyka i balet*, 94; he refers to many such instances, e.g., 159–60. Of course, many Russian noblemen maintained their own private serf theaters.
　　Both Noverre and Sumarokov — as well as Staehlin — advocated high professional standards in the arts.
63　Horst Koegler, "Dance, Western." Encyclopædia Britannica. 2003. Encyclopædia Britannica Online. Accessed May, 7, 2003. http://search.eb.com/eb/article?eu=117769
64　Giovanni-Andrea Gallini, *A Treatise on the Art of Dancing*, A Facsimile of the 1762 London Edition (New York: Broude Brothers, 1967), 174.

> The usual division for all kinds of ballets is five acts. Each act consists of three, six, nine and sometimes twelve entrées. The term entrée is given to one or more bands of dancers who, by means of their steps, gestures and attitudes, express that portion of the whole theme which has been assigned to them.[65]

In this conception, the entrée is one of the fundamental structural units of ballet, suggesting both the dance as a series of entrances (the entire ballet subdivided into mathematical segments), with each segment defined both in terms of a group formation and as a particular thematic or choreographic unit.

The dancing style of opera-ballets in the era we are discussing, in the words of Susan Leigh Foster, "drew upon, even as it aggrandized and theatricalized, social dance forms of the period."[66] Foster offers a remarkable reconstruction of the substance and inner logic of the dance styles of the era, and here and below I take the liberty of quoting from her at length. Here is her description of the pre-reform ballet as performed at the French Opera (its ballet was associated with the Royal Academy of Dance):

> The Opera's well-deserved renown for lavish visual display was surpassed only by the reputation of its ballets, whose luxurious harmony of decor, costume, and choreography achieved great notoriety throughout Europe. After periods of minimal action in which singing characters formally declared their feelings and intentions, bodies encrusted with feathers, ribbons, satin, and lace would suddenly sweep onto the stage. Each dancer, individually adorned and coiffed, contributed to the extraordinary assemblage of colors, lines, and textures that decorated the stage. The ballets involved large numbers of dancers in patterns that embroidered the space with a never-ending series of configurations. Dancers transited from pinwheel formations to columns, they processed downstage, turned away to either side, reformed in small circles, exchanged single dancers among the circles, and then suddenly reappeared in neatly spaced rows. Single dancers led others along complex paths that braided groups together in intricate assemblages, each smoothly resolving into the next...[67]

---

[65] Translated into Russian as *Tantsoval'nyi slovar'* (Moscow, 1790); quotation from 45; see also 184. The English here is taken from Noverre, *Letters on Dancing*, 12.
[66] Susan Leigh Foster, *Choreography and Narrative: Ballet's Staging of Story and Desire* (Bloomington: Indiana UP, 1996), 28.
[67] Foster, *Choreography and Narrative*, 61.

She notes that in this kind of dance,

> Dancers executed this parade of patterns invoking a moderated but dynamic energy. Phrases exemplified a range, but not the extremes, of quickness and slowness. Steps from the basic vocabulary propelled dancers along their designated paths, allowing them to make decorous contact with one another. Female dancers' bell-shaped skirts tilted from side to side, occasionally revealing the inclination and trajectory of the ankle...Men's stiff tunics (*tonnelets*), while they emphasized the entire leg's movements, still segmented the body like the female's dress into articulate periphery and composed central body.... The partially disclosed steps of the female dancer and the fully evident execution by the male created a pleasant exercise in comparison during their frequent unisons. Large circles of the leg (*ronds dejambes*); shifts of weight to the side, front, or back; jumps; turns — all signaled the dancers' synchronicity. Unison could also be deduced by tracking the precise location of the body within a vertical grid. The vocabulary of steps elaborated several heights for the body — degrees of plié and relevé — and equally subtle but precise facings for the dancer. Even when dancers directed their movements toward each other around a central point, the shifts of facing and of height confirmed their unified endeavors.[68]

There were several aspects of this "Baroque" opera-ballet dance tradition that Noverre attacked. First of all, perhaps, was the notion of the plotless dance (dance as mere entertainment) presumably of the kind described here that focused on visual effect via machine-like synchronicity and geometrical symmetry. He rejected the general notion of the visual for visuality's sake (dance "for the mere sake of dancing" [22]). Dance not only had to be beautiful, it had to tell a story and express emotions. In terms of choreographic strategy, the ballet as a *corps d'entrées* is equivalent to ballet as *divertissement*, having "no means of expression...conveying nothing," reducing the dance to merely a mathematical agglomeration of mechanical, geometrical figures (12).

REFORM VERSUS TRADITION

Noverre's most radical assertion, which gave his reform teeth well into the nineteenth century, and which could serve as a manifesto of Romantic ballet, was the right of genius to disregard the rules (or to create their

---

[68] Foster, *Choreography and Narrative*, 62.

own), and the implicit attack on all the conventions of dance. Despite such declarations, however, reform ballet nonetheless remained one of the most convention- and tradition-bound of all art forms (indeed this may be precisely what made Noverre's in retrospect rather mild reforms seem so radical). Practically all of the elements of court dancing Noverre criticizes reappear in his own reform ballet, with slightly different emphasis, and much of what he has to say about dance dovetails with earlier practices. In many cases it seems that Noverre's criticism of the older norms has to do simply with the degree of excellence, i.e., with how well the dance is performed, rather than an attack on the older balletic techniques per se. His conception of the dance, despite the demand that dance express the entire gamut of human emotion, upheld the already established canon of steps, genres, and ideals of court dancing.

Noverre's conception of the ballet was thoroughly normative in the Classicist sense. Noverre acknowledges the already universal canon of five core ballet positions (plus five "false" positions) codified by Pierre Beauchamps, the first director of Louis XIV's Royal Academy of Dance, and he agrees that learning them is a necessary part of training, although he adds that "these positions are good to know and better still to forget... it is the art of the great dancer to neglect them gracefully" (105). Yet when it comes to the basic types of dance permissible in ballet, Noverre admits only three: serious or heroic; the semi-serious or "demi-charactère" (of high comedy); and the grotesque (of low comedy). These three categories of ballet accord to a hierarchy of genres — high, middle, and low — although Noverre does not spell this out fully. At the top, serious ballets concern history, mythology, or national dances; the pastoral would appear to fall in the high-to-middle range, and the comedic into the middle or low, depending on whether it is of the classical type or boorish and rustic.

These three categories also correspond to three normative body types, facial features, and temperaments or "types of mind": the serious or heroic dancer must be tall, of elegant stature, and noble in mind; the semi-serious — of medium build and "agreeable proportion," with voluptuous and elegant bearing; and the grotesque of shorter stature, fewer physical perfections, and comic mien (88–9). Foster comments: "The three genres, like the spatial and temporal forms of the dancing, existed as predefined roles into which the dancer's body was cast. They collated movement qualities and physical attributes so as to fashion character types that represented three categories of being. Although differences in execution were permitted, they were perceived as variations on a standard type rather than as unique contributions by an exceptional artist. Artistic achievement was measured in terms of how well one exemplified the genre rather than how well one interpreted one's role."[69]

Thus despite Noverre's summons for the free play of genius, and his suggestion that the dancer (and choreographer) follow their natural inclination, ballet that is noble, elevated, and tragic occupies the privileged niche. "The style most suitable for expression in terms of dancing is tragic" because it "offers fine pictures, noble incidents and excellent theatrical effects; moreover, the imitation of them is easier and the pantomimic action more expressive, more natural and more intelligible" (21). Similarly, Noverre is predisposed against the comic; as in the case of defining "national" dance, there is a need to distinguish between the low that is too low, beyond the pale of art, like folk dancing, and that which may be justified in terms of classical models. This is evident in Noverre's comments on Fossan (aka Fussano or Fuzano; stage name of Antonio Rinaldi), whom he praises as "that excellent comic dancer who introduced into France the rage for high jumping" (42), but whose influence he also castigates as setting a bad example (49–50) that is harmful to the serious style. Noverre banishes "thrilling and perilous jumps, and feats of strength" from the ballet, and also rejects steps or movements that involve too much violence, extreme difficulty, or danger (as things that distract both dancer and spectator) (106). In general, jumping and acrobatics was rejected, including *cabrioles* (capers) and *entrechats* ("braidings," jumps with rapid leg crossings in the air) (29). Similarly, spending too long on tip-toe or in pirouettes was discouraged (164), as were any steps considered overly complicated (102).[70] Especially praiseworthy for Noverre were *pas de deux* performed with "judgment and sense" (29). And, despite Noverre's insistence on the new dance as ballet of action, he nevertheless asks us to "Remember that *tableaux* and groups provide the most delightful moments in a ballet" (30). (Notably, one of Noverre's consistent parallels to ballet is the art of painting, which he considers "a brother art" [!], and as in the present

---

69 Foster, *Choreography and Narrative*, 73. This normative, supra-personal view of the dance closely parallels the Russian Classicist notion of genre as described by G. A. Gukovskii. See his *Rannie raboty…*, 277–278f.

70 Some of Hilferding's innovations as a choreographer were the *entrechat quatre* and the *pirouette*, which he brought to Russia (Deryck Lynham, *Ballet Then and Now: A History of the Ballet in Europe*. [London: Sylvan Press, 1947], 68); but as noted, his position on dance is considered basically identical to Noverre, although of course this would not extend to every move and step.

instance, suggesting the more or less static nature of his visual conception of the stage, with the dancers as figures filling up the stage-canvas.)

In general, Noverre puts the center of attention in the ballet not on the legs but on the arms and upper part of the body (88), stressing the crucial role of facial expression and of gesture, which he refers to as "the countenance of the soul" (100). Noverre argues for a kind of proto method acting: the dancer must get into the character's emotion in order to communicate it to the spectator, and must develop the "intelligence and facility of [facial] expression" (107–8). This was one basic reason that Noverre did not approve of dance notation as it existed in his day. Dance notation—known then as "chore(o)graphy" ("dance writing")—had been developed under Louis XIV, by Raoul-Auger Feuillet, whose manual of 1700 is thought to record Beauchamps' system.[71] The "Feuillet system," which was used generally to teach social dancing, records the dancer's horizontal steps across the dance floor, tracing a linear "track" of symbols that roughly resemble footprints. Because of his emphasis on the upper body and facial expression, Noverre rejected this notation system as inadequate for recording ballets d'action.[72]

While Noverre's notion of following nature—as in Sumarokov—may at times suggest a radical rejection of conventions (something that helped inspire Romantic ballet), this was far from the case in regard to specific practices. On a broader theoretical level too, in Enlightenment terms the ideal of "nature," far from justifying the rejection of rules, took for granted a normative, hierarchical system whose precepts accord with reason and common sense. However fundamentally oxymoronic it may seem to us today, this ideal of nature was associated with Versailles as a model of civilization. This dual ideal—Versailles and *la belle nature*—was shared by Sumarokov and Noverre alike.

Noverre, like Sumarokov, was defining a new art by systematizing and regularizing an older one, and providing an aesthetic rationale based on taste and good sense, what we may describe as "classicizing" a Baroque art form, toning down its excesses and elevating its noble status. As in Foster's description above of pre-reform ballet at the French Opera, Noverre's

---

[71] Raoul-Auger Feuillet, *Choregraphie, ou L'art de de'crire [i. e. décrire] la dance*. A facsimile of the 1700 Paris ed. (New York, Broude Bros. [1968]). On this see Ann Hutchinson Guest, *Dance Notation: The Process of Recording Movement on Paper* (New York: Dance Horizons, 1984), 63.

[72] His rival Angiolini on the other hand defended this system "as it contained all principles of the ballet of the period" (Guest, *Dance Notation*, 67). See also Sandra Noll Hammond, *Ballet Basics*. 2nd ed. (Palo Alto, CA: Mayfield, 1984), 17–18.

Chapter 7. "The First Russian Ballet"

ideal of ballet was also one which avoided extremes, one of ease, grace and subtlety. He wanted the excessive gaudiness and "extraordinary assemblage of colors, lines, and textures that decorated the stage" to be reduced and subordinated to a greater aesthetic hierarchy and unity of purpose; for example, he advocated a greater contrast between stage scenery and the actors' costumes, and promoted subtlety and variety of expression over overwhelming effect (22 and 43). Despite Noverre's disparaging comments about older symmetrical and geometrical choreographic formations, he still prized ballet's precision, accuracy, and formal geometry (see, for example, 23). Indeed he embraced the generally accepted idea of the ballet as machinery, which corresponds to Foster's description quoted above of the "complex geometries" of opera-ballet, with the dancers' "symmetrical hierarchies" and "the geometrical patterning." He wrote:

> A ballet is a type of more or less complicated machinery, the different effects of which only impress and astonish in proportion as they follow in quick succession; those combinations and sequences of figures, those movements which follow rapidly, those forms which turn in opposite ways, that mixture of *enchaînements,* that *ensemble,* and that harmony which presides over the steps and the various developments — do not all these afford you an idea of an ingeniously contrived machine? (33)

Noverre's essentially formalist description of ballet here on some level contradicts — or at least moderates — his insistence on the mimetic and emotional mission of dance, and on his downplaying of convention. Foster notes that Noverre's was simply a *"more sensible* machine":

> As radically as the action ballet diverged from the opera-ballets, it shared an aesthetic interest in surfaces and in the machinelike workings of theatrical spectacle that made surfaces lustrous. Noverre and others hoped to reposition the choreographer at the origin and center of ballet production, but this centralization of authority was construed as improving the efficiency with which plot, virtuosity, and scenic liveliness might interface. They intended that dancers extend their repertoire to include the pantomimic, but this challenge to dancers' skillfulness constituted an augmentation more in amount than in kind of expertise. The pantomimic vocabulary itself emphasized the appearance of passions, not the process of their development. The crystalline display of each feeling mattered in a way that either the evolution from one feeling to the next or the difficulty in expressing a feeling did not. The contiguity of perfectly painted images was what counted, making the transformation into and out of those images register only in the efficiency and cleverness with which they facilitated change.

In the social world as in the world of art, the body — wigged, painted, beauty-marked, and jeweled — reveled in contiguous surfaces. Fashionable dress celebrated the intersection of one richly textured surface with another — of sleeve with glove with ring, or of hem with stocking with shoe. It did not explore the play between an undisclosed interiority and an approved exteriority. The woman's bosom, for example, largely exposed, was treated as another surface where the cut of each neckline spoke more significantly than the disclosure of an expanse of powdered flesh. The man's waistcoat and vest framed the groin area, but as a series of openings of one surface onto the next. Bodies, whether on stage or in the salon, intercoursed with one another like parts in a complicated machine. The perfection of mechanical dolls, so much an interest at mid century, set standards for bodily appearance and aplomb which live bodies aspired to meet.

Proponents of the action ballet hoped to deepen the appearance of bodies, to render them more vivid and more sensible, and to orchestrate a causal logic for their interactions. They did not intend to alter the clocklike timing or spatial precision that the opera-ballets had attained or to sacrifice a single moment of spectacle. The careful sequencing of a range of feelings would draw the viewer further into the action, making all the more miraculous the transitions from one compelling scene to the next. The project of representing the passions, like the construction of the stage machinery responsible for changing scenes, required choreographers to coordinate looks and gestures for each dancer and to fit all bodily postures and motions together using the plot as blueprint. The plot gave their motions coherence and integrity just as mechanical drawings elucidated the machine's purpose. Exhibiting their purpose, dancing bodies would thereby continue to signal their horizontal and vertical perfectibility even as they began to stand at the center of the grid that measured them.[73]

CLASSICISM IN DANCE AND LITERATURE

Noverre's ideas on reform of the dance parallel Sumarokov's views on the new literature to a remarkable extent, from the issue of rules and generic norms, to the (somewhat problematic) status of low art forms, to the classical and classicist cultural models on which they grounded their ideas. Like Noverre, Sumarokov insisted on the strict correlation of genre and style, as tempered by two things: the need for each artist to find the genre best suited to his or her temperament, and the demand that the artist fully

---

[73] Foster, *Choreography and Desire*, 78–9.

feel the passions he or she would communicate. In the final analysis, every genre (even the lowest) is good if it's done well. As Sumarokov warned the aspiring love poet in his "Epistle on Russian Poetry," written in emulation of Boileau's *L'Art poétique*,

Но хладен будет стих и весь твой плач — притворство,
Когда то говорит едино стихотворство;
Но жалок будет склад, оставь и не трудись:
Коль хочешь то писать, так прежде ты влюбись!..

Коль хочешь петь стихи, помысли ты сперва,
К чему твоя, творец, способна голова.
Не то пой, что тебе противу сил угодно,
Оставь то для других: пой то, тебе что сродно…

Всё хвально: драма ли, эклога или ода —
Слагай, к чему тебя влечет твоя природа;
Лишь просвещение писатель дай уму:
Прекрасный наш язык способен ко всему.[74]

(But your verse will be cold and your lamentation simulation, / If it is only versification speaking; / And your style will be pitiful, so quit, and do not labor: / If you want to write, then first fall in love!..

If you want to write [sing] poetry, first give a thought / What your head is good for, creator; / Do not try and sing if it is not in your power; / Leave it forthers; sing only what is natural to you…

Everything is praiseworthy: drama, or ode, or eclogue — / Compose that which your nature leads you to compose; / Only let enlightenment touch your spirit, writer; / Our beautiful language is capable of anything.)

This brings us back to our starting premise, and the larger parallel between the establishment of reform ballet with the assertion of a modern literature. Sumarokov wrote that

Довольно наш язык в себе имеет слов,
Но нет довольного числа на нем писцов.

(Our language has enough words in it, / But there aren't enough writers using it!)

---

74 A. P. Sumarokov, *Izbrannye proizvedeniia*, ed. P. N. Berkov, Biblioteka poeta, Bol'shaia seriia (Leningrad: Sovetskii pisatel', 1957), 118, 124 and 125. Cf. Noverre, 30–1.

In his defense of the new ballet art form, Noverre made a similar claim: that ballet amounts to a new language, that it is an art form that can communicate in new and exciting ways, and that all that is needed is great ballet masters to do so.

> It may be concluded...[he wrote] that dancing is possessed of all the advantages of a beautiful language, yet it is not sufficient to know the alphabet alone. But when a man of genius arranges the letters to form words and connects the words to form sentences, it will cease to be dumb; it will speak with both strength and energy; and then ballets will share with the best plays the merit of affecting and moving, of making tears flow, and in their less serious styles, of being able to amuse, captivate and please. And dancing, embellished with feeling and guided by talent, will at last receive that praise and applause which all Europe accords to poetry and painting, and the glorious rewards with which they are honored. (20)

Noverre nevertheless gravitates toward a more or less proscriptive definition of this endeavor, insisting — like Sumarokov and his cohort — on a program of linguistic purism. While this "beautiful language" may be "capable of anything," as Noverre writes elsewhere,

> By dancing, I mean the serious style which is the true foundation of ballets.... If he [the dancer or dance-master] ignores its principles his resources will be limited, he must renounce the grand style, abandon history, mythology and national dances, and confine himself solely to ballets founded on peasant dances with which the public is surfeited and wearied since the arrival of Fossan, that excellent comic dancer who introduced into France the rage for high jumping. I compare fine dancing to a mother tongue, and the mixed and degenerate style derived from it to those rough dialects which can be hardly understood, and which vary in proportion to the distance from the capital where the language is spoken in its greatest purity. (42)

Noverre — like Sumarokov — seems to be continually fighting a losing battle against the intrusion of bad taste, and those manifestations of popular culture which like an *impurity* or "an alloy...lowers the worth of ballet" (50). The status of Fossan's dancing seems uncomfortably contradictory in Noverre's description — he is an "excellent comic dancer" but his "mixed and degenerate style" is compared to "rough dialects" spoken far from the capital "which can be hardly understood." (Yet if the peasant dances of the distant provinces can hardly be understood, why are they so popular with the public, to the point of surfeit and weariness?)

Chapter 7. "The First Russian Ballet"

The flip side of Noverre's argument is that this *pure* language — the reform ballet, ballet of action or ballet-pantomime — as in Vaugelas' linguistic program, manifests the extremely optimistic faith that the court culture of the capital (the "ideal of Versailles") totally accords with Nature. The ballet, that most conventional and stylized of art forms, is, like the native tongue, thus felt to be transparent, universally comprehensible, *natural*. While the rough dialect of the countryside is only privy to the few, the universal language of ballet pantomime — like that of the arts in general — is perceived to need no translation:

> The arts are of all countries, let them assume a voice suitable to them; they have no need of interpretation, and will affect equally both the connoisseur and the ignoramus. If, on the contrary, their effect be limited to dazzling the eyes without moving the heart, without rousing the passions, without disturbing the soul, from that moment they will cease to be pleasing; the voice of nature and the faithful expression of sentiment will always transport emotions into the least sensitive souls; pleasure is a tribute that the heart cannot refuse to the things which matter and interest it. (103)

In retrospect, it seems somewhat of a paradox that ballet, born of an Enlightenment, Neoclassical aesthetic, and arguably one of the most technically challenging, convention-laden of theatrical pursuits, was to become a premier Romantic art form, the ideal blend of nature and artifice. "The arts are of all countries, let them assume a voice suitable to them; they have no need of interpretation…" The notion of a language of movement that needs no interpretation, immediately comprehensible to all people of all nations, that touches, transports, delights and transforms — was this not the utopian dream of avant-garde ballet as well?

WAS SUMAROKOV A LOCKEAN SENSUALIST?
On Locke's Reception in Eighteenth-Century Russia

Despite the fact that Locke occupied a central place in European Enlightenment thought, his works were little known in Russia. Locke is often listed among those important seventeenth-century figures including Bacon, Spinoza, Gassendi, and Hobbes, whose ideas formed the intellectual background for the Petrine reforms; Prokopovich, Kantemir, Tatishchev and perhaps Peter himself were acquainted with Locke's ideas, but for most Russians in the eighteenth century Locke was little more than an illustrious name. Locke's one book that did have a palpable impact was his *Some Thoughts Concerning Education*, translated by Nikolai Popovskii from a French version, published in 1759 and reprinted in 1788.[1] His draft of a textbook on natural science was also translated, in 1774.[2] Yet though Locke as pedagogue was popular, his reception in Russia, as Marc Raeff has noted, was overshadowed by the then current "infatuation with Rousseau's pedagogical ideas."[3] Toward the end of the century some of Locke's philosophical ideas also held an attraction for Russian Sentimentalists, with their new interest in subjective

---

[1] The edition of 1760 was merely the 1759 printing with a new title page (a so-called "titul'noe izdanie"). See the *Svodnyi katalog russkli knigi grazhdanskoi pechati*, 5 vols. (Moscow: Gos. biblioteka SSSR imeni V. I. Lenina, 1962–674), II, 161–2, no. 3720.

[2] *Elements of Natural Philosophy*, translated from the French as *Pervonachal'nyia osnovaniia fiziki* (*Svodnyi katalog*, II, 62, no. 3721). See *The Works of John Locke: A Comprehensive Bibliography from the Seventeenth Century to the Present*, comp. J. C. Attig (Westport, CT and London, 1985), 127–28.

[3] Marc Raeff, "The Enlightenment in Russia and the Russian Enlightenment," in J. G. Garrard, ed., *The Eighteenth Century in Russia* (Oxford, 1973), 42–3. See also E. J. Simmons, *English Literature and Culture Russia (1553–1840)* (Cambridge, MA, 1935), 91–2.

Chapter 8. Was Sumarokov a Lockean Sensualist?

epistemology, but familiarity with Locke's ideas mostly came second hand via such writers as Addison and Sterne.[4]

An often cited exception to the Russian neglect of Locke as a philosopher was the short article which appeared in the May, 1759, issue of Sumarokov's journal *The Industrious Bee* (*Trudoliubivaia pchela*) entitled "On Human Understanding According to Locke" (O chelovecheskom razumenii, po mneniiu Lokka). It was the first work in Russia concerning Locke's most important philosophical opus, *An Essay Concerning Human Understanding,* which argued the sensual basis of human cognition.[5] On the basis of this article many scholars have declared Sumarokov to be a follower of Locke and a philosophical sensualist.[6] We should state from the start that this in a gross

---

[4] Addison's series of essays from the *Spectator* (no. 411–21) on "Pleasures of Imagination," based on the *Essay Concerning Human Understanding,* were translated in the journal *Chteniia dlia vkusa, razuma i chuvstvovanii* in 1791–93 (no. 10, 484–507; no. 11, 183–99; no. 12, 3–28 and 207–26). See Iu. D. Levin, *Vospriatie angliiskoi literatury v Rossii: Issledovaniia i matertialy* (Leningrad: Nauka, 1990), 70 and 88. On Locke and Sterne, see in particular E. Tuveson, "Locke and Sterne," in S. P. Rosenbaum, ed., *English Literature and British Philosophy* (Chicago: University of Chicago Press, 1971), 86–106, and K. MacLean, *John Locke and English Literature of the Eighteenth Century* (1936; reprint. New York: Garland, 1984), passim.

Locke's ideas did have an impact on aesthetic thought earlier in the century, on such as L'Abbé du Bos in France and Johann Christian Gottsched in Germany, but there is no evidence of such impact in Russia. On German Classicist interest in Locke as reflected in a Russo-German journal of the 1730's and 1740's see V. P Stepanov, "Kritika man'erizma v 'Primechaniia k vedomostiam,'" *XVIII vek,* 10 (1975), 39–48. While Stepanov sees affinities between the ideas expressed here with early Classicism, he finds no evidence of a direct link.

[5] On August 26, 1778, P. I. Bogdanovich received 100 rubles from the Translation Society as a down payment toward a translation, but if he completed the book it was never published (V. P. Semennikov, *Sobranie, staraiushcheesia o perevode inostrannykh knig, uchrezhdennoe Ekaterinoi II, 1768–1783 gg.: Istoriko-literaturnoe issledovanie* [St. Petersburg, 1913], 86, no. 5). A translation of Book IV, chap. 10 appeared in 1782 (see below).

The first full Russian version of Locke's *Essay,* entitled *Opyt o chelovecheskom razuma,* only appeared in 1890, in A. N. Savin's translation. This translation, newly edited by M. I. Itkin, was republished in D. Lokk, *Izbrannye filosofskie proizvedeniia,* vol. 1 (Moscow, 1960). A more recent translation appeared in D. Lokk, *Sochineniia,* vol. 1 (Moscow, 1985). See also note 32 below.

[6] See, for example: P. N. Berkov, "Zhiznennyi i literaturnyi put' A. P. Sumarokova," in A. P. Sumarokov, *Izbrannye proizvedeniia* (Leningrad, 1957), 11–12; G. A. Gukovskii, "Russkaia literaturno-kriticheskaia mysl' v 1730–1750 gody," *XVIII vek,* 5 (Moscow, Leningrad, 1962), 122; *Istoriia filosofii v SSSR,* vol. 1 (Moscow, 1968), 530; W. E. Brown, *A History of 18th Century Russian Literature* (Ann Arbor, 1980), 113–14; and H. M. Nebel, Jr., *Selected Aesthetic Works of Sumarokov and Karamzin* (Washington, DC, 1981), 29–30.

exaggeration, or at best a misleading generalization, insofar as the complex philosophical and theological context that made Locke's ideas controversial (and, indeed, fully comprehensible) in Western Europe was absent in Russia. The question here, as with many cases of borrowing, translation and adaptation, becomes: what was the nature of Sumarokov's interest in Locke? How did Sumarokov interpret Locke's ideas, and to what extent did Locke's ideas coincide with his own? In this paper, after briefly comparing the texts, I will attempt to put the article on Locke into the context of Sumarokov's journalistic activity, and then consider Sumarokov's attitude toward the theological problem raised by Locke's sensualism. This had been dramatically posed by Voltaire, and his well known interpretation of Locke, with which Sumarokov must have been familiar, provides a context in which to gauge Sumarokov's views.

The first and perhaps insurmountable problem we face in drawing links between Locke's ideas and Sumarokov is the nature of Sumarokov's essay itself. "On Human Understanding" is less than two pages long in modern print. Its two long paragraphs basically summarize Book I, chapters 2 and 3 of Locke's *Essay Concerning Human Understanding*.[7] Few sentences or even phrases are translated word for word, but Sumarokov's essay recognizably reproduces arguments from Locke's text in the order they appear there, although there are also references to the start of Book II, chapter 1, which reviews earlier arguments. Starting with its title, "On Human Understanding According to Locke," the *Trudoliubivaia pchela* article is presented as a statement of Locke's opinion rather than Sumarokov's; the essay is not signed, or otherwise labeled, although the May issue ends with the note that Sumarokov composed the entire installment.[8] The article is written in the third person, beginning with the first sentence ("Locke denies innate ideas [Lokk otritsaet vrozhdennye poniatia])," although this also implies an approving first person presence, as when "Locke's incontrovertible opinion

---

[7] In the French and German translations cited below these are chapters I and 2, with the introduction to Book I (chapter 1 in the original) presented as the introduction to the entire work. Citations from Locke's English text in this article refer to book, chapter and section number as given in John Locke, *An Essay Concerning Human Understanding*, ed. P. H. Nidditch (Oxford: Clarendon Press, 1975).

[8] *Trudoliubivaia pchela*, 1759, Mai, 320. The essay on Locke may also be found in: A. P. Sumarokov, *Polnoe sobranie vsekh sochinenii*, ed. N. I. Novikov. Vol. 7 (Moscow, 1781), 322–25 (hereafter cited as PSVS followed by volume and page number); and in *N. Novikov i ego sovremenniki* (Moscow: AN SSSR, 1961), 350–51. In transcribing the text I have changed ѣ to *e*, *i* to *u*, and eliminated hard signs after final hard consonants.

(neoprovergaemoe Lokkovo mnenie)" is cited. The line between alien and authorial speech, between translation and commentary, is blurred; nowhere does an actual narratorial "I" appear, as it occasionally does in Sumarokov's moralistic essays. Further complicating the picture, the article was followed by the statement that "A continuation will follow (Prodolzhenie vpred' budet)," but none ever appeared.

Hence there are no clear grounds for considering the essay anything more than a translation-summary, that may or may not reflect the ideas of its translator. As with the other English materials which appeared in *Trudoliubivaia pchela,* it was most likely based on a French or German intermediary[9] (there is little evidence Sumarokov knew English[10]). Various abridgements of the *Essay* were also available, although most omitted the first book, and there were many discussions of Locke's ideas in European journals, but it appears as if Sumarokov prepared this summary of Locke's ideas himself.

Keeping these things in mind, we may speculate on some of the subtle changes of emphasis apparent in Sumarokov's reading of Locke, although the differences may be due mostly to the simplifications necessary in a condensation on a scale of something like 23:1. While Sumarokov represents Locke's arguments rather closely, he puts more exclusive emphasis on the sensual basis for human understanding, mostly skipping over Locke's references to the processes by which the understanding functions (which form the main subject of Book II). In the chapters under discussion, Locke makes his famous case against the notion of innate ideas, "clearing the ground a little" (as he puts it in the prefatory epistle) in order to analyze the operations of the mind, which he insists begin with the famous "tabula rasa." Sumarokov shifts Locke's emphasis from the contrast between innate and acquired notions to a continuing opposition between *razum* (*"reason"*) and

---

9   On Locke's *Essay* and translations of it (not including those in Russian), see *The Works of John Locke,* 58–70. J. W. Youlton, *Locke and French Materialism* (New York: Oxford UP, 1991), mentions pirated editions (p. 2). In Sumarokov's case the main candidates as intermediaries are Pierre Coste's French translation which underwent nine editions between 1700 and 1759, and two German editions: *Antleitung des menschlichen Verstandes zur Erkenntniss der Warheit nebst desselben,* trans. G. D. Kyupke (Königsberg, 1755); and *Versuch vom menschlichen Verstande,* trans. and ed. H. E. Poley (Altenburg, 1757).

10 On the general issue, see M. P. Alekseev, "Angliiskii iazyk v Rossii i russkii iazyk v Anglii." *Uchenye zapiski Leningradskogo universiteta,* 72, Seriia filologiceskikh nauk, 9 (1944): 77–137; on Sumarokov's English, see the discussion in my "Sumarokov's Russianized 'Hamlet': Texts and Context" in this volume.

chuvstva ("feelings"). What precisely these terms signify is by no means clear, and in general, the terminology with which Sumarokov translates Locke's linguistically innovative theory (further muddied by the probable French or German intermediary) often leaves a confused impression. *Razum* usually appears to stand for the faculty of reason, but at times also seems to denote Locke's "mind"; at others Sumarokov equates *razum* with understanding (*razumenie*), reasoning (*rassuzhdenie*), and even perhaps intelligence.[11] Sumarokov writes:

> Разумение просвещается чувствами, и что больше они укрепляются, то больше оно просвещается... Разсуждение кроме данных ему чувствами ни каких оснований не имеет. Разсуждение без помощи чувств ни малейшаго движения в изследовании зделать не может. Разум ни что иное как только действия души, в движение чувствами приведенныя... Мог ли бы человек постигнуть что сладко, и что горько, ежели бы он не имел вкуса? Может ли кто постигнуть, что бело и что красно, разумом, слеп родившися? Кто глух родился, тот о музыке ни малейшаго понятия не имеет... Разум ни чему нас не научает, чувства то делают. Все движения души — от них... Разум есть ни что иное, как только содержатель вображений, порученных ему чувствами. (PSVS, 6, 322–23)[12]

Sumarokov here emphasizes the fundamental importance of the senses in providing the foundation, the primary material, with which and upon which the mental faculties operate. The discussion here, based on Book I, chapter 2, also echoes Book II, chapter 1, and possibly also chapter 2, which appears to be the starting point in Locke for Sumarokov's opposition between *razum* and *chuvstva*. At the end of 2.1.25 Locke emphasizes the passive nature of the "understanding" as receptor of sensory ideas, "as it were the materials of knowledge," which must come first. In this sense, *razum* (understanding)

---

[11] For example, Sumarokov contrasts an educated person to a savage (*dikii*), noting that they differ not in their *razum* but in their "*upotreblenie chuvstv.*" Here *razum* appears to mean a capacity to reason, some kind of basic intelligence or power of logic (which, as Sumarokov writes elsewhere, even animals and insects have). By contrast, for Locke "reason" signifies the acquired ability to manage sensory and other ideas (perhaps the "*upotreblenie chuvstv*"). Sumarokov continues, however, asking, "If *razum* was innate, what would we need science (*nauki*) for?" *Razum* here appears to mean not a faulty of reasoning but some sort of innate knowledge itself, those "innate principles" that Locke denies.

[12] Note the additional problems in translating such basic terms as "idea" (in Sumarokov's article variously as *vo(o)brazhenie, prosveshchenie, poniatie*). Because of this, I have not attempted to translate the cited passages from Sumarokov's essay.

represents or includes the faculty of retention, more precisely described later in Book II as the faculty of memory. However, Sumarokov ignores Locke's repeated contrasts of sensation to "reflection," which Locke describes as the second of the two basic operations of the understanding.

This imbalance is clarified somewhat in the next paragraph, where it becomes more explicit that the first section refers to the initial impressions we receive; reason comes into play at a later stage:

> Ежели бы врожденное было нравоучение; оно бы вдруг постигнуто быть долженствовало, а мы оному научаемся, и сложением многих воображений, до него доходим. Одни несложныя просвещения, чувствами, разом понимаются. Рабенок то, что темняе и что светляе, равно как и большой человек постигает. Большой слагая понятие с понятием, и воображение с воображением, о свете разсуждает, а перьвое воображение, не больше младенца чувствует. (PSVS, 6, 324)

Here Sumarokov contrasts simple and complex ideas (discussed by Locke in Book II), and juxtaposes the immediate comprehension of simple sensual input to the processes by which an adult learns and reasons in a more complex way by comparing and combining ideas.

On the other side of the *razum — chuvstva* opposition, Sumarokov's understanding of *chuvstva* at times also appears to go beyond the simple meaning of the senses, which is Locke's focus, to also appear to mean feelings, emotions, even passions. In the last section of the essay, Sumarokov categorically states that the desire for happiness is not inborn but derives from *chuvstva* (whereas Locke first admits that "the desire of happiness and an aversion to misery *are* innate practical principles" [my italics], but then qualifies this by saying that "these are *inclinations of the appetite* to good, not impressions of truth on the understanding" [Locke's italics] — I.3.3). The next section, on innate moral feelings, pushes the argument even further:

> Спроси Християнина, для чево он опасается делать беззаконие: спроси ученика Гоббезиева; спроси языческаго Философа. Перьвой скажет: Боюся Бога. Другой: Боюся начальства. Третий скажет: Боюся стыда; так им сие узаконение чувства предписали, а не врожденное право. (PSVS, 6, 324)

Sumarokov here modifies the meaning of Locke's contrast. In Locke the differences in the Christian, Hobbesean, and pagan philosopher's reasons for behaving well argue against what he calls "universal consent," that is, Locke contends that innate moral ideas cannot logically exist because people have differing notions of morality. In Sumarokov's text, however, proper behavior in each case is laid to emotion (fear) and to the resultant "legalization of feelings (uzakonenie chuvstva)."¹³

In both of these examples, the desire for happiness and man's reasons for acting properly, Sumarokov seems to describe something more than sensations at work, but rather a more well developed manifestation of the emotional self. Sumarokov appears to be generalizing even farther than Locke from the simple input of the senses to speak of the irrational, animal, passionate self. We may speculate that Sumarokov is interpreting the opposition between *razum* and *chuvstva* along the lines of the conflict between reason vs. passion (also *razum* and *chuvstva*), which is such a central problem in his tragedies. The terms in which Sumarokov describes Locke's psychic processes then may reflect his own understanding as a playwright. His interpretation of *razum* as "nothing other than only the actions of the soul, set in motion by feelings (ne chto inoe, kak tol'koe deistvisa dushi, v dvizhenie chuvstvami privedennyia)" and the further statement that "All of the soul's movements are from them [feelings] (Vse dvizheniia dushi ot nikh [chuvstv])," as well as the metaphor of the "soul's movements" itself, seem quite appropriate to the lyric and tragic personae of Sumarokov's works.¹⁴ While Lockean epistemology and the psychology of Sumarokov's literary personae may be too disparate to allow useful juxtaposition, from a broader perspective Locke's groundbreaking emphasis on man himself and the inner workings of the mind (or "soul") may be seen as quite compatible with the innovations Sumarokov brought to the Russian theater. The potential linguistic confusion between *chuvstva* (the senses) and *chuvstva* (emotions) thus may form a bridge between Locke's empiricism and Sumarokov's *chuvstvitel'nost'* (sensibility). Moral sensibility plays a major role in Sumarokov's writings on ethics and theology,¹⁵ as it does

---

13   Locke himself speaks later of the fear of punishment as a motivation (I. 3. 13).
14   Locke does at one point use the motion metaphor, comparing "the perception of ideas...(as I conceive) to the soul, what motion is to the body" (2. 1. 10). I. Z. Serman has described the "dushevnyi golos" of his heroes and heroines as Sumarokov's main innovation as a playwright. See his *Russkii klassitsizm: Poeziia, drama, satira* (Leningrad: Nauka, 1973), chap. 6. See also Sumarokov's contrast between *razum* and *serdtse* in "O nesoglasii" (PSVS, 10, 315), in which Sumarokov refers to "movements of the heart."
15   See, for example, "O kazni" in which Sumarokov argues that capital punishment is required not only as justice, and as an example to others, but also as revenge, "in order to alleviate the sensibility (radi utoleniia chuvstvitel'nosti) of those who remain alive" (PSVS, 9, 332). Sumarokov sees this desire as grounded in God as the guarantee of justice. In Sumarokov's writings God and the necessity of an afterlife are often asserted

in his tragedies, drenched with the tears of his unhappy protagonists, whose stated goal was to "touch the hearts of the audience."[16]

Sumarokov's emphasis on the emotions rather than merely the senses may also be true of his presentation of Locke's description of the conscience:

> Совесть основана на чувствах, а не на врожденном понятии, котораго нет, и быть не может. Есть ли бы совесть врожденно изобличала; допустила ли бы она до беззакония. Воспитание, наука, хорошия собеседники и протчия полезныя наставления, приводят нас к безпорочной жизни, а не врожденная истинна. (PSVS, 6, 325)

On the one hand, Sumarokov emphasizes the importance of *chuvstva* as the basis for the conscience, whether we interpret this in the simplest sense, that conscience acts upon the basis of sensory input, or in that it represents our passionate self. On the other hand, conscience (as more explicitly stated in Locke) emerges as the product of (in Sumarokov's words) "education, schooling [science], good partners in conversation and other beneficial instruction," as the product of a process that combines experience and reason rather than as something innate. In this second view it is *nurture* rather than nature that makes us what we are and defines our moral impulses.

The insistence on "education, schooling, good partners in conversation and other beneficial instruction" as the way to a virtuous life may be taken as the central editorial concern of *Trudoliubivaia pchela*, and as such go far in explaining why Locke was chosen for translation. "On Human Understanding, According to Locke" stands virtually alone in the journal, which in its yearlong existence published no other original modern European philosophy.[17] Most of the translated prose material—including works by

---

on the basis of our unquenchable desire for justice (e.g., PSVS, 6, 218). Such a position is obviously far from Locke.

16 Sentiment and sentimentalism pervade many of Sumarokov's works. As Gitta Hammarberg writes perceptively, "Sumarokov's [Classicist] guidelines for the midstyle genres [and, we may add, many of his basic literary positions—M. L.] provide a practically complete description of Sentimentalist poetics as a whole…However, the basic and crucial difference…is the divergent function of such genres within the respective literary systems" (*From the Idyll to the Novel: Karamzin's Sentimentalist Prose* Cambridge: Cambridge UP, 1991], 45).

17 Neither the philosophical direction nor the journal's pattern of translating have been studied. The best work on *Trudoliubivaia pchela*, by V. Berzina ("Zhurnal A. P. Sumarokova 'Trudoliubivaia pchela,'" *Voprosy zhurnalistiki: Mezhvuzovskii sbornik statei*, vyp. 2, kn. 2 [Leningrad, 1960], 3–37), greatly overstresses its "oppositionist" character.

Xenophon, Lucian, Aeschines,[18] Maximus of Tyre, Livy, Cicero, Erasmus, Marc-Antoine Muret, Oxenstierna, and G. W. Rabener—falls into the general category of "practical ethics," popular moralizing philosophy often directed at a young audience. In this context, the piece on Locke represents not an exercise in technical philosophy or in philosophical method, but one of many essays arguing for the dual values of virtue and education. The variety of material also seems to reflect Sumarokov's opinion, expressed elsewhere in the same issue as the Locke essay, that

> многия знания возросли, многие изобретены, многия пали, а некоторыя, и может быть, многия изчезли. Все новыя умствования основаны на умствованиях древних. Мода меняется всегда, а природа никогда. (PSVS, 6, 335)
>
> (much knowledge has increased, much invented, and much declined, and some, perhaps much, has disappeared. All new philosophizing is based on the philosophizing of the ancients. Fashion always changes, but never nature.)

Philosophical truth, founded on nature, is unchanging, and does not represent an ongoing quest; the accumulation of knowledge is cyclical rather than в teleological march of enlightenment. In this context, Locke emerges not as the instigator of a modern epistemological revolution, not someone who (as in Voltaire's view) paved the way to a new empiricist philosophy shorn of idealist metaphysics, but as someone who was able to express traditional religious and ethical values in modern rationalist vocabulary.

Voltaire was the most obvious candidate for having introduced Sumarokov to Locke. His presentation of the English philosopher, however, sharply contrasts with that of the Russian and provides the most obvious philosophical context against which we may consider Sumarokov. The thirteenth letter of Voltaire's *Lettres philosophiques* (first published 1733-4), had played a major role in introducing and popularizing Locke's ideas on the continent.[19]

---

[18] Eskhin (Aeschines), not to be confused with Eskhil (Aeschylus), as cited in *Svodnyi katalog*, IV, 196.

[19] See G. Bonno, "The Diffusion and Influence of Locke's *Essay Concerning Human Understanding* in France before Voltaire's *Lettres philosophiques*," *Proceedings of the American Philosophical Society*, 91: 5 (December 1947), 421–25; his "La Culture et la Civilization Britanniques dévant l'Opinion Française de la Paix D'Uireeht aux *Lettres philosophiques*," *Transactions of the American Philosophical Society*, 38 (1948), 1–184 (80–96 on Locke); J. Hampton, "Les traductions françaises de Locke au XVIIIᵉ siècle," *Revue de littérature comparée*, 29 (1955), 240-51; J. W. Yolton, *Locke and French Materialism* (Oxford, 1991), chap. 6; and R. Hutchinson, *Locke in France, 1608-1734*. Studies on

Chapter 8. Was Sumarokov a Lockean Sensualist?

That Sumarokov knew the *Lettres philosophiques* is clear.[20] Even more obvious, for the August issue of *Trudoliubivaia pchela* Sumarokov translated Voltaire's *Micromégas,* in which a disciple of Locke encapsulates Voltaire's view of the English philosopher. There and in the thirteenth letter, while ostensibly praising Locke's religiosity, Voltaire somewhat disingenuously turns his incidental remark from the *Essay* concerning God's ability to make matter think into an attack on theologians who assert the immortality and immateriality of the soul.[21] Voltaire thus depicted Locke as a proponent of reason rather than revelation and turned the *Essay* into an important text for the later radical Enlightenment tradition. Locke himself, however, despite his rejection of innate ideas, took a "concordist" position, insisting that reason and revelation were fully compatible.[22] While one of Sumarokov's reasons for publishing the essay on Locke may have been to emulate Voltaire in popularizing Locke, there is no evidence whatsoever that he either took Voltaire's skepticist view of Locke seriously, or indeed that he considered Voltaire himself to be an opponent of Christianity or revealed religion. In fact throughout his career Sumarokov adamantly defended Voltaire as a believer, denying that he was an atheist or even a deist.[23]

Voltaire and the Eighteenth Century, 290 (Oxford, 1991). Hutchison concludes that Voltaire's letter "marked the final emergence of Locke as a contributor to the mainstream of that subversive movement of ideas that we call the Enlightenment" (229).

20   See my "Sumarokov's Russianized 'Hamlet': Texts and Contexts," chap. 5 in this volume, in which I demonstrate Sumarokov's use of Voltaire's version of Hamlet's famous monologue from the eighteenth of the *Lettres philosophiques.* Various opinions which Sumarokov expresses in his essays seem to stem from his reading of the thirteenth letter, for example, his echoing of Voltaire's opinion that Descartes' metaphysics made "une roman de l'âme" (cf. PSVS, 9, 323). On Voltaire's possible sources for this phrase, see Bonno, "The Diffusion and Influence," 424, and Huchinson, *Locke in France,* 211.

21   On Voltaire's arguments, and on his manipulation of Locke's ideas, see Bonno, "The Diffusion and Influence," 424–25; his "La Culture et la Civilization" 93–94; and Yolton, *Locke and French Materialism,* esp. 39–44.

22   As Richard Ashcraft has put it, Locke's belief in undertaking the *Essay* was that "once the old foundation of innate ideas is replaced by a 'surer' one, the superstructure of Christianity will stand mightier than ever" ("Faith and knowledge in Locke's Philosophy," in *John Locke: Problems and Perspectives,* John W. Yolton, ed. [London: Cambridge UP, 1969], 202). On Locke as a philosopher of ethics, see John Colman, *John Locke's Moral Philosophy* (Edinburgh: Edinburgh UP, 1983); and John A. Passmore, *Locke and the Ethics of Belief* (London: Oxford UP, 1980).

23   See his "Mnenie vo snovidenii o frantsuzskikh tragediiakh," PSVS, 4, 325–54, and my remarks in "Sumarokov's Drama 'The Hermit': On the Generic and Intellectual Sources of Russian Classicism," chap. 6 in this volume.

The theological problem concerning Locke's sensualism as it appears in Book I of the *Essay* arises after the passage contrasting the Christian, Hobbesean, and pagan philosophers reasons for behaving virtuously cited above. The issue is: if morality and conscience are not innate but determined by experience and custom, does this not eliminate God's role in human affairs? (Locke I. 3. 6). Sumarokov states the problem and answers it in one rhetorical period:

> Уменьшается ли тем премудрость нашего Создателя, что нравоучение основано на чувствах, а не на разуме! (PSVS, 6, 324–25)
>
> (Does the wisdom of our Creator really decrease if moral doctrine is based on the feelings and not on reason!)

This half question, half assertion that rhetorically confirms God's wisdom is as far as Sumarokov sees fit to acknowledge the issue, like Locke (and unlike Voltaire) presenting the sensualist and theist positions as in no way opposed. Like Locke, Sumarokov held to a middle, "compromise position," and believed in reconciling rationalism and religion. In this fundamental "concordism" Sumarokov adhered to the early Enlightenment tradition represented in part by Locke. Following Feofan Prokopovich, this tradition had a decisive influence on Russian Orthodox Enlightenment theology, which in turn, as I have argued elsewhere, is of crucial importance for understanding the new secular Russian literature.[24] Like Locke, Sumarokov accepted the divine revelation of Holy Writ as the highest authority on questions that are beyond the grasp of reason. Whenever philosophical questions appeared to challenge dogma, Sumarokov, like Locke, tended to move from professions of ignorance to references to Holy Writ. Like Locke, Sumarokov rejected "narrow sensualism," that is, a purely materialist view of the senses. Sumarokov defended the primacy of the soul over the body and decried those "madmen" (bezumtsy) who say that the soul is but an "outgrowth of our bodily composition (otrosl' nashego telesnogo sostava)," like the result of clanging two heavy material bodies together (PSVS, 6, 286). This comment is from Sumarokov's posthumously published essay "The Basis of Philosophy" (Osnovanie liubomudriia) of 1772. In it he attacked a new unnamed "philosophical sect" which accepted the following planks that might well have followed from a skepticist reading of Locke:

---

[24] Until the very recent past, Russian Orthodox Enlightenment theology has hardly been acknowledged, let alone studied. See my discussion in "Sumarokov's Drama 'The Hermit'" and other articles in this volume.

Chapter 8. Was Sumarokov a Lockean Sensualist?

Любити основание разсуждения, и ни какова в нем основания не иметь...
Ни о чем не имети понятия, полагая что все на свете сем не понятно...
(PSVS, 10, 143)

(To love the basis of discussion but having no basis at all for it... To have no notion about anything, presuming that everything in this world is incomprehensible...)

In the same passage Sumarokov further rejects arguments which lead either from human ignorance or from God's immensity to the conclusion that morality does not exist or is a figment of the imagination.

Like Lomonosov and the majority of his Russian contemporaries, Sumarokov firmly embraced the notion (in Locke's words) that God is

> naturally deducible from every part of our knowledge... For the visible marks of extraordinary wisdom and power appear so plainly in all the works of the creation, that a rational creature, who will but seriously reflect on them, cannot miss the discovery of a Deity. (I.4.9)

In "The Basis of Philosophy" Sumarokov takes an explicitly theist position, and similarly describes God's wisdom as revealed in the natural world, in terms which seem to paraphrase Lomonosov's well known "Morning Meditation," and his own and later variations on the theme, including Derzhavin's "God"[25]:

> Кто может сумневаться о бытии Божием! Хотя бы и не вошли в самую глубину пространства небеснаго; но только бы до солнца зрением возлетели, и оттоле возвратившиися простерли по земле очи наши, и свой собственный состав разсмотрели; какия чудеса и виды премудрости божией и его к родам животных милосердие!... Не ужели Создатель одних ради премудрых явил в устроении нашего мира, премудрость ко славе своей? Солнце составленное всемогуществом божиим из Ефира, плавающее в нем и питающееся им, дает, человекам, скотам, зверям, птицам, рыбам, гадам, древесам, цветам и траве жизнь. Вот и всемогущество, и премудрость, и милосердие Божии... Солнце, говоря пиитически, погружается в Окияне, к пользе нашей. Разсмотрим со естествословами единый глаз, или едино ухо, вашего состава. Чувства наши и все наши члены, с коликою премудростию, ко крайней нашей пользе устроены! (PSVS, 6, 287–88)

---

25   In my subsequent work I identify this idea as "physico-theology"; see "The Theological Context of Lomonosov's 'Evening' and 'Morning Meditations on God's Majesty,'" chap. 15 in this volume.

(Who can doubt God's being! Even if one can't enter the very depths of heavenly space, if we could only fly up to the sun with our vision, and from there, returning, raise our eyes to the earth, and examine our own constitution, what miracles and views of God's wisdom and His mercy to the races of animals [we would see]!... Did the Creator really manifest His wisdom (to His glory) in the structure of our world for the sake of sages alone? The sun, composed by divine omnipotence out of ether, floating in it and nourished by it, gives life to people, cattle, beasts, birds, reptiles, trees, flowers and grass. Here is God's omnipotence and wisdom and mercy!... The sun, speaking poetically, plunges into the ocean, for our benefit. Let us look with the naturalists (estestvoslovami) at only a single eye, or at a single ear, that are part of our make-up. With what wisdom are our senses and all of our members organized, to our great benefit!)

As in Lomonosov's poem, for all the miraculous power our senses, and the power which they and reason confer upon as, they are severely limited when seen from the perspective of the Maker of all things. Far from adopting an empiricist approach to strictly material reality, the natural scientist (estestvoslov) is called to poetic ecstasy at an intuitive or revelatory realization of the goodness and utility of God's universe. The senses here are not so much tools with epistemological limits as gifts to rejoice in. We are to some extent obviously comparing apples and oranges here in trying to compare a poet's perspective to that of a philosopher,[26] but the basic difference in epistemology, in defining the sources of knowledge, remains. Sumarokov's basic philosophical concern was with the nature of virtue and the working out of divine justice on earth rather than with a clinical understanding of the processes of reason.

The question here is one of emphasis, for in the *Essay* Locke also refers to God as the "true ground" of morality, but that emphasis is a crucial one. Certainly, there is a fine line between seeing God in nature (or deducing his presence there), which Locke did, and acknowledging the existence of "innate principles," which he did not.[27] But Sumarokov crossed that line, that is, he often expressed faith in the existence of innate morality. This is evident from Sumarokov's prose writings, from his two most "religious" plays, "Hamlet" (1749) and "The Hermit" (1757), as well as from the other materials Sumarokov published in *Trudoliubivaia pchela*. In "Hamlet,"

---

[26] Cf. Sumarokov's contrast between poets and philosophers, PSVS, 9, 323.

[27] For both, we should note, the existence of morality itself, whether discovered by reason or faith, whether innate or not, was an objective truth. The solipsism and potential moral relativism of later Russian Sentimentalists was foreign to Locke, although the Sentimentalists shard a basic emphasis on epistemology.

Chapter 8. Was Sumarokov a Lockean Sensualist?

for example, as I have shown, Sumarokov demonstrates the benevolent workings of the divine agency within nature, thus changing the emphasis of Shakespeare's play.[28] Here and elsewhere Sumarokov depicts conscience as a kind of innate, divine knowledge inscribed in human nature by God, a "divine spark given to us (danaia nam iskra Bozhestva)" that "demands that we fix our gaze on nothing except virtue (trebuet togo, chto by my ni na chto ne ustremliailisia vziraia ko dobrodeteli)" (PSVS, 6, 249).[29] Sumarokov's view of the God-given conscience inscribed in nature was shared by Russian Orthodox enlightenment theologians of his day such as Platon (P. E. Levshin), who also believed that the feelings of conscience "must originate from some *innate powers*" and took this, together with "our innate desire for a chief good" to be proofs of God's existence (positions which Locke explicitly rejected).[30]

Furthermore, most of the other philosophical works chosen for inclusion in *Trudoliubivaia pchela* present similar traditional Platonic metaphysical arguments about virtue (in contrast to Locke's anti-Platonic, pro-Aristotelean stance), arguments which stress the divine nature of the soul and the afterlife as basic arguments for virtuous living.[31] Yet it should be noted that for many eighteenth-century readers of Locke, he himself was seen as an important defender of God. Indeed Locke's chapter proving God's existence from Book IV of the *Essay* appeared in Russian translation in 1782 (although it has not been identified as such until now) — the only other translation from the *Essay* to appear in Russian before 1898.[32]

---

28   See my article "Sumarokov's Russianized 'Hamlet,'" chap. 5 in this volume, and esp. the description of the workings of conscience, p. 93.

29   In "O nespravedlivykh osnovaniiakh," however, Sumarokov's discussion of conscience and the way people may deceive themselves and not suffer pangs of regret might seem to contradict this, or at least offer a less rosy picture (PSVS, 6, 334–39).

30   Platon, Metropolitan of Moscow, *The Present State of the Greek Church in Russia*, trans. Robert Pinkerton (1815; reprint New York, 1973), 30–31; Platon's emphasis. This is a translation of of Platon's popular textbook in theology *Pravioslavnoe uchenie, ili Sokrashchennaia khristianskaia* of 1765, which underwent several editions in the eighteenth century (see *Svodnyi Katalog*, 2, 422–28). I briefly discuss the similarity in Sumarokov's and Platon's views in "Sumarokov's Drama 'The Hermit.'"

31   These include: an article from the *Spectator* on the immortality of the soul (March, 180–87); Oxiensterna's essays (September, 549–67); and a Socratic dialogue by Aeschines which argues that virtue stems not from learning or nature but is "a certain kind of divine gift (bozhestvennoe nekoe darovanie)" (December, 722–33).

32   It was entitled "O poznanii Bozhiia bytiia," *Vecherniaia zaria*, 3 (1782): 18–42; wrongly cited as being from Locke's *The Reasonableness of Christianity* in Simmons, *English*

Do all these things make Sumarokov a Lockean sensualist? By now the myriad problems involved in both defining the term and applying it to Sumarokov should be apparent enough. The fundamental "proof" of this contention is for all practical purposes a translation, and even if Sumarokov may have found Locke's ideas to be correct, or compatible with his own, this is hardly the definition of a disciple.[33] For all his significant differences from Voltaire, there is far more reason (for example) to consider Sumarokov a follower of that writer. In the case of Locke and Sumarokov, we are dealing with a general cultural amenability, a common broad intellectual and religious outlook (which historically Locke admittedly had done much to shape). If we do choose to refer to Sumarokov as a Lockean, it is important to keep in mind that in the areas that were most important for the subsequent history of Enlightenment thought such as Locke's empirical method, his exploration of the functioning of the mind, and his attack on scholasticism, Sumarokov and the Russians were hardly interested. Sumarokov's view of the senses was far less sophisticated than Locke's, and he seems to have taken the conclusions of sensualist arguments to be obvious rather than as something to be debated. What were obvious were both the sensual origins of all the things that pass through one's mind, but also the divine rationality of God's world which was the mission of Russian literature to celebrate.

Literature, 130. This is a translation from Latin by Mikhailo Antonskii of the *Essay Concerning Human Understanding*, Book IV, chap. 10, "Of the existence of a GOD." The *Essay Concerning Human Understanding* had appeared in several Latin translations, both the full text (by E. Burridge, 1701; by G. H. Theile, 1742) and Book IV alone (in 1709, 1729, 1741, 1758). See *The Works of John Locke*, 12–13, 68–9, 183.

[33] Sumarokov hardly even mentions Locke in his other writings. In the article "O sueverii i litsemerii" he is cited as a great man (PSVS, 10, 162) and in the fable "Dva povara" (1765) he is included in a list with ten other great men including Virgil, Cicero, Descartes and Newton.

9

BARKOVIANA AND RUSSIAN CLASSICISM

Vladimir Stepanov, writing in 1988, acknowledged the undeniably important place of "barkoviana" in Russian poetry during the second half of the eighteenth through at least the first third of the nineteenth century (from Maikov, Bogdanovich, Krylov and Derzhavin, to Pushkin — V. L. as well as A. S. — Lermontov and Polezhaev). In the highly exaggerated formulation of Andrei Voznesenskii, "Pushkin equals Derzhavin plus French literature and Barkov"! (Barkov 1992, 14). On the other hand, Stepanov rightfully complained of the "complete scholarly neglect of 'barkoviana' in its typological, historical-cultural, as well as its literary-historical aspects (its circle of authors, their literary positions, text attribution, connection with the satirical tradition, and so on)" (Stepanov 1988, 61). A giant step in making this material available for study was the appearance of the first full, uncensored, critical publication of *Devich'ia igrushka, ili Sochineniia gospodina Barkova* (*A Maiden's Plaything, or Works of Mister Barkov*) which took place only in 1992, under the editorship of Andrei Zorin and Nikita Sapov. Still, Stepanov's words still basically hold true, and there remains a dearth of research and information about basic aspects of this literature. The goal of this article is to examine some of the sources of barkoviana and to speculate on some of the reasons for the appearance of this kind of poetry in mid-eighteenth century Russia, at a time when modern Russian poetry was still in the process of taking shape. The article has two parts. The first considers *A Maiden's Plaything* as an example of classical Latin "priapeian" verse, and suggests that Russian "priapeia" follows a pattern of reception common to other poetic genres of Russian Classicism. The second part analyzes *A Maiden's Plaything*'s dedication piece, "An Offering to Belinda" (Prinoshenie Belinde), and considers the question why the heroine of Alexnder Pope's *The Rape of the Lock* was adopted as the addressee for Russian obscene poetry.

There is a basic consensus among scholars that "the invention of pornography" — the social, economic, intellectual, and sexual circumstances that gave rise to this peculiar phenomenon — took place in eighteenth century, within the context of "the origins of modernity" and the development of the public sphere (Hunt 1996). To what extent the circumstances that gave rise to pornography in the West are also applicable to eighteenth-century Russia is open to debate, but it is certainly arguable that the history of Russian "pornography" begins with barkoviana (e.g., Hopkins 1977, 70–1). On the other hand, it seems obvious that there are basic differences between the highly literary barkoviana and the type of materials that began to be labeled with the term "pornographic" in the nineteenth century, when the word acquired its modern connotations. Furthermore, as Manfred Schruba has rightly noted (1996 and 1999), there is a basic distinction to be made between pornographic poetry and pornographic prose; the later was apparently not produced in Russia until the next century, by which time "pornography" was far more sharply segregated from mainstream literary culture, both culturally and legally.

This article suggests that barkoviana may best be understood within the literary context of early Russian Classicism. Goulemot, writing about French pornography (primarily novels), recently noted that "it was under Classicism that erotic literature was invented, with its rules of production, its means of dissemination and the modes of consumption" (Goulemot 1994, 12). The same, I would assert, is fundamentally true of Russian pornographic poetry. To account for the phenomenon either as an *attack* on Russian Classicism (Makagonenko 1987), or primarily as an extension of indigenous folk erotica (e.g., Iliushin 1991; Hopkins 1977, 148–53) are insufficient and, it seems to me, misleading. While elements of folk erotica are undoubtedly present, I would argue that they are of secondary importance in accounting for the genesis and basic nature of barkoviana.

Goulemot's further observation — that pornographic literature had a special status in Classicism, as formally forbidden yet broadly known, tolerated, and even practiced, a "cohabitation" which ended with the eclipse of Classicism as a movement — also applies to barkoviana. The production of pornographic verse follows a pattern typical for other types of Russian Classicist poetry. Models for poetic genres generally came from two sources: one classical (usually Roman) and one modern (seventeenth and eighteenth century Classicism, primarily of the French type); in the latter case, if the models were in another language, e.g. German or English, they often entered Russia via French translations, and when there was a non-French

Chapter 9. *Barkoviana* and Russian Classicism

intermediary (as in the case of the ode, the "German School of Reason" [Pumpianskii 1937 and 1983]), it adhered to French Classicist standards (Levitt 2002). Furthermore, in many genres of Russian Classicism there was one particular *ur-text* that basically defined the genre (e.g., Boileau's "Ode de la prize de Namur" [Zhivov 1996: 249–54] or Des Barreaux's sonnet "Grand Dieu! tes jugements sont remplis d'équité" [Berdnikov 1997: 24–36 and passim]). Barkoviana, I am suggesting, follows just such a typical high Classicist pattern.

Schruba's work has enriched our appreciation for Piron's "Ode à Priape" (1710) as the basic *ur-text* for barkoviana and the prototype for barkoviana's burlesque method (1995, 1997). Piron's poem itself belongs to an ancient type of poetry, the so-called "*priapeia*," that is, obscene poetry dedicated to the god Priapus. According to Greek mythology, Priapus was the son of Venus or a nymph and Bacchus, and the god was symbolized (and often depicted "ithyphallically") as an erect phallus, or as a big phallus with a small body; this image is fairly common in modern Russian erotic art (e.g., Sergei Eisenstein [Eizenshtein]'s portrait of Maliutin, *Literaturnoe obozrenie* 11 [1991], inside cover). The most famous model of classical Roman *priapeia* is the anonymous collection of 80 poems, known variously as *Priapeia, Carmina Priapeia, Lusus in Priapum* (Joking about Priapus), or as the *Grand Priapeia*. This collection is thought to have been composed and compiled during the Augustan period—the golden age of Latin poetry, which was the primary inspiration for *all* classicist literature (the *Carmina Priapeia* also helped earn the Augustan period the reputation of the golden age of *obscene* poetry). Statues of Priapus, usually of the small god holding his huge penis in his hands as a weapon, were commonly placed in Roman gardens to serve the dual function of guardian deity and scarecrow (OCD 1970, 876), and a unifying conceit of the *Carmina Priapeia* (which may or may not be factually true), is that when poets arrived at their patron Maecenus' garden in Rome, which had its own a totem of the god, they would write poetic invocations to him on the walls; these are assumed to have been collected and published, presumably by one of the poets, not long after their composition. While the *priapeia* in this collection are anonymous, many are of good literary quality, and thought to include works by Virgil, Ovid, Horace, Domitis Marsus, Cinna, and even perhaps the Emperor Augustus himself (Alexandrian 1989, 23; for the scholarly literature, see Richlin 1983, 141–43 and O'Connor 1989, 37).

The *Carmina Priapeia* thus offered Barkov and his confreres a striking model, both as a collection of obscene, burlesque verse and as an example of leading poets getting together to indulge in a collective escapade. The foreword to most versions of *Devich'ia igruska* contains the following crucial admission:

> But in entrusting you, incomparable Belinda, with this book, I am entrusting not only myself to your good will, but many people, for I am not the only author of the works found in it, nor did I alone collect them. (Barkov 1992, 41)

The issue of the *Carmina Priapeia*'s unity as a collection has been posed by scholars primarily as a question of determining authorship of various poems, but is typologically relevant for Russian eighteenth-century poetry insofar as recent scholarship has emphasized the importance of the poetry book as a unified collection (Vroon 1995/96; Levitt 2002). Scholars have noted the presence within *A Maiden's Plaything* of poetic competitions, starting with dual translation-transpositions of the "Ode à Priape" by Elagin and Barkov (Hopkins 1977, 141–42, Barkov 1992, 389–90, Schruba 1996, 46), and have cited this as a clear indication of barkoviana's roots in Russian Classicist practice (citing Gukovskii's well-known article of 1928). Notably, the *Carmina Priapeia* itself suggests an extended poetic competition (although there is room for much scholarly debate over the question of authorship, and some have even argued for a single author — Richlin 1983, 141–43, O'Connor 1989, 37). In their recent edition of *A Maiden's Plaything* Zorin and Sapov record the names of the various Russian poets to whom particular poems in the collection have been, or may be attributed, and these include, apart from Barkov himself, Chulkov, Sumarokov, Lomonosov, I. P. Elagin, Fonvizin, F. Mamonov, I. D. Osipov, and A. V. Olsuf'ev. As in the case of *Carmina Priapeia*, we seem to have a case of a group of leading poets getting together to burlesque their own work. (The roster of authors also puts the lie to the notion of the collection as meant to destroy Classicism.) In the case of both collections, the reasons for anonymity are obvious, although part of the game here seems also to involve both guessing at the authorship of particular poems and enjoying the opportunity to burlesque a particular author's characteristic style. In general terms, a parallel can also be drawn between the *Carmina Priapeia* as a multi-authored collection work and the tendency in both eighteenth-century Western and Russian literary practice toward anonymous collective authorship (see Levitt 1999).

The *Carmina Priapeia* thus presents two important models for barkoviana, both as a model of obscene verse, and as a model of a *collection* of obscene verse. These two complex aspects deserve in-depth study, but we should note both that Barkov (acknowledged author of at least a good number of poems

Chapter 9. *Barkoviana* and Russian Classicism

in *A Maiden's Plaything*) was a specialist in Latin literature, and that among other things he translated Horace's satires (published 1762). These include an important priapic text, satire I. 8, which is related by Priapus himself. The little god (or rather, his statue) notes that he started out as a fig tree, and

> Приапа сделала художная рука.
> С тех пор я, став божком, воров и птиц пугаю;
> Имея в правой жердь руке, тех отгоняю,
> Стращаю наглых птиц лозою от плодов,
> Чтоб, роя семена, не портили садов...
> (Barkov 1992: 341)

> (An artist's hand made Pripapus. / From that time, having become a little god, I frighten thieves and birds; / With a pole in my right hand, I drive them away, / Scaring impudent birds away from the fruit with a vine, / So they don't spoil the garden by digging for seeds.)

Notably, Barkov has muted Horace's reference to a "red stake sticking out indecently from my loins" (*obscenoque ruber porrectus ab inguine palus*; note that "palus" echoes the Greek "phallos" [Horace 1993: 72–73, 170 n.]) into the euphemistic "pole" (*zherd'*). The image of Priapus holding his penis in hand is one of many borrowings from the *priapeia* to be found in barkoviana (and not in Piron's ode). Without a full study of the relationship between *A Maiden's Plaything* and classical *pripaeia* it is hard to draw conclusions about their relationship, and to understand the differences in the function of the obscene. Still, apart from specific images and borrowings, one can point to many ways in which barkoviana probably refers back to classical obscene verse — if not in a direct genetic way then at least typologically. Both are mock heroic, and are built on or contain burlesque and comic elements, and feature numerous references to the mythological gods and their sexual escapades, to characters from Homer, as well as to the religious cult of Priapus. (It remains a question as to whether, and to what extent, the religious and mock-heroic literary aspects of classical pripaeia may be separated; in barkoviana the religious references [e.g. to temples, sacrifices, sexual rites, etc.] are more obviously part of the secular literary game.)

As noted earlier, classical poetic forms were adopted in Russia via modern Classicist writers (usually in French or French translations), and from classical Latin writing (in most cases also via French intermediaries). Renaissance and Baroque intermediaries (in the present case, for example, fifteenth century Italian priapic poetic collections by Antonio Beccadelli and Pacifico Massimo), were virtually unknown in Russia (on pripaeia in the Renaissance, see Paula Findlen in Hunt 1996: 79–86). As also noted, the modern French Classicist model was reinforced or sometimes transmitted into Russia via a different modern national intermediary. In the present case Alexander Pope's *The Rape of the Lock*, which was accepted in Russia as a worthy emulation of the mock-heroic poem as established by Boileau, and which was well-known in Russia in French translation, helped serve this intermediary function (on Pope and Boileau, see Broich 1990: part 2; on the Russian mock epic and its sources, see Tomashevskii 1933 and Schruba 1997: chap. 6).

One of the first riddles which most manuscript collections of *A Maiden's Plaything* present is the unique dedicatory piece entitled "Prinoshenie Belinde." In the words of Sapov and Zorin, this preface "occupies a most important place (vazhneishee mesto) in its composition, uniting various works into one book" (Barkov 1992: 389). As noted, the dedication definitively presents the work as a collection, composed by many authors, but also having a common goal and presumably some degree of literary unity. Further, the dedication not only explains the collection's title metaphor (Belinda is the *devitsa* to whom the *igrushka* [the book] is offered), but acts as a colophon, characterizing its motivation (*motivirovka*), its authors and readers. It also suggests various literary and discursive contexts in which the works within may be read. The remainder of this article will center on the connection between "An Offering to Belinda" and Pope, and on sketching out some of these literary and discursive contexts which frame *A Maiden's Plaything*.

That Belinda is a reference to Pope's heroine is confirmed by several pieces of textual evidence, which also provide some clues as to the collection's origins and to nature of Russian obscene verse in general. The reference to Pope's heroine directly connects the genesis of *A Maiden's Plaything* to the verse polemics that raged in Russian letters in the early 1750s (Berkov 1936, Serman 1964, Moiseeva 1973). This polemic involved virtually all of the major writers (and many minor ones) in Russian poetry of the day (although much of this verse is anonymous). By this period, the early literary legislators of Russian Classicism had already staked out their basic initial positions — Sumarokov with his *Two Epistles* of 1748 and his first published tragedies; Lomonosov with his *Rhetoric*, also of 1748, his *Collection of Various Works in Verse and Prose* of 1751, as well as his many published odes; and Trediakovskii with the revised version of his 1735 *New and Short Method to Composing Russian Verse* and the *Works and Translations* of 1752. A new generation of poets (including Popovskii, Chulkov, Kheraskov, and Barkov) were just starting out. Barkoviana thus appeared at a moment when Russian literature was in the process of establishing its new institutional status and dividing up into schools, taking the theoretical descriptions of various poetic genres and working them out in practice, and also working out behavioral etiquette among writers. By the early 50's the relative harmony of the mid to late 40's had significantly soured, but in the absence of literary journals there was still no forum for debate apart from privately circulated manuscripts. This was the context for both the manuscript verse polemics of the time and for the parallel phenomenon of barkoviana, which has numerous but as yet unexplored connections to them.

One of the main starting shots in the polemic of c. 1751–53 was Ivan Elagin's "Epistle of Mr. Elagin to Mr. Sumarokov" (Epistola g. Elagina k g. Sumarokovu), alternatively known in manuscript copies as "Satire on Fop and Coquettes" (Satira na petimetra i koketok) (*Poety XVIII veka* 1972, II, 372–77). As the two titles suggest, this was both an epistle in praise of Sumarokov and his school (the poem begins "You who revealed the secrets of the amorous lyre to us" [Otkrytel' tainstva liubovnyia nam liry...], and Sumarokov is referred to as "Good teacher" [Blagii uchitel']), and also a satire; scholars agree that Elagin's poem was primarily directed against Lomonosov and his patron Ivan Shuvalov, a great Francophile and fashion plate of Empress Elizabeth's court (Berkov 1936, 114, 119–25). In his epistle-satire Elagin directly apostrophizes Pope, naming the *Rape of the Lock* and its heroine directly:

Ты, остроумный Поп, любимец Аполлонов,
Честь аглицких стихов, поборник их законов, [...]
Скажи мне ты, творец Отрезанных власов
Скажи мне, где ты брал воздушных тех богов,
Которыми свою Белинду несравненну...
(Berkov 1936: 123; *Poety XVIII veka* 1972: II, 372–77)

(Tell me, witty Pope, darling of Apollo, / Honor of English verse, defender of its laws,... / Tell me, creator of the Stolen Locks, / Tell me, where did you take those aerial gods / With whom your incomparable Belinda...)

This passage appears to be the direct source for "An Offering to Belinda," suggested by the fact that the dedication, in its first sentence and once again later, repeats Elagin's phrase "incomparable Belinda" (Belinda nesravnenna). This phrase or its equivalent does not appear either in Pope's original poem or in the French prose translation by Caylus, translated into Russian in 1748 (pub. 1761), which was most likely the version Elagin read.

Why appropriate Pope and his heroine for the purposes of defending Russian obscene verse? For one thing, Pope's poem offered an additional justification of the mock-heroic parodic procedure described in Sumarokov's epistle on versification (from which Elagin also took his reference to "witty Pope" cited above):

> В сем складе надобно, чтоб муза подала
> Высокие слова на низкие дела.
> (Sumarokov 1957: 123)

(In this type of verse, the Muse must use / High words for low deeds.)

Barkoviana represents an extended exercise in this type of burlesque (Schruba 1995, 1997). What could be more "low" than inserting Russian *mat* into the highest of (Russian Classicist) genres? That Pope could serve as an additional justification of this procedure also suggests the elitist, literary nature of barkoviana; low and carnivalesque folk material had shock value in the context of a "high" ludic literary strategy.

However, *The Rape of the Lock* itself is by no means pornographic. The poem, certainly, is sexually charged and gently titillating, full of sexual metaphor, double entendre and innuendo. Pope's ironic use of a (somewhat modified) Latin epigraph from Martial[1] (eliminated from the French and Russian translations of the poem) also suggests his work's not-so-hidden sexual import and his own orientation on classical Latin models (Wasserman 1980: 244–45). Still, *The Rape of the Lock* is self-consciously a work of "high" literature, both indebted to yet distancing itself from, for example, soft-core Restoration sex comedies, such as George Etherege's *The Man of Mode*, William Congreve's *The Old Bachelor* (1693), or John Vanbrugh *The Provok'd Wife* (1697), which served as some of the work's obvious and well-documented sources (Pope 1940: 143n). Indeed these plays all have characters named Belinda, and evidently supplied the name (and somewhat equivocal literary satirical background) for Pope's heroine. The fact that Pope's thinly veiled sex comedy insisted on (and received) general recognition as a work of high literary status, may also have played a role in the choice of his heroine as addressee for Russian erotic verse. As we have seen,

---

[1] Pope cites the first couplet of Martial's epigram XII: 84, substituting "Belinda" for "Polytime," the male addressee of the original verse. Pope's version goes: "Nolueram, *Belinda*, tuos violare capillos, / Sed juvat hoc precibus me trebuisse tuis" (I do not wish, Belinda, to violate your hair, / But it pleases me to have granted your wish).

Chapter 9. *Barkoviana* and Russian Classicism

Elagin's satire explicitly describes Pope as "Honor of English verse, defender of its laws." On the other hand, the dedication to Belinda may also suggest a commentary on Pope's attempt to dress up its plainly erotic content in the clothes of high literature. It continues:

> …ты любишь сии увеселения, но любишь для того, что в них или представляется или напоминается или случай неприметный подается к ебле. (Barkov 1992: 39)
>
> (You love these amusements [going to balls, on promenades, to the theater], but you love them because they represent, or remind you, or offer you an unobtrusive opportunity for fucking.)

Indeed "An Offering to Belinda" offers a defense (albeit tongue in cheek) of the acceptability and worthiness of sex as the subject for poetry. At the same time, we should keep in mind that definitions of the obscene (as of the pornographic) are also permeable, and that the comic has always included the risqué or obscene, starting with Aristophanes. Notably, in eighteenth-century French literary discourse the same terms — *badine, badinage* — were used both for Pope's decorous satire and for collections of obscene verse (like Piron's); the title also obviously recalls *Lusus in Priapum* (Joking about Priapus).

On the level of character, there are clear connections between the image of the *petit-maître* or coquette sitting before a mirror putting on make-up, as found in the first canto of *The Rape of the Lock* (as well as in Elagin's epistle-satire) and in "An Offering to Belinda," which begins:

> Цвет в вертограде, всеобщая приятность, несравненная Белинда, тебе, благосклонная красавица, рассудил я принесть книгу сию, называемую «Девичья игрушка», ты рядишься, белишься, румянишься, сидишь перед зеркалом с утра до вечера и чешешь себе волосы, ты охотница ездить на балы, на гулянья, на театральные представленьи затем, что любишь забавы, но естли забавы увеселяют во обществе, то игрушка может утешить наедине, так, прекрасная Белинда! (Barkov 1992, 39)
>
> (It is to you, garden flower, universal joy, incomparable Belinda, to you, gracious beauty, that I have decided to dedicate this book, entitled A Maiden's Plaything. You dress yourself up, put on powder and rouge, and sit in front of the mirror from morning til night brushing your hair, you are a great enthusiast of balls, promenades, theatrical presentations, because you love amusements. But if these things amuse you in society, this plaything can amuse you when you are alone, yes, beautiful Belinda!)

This image of Belinda is immediately recognizable as a standard depiction of the fop and coquette in English satirical literature, especially in Addison and Steele's journalistic satires, which are another major documented source for *The Rape of the Lock* (Pope 1940 passim, Kinsley 1979, chap. 6). The "fop in front of the mirror" also became a commonplace in Russian literature, from the satirical journals of Catherine the Great's day (themselves modeled on Addison and Steele) to the first canto of *Eugene Onegin*. Many passages of the dedication, starting with the coquette at the mirror noted above, suggest connections with the satirical literature that was already gaining popularity in Russia (see below).

The dedication of *A Maiden's Plaything* to Belinda also raises the question of the audience for barkoviana. The dedication of Pope's poem is a letter to Arabella Fermour, presented as the real-life prototype for Belinda (but who, the author notes, "resembles You in nothing but in Beauty"). It states that the poem "was intended only to divert a few young Ladies, who have good Sense and good Humor enough, to laugh not only at their Sex's little unguarded Follies, but at their own" (Pope 1940, 142). To what extent the implied and real readers of Pope's poem were meant to be female, and to what extent the work imposes a coercive masculinist master narrative upon women are both open to debate; there are contemporary American feminist critics who see the work in virtually pornographic terms (see Pollak [1985] 1996 and Claridge's response [1988]). It should also be noted that there is also a spectrum of opinion on the extent to which pornography itself is or must be misogynist (for a defense of pornography, for example, see Carter 1978). Similar questions apply to *A Maiden's Plaything*, and are equally if not more difficult to resolve, given the general dearth of data not only on this specific material but on Russian gender relations in the eighteenth century in general.

That said, dedicating *A Maiden's Plaything* to a woman is a brilliant rhetorical move. It functions as an apologia for pornographic verse, but couches its arguments in ambiguous satirical discourse which allows the whole enterprise to be taken as a clever spoof. Belinda serves both as sympathetic heroine, to be won over by the writer's arguments, and also as its potential satirical target. On the one hand, this is a brazen defense of the book and its authors in advance against the threat of anathema (Barkov 1992, 40), admitting openly that "nothing is written about in this book except cunts, pricks, and fuckings" (Barkov 1992, 39). The author urges:

> …оставь, красавица, глупые предрассуждения сии, чтоб не упоминать о хуе, благоприятная природа, снискивающая нам и пользу и утешение, наградила женщин пиздою, а мущин хуем: так для чего ж, ежели подьячие

Chapter 9. *Barkoviana* and Russian Classicism

говорят открыто о взятках, лихоимцы о ростах, пьяницы о попойках, забияки о драках, без чего обойтись можно, не говорить нам о вещах необходимых — «хуе» и «пизде». Лишность целомудрия ввела сию ненужную вежливость, а лицемерие подтвердило оное, что заставляет говорить околично о том, которое все знают и которое у всех есть. (Barkov 1992: 39–40)

(…Abandon, my beauty, those stupid prejudices against mentioning pricks; gracious nature, in an attempt to bring us utility and pleasure, rewarded women with cunts and men with pricks; and so, if clerks can speak openly about bribes, usurers about interest rates, drunkards about drinking sprees, and brawlers about fist-fights — things which one can certainly do without — then why should we not speak about things which are necessary — "pricks" and "cunts"? Excessive chastity initiated this unnecessary fastidiousness, and hypocrisy confirmed it, so that we have to speak in roundabout ways about things which everybody knows and everybody has.)

The references to bribe-taking clerks, usurers, drunks and fist-fighting brawlers mark another connection between barkoviana and Russian satirical literature. But the language here also appeals to (and parodies) Enlightenment values. We should shed our "stupid prejudices" and speak honestly about what we all *really want*. "An Offering to Belinda" to some extent echoes the discourse of what Margaret Jacobs has called "materialist pornography" (1996) reflected in such well-known European porn classics as *Thérèse philosophe*, which reflected the new eighteenth century rationalist, mechanist view of physical reality. Such pornography depicted atomized human bodies and the pleasure derived from their various chance collisions and couplings. These books justified their obscene content using (more or less tongue in cheek) enlightenment argumentation, whose greatest (and most serious) exponent was of course de Sade.

"An Offering to Belinda" makes several quite outlandish arguments in favor of the kind of sex education that *A Maiden's Plaything* provides. One is that a young virtuous woman can only benefit from reading the book, insofar as it will give her a notion of what to avoid ("poniatie o vsekh pakostiakh, daby izbegnut' onykh"), although the author argues in the same breath that the book will also serve as a "foretaste" (predvoobrazhenie) of delights to come. One who has already tasted the joys of sex — it continues — will cherish the book as a happy reminder! More than the discourse of "materialist pornography" per se, and more directly relevant for Russia (where materialist philosophy was yet to make significant inroads), the preface echoes and parodies the familiar discourse of enlightenment virtues — openness, honesty, reason, the ridicule of vice, etc. — as in the following passage:

Ты... рассудительна без глупого постоянства, ты тиха без суеверия, весела без грубости и наглости, а здесь сии пороки осмеяны, а потому, ни превосходя, ни восходя степеней благопристойности, ты будешь разуметь оную... (Barkov 1992: 40)

(You... sensible without stupid tenacity, you are calm and without superstition, gay without coarseness or effrontery. Here all these vices are ridiculed, and therefore, without exaggerating or minimizing the [proper] level of decorum, you will [be able to] understand it [the book]...)

This kind of argument is clearly meant to disarm the reader (in the person of Belinda), both by frankness and logic, and by flattery. At the same time, it can't mask a carnivalesque, satirical inversion — defending the rational use of obscene verse on the basis of its alleged effects on the reader, allegedly bolstering *blagopristoinost'* (decorum or decency), morality ("all vices are ridiculed"), and the lack of coarseness or vulgarity (an argument which is itself the height of effrontery!). In these passages the dedication suggests the satirical genre of the *lozhnaia panegirika*, the praise of things unpraiseworthy (see also Berdnikov's discussion of mock dedications, 1997, 162–74).

The other marked satirical theme in the dedication that may also signal indebtedness to French pornographic literature is its marked anti-clericalism. Apart from the sheer shock value of sexualized priests and nuns, depictions of the clergy in French pornography served both philosophical ends — as part of the "materialist" attack on idealist "superstition" — and also as an institutional attack on the church. In "An Offering to Belinda" clerics are targeted as the primary enemies of barkoviana, and are even offered as an additional reason for Belinda to read the book carefully:

Посмотри ты на облеченную в черное вретище весталку, заключившуюся добровольно в темницу, ходящую с каноником и четками, на сего пасмурного пивореза с седою бородою, ходящего с жезлом смирения, они имеют вид печальный, оставивши все суеты житейские, они ничего не говорят без четок и ничего невоздержного, но у одной пизда, а у другого хуй, конечно, свербится и беспокоят слишком; не верь ты им, подобное тебе имеют все, следовательно подобные и мысли, камень не положен в них на место сердца, а вода не влиянна на место крови, они готовы искусить твою юность и твое незнание. (Barkov 1992: 40)

(Just look at the vestal wrapped up tightly in black sackcloth, who has locked herself away voluntarily in a dungeon, walking about with a prayer book and rosary, [look at] that gloomy beer-guzzler [?] with his gray beard, walking about with his staff of humility — they put on a sad look, having abandoned

Chapter 9. *Barkoviana* and Russian Classicism

all of life's vanities, and only speak with the help of rosaries, and say nothing unrestrained. But the one has a cunt, and the other a prick, which of course causes them great pangs and disturbance — don't believe them, they have exactly what you do, and hence similar thoughts... [T]hey are ready to take advantage of your youth and inexperience.)

It is difficult to judge to what extent the anti-clerical theme here derives from French pornography, and to what extent it had an indigenous Russian resonance. Priests, monks, nuns and their family members had long been common characters in popular obscene literature, in Russia and elsewhere, whether for simple shock value or as implied criticism of officialdom, and *A Maiden's Plaything* also has its share of sexually ravenous clerics. However, the situation depicted here — of nuns and priests hypocritically using their feigned piety to prey upon the young and sexually innocent — was a major motif of French "materialist pornography." The fact that this situation does not occur elsewhere in barkoviana, together with the very vehemence of the language, suggest that at least this part of "An Offering to Belinda" may have been adapted or translated from a foreign (most likely French) source.[2]

The dedication ends with a further sharp attack on clerics, those "bearded goats, horned sheep, wooden posts and tame horses" who "will condemn

---

2 Alexandrian (1989, 23) writes of "an adresse liminaire" by "un poëte latin" to the *Priapea* entitled "Au lecteur," which suggests a separate poetic preface, but I have not been able to locate such a work in Latin or in French. In fact, the fundamental bibliography of pornographic literature in France (held in the Bibliotheque Nationale) lists no collections or translations of priapeia at all published before the mid-nineteenth century (Pia, 1978: II, col. 1089–96). It seems likely then that such collections, if they existed, remained in manuscript, like *A Maiden's Plaything*. There are several editions of obscene poetry by Francois de Maynard (1582?–1646) listed from the later period, including his *Les Priapeés*. The edition I was able to consult (Paris, 1909; Pia 1978: II, col. 1091) does include a short untitled preface in verse starting "Lecture, dont le grave sourcy...", but this has nothing in common with "An Offering to Belinda." Note: Since this article was published, A. A. Dobritsyn (2002) has suggested that the seventeenth-century poetic miscellany *Cabinet Satyrique* (1618 and many other editions) was a French source for some of the poems in *A Maiden's Plaything*. He also describes its anonymous preface as "extraordinarily similar" to "An Offering to Belinda," citing its "parodically-hypociritcal rhetoric" (376). However, my own examination of the preface (*Le Cabinet satyrique; première édition complète et critique d'après l'édition originale de 1618, augmentée des éditions suivantes...*, ed. Fernand Fleuret and Louis Perceau. 2 vols. [Paris: J. Fort, 1924], 1: 5–11 [second pagination]), finds no evidence of direct borrowing. From our point of view conspicuously absent are the address to a female reader and references to religious hypocrisy (or any other specific details) that we might expect to be present in the source for "An Offering to Belinda."

this [book] as well as its creators to anathema." We should not discount the possibility that the vehement language here reflects not a foreign source (or: not merely a foreign source) but that it may be in response to a genuinely perceived threat. At this period, the Synod as censor often posed greater obstacles to Russian writers than the secular authorities, at least, it not only periodically halted publication of particular works but threatened serious punishment for unacceptable writings. A well-known example are threats directed against Lomonosov for his satirical "Hymn to the Beard" (Gimn borode) of c. 1756 (Lomonosov 1953–83, VIII, 1060–69), which itself spawned a verse polemic. Notably, this poem was included in many manuscript collections of barkoviana, and may even be loosely considered part of it. The "Hymn to the Beard" is more clearly anti-clerical than most other works which comprise barkoviana, although its blasphemy substantially derives from sexual references, in particular, its comparison of beards and pubic hair (Lomonosov 1953–83, VIII, 619–626). It may also be significant that in one poem from *A Maiden's Plaything* ("Monakh," Barkov 1992, 185) these two images are further associated with "bearded goats," one of the epithets we have seen also used for priests in "An Offering to Belinda" (it is also found in Lomonosov's anti-clerical verse, e.g., Lomonosov 1953–83, VIII, 628–29). Lomonosov also makes fun of the Synod's inability to act (e.g., "O strakh! O uzhas! Grom!..." [627]), making jocular references to threats of being beaten and burned at the stake (628; 826–29; 835; cf. the poem by Barkov, "Pronessia slukh: khotiat kogo-to budto szhech'" [*Poety XVIII veka* 1972, II, 400]). As Lotman has noted, Lomonosov was very well aware of religious persecutions in Germany and elsewhere in the West, and it wasn't so long since Peter I's reign, when a number of heretics had been burnt at the stake in Russia (Lotman 1992, 36). Despite the fact that Lomonosov could be relieved that (in the words of Barkov's poem) "vremia to proshlo, chtob nashe miaso pech'" (the time has passed for baking our meat) (*Poety XVIII veka* 1972, II, 400), the very suggestion of fiery inquisition suggests a fear of persecution by the ecclesiastical authorities, whether real or imagined. If "pornography" is a concept determined by the regulatory discourse that defines it, as something to be disciplined and punished, then it might be this very fear of persecution (which only manifested itself explicitly in a later period in Russia) that qualifies barkoviana as pornographic in the modern sense. On the other hand, despite the fact that it remained in manuscript, and almost all anonymous, the very creation of *A Maiden's Plaything* testifies to a significant degree of tolerance and creative freedom, as well as to the cultural prestige of Russian Classicism.

Chapter 9. *Barkoviana* and Russian Classicism

Works Cited

Alexandrian 1989 — Alexandrian, [Sarane]. *Histoire de la littérature érotique*. Paris: Seghers, 1989.

Barkov 1992 — Barkov, Ivan. *Devich'ia igrushka ili sochineniia gospodina Barkova*, ed. A. Zorin and N. Sapov. Moscow: Ladomir.

Berdnikov 1997 — Berdnikov, L. I. *Schastlivyi feniks: Ocherki o russkom sonete i o knizhnoi kul'ture XVIII — nachala XIX veka*. St. Petersburg: Akademicheskii proekt.

Berkov 1936 — Berkov, P. N. *Lomonosov i literaturnaia polemika ego vremeni, 1750–1765*. Moscow-Leningrad: AN SSSR.

Broich 1990 — Broich, Ulrich. *The Eighteenth-Century Mock-Heroic Poem*. Trans. David Henry Wilson. New York: Cambridge University Press, 1990.

Carter 1978 — Carter, Angela. *The Sadeian Woman and the Ideology of Pornography*. New York: Pantheon.

Claridge 1988 — Claridge, Laura. "Pope's Rape of Excess." In *Perspectives on Pornography: Sexuality in Film and Literature*. Ed. Gary Day and Clive Bloom. New York: St. Martin's Press, pp. 129–43.

Dobritsyn 2002 — Dobritsyn, A. A. "'Devich'ia igrushka' i 'Cabinet Satyrique': O frantsuzskikh istokakh russkoi obtsennoi epigrammy," in *Ten' Barkova: Teksty, kommentarii, ekskursy*, ed. I. A. Pilshchikov and M. I. Shapir. Moscow: Iazyki slavianskoi kul'tury, 2002, pp. 375–88.

Goulemot 1994 — Goulemot, Jean Marie. *Forbidden Texts: Erotic Literature and its Readers in Eighteenth-century France*. Translated by James Simpson. Philadelphia: University of Pennsylvania Press.

Gukovskii 1928 — Gukovskii, G. A. "K voprosu o russkom klassitsizme: Sostiazaniia i perevody." *Poetika*, 4 (1928): 126–148.

Hammond 1996 — Hammond, Brean, ed. *Pope*. London: Longman.

Hopkins 1977 — Hopkins, William Hugh. "The Development of 'Pornographic' Literature in Eighteenth- and Early Nineteenth-Century Russia." Diss. Indiana University.

Horace 1993 — Horace. *Satires I*. Ed. and trans. P. Michael Brown. Warminster,, England: Aris & Phillips.

Hunt 1996 — Hunt, Lynn, ed. *The Invention of Pornography: Obscenity and the Origins of Modernity, 1500–1800*. New York: Zone Books.

Iliushin 1991 — Iliushin, A. A. "Iarost' pravednykh: Zametki o nepristoinoi russkoi poezii XVIII–XIX vv." *Literaturnoe obozrenie* 11 (1991): 4–14.

Jacobs 1996 — Jacobs, Margaret. "The Materialist World of Pornography." In Lynn Hunt, ed. *The Invention of Pornography: Obscenity and the Origins of Modernity, 1500–1800*. New York: Zone Books, pp. 157–202.

Kinsley 1979 — Kinsley, William. *The Rape of the Lock: Contexts 2*. Hamden, CT: Archon Books.

Levitt 1999 — Levitt, Marcus C. "Catherine the Great," in Christine Tomei, ed. *Russian Women Writers*, vol 1. New York: Garland, 1999, pp. 3–10.

Levitt 2002 — Levitt, Marcus C. "Sumarokov and the Unified Poetry Book: *Ody toržestvennyia* and *Elegii ljubovnyja* Through the Prism of Tradition." *Russian Literature* (North Holland). Special Issue: Eighteenth Century Russian Literature. LII: I/II/III (1 July — 15 August — 1 October 2002), pp. 111–139. (Also in this volume)

Lomonosov 1953-1983 — Lomonosov, M. V. *Polnoe sobranie sochinenii*. 11 volumes. Moscow: AN SSSR, 1950–1983.

Lotman 1992 — Lotman, Iu. M. "Ob 'Ode, vybrannoi iz Iova' Lomonosova." In his *Izbrannye stat'i*, vol. 2. Tallinn: Aleksandra, pp. 29–39.

Makagonenko 1987 — Makogonenko, G. P. "'Vrag parnasskikh uz' (O poezii Ivana Barkova." *Izbrannye raboty*. Leningrad: Khudozhestvennaia literatura, pp. 149–70.

Marker, Gary. *Publishing, Printing, and the Origins of Intellectual Life in Russia, 1700–1800*. Princeton: Princeton UP, 1985.

Modzalevskii 1958- Modzalevskii, L. V. "Lomonosov i ego uchenik Popovskii (O literaturnom priemstvennosti)." *XVIII vek*, 3 (1958): 111–169.

Moiseeva 1973 — Moiseeva, G. N. "K istorii literaturno-obshchestvennoi polemiki XVIII veka." In *Iskusstvo slova: Sbornik statei k 80-letiiu... D. D. Blagogo*. Moscow: Nauka, pp. 56–64.

O'Connor 1989 — O'Connor, Eugene Michael. *Symbolum salacitatis: A Study of the God Priapus as a Literary Character*. Studien zur klassischen Philologie Bd. 40. Frankfurt am Main, New York: Lang.

OCD 1970= *The Oxford Classical Dictionary*. Edited by N. G. L. Hammond and H. H. Scullard. 2d ed. Oxford: Clarendon Press.

Pekarskii 1870-73 — Pekarskii, P. P. *Istoriia Imperatorskoi akademii nauk v Peterburge*. 2 vols. St. Petersburg: Imp. Akademiia nauk.

Pia 1978 — Pia, Pascal. *Les Livres d'Enfer: Bibliographie critique des ouvrages érotiques dans leurs différents éditions du XVIe siècle à nos jours*. 2 vols. Paris: C. Coulet et A. Faure.

Piron 1928 — Piron, Alexis. *Oeuvres complètes illustrées*. Publiées... par Pierre Dufay. 10 vols. Paris: Francis Guillot.

Poety XVIII veka 1972 — *Poety XVIII veka*, ed. G. P. Makagonenko and I. Z. Serman. 2 vols. Biblioteka poeta, bol'shaia seriia. 2nd ed. Leningrad: Sovetskii pisatel'.

Pollak 1996 — Pollak, Ellen. "*The Rape of the Lock*: A Reification of the Myth of Passive Womanhood." In *Pope*, ed. Brean Hammond. London and NY: Longman, pp. 64–87; this is a slightly modified version of chapter 3 of her *The Poetics of Sexual Myth: Gender and Ideology in the Verse of Swift and Pope*. Chicago: University of Chicago Press, 1985.

Pope 1728 — Pope, Alexander. *La boucle de cheveux enlevée; poeme heroico-comique de Monsieur Pope*. Traduit de l'Anglois par Mr. xx. Paris, F. Le Breton.

Pope 1940 — Pope, Alexander. *The Poems of Alexander Pope*, vol. 2: *The Rape of the Lock, and Other Poems*. Edited by Geoffrey Tillotson. London, Methuen.

Pumpianskii 1937 — Pumpianskii, L. V. "Trediakovskii i nemetskaia shkola razuma." *Zapadnyi sbornik*, 1 (1937): 157–186.

Pumpianskii 1983 — Pumpianskii, L. V. "Lomonosov i nemetskaia shkola razuma." *XVIII vek*, 14 (1983): 3–44.

Reichard 1969 — Reichard, Hugo M. "The Love Affair in Pope's *Rape of the Lock*." In *Alexander Pope, The Rape of the Lock*, ed. David G. Lougee and Robert W. McHenry, Jr. The Merrill Literary Casebook Series. Columbus, OH: Charles E. Merrill, pp. 83–100; originally published in *PMLA* 69: 4 pt. 1 (1954): 887–902.

Richlin 1983 — Richlin, Amy. *The Garden of Priapus: Sexuality and Aggression in Roman Humor*. New Haven: Yale University Press.

Schruba 1995 — Schruba, Manfred. "Barkov i Maikov." *Novoe literaturnoe obozrenie*, 14 (1995): 139–144.

Schruba 1996 — Schruba, Manfred. "O frantsuzskikh istochnikakh barkoviany." *Study Group on Eighteenth-century Russia Newsletter*, 24 (1996): 46–61.

Schruba 1997 — Schruba, Manfred. *Studien zu den burlesken Dichtungen V. I. Majkovs*. Slavistische Veroffentlichen, Band 83. Wiesbaden: Harrasowitz Verlag.

Schruba 1999 — "K spetsifike barkoviany na fone frantsuzskoi pornografii." In *Eros i pornografiia v russkoi kul'ture / Eros and Pornography in Russian Culture*, ed. M. Levitt and A. Toporkov. Russkaia potaennaia literatura. Moscow: Ladomir, 1999, pp. 200–218.

Serman 1964 — Serman, I. Z. "Iz literaturnoi polemiki 1753 goda." *Russkaia literatura*, 1 (1964): 99–104.

Stepanov 1988 — Stepanov, V. P. "Barkov (Borkov), Ivan Semenovicha." *Slovar' russkikh pisatelei XVIII veka*, ed. N. V. Kochetkova, et al. Lenengrad: Nauka, pp. 57–62.

Sumarokov 1957 — Sumarokov, A. P. *Izbrannye sochineniia*. Biblioteka poeta, bol'shaia seriia. 2nd ed. Leningrad: Sovetskii pisatel'.

Tomashevskii 1933 — Tomashevskii, B. "Iroi-komicheskaia poema." In *Iroi-komicheskaia poema*. Biblioteka poeta. Leningrad: Izd. pisatelei v Leningrade, pp. 77–87.

Verèb 1997 — Verèb, Pascal. *Alexis Piron, poète (1689–1773) ou la difficile condition d'auteur sous Louis XV*. Studies on Voltaire and the Eighteenth Century, 349. Oxford: Voltaire Foundation.

Vroon 1995/96 — Vroon, Ronald. "Aleksandr Sumarokov's *Ody torzhestvennye* (Toward a History of the Russian Lyric Sequence in the Eighteenth Century)." *Zeitschrift für slavische Philologie*, 55: 2 (1995/96): 223–263.

Wasserman 1980 — Wasserman, Earl R. "The Limits of Allusion in *The Rape of the Lock*." In *Pope: Recent Essays*, ed. Matnard Mack and James A. Winn. Hamden CT: Archon Books, pp. 224–246; originally appeared in: *Journal of English and Germanic Philology* 65 (1966): 425–444.

Zhivov 1996 — Zhivov, V. M. *Iazyk i kul'tura v Rossiii XVIII veka*. Moscow: Iazyki russkoi kul'tury.

10

THE ILLEGAL STAGING OF SUMAROKOV'S *SINAV AND TRUVOR* IN 1770
and the Problem of Authorial Status in Eighteenth-Century Russia

Authors and authorship had little formal legal status in eighteenth-century Russia. Over the course of the century the basic elements and institutions of literary life — from writer and audience, to the text, means of dissemination, and their very linguistic medium — underwent dramatic changes (Levitt, Introduction, ix-xviii). If William Todd, in his ground-breaking study of literary institutions in the age of Pushkin, could refer to a "vexing multiplicity" of institutional choices facing the writer (46), for Alexander Sumarokov (1717–1777) the situation was sooner the reverse: he struggled to define the emerging role of the writer in what often seemed a vacuum. The fact that scholars have awarded such titles as "first modern Russian poet" and "first professional Russian writer" to such disparate figures as Simeon Polotskii (Hippisley 1–2); Antiokh Kantemir (Gukovskii 51); the trio of Lomonosov, Trediakovskii and Sumarokov (Pypin 433); the cohort of Matvei Komarov, Fedor Emin and Andrei Bolotov (Grits, Trenin, Nikitin, ch. 3), as well as to Pushkin (Gessen; Meynieux 85-6); testifies not only to the various shades of meaning implied by these terms but also to the changing nature of Russian letters between the late seventeenth and early nineteenth centuries.

Sumarokov's claim to these titles is based on the fact that for much of his adult life he was occupied exclusively with literature, and on his strong belief that he was laying the groundwork for what he called his "professiia" (Pis'ma 131). Among his other firsts was the publication of original Russian *belles-lettres* as individual books (excluding individually published odes). In addition, he published, edited, and largely wrote Russia's first private literary monthly, *Trudoliubivaia pchela;* he was the first director and principal playwright of the national theater, founded by Empress Elizabeth in 1756 in St. Petersburg; and he introduced many of what were to be staple genres of modern Russian literature (Levitt, "Sumarokov," 370–381). As a writer on

Chapter 10. The Illegal Staging of Sumarokov's *Sinav and Truvor* in 1770

the cutting edge of literary development, Sumarokov was acutely aware of the difficulties in establishing his new profession and defining the status — legal, financial, political, cultural — of the author. In early 1770 Moscow's commander-in-chief, P. S. Saltykov, ordered the staging of Sumarokov's tragedy *Sinav and Truvor* against the author's will and despite the theater's contractual obligation not to stage his plays without his expressed assent. This incident, alleged by some to be a turning point in Sumarokov's career, dramatically laid bare the limitations, legal and other, of the author's position.

The incident came at a moment when Sumarokov appeared to be at the height of his powers and repute. Up to this point at least, Sumarokov seemed to enjoy a position of favor under Catherine II, although their relationship as patron and client was never comfortable and is open to various interpretations (e.g., Gukovskii, Ocherki; Gleason). A supporter of the empress several years before the coup that brought her to the throne, upon her ascension in 1762 he had been rewarded with, among other things, the unique lifelong privilege of having his works published at her expense. This meant that at times Catherine took the role of Sumarokov's personal censor, which led to minor clashes. Despite such incidents, Sumarokov continued to enjoy her ostensible support, and in 1769 he was apparently granted a modest "derevushka" near Moscow where he could write in peace. He also made ample use of having the empress' ear, often (as she put it) "bombarding" her with letters. He excused his "impertinence" by arguing that he spoke not merely as an individual petitioner but in the name of Russian literature. When pleading the case for establishing a Russian theater in Moscow in the late 1760s, he explained that he had taken upon himself the role of "advocate (advokat) for Melpomene and Thalia," a role for which he claimed himself uniquely worthy (Pis'ma 123).

Still, Sumarokov's position was far from secure. After leaving the Russian theater in 1761, he had been allowed to keep his annual stipend, on top of his military salary, for which he had earlier been excused from duties. However, both sums gave him a relatively small income, and Sumarokov continued to be strapped for money and often in debt. He acutely felt the anomaly of the writer's position in rank-conscious Russia and was frustrated by the privations that the profession forced upon him and his family. On May 3, 1764, for example, he wrote to Catherine asking her to fund a trip to Italy and France so that he could produce travel notes that he felt would be of use to the country. At the same time he begged the empress, whether or not she accepted his proposal (and she did not), to let him know "what I am: in the service, and if so, in which?" (Pis'ma 97). He complained that he was without clear institutional affiliation or responsibilities, and hence without the possibility for normal career advancement and salary increases: "Moreover I have no place or position at all. I am neither with the military, nor the civil service, nor with the court, nor with the Academy, nor in retirement. I make so bold as to make this request of Your Imperial Majesty, so that something will be determined for me, so that I will know what I am" (Pis'ma 96).

The episode with Saltykov in 1770 reveals in a dramatic way just how precarious his position was. It offers a compelling starting point for discussing the problem of what Foucault calls the "author function" in eighteenth-century Russia, a complex and little studied subject (see: Jones, "The Image"; Serman; Stepanov; Zhivov, "Pervye"). In this article I will describe what is known about the incident, try to clarify Sumarokov's murky legal position, and analyze two cultural models (patronage and personal honor) that, given the limited possibility of legal redress, Sumarokov invoked to define and defend "who he was."

AN ACCOUNT OF THE DEBACLE

In March 1769, the writer had moved to Moscow, where he became involved in protracted negotiations to set up a permanent theater there. With the support of Moscow's commander-in-chief, Count P. S. Saltykov, and the city's police office (which at that time had jurisdiction over theatrical matters and censorship), he had helped the Italians Giovanni Belmonti and Giuseppe Cinti (variously spelled Chinti, Tchougi, Chuzhi; see Mooser 89–90, 135, 144) assume the privilege to stage plays in Russian (a privilege previously held by N. S. Titov, whose company, founded in 1766 with actors from Moscow University, had gone bankrupt). "The Muses, the local governor-general (*namestnik*), chief of police (*politseimeistr*), entrepreneurs and actors are all in complete agreement with me," he wrote to the empress on July 24, 1769 (Pis'ma 125). Sumarokov himself signed a personal contract with Belmonti giving Belmonti the right to stage his plays, but only with his permission and under his supervision.

The reasons for Sumarokov's debacle are not clear; some scholars assert that there was a large-scale conspiracy to publicly embarrass the writer. On about January 24, 1770, a few days before the advertised opening of his popular tragedy *Sinav and Truvor*, together with his new comedy *Tri brata sovmestniki*, the playwright contacted the head of the police department (*ober-politseimeistr*), Count V. I. Tolstoi, to let him know that the play had to be postponed because the leading actress, Elizaveta Ivanova, was getting

Chapter 10. The Illegal Staging of Sumarokov's *Sinav and Truvor* in 1770

drunk and not coming to rehearsals; he asked Tolstoi's help in ensuring that she appear. Earlier, on January 18, Saltykov and his son themselves had come to Sumarokov to ask him to have the theater directors "restrain" the actress, with whom Saltykov had formed a special attachment, apparently as a drinking companion. Then, while Sumarokov was away at his estate, she had run away, and been subsequently sent back, but ran off again, with Count M. F. Apraksin, who (according to Sumarokov) "made a drunkard of her (*s kruga spoil*), so that every day she would quarrel with her comrades" (presumably the other actors; Pis'ma 126).

Sumarokov's request to police chief Tolstoi for help offended the seventy-year-old war hero Saltykov. This is Sumarokov's version of what then transpired:

> Count Tolstoi, a good and conscientious person, wanted to send her [to the theater], but could not, because Count Saltykov had told him that *he* would assign the actors their roles, and that *he* would order what they would play and how they would perform. Count Tolstoi told me to speak with Count Saltykov myself. I went to his house, but he was not in. I went to his son's house to make him a *contre-visite* (since he had been to visit me). His father also arrived. He came in and started shouting at me with exceedingly great anger and with even greater disdain. "Why are you sticking your nose into putting on plays?" "So that they be performed well," I answered, my heart in my shoes. "Why are you sending orders to the police?" — "I am in no position to send orders anywhere, except perhaps to the villages I own, and the chief of police is witness to my innocence." "You have no business with performances and actors, so don't you tell them what and how to act. *I* will give the orders. So there!"

The next day, Sumarokov continued, Saltykov came up to him at the theater during a performance and demanded to know why they were putting on a comedy and not *Sinav and Truvor* as advertised:

> "Was it you who forbade it?" "No," I answered, "I haven't seen the actors, but they don't know their parts, that's why the play was postponed." "To spite you (*nazlo tebe*)," he responded, "1 order that 'Sinav' be played tomorrow," and he ordered that this be announced... (Pis'ma 127)

Sumarokov immediately left the theater, and Saltykov, apparently under the influence of Prince Aleksei Golitsyn, a long-time foe of the playwright's, led Ivanova out off the stage and into the theater during the performance, to the audience's glee. Sumarokov's further protests to Tolstoi, Saltykov,

Belmonti, and other officials had no effect. Sumarokov took to his bed, and on January 31, 1770, the presentation of *Sinav and Truvor* took place.

In an apologetic note to Sumarokov from Ivanova written before the performance, she wrote that "in my illness they are almost forcing me to perform" (*v bolezni moei pachti* [sic] *nasil'no menia prinevolivaiut igrat'* [Pis'ma 130]) and that she would perform only to protect him from further unpleasantness, including the suspicion that he had put her up to feigning illness. She added that Il'mena (the character she was playing) "will be emotionless to the same degree as the play is being presented against the author's will" (*stol'zhe bezchuvstvitel'na budet, skol' i bez zhelaniia sochineleva predstavliaetsia* [130]). Whether or not the play was intentionally travestied is unclear. Theatrical cliques set on demolishing a rival playwright's plays by rowdy behavior (something fairly common in London and Paris) were not unheard of in the Russian theater. In the foreword to his *Prodigal Reformed by Love* (*Mot liubov'iu ispravlennyi*), for example, V. I. Lukin described efforts at sabotaging the comedy's premiere on January 19, 1765, and in another comedy, *Constancy Rewarded* (*Nagrazhdennoe postoianstvo*), a character describes the "science" (*nauka*) of disrupting plays via organized cliques (Lukin 14, 146–47, qtd. in Maikov 317–20). In Sumarokov's letters of 1770, however, he only complained about "untrained actors, not only ignorant of declamation, but not even knowing their roles by heart" and about the main male lead being played by "someone who has never even been in a theater [before]." He continued, "All of Moscow gathered, not to see *Sinav*, but a mockery of its author — that is, everyone gathered but me, for I was home in bed, sick with despair." At the same time, he alluded to the sympathy of "all of [my] clerical and high placed secular friends" (Pis'ma 139, 131). The performance must have been, he concluded, "so miserable as to defy description" (*tak skaredno, chto opisat' ne mozhno* [131]). To his letter to Catherine Sumarokov was appended an elegy which began:

> Все меры превзошла теперь моя досада;
> Ступайте фурии, ступайте вон из ада,
> Грызите жадно грудь, сосите кровь мою!
> В сей час, в который я терзаюсь вопию,
> В сей час среди Москвы Синава представляют,
> И вот так Автора достойно прославляют:
> Играйте, говорят, во мзду его уму,
> Играйте пакостно за труд на зло ему.
> Збираются ругать меня враги и други;
> Сие ли за мои, Россия, мне услуги!... (PSVS, 9, 93)

Chapter 10. The Illegal Staging of Sumarokov's *Sinav and Truvor* in 1770

(My vexation has now overleaped all bounds; / Come, furies, come up from hell, / Greedily bite my breast, suck my blood! / At this moment, in which I wail in torment, / At this moment "Sinav" is being performed in Moscow. / So that's how they fittingly honor an author: / "Perform it," they say, as a reward for his cleverness. / "Perform it wretchedly to spite his labor." / Both friends and foes gather to mock me; / Is this what I get, Russia, for my services!)

Whatever actually took place in the theater, Sumarokov's disgrace did not end there. On February 15, Catherine responded to Sumarokov's two voluminous complaints of January 28 and February 1, but did not give him satisfaction. She wrote:

> The Fieldmarshal [Saltykov] wanted to see your tragedy — that does you honor. It would be fitting to satisfy the request of the first man in Moscow. If Count Saltykov thought it fitting to order the play performed, it was thus appropriate to carry out his will without objections. You more than others, I should think, know how much honor is due such men, who have earned glory, and whose heads are covered with grey, and hence I advise you not to enter into such disagreements, and in this way you will preserve your equilibrium for writing, and it will always be more pleasant for me to see the presentation of passions in your dramas rather than to read them in your letters. (Pis'ma 211)

On the explanatory note from her secretary G. V. Kozitskii, through whom Sumarokov had sent his letters, Catherine wrote (punning on the phrase *soiti s uma*, to go mad): "Sumarokov is and will be crazy" (*Sumarokov bez uma est' i budet*). It is clear from his next two letters to the empress that Sumarokov, even while expressing his gratitude, felt ever more defensive, needful of protecting himself both against Saltykov, whom he had allegedly insulted, and against Catherine's own evident displeasure. Even worse, within a day after receiving her letter he discovered that it had been circulated all over Moscow, in what he said were more than 1000 copies made from the one the empress had sent Saltykov. (Within the year, the letter made it to Paris in a French version, from which later published source [Grimm 9, 186–88] the letter made it back into nineteenth-century Russian literary histories.) Sumarokov complained that the empress' letter was being interpreted as an "angry reprimand" (Pis'ma 139) and that he had become a "universally reprimanded person" (136). Sumarokov wrote an epigram titled "Kukushki" (Cukoo Birds) (PSVS, 7, 331) on his detractors, attacking those who "interpret Diana's favor as anger" (*gnevom milosti Diianiny tolkuiut*), but this in turn provoked new mockery against him, including an epigram by the as yet unknown Derzhavin. Catherine declined to answer Sumarokov's further letters, letting him know coyly via Kozitskii that this was "so that copies of the letters won't cause him new vexation" (Pis'ma 212).

Various hypotheses have been put forward about who was ultimately responsible for Sumarokov's embarrassment. Some have alleged a conspiracy, instigated variously by Belmonti, Apraksin's circle, or some of Sumarokov's many literary (and other) ill-wishers. Sumarokov's nineteenth-century biographers (Glinka; Bulich; Longinov, "Poslednie gody") saw the incident as a purposeful plot to destroy his name, and believed that it led directly to Sumarokov's alcoholism, penury, and death in 1777. Some have tried, unconvincingly, to connect the incident to Sumarokov's campaign against "tearful dramas," and specifically against the staging of Beaumarchais's *Eugénie* in Russian at Belmonti's theater (Longinov, "Poslednie," col. 1671). Gukovskii accounted for the incident as part of Catherine's campaign against the Panin faction, with whom Sumarokov was probably in sympathy (*Russkaia* 186; for a critique of Gukovskii's "Fronde" theory, see Ransel, *Politics*, esp. 1–8), but again, there is no hard evidence to support this view. To these possibilities more may be suggested. The incident came at the height of the short-lived satirical journals (1769–1774), and even though Sumarokov was not much involved with them, Catherine's patience with unruly Russian men of letters may have been wearing thin. She had recently acquired her own "pocket versifier" and court poet Vasilii Petrov, arch-enemy of Sumarokov and Novikov (Shliapkin); the literary landscape in Russia was changing, and she no longer needed to rely on the unmanageable and ill-tempered Sumarokov to sing her praises. Be that as it may, Sumarokov did continue for several years to write, publish, pen letters to Catherine, and negotiate the fate of the Russian theater with her. Sumarokov's letters do not suggest that he suspected any kind of conspiracy, but indicate, rather, that it was a conflict between himself and Saltykov, with Ivanova caught in between. As he wrote to Catherine, "the affair was not caused by my disobedience to the count — although my muse does not depend on his orders — but on account of the actress, because she did not want to come to the theater for rehearsal and because I made that known to the chief of police with all proper decency" (Pis'ma 138).

From the perspective of Sumarokov's authorial rights, however, such speculations about who else might have been involved in the incident and what their motives were — questions which will probably never be answered — are not relevant. An assault had been made on his position as author, and he struggled to define and defend his "rights." My focus in the subsequent discussion is to try and understand Sumarokov's legal position as

Chapter 10. The Illegal Staging of Sumarokov's *Sinav and Truvor* in 1770

author and how he understood his own legal status (what Nancy Kollman has termed a "legal imaginary"), and to analyze some of the terms and rhetorical strategies with which he tried to present his case.

LEGAL PRIVILEGE AND AUTHORIAL RIGHTS

Sumarokov defended his position on the basis of his contract with Belmonti and Cinti, who in a public announcement of December 22, 1769, had "pledged in writing not to present [Sumarokov's] works without his permission." The nature of Sumarokov's contract, its substance as well as its legal status, presents us with a tangle of problems. First of all, there is the issue of what was being contracted: an author's control over literary property. With the exception of England, in eighteenth-century Europe authors did not have basic control over the production or reproduction of their writings. Russia's first copyright law only went into effect in 1828, stimulated in part by Pushkin's clash with the bookdealer August Oldekop (Avgust Ol'dekop), who in 1824 had sold a pirated version of "Kavkazskii plennik" (Pereselenkov, Oksman, Gessen 41-49). Before copyright, "property in literature was not in the writing but in the right to make copies, and the right to make copies belonged to the owner of the press" (Wittenberg 13; see also Patterson, Rose, Woodmansee, Woodmansee and Jaszi, and Sherman and Strowel). A press's right over textual reproduction was based on "privileges" (from the Latin *privilegio*, "private law") which were delegated by the crown as a matter of royal prerogative and patronage; privileges were essentially licenses that were defined by the state and delegated to specific persons or institutions, including typographies, theaters, and factories (Armstrong 1-20).[1] The

---

[1] There is a distinction which may need to be made between specifically noble privileges and the commercial sort I am describing here. On the former see Bush. On the complexities of old regime French political privilege, including trade and corporate privilege, see Bossenga. Notably, Sumarokov was able to obtain the honorific noble privilege of wearing swords (*shpagi*) for the actors of his Russian theater in St. Petersburg despite their non-noble origins. This privilege was also accorded the "most worthy" of the actors from Moscow University who were contracted to the entrepreneur Lokateli in the early 1760's. According to Gorbunov (99), this sign of nobility was given to the actors in order to discourage them from taking part in fist fights with gymnasium and seminary students. Catherine rewarded Petrov, a clergyman's son, with a gold snuffbox with 200 gold coins and the right to carry a sword for his "Oda na velikolepnyi karusel'" (1766), his first marks of recognition from the empress (Shliapkin 383).

crown, Pope, or other local authority granted publishing privileges over specific titles, categories of books, and presses. In Russia, such privileges were first given to the Academy of Sciences and Holy Synod typographies in 1727, and between 1752 and 1774 to eight new institutional presses; in the decade before the "free press" law of 1783 that gave individuals the right to own and operate presses without grants of privileges, select private persons also received official permission to publish, as well as the right to lease institutional presses (e.g., Novikov's famous ten-year lease of the Moscow University typography from 1779–89; Marker 44–45, 76f, 103–5). Legally conferred book publishing privileges did not seem to have become a source of contention in Russia, although there were occasional turf conflicts between the Academy and Synod presses over the rights to print particular works (Marker ch. 2).² Under the system of privileges, power derived from the throne, and not from any notion of a legally empowered or philosophically autonomous self. In his recent study of eighteenth-century English debates over copyright, Mark Rose calls attention to the widespread metaphor (and legal tradition) equating the author's right to control texts to an individual's landowning rights, the defense of which is commonly traced to John Locke's *Two Treatises on Government* of 1690 (Rose 5). In Russia, however, where there were no private property rights, there were neither a clear notion of literary property nor a clear legal framework within which such rights could be exercised or enforced.

It is significant in the present context that it was during the reigns of Peter III and Catherine that the legal basis for private property was

---

² The Holy Synod was given its privilege to control religious publishing simultaneously with the Academy of Sciences in 1727; on the tensions between secular and religious publishing, see Marker, ch. 2. Contention was primarily over content (censorship) rather than property rights.

The single incident of copy-privilege infringement that I have come across occurred in 1784 when the Imperial National Schools Commission appealed to uphold their right to publish a series of textbooks, for which they had signed a six-year contract with the publisher Bernard Breitkopf. They complained against Novikov, who had issued reprints of the textbooks at the request of Moscow's commander in chief Z. G. Chernyshev (to whom the Commission's appeal was addressed). The Commission cited Breitkopf's exclusive right based on his publisher's privilege, and asked that Novikov's remaining copies of the books be confiscated and that he turn over the money collected for copies already sold (Longinov, *Novikov*, 24–29). W. Gareth Jones asserts that the Commission's request was fulfilled, and that the incident reflected the start of an official campaign against Novikov, but the published documents do not indicate that any action was actually taken (Jones, *Nikolay*, 183–284; "Dlia biografii" 521–24).

Chapter 10. The Illegal Staging of Sumarokov's *Sinav and Truvor* in 1770

established in Russia. Peter III's Manifesto on the Freedom of the Nobility of 1762, which explicitly separated landholding from state service, which was now made voluntary, was a significant step towards establishing private property (on the manifesto: Romanovich-Slavatskii, Dukes, Jones; on the status of property in eighteenth-century Russia: Weickhart, Pipes, Farrow). Article 11 of Catherine's 1785 Charter to the Nobility proclaimed that "A noble's property is not to be taken away or destroyed without due process of law" (Dukes, *Russian*, 66); noble Russians were now freed from the threat of having their estates confiscated by administrative fiat (as had been the fate of innumerable fallen "favorites" as well as many others earlier in the century [Andreevskii, Meehan-Waters]). Even the lands of those nobles convicted of serious crimes would not revert to the state but were now to be transferred to their legal heirs. Hence whereas the playwright Iakov Kniazhnin had been stripped of his noble title and rank and lost his estates when convicted of gambling away state funds in 1773, neither Radishchev or Novikov, nor later the Decembrists, lost their estates when charged with far more serious crimes. It is problematic, however, to consider the expansion of property rights in Russia in the context of liberal or Enlightenment theory. There were those (like M. I. Vorontsov, an author of Peter's manifesto, and under Catherine, N. I. Panin) who were conscious ideologists of noble rights, but the "emancipation of the Russian nobility" in the eighteenth century was rather a case of noble prerogatives granted by the crown often at the expense of other estates rather than an ideal of possessive individualism (see the discussion of rights and privileges in Griffiths 1991). Sumarokov was the first writer in Russia to confront the problem of control over intellectual property, although his main concern was over his reputation and not with copy rights as such. While Sumarokov knew Panin and shared some of his views on the nobility, distinctions between noble prerogatives and literary rights, of both a legal and financial nature — so clear, for example, in the later case of Pushkin — do not seem clearly conceptualized in his thinking. In the November edition of his 1759 journal *Industrious Bee* (*Trudoliubivaia pchela*; hereafter: TP), Sumarokov published some of his songs, which he said had not only been pirated but published anonymously in defective versions and with strange titles (by G. N. Teplov in his *After Work, Idleness, or a Collection of Various Songs* [*Mezhdu delom bezdel'e iii sobranie raznykh pesen*] of earlier that year; Livanova 66–7). He did so, he said, not only to establish the true texts but also in the hope that "this audacity of publishing someone else's works without the authors' permission will not multiply, not to speak of spoiling that which others have composed with care and imposing indecent titles on others' works, something which is nowhere practiced, and nowhere permitted" (TP, May, 1759, 678). The issue here certainly was not control over financial property, insofar as Sumarokov himself published very few of his songs, which circulated in manuscript and by memorization; he did so now only to counter the defects of the pirated edition. Furthermore, the literary marketplace (especially for highbrow literature, which was often produced at a loss) had not reached a level of profitability to make property rights a major issue. Sumarokov's assertion that the pirating of literary works was nowhere practiced or permitted was wishful thinking, and indeed M. D. Chulkov repeated Teplov's offense ten years later in his four-volume *Collection of Various Songs* (*Sobranie raznykh pesen*; Semennikov 134). As A. V. Kokorev discovered, a series of Sumarokov's texts (mostly epigrams and fables) were also pirated for use in *lubki*, the one area of Russia publishing which was starting to become commercially successful. In the foreword to *Dimitrii the Impostor* (*Dimitrii Samozvanets*) Sumarokov again attacked such abuses, connecting them to the staging of his plays without his permission. He decried those who dared "to spoil, print, and sell my songs against my will, or to spoil the dramas of an author who is still living, and to collect money for that disfigurement" (PSVS, 6, 63). The emphasis, again, is on the personal affront from the defacing of his works; making money from them is a final insult, not the primary violation or concern.

Authorial rights over control of theatrical productions (as opposed to publishing rights) was an even thornier issue, and across Europe dramatic works did not come under copyright protection until a much later date. In France before the revolution playwrights most often had little remuneration and virtually no control over production after the original decision to have their plays produced. Even in England, with its long tradition of copyright law, performance rights were not established until 1833 with the Dramatic Copyright Act (Barber 149–54; see also Boncompain, Bonnaisses 1874 and 1970). In the era before copyright, a playwright could protect his work in two ways: he could obtain a personal privilege over it or negotiate an agreement with theatrical management before the initial production. I know of no case in Russia where a playwright obtained his own personal privilege, and negotiated agreements (of the kind Beaumarchais was famous for demanding) were extremely rare. Not long after the episode with *Sinav and Truvor*, Sumarokov sold Belmonti the rights to produce *Dimitrii the Impostor*, which was to be his most popular and long-lasting play, for the sizable sum of 1600 rubles (Pis'ma 176; the contract stipulated that it would only be produced with the author's permission, on pain of returning all monies collected at the door to the author [219, п. 2]). As far as I know this was the only time Sumarokov was ever directly paid for a play. (It also undercuts the assertion that the episode with Saltykov directly resulted in the author's moral and financial ruin.)

Like a text in the control of a printer, once a play was out of the author's hands and on stage, it was essentially in the public domain. "For they reason like this," Sumarokov complained in a letter to Catherine in 1773, "if, they say, a play has been performed at court and published, then one can perform it [without any constraint]" (Pis'ma 162). As Bulwer-Lytton put it in a famous speech to the House of Parliament defending the Dramatic Copyright Act sixty years later: "The instant an author publishes a play, any manager may seize it, mangle it, act it, without consent of the author, and without giving him one sixpence of remuneration" (Scarles 229). Thus when Prince P. V. Urusov and Melchior Groti acquired Belmonti's privilege after he died in the plague of 1772 (at which time Saltykov was fired from his job as governor-general for mishandling the disaster) *Dimitrii the Impostor* was produced without Sumarokov's permission. Groti "began to treat the dramatic works of the Russian Racine as his own property; not only did he not invite him to rehearsals but did not [even] obtain his permission to present the plays on stage" (Gorbunov 105). Sumarokov complained that his plays were being produced badly and "without contracts," and argued that it would be preferable if the profits from the Russian theater in Moscow went to the state rather than unscrupulous entrepreneurs (Pis'ma 175–76; 154). Sumarokov complained in 1775 that after all he had done for the Russian theater in Moscow, Urusov, adding insult to injury, had deprived the elderly author of the box in the theater that Belmonti had put at the disposal of his family.[3] "And so he will collect money for my tragedy, while I will have to pay six rubles for the performance of my own tragedy, even though I don't even have a kopeck at home" (Pis'ma 176).

Sumarokov was also well acquainted with the problem of attaining privileges to run a theater, as well as the conflict of interest between imperial theaters, which enjoyed a special status and security, and private ones (cf. the analogous struggles against the monopoly of the Comédie Française or with the King's Men of Drury Lane, both of which had long and complex

---

[3] This was not only accepted practice, but at the Comédie Française this had been a legal requirement since 1719 — with the proviso that authors behave themselves (Boncompain 98).

histories). Sumarokov himself had been on both sides of the fence. In the late 1750s he had arranged that the Russian language theater established by Elizabeth in St. Petersburg with himself as director become a court (*pridvornyi*) theater as a way of ensuring its survival, and as we have seen, he acted as intermediary with Catherine in attempts to establish a private Russian theater in Moscow. In 1769, when Sumarokov argued Belmonti's worthiness to be accorded the Moscow privilege to stage Russian plays and his Petersburg rival I. P. Elagin (then head of the official theater) argued that Moscow theaters should not be given privileges on the grounds that that would put them on a level with factories, Sumarokov countered (on a Maiakovskian note): "The theater *is* a factory, and of the most useful kind" (Pis'ma 122).

Just as the center delegated its authority to select institutions through privileges, the bearers of imperial privileges could contract them out, thus passing privileges down the line. Hence theatrical entrepreneurs could make agreements with actors and other necessary theatrical personnel. Presumably the same legal principle that made a privilege valid and gave a theater the power to contract actors, artists and stagehands, might also extend to contracting with authors to produce their plays. If in the cases of Sumarokov's pirated songs, fables, and epigrams Sumarokov had no legal basis for complaint, insofar as these were works which had not been published earlier, and hence did not fall under a typographer's privilege, in the case of *Sinav and Truvor*, Sumarokov had an explicit agreement with Belmonti.

Sumarokov was acutely aware that the violation of this agreement meant both an affront to his reputation and potential financial inequity, although according to the original agreement Sumarokov was to expect no remuneration. He charged Belmonti with illegally violating their contract, arguing that Saltykov had no legal right to make Belmonti stage the play against its author's will. He insisted that that "even if I had argued with His Excellency [in insisting] that the unrehearsed play be learned before it is performed, I would still not have been at fault, since I have the right [to do so] as author, and on top of that have a contract" (Pis'ma 136). He further asserted a claim to the ill-gotten proceeds from the performance:

> The money collected for "Sinav" should go to me, because my contract with Belmonti was violated against my will. For the person who sells my horse without my knowledge should not receive the money for it, I should; and the law, both civil and natural, maintain that. And the fact that P. S. Saltykov ordered the contract violated is no excuse either; even if Belmonti was not at fault, he should not hold onto the money, because it belongs to me. (Pis'ma 132)

Chapter 10. The Illegal Staging of Sumarokov's *Sinav and Truvor* in 1770

Sumarokov was making one of the basic financial arguments in favor of copyright protection, whether for publishing or production. In 1773 Samuel Johnson made the same point in a discussion with Boswell, also equating the control over a text to the ownership of an animal. When Boswell cited Lord Monboddo's claim that memorization of someone else's work gives one the right to print it, Johnson responded: "No, sir, a man's repeating it no more makes it his property, than a man may sell a cow which he drives home" (Boswell 286). Nonetheless, Sumarokov's basic concern remains with his reputation and status, not for the money as the rightful fruit of his labor, but as a penalty for Belmonti and a mark of his vindication as author.

A legal question arises here however: may a contract be considered valid if the rights being contractually guaranteed are not legally recognized? A contract alone is most likely insufficient to confer rights. Be that as it may, the validity of Sumarokov's contract never came into question. The issue was, rather, whether and by whom it could be enforced. This problem was directly addressed in Sumarokov's account of the argument he and Moscow's senior policemaster (*ober-politseimeistr*) V. I. Tolstoi had with Saltykov over the breach of contract:

> Count Tolstoi declared that it was not permissible to break the contract which was given and published by the police. Belmonti had no intention of breaking the contract, for he had given his honest word not to present my plays without my permission. And indeed it's more profitable for him when they are presented well under my direction. I have stated this to many senators and will write to the main office of the police (*glavnuiu politsiiu*) by the first mail; and the senior policemaster also wanted to write out of a sense of responsibility (*radi svoei ochistki*)... The entrepreneurs bound themselves in writing not to put on my plays without my permission, and this commitment was registered (*iavleno*) in the Moscow police [department]; but he [Saltykov] did not pay any attention either to my request, nor to the entrepreneurs' objections (*otgovorki*), nor to the actors' inconvenience, nor to the sanctity of my contract, but cried out publicly to the senior policemaster: "I'll rip your contracts to shreds!" And when the senior policemaster declared — I, that I would send a complaint to Your Highness, and he that he would write to police headquarters (*v glavnuiu politsiiu*), because the sanctity of contracts and the due process of law (*ustanovienie zakonov*) were being violated — he replied: "Write wherever you want" (*Pishite, kuda khotite*), quite an offensive response. (Pis'ma 128 and 131)

The issue came down not to legal arguments but simply to one of authority — a conflict between an "all-powerful" governor-general, whose office gave him "full command of the police" and in whose hands "the totality of judicial power was vested" (LeDonne 43–44), and his second in command, the senior policemaster, the highest representative of the police in Moscow. Still, Tolstoi was not only below the governor in military rank but also administratively and politically subordinate to him. The senior policemaster was answerable to "both his superior in Petersburg [the *"glavnaia politsiia"* or office of the Policemaster General, referred to here] and to the governor general" himself (LeDonne 90). The police office, which had jurisdiction over both contracts and theaters, was the logical authority to which Sumarokov could appeal, apart from the senate in Petersburg (which functioned as court of last appeal, and to which Sumarokov here alludes ["1 have stated this to many senators…"]), that is, apart from an appeal to the empress herself.

From Sumarokov's point of view, the issue, then, was a clash between legality and raw political power. He argued that "he [Saltykov] has authority (*polnomochie*); however, his authority is under the law and not above it, and he is giving orders not based on the laws but in violation of them, and hence I am not obliged to respect them, [for] the law does not permit contracts to be ripped up and violated" (Pis'ma 132). Despite this and other eloquent appeals to law and due process, in the end Sumarokov was forced to make personal entreaty to the Empress herself to fulfill the promise of legality. He requests a personal ruling from her on his behalf, not only to right the wrong in the case of *Sinav and Truvor* but also to guarantee the inviolability of his forthcoming tragedy *Dimitri Samozvanets*. He asserts that he would rather consign the four completed acts of the play to the fire than to face such interference again, and asks Catherine for a "personal order, so that it will not be performed in any fashion against my will; for when contracts are not enforceable (*nedeistvitel'ny*), then on what can one depend except personal decrees…?" (Pis'ma 140).

The problem clearly rested in the personalized nature of legal power and the amalgam of executive and judiciary functions in absolutist Russia. Sumarokov's dilemma is characteristic of a period in which the lines between "rights" as privileges contingent on the throne and "rights" as inalienable ethical and political prerogatives were not clearly drawn or conceptualized; to most, Catherine's enlightened rule made (or should have made) the issue moot. As Richard Wortman has shown in *The Development of a Russian Legal Consciousness*, the ideal of law never achieved institutional embodiment in Russia, where absolutist tendencies undermined the development of a legal consciousness. Notions of justice ultimately (and traditionally) devolved upon the person of the monarch, as in the present case. The monarch was not merely (or primarily) the

Chapter 10. The Illegal Staging of Sumarokov's *Sinav and Truvor* in 1770

embodiment and upholder of law and justice (*pravosudie*), a view which Catherine herself promoted and to which Sumarokov appealed, but a divine mother and protector.

Indeed when legal arguments fail, Sumarokov makes a plea for maternal compassion. He told Catherine that his daughter was in such terror of Saltykov that she feared to use the family box at the theater because it was too near his. He continued, "1 am not asking that you put in a good word for me (*rekomendovali*) with Saltykov; that would be like one of my peasants asking that I put in a good word for him with the bailiff; for monarchs do not recommend some of their subjects to others. We are all the children and subjects of Your Majesty, and you are mother and sovereign to us all" (Pis'ma 132). Sumarokov falls back on a sentimental notion of the state as a family to conceptualize his position: Catherine's role as "mother and sovereign to us all" erases hierarchies of power and creates equality among her subjects if not under the law, then under her parental protection. (In this scenario Sumarokov casts himself in the role of a peasant appealing for help against an overseer, though explicitly denying the analogy.) In formal odes and celebratory address it was common to refer to Russian empresses as Mother, Mother of the Fatherland (*mat' otechestva*), and even Mother Russia, and Sumarokov resorts to what was both a traditional paternalistic image and a utopian trope to make his plea (on the utopian mother image, see Baehr ch. 4). As we will see below, this is a common rhetorical tactic Sumarokov uses in his attempts to persuade Catherine: he contrasts an ideal of imperial behavior to his own pitifully unjust treatment—which casting himself as an oppressed peasant emphasizes.

PATRONAGE AND PERSONAL HONOR

Sumarokov's conflict with Saltykov may thus be seen as a clash between autocratic political privilege and privileges in the contractual sense discussed above. Catherine upheld the Moscow commander-in-chief's power to treat Moscow as his fiefdom over Sumarokov's legal rights, choosing to extend her patronage to an important political client rather than to an unruly literary one. From this perspective the incident demonstrates the conflict between autocracy and legality inherent within the system of privilege. It also lays bare just how important patronage was.

In the middle of the eighteenth century it was almost unheard of for writers anywhere, including England or France, to make a living from the sale of their books (Dawson 301; Korshin 456), and this most often made patronage an overriding concern in a writer's career. In his study of the literary institutions of France's "classical age," Alain Viala distinguishes two alternative models of what in English unfortunately both fall under the term "patronage": clientism (le clientélism) and maecenasism (le mécénat).[4] Clientism follows the logic of service and defines the mutual, hierarchical obligations between client and patron; clients are often in the direct employ of their patron (e.g., Petrov, Elagin, Kozitskii's positions in Catherine's personal *kabinet*, or Fonvizin, who worked for N. I. Panin in the department of foreign affairs). Clientism is part of a larger pyramidal network which involves some combination of political, ideological, and clan loyalties. In contrast, maecenasism — named for the Augustan nobleman who supported Horace — represents altruistic support of the arts for their own sake, and assumes no material interest or obligation on either side; artists are supported, for example, by long-term state pensions (as under Louis XIV and Colbert) rather than for specific services, and the utilitarian aspect of the relationship is downplayed. Maecenasism advertises itself as "an exchange of affirmations" not between Client and Patron but between Artist and Great One, "for the glory of each," although such glory is obviously a way the rich and powerful gain status and legitimization in the eyes of society (Viala 55). I. I. Shuvalov's support for Lomonosov is a good example of such a relationship in mid-century Russia. Maecenasism reflects the attitude, inherited from ancient Greece and Rome, that "artists and poets should not be regarded as paid laborers, but should be free to carry out their work without any thought whatsoever for financial concerns" (Gold 1). However, in all but the purest of maecenasist models, the two modes of patronage are to some extent intertwined, insofar as they may be seen to represent two basic aspects of art in society: its ideal, altruistic aim as opposed to its instrumental, utilitarian function. At one extreme is the ideal of the free and independent creator, at the other, the writer as sycophant or hireling.

Viala's distinction between maecenasism and clientism is particularly relevant to Catherinean Russia, whose major political struggle (as described by David Ransel 1973, 1975) was a clash between Petrine political ideals of merit and legality, on the one hand, and the power of shifting "familial patronage cliques" or "clientelle groups" on the other. Sumarokov's relation-

---

[4] The Russian equivalents of these terms are *patronazhestvo* (also: *pokrovitel'stvo, patronat, odobrenie*) and *metsenatstvo*, although these terms are often used interchangeably and do not necessarily reflect Viala's distinction.

Chapter 10. The Illegal Staging of Sumarokov's *Sinav and Truvor* in 1770

ship with Catherine in terms of literary patronage reveals a similar tension or confusion of models. While he turned to Catherine for support as from a Client to a Patron, Catherine responded as a Great One to an Artist, reaffirming her overall support for the arts as a Maecenas but rejecting Sumarokov's repeated specific and irritating demands that she make good on her obligations to him. On the surface, Sumarokov appealed to the altruistic logic of maecenasism. He cited Voltaire's recent letter to him in which he had praised Catherine's glorious support of the literary arts, noting that "les têtes couronées mêmes ne forcent point les Muses et encouragent les poëtes, s'ils veulent que les beaux arts fleurissent dans leurs pays et portent les fruits pour la gloire de ceux qui les protègent." (Pis'ma 131) Art should be allowed to freely develop and flourish, bringing rulers and their nations glory (and to the Artists as well). The main example of such patronage was the golden age of Louis XIV, when as Viala notes, state maecenasism was at its height. Perhaps no one had done more to celebrate Louis than Voltaire, although it is worth noting that Voltaire himself may be considered one of Catherine's most illustrious Clients (Wilberger, Lentin). Sumarokov repeatedly invoked the sun King as a paradigm in his appeals to Catherine. In a petition of 1767, he wrote, for example, that "no one can deny that Racine, La Bruyère and de La Fontaine increased the honor of France and the honor of Louis' reign, and no less than his victorious arms" and asserted his own (he thought acknowledged) right to such a role in Russia, since "Voltaire himself along with Metastasio is the only one worthy of me among contemporaries" (Pis'ma 108).

However, the logic of Sumarokov's case was that of a loyal Client appealing to his Patron for support in a hierarchical power struggle; he was using maecenasist arguments to assert a quid pro quo which was essentially clientist. Sumarokov's letters to Catherine emphasize not only the empress' responsibilities as dispenser of justice and as protector of the arts but the reciprocal (rather than disinterested) nature of their relationship. Sumarokov argues both that he deserves Catherine's support and that it is advantageous for her to support him — more profitable than supporting Saltykov because he is able to bring more glory to her and to Russia than the military success of Saltykov, who had made his name as commander-in-chief during the Seven Years' War. He recognized, he said, again at times slipping into French,

> that he is respected for his fame and services to Russia, distinguished in rank and worthy for his esteemed old age... but he too should not forget that I am already fifty-two years of age and that to the honor of my fatherland have earned

no little amount of glory in Europe... Sophocle, le prince des poëtes tragiques qui était en même temps le général des Atheniens et camarade de Pericles, est encore plus connu sous le nom de poëte qu'en qualité de général. Rubens était ambassadeur; mais il est plus connu sous le titre de peintre; d'être un grand capitaine et vainqueur est un grand titre, mais d'être Sophocles est un titre qui n'est pas moins — and especially in an age and among a people where the arts and sciences have hardly been sown. (Pis'ma 138–39)

A further enticement to Catherine from Sumarokov's point of view was his next tragedy *Dimitrii the Impostor*. The Parisian *Journal étranger* had recently declared *Sinav and Truvor* (the very play disfigured by Saltykov) to be "un monument de la gloire du regne de l'impératrice Elisabeth," and Sumarokov said that he had wanted "to produce something new upon the Russian stage during your reign as well, and so I tried to write a new tragedy 'Psewdo Demetrius,' but that menacing Count Saltykov interrupted me right at the dénouement — that was a new insult to me" (Pis'ma 128). In a note to Kozitskii accompanying his next letter to Catherine, Sumarokov claimed that the new play would "show Russia Shakespeare" (Pis'ma 133), and this and his threat to incinerate the unfinished play were clearly meant to underscore what Catherine would lose in not supporting the playwright. According to the logic of clientism, Sumarokov felt that he still had bargaining power.

Sumarokov's admitted *"samokhval'stvo"* (self-advertisement) may also be seen as an important element in this reciprocity: Sumarokov advertises the goods, as it were. Sumarokov also played on Catherine's desire to make Russia part of Enlightened European civilization as well as her obsessive "pursuit of immortality" (Griffiths 1986). Sumarokov drew on the Voltairean theme of enlightened European maecenasism, emphasizing Saltykov's coarse behavior by again switching from Russian (here in English translation) into French:

> However, Count Saltykov ordered with a shout: "That's how I want it! Go ahead and play, never mind the author!" Est-ce une chose usitée dans quelque endroit dans l'Europe? Est-ce seconder la protection de votre majesté que vouz avez pour les beaux arts? Est-ce encourager les poëtes? (Pis'ma 128)

The positive paradigm of a Louis XIV becomes grounds for complaint against Saltykov, and by extension, also against Catherine. From this perspective Sumarokov's subsequent comparison of Saltykov's behavior to that of Nero seems particularly audacious: "they [i.e., Saltykov] are treating a well-known poet more despotically and cruelly (*samovlastnee i zhestoche*) than Nero did," he charged. Sensing that he was on thin ice, Sumarokov added, "But he was a Roman emperor," thus perhaps blunting the comparison, but then noting, "however, even he [Nero] took care of (*odobrial*) all of the poets, except for Lucan," thus throwing the ball back into Catherine's court (Pis'ma 128–29).

The comparison to Nero may have been a surprising impertinence, but the parallel between imperial Russia and imperial Rome was a commonplace of the age (Kahn 754–55). The reference to Nero was obviously something of a warning, the anti-type of how poets should be treated. Again, while the ideal invoked here was that of Augustan Rome, the model of maecenasism, its invocation marks the consciousness of a faithful Client. In several of his later letters Sumarokov offers to put his muse directly at the service of his patrons (Catherine and Potemkin), offering to write a history of Russia's victory over the Turks and a tragedy in blank verse (neither of which he did). He nominates himself for the role of a Horace or Virgil to Catherine's Augustus, directly offering his services to glorify her reign, perhaps as an alternative to Petrov. As noted above, Petrov was Catherine's most visible (and highly criticized) poet-Client, her "pocket versifier," who with his translation of the *Aeneid* (cantos 1–6) hoped to assume the mantle of Catherine's Virgil (Kahn 753–57, Shliapkin 397).

Whereas Augustus and Louis XIV personified the ideal of the Maecenas, Sumarokov's offers to write on demand demonstrate not only his sense of being Catherine's servitor, but also his increasing desperation. Having helped to champion the empress as the ideal enlightened monarch, and having put himself at her service, he had little grounds to criticize any of her actions, apart from insistent references to the cherished ideal she allegedly embodied.[5] At the same time as he offered to put his pen at the disposal of his patrons, however, Sumarokov insisted on his contempt for servility (*laskatel'stvo*) and on his honor as a gentleman (e.g., Pis'ma 142–44; 175–6). Although clientism did not necessarily spell a sell-out — Fonvizin's relationship to

---

[5] Catherine's own view — and practice — of patronage is harder to gauge, and deserves in-depth study. Allen McConnell has challenged the traditional view of her motives as patron of the arts as being exclusively and "crassly political" (37), but he also chronicles her in many ways dismal record of failing to support native Russian talent, citing the sad cases of the sculptor F. I. Shubin and the painter A. P. Losenko (46–47, 51). Several talented writers of Catherine's era including A. A. Rzhevskii and Mikhail Chulkov abandoned literary pursuits for lack of support. Catherine's extremely important role as patron of Russian letters has not been the subject of special scrutiny, but seems to have followed a similar rather conservative and pragmatic pattern as in her patronage of the fine arts.

Panin is a case in point—the dangers were obvious. The cultural paradigm of the "honnête homme," the ideology of civilized society which the age of Louis XIV had done so much to propagate, played an important mediating function here, cushioning the tensions between service and independence. In his letters of 1770, Sumarokov staunchly defends his *chest'*, his honor and his honesty, both as citizen and subject, as well as a writer. In his letter to Belmonti, together with his legal complaint, Sumarokov noted caustically that "votre honneur n'est plus honneur; vouz l'avez perdu en donnant parole d'honneur que vous avez rompue" (Pis'ma 129); the entrepreneur had broken his word of honor and could no longer be treated as a gentleman. The code of honor, however, also serves as a defense of Sumarokov's position as author, as when in May 1758 he had been insulted by Count I. G. Chernyshev, and he complained to Shuvalov (in his characteristic mix of Russian — here English — and polite society French):

> However, de traiter les honnêtes gens d'une tel façon and say: you are a thief — ce peut allarmer tout le genre humain and all those qui n'ont pas le bonheur d'être les grands seigneurs comme son excellence mr. le comte Tchern. qui m'a donné le titre d'un voleur, titre trés honorable pour un brigadier et encore plus pour un auteur des tragédies, a présent je vois, monseigneur, que c'est peu d'être poëte, gentilhomme et officier. (Pis'ma 78)

Gukovskii comments that Sumarokov was caught here between the new code of aristocratic honor (which by the early nineteenth century produced the golden age of dueling in Russia) and what Gukovskii calls "old-fashioned slavishness" (*starozavetnoe rabstvovanie* [*Ocherki*, 50]). It may also be seen as a moment when the role of *gentilhomine* mediates between that of *poëte* and *officier*, and when the notion of spiritual nobility (its special calling and prerogatives, as advocated by Sumarokov and the Panin party) begins to contribute to a new notion of authorship and its special status. The notion of nobility as an ideal was one which transcended social classes. In the forward to *Dimitrii the Impostor* Sumarokov rejected the facile opposition of "noble" and "plebian" (*dvorianin* versus *chern'*), arguing that "according to this stupid definition, theologians, natural scientists, astronomers, orators, painters, sculptors, architects" are indiscriminately lumped together with "the rabble...Oh, intolerable aristocratic pride, worthy of disdain and outrage! The true rabble are the ignorant, even if they have great rank, the wealth of Croesus, and trace their clan from Zeus and Juno..." (Sumarokov PSVS VI: 61). In elaborating on Voltaire's notion of "the public," Sumarokov presents a polite society ideal of cultured nobility ("people who are educated

Chapter 10. The Illegal Staging of Sumarokov's *Sinav and Truvor* in 1770

and have taste" [*liudei znaiushchikh i vkus imeiushchikh*]), not dependent merely or primarily on birth for status. Implicitly, Sumarokov included poets and playwrights in his list of what may be seen to constitute an eighteenth-century version of the intelligentsia.

As in his earlier run-in with Chernyshev, Sumarokov was outraged at Saltykov both for treating him like a social inferior and for insulting him as a poet: "He may get angry at his valet over a wig, but not at me and over my works — at someone whose name will endure longer on this earth than his" (Pis'ma 128; cf. 135, 140). In the letter to Belmonti cited above, the voice of poet as man of honor defending the republic of letters rings out:

> Si vous dites que c'était par ordre du maréchal: le maréchal est sous les lois, mais non pas les lois sous lui en mere temps. *Ii est le premier seigneur dans la ville de Moscou; mais les Muses ne soft pas sous ses commandements*...Montrez-lui, si vous voulez, cette lettre. Je le respecte comme grand gouverneur de la ville capitale, mais non pas comme le gouverneur des muses, et par consequence du côté de la place qu'il occupe je le respecte, et du côté de la poésie, je m'estime plus que lui. (Pis'ma 129; italics mine)

Here sounds the voice of the independent Russian poet, so striking in the later history of Russian poetry, from Derzhavin on (Crone).

At the heart of Sumarokov's view of authorship is the notion of honor, a combination of the "honnête homme"'s desire for respect, the Enlightenment cult of public glory (Griffiths 1986), and classical notions of the mission of the poet. At the same time, the practical exigencies of being a writer repeatedly clashed with these altruistic ideals. Hence for example Sumarokov could simultaneously complain and boast to Catherine that "'Merope' alone brought Voltaire a lot of money. But I have nothing from my dramas except for naked honor; so why try and take that away from me as well? What reason do I have to oppose Count Saltykov?" (Pis'ma 139). "Naked honor" was both Sumarokov's badge of righteousness and mark of his helplessness. Without honor, without recognition for his labors, Sumarokov repeatedly argues, what sense in being a writer all?

Sumarokov's desperate need for validation and recognition led him to ever more rarefied arguments — from contractual commitments, to patronage obligations, to questions of honor, and finally, to an invocation of the court of last appeal: posterity. Sumarokov invoked the Horatian theme of "exegi monumentum," which was to become so familiar in the later Russian tradition (Alekseev; Levitt *Russian* 23–26) — asserting that his name would outlast that of Saltykov and that his fame would live on:

> And I who have striven up Parnassus, being in circumstances in which I could have made a good living even without dishonesty, leave behind only poverty, debts, and naked honor, which my ashes in the grave will not enjoy, but which in posterity will bring just as much praise to my name, as His Excellency was gracious enough to cause me grief. (Pis'ma 136–37)

He told Catherine that if he died from the incident,

> I desire that at least those people who labor in the verbal arts will represent my death in this way, [asking] whether or not it is possible for the free arts to flourish in Russia, given such ignorance, stubbornness, stubbornness and coarseness of those in charge. (Pis'ma 131)

Sumarokov here tries to frame the way in which posterity should view him, trying on a martyr's crown, picturing himself as victim to Russian ignorance and the oppression of "those in charge."

The image Sumarokov describes for himself here, so familiar in the later Russian literary tradition, cannot, however, be said to be much more convincing or successful than his earlier ones as legal complainant, poet-client, and man of honor. (He had threatened to die or stop writing too often!) Sumarokov's words indicate a consciousness of the institutional aspect of his problem, summoning "those who labor in the verbal arts" to consider the fate of the "free arts" (*svobodnye khitrosti*) in Russia, yet he is forced to address himself to an imagined future when these institutions will be able to render more real authority to authorship. Both Sumarokov's quest for authorial rights and his hoped for posthumous rehabilitation came to naught. Symptomatically, when his correspondence (upon which much of this article was based) did begin to be published, piecemeal, in the nineteenth century, the first item to appear was Catherine's "reprimand"; the second was Sumarokov's desperate letter of 1775 to Potemkin offering to fulfill his "order" for a tragedy in blank verse, together with one of his complaints to Shuvalov against Lomonosov.[6] These publications reflected

---

[6] Catherine's letter was published by P. A. Viazemskii in *Syn otechestva*, 49 (1818): 170–173, from the French version that had appeared in Grimm's *Correspondance littéraire*, first published for public consumption in 1812 (in its day the *Correspondance littéraire* was a unique, elite private journal addressed primarily to the courts of Europe). Her letter was republished in *Chteniia v Obshchestve istorii i drevnostei rossiiskikh*, 2 otd. 5 (1860): 238, and again in Viazemskii 61–64. Sumarokov's letters to Potemkin and Shuvalov were also published by Viazemskii, in *Literaturnaia gazeta*, no. 28, May 16, 1830, 222–225 (and Viazemskii II: 16–74). According to Stepanov, it was not considered proper

Chapter 10. The Illegal Staging of Sumarokov's *Sinav and Truvor* in 1770

a strikingly negative image of eighteenth-century literary life as debased clientism, and no doubt helped contribute to the repudiation of the entire earlier Russian literary tradition. For many, Sumarokov came to personify everything that modern Russian literature was rejecting. Yet as with so many other aspects of his career, Sumarokov marked out many of the paths (and pitfalls) that were later traveled by his more illustrious successors. They gained ample recognition for what during Sumarokov's lifetime may have seemed undeservedly inflated claims for the special role of the Russian author and poet.

Work Cited

Alekseev, M. P. *Stikhotvorenie Pushkina "a pamiatnik sebe vozdvig..."* Leningrad: Nauka, 1967.

Andreevskii, I. E. "Kantseliariia konfiskatsii 1729–1780 gg.," *Russkaia starina*, 31:6 (1881): 167–186.

Armstrong, Elizabeth. *Before Copyright: The French Book-Privilege System 1498–1526*. Cambridge: Cambridge UP, 1990.

Baehr, Stephen L. *The Paradise Myth in Eighteenth-Century Russia: Utopian Patterns in Early Secular Russian Literature and Culture*. Stanford: Stanford UP, 1991.

Barber, M. Elizabeth, "Copyright in a Dramatic Work." *The Oxford Companion to the Theatre*. Ed. Phyllis Hartnoll. 2nd ed. London: Oxford UP, 1957. 149–154.

Berkov, P. N., ed. *Istoriia russkoi literatury XVIII veka: Bibliograflcheskii ukazatel'*. Comp. V. P. Stepanov and Iu. V. Stennik. Leningrad: Nauka, 1968.

Boncompain, Jacques. *Auteurs et comédiens au XVIIIe siècle*. Paris: Perrin, 1976.

Bonnassies, Jules. *Les Auteurs dramatiques et la Comédie Française aux XVIIe et XVIIIe siècles*. 1874; repr. Paris, 1970.

Bonnassies, Jules. *Les Auteurs dramatiques et les theatres de Province aux XVIIe et XVIIIe siècles*. Paris: Leon Willem and Paul Daffis, 1874.

Bossenga, Gail. *The Politics of Privilege: Old Regime and Revolution in Lille*. Cambridge: Cambridge UP, 1991.

Boswell, James. *Boswell's Life of Johnson, Including Their Tour to the Hebrides*. ed. J. W. Croker. Revised ed. London: John Murray, 1860.

Bulich, N. *Sumarokov i sovremennaia emu kritika*. St. Peterburg, 1854.

Bush, M. L. *Noble Privilege*. New York: Holmes and Meier, 1983.

---

to reveal (or make copies of) correspondence with an empress (Pis'ma 185), although clearly Saltykov did not heed this stricture! Sumarokov's letters to Catherine only began to be published in the 1860's. See Berkov 368–69, no. 7011.

Crone, Anna Lisa. *The Daring of Deržavin: The Moral and Aesthetic Independence of the Poet in Russia*. Bloomington, IN: Slavica, 2001.

Dawson, Robert L. *The French Book Trade and the "Permission Simple" of 1777: Copyright and Public Domain.* Studies on Voltaire and the Eighteenth Century, 301. Oxford: The Voltaire Foundation, 1992.

"Dlia biografii N. I. Novikova," *Moskvitianin* [2:] 2 (1842): 521–524.

Dukes, Paul. *Catherine the Great and the Russian Nobility: A Study Based on the Materials of the Legislative Commission of 1767*. Cambridge: Cambridge UP, 1967.

Dukes, Paul, ed., trans. *Russian Under Catherine the Great: Select Documents on Government and Society*. Vol. 1 Newtonville, MA: Oriental Research Partners, 1978.

Farrow, Lee A. "The Control of Property in Eighteenth-Century Russia." Presentation, AAASS National Conference. 17 Nov. 1996. Boston.

Gessen, Sergei. *Knigoizdatel' Aleksandr Pushkin*. 1930; rpt. Moscow: Kniga, 1987.

Gleason, Walter J. *Moral Idealists, Bureaucracy, and Catherine the Great*. New Brunswick, NJ: Rutgers UP, 1981.

Glinka, Sergei. *Ocherki zhizni i izbrannye sochineniia Aleksandra Petrovicha Sumarokova*. Vol. 1. St. Petersburg, 1841.

Gold, Barbara K. *Literary Patronage in Greece and Rome*. Chapel Hill, NC: University of North Carolina Press, 1987.

Gorbunov, I. E. "Moskovskii tear v XVIII–XIX stoletii." *Sochineniia*. St. Petersburg, 1910, III, chast' 5, 98–129.

Griffiths, David. "To Live Forever: Catherine II, Voltaire and the Pursuit of Immortality." *Russia and the World of the Eighteenth Century*. Ed. R. P. Bartlett, A. G. Cross, and Karen Rasmussen. Columbus: Slavica, 1986. 446–468.

Griffiths, David. "Of Estates, Charters and Constitutions." *Catherine II's Charters of 1785 to the Nobility and the Towns*. Ed. David Griffiths and George E. Munro. Bakersfield, CA: Charles Schiacks, Jr., 1991. xvii–lxix.

Grimm, Jacob. *Correspondence littéraire, philosophique et critique par Grimm, Diderot, Raynal, Meister, etc...* Ed. Maurice Tourneux. Vol. 9. Paris: Gamier Frères, 1879.

Grits, T., V. Trenin, M. Nikitin. *Slovesnost' i kommertsiia (knizhnaia lavka A. F. Smirdina)*. Moscow: Federatsiia, [1929].

Gukovskii, G. A. *Ocherki po istorii russkoi literatury XVIJI veka: Dvorianskaia fronda v literature 1750-kh — 1760-kh godov*. Moscow, Leningrad: AN SSSR, 1936.

Gukovskii, G. A. *Russkaia literatura XVIII veka*. Moscow: Uchpedgiz, 1939.

Hesse, Carla. *Publishing and Cultural Politics in Revolutionary Paris, 1789–1810*. Berkeley: University of California Press, 1991.

Hippisley, Anthony. *The Poetic Style of Simeon Polotsky*. Birmingham Slavonic Monographs, 16. Birmingham: Dept. of Russian Language and Literature, University of Birmingham, 1985.

Jones, Robert. *The Emancipation of the Russian Nobility 1762–1785*. Princeton: Princeton UP, 1973.

Jones, Gareth W. "The Image of the Eighteenth-Century Russian Author." *Russia in the Age of Enlightenment: Essays for Isabel de Madariaga*. Ed. Roger Bartlett and Janet M. Hartley. London: Macmillan, 1990. 57–74.

Jones, Gareth W. *Nikolay Novikov: Enlightener of Russia*. Cambridge: Cambridge UP, 1984.

Kahn, Andrew, "Readings of Imperial Rome from Lomonosov to Pushkin." *Slavic Review*, 52:4 (1993): 754–55.

Kokorev, A. V. "Sumarokov i russkie narodnye kartinki." *Uchenye zapiski Moskovskogo Gos. Universiteta*, 127. Trudy kafedry russkoi literatury (1948): 227–36.

Kollmann, Nancy Shields. "The Legal Process: Insult and Community in Seventeenth-Century Russia." Presentation, Annual AAASS Conference. 16 Nov. 1996. Boston.

Korshin, Paul J. "Types of Eighteenth-Century Literary Patronage." *Eighteenth-Century Studies*, 7: 4 (1974): 453–73.

LeDonne, John P. *Ruling Russia: Politics and Administration in the Age of Absolutism, 1762–1796*. Princeton: Princeton UP, 1984.

Lentin, A. Introduction. *Voltaire and Catherine the Great: Selected Correspondence*. Cambridge: Oriental Research Partners, 1974. 4–32.

Levitt, Marcus C. "An Antidote to Nervous Juice: Catherine II's Response to Chappe d'Auteroche." *Eighteenth Century Studies*, 32:1 (1998): 49–63. (Also in this volume.)

Levitt, Marcus C. "Aleksandr Petrovich Sumarokov." *Early Modern Russian Writers, Late Seventeenth and Eighteenth Centuries. Dictionary of Literary Biography*. Vol. 150. New York: Bruccoli Clark Layman, and Gale Research, Inc., 1995. 370–381. (= "Sumarokov: Life and Works" in this volume.)

Levitt, Marcus C. Introduction. *Early Modern Russian Writers, Late Seventeenth and Eighteenth Centuries. Dictionary of Literary Biography*. Vol. 150. New York: Bruccoli Clark Layman, and Gale Research, Inc., 1995. ix–xviii.

Levitt, Marcus C. *Russian Literary Politics and the Pushkin Celebration of 1880*. Ithaca: Cornell UP, 1989.

Livanova, T. *Russkaia muzykal'naia kul'tura XVIII veka v ee sviaziakh s literaturoi, teatrom i bytom: Issledovaniia i materialy*. Vol. 1. Moscow: Gos. muz. izdat, 1952.

Longinov, M. N. *Novikov i Shvarts: Materialy dlia istorii russkoi literatury v kontse XVIII veka*. 2nd ed. Moscow, 1858.

Longinov, M. N. "Poslednie gody zhizni Aleksandra Petrovicha Sumarokova (1766–1777)." *Russkii arkhiv* (1871): col. 1637–1717 and 1955–59.

Lukin, V. I. *Sochineniia i perevody*. St. Petersburg, 1768.

Maikov, L. N. *Ocherki iz istorii russkoi literatury*. St. Petersburg, 1889.

McConnell, Allen. "Catherine the Great and the Fine Arts." *Imperial Russia 1700–1917: State, Society, Opposition*. Ed. Ezra Mendelsohn and Marshall S. Shatz. Dekalb, IL: Northern Illinois UP, 1988. 37–57.

Meehan-Waters, Brenda. *Autocracy and Aristocracy: The Russian Service Elite of 1730*. New Brunswick: Rutgers UP, 1982.

Meynieux, André. *La literature et le métier d'écrivain en Russie avant Pouchkine.* Paris: Librarie des cinq continents, 1966.

Mooser, R.-Aloys. *Annales de la Musique et des musiciens en Russie au XVIIIe siècle.* Vol. 2. Geneva, 1951.

Oksman, Iu. "Narushenie avorskikh prav ssylnogo Pushkina v 1824 g. (Po neizdannym materialam)." *Pushkin: stat'i i materialy,* I (Odessa, 1925): 6–11.

Patterson, Lyman Ray. *Copyright in Historical Perspective.* Nashville: Vanderbilt UP, 1968.

Pereselenkov, S. "Pushkin v istorii zakonopolozhenii ob avtorskom prave v Rossii." *Pushkin i ego sovremenniki,* XI (St. Petersburg, 1909): 52–63.

Pipes, Richard. "Was There Private Property in Muscovite Russia?" *Slavic Review,* 53.2 (1994): 524–530.

Pis'ma — Sumarokov, A. P. "A. P. Sumarokov." Ed. V. P. Stepanov. *Pis'ma russkikh pisatelei XVIII veka.* Ed. G. P. Makagonenko. Leningrad: Nauka, 1980. 68–223.

PSVS — Sumarokov, A. P. *Polnoe sobranie vsekh sochinenii, v stikhakh i proze.* Ed. N. I. Novikov. 10 Vols. Moscow: Universitetskaia tipografiia, 1781–82.

Pypin, A. N. *Istoriia russkoi literatury.* 4 vols. 2nd ed. 1902; rpt. The Hague: Mouton, 1968.

Ransel, David L. *The Politics of Catherinean Russia: The Panin Party.* New Haven: Yale UP, 1975.

Ransel, David L. "Bureaucracy and Patronage: The View from an Eighteenth-Century Russian Letter Writer." *The Rich, the Well Born, and the Powerful: Elites and Upper Classes in History.* Ed. Frederic Cople Jaher. Urbana: University of Illinois UP, 1973. 154–178.

Romanovich-Slavatinskii, A. *Dvorianstvo v Rossii ot nachala XVIII veka do otmeny krepostnogo prava.* 1870; rpt. The Hague: Mouton, 1968.

Rose, Mark. *Authors and Owners: The Invention of Copyright.* Cambridge: Harvard UP, 1993.

Scarles, Christopher. "Dramatic Copyright." *The Cambridge Guide to Theatre.* Ed. Martin Banham. Cambridge: Cambridge UP, 1992.

Semennikov, V. P. *Materialy dlia istorii russkoi literatury i slovaria pisatelel epokhi Ekateriny II.* St. Petersburg, 1914.

Serman, Ilya. "Le statute de l'écrivain au XVIIIe siècle." *Histoire de la littérature russe: Des origines aux Lumières.* Ed. Efim Etkind, Georges Nivat, Ilya Serman and Vittorio Strada. Paris: Fayard, 1992. 681–89.

Sherman, Brad, and Alain Strowel, eds. *Of Authors and Origins: Essays on Copyright Law.* Oxford: Clarendon Press, 1994.

Shliapkin, I. "Vasilii Petrovich Petrov, 'karmannyi stikhotvorets' Ekateriny II (1736–1799)." *Istoricheskii vestnik,* 22:11 (November 1885): 381–405.

Stepanov, V. P. "K voprosu o reputatsii literatury v seredine XVIII v." *XVIII vek,* 14 (Leningrad: Nauka, 1983): 105–120.

Todd, William Mills III. *Fiction and Society in the Age of Pushkin: Ideology, Institutions, and Narrative.* Cambridge: Harvard UP, 1986.

Viala, Alain. *Naissance de l'écrivain: Sociologie de la littérature à l'âge classique.* Le sens commun. Paris: Les Editons de Minuit, 1985.
Viazemskii, P. A. *Polnoe sobranie sochinenli.* Vols. 1–2. St. Peterburg, 1878–79.
Weickhart, George. "The Pre-Petrine Law of Property." *Slavic Review,* 52: 4 (1993): 663–679.
Weickhart, George. [Reply to Pipes.] *Slavic Review,* 53: 2 (1994): 531–38.
Wilberger, Carolyn. *Voltaire's Russia.* Studies on Voltaire and the Eighteenth Century, 164. Oxford: The Voltaire Foundation, 1976.
Wittenberg, Philip. *The Protection of Literary Property.* Rev. ed. Boston: The Writer, 1978.
Woodmansee, Martha. "The Genius and the Copyright: Economic and Legal Conditions of the Emergence of the 'Author.'" *Eighteenth-Century Studies,* 17 (1984): 425–448.
Woodmansee, Martha, and Peter Jaszi, eds. *The Construction of Authorship: Textual Appropriation in Law and Literature.* Durham and London: Duke UP, 1994.
Wortman, Richard. *The Development of a Russian Legal Consciousness.* Chicago: University of Chicago Press, 1976.
Zhivov, Viktor. "Pervye russkie literaturnye biografii kak sotsial'noe iavlenie: Trediakovskii, Lomonosov, Sumarokov." *Novoe literaturnoe obozrenie,* 25 (1997): 24–83.

11

SUMAROKOV AND THE UNIFIED POETRY BOOK:

His Triumphal Odes *and* Love Elegies *Through the Prism of Tradition*

The goal of this article to consider the classical and European precedents for Sumarokov's *Triumphal Odes* (*Ody torzhestvennyia*) and *Love Elegies* (*Elegii liubovnyia*) of 1774 when considered as unified poetry books, and to outline the place of these experimental collections within the larger cultural traditions that formed these genres.[1] In discussing precedents we will analyze examples of poetry books which were available (and, if possible, actually known) to the Russian poet in 1774. The problem here involves not only identifying or defining a particular corpus of unified poetry books that developed over the course of European literature, but, even more importantly, understanding how they were *perceived* as models by the later tradition and by Sumarokov in particular.

Any modern critic would probably agree that our reading of a particular poem is shaped by its position and context within a larger body of texts, although the precise nature and extent of that shaping may give rise to significant theoretical and practical disagreement (for a discussion of the problem as it relates to modern poetry, see for example: Rosenthal and Gall 1983; Fraistat 1985, 1986; Fenoaltea and Rubin 1991; see also the recent scholarship on classical poetry books cited below). Before the nineteenth century, however, there is hardly any evidence that either poets or scholars considered the "poetry book" an issue worthy of special attention.[2] In Russian

---

[1] This article was prepared in conjunction with a scholarly edition of these two collections (Vroon 2009). On their status as unified poetry books see Vroon 1995–96 and 2000.

[2] There are some notable exceptions to this, for example, Ronsard's architecturally-constructed books of odes (Fenoaltea 1990 and 1991), although as I point out below, even French Renaissance scholarship, within the context of which Ronsard's views were clearly shaped, did not seem to have considered the issue of the poetry book worthy of special attention.

scholarship there has been virtually no attention to the cycle or unified collection of poetry before this century (Sloane 1987; Berdnikov 1997; Darvin 1988 reviews the Russian scholarship). In modern literary consciousness, and especially in Russia, the concept of the "cycle" and the unified poetry collection have been associated primarily with Romanticism, and even in classical studies the poetry book was not identified as a phenomenon worthy of any serious attention until the end of the nineteenth century.

The obstacles to talking about the historical development of the unified poetry book within which we might place Sumarokov's collections are formidable. We lack the basic groundwork for even a simple history of the poetry book as a phenomenon in the Western tradition (or in Russia), not to mention a historical typology which would encompass its basic types and traditions — assuming that such an overarching typology is possible or justifiable at all. Indeed the very complexity of the organizational principles that govern any poetry book which would be judged as purposefully unified (as opposed to chance grouping or ordering by some externally imposed principle such as alphabetical or chronological order) is such as to make broad typological connections problematic, although there do exist relatively well-defined traditions in which patterns may identified, as in the development of the Augustan poetry book.

Furthermore, we should also state at the outset that the exercise of "hunting for sources" may be misleading, as it unjustifiably assumes the derivative and unoriginal nature of Sumarokov's approach to literature. Certainly, Russian Classicism put great value on the doctrine of imitation, and promoted the emulation of models whose authority was believed to be objectively grounded in "Nature," but at the same time there was an equal if not greater desire to rival and surpass those models, and to transform classical and European exemplars so that they conformed to specific Russian cultural standards (Gukovskii 1927 and 1929). This is borne out by various examples of Sumarokov's "borrowing" and adapting, in which, while one certainly may often isolate elements of a source work or works (which Sumarokov at times practically invites us to do), the end result is fundamentally new. For example, by naming his second tragedy "Hamlet" (*Gamlet*), Sumarokov called attention to his *improvement* on Shakespeare's famous play, which functioned as a mere foil and starting point for his own work (Levitt 1994b; other sources for the play include Racine, Voltaire, and Corneille). Indeed apart from directly acknowledged translations or paraphrases, few of Sumarokov's original works can be traced to a single source. Nevertheless, the exercise of placing Sumarokov's two poetry collections of 1774 onto a cultural and generic map seems to us to be useful for understanding the nature of Sumarokov's experiment. Such a preliminary mapping is attempted here.

* * *

With some justification, we may outline four periods in the history of the poetry book before 1774 which seem relevant for a consideration of Sumarokov's collections.

The earliest period is that of the Greek Alexandrian poets and critics (c. 325 B.C. – c. 30 B.C.) who created, edited, and passed on the first poetry books. Very little of the canon of poets and texts they bequeathed to the later tradition survived, however, and the questions of both defining the texts (distinguishing the originals from the work of later copyists, editors and scholars) as well as gauging the influence of Alexandrian collections on the later Latin tradition are thorny and still debated. The second, and perhaps richest period in the history of the poetry book is the extraordinary half-century of the Augustan poets (roughly, the last three decades of the first century B.C. and first two of the new millennium). This famous cohort left the first surviving examples of entire poetry books. Virgil, Ovid, Horace, Tibullus, Propertius and others published separate "books" (*libri*, actually, scrolls) of their poetry in individual genres or types in more or less unified and organized form. Not only Sumarokov, but most any post-classical European poet would certainly have turned to the Roman tradition as a precedent, although if and in what sense Augustan poetry books were appreciated as integrated collections remains a question. It may be significant that in his own poetry books of 1774 Sumarokov replicated the four major genres in which the Augustans created poetry books — eclogues, elegies, satires, and odes[3] (other classical poetry books include epodes and epigrams). Notably, along with the *Love Elegies* and *Triumphal Odes*, Sumarokov also published collections of *Eklogi* (*Eclogues*) and the first volume of his *Satiry* (*Satires*); to this list we may also add his paraphrase of the Psalter, the *Stikhotvoreniia dukhovnyia*, also of 1774. Might Sumarokov have been consciously emulating the Roman achievement in trying to establish a national tradition of poetry books in discrete genres? As unified collections, however, neither Sumarokov's collection of satires or eclogues appear to have been put together with the same degree of organization as his odes and elegies.[4]

---

[3] The designation "ode" is post-classical. See the discussion which follows.

[4] The *Eklogi* and *Satiry* have not been investigated as unified collections. Joachim Klein (1988) indicates no evidence for unity in his comprehensive study of Sumarokov's eclogues, although as he noted (in personal correspondence) this issue did not come

Chapter 11. Sumarokov and the Unified Poetry Book

The next significant stage in the development of the poetry book is the Renaissance, when poetic traditions in the vulgar tongue developed concurrently with the rediscovery, republication, and study of the classical texts. Writers from the fifteenth century onward turned to the Augustans both for specific generic models from which to build and for inspiration in the more general task of creating a national tradition. Just as the Roman poets built upon the Greeks, modern European poets (including the Russians) were consciously trying to create a poetry in the vulgar tongue by adapting earlier (classical, primarily Roman) precedents. Even though the argument has sometimes been made that Russian culture of the seventeenth, eighteenth, or early nineteenth century functioned as a kind of Renaissance, Renaissance literary traditions themselves had minimal importance for Russia, at least for eighteenth century Russian poetry. Russian poetry saw itself as starting virtually from scratch and took its cue primarily from the more recent French classicist example.[5] Indeed, as we argue below, Sumarokov and his contemporaries tended to view both the classical past as well as the Renaissance (and later) tradition through eighteenth century French eyes, although this should not blind us to the cases where there might have been direct influence of Renaissance poets. In any case, the Latin classical poets were certainly far more important as models than poets of the Renaissance; the latter were hardly translated (or even mentioned), and tended to be seen merely as historic forerunners rather than of particular interest in their own right.[6]

---

up during the course of his research. On the connection between Psalm paraphrases and cyclization, see the discussion below.

[5] This does not mean that the earlier Baroque Slavonic poetic tradition of Simeon Polotskii and his followers was not felt, but it provided more the linguistic and cultural background which was to be reshaped and reformed rather than a conscious model to be emulated (indeed in most cases it was a tradition that was to be rejected, at least on paper, for ideological reasons — like Boileau's rejection of the Baroque tradition, discussed below). On this issue, see esp. Robinson 1989, and Zhivov 1990, 1996. Furthermore, it is clear that the Baroque and the Jesuit-influenced Latin traditions of the Kiev Academy served as an important conduit for the classical tradition into Russia, although the lines of influence are complex.

[6] *Istoriia russkoi perevodnoi literatury* (II, 1996) which covers poetry translated during the eighteenth century lists virtually no Renaissance poets at all — as opposed to a very full listing of classical Latin and Greek and seventeenth and eighteenth century French ones. Missing, for example, are: Dante, Petrarch, Michelangelo, Ronsard, Malherbe, Villon, du Bellay, Opitz. Those few poets of before 1600 who were translated (Tasso, Shakespeare) were mostly translated from French versions into prose, and even then very selectively (this is confirmed by the *Svodnyi katalog* 1962–67). On Malherbe's special role in the odic tradition, see below.

The final, and least studied period, at least from the perspective of the poetry book, is that broadly contemporary to Sumarokov, the seventeenth and eighteenth centuries. Despite scholars' repeated acknowledgment of the importance of classical models during this period, their corresponding insistence on the individual poetic work as emulation of an ideal generic exemplar (as in Gukovskii's well known essay [1929]) has served to obscure the links with earlier traditions in which the poetic cycle and poetry book played a role.

This thumbnail sketch of the history of the poetry book, upon which I will expand below, has left out the crucial consideration of the role that generic traditions have played in the creation of poetry books. These traditions have their own inner logic that may modify or even override reigning literary prescriptions. The shape of any particular poetry book depends upon the poet's relationship toward his predecessors and to the specific generic traditions that come into play in the given instance. Two clear examples of genres whose collections have been subject to specific Russian poetic and cultural traditions are the psalm paraphrase and the sonnet. Paraphrases of the Psalter, whether full or partial, had a distinguished history in both European and Russian poetry, and the ordering of Psalms could follow traditional rhetorical or liturgical patterns (Levitsky 1981–85; Sloane 1987, 66–76; Vroon 2000). Since the Renaissance, and especially after Shakespeare, the sonnet was associated with cycles and to some extent with the unified collection. Sumarokov himself left precedent-setting examples of the sonnet cycle (a translation-adaption of three sonnets by the German Baroque poet Paul Fleming which Sumarokov turned into a cycle, as well as his own original sonnet cycle [both of 1755; see Berdnikov 1997]), and he also created a complete paraphrase of the Psalter. M. N. Darvin, one of the few scholars to recognize the cycle as a basic component of Russian eighteenth-century poetry, observes not only a tendency towards "active cyclization" in certain genres [aktivno tsiklizuiushchie zhanry] and the unified nature of particular Russian poetry books, but also suggests that it was the more "imitative genres" (in which he includes psalm paraphrases and Anacreontic odes) that inclined more towards cyclization (1988, 45).[7]

---

[7] At the same time Darvin notes that in the eighteenth century what may seem to be most "imitative" may be imbued with the most personal and original elements. While Darvin is certainly correct in connecting issues of cyclization with the historical development of genres, his hypothesis seems doubtful to us. First of all, the very notion of a "more

Chapter 11. Sumarokov and the Unified Poetry Book

In the analysis below I attempt to place the Russian love elegy and triumphal ode as Sumarokov practiced them within the history of the unified poetry book, although it should be noted that despite the considerable work on these genres their early history in Russia and the literary and cultural traditions they represent are still only imperfectly understood (on the elegy: Gukovskii, 1927, 48–102; Kroneberg 1972; Frizman 1973; Vroon 1996; among many works on the ode: Gukovskii 1927; Pumpianskii 1935, 1937, 1983a, 1983b; Alekseeva 1996 [on its German sources]; Zhivov 1996, 243–64 [on the Church-Slavonic tradition]). At the same time, we also need to keep in mind the real possibility of inter-generic crossover—that a unified collection of poems in one genre set the precedent for one in another. The best documented cases of this are from the Augustan poetry books, among which there was clearly much cross-fertilization among the published examples (eclogues, elegies, satires, and epodes; on this see, for example, Leach 1978). Conversely, it was often and more obviously the case that a particular well known text rather than an entire collection served as the generic exemplar, especially in the case of presentation odes, which were commonly published individually. For example, Boileau's "Ode sur la prise de Namur," which was the only important ode he published, became the model for the genre in Russia, and such was also the case with works in other genres, for example, Des Barreaux's sonnet "Grand Dieu! tes jugements sont remplis d'équité," which was repeatedly translated in eighteenth century Russia as a programmatic text (Lauer 1975, 51–4, 75–7, 94, 96–7, 279, and passim; 1997).[8]

Lastly, there is the additional possibility that the inspiration for Sumarokov's collections was not one or more poetry books, but shorter poetic

---

imitative" genre seems to us problematic. Other of Darvin's attempts to account for cyclization also seem questionable. For one, he connects literary cycles with changing perceptions of time. More specifically, he analyzes Kheraskov's anacreontic *Novyia ody* of 1762 — in which he sees significant elements of unity — in terms of the notion of the "anthology," based on a discussion of the Greek (Palatine) Anthology. This seems unfounded, insofar as this work does not seem to have been well known in Russia in the eighteenth century, and it was not translated until the 1820's (1988, 34–43); the influence of an earlier Baroque anthological tradition seems much stronger in the case of Simeon Polotskii's collections, which Darvin also discusses. Still, Darvin makes a strong case that cyclization (if not always cycles) was a fundamental characteristic of eighteenth-century Russian poetry (1988, chap. 2).

8   Similarly, Alexis Piron's "Ode à Priape" played a central role as model for Russian obscene verse ("Barkoviana"); in this case burlesque odes led to the "burlesquing" of a whole range of other genres.

sequences or cycles that appeared in books or journals. Darvin has noted that in the Russian eighteenth century what appeared first as a separate book of poems in one genre could later reappear as a subsection of a poet's larger multi-generic collected works (1988, 32). We should note in this context that the very notion of a "book" does not necessarily signify a discrete object, in the sense of a separate, free-standing publication; in the European poetic tradition, it was common for a single volume of verse to contain several "books," often, but not necessarily, grouped by genre. At the same time, the very notion of a "book" (or "collection") implies a certain degree of unity, although that does not relieve us from the task of discriminating between a merely mechanical, formal compilation and a more purposeful unity which helps define the poems within it (see Darvin 1988, 30f for a brief discussion on the ordering of eighteenth-century Russian collections). Notably, neither Sumarokov's triumphal odes nor his love elegies are divided into "knigi." In only two genres did Sumarokov employ this rubric — in his collections of fables (*pritchi,* published in three "knigi" — separate volumes — between 1762 and 1769[9]) and in his *Stikhotvoreniia dukhovnyia* of 1774, in which most of the psalm paraphrases were divided into twenty "books" consisting of one to fifteen poems. The psalm transpositions are numbered consecutively despite these divisions, although in other cases of Sumarokov's poetry publications, in journals as well as individual volumes, works were mostly numbered separately within a usually generic rubric. Hence while in some cases numeration may serve as a linking element, contributing to the creation of a lyric sequence, the evidence remains ambiguous and needs to be examined on a case to case basis.

Sumarokov and his contemporaries left no statements or other external evidence concerning the unity of his poetry books of 1774 nor about the models he may have been emulating in creating them, and as Vroon has noted in making the case for their unity, relying on the intrinsic evidence of the texts alone can be extremely precarious (Vroon 2000). Keeping this and the complexities traced above in mind we may attempt to reconstruct Sumarokov's perception of the ode and elegy book, and to place these genres within traditions of the unified poetry book.

---

[9] In the posthumous full works edited by N. I. Novikov (Sumarokov 1787 [first edition 1781–82]), these were augmented by three more books of fables, for a total of six books which were published together in the seventh volume.

Chapter 11. Sumarokov and the Unified Poetry Book

* * *

> quis tamen exiguo elegos emiserit auctor
> grammatici certant, et adhuc sub iudice lis est.
>
> Horace, *Ars Poetica*, 77–8
>
> (But the critics dispute who was the first to produce slender elegies, and the controversy has not yet ended.)

In Trediakovskii's *Guide to Composing Russian Verse* (*Sposob k slozheniiu rossiiskikh stikhov*) of 1752, the revised version of the *New and Short Method for Composing* (*Novyj i kratkii sposob*) of 1735, both of which Sumarokov knew extremely well, he names the Greek poet Philetas (c. 330 B.C.–c. 270 B.C.) and the Augustan poet Gaius Cornelius Gallus (c. 70 B.C.–26 B.C.) as model elegiac poets. However, Trediakovskii was merely repeating a commonplace of the Alexandrian critics and of the Augustan poets themselves. Only 43 lines by Philetas survived to modernity, fragments from works in diverse genres (Day 1938, 14–19, 25; Luck 1959, 25–29). Similarly, though Gallus was known to have written four books of love elegies, he died in disgrace, and all of his works were lost (except for one single attested line, and echoes of his verse in Virgil's tenth eclogue [Day 1938, 77–79; Luck 1959, 44]). For Sumarokov's cohort then, Philetas and Gallus were no more than great names, and if nothing else, this warns us that we should not take Russians' pronouncements about literary authorities and predecessors at face value.

During Sumarokov's day, as Gukovskii noted, the thematic content of the elegy as inherited from the classical Latin tradition was "extremely indistinct" (ves'ma rasplyvchata), and neither was the genre clearly defined by later Classicist theory (1927, 48; Potez 1898, chap. 1). Ancient "elegiac verse" could embrace a wide variety of subject matter, including war, politics, mythology, death, love, and friendship, and in a variety of tonalities (Luck 1959, 11; Day 1938, 138).[10] No Greek elegiac poetry has survived except in fragments; Roman poets left several examples of dedicated books of elegies, although the genre, of disputed origins (as Horace noted), was defined only by its meter (the so-called elegiac distich, consisting of alternating lines of dactylic

---

[10] The question of the debts of the Augustan elegiac poets to their Greek predecessors remains a rich one in classical scholarship. While the Latins clearly knew the Greek material very well, the surviving evidence concerning the precise nature and extent of the influence is slight and difficult to judge.

hexameter and pentameter). Up at least until Romanticism, later European poets continued to struggle both with the problem of an accepted meter and of verse form for the elegy, as well as with the issue of its appropriate content.

In Augustan Rome, the elegy became the preferred vehicle for love poetry, although this was not the only use for elegiac verse. Ovid, Tibullus, and Propertius all wrote collections of what are known as "love elegies" and while there has never been any question but that these books were created as whole collections, what this might mean for an interpretation of the poems within them did not become a subject of discussion among scholars until the later nineteenth century. The lack of attention was partly due the fact that (as in Sumarokov's case) there is virtually no meta-literary evidence or commentary that would bear witness to purposeful organizational design, apart from what may be gleaned from the evidence of the texts alone. While there is a general consensus that these collections *were* meant as wholes, the question of the extent and nature of their unity has been the focus of much controversy, one that has been renewed in the past twenty-five years, with a group of critics making quite aggressive (and disputed) cases for specific and purposeful kinds of poetic structure. (For two radically different perspectives, see Dettmer's broad positive claims [1983] and Anderson's skeptical survey of recent theories [1986]).

Sumarokov was familiar with all of the Latin elegists, as indicated by his "Epistle on Poetry" and the accompanying notes. More specifically, we know that Sumarokov borrowed several volumes of these poets' works from the Academy of Sciences Library in 1755 (Levitt 1995). Among these was an edition of the works of Catullus, Tibullus and Propertius, edited by Joseph Scaligeri (Amsterdam, 1582) (ibid, 54–55). This contained Catullus' surviving works; four books of elegies by Tibullus (modern scholars consider only the first two his); and Propertius' four books of elegies. The poetry and commentaries are all in Latin, a language we have no reason to think Sumarokov knew particularly well (see Trediakovskii's censure of Sumarokov for ignorance of both Latin and Greek [Kunik 1865, II, 496 and 486]). Still, the fact that Sumarokov borrowed the book indicates some degree of familiarity with these poets' corpus, as do his notes to the "Two Epistles." The surviving poetry by Catullus (c. 84–54 B.C.) contains some elegiac verse, and since the later nineteenth-century scholars have begun to discern groups of poems that form cycles, but it is only quite recently that some of them have tried to make the case that his surviving body of 116-odd poems may be seen as a unified whole, planned by the author rather than as a chance melange forged by a combination of later editors and historical happenstance (see *Classical World*, 81: 5 [1988], especially the articles by Skinner and Dettmer,

Chapter 11. Sumarokov and the Unified Poetry Book

and the literature cited on 338 n.1). The allegedly highly unified structure of the elegiac books by Tibullus and his rival Propertius, which are indisputably discrete collections of elegies, has also been the subject of significant debate (on Tibullus: Littlewood, 1970; Leach, 1978 and 1980; Dettmer, 1983, 14–22; on Propertius: Skutsch, 1963; Otis, 1965; Putnam, 1980; Dettmer, 1983, 22–32). Ovid's *Amores*, the last in the series of Augustan elegy books, is in a sense the closest to Sumarokov's collection, in that Ovid shortened the second (and only surviving) edition of his love elegies down from five books, which had been published individually over the course of several years, to three, which were published simultaneously — in other words, with the conscious purpose of forming a new whole. That noted, however, many critics have tended to see *less* organization in the *Amores* than in other Augustan poetic collections, including Ovid's own earlier ones (Port, 1926; Cameron, 1968, 329; Dettmer, 1983, 49–63, gives the argument for total unity).

In considering the ancient models of the elegy book, however, it is probably misleading to consider them out of the larger context of the Augustan poetry book as a whole. Tibullus' first book of elegies, for example, may be seen to have followed the model set by Virgil's *Eclogues*, "the earliest surviving [poetry] book" (Anderson 1986, 47), and by Horace's first book of satires, each of which contained ten poems (on their similarities of arrangement, see Leach, 1978). As noted, a poetry book in one genre may set the precedent for one of another type. This should also be kept in mind in Sumarokov's case.

There do not appear to be any modern European precedents for Sumarokov's collection of love elegies. In marked contrast to the ode, no modern poetic collections were dedicated to the elegy, nor was it a genre favored by French Classicism (on the elegy in eighteenth-century France, see Potez 1898, chap.1). Trediakovskii, whose formative years as a man of letters were spent in Paris, was well acquainted with the *précieuse* poetry of French salons, and in his *New and Short Method* cites the works of Madame (la Comtesse) de la Suze (Henriette de Coligny, 1618–1673) alone as the model for the modern love elegy. In his "Epistle on Poetry" Sumarokov follows suit, naming de la Suze alone as representative of the "tender elegy." Gukovskii traces the differences between the love elegy of de la Suze's gallant, *précieuse* type and that of Sumarokov and his contemporaries (1927); among other things, Gukovskii asserts that it was on the example of de la Suze that Sumarokov established the Alexandrine as the standard meter for the Russian elegy. However we judge the importance of de la Suze for Sumarokov's brand of love elegy, she did not provide a model either of lyric sequencing or of a unified collection of love elegies. Her elegies were published in voluminous, multi-authored, heterogeneous and multi-generic (often multi-volume) miscellanies (*recueils*) that showcased the variety of salon writing of her day. Even the famous collection which bore the title *Recueil de pièces galantes en prose et en vers de Madame La Comtesse de la Suze et de Monsieur Pellison*, which underwent at least twenty editions (regularly augmented and revised) between 1663 and 1741 (Magne 1908, 309–319; Lachèvre, 1901–1905; see also Fukui, 1964, 266–72), contained various genres by many different authors. Some of the most popular of these editions, published by Charles Sercy, were comprised of four or five volumes and contained up to 150 authors.[11] De la Suze's single poetry book that was hers alone, *Poésies de Madame la Comtesse de la Suze* of 1666, also published by Sercy, contained eighteen poems, five of which were elegies, but these were dispersed among odes, airs, stances, and madrigals (this is based on page numbers as given in Magne 1908, 290–99). Hence this seems to be a case where de la Suze's works may have provided an important precedent for Sumarokov's variant of the love elegy, but not for his collection of elegies.

Notably, Sumarokov's grouping of the elegies together in a holistic pattern came late in the poet's career, after a decade in which poets of the Sumarokov-Kheraskov school (Kheraskov, Rzhevskii, Naryshkin, Nartov, Bogdanovich, etc.) had been experimenting with poetic cycles (Vroon, 1996; Berdnikov, 1977). As early as 1735, Trediakovskii had created a cycle of two "tearful elegies" (elegii plachevnye) for his *New and Short Method* (1735), and Sumarokov's own trio of sonnet-translations from Paul Fleming in 1759 was another early, and influential, poetic cycle (Berdnikov 1997); we might also consider the collective phenomena of poetic competitions and poetic dialogues (e.g., poems in question and answer sequence) as early attempts at cyclization.

One other quite visible possible precedent for Sumarokov's collection of love elegies is F. Ia. Kozel'skii's collection of love elegies, *Elegies and Letter* (*Elegii i pis'mo*) of 1769. Kozel'skii followed in the footsteps of Sumarokov and Rzhevskii in the form and content of his elegies (Kroneberg 1972, 171–72), and his collection also made some movement toward cyclization (Kroneberg 1972, 178–82; Vroon 2000). At the same time, we should note that Kozel'skii was not taken seriously as a poet. When his elegies and tragedy "Panteia" were published in 1769 they had been subjected to devastating satire in N. I. Novikov's *Truten'*:

---

[11] Fukui (1964: 266–72) discusses the changing contents of the main editions. Notably, the version of volume three which appeared after 1680 contained Tallement's *Voyage de l'Ile d'Amour* (270). This collection may well have been the source for Trediakovskii, who translated the novel in 1730.

Chapter 11. Sumarokov and the Unified Poetry Book

Я не знаю, как то здешний воздух весьма противен аглинскому. Там умные люди с ума сходят, а здесь рассудка не имеющие разумными представляются. Кто может на рифмах сказать байка, лайка, фуфайка, тот уже печатает оды, трагедии, элегии и проч., которые, а особливо трагедию г. *, недавно напечатанную, полезно читать только тому, кто принимал рвотное лекарство, и оно не действовало. Здесь лягушка надувшись может говорить слону, что он ростом весьма мал. (Berkov 1951, 90)

(I don't know why, but the air here is extremely inimical to the English. There intelligent people go crazy, but here those without intelligence are presented as rational. Whoever can rhyme *baika, laika, fufaika* publishes odes, tragedies, elegies and the like, and especially the tragedy of Mr. *, recently published, [which] is only useful to be read by those who have had to take an emetic but it didn't work. In this case a puffed up frog can tell an elephant how short he is.)

And in Novikov's *Opyt istoricheskogo slovaria o rossiiskikh pisateliakh* of 1772 (probably written in collaboration with Sumarokov), Kozel'skii's elegies and tragedy were only somewhat more kindly described as "not particularly successful" (Efremov 1867, 53). Still, it was a typical procedure for Sumarokov to borrow and revise the work of his rivals, taking their attempts and giving them his own twist, and even reversing their significance (e.g., deliberately lowering Trediakovskii's "high" sonnet [Berdnikov 1997]). Hence if Kozel'skii gives his collection of elegies a happy ending promising future bliss in love, Sumarokov ends "on a note of absolute finality" and failure (Vroon 2000).

* * *

> Russia received the classical ideal through perhaps the greatest number of refractions; thus Lomonosov's ode was a classical work [that came] via Malherbe, Boileau, and the Germans…
>
> Pumpianskii (1983a, 305)

The opening lines of one of Sumarokov's earliest published mature odes, the "Oda na Gosudaria Imperatora Petra Velikogo" of 1755 (*Ezhemesiachnyia sochineniia* 3 [1755]; 219–222), which in shortened form (without the opening stanzas) introduced the *Triumphal Odes* of 1774, suggest the cultural genesis of the Russian triumphal ode:

> Быстры песни соплетая,
> Яко дерзостный орел,
> Пиндар, крылья простирая,
> Выше облак возлетел [...]
> О моя любезна Лира,
> Дай и мне путь в небеса: ...

Sumarokov was paraphrasing a famous passage from Horace (Book 4, ode 2, beginning "Pindarum quisquis studet aemulari..."), which in turn glorified Pindar's high panegyric style. The passage from Horace had become a commonplace in the later high ode tradition, in which, following Ronsard, Pindar and "pindarizing" had become a signal of its exalted poetics (Charmand 1898; Zhivov 1996, 255 n. 37). Sumarokov's opening also clearly recalled Boileau's "Ode sur la prise de Namur," his famous defense of the Pindaric ode; in the accompanying "Discours sur l'ode" Boileau had also cited Horace's lines. In his Russified version of Boileau's discourse, the "Rassuzhdenie o ode voobshche" of 1734, Trediakovskii had also cited the passage from Horace, although as Alekseeva has shrewdly noted, where Horace and Boileau suggest that the poet who dares to fly as high as the great Pindar is likely to meet the fate of Daedalus — have his wings of wax melt and fall down into the sea of obscurity — Trediakovskii's paraphrase of Boileau asserts the poet's ability to fly up and down at will. He thus raised Horace to an equal level with Pindar as practitioner of the ode (which also obscured the French debate over "ancients and moderns"; Alekseeva 1996a, 18–19; cf. also Zhivov 1994 and 1996, 174–6; and Rosenberg 1980, 220–228). Sumarokov's lines as it were confirm and complete the transformation, combining Pindar and Horace with Boileau and Trediakovskii, and turning Daedalus' fragile appendages into eagle's wings.[12]

This small example suggests the complex cultural pedigree of the triumphal ode in Russia, including the dual influences of Pindar and Horace, the filtering of the Latin and Greek heritage through Boileau and the French tradition, and finally Sumarokov's debt to earlier Russian predecessors in

---

[12] The image of Pindar as eagle is from Boileau's ode and the discussion of Horace's lines about Daedalus is from the "Discours" (Boileau 1966: 228 and 230). That Sumarokov followed in Trediakovskii's steps in blurring the boundaries between the two classical models for the ode is also suggested by his earlier programmatic "Epistola o stikhotvortve" of 1748, in which the writer of epic poetry is also able to swoop up and down at will ("vskidaet vsiudu vzgliad, / Vzletaet k nebesam, svergaetsia vo ad, / ... Vrata i put' vezde imeet otvorenny" [Sumarokov 1957: 118]).

Chapter 11. Sumarokov and the Unified Poetry Book

the genre.[13] As discussed above, genre history does not neatly accord with the history of the unified poetic collection, but the trajectory of the odic ideal reflected in Sumarokov's lines gives us a convenient starting point for exploring the precedents for Sumarokov's experimental collection of triumphal odes.

Sumarokov knew of the classical tradition of the ode first hand. In 1755, he borrowed editions of both Horace and Pindar from the Academy of Sciences Library (Levitt 1995, 54 and 57). As with the elegy, the poems commonly known as "odes" in both the classical and modern period cover a wide variety of poetic forms, differing in meter, stanzaic structure, and subject matter. As noted above, the specifically "triumphal (also: panegyric, political, performative) ode" traced its genealogy, first of all, to Pindar's works (although, notably, neither Pindar's nor Horace's works were called "odes" until the Renaissance). Pindar's surviving poetry — only about 25% of his estimated production — consists of four books of "epinicians" (Greek, songs of victory) plus several other odd poems and fragments. Pindar's verse came down to the later tradition in the form given to them by the Alexandrian critic-editors, who canonized the other eight classical Greek lyric poets whose work survives. This body of texts accompanies many editions of Pindar (including those of 1598 and 1600 which Sumarokov borrowed).[14] Pindar's epinicians are mostly celebratory choral hymns; each of the four books is named after the games that the poems honored (the Olympian, Nemean, Pythian, and Isthmian games) (Irigoin, 1952; Pfeiffer 1968, 183f, 205). The fact that Pindar's poems were ordered by event (an ordering done by later editors) makes it unlikely that Sumarokov would have seen them as anything more than mechanical compilations.[15] Many later collections of odes in the European tradition, as well as the Russian, seem also to have been arranged mechanically. Russian collections by other authors which included sets of panegyric odes that appeared before 1774 — Lomonosov's *Sobranie raznykh sochinenii* of 1751 and 1757–59 and volume 2 of Trediakovskii's *Sochineniia*

---

13 We would also add to this that the tradition of the Boileau ode came into Russia by way of German poetry, as discussed below.

14 The other eight poets are: Alcman, Alcaeus, Sappho, Stesichorus, Ibycus, Anacreon, Simonides and Bacchylides, poets who also played a role in establishing other later variants of the ode.

15 Despite the fact that the books of epinicians may have survived mostly complete, nowhere have I seen it suggested that there was any vestige of earlier authorial organization among the poems; the existant order is that of the mechanical, systematizing kind imposed by Pindar's later editors.

i perevody of 1752, which contained six odes — were also apparently ordered in a fundamentally mechanical, chronological fashion.[16]

In contrast to Pindar and such later compilations, Horace's odes (known in the Latin tradition as "carmina," or simply "lyrics") offered at least the potential example of an organically unified collection, and while the nature of their unity may be debated, their importance as the prototype of the unified poetry book seems undeniable. Horace's odes are the only existent Augustan ode collections; furthermore, apart from Ovid's *Amores*, the first three books are the only surviving example of ancient poetry books published together as an ensemble (the nature and degree of their unity has been the subject of much discussion — see Dettmer 1983; Santirocco 1980, 1986; Anderson 1986). Horace's books of odes arguably have the most complex inner unity of Augustan collections, both in terms of the number of works they contain (38, 20, and 30 poems in the three books, respectively — as opposed to Virgil's ten eclogues per book, Tibullus' ten elegies, and Horace's own previous books of ten satires and seventeen epodes), as well as in their variety of meters, stanzaic forms, and subject matter. However, for all of Horace's profound influence in eighteenth century Russian poetry (Berkov 1935; Busch 1964; Morozova 1990), there is no evidence of any interest in, or consciousness of, his books as unified collections. This lack of interest is also true of Europe, as evident, among other places, in the edition of Horace's full works (Amsterdam, 1735, in Latin with parallel French translation, with commentary by N. E. Sanadon and André Dacier) which Sumarokov borrowed from the Academy of Sciences' library in 1755 (Levitt 1995, 54).

---

[16] Darvin reminds us, however, that in many cases what might seem at first to be formal and mechanical groupings — both within sections of poetic collections and in poetic collections as whole books — often actually have their own clear logic. On the level of the poetic collection as a whole he cites Sumarokov's *Raznyia stikhotvoreniia* of 1769, which he notes is organized according to the "hierarchichal and logical thinking of the epoch" (ierarkhicheski-logicheskomu myshleniiu epokhi), divided into four sections moving from religious verse (dedicated to God), to panegyric odes (dedicated to the tsar), to elegies (dedicated to man) to eclogues (from man to himself) (Darvin 1988: 32). Within subsections (or in collections as a whole) he notes such important ordering elements as dedicatory poems, opening and closing verses, and poems in dialogic juxtaposition (in Kheraskov's *Novyia ody* he sees an ongoing clash between poems concerning "pure" and "impure" reason ("chistyi" vs. "zarazhennyi razum") (Darvin 1988: 32–45). Darvin goes on to distinguish between eighteenth and nineteenth century poetic cycles and cyclization, contrasting the "khudozhestvennaia obraznost'" of the latter, which "otlichaetsia nerazryvnoi slitnost'iu i edinstvom," to the "drobnyi i statichnyi kharakter" of the former, which "ob"ediniaiutsia...ne stol'ko vnutrennim razvitiem, skol'ko logikoi soediniaiushchei ikh avtorskoi mysli" (1988: 45).

Chapter 11. Sumarokov and the Unified Poetry Book

Boileau's defense of the Pindaric ode played a decisive role in defining the triumphal ode and its classical canon in Russia, and it was primarily through his prism that Sumarokov and the Russians viewed the tradition of panegyric ode writing. In his *L'Art poétique,* Boileau credited Malherbe with providing the first acceptable modern model for the high pindaric ode, a role which Sumarokov in the Russian context had accorded to Lomonosov (in the "Epistola o stikhotvorstve": "On nashikh stran Mal'gerb, on Pindaru podoben" [Sumarokov 1957, 125]). According to Boileau, Malherbe was "le premier en France, / Fit sentir dans les verses une jûste cadence [...] / Et reduisit la Muse aux regles du devoir. / Par ce sage Ecrivain la Langue reparée / N'offrit plus rien de rude à l'oreille épurée" (*L'Art poétique*, I, lines 131–36; Boileau 1966, 160). Malherbe's reform of the ode was an important precursor to Boileau and through him to the Russian *torzhestvennaia oda*, both in technical terms (Malherbe and his disciple Racan canonized Ronsard's ten line stanza and the 7–8 syllable line as the norm [Maddison 1960, 281; Viëtor 1961, 50]) and as an exclusively serious, celebratory, political, court-oriented genre.

Important as they may have been for the codification of the ode as a poetic genre, neither Malherbe nor Boileau published any collections of odes. Indeed, apart from the "Ode sur la prise de Namur," Boileau only wrote one other ode (and that was a very early poetic attempt) (see Magne 1929, I, 46–8, 175–77).[17] Malherbe never published an entire volume of verse (Malherbe 1936, I, v), and of his thirteen odes, only two were published as separate works during his lifetime; when they appeared in *recueils*, the odes were grouped together with other genres (stances, sonnets, and epigrams, etc.), as they were in later collections of Malherbe's works, in which they were included as parts of "books" composed of heterogeneous genres (Maddison 1960, 277–85; Malherbe 1936, I, xx-xxv). Similarly, Voltaire did not publish collections of his odes; his twenty odes (not all of the panegyric type) came out individually over the course of sixty years; they were republished in various combinations in a variety of collected and selected works before 1774 (Bengesco, I, 141–49 and IV, 1–105; 205).

In contrast, Malherbe's illustrious predecessor, Ronsard, had attempted not only to resurrect the classical ode, but to recreate the classical poetry book. Indeed, Ronsard began the modern tradition of ode-writing and books of odes which from the mid-sixteenth century became a prominent fixture in

---

17 Despite its crucial role in Russia, the Namur ode was not held in high regard in France. On the reasons for its success in Russia, see Zhivov's analysis of the role it played in legitimizing the Church-Slavonic linguistic and poetic heritage (1990; 1996).

Latin, French, German, Italian, Polish and other poetic traditions (Stemplinger 1906, 1921; Viëtor 1923; Maddison 1960, 275–76; Schmitz 1993). In his four books of *Odes* published in 1550, Ronsard claimed (with some exaggeration) that "Le premier de France / J'ai pindarizé" (Book 2, ode 2) and that "J'allai voir les étrangers, et me rendi familier d'Horace, et...osai le premier des nostres enrichir ma langue de ce nom Ode" (Stemplinger 1921, 103–104; on the problem of who was first to use the term "ode" in France, see Charmand 1898). In the architectonics of his collections and their larger conception as four "books of odes," Ronsard called explicit attention to the fact that he was emulating Horace. According to Fenoaltea, Ronsard purposefully "recognized and used principles of arrangement...discernible in the works of the Latin lyric poets," in order to create "a formal and architectural unity similar to that found in the work of the poets of Augustan Rome" (Fenoaltea bases her argument about the unity of Horace's poetry books on Dettmer 1983; see Fenoaltea 1990, 54 and 1991). For Ronsard, we may presume the influence of the scholar, editor and poet Jean Dorat in asserting the formal design of Horace's poetry books (e.g., Fenoaltea 1991, 33 note 7), yet Fenoaltea notes in passing that there is a strange dearth of evidence to indicate that classical scholarship considered the unified poetry book an issue, at least they left no written trace if they did (Fenoaltea 1991, 34 note 8). Fenoaltea demonstrates that Ronsard's inspiration for his poetry collections came almost exclusively from the realm of Renaissance architecture rather than literature or literary scholarship. Furthermore, while the *Odes* of 1550 were a turning point for French poetry, initiating a new interest in the classics, they were never popular, and after Malherbe (c. 1558–1628) Ronsard's reputation was in almost total eclipse (Maddison 1960, 226, 250, 272–77; Sainte-Beuve helped bring him back into vogue in the 1830's). Hence Ronsard's experiments in the poetry book did not seem to have left much impression (as noted above, Boileau gave Malherbe the credit for introducing the ode).

When Boileau spoke of Malherbe as "the first" correct poet, and referred to his "repairing" or "restoring" and "purifying" the language, he was explicitly rejecting, not so much Ronsard, as the subsequent tradition of Baroque ode writing. Boileau was outspoken in his rejection of the Baroque as a period of total decline ("un retour grotesque, / Tomber de ses grands mots le faste pedantesque" [Boileau 1966, 160]), although he did allow some praise to those who came before, including Ronsard, whose "French Muse" could also "speak Greek and Latin." While in principle Sumarokov and his contemporaries seconded Boileau's rejection of the Baroque poetic tradition and adhered to Vaugelas' linguistic purist doctrine, this "first generation" of Russian poets had

Chapter 11. Sumarokov and the Unified Poetry Book

far fewer alternatives in their choice of native predecessors and a far smaller range of poetic texts to work from. As Zhivov has brilliantly shown, the high Pindaric ode as interpreted by Boileau became a vehicle for legitimizing some aspects of the older, Baroque, Church-Slavonic, syllabic tradition (1990; 1996). While it is clear that Sumarokov's theoretical views about the high ode (as well as those of his Russian contemporaries) took its basic departure from Boileau (Alekseeva 1996a, 1996b), there is clear evidence that he and his generation were also familiar with aspects of the Baroque tradition, not only the indigenous Slavonic tradition of Simeon Polotskii and Feofan Prokopovich, but also that of the German Baroque. This is not the place to attempt a consideration of this difficult topic, but we may note in passing that Sumarokov knew German fluently and was familiar at least with the poetry of Paul Fleming (he borrowed three collections of his poetry from the library in 1755, most likely in connection with his translation of the three "Moscow" sonnets that he published that year [Levitt 1995, 49, 55–56]).

While the Russian Baroque panegyric tradition presented some literary and linguistic precedent, the "German School of Reason" (nemetskaia shkola razuma, as defined by Pumpianskii 1937, 1983a) offered the specific generic model of the Classicist triumphal ode, the model of the "Pindaric" ode canonized by Malherbe and defended by Boileau. Pumpianskii was the first to note that the tradition of this ode was assimilated into Russia via the German poets who were brought to Russia in the late 1720's and 30's to staff the newly opened Academy of Sciences in St. Petersburg, and who supplied the court with ceremonial verse. The Germans had a rich tradition of ode writing going back to Martin Opitz, who, following Ronsard, had assimilated the term "ode" to modern poetic usage (Stemplinger 1921, 104; Viëtor 1923, 59f); like Boileau, the Petersburg Germans rejected earlier Baroque traditions in odic verse. While Pumpianskii emphasized Lomonosov's original contribution to Russian poetry in the area of stylistics, and other scholars have focused on the German Petersburg poets as a source for Russian syllabo-tonic verse reform (see the literature cited in Klein 1995), Alekseeva has recently stressed that it was precisely here—in the presentation odes of G. F. W Juncker (V. F. Iunker) and Jakob von Staehlin (Ia. Ia. Shtelin)—that the very genre of the triumphal ode entered Russian poetry. Pumpianskii himself outlined the Russian ode's broad debt to the Germans:

> What was it that the Petersburg Germans contributed? First of all the practices relating to the court and ceremonial side of the ode..., the technique of presenting the ode, its recitation, its consideration of the theatrical, ceremonial

aspect... [but also] their adapting of the ode's meter, structure, style, and words to this its primary function... (1983a, 19)

From the Petersburg Germans, then, came the standard "Boileau" eight or ten-line odic stanza (in subsequent Russian literary history the "Lomonosovian" stanza); the meter (iambic tetrameter); as well as the "narrowed" thematic diapason of this special type of political, panegyrical, presentation ode.[18]

Pumpianskii and Alekseeva draw our attention to the specific courtly function of the triumphal ode of this type as the primary factor in its ascendance in Russia.[19] This issue also returns us to the problem of the unified poetry book, and the fundamental tension (even potential contradiction) that exists between a "one-time" genre whose ostensible purpose was to be declaimed or presented on the occasion of a ceremonial event, on the one hand, and as a written text meant to be read and re-read in private, on the other (on the ode as an oratorical,

---

[18] Although Sumarokov's connections to the "German School of Reason" have not been systematically examined, that there were many such connections with it, and its main representatives — the Leipzig Deutsche Gesellschaft der freyen Künste that J. Chr. Gottsched had founded in 1727 — is well established (see Gukovskii 1958; Lehman 1966a: 93–4; 1966b via index). Among other things, his *Sinav and Truvor* and a love ode were translated into German in the 1750's by members Gottsched's society, and these works were praised in Gottsched's journal *Das Neueste aus der anmuthigen Gelehrsamkeit* (Gukovskii 1958: 387–89 and passim); Sumarokov was chosen "honored member" of the Leipzig society in 1756 (Iazykov 1885: 445–46; Gukovskii 1958: 399–400). In general, Sumarokov's literary program was in many ways the same as that of Gottsched and the Germans, who also admired French Classicism.
For the most through and recent study of the Petersburg Germans' influence on the Russian ode (which appeared after this article was published) see Alekseeva 2005.

[19] There is also an obvious connection here between the new imported classicist ode and earlier baroque traditions in court poetry, which had become a regular feature of Russian ceremonials starting with Simeon Polotskii. The thematic and imagistic connections between syllabic panegyrical verse and the triumphal ode have often been noted (see the works cited in Sazonova 1987; see also Zhivov and Uspenskii 1987; L. I. Sazonova in Robinson, 1989:188–200; Baehr 1988, 1991). Polotskii's encyclopedic *Rifmologion* was a collection of poetry written for court ceremonials, and included five panegyric proto-odes called *knizhitsy* ("booklets" that had been presented to the tsar in manuscript copies) (Hippisley 1985: 10, 32–36; Vroon 1995: 301). As a collection of ceremonial poetry, then, the *Rifmologion* may be considered a precedent for later Russian collections of panegyric odes, including Sumarokov's, although it was never published, and hence mostly lost to the later tradition. On Polotskii's works as unified collections, see Darvin 1988: 27–31, and Vroon 1995–96. Darvin concludes that "On the whole, in the early stages of Russian poetry's development *cyclization occurred within the bounds of the book form. This tendency... was also clearly manifested in the subsequent period, in the eighteenth century*" (31; Darvin's italics). On the issue of performance, see note 20.

Chapter 11. Sumarokov and the Unified Poetry Book

performative genre and on its place in court ceremonial, see Tynianov 1985 and von Geldern 1991; on the ceremonials themselves see Baehr 1979; Wortman 1995, 87).[20] To some extent, these two aspects of the ode correspond to the "Pindaric" and "Horatian" varieties of ode, the first presented from a lofty, ornamental, "baroque," public, "loud" oratorical standpoint, and the latter assuming a more rational, calm, meditative, controlled, private, philosophizing stance. To edit a one-time, performative ode with an eye to its inclusion within a larger whole, as Sumarokov did with the *Triumphal Odes,* is to change its fundamental nature, and as Vroon has argued, to undermine "the generic integrity of the constituent texts" (Vroon 1995–96, 262).[21] The unified poetry book implicitly demands a reader rather than listener who is able to appreciate the complex relationship of each particular text within the larger whole (see Anderson's objections [1986, 49–55] to schemes for complex unity precisely from the point of view of the reader). In Sumarokov's case, even while the larger pathos of his career as a poet was to create a simple, clear, comprehensible poetic language (defining his "classicist" poetics in opposition to the more "baroque" Lomonosov) — and he may also have been to some extent trying to create a new, "rationalized" ("Horatian") variant of the ode (as Tynianov argued in his classic essay "Oda kak oratorskii zhanr"(1929) [1985, 69–74]) — on the other hand he was clearly offering his collection as the culmination of his career's work in the ode of the "Pindaric,"performative type. All but the first five odes included in the *Triumphal Odes* had originally been published separately as standard, free-standing presentation works, and despite all of the changes Sumarokov made in them, as Vroon has shown, the radical editing was not aimed at changing their basic stylistic nature (Vroon 1995–96, 230–35).[22]

---

20   While Tynianov and von Geldern have convincingly described the "performative" nature of the genre (see also Smoliarova 1999: 10–13), there is no evidence that Russian triumphal odes actually were declaimed (see Panov and Ranchin 1987: 176–177 on Lomonosov's odes). These were, however, clearly "presentation" (podnesennye) odes, published separately to commemorate particular events, and to be offered as ceremonial gifts. On the other hand, precedents for both declamation of court poetry and presentation verse (which do not necessarily coincide) go back at least to Simeon Polotskii (see Vroon 1995, esp. 301–302). The place of the triumphal ode in court ceremony awaits full study.
21   Of course, this does not mean that there may not be unified collections of the "Pindaric" type, or that all collections of "Horatian" odes will be unified.
22   The first five odes appeared first in *Ezhemesiachnyia sochineniia* and *Trudoliubivaia pchela.* We may offer as a way of overcoming this paradox the hypotheses that if Sumarokov was undermining the generic integrity of individual texts within the collection, the collection of odes itself as a whole may be seen as tending toward the creation of a single unified "super ode."

Although Sumarokov's odes adhere to the "Pindaric" mode stylistically (contrary to the view of those scholars who would assign them to the "middle style" in opposition to Lomonosov's high odic practice [e.g., Gukovskii 1927, 9–47; Tynianov 1985]), we should note that during the decades prior to the *Triumphal Odes* of 1774, Russian poets of the Sumarokov-Kheraskov coterie had been experimenting with many other types of non-performative odes which were created to be read in books and in the new literary journals by an emerging aristocratic rather than courtly reading public. These alternative odic genres, in which Sumarokov actively experimented, include Sapphic, Anacreontic, and more properly Horatian odes, as well as the related "stansy," and were clearly opposed to a greater or lesser to degree to the "Lomonosov ode." In terms of the poetry collection, Kheraskov's *Novyia ody* of 1762 is the most important Russian monument of this type (see Gukovskii 1927, 126; Vroon 1995–96, 261–2).

An important link between Kheraskov's new type of philosophical ode and Sumarokov's *Triumphal Odes* of 1774 as a unified collection were the odes of Jean-Baptiste Rousseau. While the lines of cultural influence are somewhat tangled, this is perhaps the closest thing to an actual precedent for Sumarokov's collection that there is, although we can only speak of it as such with qualifications. Rousseau played an important role in popularizing Boileau's type of "Pindaric" ode that the "Ode de la prize de Namur" represented, in part by his psalm paraphrases ("sacred odes"). Like Boileau, Rousseau took the side of the "ancients," and specifically against Antoine Houdar de la Motte and his more rationalized, Malherbean *Odes* of 1707.[23] At the same time, Rousseau used the term "ode" in a loose sense to embrace a variety of verse forms, among them the "middle style" Horatian ode, which became a popular alternative to the "high" ode in Russia.

---

[23] There were further editions of La Motte's *Odes* in 1709, 1711, and 1713–14 (in 2 vols.), each enlarged, plus a parallel French and Latin edition (*Catalogue général* 1939, LXXXVII: col. 747–772; Cioranescu 1965–66, II: 1018). The influence of La Motte's odes and the accompanying "Discours sur la poésie en général et l'ode en particulier" in Russia has not been studied; they were a strong influence on the Gottsched circle, which published a German version of the discourse and of his ode "L'Homme" in the 1728 *Oden Der Deutschen Gessellschafft in Leipzig* (Leipzig: Joh. Friedr. Gleditschens), a collection which Alekseeva cites as important for helping to establish the "Namur" type "Boileauesque" ode in Russia (1996b). Alekseeva's excellent article on the sources for Trediakovskii's "Rassuzhdenie o ode voobshche" (1996a), however, overlooks the connection with La Motte, whose work is suggested even by the title of Trediakovskii's discourse.

Chapter 11. Sumarokov and the Unified Poetry Book

Rousseau published his odes in three "books" of ten poems each (as parts of larger volumes that made up his Oeuvres[24]), a division which would seem to recall the Augustan poetry books; his broad definition of the ode was also probably an attempt to emulate Horace.[25] The first "book" contains psalm paraphrases; the second and third include a variety of stanza forms, meters, subjects and tonalities (Grubbs 1941, 236). The precise nature of Rousseau's use of classical sources and the poetry book has not been studied. He states in the preface that "Je me suis attaché sur toutes choses à éviter cette monotonie [of the psalm paraphrases] dans mes odes du second livre, que j'ai variées à l'exemple d'Horace, sur lequel j'ai tâché de me former, comme lui-même s'était formé sur les anciens lyriques" (Rousseau 1795, xxii). In other words, he understood the Horatian constructive principle as (if nothing more complex) that of the ancient commonplace notion of "variety" (Latin, "variatio" or "varietas"; Greek, "poikilia") (see Kroll 1924, chap. 10; Port 1925; and the use of the notion in Santirocco 1986, 7, 10, 11, 42, and passim). The notion of "variety" as a critical term to describe the poetry book derives from Ovid's *Epistulae ex Ponto*, but as Anderson notes (1986, 45–49), if we look to this idea for clues about the arrangement of specific collections we are in for "serious disappointment." It is clear, nevertheless, that Rousseau was openly claiming his connections both to the (to some extent unified) Augustan poetry book, as well as to the French ode from Malherbe (to whom an ode in the second book is addressed) to Boileau.

While only a few of Rousseau's *Odes* were of the high Pindaric type, the book nonetheless provided an example of a collection of odes that was explicitly meant as a collection. Furthermore, the parallels with Sumarokov's *Triumphal Odes*, are, at least at first glance, substantial. Sumarokov also included thirty poems in his collection, and, in it, similar to Rousseau's, the poems may be seen as falling into three chronological groups (Vroon 1995–96, 244). According to a biographer of the poet, Rousseau's three books of odes correspond chronologically to the three main stages of his life (odes of full maturity, middle and old age), although he makes no claim

---

[24] These included *Oeuvres* (1712), *Oeuvres diverses* (at least six editions between 1712 and 1719, plus 3-volume editions of 1731 and 1732); *Oeuvres choisies* (ten editions between 1714 and 1774) — at least thirty one editions in all through 1753 (*Catalogue général* 1939, CLVII: col. 747–772; Cioranescu 1965–66, II: 1018).

[25] Notably, later eighteenth and nineteenth century editors did not preserve Rousseau's order, including odes from his "poésies diverses" among the others to make up four books of uneven length (e.g., the *Oeuvres* of 1795, which contain four books of 15, 10, 9, and 10 odes; see also Grubbs 1941: 235 n. 28).

that this is reflected in the texts themselves (Grubbs 1941, 235). Vroon has demonstrated significant intrinsic thematic justification for Sumarokov's groupings, which cannot apparently be said for Rousseau; moreover, Sumarokov does not emphasize the larger symmetry of his collection and its antique or modern precedents by dividing it into three obvious and equal parts, which Rousseau does. (According to Vroon, Sumarokov's odes in *Torzhestvennye ody* fall into groups of 6, 14 and 10 [Vroon 1995/96, 244].) Sumarokov does not advertise any structural symmetry of his collection by dividing it into books or any other orderings (apart from simply numbering the poems).

Rousseau's connection to Sumarokov is strengthened by several other secondary factors. First, there is the fact that Sumarokov translated one of the most popular of Rousseau's odes (Grubbs 1941, 238), the "Ode à la Fortune," from the second book of his collection. Sumarokov and Lomonosov published parallel verse translations of Rousseau's ode, anonymously, in the January, 1760, issue of Kheraskov's *Poleznoe uveselenie;* Sumarokov's was in trochaic verse, and Lomonosov's in iambic (see also Rousseau n.d.). At least one scholar has suggested that this publication continued the old debate over the appropriate meter for Russian poetry (Morozov 1986, 532), although in their earlier competition of 1744 (*Tri ody parafrasticheskiia psalma 143;* Kunik, 1865, 2, 419–434), in which Sumarokov, Lomonosov and Trediakovskii each paraphrased Psalm 143, both Sumarokov and Lomonosov had used iambic, as opposed to Trediakovskii's trochaic, and this issue was hardly relevant any more in 1760. In the same issue which contained Sumarokov's and Lomonosov's translations, Kheraskov published the "stans" "Vse na svete sem prexodit" — a free version of Rousseau's "Ode sur un commencement d'anneé" [Levitsky 1995, 160; Lauer 1975, 139–42]. What was much more obviously important for the Russian poets were Rousseau's experiments with a new "middle style" ode, which Rousseau himself had described as "une autre espèce d'odes toute nouvelle parmi nous" (1795, xxii, referring to the works of the second book; on the function of the "stans" as a "reduced" or "non-canonical ode," see Lauer 1975, 25–26). Even more suggestive is that, as Darvin has shown, Kheraskov's 28-ode collection, the *Novyia ody* of 1762, was a consciously organized, unified poetry book (Darvin 1988, 34–41; see note 5 above).[26] However, there are no obvious

---

[26] On the basis of his analysis of Kheraskov's collection, Darvin over-generalizes that *all* Russian poetic collections of the eighteenth century "were characterized both by careful planning (obdumannost') in the ordering of individual works as well as by compositional balance (kompozitsionnaia stroinost')"(Darvin 1988: 41).

structural connections between Kheraskov's *Novyia ody* and Sumarokov's *Torzhestvennye ody* as unified poetry books (or between these collections and the ordering of Rousseau's *Odes*, which may simply have offered the precedent of a poetry book with its own unique organization). While future research may uncover further connections, what is clear at present is that these varied attempts to create unified poetry collections were remarkable experiments for their time — albeit ones that took over two hundred years to be acknowledged.

Works Cited

Alekseeva, N. Iu. 1996a. "'Rassuzhdenie o ode voobshche' V. K. Trediakovskogo." *XVIII vek*, sb. 20. Pp. 13–22.

Alekseeva, N. Iu. 1996b. "Podnosnye stikhi peterburgskikh nemtsev 1720–1730 gg." Lecture at the Conference "Berkovskie chteniia," Institute of Russian Literature, St. Petersburg, Dec. 18, 1996.

Anderson, William S. 1986. "The Theory and Practice of Poetic Arrangement from Vergil to Ovid." In Neil Fraistat, ed., *Poems in Their Place: The Intertextuality and Order of Poetic Collections*. Chapel Hill, NC: University of North Carolina Press. Pp. 44–65.

Baehr, Stephen L. 1979. "'Fortuna redux': The Iconography of Happiness in Eighteenth-Century Russian Courtly Spectacles." In A. G. Cross, ed. *Great Britain and Russia in the Eighteenth Century: Contacts and Comparisons*. Newtonville, MA: Oriental Research Partners. Pp. 109–122.

Baehr, Stephen L. 1988. "The 'Political Icon' in Seventeenth- and Eighteenth-Century Russia." *Russian Literature Triquarterly*, 21: 61–79.

Baehr, Stephen L. 1991. *The Paradise Myth in Eighteenth-Century Russia: Utopian Patterns in Early Secular Russian Literature and Culture*. Stanford: Stanford University Press.

Bengesco, Georges. 1882–1890. *Voltaire: Bibliographie de ses oeuvres*. 4 vols. Paris: É. Perrin.

Berdnikov, L. I. 1997. *Shchastlivyi feniks: o russkom sonete i knizhnoi kul'ture XVIII — nachala XIX v.* St. Petersburg: Akademicheskii proekt, 1997. [Contains his: *Stanovlenie soneta v russkoi poezii XVIII veka (1715–1770)*. Dissertatsiia. Moscow: Moskovskii oblastnoi pedagogoicheskii institut imeni N. K. Krupskoi, 1985.]

Berkov, P. N. 1935. "Rannie russkie perevodchiki Goratsiia (K 2000-letiiu so dnia rozhdeniia Goratsiia)." *Izv. AN SSSR, otd. obshch. nauk*, 10 (1935): 1039–56.

Berkov, P. N., ed. 1951. *Satiricheskie zhurnaly N. I. Novikova*. Moscow—Leningrad: AN SSSR.

Boileau [Nicolas Boileau Despréaux]. 1966. *Oeuvres complètes*. Ed. Françoise Escal. Paris: Gallimard.

Busch, Wolfgang. 1964. *Horaz in Russland: Studien und Materialien.* Forum Slavicorum, Bd. 2. München: Eidos Verlag.

Catalogue général = Catalogue général des livres imprimés de la Bibliothèque Nationale. 1897–1981. 231 vols. Paris: Impr. Nationale.

Cioranescu, Alexandre. 1965–66. *Bibliographie de la littérature française du dix-huitième siècle.* 3 vols. Paris: Éditions du Centre national de la recherche scientifique.

Classical World, 81: 5 (May-June 1988). Special issue devoted to Catullus and the problem of the arrangement of his poetry.

Cameron, Alan. 1968. "The First Edition of Ovid's *Amores*." *Classical Quarterly* 18 (1968): 320–333.

Charmand, Henri. 1898. "L'Invention de L' 'Ode' et Le Différend de Ronsard et Du Bellay (Contribution à l'histoire de la Pléiade)." *Revue d'Histoire littéraire de la France*, 6 (1898): 21–54.

Courtney, Edward. 1968. "The Structure of Propertius Book 1 and some Textual Consequences." *Phoenix*, 22 (1968): 250–58.

Darvin, M. N. 1988. *Russkii liricheskii tsikl: Problemy istorii i teorii.* Krasnoiarsk: Krasnoiarskii universitet.

Day, Archibald A. 1938. *The Origins of the Latin Love Elegy.* Oxford: Basil Blackwell.

Demerson, Geneviève. 1983. *Dorat et son temps: culture classique et présence au monde.* Clermont-Ferrand: Adosa.

Dettmer, Helena. 1988. "Design in the Catullan Corpus: A Preliminary Study." *Classical World*, 81: 5 (1988): 371–81.

Dettmer, Helena. 1983. *Horace: A Study in Structure.* Altertumswissenschaftliche Texte und Studien, Bd. 12. Hildesheim: Olms — Weidmann.

Efremov, P. A. 1867. *Materialy dlia istorii russkoi literatury.* St. Petersburg.

Fenoaltea, Doranne. 1990. *Du palais au jardin: L'architecture des Odes de Ronsard.* Études ronsardiennes, 3; Travaux d'humanisme et Renaissance, 241. Geneva: Droz.

Fenoaltea, Doranne and David Lee Rubin, eds. 1991. *The Ladder of High Designs: Structure and Interpretation of the French Lyric Sequence.* Charlottesville, VA: University Press of Virginia.

Fraistat, Neil. 1985. *The Poem and the Book: Interpreting Collections of Romantic Poetry.* Chapel Hill, NC: University of North Carolina Press.

Fraistat, Neil, ed. 1986. *Poems in Their Place: The Intertextuality and Order of Poetic Collections.* Chapel Hill, NC: University of North Carolina Press.

Fukui, Y. 1964. *Raffinement précieux dans la poésie française du XVIIe siècle.* Paris: A. G. Nizet.

Grasshoff, Helmut. 1973. *Russische Literatur in Deutschland im Zeitalter der Aufklärung: Der Propagierung russischer Literatur im 18. Jahrhundert durch deutsche Schriftsteller und Publizisten.* Berlin: Akademie-Verlag.

Grubbs, Henry A. 1941. *Jean-Baptiste Rousseau: His Life and Works.* Princeton: Princeton University Press.

Gukovskii, G. A. 1927. *Russksaia poeziia XVIII veka.* Leningrad: Academia; rpt. Slavische Propyläen, Bd. 136. München: Wilhelm Fink Verlag, 1971.

Gukovskii, G. A. 1929. "O russkom klassitsizme." *Poetika*, 5 (1929): 21–65.

Gukovskii, G. A. 1958. "Russkaia literaura v nemetskom zhurnale XVIII veka." *XVIII vek*, 3 (1958): 380–415.

Hippisley, Anthony. 1985. *The Poetic Style of Simeon Polotsky*. Birmingham Slavonic Monographs, no. 16. Birmingham: Dept. of Russian Language and Literature, University of Birmingham.

Iazykov, D. D. 1885. "Novye materialy dlia biografii A. P. Sumarokova." *Istoricheskii vestnik*, 5 (1885): 442–47.

Irigoin, Jean. 1952. *Histoire du texte de Pindar*. Paris: C. Klincksieck.

Istoriia russkoi literatury X–XVII vekov. 1980. Ed. D. S. Likhachev. Moscow: Prosveshchenie.

Istoriia russkoi perevodnoi literatury. Drevniaia rus'. XVIII vek. / Schöne Literatur in russischer Übersetzung: von den Anfängen bis zum 18. Jahrhundert. 1995–96. Ed. Iu. D. Levin. 2 vols. Köln: Böhlau / St. Petersburg: D. Bulanin.

King, Joy K. 1975–76. "Propertius' Programmatic Poetry and the Unity of the Monobiblos." *Classical Journal*, 71 (1975–76): 108–24.

Klein, Joachim. 1988. *Die Schäferdichtung des russischen Klassizismus*. Veröffentlichungen der Abteilung für Slavische Sprachen und Literaturen des Osteuropa-Instituts (Slavisches Seminar) an der Freien Universität Berlin, Bd. 67. Wiesbaden: O. Harrassowitz.

Klein, Joachim. 1995. "Reforma stikha Trediakovskogo v kul'turno-istoricheskom kontekste." *XVIII vek*, 19 (1999): 15–42.

Kroll, Wilhelm. 1924. *Studien zum Verständnis der römischen Literatur*. Stuttgart: J. B. Metzler.

Kroneberg, Bernhard. 1972. *Studien zur Geschichte der russischen klassizistischen Elegie*. Osteuropastudien der Hoschschulen des Landes Hessen Reihe 3: Frankfurter Abhandlungen zur Slavistik, Bd. 20. Wiesbaden: Steiner-Athenäum.

Kunik, A. 1865. *Sbornik materialov dlia istorii imperatorskoi Akademii nauk v XVIII veke*. 2 vols. St. Petersburg.

Lachèvre, Frédéric. 1901–1905. *Bibliographie des recueils collectifs de poésies publiés de 1597 à 1700*. 4 vols. Paris, H. Leclerc.

Lauer, Reinhard. 1975. *Gedichtform zwischen Schema und Verfall: Sonett, Rondeau, Madrigal, Ballade, Stanze und Triolett in der russischen Literatur des 18. Jahrhunderts*. München: Wilhelm Fink Verlag.

Leach, Eleanor W. 1978. "Vergil, Horace, Tibullus: Three Collections of Ten." *Ramus*, 7: 1 (1978): 79–105.

Leach, Eleanor W. 1980. "Poetics and Poetic Design in Tibullus' First Poetic Book." *Arethusa*, 13 (1980): 79–86.

Lehmann, Ulf. 1966a. "Der Gottschedkreis und die Moskauer und Petersburger Aufklärung," *Studien zur Geschichte der russischen Literatur der 18. Jahrhunderts*, ed. Helmut Grasshoff and Ulf Lehmann. Berlin: Akademie-Verlag. Pp. 86–95.

Lehmann, Ulf. 1966b. *Der Gottschedkreis und Russland: Deutsch-russische Literaturbeziehungen im Zeitalter der Aufklärung*. Berlin: Akademie-Verlag.

Lesky, Albin. 1963. *A History of Greek Literature.* Trans. James Willis and Cornelis de Heer. New York: Thomas Y. Crowell.

Levitsky, Alexander. 1981–85. "M. V. Lomonosov's Psalms of 1751 as an Encoded Syllogistic Medium (With Additional Comments on the Ordering of Psalms by Sumarokov and Derzhavin)." *Byzantine Studies/Etudes Byzantines,* 8, 11 & 12 (1981, 1985, 1985): 215–229.

Levitsky, Alexander. 1995. "Mikhail Matveevich Kheraskov." In *Early Modern Russian Writers, Late Seventeenth and Eighteenth Centuries,* ed. Marcus C. Levitt. *Dictionary of Literary Biography,* vol. 150. Detroit, Washington, D.C., London: Bruccoli Clark Layman, Gale Research, Inc. Pp. 156–166.

Levitt, Marcus. C. 1993. "Drama Sumarokova 'Pustynnik': k voprosu o zhanrovykh i ideinykh istochnikakh russkogo klassitsizma." XVIII vek, 18 (1993): 59–74. (= "Sumarokov's Drama 'The Hermit': On the Generic and Intellectual Sources of Russian Classicism" in this volume.)

Levitt, Marcus C. 1994a. "Sumarokov's Russianized 'Hamlet': Texts and Contexts," *The Slavic and East European Journal,* 38: 2 (Summer 1994): 319–341. (Also in this volume)

Levitt, Marcus C. 1994b. "K istorii teksta 'Dvukh epistol' A. P. Sumarokova. In Marginalii russkikh pisatelei XVII veka, ed. N. D. Kochetkova. Studiorum Slavicorum Monumenta, 6. St. Petersburg: Dmitrii Bulanin. Pp. 16–32. (= "Censorship and Provocation: The Publication History of Sumarokov's 'Two Epistles'" in this volume)

Levitt, Marcus C. 1995. "Sumarokov — chitatel' Peterburgskoi biblioteki Akademii nauk," XVIII vek, 19 (1995): 43–59. (= "Sumarokov's Reading at the Academy of Sciences Library" in this volume)

Levitt, Marcus C. 1997. "Paskvil', polemika, kritika: 'Pis'mo pisannoe ot priiatelia k priiateliu' (1750 g.) Trediakovskogo i problema sozdaniia russkoi literaturnoi kritiki." XVIII vek, 21 (1997): 62–72. (= "Slander, Polemic, Criticism: Trediakovskii's 'Letter... Written from a Friend to a Friend' of 1750 and the Problem of Creating Russian Literary Criticism" in this volume)

Littlewood, R. J. 1970. "The Symbolic Structure of Tibullus, Book I." *Latomus,* 29 (1970): 661–69.

Luck, Georg. 1959. *The Latin Love Elegy.* New York: Barnes and Noble.

Maddison, Carol. 1960. *Apollo and the Nine: A History of the Ode.* London: Routledge and Kegan Paul.

Magne, Émile. 1908. *Madame de la Suze (Henrietie de Coligny) et la société précieuse. Documents inédits.* Femmes galantes du XVIIe siècle. Paris, Société du Mercure de France.

Magne, Émile. 1929. *Bibliographie générale des ouvres de Nicolas Boileau-Despréaux et de Gilles et Jacques Boileau, suivie des luttes de Boileau, essai bibliographique et littéraire, documents inédits.* 2 vols. Paris, L. Giraud-Badin.

Malherbe. 1939. *Les poésies de M. de Malherbe.* Ed. Jaques Lavaud. Paris: E. Droz.

Maury, P. 1944. "Le secret de Virgile et l'architecture des Bucoliques." *Lettres d'Humanité,* 3 (Paris, 1944): 71–147.

Morozova, G. V. 1990. "Ody Goratsii v russkikh perelozheniiakh XVIII v. (Chast 1)." In *Zhanr, stil', metod: Sbornik nauchnykh trudov*. Alma-Ata. Pp. 56–58.

Omilianchuk, S. P. 1969. "Problemy tipologii sobranii sochinenii." *Kniga: Issledovaniia i materialy*, 18 (1969): 20–43.

Otis, T. Brooks. 1965. "Propertius' Single Book." *Harvard Studies in Classical Philology*, 70 (1965): 1–44.

Panov, S. I. and A. M. Ranchin. 1987. "Torzhestvennaia oda i pokhval'noe slovo Lomonosova: obshchee i osobennoe v poetike," *Lomonosov i russkaia literatura*, ed. A.S. Kurilov. Moscow: Nauka. Pp. 175–89.

Pekarskii, P. 1870–73. *Istoriia Akademii nauk v Peterburge*. 2 vols. St. Petersburg.

Pfeiffer, Rudolf. 1968. *History of Classical Scholarship from the Beginnings to the End of the Hellenistic Age*. Oxford: Clarendon Press.

Port, Wilhelm. 1926. "Die Anordnung in Gedichtbuchern augusteischer Zeit." *Philologus*, 81: 3 (1926): 280–308 and 81: 4 (1926): 427–468.

Potez, Henri. 1898. *L'Elégie en France avant le romantisme (de Parny à Lamartine)*. Paris, 1898; reprint Geneva: Slatkine Reprints, 1976.

Pumpianskii, L. V. 1935. "Ocherki po literature pervoi poloviny XVIII veka (Kantemir i ital'ianskaia kul'tura.—Lomonosov v 1742–43 gg.—Lomonosov i Malerb)." *XVIII vek*, [1] (1935): 83–132.

Pumpianskii, L. V. 1937. "Trediakovskii i nemetskaia shkola razuma." *Zapadnyi sbornik*, 1 (1937): 157–186.

Pumpianskii, L. V. 1983a. "Lomonosov i nemetskaia shkola razuma." *XVIII vek*, 14 (1983): 3–44.

Pumpianskii, L. V. 1983b. "K istorii russkogo klassitsizma (poetika Lomonosova)." *Kontekst 1982: Literaturno-poeticheskie issledovaniia*. Moscow. Pp. 303–331.

Putnam, M. C. J. 1980. "Propertius' Third Book: Patterns of Cohesion." *Arethusa*, 13:1 (1980): 97–114.

Robinson, A. N., ed. 1989. *Razvitie barokko i zarozhdenie klassitsizma v Rossii XVII — nachala XVIII v*. Moscow: Nauka.

Rosenthal, M. L. and Sally M. Gall. 1983. *The Modern Poetic Sequence: The Genius of Modern Poetry*. New York: Oxford University Press.

Rousseau, Jean Baptiste. [Zhan Batist Russo] *Oda na shchastie sochineniia gospodina Russo, perevedennaia g. Sumarokovym i g. Lomonosovym* [St. Petersburg]: n.d.

Rousseau, Jean Baptiste. 1795. *Oeuvres de Jean-Baptiste Rousseau*. Rev. ed. Vol. 1. Paris.

Rousseau, Jean Baptiste. 1774. *Perevody iz tvorenii Zan Batista Russo i g. Tomasa*. St. Petersburg: [tip. Akademiia nauk].

Santirocco, Matthew S. 1980. "Horace's *Odes* and the Ancient Poetry Book." *Artheusa*, 13:1 (1980): 43–57.

Santirocco, Matthew S. 1986. *Unity and Design in Horace's Odes*. Chapel Hill, NC: University of North Carolina Press.

Sazonova, L. I. 1987. "Ot russkogo panegirika XVII v. k ode M. V. Lomonosova." *Lomonosov i russkaia literatura*, ed. A.S. Kurilov. Moscow: Nauka. Pp. 103–126.

Schmitz, Thomas. 1993. *Pindar in der französischen Renaissance: Studien zu seiner Rezeption in Philologie, Dichtungstheorie und Dichtung*. Hypomenata: Untersuchungen zur Antike und zu ihrem Nachleben, Heft 101. Göttingen: Vandenhoeck & Ruprecht.

Segal, Charles P. 1968. "The Order of Catullus, Poems 2–11." *Latomus*, 27: 2 (April-June 1968): 305–321.

Skinner, Marilyn B. 1988. "Aesthetic Patterning in Catullus: Textual Structures, Systems of Imagery and Book Arrangements: Introduction." *Classical World*, 81: 5 (May-June 1988): 337–40.

Skutsch, Otto. 1963. "The Structure of the Propertian *Monobiblos*." *Classical Philology*, 58 (1963): 238–39.

Sloane, David. 1987. *Alexander Blok and the Dynamics of the Lyric Cycle*. Columbus, OH: Slavica.

Smoliarova, T. I. 1999. *Parizh 1928: Oda vozvrashchaetsia v teatr*. Chteniia po istorii i teorii kul'tury, vyp. 27. Moscow: Rossiiskii gosudarstvennyi gumanitarnyi universitet.

Stemplinger, Eduard. 1906. *Das fortleben der horazischen lyrik seit der renaissance*. Leipzig: B. G. Teubner.

Stemplinger, Eduard. 1921. *Horaz im Urteil der Jahrhunderte*. Leipzig: Dieterich.

Sumarokov, A. P. 1787. *Polnoe sobranie vsekh sochinenii, v stikhakh i proze*. Ed. N. I. Novikov. 10 vols. 2nd rev. ed. Moscow: Universitetskaia tipografiia.

Sumarokov, A. P. 1957. *Izbrannye proizvedeniia*. Ed. P.N. Berkov. Biblioteka poeta, Bolshaia seriia, 2nd ed. Leningrad, Sovetskii pisatel'.

Svodnyi katalog russkoi knigi XVIII veka, 1725–1800. 1962–67. 5 vols. Moscow: Kniga.

Tri ody parafrasticheskiia psalma 143 = [Sumarokov, Trediakovskii, Lomonosov] 1744. *Tri ody parafrasticheskiia psalma 143, sochinennyia chrez trekh stikhotvortsev, iz kotorykh kazhdyi odnu slozhil osoblivo*. St. Petersburg: Akademiia nauk, 1744; rpt. A. Kunik, *Sbornik materialov dlia istorii Imperatorskoi Akademii Nauk v XVIII veke*, vol. 2. St. Petersburg, 1865, pp. 419–434.

Tynianov, Iu. 1985. "Oda kak oratorskii zhanr." In *Arkhaisty i novatory*, 1929; rpt. Ann Arbor: Ardis, 1985. Pp. 48–86.

Van Sickle, John. 1978. *The Design of Virgil's Bucolics*. Rome: Edizioni Dell' Ateneo & Bizzarri.

Viëtor, Karl. 1961. *Geschichte der deutschen ode*. 1923; rpt. Hildesheim: Georg Olms, 1961.

von Geldern, James. 1991. "The Ode as a Performative Genre." *Slavic Review*, 50:4 (Winter 1991): 927–39.

Vroon, Ronald. 2000. "Aleksandr Sumarokov's *Elegii liubovnye* and the Development of Verse Narrative in the Eighteenth Century: Toward a History of the Russian Lyric Sequence." *Slavic Review*, 59: 3 (Fall 2000): 521–46.

Vroon, Ronald. 1995–96. "Aleksandr Sumarokov's *Ody torzhestvennye* (Toward a History of the Russian Lyric Sequence in the Eighteenth Century). *Zeitschrift fur Slavische Philogie*, 55: 2 (1995–96): 223–263.

Vroon, Ronald.. 1995. "Simeon Polotsky." In *Early Modern Russian Writers, Late Seventeenth and Eighteenth Centuries*, ed. Marcus C. Levitt. *Dictionary of Literary*

Biography, vol. 150. Detroit, Washington, D.C., London: Bruccoli Clark Layman, Gale Research, Inc. Pp. 291–307.

Wortman, Richard S. 1995. *Ceremonials of Power: Myth and Ceremony in Russian Monarchy*. Vol. 1: *From Peter the Great to the Death of Nicholas I*. Princeton: Princeton University Press.

Zhivov, V. M. and B. A, Uspenskii. 1987. "Tsar i Bog: Semioticheskie aspekty sakralizatsii monarkha v Rossii." In B. A. Uspenskii, ed., *Iazyki kul'tury i problemy perevodimosti*. Moscow: Nauka. Pp. 47–152.

Zhivov, V. M. 1990. *Kul'turnye konflikty v istorii russkogo literaturnogo iazyka XVIII — nachala XIX veka*. Moscow: Institut russkogo iazyka AN SSSR.

Zhivov, V. M. 1994. "Tserkoslavianskaia literaturnaia traditsiia v russkoi literature XVIII v. i retseptsiia spora 'drevnikh' i 'novykh'" In *Istoriia kul'tury i poetika*. Moscow: Nauka. Pp. 62–195.

Zhivov, V. M. 1996. *Iazyk i kul'tura v Rossii XVIII veka*. Moscow: Shkola "Iazyki russkoi kul'tury."

12

THE BARBARIANS AMONG US, OR SUMAROKOV'S VIEWS ON ORTHOGRAPHY

This paper is an attempt to characterize Alexander Sumarokov's views on orthography and to situate them in regard to contemporary practice (in connection with preparatory work to publish a new critical edition of the author). Establishing the new literary language in eighteenth-century Russia was a long and painful process, and the assertion of orthographic norms (especially spelling, but also grammatical endings, punctuation, etc.) was both a major concern and a hotly contested domain. An Academy of Sciences translator complained in 1773 that "great disagreements, uncertainties and difficulties [make] the spelling of almost every writer or translator in some way different from the rest."[1] Sumarokov's views on spelling and orthography are embedded in several essays that are far from systematic and straightforward. The most important for us are "To Typographical Typesetters" (K tipografskim naborshchikam), which appeared in *The Industrious Bee* (*Trudoliubivaia pchela*) in May, 1759, and two posthumously published articles, "On Spelling" (O pravopisanii) and "Notes on Spelling" (Primechaniia o pravopisanii) that appeared in the Novikov edition.[2] "To Typographical Typesetters" was one

---

[1] V. P. Svetov, *Opyt novogo rossiiskogo pravopisaniia* (St. Peterburg, 1773), 7.
[2] Among other relevant writings, see Sumarokov's other essays in *Trudoliubivaia pchela*, for instance "O kopiistakh," "K nesmyslennym rifmotvortsam," "K pod"iachemu, pistsu ili pisariu, to-est', k takomu cheloveku, kotoryi pishet, ne znaia togo, chto on pishet," "O istreblenii chuzhikh slov iz russkogo iazyka," "O korennykh slovakh russkogo iazyka" and "Istolkovanie lichnykh mestoimenii." The "Epistola o russkom iazyke" and other works in verse also contain relevant material. On the development of Russian orthography in the eighteenth century, and Sumarokov's position, see also V. M. Zhivov's fundamental study *Iazyk i kul'tura v Rossii XVIII veka* (Moscow: Iazyki russkoi kul'tury, 1996) (forthcoming English translation: Victor Zhivov, *Language and Culture in Eighteenth Century Russia* [Boston: Academic Studies Press, 2009]).

Chapter 12. The Barbarians Among Us, or Sumarokov's Views on Orthography

of Sumarokov's most famous public journalistic tirades, while "On Spelling," which we may date by internal evidence to the early 1770s,³ is Sumarokov's most thorough and systematic discussion of orthography.

The question of defining Sumarokov's ideas about orthography as a "system" turns out to be a very difficult one, insofar as a basic thrust of Sumarokov's position as a critic was *anti-systematic*. In stating his position in "To Typographical Typesetters" on masculine plural adjective endings — perhaps the most evident marker of his orthography — Sumarokov explains that

> я по единому только собственному моему произволению [т.е., произволу — М.Л.] ни каких себе правил не предписиваю, и не только другим но и самому себе в грамматике законодавцем быть не дерзаю, памятуя то, что Грамматика повинуется языку, а не язык Грамматике...⁴

(I do not prescribe any rules for myself [that derive] solely from my own arbitrary assertion, and I do not presume to be a lawgiver in grammar, either to others or even to myself, remembering that grammar is subservient to language and not language to grammar...)

---

3   The article discusses A. A. Barsov's *Azbuka tserkovnaia i grazhdanskaia* (Moscow, 1768), which Sumarokov might also have known from its inclusion in his *Kratkie pravila rossiiskoi grammatiki* (1771 or 1773). See V. P. Stepanov, "Barsov, Anton Alekseevich," in *Slovar' russkikh pisatelei XVIII veka*, vyp. 1 (Leningrad: Nauka, 1988), 66. Sumarokov also refers to the taking of Bender which occurred in September 1770. "On Spelling" also most probably preceded "Notes on Spelling," which took as its starting point a critique of Svetov's *Opyt novogo rossiiskogo pravopisaniia* of 1773, cited in note 1.
It is possible that Svetov's remark of 1773 in *Opyt novogo rossiiskogo pravopisaniia* (5–6) in which he urges an unnamed "velikii vitiia" to publish his "orthographic rules" refers not to G. V. Kozitskii but to Sumarokov and his "On Spelling." On the attribution to Kozitskii see M. I. Sukhomlinov, *Istoriia rossiiskoi akademii*, vyp. 4 (St. Petersburg, 1878), 308. Svetov writes that "O izriadstve ikh [the unpublished rules] chitatel' mozhet napered rassuzhdat' iz ezhenedel'nykh listov Vsiakiia Vsiachiny (Concerning their excellence the reader may judge beforehand from the weekly sheets of Vsiakaia Vsiachina)." As an insider, Svetov probably knew of Kozitskii's important (anonymous) role editing *Vsiakaia Vsiachina*, but his words may not necessarily refer to him. Kozitskii was a close literary associate of Sumarokov, to whom the latter entrusted the publishing of some of his works, and it seems possible that Svetov may be suggesting Sumarokov's influence on the journal's practices. Svetov's remark seems to be the only basis for the opinion that Kozitskii had composed orthographic rules. It is repeated by V. P. Stepanov, "Kozitskii, Grigorii Vasil'evich," in: *Slovar' russkikh pisatelei XVIII veka*, vyp. 2 (St. Petersburg: Nauka, 1999), 97.
4   *Trudoliubivaia pchela*, mai, 1759, 266 (further reference to this edition will be to "TP"); also in A. P. Sumarokov, *Polnoe sobranie vsekh sochinenii, v stikhakh i proze*, 10 vols, ed. N. I. Novikov, Moscow, 1781–82 (henceforth: "PSVS"), 6, 327. References to "On Spelling" and "Notes on Spelling" are to the second, 1787, edition. This reluctance to issue rules seems a likely reason why Sumarokov did not publish "On Spelling."

Sumarokov's starting position is that orthography (a subset of grammar) "is subservient to language," and in spurning the role of lawgiver-grammarian, Sumarokov speaks as a practitioner. The authority for his own prescriptions derives from his assumed superior understanding and feel for the language. His attitude toward orthography thus fits seamlessly into Amanda Ewington's pioneering study of Sumarokov's literary critical stance as "grounded in a specifically Voltairean conception of taste."[5] As she notes about attempts to codify Sumarokov's aesthetics, "the notion of a Sumarokovian 'aesthetics' falls apart on the very notion of system...Rather than an aesthetics, his literary position is best understood as an applied criticism."[6] A fundamental error, in Sumarokov's view, is to hold fast to one extreme position or another, to fall back on either "arbitrary assertion" or abstract logic. Like Voltaire, Sumarokov is opposed in principle to the systematizing linguistic rationalists—those whom Voltaire labeled *géomètres* (geometricians), and as Ewington notes he came to share with the French writer "a deep hostility to academic abstraction."[7]

As Victor Zhivov has written, "the most important difference of Sumarokov [from the "classicizing purism" of Trediakovskii and Lomonosov] is his skeptical attitude toward rules," although as he rightly notes, Sumarokov

---

[5] Amanda Ewington, "A Voltaire for Russia? Alexander Petrovich Sumarokov's Journey from Poet-Critic to Russian Philosophe" (Diss. University of Chicago, 2001), 54.

[6] Ewington, "A Voltaire for Russia?," 55–56. Ewington adds that the very notion of an "aesthetics" is "somewhat of an anachronism" in reference to Voltaire and Sumarokov.

[7] Ewington, "A Voltaire for Russia?," 62. "Linguistic rationalists" refers to the French Cartesian grammatical "Port-Royal" school of the seventeenth century (Antoine Arnauld, Bernhard Lamy, Claude Lancelot) and their later followers who believed that language (and grammar) follow the laws of universal reason. There is some indirect evidence that Sumarokov took Voltaire as a model or precedent for his orthographic position. In his "Letter...from a Friend to a Friend" of 1750 Trediakovskii charged Sumarokov with trying unjustifiably to play the role of Voltaire in regard to his orthographic innovations, without, in Trediakovskii's opinion, having the talent and authority to do so. See his "Pis'mo, v kotorom soderzhitsia rassuzhdenie o stikhotvorenii...ot priiatelia k priiateliu," in *Sbornik materialov dlia istorii Imperatorskoi Akademii Nauk v XVIII veke*, ed. A. Kunik, 2 vols. (St. Petersburg, 1865), 2, 435–500; the passage cited is on 82, and refers to Voltaire's well-known 1737 preface to *Le Henriade* which defended the author's spelling of "Français" instead of "François" on the grounds of pronunciation, and also in order to avoid confusion with the man's name (*Oeuvres complètes de Voltaire*, ed. Ulla Kölving et al. [Geneva, Banbury, Oxford, 1968–], 2, 323). Notably, the French Academy retained the older orthography through the end of the century. Trediakovskii's "Letter" has recently been reprinted in A. M. Ranchin and V. L. Korovin, eds., *Kritika XVIII veka*. Biblioteka russkli kritiki (Moscow: Olimp, AST, 2002), 29–109.

Chapter 12. The Barbarians Among Us, or Sumarokov's Views on Orthography

was far from rejecting grammar and grammatical rules per se.[8] Sumarokov acknowledges the existence of the rules of the language that stem from its nature, at the same time insisting on the necessity of exceptions to them. "Nature" here itself is a slippery concept, as it spans the ideal utopian truth of "la belle nature" and empirical linguistic reality. Other factors that inform Sumarokov's conception of the nature of the language include its "ancient character" (*drevnost'*), continuity with the language of "our ancestors" (its Slavonic roots), as well as, in some cases, general usage; although each of these categories — like the notion of "nature" itself — is problematic. One is forced time and again to consider the complex interactions of these factors as they refer to the particular case. "Taste" — the authority of the poet-practitioner — offers a way of mediating between these often competing factors.[9]

This mediating function of taste had both a philosophical and an aesthetic correlative. Writing of Trediakovskii's proposed orthographic reform, Sumarokov comments:

> Г. Тредьяковской в молодости своей, старался наше правописание испортити простонародным наречием, по которому он и свое правописание располагал: а в старости глубокою и еще учиненною самим собою глубочайшею Славенщизною[10]: тако пременяется молодых людей неверие в суеверие; но истинна ни какая крайности не причастна. Совершенство есть центр, а не крайность: такова Премудрость Божия: а человеческая тем более, колико ближе к сему подходить центру, котораго она ни когда не коснется; ибо совершенная премудрость принадлежит единому Богу. (PSVS, 10, 15)

> (In his youth Mr. Trediakovskii wanted to spoil our spelling by following the usage of the simple folk, while in his old age he turned to a most profound Slavonicizing that he devised by himself; thus the unbelief of the young changes into superstition; but the truth is never privy to extremes. Perfection is the center, not an extreme: such is Divine Wisdom, and all the more so as regards human [wisdom], which, however close it may get to that center, never reaches it, for perfect wisdom belongs to God alone.)

In terms of a working principle for orthographic usage, Sumarokov advocates a middle way, "moderate difficulty." Writing as a practitioner, he preserves for

---

[8] Zhivov, *Iazyk i kul'tura*, 350, 357.
[9] See Zhivov's discussion in *Iazyk i kul'tura*, 344–50.
[10] This is an ironic reference to Trediakovskii's well-known preface to his translation of Paul Talleman, *Ezda v ostrov liubvi* (St. Peterburg, 1730), in which he refers denigratingly to "glubokoslovnaia...slavenshchizna" (profound Slavonicizing), a rejection of the Slavonic linguistic heritage in favor of vernacular Russian letters.

himself the freedom of poetic license (*vol'nost'*) and defends linguistic variety (*variativnost'*) as basic to the expressiveness and beauty of the language:

> Мне думается, что в умеренной тягости языка больше найти можно достоинства, по тому что от того больше разности, а где больше разности, там больше приятности и красоты, ежели разность не теряет согласия. Трудность в языке к научению больше требует времени, но больше и принесет удовольствия. (TP, 268; PSVS, 6, 329)

> (I think that one may find more value in moderate linguistic difficulty because this leads to greater variety, and where there is greater variety, there is more that is pleasing and beautiful, if variety does not spoil harmony. Difficulty in language makes learning take more time, but it also results in more satisfaction.)

The often ambiguous criterion of "taste" — having to distinguish between pleasing variation and disharmony — goes hand in hand with Sumarokov's animus toward system. One of the main difficulties of making sense of Sumarokov's writings on orthography as a practical and theoretically coherent body of material is well illustrated by "To Typographical Typesetters." While this was an outspoken, public statement of Sumarokov's views, they are deeply embedded in what amounts to one continuous 1800-word, eleven-page paragraph whose heavily ironical discourse has the effect, and perhaps paradoxical intent, of frustrating linear logic, and thus illustrating Sumarokov's argument that grammar rules follow language. To cite one short example:

> Лутче ставить силу над словами чужестранными, в которых нам нет нужды, и которыя присвоены быть не могут, и для того их силою почтить, что они силою въехали в язык наш и которыя трудно выжить, потому что десять человек выталкивают, а многия их тысячи ввозят. (TP, 265; PSVS, 6, 327)

> (It's better to put stress marks [*stavit' silu*] on foreign words that we have no need of, and which cannot be assimilated, and to honor them with stress for the reason that they have forced themselves into our language under stress [*oni siloiu v"ekhali*], and are hard to get rid of [or: to survive] because ten people try to keep out what many thousands are bringing in.)

Writing like this turns the attempt to clarify Sumarokov's position into an exercise in close reading. Given the string of clauses without precise conjunctions, pinpointing changes in tone and inflection becomes crucial. It is common, as in this sentence, that the opening proposition — *Lutche stavit' silu nad slovami chuzhestrannymi* — seems clear and straightforward, but is then seriously undercut if not totally reversed by what follows.

Chapter 12. The Barbarians Among Us, or Sumarokov's Views on Orthography

Putting stress marks on foreign words that might at first be disregarded as unassimilatabile turns out to ease their ability to infiltrate and cause violence to the language. The switch in tone and sentiment is marked by a play on works — *sila* as referring to both accent marks and violence. What at first might seem a contradiction within the essay, insofar as the first pages offer a detailed rejection of the use of stress marks, becomes an exercise in irony.[11]

The fundamental linguistic problem that this passage describes — the intrusion and assimilation of foreign forms — also highlights Sumarokov's problematic role in trying to assert orthographic good taste. He positions himself as someone who would stem the tide of linguistic deterioration, as one of the few persons of taste striving against the "many thousands." This issue points not only to the inherent social elitism implied by the doctrine of "taste"[12] but to the broader structural problem inherent in the Russian linguistic situation. Ewington has identified the paradoxical nature of Sumarokov's adoption of Voltairean taste — something that "emerges as the crowning glory of highly evolved civilizations" — in the context of a fledgling modern Russian literature. Voltaire's doctrine of taste emerges as a defensive reaction to a perceived decline in already well established literary and cultural standards:

> Years after the break-up of classicism in France, Voltaire creates the notion of "classicism." He defines a new canon, discerns fundamental artistic principles, and then consciously perpetuates them in his own work. In the same way, the decline of good taste in France sparks his crusade to define, defend, and promote the "grand goût" of his predecessors.
> Sumarokov without question places himself among those preserving good taste far from the crowd. In his later years he begins to voice Voltaire's dire predictions of a disappearing age of perfection, but with an interesting twist: He posits Russia herself as a grand culture in decline.... His grief is compounded by a rather peculiar consequence of Russia's rapid assimilation of European culture: He defines himself as simultaneously guardian and founder of the Russian classical "tradition." He mourns the loss of a "tradition" initiated not by literary predecessors, but by two decades of his own unflagging labor.[13]

---

11 There are many places in Sumarokov's writings on orthography which may lead to similar confusion, for example, where he argues (facetiously) that all nouns ending in a soft sign should be feminine (TP, 268; PSVS, 6, 329) or where he seems to argue seriously that all literate people need to study grammar except poets (PSVS, 10, 20–21).

12 However, Sumarokov consistently criticizes the bad taste of poorly-educated nobles (e.g. PSVS, 9, 38). See further Ewington, "A Voltaire for Russia?," 97–98, and Zhivov, *Iazyk i kul'tura*, 357, who criticizes M. S. Grinberg and B. A. Uspenskii on this point.

13 Ewington, "A Voltaire for Russia?," 58 and 102–03.

The paradoxical nature of Sumarokov's situation is even more sharply highlighted in reference to Russia's chaotic orthographic situation, insofar as one can speak of "traditions" only as at best provisional and at worst as self-serving fictions, given the acknowledged lack of generally accepted usage. Sumarokov finds himself working practically in a vacuum:

> чем пособить, когда Россия ни какова не имеет собрания пекущагося о языке и словесных науках: да и в школах ни Российскому правописанию ни Грамматике Российской не учат. Ето удивительно, и достойно великаго примечания.
>
> Как учить людей Грамматике и Правописанию; ибо де о том исправно не писано; так на что же следовати Грамматике Г. Ломоносова? а Грамматика во всех народах есть во естестве: и всегда писатели весьма хорошия предшествовали Грамматике; ибо люди говорят и пишут не Грамматике следуя, но разуму основанному на естестве вещи: а Грамматика уставливается по народу и паче по авторам. Когда писал Гомер, тогда у Еллин еще не было написанной Грамматики, но сей великий Пиит и отец Пиитов Грамматику знал.
>
> Мы ни Грамматики не имеем, ни знания о Грамматике показаннаго естеством и употреблением, ни исправных авторов, а писателей, да и Пиитов излишно много: и еще больше худых переводчиков; так чево ожидати нашему прекрасному языку? (PSVS, 10, 37)

(what can alleviate [the situation], when Russia has no assembly concerning itself with language and the verbal arts; and when even in schools they do not teach either Russian spelling or even Russian grammar. This is surprising, and worthy of serious attention.

How can we teach people grammar and spelling; as people say, no one has written about this correctly; so why then should we follow Mr. Lomonosov's Grammar? But in all peoples grammar exists in nature; and outstanding writers always preceded grammar; because people speak and write not according to grammar, but according to reason founded on the nature of the thing; and grammar is established on the basis of the language and even more so on the basis of authors. When Homer wrote, the Greeks still had no written grammar, but this great poet and father of poets knew grammar.

We have neither a grammar nor knowledge of grammar demonstrated on the basis of nature and usage, nor model [*ispravnye*] authors — although there are all too many writers and poets, and even more bad translators. So what can one expect will happen to our beautiful language?)

Sumarokov bemoans not only the lack of institutions that could establish and regulate orthographic norms — a language assembly, schools, the lack of authoritative dictionary and grammar textbook — but the structural

Chapter 12. The Barbarians Among Us, or Sumarokov's Views on Orthography

dilemma in which he finds himself. This passage well illustrates the conflict between "grammar" as an ideal existing in nature and its concrete (human, debased) incarnation (e.g., Mr. Lomonosov's Grammar), as well as the kind of "catch-22" situation Sumarokov found himself in as one who would correct this disparity. Grammar exists in nature, "in all peoples," it is inherent in them and in language as a natural phenomenon. This ideal of grammar is reflected or embodied in the language of great writers, and can only then be retrospectively codified into grammar-books and rules. Sumarokov's problem, then, is in trying simultaneously to position himself at two points in the process — as founder and guardian, great writer and as codifier. However we interpret the last paragraph, it is clear that Sumarokov both puts himself forward as candidate for the role of "model author" and to some extent also acknowledges his failure; his works may reflect grammar based on genuine "nature and usage" but this model has not been taken up in grammar books.

"So what can one expect will happen to our beautiful language?" This structural problem helps to explain one of the most striking aspects of Sumarokov's views on orthography in "On Spelling," his extreme pessimism. The argument about decline and "literary decadence," which, as Ewington shows, is inherent in the notion of good taste, approaches apocalyptic proportions in the context of Russia's dilemma. "On Spelling" might easily have been called "On Lousy Spelling" or "On Misspelling" ("O krivopisanii").[14] By the time Sumarokov wrote it, both Lomonosov and Trediakovskii were gone from the scene, and the article sums up Sumarokov's criticism of their orthographic views. Together with the lack of institutions that could establish and regulate orthographic norms, Sumarokov also inventories the many groups of people who contribute to the problem and their various motives. These include clerks (*pod"iachie*),[15] copyists; typesetters; "pedant-scholars" and "pseudo-scholars"; clergymen, Ukrainian scholastics and ignorant Russian sextons, as well as choristers (*pevchie*); fops (*petimetry*); noble and peasant women (*baby*); and, not least, the growing numbers of bad writers and translators he sees, who are perhaps his main concern.

---

14   The word *kriovopisanie* (*krivopis'*) as an antonymn to *pravopis'* is actually Trediakovskii's coinage, which he had used against Sumarokov twenty years earlier in his "Letter...from a Friend to a Friend" (see note 7). See the entry for "krivopis'" in the *Slovar' russkogo iazyka XVIII veka*, vyp. 1 (St. Petersburg: Nauka, 2000), 15.

15   These were a constant satirical target for Sumarokov, and the satirical link between linguistic and other kinds of corruption is strikingly clear when in "On Spelling" Sumarokov compares the attempt to champion correct orthographic practice (in regards to spelling the prefix "pri-") to seeking justice in a corrupt court (TP, 267–8; PSVS, 6, 329).

...так пишут они, чтобы им и стен стыдиться надлежало; а они просвещенных людей не стыдятся. Жаль того что со врак не положено пошлины а из стихотворцев не берут в рекруты; ибо полка два из них легко составить можно: а когда изо всех и сочинителей и переводчиков набирать рекрутов; так в один месяц целая великая армия на сражение будет готова; но ежели они такия будут солдаты, каковыя писатели так не прогоним ни Визиря, ни возмем Бендера. (PSVS, 10, 25)

(...the way they write should make the walls blush, but they aren't even ashamed before educated people. It's too bad that they don't slap a tax on this rubbish and draft poets as recruits; for it would be easy to form a regiment or two; and if you made soldiers out of all of the scribblers and translators, you could have a whole entire army ready for battle; but if they are equally good soldiers as they are writers, we'll never defeat the vizier, nor take Bender.)

Although "On Spelling" begins as a systematic discussion of the Russian alphabet in a basically neutral tone, on the order of Lomonosov's *Russian Grammar*, as it continues this heavily satirical tone and the theme of the destruction of the language — its *porcha, pogibel', padenie* — gets progressively stronger. This is illustrated by a variety of metaphors, some satirical, like the army of bad writers, and some suggesting the apocalyptic destruction of the language. For example, Sumarokov likens Trediakovskii's translation of Rollin's *Ancient History* which finished publication in 1762 (1749–62, 10 vols.) to the bubonic plague that hit Moscow in 1771:

...старанием несмысленных и безграмотных писцов, лишаемся мы ежедневно и оставших красот нашего языка: а со временем и всех лишимся. Еллин и Римлян лишили Варвары языков, а мы лишим себя нашего прекраснаго языка сами. Вот ожидаемая польза от умножения сочинений и переводов, которыми нас невежи обогащают! Вредно ободряти вралей похвалами, чтобы они больше врали; ибо де не писав худо, не льзя писать и хорошо; но враки должно ли издавать на свет? Древняя История неоцененнаго Роллина, в переводе нашем, подает читателю не знающему чужих языков некоторое ему познание, к малому просвещению, без других знаний, и ко прогнанию скуки: а язык наш как моровая заражает язва. (PSVS, 10, 23)

(...due to the efforts of senseless and illiterate scribblers, we are daily losing what remains of the beauty of the language, and in time it will all be lost entirely. The barbarians deprived the Greeks and Romans of their languages, while we ourselves are causing the loss of our beautiful language. This is the expected benefit of the increase of writings and translations with which ignoramuses enrich us! It is dangerous to encourage those who produce rubbish (*vralei*), because they will just produce more of it; they say that without writing badly

Chapter 12. The Barbarians Among Us, or Sumarokov's Views on Orthography

there won't be good writing; but must all this trash (*vraki*) be published for the world to see? The Ancient History by the invaluable Rollin in our translation may give the reader who doesn't know foreign languages some information, a small degree of enlightenment [if he has] no other knowledge, and a way to avoid boredom; but it infects our language like the bubonic plague!)

As Zhivov has noted, Sumarokov employs a well-known historical scheme here that attributes the destruction of the classical linguistic heritage to barbarian linguistic invasion that divides linguistic history into "ancient" and "modern." (Here Sumarokov is definitely on the side of the ancients.) It is perhaps purposeful irony on Sumarokov's part that he chooses a book entitled *Ancient History*, written by Rollin — one of those who articulated this scheme of linguistic rise and fall, and whom Sumarokov praises highly — to illustrate how defective translations may themselves become carriers of barbarian "infection" that dooms the ancient heritage. In the Russian case, as Sumarokov notes, the awful rub is that we ourselves are the barbarians — "we ourselves are causing the loss of our beautiful language."

The word "ancient" used by Sumarokov in this linguistic context is a central and multivalent term of approbation, as it conflates the problem of historical development (continuity and tradition) and the notion of "classic" in the meaning of an unchanging ideal. On the one hand, it suggests the ancient historical heritage of Greece and Rome, the heritage that was passed down to Russia as to a "grand culture." On the other hand, "ancient" suggests the existence of a timeless linguistic ideal, the "natural" character of the language that serves as a basic pillar of correct spelling and orthography. This dual notion of "ancient" allows the linguistic-historical scheme that equates the barbarians who destroyed Rome with the imagined hordes of bad poets and translators in Catherinean Russia.

Sumarokov feels that the current state of affairs teeters on the brink of irreparable disaster. He finds the orthographic practices of another recent work — Lomonosov's two-volume posthumous *Works* published in 1768 — even more shocking: not Lomonosov's works, but the way they are edited. Sumarokov mentions the posthumous edition several times as an especially disturbing sign of the times.

> Но бывало ли от начала мира, в каком нибудь народе, такое в писании скаредство, какова мы ныне дожили. *Возток, източник, превозходительство*! [i.e., spelling forms he abhors — M.L.] Конечно падение нашего языка скоро будет, когда такая нелепица могла быть восприята.

Part One. Sumarokov and the Literary Process of His Time

> О Ломоносов, Ломоносов, что бы ты сказал, когда бы ты по смерти своей сим кривописанием увидел напечатаны свои сочинении! [...] Были врали и при жизни твоей; но было их и мало, и были они поскромняе: а ныне они умножилися за грехи своих прародителей... (PSVS, 10, 25)

(But has there ever been such a lousy state of affairs [*skaredstvo*] since the beginning of time, among any other nation, like that which we have lived to see? *Возток, източник, превозходительство*! [i.e., spelling forms he abhors]. Of course the fall of our language is not far off when such idiocy can pass muster.

Oh, Lomonosov, Lomonosov, what would you have said if you had seen with what kind of distorted spelling (*krivopisanie*) your works would be published after your death! [...] There were writers of rubbish even in your lifetime, but they were few, and they were a bit more modest; but now they have proliferated, due to the sins of the forefathers...)

We will return to "the sins of the forefathers" below. The picture Sumarokov draws is of a serious qualitative change in literary affairs, which, as stated in "Notes on Spelling," presages a coming end:

> да не только портим, но уже и произношением и письмом и испортили: и есть ли не приложим мы труда; то нашему прекрасному языку будет погибель, а после он не воскреснет никогда. (PSVS, 10, 41)

(indeed we are not only spoiling [our language], but both in pronunciation and in writing have already spoiled it, and if we do not make an effort, then our beautiful language will perish, and never be resurrected thereafter.)

Sumarokov held that post-Lomonosovian Russian orthography had reached a point of no return. The root of the problem, it turns out, was the "reformed" alphabet itself, the very adoption of the civil script. Sumarokov discusses this historical moment in the context of his rejection of Trediakovskii's orthographic ideas (e.g, the *Conversation...About Orthography* [*Razgovor...ob orfografii*] of 1748), and offers his own perspective on the Petrine alphabet reform:

> ...А г. Тредьяковской извергал литеру З. и вводил S. оснуяся на Азбуке выданной при Государе Петре I, но сей Азбуке соображающейся с начертанием Латинских литер во Типографиях хотя и следовали; однако отошли от не свойственнаго нам Латинскаго начертания нечувствительно, и пристали ко своему, данному нам от Греков, откуда и Римляня свое начертание получали, и прилепилися мы к подлиннику, отстав от преображеннаго списка. От сего произошла у нас другая Азбука, которую мы гражданскою нарицаем печатью: а от того у нас две грамоты к великому и безполезному затруднению читателей...

Chapter 12. The Barbarians Among Us, or Sumarokov's Views on Orthography

> В Азбукѣ выданной при преображеніи Россіи, и можетъ быть напечатанной въ Амстердамѣ, научились мы писати тако: Пріимі sа Имѣніе sлата: вмѣсто приими за имѣніе злата. Всѣ начертанія сообразовались Латинской Азбукѣ: словомъ: украшеніемъ искали мы безобразія и самой нашему начертанію гнусности. Съ новою модою вошло было къ намъ и новомодное кривописаніе, какъ вошли въ нашъ языкъ чужія слова: а особливо Нѣмецкія и Французскія, и складъ ихъ: а то еще и по нынѣ не очистилось: а можетъ быть и еще лѣтъ двѣсти не очистится; ибо скаредныя стихи и гнусныя переводы оное вкореняютъ: а простый народъ почитаетъ то все закономъ, когда что хотя и къ безчестію автора напечатано. (PSVS, 10)

(Mr. Trediakovskii rejected the letter з and introduced s, basing this on the alphabet book [*azbuka* (= both "Alphabet" and "Primer")] published under Emperor Peter I, but although typographies followed this alphabet book, which was based on the contours of Latin letters, they imperceptibly departed from these uncharacteristic Latin contours and adhered to our own, given to us by the Greeks (and from which the Romans also received their contours), and we persisted with what was genuine, rejecting the transformed script. [It was] from this [version] that the other alphabet derived, which we call civil print, and because of this we now have two writing systems (*gramoty*), to the great and unnecessary nuisance of readers....

In the alphabet book issued during the reform of Russia, and perhaps printed in Amsterdam, we learned to write like this: 'Пріимі sа Имѣніе sлата' instead of 'приими за имѣніе злата'. The tracing [*nachertanie*] [of the letters] conformed to the Latin alphabet, [and] in a word, we sought beautification in deformity and in what is offensive to our writing. With the new fashions, new-fashioned misspelling [*krivopisanie*] was about to come to us, just as foreign words entered our language, especially German and French, and their forms [*sklad*]; and if [our language] hasn't been cleansed of them by now, it probably won't be purified for another 200 years, because miserable verses and abominable translations cause them to take root; and the simple folk take them as the law, when (even if to the infamy of the author) these things are printed.)

Sumarokov's criticism of Peter's alphabet reform should be placed in the context of the broader mid-century Russian critique of the Petrine transformation as excessive, uncivilized, too violent and extreme. Despite the fact that Sumarokov was a major figure in the cult of Peter the Great, he nevertheless may have had Peter in mind when he alluded to "the sins of the forefathers" in the passage cited earlier, a reference to those who took Latin letters too much as a model and sinned against the nature of the native tongue.[16] Latinizing

---

[16] On Sumarokov and the cult of Peter, see Nicholas Riasanovsky, *The Image of Peter the Great in Russian History and Thought*, Oxford, 1985; and Ewington, "A Voltaire

the alphabet, as it were, opened the door to foreign borrowings and new-fashioned pseudo-spelling.

According to Sumarokov, the Petrine alphabet diverged "imperceptibly" from its Latin model and adhered to the older Greek-inspired orthography which he describes as "our own," that which was "genuine" (*podlinnik*); it "rejected the transformed script" (*otstav ot preobrazhennogo spiska*). The ancient Greek heritage — which Sumarokov states also served as the basis for the Latin alphabet — remained palpable. Sumarokov not only makes a sharp differentiation here between, on the one hand, what is ancient / Slavonic / Greek-oriented / genuine / native, and on the other, what is new-fashioned / Latinate / artificially imported / alien / barbarian, but, even more radically, suggests that the reform was fundamentally flawed because it established two ways of writing, two alphabets (*dve gramoty* — "two literacies"), suggesting that there should be only one. To repeat:

> От сего [порочного преображеннаго списка — М.Л.] произошла у нас другая Азбука, которую мы гражданскою нарицаем печатью: а от того у нас две грамоты к великому и безполезному затруднению читателей. (PSVS, 10, 11)
>
> ([It was] from this [version] that the other alphabet derived, that which we call civil print, and because of this we now have two writing systems [*gramoty*], to the great and unnecessary nuisance of readers.)

Sumarokov does not take this point too much further, but it basically echoes the sentiment he expressed at the end of his "Epistle on the Russian Language" of 1747:

> Не мни что наш язык, не тот, что в книгах чтем,
> Которы мы с тобой, не Русскими зовем.
> Он тотже... (PSVS, 1, 333)
>
> (Don't imagine that our language is not the same as that which we read in books, / Those that you and I call "not Russian." / It's the same!...)

Just as Sumarokov objected to the idea that there could be such thing as an author's individual spelling system ("*my* spelling"), insofar as "spelling has to be for everyone (*obshchee*) and according to the nature of the matter" (PSVS, 10, 32), he also objected to the idea that one could speak of two

---

for Russia?," 183–201. In the development of his views on Peter, Ewington sees Sumarokov reacting against Voltaire.

Chapter 12. The Barbarians Among Us, or Sumarokov's Views on Orthography

separate literary languages. For these reasons he had a double objection to Svetov's terminology, both the notion of a "new" Russian spelling (*Opyt novogo rossiiskogo pravopisaniia* [Attempt at a New Russian Spelling]) and also his references to a "new" Russian language:[17]

> § 1. Новаго Правописания у Россиян никогда не было…
> §. 6. Странно ето титло нашему языку: Новороссийской язык, ибо мы тем же языком говорим, которым говорили и предки наши, и наваго Правописания почти нет. (PSVS, 10, 38 and 39)
>
> (§. 1. Russians never had [such a thing as] new spelling…
> §. 6. This title for our language, "the New Russian Language," is strange, because we speak the very same language that our ancestors spoke, and there is almost no [such thing as] new spelling.)

There are several interesting problems here, including the slippage between the spoken and written language, and the rhetorically uncomfortable "almost" that attempts to cover over the gap between Sumarokov's view of language as something "natural," static, and timeless, and the chaotic and ever-changing linguistic reality to which he himself amply testifies.

Sumarokov's objection to Western European usage (French and German, via Latin) that crept into Russia with the new-fashioned alphabet may also be correlated with his other major criticism of Petrine usage, associated for example with Prokopovich, that is, the clerical scholastic influence. This usage was tarnished by various kinds of impurity, especially the influence of Ukrainian (associated either with the provincial or low usage, and contrasted to the Muscovite norm) and scholarly pedantry. He identified several of these problems in Lomonosov, and offered as an alternative the writing of the new generation of "our sensible preachers (nashi razumnye Propovedniki)" like Platon (Levshin), who were native Russians and well educated in Latin grammar. By referring to his orthographic program as that of "our ancient Slavonic forefathers,"[18] Sumarokov seems to be suggesting continuity not with the historically ancient medieval Slavonic tradition, but with the immediate

---

[17] Svetov explained his terminology in "Nekotorye obshchie zamechaniia o iazyke rossiiskom," *Akademicheskie izvestiia*, chast' 3 (1779), 77. According to Sukhomlinov this was: 1) *slavianskii*, referring to the pre-literate oral language; 2) *slavianorusskii*, the language of church books and chronicles; and 3) *novorossiiskii*, the language spoken and written by contemporary educated Russians (*Istoriia akademii rossiiskoi*, 314).

[18] Cf. references to '*drevnie*', '*nashi praroditelei*', '*predki nashi Slaviania*': e.g., PSVS, 10: 7, 9, 39, 40.

pre-Petrine period, thus skipping over and rejecting the "hybridizing" linguistic stage of the Baroque.[19] In this context, "ancient" means "pre-Petrine." Russia of the 1770's, as Sumarokov lamented in his aside on Lomonosov, is reaping the sins of the grandparents' generation (that of the *praroditelei*). It was Peter's reform itself, it seems, that opened the gates to the barbarians.

Sumarokov's pessimism deepens in his later works, as various possible lines of defense against bad usage seem to collapse. Ewing has chronicled, for example, Sumarokov's growing negativity toward the Academy of Sciences, connected with his own frustrated efforts to become a member, and bolstered by Voltaire's anti-academic stance. In regard to the issue of usage as a criterion for grammatical and orthographic norms, Sumarokov's attitude also seems to become more skeptical, as the barbarian invasion of bad taste not only obscures the true nature of the language but may also do permanent damage to it, and at the same time undercut the very grounds for a critique based on taste. While the following might be taken as one more example of Sumarokov's rejection of consistency, or of the potentially contradictory nature of "taste" as a criterion, it may also suggest the more sinister process by which social evil perverts the "natural" ideal itself, reducing language to corruptible human conventions. After the rejection of grammatical lawgiving from "To Typographical Typesetters" cited earlier in this article, Sumarokov had defended his recommendation of masculine plural nominal adjective endings by referring to common usage ("I should declare to you why I use this ending for all adjectives. The reason is that everyone pronounces them this way" [TP, 266; PSVS, 6, 327]). Yet in "On Spelling" he more than once rejects this kind of argument, on the grounds that "it is not the numbers that decide, but the truth" (PSVS, 10, 7). The problem comes when bad practice becomes rooted in the "basis" or nature of the language. In speaking of the iotization of e he writes:

Чаятельно мне, что литеру Е во слиянную литеру наши предки, древния Славяня, претворили употреблением; но древнее употребление есть правило, хотя и не всегда: а здесь оно не опровергаемо; ибо оно вошло во

---

[19] On "hybrid Church Slavonic" see V. M. Zhivov, "Iazyk Feofana Prokopovicha i rol' gibridnykh variantov tserkoslavianskogo v istorii slavianskikh literaturnykh iazykov," *Sovetskoe slavianovedenie*, 3 (1985), 70–85. If pre-Petrine writers attempted to make Slavonic a modern literary vehicle by means of hybridizing (Russianizing Slavonic), the Petrine reform reversed the poles and, as Zhivov has shown in *Iazyk i kul'tura*, posed the problem as one of legitimizing the Slavonic heritage of the vernacular Russian literary tongue (Slavonicizing Russian).

Chapter 12. The Barbarians Among Us, or Sumarokov's Views on Orthography

основание языка, вкоренилося и утвердилося, и отменити того не удобно. (PSVS, 10, 8)

(I suppose that the letter E was turned into a combined letter by our forefathers, the ancient Slavs, through usage; ancient usage is a rule, although not absolute; but here it is incontrovertible, because it became part of the basis of the language; it became rooted and was established in it, and it is not practical to repeal this.)

In this case bad or unnatural usage was elevated to the norm — "became part of the basis of the language" — simply by repeated usage. Sumarokov even begrudgingly concedes that "age (drevnost')" renders even ugly expressions attractive," wondering "whether our descendants will employ these strange depictions [usages]. They will [lead] to the ruination of the language if illiterate copyists do not cease defacing paper" (PSVS, 10, 14). The issue of bad usage, its effects and the difficulty of eradicating it once established, is a constant concern. In some places Sumarokov speaks of usage so bad and contrary to the nature of the language that it cannot possibly hold, as people of the future (*potomki*) will abolish it (PSVS, 10, 6). On the other hand, he concedes "that we have sufficient number of examples that a clear corruption of the language can become rooted in it forever" (PSVS, 10, 24).

This is a problem not only caused by bad writers but by the general lack of discriminating readers, that is, the lack of those linguistic traditions in Russia that would give traction to a critique based on Voltairean taste. In the vacuum-wasteland of Russian letters, grammar itself as an eternal ideal seems doomed:

а Стихотворцев довольно, которыя не только правил онаго, но и Грамматики не знают; ибо колико автор ни несмыслен и колико сочинение ево ни глупо; но сыщутся и читатели и похвалители онаго, из людей которыя еще ево несмыслянняе; безумцы от начала мира не переводилися, и ни когда не переведутся. Да и болышия умы омраченныя невежеством ни истинны не достигают, ни вкуса не получают. Сверьх того по большей части вещи утверждаются большинством [sic] голосов: а невеж больше нежели просвещенных людей; так и ето тамо где много невежества помогает марать бумагу, и обезображая себя, обезображать бедных читателей, и приводить согражан ко скаредному вкусу. (PSVS, 10, 21)

(and there are many poets who not only do not know the rules, but not even grammar; for however inane [nesmyslen] an author and however stupid his writing, there will be found readers and admirers among those who are yet more empty-headed; there have been brainless people ever since the start of creation and they will never go away. And indeed even great minds that have been shrouded by ignorance cannot attain either the truth or [good] taste. Moreover, for the most part things are decided by majority vote; and there are more ignorant people than enlightened ones, so that the fact that there is much ignorance helps people to deface paper and, in disfiguring themselves, disfigure poor readers, and lead their fellow citizens to awful taste.)

While Sumarokov here generalizes the problem into one relevant to all humanity, the Russian problem is particularly acute, as the vital connection between *narod* as nation and as carrier of the "natural" language may be broken. Far from what was to be Karamzin's well-known position, formulated by Sumarokov as "without bad writing it's impossible to write well (ne pisav khudo, ne l'zia pisat' i khorosho)" (PSVS, 10, 23), Sumarokov holds that the deterioration of linguistic standards and literary taste precludes the development of good writers, even from "great minds."

Part Two

VISUALITY AND ORTHODOXY IN EIGHTEENTH-CENTURY RUSSIAN CULTURE

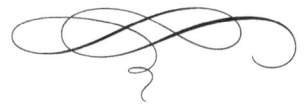

Preface

The title I have given this section may puzzle many readers, insofar as cultural historians have paid scant attention either to the importance of the visual in eighteenth-century Russia (in striking contrast, for example, to its role in Russian Modernism) or to the vital place of religion in that period, which is often written off as a time of secularization and of total state domination over the church. The articles in this section challenge both of these views and in some cases investigate their interconnection.

The Enlightenment privileged vision as the principle means of understanding the world, and this view played a uniquely important role in the development of early modern Russian culture.[1] We may connect this to the country's post-Petrine self-perception as "new" and newly European and to the early modern cultural-psychological imperative to be seen and acknowledged. Several of the articles here explore the Russian Orthodox underpinnings of eighteenth-century Russian "occularcentrism" (Martin Jay's term). The more general argument being put forward in this section is that eighteenth-century Russian culture was faith-based and far more permeated by religious traditions than is usually recognized. Despite the fact that Peter the Great clearly broke with the world of *Slavia Orthodoxa*, reorienting Russia toward Western culture and claiming state hegemony over the church, I agree with Harvey Goldblatt's characterization of the eighteenth century not as a wholesale rejection but as a "resystematization of the [medieval] Orthodox Slavic tradition." Victor Zhivov's pioneering work on the literary language has also shown that the mid-century "Slaveno-rossiiskii" cultural and linguistic synthesis heralded a more conscious attempt to integrate secular

---

[1] This is he starting point for my forthcoming monograph provisionally entitled *Making Russia Visible: The Visual Dominant in Eighteenth-Century Literature and Culture*.

and religious culture, which was reflected in the new literary institutions and production of the era—the period that gave birth to the "new" Russian literature. Denigrating or ignoring Russian eighteenth-century culture in general and its religious features in particular has been due largely to two major historiographical biases: the nineteenth-century "Slavophile" tradition that narrowly defined a certain type of Orthodox religiosity and denied the validity of what we may call "Enlightenment Orthodoxy," and to Soviet scholarship that rejected a priori the notion of religion as the basis of culture and focused on aspects of eighteenth-century Russia that could be seen as politically oppositionist.

In these essays I have tied the occularcentric argument not only to the ideology of the "Century of Light" (as argued, e.g., by Jean Starobinski, Martin Jay and others) as interpreted by the Russians but also to specific traditions of Russian Orthodoxy that I argue were still alive, if latent or reformulated, in eighteenth-century literary and cultural consciousness. On the one hand, I examine the mystical, ascetic view of vision (linked to the defense of icons and Hesychasm) as a basic element of Russian cultural memory, and specifically as an underlying visual paradigm for Lomonosov's panegyric odes. On the other hand, I argue for a more explicitly expressed and generally accepted eighteenth-century Russian belief in "physico-theology"— the view that the visual evidence of God's existence is manifested in the physical world. This was part of a broader early modern European trend that harmonized Christian theology (including Eastern Orthodox patristics) of a "moderate rationalist" type with Enlightenment views. In this section I have also included several articles in which the occularcentric argument is implicit but not emphasized, one on Catherine II's polemic with Chappe d'Auteroche over Russia's self-image as an Enlightened state, and one on Princess Urusova's *Polion* (itself a thoroughly occularcentric work) that interrogates its status as a piece of "women's writing."

13

THE RAPPROCHEMENT BETWEEN "SECULAR" AND "RELIGIOUS" IN MID TO LATE EIGHTEENTH-CENTURY RUSSIAN CULTURE

In 1761 Lomonosov made a special addition to his report on the astronomical observations made earlier that year when Venus crossed the sun's path (a moment of international scientific interest). In it he defended the study of astronomy, and of science itself, addressing one of the central issues in Enlightenment culture:

> Reason [truth] and faith are sisters, daughters of one all-supreme parent, and they can never come into conflict unless someone out of vanity and the desire to flaunt his cleverness tries to latch enmity onto them. Good and sensible people, however, must strive to see what means may be found to explain and avert any seeming strife between them, as the most wise pastor of our Orthodox Church [Basil the Great] taught.[1]

While it is true that Lomonosov was in the midst of a conflict with members of the Synod over issues of censorship,[2] his excursus on the concord of reason and faith, offered as appendix to a scientific paper, is a good starting point for describing the new cultural synthesis that emerged in the mid eighteenth century, and to argue that a basic reconceptualization concerning Russian culture in the period is in order. This article, taking its cue from Victor Zhivov's path-breaking *Iazyk i kultura v Rossii XVIII veka* (*Language*

---

1 M. V. Lomonosov, *Polnoe sobranie sochinenii*, 11 vols. (Moscow, Leningrad: Akademiia nauk SSSR, 1950–83), 4: 373. Compare 5: 618–19.
2 See B. E. Raikov, *Ocherki po istorii geliotsentricheskogo mirovozzreniia v Rossii: iz proshlogo russkogo estestvoznaniia*, 2nd ed. (Moscow: Akademiia nauk SSSR, 1947), chap. 11. Raikov argues that Lomonosov insists on the separate and independent status of scientific truth and does not accept the "reactionary" position of "a hypocritical reconciliation of science and religion" (311); to him the speech thus represents "a pamphlet against the clerics" rather than a straightforward statment of belief.

and Culture in Eighteenth Century Russia),³ suggests that there was a distinct rapprochement between ecclesiastical and secular culture during the fifty-year period from the mid 1740's through the 1790's, corresponding to the reigns of Elizabeth and Catherine II.

Before this argument can be made, there is a lot of historiographical debris that should probably be cleared away. Historians have generally denied the institutional and intellectual viability of the Russian Church in the eighteenth century, asserting that it was fully under the administrative thumb of the secular state (a view challenged most notably by Gregory Freeze⁴), and have never seriously considered the existence of what we may refer to as a Russian brand of "Enlightenment Orthodoxy."⁵ Slavophile-oriented

---

[3] See the forthcoming translation, *Language and Culture in Eighteenth Century Russia*, trans. Marcus C. Levitt (Boston: Academic Studies Press, 2009). *Iazyk i kultura* is a revision and expansion of Zhivov's *Kulturnye konflikty v istorii russkogo literaturnogo iazyka XVIII — nachala XIX veka* (Moscow: Institut russkogo iazyka, AN SSSR, 1990). For a discussion of *Kulturnye konflikty*, see my review in the *Study Group on Eighteenth-Century Russia Newsletter*, 19 (1991): 53–57.
This article was first presented as a conference paper at the Tenth International Congress of the Enlightenment, Dublin, July 28, 1999.

[4] Gregory Freeze, "Haidmaiden of the State? The Church in Imperial Russia Reconsidered, "*Journal of Ecclesiastical History* 36, no. 1 (January 1985): 82–102; see also his remarks, passim, in *The Russian Levites: Parish Clergy in the Eighteenth Century* (Cambridge: Harvard UP, 1977). For example: "the triumph of secular absolutism did not mean a sudden eclipse of Church authority and influence. To the contrary, precisely because secular absolutism was evolving, it still allowed for a dynamic change in Church-state relations" (15).

[5] This is true of the standard histories of the Russian Church, for example Georgii Florovskii's *Puti russkogo bogosloviia* (Paris: YMCA Press, 1937), chap. 4, and A. V. Kartashev, *Ocherki po istorii russkoi tserkvi* (Paris: YMCA Press, 1959), vol. 2, which take what we may consider a basically "slavophile" approach. I have also raised this issue in "Sumarokov's Drama 'The Hermit'," chap. 6 in this volume.
In recent years there have also been a series of excellent monographs on leading "Enlightened" clergymen in Russia: Stephen K. Batalden, *Catherine II's Greek Prelate: Eugenios Voulgaris in Russia, 1771–1806* (Boulder: East European Monographs; New York: Distributed by Columbia UP, 1982); K. A. Papmehl, *Metropolitan Platon of Moscow (Petr Levshin, 1737–1812): The Enlightened Prelate, Scholar and Educator* (Newtonville, Mass.: Oriental Research Partners, 1983); Gregory L. Bruess, *Religion, Identity and Empire: A Greek Archbishop in the Russia of Catherine the Great* (Boulder: East European Monographs; New York: Distributed by Columbia UP, 1997).
On eighteenth-century Orthodox writers, see also the recent reprint of Evgenii (Bolkhovitinov), Metropolitan of Kiev, *Slovar istoricheskii o byvshikh v Rossii pisateliakh dukhovnogo china greko-rossiiskoi tserkvi* [first published in 1818], 3rd rev. ed. (Moscow: Russkii dvor; Sviato-troitskaia Sergieva lavra, 1995), a work which, as

Chapter 13. The Rapprochement between "Secular" and "Religious"

historians who have chronicled the history of the church, as well as Soviet and Western scholars, have tended to write off official ecclesiastical culture of the period by referring to such generalizations as secularization, Westernization (that is, as a turning away from "genuine" orthodoxy), rationalism, and the state's allegedly complete hegemony over the church.[6]

A reevaluation of these ideas has important ramifications for the way we understand eighteenth-century Russian culture. It is central, for example, in evaluating the new type of "early modern" national consciousness that developed in Russia. Harvey Goldblatt has meditated on the problem in these terms:

> ...what remains unclear is whether the new type of state patriotism established by Peter I was actually in contradistinction to the older ideological patrimony of Orthodox Slavdom. A careful analysis of the literary works of important eighteenth-century authors such as Feofan Prokopovyč, Vasilij Tredjakovskij, and Mixail Lomonosov tends to suggest that the survival and resystematization of the Orthodox Slavic tradition played a central part in the 'new secular nationalism' of post-Petrine Russia.[7]

P. V. Kalitin writes in the foreword, testifies to "a flowering epoch of church culture, forgotten today" (11). Filaret (Gumilevskii) augmented Evgenii's dictionary with his *Obzor russkoi dukhovnoi literatury, 862–1863*. 3rd rev. ed. (1884; rpt. Oxford: Willem A. Meeuws, 1984), noting that to the 90 writers Evgenii discussed who were active between 1720–1826 he added 150 more (see 279) Curiously, he included among these such non-clerical writers as Mikhail Lomonosov, noting his spiritual odes and the theme of "the harmony of natural science and religion" in his prose works (citing the passage with which we began this article, 336). Among the many other lay writers discussed include Nikolai Popovskii, Grigorii Kozitskii, Vasilii Ruban, Vasilii Petrov, and Gavrill Derzhavin.

The work of Batalden and Breuss testifies to the active Orthodox Enlightenment in Greece, on which see also: Raphael Demos, "The Neo-Hellenic Enlightenment (1750–1821): A General Survey," *The Journal of the History of Ideas*, 19: 4 (October 1958): 523–41. Demos notes that (as in Russia), "The [Greek Orthodox] Church, at first tolerant and even friendly to such [Enlightenment] views, then neutral, became abruptly (circa 1790) and finally uncompromising in its hostility" (527).

6   For a discussion of the historiography see Freeze, "Handmaiden," and David M. Griffiths, "In Search of Enlightenment: Recent Soviet Interpretation of Eighteenth-Century Russian Intellectual History," *Canadian-American Slavic Studies* 16, nos. 3–4 (Fall-Winter 1982): 317–56; see 354–56 for the issue of religious enlightenment.

7   Harvey Goldblatt, "Orthodox Slavic Heritage and National Consciousness: Aspects of the East Slavic and South Slavic National Revivals," *Harvard Ukrainian Studies*, 10: 3–4 (December 1986): 347. Goldblatt draws special attention to the crucial role of the "language question," and suggests that linguistic self-definition in the Slavic world offers a paradigm for the development of national consciousness. His argument dovetails in many ways with V. M. Zhivov's views, discussed below.

Goldblatt goes as far as to assert "the existence of a premodern type of supranational spiritual solidarity...based on the common Orthodox Slavic heritage," which he describes as Petrine Russia's "Orthodox revival" (347 and 353). Goldblatt's argument suggests that a purely "Westernizing" perspective on Russian nationalism that ignores Russia's unique place in Slavic civilization may be seriously distorted.[8] Furthermore, the status of religious culture also has direct significance for the issue of defining (and defending the very existence of) a Russian Enlightenment.[9] Such redefinition may be seen as part of a broad attempt among scholars of modern European culture to pluralize *the* Enlightenment into a series of local Enlightenments.[10]

---

[8] For a brilliantly argued example of the first type of argument that sees Russia as one pole in an all-European spectrum, see Martin Malia, *Russia Under Western Eyes: From the Bronze Horseman to the Lenin Mausoleum* (Cambridge, MA: The Belnap Press of Harvard UP, 1999), chap. 1. A striking example of the importance of the Orthodox Slavic heritage for late eighteenth century Russian national identity and politics was Catherine's "Greek project," which Andrei Zorin argues played a key role in the development of subsequent Russian state ideology. See his *Kormia dvuglavogo orla...: Literatura i gosudarstvennaia ideologiia v Rossii v poslednei treti XVIII — pervoi treti XIX veka* (Moscow: Novoe literaturnoe obozrenie, 2001), chap. 1.

[9] For a useful discussion of this question, see Griffiths, "In Search of Enlightenment."

[10] In the introduction to *Barbarism and Religion* (Cambridge, UK: Cambridge UP, 1999), vol. 1, for example, J. G. A. Pocock makes the argument for a plurality of Enlightenments. He defines Enlightenment as characterized by two factors: "first, as the emergence of a system of states, founded in civil and commercial society and culture, which might enable Europe to escape from the wars of religion without falling under the hegemony of a single monarchy; second, as a series of programmes for reducing the power of either churches or congregations to disturb the peace of civil society by challenging its authority. Enlightenment in the latter sense was a programme in which ecclesiastics of many confessions might and did join..." (7). Russia, I would argue, fits this description.

Among the large number of works considering the religious roots of Enlightenment thought in various European religious traditions, see: Derek Beales, "Christian and *philosophes*: the case of the Austrian Enlightenment," in *History, Society, and the Churches: Essays in Honour of Owen Chadwick* (Cambridge, UK: Cambridge UP, 1985), 169–194; *The Margins of Orthodoxy: Heterodox Writing and Cultural Response, 1660–1750*, ed. Roger D. Lund (New York: Cambridge UP, 1995); Joseph P. Chinnici, *The English Catholic Enlightenment: John Lingard and the Cisalpine Movement, 1780–1850* (Shepherdstown, W. Va.: Patmos Press, 1980); S. J. Barnett, *Idol Temples and Crafty Priests: The Origins of Enlightenment Anticlericalism* (New York: St. Martin's, 1999); Bernard Plongeron, *Théologie et politique au siècle des lumières (1770–1820)* (Geneva: Droz, 1973); Monique Cottret, *Jansénismes et Lumières: pour un autre XVIIIe siècle* (Paris: Albin Michel, 1998); David Sorkin, *Moses Mendelssohn and the Religious Enlightenment* (Berkeley, CA: University of California Press, 1996) and *The*

Chapter 13. The Rapprochement between "Secular" and "Religious"

While it is possible to describe the new Russian cultural synthesis in traditional period terms, linking it to specific cultural, political, social and institutional changes, it is perhaps less problematic to define it as a regnant discourse. To use Keith Baker's formulation, discourses are "fields of social action symbolically constituted, social practices, 'language games'[,] each subject to constant elaboration and development through the activities of the individual agents whose purposes they define."[11] Discourse thus occupies a mediating position between cultural mythology (the symbolic plane) and the embodiment of these conceptions (to whatever degree) in concrete institutions, actions, political or social formations. While the discourse in question may never have achieved full and successful embodiment in institutional terms, its existence and influence as a dominating mode of thought seems unquestionable. To describe the cultural rapprochement in terms of discourse seems particularly pertinent insofar as the discourse under consideration is more than simply one of many competing philosophical and other discourses that may be said to constitute culture or history as a whole. The discourse in question was embodied in — and in a basic sense equivalent to — the *very vehicle of communication itself*— the new and self-consciously developing literary language. In the Petrine period there had been a sudden sharp linguistic differentiation between the secular and religious literary tongues, as Peter demanded the rejection of Slavonic in favor of a (as yet non-existent) literary language in Russian, for which he created a new "civil" script. Slavonic was thus narrowly re-defined as ecclesiastical and outdated, as indicated by its subsequent classification as "Old" and "Church" Slavonic.[12] Yet by the 1740's–90's the Slavonic linguistic heritage was re-

---

Berlin Haskalah and German Religious Thought: Orphans of Knowledge (Portland, OR: Vallentine Mitchell, 2000); Claudio Manzoni, *Il "cattolicesimo illuminato" in Italia tra cartesianismo, leibnizismo e newtonismo-lockismo nel primo Settecento (1700–1750): note di ricerca sulla recente storiografia* (Trieste: Università degli studi di Trieste, Facoltà di lettere, Dipartimento di filosofia: Edizioni LINT, 1992). For a general overview see James M. Byrne, *Religion and the Enlightenment: From Descartes to Kant* (Louisville, KY: Westminster John Knox Press, 1997); for an introduction to historiography of the question of national Enlightenments, see Dorinda Outram, *The Enlightenment* (New York: Cambridge UP, 1995), chap. 1. My thanks to Olga Tsapina for help with this list, and for her generous help and advice during my work on this article.

11 *Inventing the French Revolution: Essays on French Political Culture in the Eighteenth Century* (New York: Cambridge UP, 1990), 16. Pocock's works, including that cited above, are exemplary explorations of Enlightenment discourse.

12 The first appearance of the combination "tserkovnyi slavianskii" may be traced as far back as a letter by Gavriil Buzhinskii to Thomas Consett in 1726 (see *For God and*

accepted as part of a new synthetic discourse which came to be known as "Slaveno-rossiiskii" (Slaveno-Russian). As the label suggests, the fundamental conception was of a literary language that subsumes both Church Slavonic and vernacular elements into a single, unified tongue.[13]

My argument here rests upon—and elaborates—Victor Zhivov's analysis, which brilliantly demonstrates how the debates over the creation of a new literary language, which seemed so arcane and pedantic to later generations, reflected the fundamental cultural self-consciousness of the era.[14] Zhivov's study, in essence, the history of the rise and fall of the Slaveno-rossiiskii discourse, provides a powerful framework from which to examine the changing cultural status of religion. The new "Slaveno-rossiiskii synthesis" was to be, in Zhivov's formulation, "the single language for a single unified culture" (edinyi iazyk edinoi kulk'tury). As opposed to the sharp cultural and linguistic differentiation of the Petrine era (which reasserted itself again in the nineteenth century), Russian intellectuals of the period believed—following prevailing European linguistic theory—that a modern literary language had to be polyfunctional and to unite all sectors of society.[15] Trediakovskii imagined the new linguistic situation in this way:

Peter the Great: the Works of Thomas Consett, 1723–1729, ed. James Cracraft [Boulder: East European Monographs, 1982], 369, and V. M. Zhivov, *Iazyk i kultura v Rossii XVIII veka* [Moscow: Iazyki russkoi kultury, 1996], 125). On the usage of the terms "staroslavianskii" and "tserkovnoslavianskii," see also V. M. Zhivov, "Pervyi literaturnyi iazyk slavian," *Ricerche slavistiche*, 40–41 (1998–99): 99–136, and H. Keipert, "Tserkovno-slavjanskij: eine Sprachbezeichnung als Problem der Wortbildungslehre," in *Liki iazyka: K 45-letiiu nauchnoi deiatel'nosti E. A. Zemskoi* (Moscow: Nasledie, 1998), 143–52.

[13] I do not mean to suggest that this term was universally accepted, or used consistently; terminology of the epoch was notoriously loose. Neither was "slaveno-rossiiskii" a new coinage, but had been used before in other contexts, sometimes, for example, to describe the Russian recension of Slavonic, at others to mean something like Common or Proto-Slavic. See the discussion of the term in Myriam Lefloch, "'Sovereign of Many Tongues': The Russian Academy Dictionary (1789–1794) As A Socio-Historical Document" (Diss. University of Southern California, 2002), chap. 4.

[14] Zhivov's provides a corrective to the work of Iuri Lotman and Boris Uspenskii, which focused primarily on the Karamzinian linguistic reform of the early nineteenth century. See esp. their "Spory o iazyke v nachale XIX veka kak fakt russkoi kul'tury," *Uchenye zapiski Tartusskogo gos. Universiteta*, vyp. 358: *Trudy po russkoi i slavianskoi filologii*, XXXIV (Tartu, 1975): 168–322 and B. A. Uspenskii, *Iz istorii russkogo literaturnogo iazyka XVIII—nachala XIX veka: iazykovaia programma Karamzina i ee istoricheskie korni* (Moscow: Moskovskii universitet, 1985).

[15] See also V. M. Zhivov, "Svetskie i dukovnye literaturnyi iazyki v Rossii XVIII veka: vzaimodeistvie i vzaimootalkivanie," *Russica Romana*, 2 (1995): 64–81.

Chapter 13. The Rapprochement between "Secular" and "Religious"

...wherever anyone goes in a well-ordered city one may hear one's native language. If a great bell calls someone to church, he may hear prayers flowing there as well as the word of God preached in his native tongue. If, on business or for curiosity, he goes down to the palace of the supreme Autocrat, there everyone...speaks the native language and congratulates each other in it, expresses their good wishes, greets one another, and so on, conversing in the native tongue, sincerely or hypocritically as the case may be. But it is *this* language which he hears and wants to speak for his own self-respect...If he enters the courtroom to appear before a Judge, he will likewise defend himself, present evidence...or be charged...in his native tongue. Does he wish to go out on the street? There too he can speak his native language and understand... the speech he hears spoken. Let him go see a comedy during a holiday; at the theater too they are putting the show on in the native tongue...What else? [He can]...hire a worker — in his native tongue; greet his friends — in his native tongue; scream at his servant — in his native tongue; give his children a lesson — in his native tongue; utter affectionate words to his better half or speak to her in anger — [all] in his native tongue.[16]

A modern literary language could thus accommodate all spheres of activity, from the palace, to the street, to the law courts — and to the church. This was not merely a new literary language to replace the old but a fundamentally altered socio-linguistic model. The situation Trediakovskii envisages bridges the gap not only between traditionally separate arenas of social activity, secular, civil and religious, but also overcomes traditional diglossia and the very separation of written (literary) and spoken linguistic spheres. The spoken language — a new, informed, educated discourse — establishes the norm, as was accepted in mainstream French linguistic theory (to write as one speaks). However immediately impractical this may have been in Russia at the time of Trediakovskii's writing (1745), his scenario pointed the way towards accepting a modern, polyfunctional literary discourse which would close the gap between secular and religious culture.[17]

This discourse of synthesis both continued and to some extent reversed the Petrine position. On the one hand, the "concordist" discourse so

---

[16] *Slovo o bogatom, razlichnom, iskusnom i neskhotstvennom vitiistve* (St. Petersburg, 1745), 57–59; quoted in Zhivov, *Iazyk i kul'ture*, 275.

[17] This analysis is based on Zhivov. As he points out, despite the theoretical call to write as one speaks, the assimilation of the written Slavonic heritage was necessitated by the lack of a normative spoken tongue (177–83, 216–21). By the time of Karamzin's reform at the end of the century, such an educated spoken Russian — the language of the salons — had already begun to form, and could potentially serve as a starting point for literary usage.

eloquently expressed by Lomonosov above that saw no clash between reason and faith (a position elaborated by a host of Enlightenment thinkers of the late seventeenth and early eighteenth century — including Locke, Leibniz, and Wolff) informed Petrine ideology, as articulated, for example, by the works of Feofan Prokopovich. In the larger context of the Petrine reforms, however, the idea of concord could also play the somewhat paradoxical role of justifying a rationalist, anti-clerical position, which dictated Peter's assault on medieval, Muscovite culture.[18] Thus Peter rejected the type of linguistic synthesis Feofan had attempted — a "hybridization" of Church Slavonic, that is, an attempt to Russianize Slavonic[19] — in favor of the creation of a completely new and distinct vernacular literary language. As opposed to Feofan's attempt to incorporate vernacular elements into Slavonic, Slaveno-rossiiskii discourse reflected the attempt of the new, post-Petrine, generation to create a new literary discourse which could incorporate the Slavonic tradition into the fledgling vernacular. This discourse thus validated the Slavonic literary and religious heritage, bringing it into harmony with the secular. In the remainder of this article I will examine the Slaveno-rossiiskii synthesis by considering its literary production from the perspective of its two constituent elements, the secular and ecclesiastic, with some comments on their respective institutional contexts and orthographic differentiation; and in the last section consider the *Dictionary of the Russian Academy* (*Slovar' Akademii Rossiiskoi*) as a crowning monument to this unique discursive synthesis.

The efforts of the first generation of modern literary professionals, led by the trio of Trediakovskii, Lomonosov and Sumarokov, to create a "new literature" are relatively well known and need not be repeated

---

[18] Feofan Prokopovich's "tragi-comedy" *Vladimir* (1705) may be taken as an example of this basic tension. The Enlightened, concordist position that the Greek Philosopher propounds to Vladimir in the third act is juxtaposed to the ignorant, grotesque and superstitions of the pagan priests, who in the given context stand for the Muscovite-oriented Orthodox clergy. See Feofan Prokopovich, *Sochineniia*, ed. I. P. Eremin (Leningrad: AN SSSR, 1961), 181–87.
Francis Butler disputes the generally-held assumption that *Vladimir* was meant as an allegory for the Petrine reforms, although he confirms that the parallel between the two rulers became a durable part of the Petrine mythology. See his *Enlightener of Rus': The Image of Vladimir Sviatoslavich Across the Centuries* (Bloomington, IN: Slavica, 2002), chap. 6.

[19] V. M. Zhivov, "Iazyk Feofana Prokopovicha i rol' gibridnykh variantov tserkovno-slavianskogo v istorii slavianskikh literaturnykh iazykov," *Sovetskoe slavianovedenie*, 3 (1985): 70–85.

here.²⁰ Yet it should be emphasized that although commonly referred to as "Russian," the tradition they founded — and the discourse they developed and defended — was quite explicitly "Slaveno-rossiiskii," as exemplified in essays, treatises, manuals and many other works (see note 12; the terms "russkii," "ruskii," "ross(iis)kii," and "slaveno-rossiiskii" were often interchangeable). The fact that the second element of the formula was "rossiiskii" and not "russkii" is suggestive of the role that the literary language was to play as the language of an empire, as opposed to an ethnos.²¹

Assertions about the richness, abundance and ancient roots of the Slavonic literary tradition buttressed the hope of creating a fully functional, independent national literature, and even suggested the superiority of the Russian over the European position, insofar as Slavonic was said to be "of one nature" with Russian, as opposed to the greater distance between European vernacular languages and Latin. Lomonosov's well-known "Foreword on the Use of Church Books in the Russian Language" (Predislovie o pol'ze knig tserkovnykh v rossiiskom iazyke), which Ricchardo Picchio has characterized as "a manifesto of confessional [i.e., Orthodox] patriotism,"²² was just such an apologia for the Orthodox Slavonic element in Slaveno-rossiiskii. The entire literary production from Trediakovskii to Fonvizin, Derzhavin and Radishchev, and through the "archaists" of the early nineteenth century, that is, up until Karamzin's reform took hold, reflects this linguistic self-consciousness.

Lomonosov's essay on Venus — with which this article opened — indicates the direct connection in his mind between science and rhetoric, and also implies that the primary mission of literature was to glorify God's rational goodness, as embodied among other things in the enlightened well-ordered state. Significantly, Lomonosov explicitly grounds his "concordist" philosophical position not only upon contemporary science and

---

20 See for example G. A. Gukovskii, *Russkaia literatura XVIII veka* (Leningrad: Khudozhestvennaia literatura, 1937), chap. 2–4; *Istoriia russkoi literatury*, vol. 3, ed. G. A. Gukovskii and V. A. Desnitskii (Moscow: Akademiia nauk SSSR, 1941), part 3; Irina Reyfman, *Vasilii Trediakovsky: The Fool of the "New" Russian Literature* (Stanford, Calif.: Stanford UP, 1990); Viktor Zhivov, "Pervye russkie literaturnye biografii kak sotsial'noe iavlenie: Trediakovskii, Lomonosov, Sumarokov," *Novoe literaturnoe obozrenie* 25 (1997): 24–83.
21 On the distinction between *russkii* and *rossiiskii*, see M. N. Tikhomirov, "O proiskhozhdenii nazvaniia 'Rossiia,'" *Voprosy istorii*, 11 (1953): 93–96.
22 "'Predislovie o pol'ze knig tserkovnykh' M. V. Lomonosova kak manifest russkogo konfessional'nogo patriotisma," in *Sbornik statei k 70-letiiu prof. Iu. M. Lotmana* (Tartu, 1992), 142–52.

those Western thinkers mentioned above by whom the Petrine reform had been justified, but also upon Orthodox patristic thought.[23] The religious aspects of Russian Classicism have been almost completely ignored, and I am tempted to offer "Slaveno-rossiiskii literature" as a less problematic designation for this literary formation than "Russian Classicism," insofar as it signals not only the inclusion of the Baroque poetic (Slavonic linguistic) heritage, but also much of its religious ideals, which both reflected and fed into the new discourse.[24]

A tremendous amount of material could be cited here in support of this proposition. Here we may simply suggest several major areas of literary production that call for further investigation and reconceptualization. Russian dramaturgy, which developed out of school drama and the traditions established by Polotskii, in many cases exhibits Orthodox religious underpinnings.[25] Furthermore, secular writers produced a massive amount of religious poetry, which is hardly considered, or even acknowledged, in literary histories, and yet which played a primary role in the development

---

[23] On this issue see my "The Ode as Revelation: On the Orthodox Theological Context of Lomonosov's Odes," chap. 16 in this volume.

[24] Much of later Soviet scholarship on eighteenth-century Russian literature was taken up with (mostly inconclusive) debates over "period style" classifications such as "Baroque," "Classicism," and "Sentimentalism." See the debate in *Russkaia literatura* in the mid 1970's, for example, P. P. Okhrimenko, "Gde zhe konets ili nachalo (K voprosu o periodizatsii russkoi literatury)," *Russkaia literatura* 1 (1974): 94–99. Zhivov discusses the crucial place of the ode in legitimizing aspects of the Baroque, Slavonic linguistic heritage in *Iazyk i kul'tura*, chap. 2.

P. E. Bukharkin, in his recent monograph *Pravoslavnaia tserkov' i russkaia literatura v XVIII–XIX vekakh: Problemy kul'turnogo dialoga* (St. Petersburg: Izd. S.-Peterburgskogo universiteta, 1996), attempts to qualify traditional views (recently developed by V. A. Kotel'nikov) of the fundamental rift between Church and secular literature in the eighteenth century (50). Bukharkin concludes that there was no such basic break with the older Orthodox tradition, and that "Despite all perturbations, as before, at the basis of [eighteenth-century Russian] art lay Orthodox traditions" which "preserved the possibility of a fruitful dialogue between Church and literature" (80). Nevertheless, his analysis does not go very far beyond asserting the *possibility* of a fruitful dialogue and, it seems to me, remains hampered by an overall "slavophile" framework (discussed above). An earlier work which frames the dialogue as that between the modern secularized "Academy" and the traditional, monastic, manuscript culture of the "Church" is Hans Rothe, *Religion und Kultur in den Regionen des russischen Reiches im 18. Jahrhundert: erster Versuch einer Grundlegung* (Opladen: Westdeutscher Verlag, 1984).

[25] See my discussions in "Sumarokov's Drama 'The Hermit': On the Generic and Intellectual Sources of Russian Classicism" and "Sumarokov's Russianized 'Hamlet': Texts and Contexts," chap. 5 and 6 in this volume.

of modern Russian poetry and poetics. This includes the rich tradition of psalm paraphrases and spiritual odes, genres practiced by virtually every poet of any stature from Polotskii and Trediakovskii to Kheraskov and Derzhavin. Furthermore, the spiritual ode and psalm paraphrase constitute a crucial link to the far better studied secular, panegyric ode.[26] There exists an extensive corpus of explicitly religious literature by "secular" writers, including many longer works in prose and verse, but practically none of this material has been published since its original appearance, and has completely fallen out of the purview of scholars and the canon of "Russian literature."[27]

Slaveno-rossiiskii discourse was also taken up and developed by a new generation of clergymen who were transforming the face of the Orthodox Church, and advocating a new trend which may be described as Enlightened or Enlightenment Orthodoxy.[28] In institutional and sociological terms,

---

[26] Lomonosov's famous "Evening" and "Morning Meditations on God's Majesty..." and Derzhavin's "God" are notable exceptions to this rule of neglect, although these works are virtually always treated in isolation from an Orthodox or religious context. On this see chaps. 15 and 16 in this volume. On the tradition of eighteenth-century religious poetry, see Alexander Levitsky, "The Sacred Ode in Eighteenth Century Russian Literary Culture" (Diss., University of Michigan, 1977); his publication of Trediakovskii's *Psalter 1753*. Ed. Alexander Levitsky. Russische Psalmenübertragungen; Biblia Slavica, Ser. 3; Ostslavische Bibeln, Bd. 4b (Paderborn: Ferdinand Schoningh, 1989); and L. F. Lutsevich, *Psaltyr' v russkoi poezii* (St. Petersburg: D. Bulanin, 2002).

[27] Just to name a few of the longer works: Mikhail Kheraskov's poems *Pocherpnutye mysli iz Ekklesiasta* (an adaption from Voltaire, three editions 1765–86), *Uteshenie greshkykh* (1783 and 1800) and Christian verse epic *Vselennaia* (1790); the novelist Fedor Emin's *Put' k spaseniiu, ili Raznyia nabozhnyia razmyshleniia* (eight editions between 1780–1798); Andrei Bolotov's *Chuvstvovaniia khristianina, pri nachale i kontse kazhdogo dnia v nedele, otnosiashchiiasia k samomu sebe i k Bogu* (1781), which was one of the works confiscated in Catherine's raids of Moscow bookstores in 1787; the poet Vasilii Ruban's translation of St. John Damascene, *Kanon Paskhi prelozhennyi stikhami* (four editions from 1769–1821, the last by the Synod typography); and Semen Bobrov's monumental poem *Drevniaia noch' Vselennoi, ili stranstvuiushchyi slepets* (2 vols., 1807–1809).

[28] As noted earlier and in my articles cited in note 24, as of the time of writing this piece (1999) there had been almost no work done on Enlightenment Orthodoxy as an intellectual or theological trend. (Various aspects of the larger phenomenon of Orthodoxy and Enlightenment — especially the politics of religion — were the subject of a dual panel at the AAASS National Convention in Denver, November, 2000.) In recent years, the historians Gregory Freeze and Olga Tsapina have been challenging regnant clichés about the institutionalized church as passive "handmaiden of the state" and about its alleged uniformity and intellectual stagnation. See the works by Freeze cited above and Olga Tsapina, "Iz istorii obshchestvenno-politicheskoi mysli

just as a new generation was creating a modernized Russian literature, a new generation of leaders was changing the face of the Russian Orthodox Church. This new clerical cohort, whose representative figures I will take as Gedeon (Krinovskii), Gavriil (Petrov), Platon (Levshin) and Damaskin (D. E. Semenov-Rudnev), shared "a common 'enlightened' outlook" and were totally dedicated to the post-Petrine Orthodox Church[29]; according to Freeze (ibid) they established the basic career profile for high churchmen in imperial Russia. These men had grown up within the new, post-Petrine reformed church, and for them the new cultural situation was already a given. As with Lomonosov's cohort, they were moved by patriotic national and "confessional" goals, and strove to systematize and spread Enlightenment. This new generation of clergymen were almost all Russians and graduates of the Moscow Slaviano-Greko-Latino Academy, and Elizabeth and Catherine appointed them to replace the mostly ethnic Ukrainians who had come from the Kievan Mohyla Academy, and who had occupied the top positions since Peter's time.[30] In the words of Freeze,

---

Rossii epokhi Prosveshchenia: Protoierei P. A. Alekseev (1727–1801)" (Diss. Moscow State University, 1998) and her articles "Secularization and Opposition in Times of Catherine the Great," *Religion and Politics in Enlightenment Europe*, ed. James E. Bradley, Dale K. Van Kley (Notre Dame, IN: University of Notre Dame Press, 2001): 355–392; and "Pravoslavnoe Prosveshchenie — oksiumoron ili istoricheskaia real'nost'?" *Evropeiskoe prosveshchenie i tsivilizatisia Rossii*, ed. S. Ia. Karp and S. A. Mezin (Moscow: Nauka, 2004), 301–13.

Among other things, these and other scholars have begun to reconsider the political position of the Synod; the significance and effects of the nationalization of church property of 1764; the problem of the clergy's legal and social status; ecclesiastical versus secular censorship; and attitudes toward such sensitive issues as religious toleration (e.g., the position of the Old Believers); relating these issues both to Elizabeth's and Catherine's policies and to conflicts within the Church.

[29] Useful surveys of the life and works of Gedeon Krinovskii, Gavriil Petrov, and Platon Levshin, including lists of their works and of basic secondary material, may be found in: *Dictionary of Literary Biography, Volume 150: Early Modern Russian Writers, Late Seventeenth and Eighteenth Centuries*, ed. by Marcus C. Levitt. (Detroit, Washington, D.C., London: Bruccoli Clark Layman, Gale Research, Inc., 1995). See also Evgenii (Bolkhovitinov), *Slovar' istoricheskii*, and Filaret, *Obzor russkoi dukhovnoi literatury*.

[30] My argument here stresses the differences between these generations and cohorts, but we might also note the crucial role of the earlier generation of "Latinizing" churchmen both in laying the ideological groundwork for Enlightened Orthodoxy and in advancing poetry and rhetoric (two of the seven liberal arts) into the center of the new academic curriculum that became standard in Russia in the later seventeenth century. Both of these aspects unquestionably contributed in a major way to Slaveno-rossiiskii discourse and literary culture.

Chapter 13. The Rapprochement between "Secular" and "Religious"

"a new episcopal elite took shape — Russian in nationality, clerical in social origin, elite in its advanced theological training."[31] (Notably, the Moscow Academy, which was the city's only institution of higher learning before Moscow University was founded, graduated a stream of leading political, military, academic, and literary as well as ecclesiastic figures; illustrious graduates included the geographer Stepan Krasheninnikov, mathematician Leonid Magnitskii, professor of medicine Semen Zybelin, and the poets Kantemir, Trediakovskii, Lomonosov, Kostrov, Popovskii, and Vasilii Petrov. The cream of educated Russia, ecclesiastic and civil, thus shared a common educational background and literary culture.)

Gedeon (c. 1730–63), the Bishop of Pskov was the first to preach in Slaveno-rossiiskii; his sermons brought him great fame, especially after he was appointed court preacher by Elizabeth in 1753. Gedeon's sermons were also marked by his use of use classical rather than biblical sources. (Lavished by presents from the empress, Gedeon acquired the reputation of a court grandee, and reputedly owned shoes with diamond buckles worth 10,000 rubles!) Gavriil (1730–1801) and Platon (1737–1812) were his disciples, and carried on his tradition in preaching. Gavriil, Metropolitan of St. Petersburg and Novgorod, though an ascetic in private life, played a visible role as court figure, scholar and theologian, and in his writing and public persona asserted the compatibility of Orthodox and Enlightenment thought. He was an accomplished linguist who knew French and German as well as the classical languages, and worked both on the Slavonic text of the bible and on the academy dictionary. Catherine dedicated her translation of Marmontel's *Belisaire* to Gavriil, and he acted as the sole representative of the clergy to the Commission for New Law Code. Platon, who served as religious tutor to tsarevich Pavel Petrovich and who later became Metropolitan of Moscow, has been called the "leading representative" of "a spiritual or ecclesiastical branch of eighteenth-century Russian literature" which aimed "to bridge the gap between the ideas and fashions currently accepted by the educated segment of society, on the one hand, and strict adherence to the precepts of Russian Orthodox Christianity, on the other."[32] He was probably the most prolific and well-known cleric publishing and preaching in Slaveno-rossiiskii in the century. He produced a great number of sermons, catechisms, treatises, historical and other pedagogical works, and was a close associate of such figures as Potemkin, N. Panin, Sumarokov, Fonvizin, Novikov, Dashkova,

---

[31] Freeze, "Handmaiden," 96.
[32] K. A. Papmehl, "Platon," *Dictionary of Literary Biography*, 289.

and Derzhavin. (In *The Brothers Karamazov* Dostoevsky immortalized an anecdote about how during Diderot's visit to Russia Platon had bested him in debate; when Diderot mocked the idea of God's existence, Platon cut him short with the line from the psalms, "The fool hath said in his heart, 'There is no God.'"[33]) Damaskin (1737–1795), Bishop of the Nizhegorod Region, was another outstanding "enlightened cleric." He studied French, German, history, science and theology for six years in Göttingen before returning to become professor and prefect of the Moscow Slaviano-Greko-Latino Academy. He was a scholar and prolific translator and editor. Among his translations were Russian chronicles into German, Platon's catechism into Latin, and classical works from Latin and Greek into Slaveno-rossiiskii. His extensive work as editor not only included editions of Prokopovich and Platon but also of Lomonosov, whose works he published in an exemplary three volume edition (1778), including much new material. This generation of clerics was involved in the cultural and literary life of their day to an extent perhaps never seen before or since.

Platon and his cohort spread the faith using the new Slaveno-rossiiskii discourse. All wrote, preached and published in this language, and several owed their career advancement to their literary skill in it, no less than did Catherine's court poet Vasilii Patrov or Derzhavin. For example, Lomonosov's patron Ivan Shuvalov originally brought Gedeon to Elizabeth's attention for his electric sermons delivered in what were described as "pure Russian speech" (that is, in Slaveno-rossiiskii, which, as noted, he was the first to use for this purpose, abandoning Prokopovich's hybrid Slavonic). Gedeon, Petrov and Platon revived the Petrine tradition of the "live" sermon (that is, interpretive preaching instead of reading from scripture), a practice that had been introduced to Moscow and St. Petersburg from Kiev by Prokopovich and his cohort, but which had fallen into some decline in the intervening period. The 1740's and 50's witnessed a boom in the Slaveno-rossiiskii sermon, with its own themes and traditions. As in Peter's day, the sermon could serve as a tribune for official policy matters, and — as in the case of the new secular poetry and dramaturgy — helped contribute to a rudimentary public sphere. An important theme of this literature — as in secular writing — was the cult

---

[33] Part I, book 2, chap. 2. According to Fedor Karamazov, who expands upon the story for buffoonish effect, Diderot thereupon immediately declared his faith and requested baptism, and Princess Dashkova and Potemkin served as his godparents. For the historical source of the episode, see F. M. Dostoevsky, *Polnoe sobranie sochinenii*. 30 vols. (Leningrad: Nauka, 1972–1990), 15: 529–30.

Chapter 13. The Rapprochement between "Secular" and "Religious"

of Peter the Great, and of enlightened state rule.[34] The official sanction no doubt helped make the sermon the most widely published genre of religious literature in the century (not including service and prayer books).[35] Under Catherine the Great sermons in Slaveno-rossiiskii were collected, edited, published and sent out to all parish priests for obligatory use, thus further endorsing and spreading this language as the discourse of the Church. This, the *Collection of Sermons for All Sundays and Holidays (Sobranie pouchenii na vse voskresnye i prazdnichnye dni)* (3 volumes, Moscow: Synod, 1775), edited by Gavriil, established the "homiletic canon which continued to be in force through the first decades of the nineteenth century."[36] It included works of the leading Russian contemporary homilists (Gedeon, Gavriil, and Platon), translations of popular modern Greek Orthodox writers like Elias Miniates, as well as sermons by a variety of contemporary European writers, Catholic as well as Protestant, and not even exclusively clerics. Non-Orthodox contemporary writers included Bernard-Joseph Saurin (1706–61), Johann Lorenz von Mosheim (1693–1755) and Louis Bourdaloue (1632–1704), and some sermons were compiled from various sources, including Salomon Gessner (soon to be famous in Russia as the author of poetic idylls). Mosheim's *Heilege Reden* of 1765 served as a model for the collection.[37] It also included works by the Church Fathers, who were themselves also being actively translated into Slaveno-rossiiskii. The Priest Ioann Sidorovskii, who was a member of Dashkova's Russian Academy, was known for his translations of John Chrysostom's sermons (published in 2 volumes, 1787; second edition, 1791), which were later celebrated in his verse epitaph:

---

[34] E. V. Anisimov, *Rossiia v seredine XVIII veka: borba za nasledie Petra* (Moscow: Mysl, 1986), 46. As Anisimov notes, they had much in common as far as both content and language—from our perspective we may say that they shared the common Slaveno-rossiiskii discourse. Both odes and sermons also came to feature extravagant praise of Peter; see V. V. Pochetnaia, "Petrovskaia tema v oratorskoi proze nachala 1740-kh godov," *XVIII vek*, 9 (1974): 331–337.

[35] T. A. Afanas'eva, "Svetskaia kirillicheskaia kniga v Rossii v XVIII veke: Problemy izdaniia, repertuara, rasprostraneniia, chteniia" (Diss. Leningradskii Institut kul'tury im. N. K. Krupskoi, 1983), 119–23; Pochetnaia, "Petrovskaia tema"; Zhivov, "Svetskie i dukhovnye literaturnyi iazyki," 68.

[36] V. M. Zhivov, "Gavriil Petrov," *Dictionary of Literary Biography*, 276.

[37] Zhivov, "Gavriil Petrov," 277. On translations of non-Orthodox theology into Russian during this period, see Horst Rohling, "Observations on Religious Publishing in Eighteenth-Century Russia," *Russia and the World of the Eighteenth Century*, ed. R. P. Bartlett, A. G. Cross, Karen Rasmussen (Columbus, OH: Slavica Publishers, 1986), 91–111.

Течение Иоанн окончил Сидоровский
Кой в церкви расплодил язык славеноросский;
Чем древле Златоуст во Греции гремел,
Он сделал чтобы росс легко то разумел...[38]

(The course of Ioann Sidorovskii's [life] has come to an end; he made the Slavenosossiiskii language fruitful in the church; that which Chrysostom thundered in Greece of old he made clearly understood to Russians...)

Notably, during the period of the Slaveno-rossiiskii synthesis the sermon was accepted as part of the Classicist generic hierarchy,[39] and sermons continued to be recognized and valued as part of "high" literature in Russia though approximately the 1830's (by which point a new split had come to differentiate "Russian" and "Church Slavonic," secular and religious, culture and language). Other important religious works in Slaveno-rossiiskii included theological textbooks, catechisms, translations and treatises, and saint's lives. This period, which produced the modern standard Slavonic version of the Bible (the so called Elizabethan Bible, begun under Peter, whose second edition of 1756 is still the basic text in use), also saw the first impulse to translate the Bible into the vulgar tongue, an undertaking that was not completed for more than another century.[40]

---

[38] M. I. Sukhomlinov, *Istoriia rossiiskoi Akademii*, 8 vols. (St. Petersburg: Akademiia nauk, 1875), 1: 273; quoted in Zhivov, *Iazyk i kul'tura*, 401. Zhivov suggests that there was a confusion between Sidorovskii's translations of Zlatoust and those of Priest Ivan Ivanov (401).

[39] In the first draft of his "Epistle on the Russian Language," Sumarokov included a section on Church oratory; for a discussion of why he did not include the passage in the published version, see my "Censorship and Provocation: The Publication History of Sumarokov's 'Two Epistles,'" chap. 3 in this volume.
At the time when the epistle was written, sermons were not yet being composed in Slaveno-rossiiskii (the passage in question refers to Prokopovich, whom Sumarokov ranks with Bourdaloue and Mosheim despite the "impurity" of his language, that is, his use of hybridized Slavonic). Sumarokov later wrote an approving literary analysis of Slaveno-rossiiskii sermons ("O Rossiiskom Dukhovnom Krasnorechii," *Polnoe sobranie vsekh sochinenii*, 10 vols. [Moscow: N. Novikov, 1781–1782], 6: 293–302). In his *Rhetoric* (*Kratkoe rukovodstvo k krasnorechiiu*, 1748), Lomonosov also included numerous examples of not only classical but Christian orators (Orthodox and non-Orthodox, patristic and modern).

[40] According to the Czech scholar Josef Dobrovský who visited Russia in the 1790s, P. A. Alekseev told him that Trediakovskii had proposed translating the Bible "into vulgar Russian" (*vulgaris russicae*), but that this idea was rejected, as was the Petersburg publisher Veitbekht's proposal to publish the Slavonic Bible in civil script. See Josef

Chapter 13. The Rapprochement between "Secular" and "Religious"

The rapprochement described here may also be traced orthographically, that is, by noting the instances when works of a religious nature appeared in civil script, and when works of non-religious content were published in *kirillitsa* ("church script"). Over the course of the century, the church's presses published approximately 1.5% of the titles that appeared in civic type.[41] Only seven of these came out between 1725 and 1755,[42] and these were of a utilitarian character (descriptions of court ceremonies and publications of government regulations); the great majority of the rest appeared either in 1765, when a series of service books (*sluzhby*) were issued,[43] or during the

---

Dobrovský, *Korrespondence Josefa Dobrovského*, ed. Adolf Patera, 2 vols. (Prague: Ceske akademie Cisare Frantiska Josefa pro Vedy, slovesnost a umeni, 1895–1913), 1: 274, and G. N. Moiseeva and M. N. Krbets, *Iozef Dobrovskii i Rossiia: pamiatniki russkoi kultury XI–XVIII vekov v izuchenii cheshskogo slavista* (Leningrad: Nauka, 1990), 222. It seems possible that the reference to Trediakovskii's proposal had to do with his Psalter, which he proved unable to publish.

Pskov Archbishop Mefodii Smirnov's 1794 translation and commentary of Paul's Letter to the Romans formed the basis for the well-known project to translate the entire Bible taken up by the Bible Society in the first quarter of the nineteenth century, that was only completed in the 1860's and 70's (*Polnyi pravoslavnyi bogoslovskii entsiklopedicheskii slovar*. 2 vols. [1913; rpt. Moscow: Vozrozhdenie, 1992], 1: 328). The 1815 edition of Smirnov's translation was published in both civic and church scripts (Evgenii, *Slovar' istoricheskii*, 220). For a general history of Bible translations in Russia, see I. A. Chistovich, *Istoriia pervoda Biblii na russkii iazyk* (St. Petersburg, 1899) and M. I. Rizhskii, *Istoriia perevodov biblii v Rossii* (Novosibirsk: Nauka, 1978).

41 A calculation based on the *Svodnyi katalog russkoi knigi grazhdanskoi pechati vosemnadtsatogo veka 1725–1800*, 5 vols. (Moscow: Gos. biblioteki SSSR imeni V. I. Lenina, 1963–67). I did not include lists of publications (*reestry*) in this calculation.

42 Gary Marker, *Publishing, Printing, and the Origins of Intellectual Life in Russia, 1700–1800* (Princeton, N.J.: Princeton UP, 1985), 63. In 1764, the Synod opened a press in St. Petersburg. See A. V. Gavrilov, *Ocherk istorii S. Peterburgskoi sinodal'noi tipografii*, vyp. 1, *1711–1839* (St. Petersburg, 1911), 191–392.

43 It is hard to judge the significance of this peculiar and brief publishing episode, arguably the most dramatic instance of the secular alphabet's inroads into the ecclesiastical domain. One possibility is the church's desire to reach a more secular audience, although as Gary Marker notes, the Slavonic script continued to be used for virtually all primary education and so remained generally comprehensible ("Faith and Secularity in Eighteenth-Century Literacy, 1700–1775," in *Christianity and the Eastern Slavs*, vol. 2: *Russian Culture in Modern Times*, ed. by Robert P. Hughes and Irina Paperno [Berkeley, Calif.: University of California Press, 1994], 3–24). Zhivov notes that the presumption of such a publication was "to reach those who could not read the old Cyrillic script. The intended addressee was thus a secularized section of society," but he adds that this intended addressee may not have existed in 1765 and may thus simply have been "constructed in a discursive practice by the very act of this publication" (personal correspondence). That is, such an intended audience was a cultural fiction, a function of an ideally polyfunctional

decade of the 1790's, when over half of the total number of Synod titles in civic type for the century were published. Of the works the Synod presses published in civil type, apart from a second edition of Catherine the Great's *Russian Primer* (*Rossiiskaia azbuka*) in 1783 and several historical works (e.g., chronicles, the *Russkaia pravda*, or A. I. Zhuravlev's historical polemic on the schism), almost all titles were on directly religious topics, though not necessarily by Orthodox writers, for example, translations of François Arnaud's "Lamentations de Jérémie," Hugh Blair's guide to rhetoric, and various religious tracts including ones by Lorenzo Scupoli (c. 1530–1610), Roberto Bellarmino (1542–1621), and Philippe Julius Liberkühn (1756–88).

Since the Petrine orthographic reform of 1708–10 the use of church script had been reserved to church typographies, but when the Synod typography was backed up with work, it did sometimes farm out the printing of books to private presses.[44] There were other occasional but rare instances when secular presses used church type; notably, the formal pretext for the arrest of Novikov in 1792 was that he was selling an Old Believer book in church script, *O stradaniakh otsev solovetskikh*, which he was also suspected of having published.[45] Orthographic overlap may be seen in terms of books' content, although judgments in this area depend on how we define the bounds between "secular" and "religious." The right to publish this or that work could spark controversy between secular and church publishers throughout the century,[46] and defining the lines may also remain a problem today. T. A. Afanas'eva's 1983 study of "secular books in church type" in the eighteenth century, for example, essentially defines "secular" relative to the

---

Slaveno-rossiiskii discourse. The publication of the *Sluzhby* might also have been prompted by the Synod Press' desire to broaden its commercial appeal. Notably, in 1764 Grigorii Teplov had proposed that the Synodal Typography be transformed into a "commercial establishment" under direct jurisdiction of "Her Majesty's Cabinet" that would print "useful books," i.e. textbooks and manuals, and although this proposal was rejected, in 1765 there was criticism that the presses' civic fonts were "lying purposelessly (lezhali bezplodno) in the Moscow Typography of the Holy Synod" (RGADA, fond 18, d. 174, l. 11). (My thanks to Olga Tsapina for this information.)

[44] Afanas'eva, "Svetskaia kirillicheskaia kniga," 97. Thus the Synod farmed out the publication of Prokopovich's sermons to the Kadetskii korpus press (4 vols., 1760–1777; the last volume was published by Novikov), although this was published in civic type (153).

[45] It was in fact published in Suprasl' by Old Believers; see A. V. Voznesenskii, *Starobriadcheskie izdaniia XVIII — nachala XIX veka: vvedenie v izuchenie* (St. Petersburg: S.-Peterburgskii universitet, 1996), 102.

[46] Marker, *Publishing, Printing*, chap. 2, passim.

Chapter 13. The Rapprochement between "Secular" and "Religious"

traditions of medieval Russian literacy, including in this category not only works of history, grammars and primers (*azbuki* and *bukvari*) and other works of pedagogical and didactic literature, but also "books for reading," which include saints lives, Prologues, Lives of the Fathers (*pateriki*), and other non-liturgical texts which, in more modern terms, we still might well consider "religious" (e.g, 138). By Afanas'eva's count, 20% of eighteenth-century books published in church type may be considered secular (193). What is especially significant here, particularly as we move from the sphere of high culture to Russia's broader experience of modernization, is that — as Gary Marker has shown — for most of the eighteenth century, despite sporadic efforts to the contrary (for example, Catherine's civil primer), the teaching of initial literacy (that is, primary education) continued to follow the pre-Petrine pattern, and remained in a traditional, religious cultural context (i.e., in Slavonic using kirillitsa). It was based on memorization of "sklady" (syllables) and of the catechism, breviary (*chasoslov*) and Psalter, all of which continued to be published primarily in church type.[47] This was one reason that despite the country's overall changeover to civic type, more than one quarter of Russian books in the eighteenth century were printed in church type[48]; somewhat less than a quarter of this figure represents books in church type published by Orthodox presses outside of Russia. The issue of orthographic changeover and of when and why which script was used is complex, and deserves further analysis. Pre-Petrine literary traditions continued to exist in parallel, in combination or in competition with the new.[49]

Throughout the second half of the century, secular presses published a great number of religious works in civic type (especially sermons, but also school texts, treatises and other works of theology, saints lives, etc.), thus like the Synod's publications in civic type, helping to spread the bounds of Slaveno-rossiisskii polyfunctional discourse. Clearly, publishing such

---

[47] See Marker, "Faith and Secularity," 9–18.
[48] Afanas'eva, "Svetskaia kirillicheskaia kniga," 192.
[49] In general, the use and function of many works in church script (apart from explicitly liturgical ones) is more complex than it might seem at first. For example, due to the fact that primary education began with memorizing church texts, the high, artificial, ecclesiastical language could be perceived as being closer to the "simple folk" than the new literary language based on the vulgar tongue, which was felt to be Europeanized and elitist. Hence the government published newspapers and regulations in both scripts, and put out some of its most urgent communications (e.g., announcements regarding the Pugachev rebellion or Napoleon's invasion) in church script, possibly also counting on local clergy to pass them on.

works in civil as well as church script were meant to help make them more accessible to the general reading public, even (or especially?) to those without formal training in the civil script.[50] Most or all sermon writers who published their works did so in dual editions, one in each type face. The well known sermonizers of the Petrine epoch, Feofan Prokopovich and Gavriil Buzhinskii, who had, like Gedeon, made their careers in the church via oratory, continued to be published in the later part of the century in civic script.[51] Over the course of the century, Afanas'eva counts approximately 550 sermon publications (*slova* and *panegiricheskie rechi*), of which 350 or almost 65% were in civic type (119). Often, individual works or entire collections of sermons could migrate between typefaces and between church and secular presses. Gedeon's *Sobranie raznykh pouchitel'nykh slov* (4 vols., 1755–59), for example, was first published by the Academy of Sciences typography in civil script but was subsequently put out by the Synod press in church type (1760, 1828, and 1855). Platon's twenty-volume collected sermons which came out over 43 years was published piecemeal by a variety of secular presses — the Moscow Senate Press, F. Gippius, Novikov, and Ridiger and Klavdiia; only volumes 13–15 and 19–20 were published by the Moscow Synod press, and also in civil type. As noted, Platon was one of the best known and most published Russian homilists in the eighteenth century, and left over 600 published sermons in Slaveno-rossiiskii (his famous sermon on the Chesme victory of 1770 was translated into several modern European languages — Princess Dashkova rendered it into French — and it was praised by Voltaire in the foreword to his *History of Russia Under Peter the Great*[52]). There were also a number of clergymen who published poetry and theatrical works in Slaveno-rossiiskii (e.g., by Amvrosii [Sereb-rennikov],[53] Antonii [Znamenskii], and Apollos [A. D. Baibakov], who among many other works wrote commentaries on the New Testament, "holy tragedies" and "holy stories" [*povesti*]).

---

[50] The issues raised in note 41 concerning the presumed audience for these works are also relevant here.

[51] T. A. Afanas'eva, "Svetskaia kirillicheskaia kniga," 124–27 and 153. See also the appropriate entries in the *Svodnyi katalog russkoi knigi*.

[52] *Sermon prêché...sur la tombe de Pierre le Grand...* (London, 1771); see also the letters from Voltaire to Catherine May 15, 1771 and Catherine to Voltaire, June 10/21, 1771 (*Voltaire and Catherine the Great: Selected Correspondence*, trans. and ed. A. Lentin [Cambridge, U.K.: Oriental Research Partners, 1974], 103 and 108).

[53] For example, his "Poema na den' vozshestviia na vserossiiskii prestol e. v. gosudaryni Ekateriny Alekseevny, samoderzhitsy vserossiiskiia, razgovor Marsa, Neptuna i Rossa predstavliaiushchaia..." (!) of 1772.

Chapter 13. The Rapprochement between "Secular" and "Religious"

The culmination and a purposeful attempt at canonizing Slaveno-rossiiskii discourse was the monumental *Dictionary of the Russian Academy* (*Slovar' Akademii Rossiiskoi*, henceforth: "SAR"), which came out in six volumes from 1789–94. The SAR was the product of the Russian Academy, an institution founded in 1783 under the presidency of Princess Dashkova, who simultaneously presided over the Academy of Sciences. Almost all of the major writers and literary figures of the later eighteenth century were members, save Nikolai Novikov; these included Mikhail Kheraskov, Gavriil Derzhavin, Denis Fonvizin, Aleksei Rzhevskii, Vasilii Petrov, Nikolai L'vov, Ivan Shuvalov, Iakov Kniazhnin, Ivan Bogdanovich, Adam Olsuf'ev, Ivan Khemnitser, Vasilii Kapnist, Dmitrii Khvostov, Nikolai Nikolev, Ivan Elagin, Mikhail Shcherbatov and Vasilii Tatishchev. Forty-seven of the Academy's sixty members took part in compiling the dictionary, and of these nineteen, or 41 percent, were churchmen (the French and German academies, in sharp contrast, excluded clergymen altogether, and the Académie française even forbade discussion of theological issues).[54] Gavriil, already Metropolitan of Novgorod and St. Petersburg, and de facto leader of the church was, after Dashkova, the Russian Academy's leading member. He occupied the president's chair during her absences, and took a central part in organizing, compiling and editing the SAR.

Lefloch has identified six main groups of source material that was incorporated into the dictionary: 1) earlier dictionaries (including P. A. Alekseev's *Tserkovnyi slovar'* of 1773, which was an important starting point for the SAR[55]); 2) the Elizabethan Bible and myriad church books — including liturgies, private and church prayer books, saints lives, as well as sermons, from John Chrysostom to Platon Levshin (i.e., Slavonic material from all periods as well as some in Slaveno-rossiiskii); 3) contemporary Russian poetry and prose (primarily the verse of Lomonosov[56] but also works by

---

[54] Lefloch, "Sovereign of Many Tongues," chap. 1. Among other things Lefloch analyzes the illustrative quotes used in the SAR's definitions which collectively illustrate and define the discourse it was promoting as normative.

[55] Alekseev published additional material for the dictionary in 1776 and a "continuation" in 1779; a second edition was published by the Academy of Sciences in 1794; see *Svodnyi katalog russkoi knigi grazhdanskoi pechati*, 1: 28. The *Tserkovnyi slovar'* was published in civil type, and included special entries "translating" letters and symbols of the church script. It had been sponsored by the Free Russian Assembly, in which Alekseev was the only member from the clergy. (Tsapina, *Iz istorii obshchestvenno-politicheskoi mysli*, 23; see also her "The Image of the Quaker and Critique of Enthusiasm in Early Modern Russia" *Russian History*, 24, no. 3 [Fall 1997], 263.)

[56] Sukhomlinov, *Istoriia rossiiskoi Akademii*, 8: 28; see the discussion in Lefloch, "'Sovereign of Many Tongues'," chap. 3.

Sumarokov, Kheraskov, Dashkova, Derzhavin, Catherine II, and others); 4) historical texts (including chronicles); 5) proverbs and other material of oral provenance; and 6) legal texts, both historical and modern.[57] According to her preliminary calculations, the ratio of religious to secular material used in the SAR is between about three or four to one.[58] The creation of the SAR thus dramatically asserted the unity of Orthodox and secular discourse, validating mainstream literary and linguistic practice, on the one hand, and on the other, demonstrating the institutional alliance of clerical and lay literary forces.[59]

Thus, as Zhivov has described the linguistic and cultural rapprochement under Catherine,

> The Petrine anti-clerical policy was replaced by the creation of a united state enlightenment culture, in which both religious and secular authors responded to [poluchaiut] the identical social demand... The empresses' confessor, the heir to the throne's tutor in religion, and the court preacher were just as much literary agents of the court as those who composed panegyric odes or

---

[57] A possible seventh category is classical texts in translation. This list of material is from a lecture she delivered at USC on Feb. 12, 1999; see also Lefloch, "'Sovereign of Many Tongues,'" which contains extensive appendices containing all of the SAR's ascertainable sources. Notably, almost all of the religious texts had to be "translated" from the Slavonic to the civil script.

[58] Ibid. This number may seem very high, but is perhaps less surprising if we keep in mind the approximately fifty-year existence of "secular" literature in comparison to the centuries'-long Slavonic tradition.

[59] This institutionalized literary unity lived on to some extent in Beseda liubitelei russkogo slova (1811–16), the organization of the "arkhaisty," which included bishops Evgenii and Amvrosii as "honored members" (Mark Altshuller, *Predtechi slavianofilstva v russkoi literature: obshchestvo "Beseda liubitelei russkogo slova"* [Ann Arbor: Ardis, 1984], 369), and in the Obshchestvoi liubitelei rossiiskoi slovesnosti, (founded 1811), whose members included Moscow Metropolitan Filaret.
The illustrious Filaret carried on Platon's legacy; he was a well known homilist, and leading member of the Bible Society. The Obshchestvo liubitelei rossiiskoi slovesnosti, which was later to organize the famous 1880 Pushkin Celebration, celebrated a memorial for Filaret upon his death in 1867 (Marcus C. Levitt, *Russian Literary Politics and the Pushkin Celebration of 1880* [Ithaca: Cornell UP, 1989], 55). Curiously, in 1880 the Ober-Prokurator of the Holy Synod, Konstantin Pobedonostsev, tried to promote Filaret as "national hero" in place of the overly-secular Pushkin! (Olga Maiorova, "Polemika vokrug Pushkinskogo prazdnika 1880 goda: Novye materialy," lecture delivered at the conference, "Alexander Pushkin and Humanistic Study," Stanford University, April 16, 1999). Thus at one end of the spectrum we have a religious-secular alliance represented by the SAR, and at the other the idea of two separate, opposing literary traditions.

Chapter 13. The Rapprochement between "Secular" and "Religious"

academic greetings... the juxtaposition of religious and secular, as in language, was no longer an issue. In Catherine's reign literary activity gained the status of an activity that had state importance, and in which the empress was herself involved. Having achieved that status, literature—like language—began to embody (not only as an intention, but in a real, functional way) the unified power of the regnant culture (edinovlastie gospodstvuiushei kul'tury), which dominated all spheres of social life. Accordingly, it was perceived as a single whole, creating a system of genres in which sermons and theological tracts took their place beside odes, elegies and comic operas.[60]

Yet by the time the SAR was completed it had already begun to outlive itself, and the cultural discourse it canonized was fast becoming obsolete by the time the companion seven-volume alphabetical version appeared in 1806-1822 (the earlier version was organized by roots).[61] The last serious debate over the viability of Slaveno-rossiiskii discourse as vehicle for secular literature was arguably that between the "archaists and innovators," terms made famous among later scholars by Iurii Tynianov's 1929 essay.[62] There

---

[60] The passages, separated by ellipses, are from Zhivov, *Iazyk i kul'tura*, 77, 370 and 403. We should note here, however, that this system of genres was still strictly hierarchical, and that low, "purely entertainment" genres (such as comic operas, novels, or popular farces [*igrishchi*]) could be rejected as falling below ethical or aesthetic standards.

[61] See Pushkin's heavily ironic comments in canto one of *Eugene Onegin* in 1825 (*Eugene Onegin: A Novel in Verse*, translated from the Russian, with a commentary, by Vladimir Nabokov, 2 vols. [Princeton, N.J.: Princeton UP, 1975], 2: 107-8), in which he describes the SAR as "an everlasting monument to the solicitudinous will of Catherine and to the enlightened labors of Lomonosov's successors, strict and trustworthy guardians of our native tongue" — a not so hidden parody of pompous slavenorossiiskii discourse! Pushkin continues by quoting an equally ornate speech by Karamzin about the SAR, delivered to the Academy in 1818.
The SAR was replaced by a new academy dictionary, significantly entitled *Slovar tserkovno-slavianskago i russkago iazyka* in 1847 (2nd ed., 4 vols. [St. Petersburg: Akademiia nauk, 1867-68]); this dictionary was published by the "Second Section" (Vtoroe otdelenie) of the Academy of Sciences which had replaced the Russian Academy. The standard Russian dictionary (analogous to Webster's in America) was to become V. I. Dal's *Tolkovyi slovar zhivago velikorusskago iazyka*. 4 vols. (1863-66), whose title is also indicative; the standard scholarly dictionary of Church Slavonic was I. I. Sreznevsky's *Materialy dlia slovaria drevne-russkago iazyka po pis'mennym pamiatnikam*. 3 vols. (St. Petersburg: Otd-niie russkago iazyka i slovesnosti Imp. Akademii nauk, 1893-1912).

[62] In the collection *Arkhaisty i novatory* ([Berlin]: Priboi, 1929); on this episode, see Altshuller, *Predtechi slavianofilstva*; and Iu. M. Lotman and B. A. Uspenskii, "Spory o iazyke." These scholars emphasize the utopian and Romantic aspects of the archaists' program, represented primarily the works of Admiral A. S. Shishkov, which

is no need here to review the epochal political and cultural circumstances that put an end to the tradition this discourse represented, and that set the stage for the new synthesis of the literary language accomplished by Pushkin, canonized anew in the later nineteenth century.[63] Zhivov himself, somewhat paradoxically, has described the cultural synthesis he so meticulously defined and the very existence of a Russian Enlightenment as a "mirage," as "illusory," a "myth" manufactured by the state (primarily Catherine) as a camouflage for hidden, "real" political purposes (with distinctly totalitarian overtones).[64] For many critics of Russian culture, both the secular as well as the religious traditions of the eighteenth century were subsequently seen as empty and bankrupt due to the interference or control of the state. In the aftermath of the French Revolution the hypocritical self-interest of old regime culture became strikingly evident as an inevitable structural problem, and destroyed the very basis of the cultural synthesis, which after all had taken place within the ideological and institutional context of imperial state culture. Slaveno-rossiiskii discourse and its normative texts were (with minor exceptions) relegated to the trash-bin of history, as relics of an archaic or pseudo-culture.

Since the early nineteenth century, practically all of Russian culture has, at one time or another, been seen as an illusion, from Chaadaev's rejection of the entire national heritage going back to Byzantium, to the leftist political and cultural avant-gardes who were ready to throw Pushkin & Co. from the ship of modernity, to those who in our day dismiss Socialist Realism as nothing more than a state-imposed sham. On the other hand, Zhivov's reservations about the status of Enlightenment in Russia do suggest substantive questions about the case I have tried to make here on the basis of the framework his own work provides. Does the material offered here allow us to speak of a true synthesis during this period? I have tried to indicate an initial positive response to this question, suggesting that especially if seen as a regnant elite discourse, and not only an institutional and literary formation, the evidence

---

put great stress on the pre-Petrine folk and Church-Slavonic aspects of the Slaveno-rossiiskii linguistic synthesis while denying the middle registers—those on which the Karamzinian program rested—as alien and "French." As Zhivov shows in *Iazyk i kul'tura*, chap. 5, the Slaveno-rossiiskii legacy was carried on in the nineteenth century by the specifically religious, Russian Orthodox literary tradition.

[63] Boris Gasparov, *Poeticheskii iazyk Pushkina kak fakt istorii russkogo literaturnogo iazyka.* (Wien: Gesellschaft zur Föderung slawistischer Studien, 1992).

[64] V. M. Zhivov, "Gosudarstvennyi mif v epokhu Prosveshcheniia i ego razrushenii v Rossii kontsa XVIII veka," *Vek Prosveshcheniia: Rossiia i frantsiia. Le siecle des lumieres. Russia. France. Materialy nauchnoi konferentsii. Vipperovskie chteniia — 1987*, vyp. 20 (Moscow, 1989), 141–65 and *Iazyk i kul'tura*, 419–25.

Chapter 13. The Rapprochement between "Secular" and "Religious"

of a Slaveno-rossisskii episode in Russian culture is hard to gainsay. At the same time, there is a great deal left to be said about many of the historical developments and cultural trends of the day that surely influenced the shape of the proposed synthesis. These include such things as: the practical differences between Elizabeth's and Catherine's cultural policies; the conflicts between secular writers and Synodal censors; the effects of the nationalization of church property; the monastic revival; Freemasonry; and other tensions within and between secular and religious realms that could not help but affect the character of the overall synthesis. Another objection might come from the very assertion of an "Enlightened," non-"traditional" Orthodoxy. Were the Slaveno-rossiiskii sermons, for example, by presuming a greater degree of human moral perfectibility by rational means contrary to "traditional" Orthodox discourse about original sin?[65] We are confronted with the problem of how to define Orthodoxy, a particularly difficult question given the rather inclusive nature of the Russian Orthodox theological tradition.[66]

More generally, this challenge to the nature of eighteenth century Russian religious doctrine raises the larger issue posed by Enlightenment culture for all traditional religious cultures of the older type (Protestant and Jewish as well as Orthodox and Catholic): does the rapprochement between faith and reason demanded by adapting to life in a modern society spell the inevitable demise of a faith-based life-style? An affirmative answer to this question would seem to come only from those on the extreme ends of the spectrum, either radical traditionalists (e.g, Slavophiles) or radical secularists (e.g., atheist revolutionaries), and would not do justice to those for whom concord or compromise, as articulated in a discourse of cultural synthesis, indicated a possible alternative path.

---

[65] See Zhivov's comments, for example, in *Dictionary of Literary Biography*, 276–77. Some have also seen the Petrine tradition in Russian Orthodoxy as essentially alien for its "Protestant" innovations.

[66] Certainly, defining and documenting Orthodox doctrine is problematic throughout the history of the church. In the 1750's and 60's, some of the main opponents of "Enlightened Orthodoxy" were those associated with the Kievan scholastic tradition, the faction which during the Petrine period had been opposed to the Moscow "Grecophiles" as "Latinizers." Does it follow that we are to define the *scholastic* tradition as traditional Russian Orthodoxy?

14

THE "OBVIOUSNESS" OF THE TRUTH IN EIGHTEENTH-CENTURY RUSSIAN THOUGHT

> For from the greatness and beauty of created things comes a corresponding perception of their Creator.
>
> — *Wisdom of Solomon* 13: 5

> First follow NATURE, and your Judgment frame
> By her just Standard, which is still the same:
> *Unerring Nature,* still divinely bright,
> One *clear, unchang'd,* and *Universal* Light,...
>
> — Alexander Pope,
> *An Essay on Criticism* (1711)

> We hold these truths to be self-evident...
>
> — Thomas Jefferson,
> *The Declaration of Independence* (1776)

> Видими нами мир сей уверяет о бесконечной мудрости Божией.
> [The world we see assures us of God's infinite wisdom.]
>
> — Phrase illustrating the word "vidimyi" (visible)
> in the *Slovar' Akademii Rossiiskoi* (1789)

The staring point for much of Russian philosophical and theological thinking in the eighteenth century is quite simple and basic: namely, that to any unbiased observer, *the truth is obvious.* The senses—particularly "the noblest of the senses," vision—offer incontrovertible proof of the rational structure of the universe, and hence of God's existence. While such ideas may seem naïve or outlandish to us today, they underwrote the age's fundamental belief in reason. On the one hand, pre-Kantian philosophy reflected a modernized version of scholastic cosmology and a quasi-Aristotelean teleological argumentation about the orderly, hierarchical nature of the universe, represented, for example, in the works of Christian Wolff.[1] On the other hand, Enlightenment thought was caught in a kind of ontological and epistemological loop, going back to the way Descartes had posed the central problems of modern philosophy. Descartes' ultimate criterion for knowledge, the well known formula of "clear and indubitable truth," is itself self-verifying, as it posits an inner faculty (e.g. "the light of nature," which in turn depended on scholastic proofs of God's existence). Thus the "proofs" of the objectivity of reason necessarily depend to some degree on individual subjective perception. Discussing Fénélon's debt to Descartes, one of his contemporaries noted that " Fénélon has fallen into the same vicious circle as his leader: Reason is to demonstrate the existence of God, and God to guarantee the validity of Reason…they presuppose what they set out to justify."[2] Reason is the only tool accepted and needed to prove God's existence and goodness, but without God's existence Reason cannot be validated (so as to extricate us from the solipsistic cul de sac of the "cogito"). Nevertheless, for many the authority of reason was just as solid and obvious as the evidence of sight.

Before I continue, I should note that the argument I am putting forward here about eighteenth-century Russian "occularcentrism"[3] contradicts most accounts of the history of Russian philosophy. Mikhail Miaitskii, one of the few scholars to examine "the problem of visuality" in Russian culture, for example, has written that

> The path of secularizing the invisible, its domestication, its justification in terms of the visible — in a word, the path that was considered Western in Russia — was unacceptable for Russian thought. This unacceptability is embodied in the anathematizing of obviousness (anafema ochevidnosti)…[4]

---

[1] On Wolff in Russia, see *Khristian Vol'f i russkoe vol'fianstvo*, a special issuer of *Filosofskii vek: Al'manakh*, 3 (St. Petersburg, 1998); and *Vol'f i filosofiia v Rossii*, ed. V. A. Zhukov (St. Petersburg: Izd-vo Russkogo khristianskogo gumanitarnogo instituta, 2001).

[2] Stafford H. St. Cyres, *François de Fénélon* (Port Washington, NY: Kennikat, 1970), 254–55.

[3] The term was coined by Martin Jay, author of the fundamental study *Downcast Eyes: The Denigration of Vision in Twentieth-Century French Thought* (Berkeley, CA: University of California, 1993).

[4] Mikhail Maiatskii, "Nekotorye pokhody k probleme vizual'nosti v russkoi filosofii," *Logos*, 6 ([Moscow] 1995), 57. Maiatskii complains of contemporary scholarship's "complete lack of consideration" of the problem of the visual in Russia (48).

Such a conclusion is understandable, insofar as — as Maitskii here holds — "Russian thought" is constituted by the philosophical school that formed in the later nineteenth century, a philosophical tradition that as a rule also rejected the eighteenth century as "un-Russian" and "Western." We take a contrary position, both that one may legitimately speak of eighteenth-century Russian thought, and that the visual played a uniquely privileged role in it. Furthermore, we would suggest that the Russian preoccupation with sight was not merely a Western import, a naïve or provincial version of Descartean metaphysics, but had deep roots in traditional Orthodox theology, in which the justification of vision (in connection with the defense of icons) played a central role.[5] Moreover, one cannot fully appreciate the later nineteenth-century philosophical and cultural tradition — that declared obviousness to be anathema — without taking into account the fact that it represented a profound *dialectical negation* of the preceding cultural configuration. Only in this light may one appreciate the very tenacity of the later tradition's "logocentrism," its turn away from Sight in favor of the Word.

In a short article, I cannot, of course, offer an extended defense of these ideas, which will be developed in a forthcoming book. In the following I will focus on what was known in the eighteenth century as "physico-theology," the idea that the existence of God and the rational structure of the universe may be demonstrated by the self-evident evidence of the visible world.[6] I will

---

[5] See, for example, Jaroslav Pelikan, "The Senses Sanctified: The Rehabilitation of the Visual," chapter 4 in *Imago Dei: The Byzantine Apologia for Icons* (Princeton: Princeton UP, 1990).

[6] For an excellent exposition of this philosophical tradition, with emphasis on Germany, see Thomas P. Saine, *The Problem of Being Modern, or, The German Pursuit of Enlightenment from Leibniz to the French Revolution* (Detroit: Wayne State UP, 1997). Perhaps the most comprehensive exposition of physic-theological ideas in eighteenth-century Russia was Trediakovskii's unpublished poem *Feoptiia ili dokazatel'stvo o bogozrenii po veshcham sozdannogo estestvo* (which we may paraphrase as "Feoptiia or Proof of God's Existence by Means of Visual Evidence from His Natural Creation"). This visual theodicy in verse, inspired by Leibniz and Alexander Pope, was largely based on Fénélon's *Traité de l'existence et des attributs de Dieu* (1712, 1718). On Feoptiia, see Breitschuh's work cited in note 11. Fénélon's *Traité* was among the most popular French expositions of physico-theological ideas, and well known in Russia. Kantemir wrote an unpublished paraphrase entitled "Letter on Nature and Man" (1743; published in 1868), and it was translated at least three times, twice in abridged versions (1766, 1778, 1793). Other physico-theological tracts that appeared in Russia include: "Razmyshlenie o velichestve bozhiem, po koliku onoe prilezhnym rasmotreniem i ispytaniem estestva otkryvaetsia," *Ezhemesiachnye sochineniia k pol'ze i uveselieniiu sluzhashchiia*, noiabr, 1756, pp. 407–38 (a translation); and Iermonakh Apollos (Baibakov), *Evgeont, ili sozertsanie*

take my main evidence from Lomonosov, and center on his adaptation of classical philosophical sources (especially Cicero). In eighteenth-century Russia the ideas of "physico-theology" were universally accepted and may be found in numerous scientific and philosophical texts, in poetry (religious as well as what is often referred to as "nature-philosophical" verse), as well as in sermons and other theological works. In Lomonosov's writing, as in many of these others, there was no clear boundary between science and theology, literature and philosophy, or between "natural philosophy" and "natural theology" ("estestvennoe" or "natural'noe" "bogoslovie"). The physico-theological tradition was thus a meeting ground and melting pot for generically heterogeneous works — of natural science, poetry, and philosophy — and for chronologically disparate trends, a peculiarly early modern blend of classical, Christian (Eastern and Western), and Enlightenment ideas.

A useful place to start is Lomonosov's *Rhetoric* (*Short Guide to Oratory*), first published in 1748, revised in 1765, and republished seven times during the eighteenth century. As an example of a "conditional syllogism" (*uslovnyi sillogizm*) Lomonosov offers a seven-page proof of God's existence as demonstrated by the visible world. While presented as an exercise in formal logic, loosely based on Cicero's dialogue *The Nature of the Gods,* the substance of Lomonosov's arguments very much reflected the thinking of the age. Cicero's work, which has been termed his *Summa theologica,* had a major impact on both the medieval Christian tradition (especially via Augustine and Thomas Aquinas), as well as on the growth of modern philosophy from Grotius and Descartes to Montesquieu, Locke and Hume.[7] The syllogistic logic concerning interlocking parts deriving from a rational being, as well as its application to the question of God's existence — the so-called "argument from design" — were accepted not only by Cicero, but also by the Early Christian world. These ideas made a dramatic comeback in the Early Modern period in the wake of the challenge of the new science to the old Medieval cosmography. As Thomas Saine has noted, with the demise of Aristotelian-

---

v nature bozhiikh vidimykh del (Moscow, 1782). Apollos lists as his main sources Fénelon, Roberto Bellarmino's *Ladder to Heaven* (Russian editions 1783 and 1786), St. Theodoritus' sermons on Providence (Russian edition, 1784), L. Euler's *Letters on Various Physical and Philosophical Materials* (Russian edition, 1768–74), and G. W. Krafft's *Geography* (*Short Guide to Mathematical and Natural Geography,* Russian edition, 1739). On physico-theology on Russia, see "The Theological Context of Lomonosov's 'Evening' and 'Morning Meditations on God's Majesty,'" chap. 15 in this volume.

[7] Paul MacKendrick, with the collaboration of Karen Lee Singh, *The Philosophical Books of Cicero* (New York: St. Martin's, 1989), chap. 20.

Ptolemaic cosmology, the even older Epicurean atomist model which it had displaced, and whose arguments had long seemed scientifically discredited as well as morally anathema, now suddenly took on dangerous new plausibility. Seemingly outmoded and long-resolved arguments against the Epicurian position assumed new relevance.[8] Texts like *The Nature of the Gods*, which iterated the position of the Sophists against the Epicureans, many of whose arguments had been taken up by the Church Fathers centuries before, also took on new importance. Cicero's detailed discussion of the various arguments proving God's existence, excerpted by Lomonosov, were typologically similar and historically connected to various aspects of the Russian Orthodox tradition that validated the occularcentric suppositions of the age.

The syllogism that Lomonosov sets out to demonstrate is the following:

> If something consists of parts, of which each one depends on another for its existence, [that means that] it was put together by a rational being. The visible world consists of such parts, of which each one depends on another for its existence. It follows that the visible world was created by a rational being.[9]

The ideas expressed in this tripartite syllogism — two premises and conclusion — had far-reaching influence in the eighteenth century, and provided a basic theological framework for its faith in the validity of the world that we see. To cite from Lomonosov's working out of the second premise of the syllogism:

> But let us take a look at the marvelous enormity of this visible world and at its parts: do we not see everywhere the mutual connection of things whose very being benefits one another? Do not the mountains' height and the valleys' inclination serve so that the water that comes together from their springs creates streams and finally unites in rivers? And rivers, which themselves stretch out over the broad earth like the manifold branches of a thick tree, small and large united, so as to water and bathe the inhabitants spread out over the land and with its movement to connect the human race for its mutual benefit? (VII: 320–321)

The discussion of water circulation continues for several pages, covering the role of the heavenly bodies, plants, seeds, and then goes on to discuss the arrangement of the human body and its sense organs. Part of the efficacy of the "mutual connection and benefits" argument evidently came from the

---

[8] Saine, *The Problem of Being Modern*, 37.
[9] M. V. Lomonosov, *Polnoe sobranie sochinenii*. 11 vols. (Moscow: AN SSSR, 1950–1983), VII: 319. Further references to this edition will be given in the text.

sheer mass of examples and rhetorical variations on a theme (often presented, as above, as a series of unanswered rhetorical questions).

One of the most popular scenarios dramatizing this second premise is that of the viewer looking out into the dark, starry sky and being overcome by the sublime order of the universe. The prototype of this epiphanic experience probably also comes from Cicero's *The Nature of the Gods*, which quotes the following passage from Aristotle's lost treatise *On Philosophy*:

> Imagine that there were people who had always dwelt below the earth in decent and well-lit accommodation embellished with statues and pictures, and endowed with all the possessions which those reputed to be wealthy have in abundance. These people had never set foot on the earth, but through rumor and hearsay they had heard of the existence of some divine power wielded by gods. A moment came when the jaws of the earth parted, and they were able to emerge from their hidden abodes, and to set foot in this world of ours. They were confronted by the sudden sight of earth, seas, and sky; they beheld towering clouds, and felt the force of winds; they gazed on the sun, and became aware of its power and beauty, and its ability to create daylight by shedding its beams over the whole sky. Then, when night overshadowed the earth, they saw the entire sky dotted and adorned with stars, and the phases of the moon's light as it waxed and waned; they beheld the risings and settings of all those heavenly bodies, and their prescribed, unchangeable courses through all eternity. When they observed all this, they would certainly believe that gods existed, and that these great manifestations were the works of gods.[10]

The episode described here is something like the parable of the cave in *The Republic*, only in this one people escape not into the transcendent realm of Truth and Light but out into the physical world, whose constant natural movements embody eternal truth. Aristotle's underground visitors experience a sudden vision of divine power and beauty. The truth is something to be physically felt (here: the force of the wind, presumably the heat of the sun), especially through the sense of sight. This illustration of the second premise — the sudden revelation of the glory of the physical universe, often taking place when gazing up into the night sky — is one of the most widespread scenarios in eighteenth-century Russian religious and meditative poetry (e.g., Lomonosov, Trediakovskii, Kheraskov, Derzhavin and others); much of this mostly well-known verse, I would suggest, belongs to the "physico-theological" category.

---

[10] Cicero, *The Nature of the Gods*, trans. P. G. Walsh (New York: Oxford UP, 1997), 81.

Lomonosov's syllogism ends with a formal "Conclusion":

> Hence there is no doubt at all that this visible world has been constructed by a being possessing reason and that, apart from this most marvelous and magnificent enormity, there is some force that has delimited (sogradila) it, a force that is immeasurably great, so as to create such an immeasurable edifice; a force so inconceivable and most wise so as to make it so well shaped, so harmonious, so magnificent; a force so inexpressibly generous that it established and confirmed the mutual utility of all these creations. Is not this immeasurably great, inconceivably wise, inexpressibly generous power none other than that which we call god and revere as immeasurably great and all-powerful, inconceivably wise, inexpressibly generous?... And you who are privileged to gaze into the book of unshakable natural laws, raise up your minds to the one who constructed them, and with extreme reverence thank the one who revealed to you the theater of his most wise deeds, and the more that you comprehend of them, the greater the awe with which you will extol him. The tiniest of vermin (gady) proclaim His omnipotence to you, and the vast heavens announce, and the numberless stars demonstrate, his greatness that passes understanding. O how blind you are, Epicurus, that in the presence of so many luminaries you do not see your creator! Sunk because of barbaric ignorance or carnal pleasures in the depth of unbelief, rise up, bethink yourself, having considered that the one who once shook the earth's foundations may throw you down alive into hell, the one who caused seas and rivers to overflow will drown you with his waters, the who set mountains aflame with His touch will exterminate you with fire, the one who covers the heavens with storm clouds will strike you down with lightning. The One Who casts down lightning, He Is. Atheists, tremble! (VII: 324–26)

Cicero's dialogue, which presents viewpoints both pro and con, does at moments include some invective, but generally strives to be straightforward and undogmatic. In contrast, this final apostrophe to Epicurus that culminates Lomonosov's syllogism suggests the more or less explicit Christian and polemical eighteenth-century context. The last (imperfectly preserved) section of Cicero's dialogue is comprised of criticism of the Stoics' proofs of God, but there is nothing comparable in fervor to Lomonosov's fire-and-brimstone condemnation of atheists, which recalls a sermon rather than an imitation of classical philosophy.

Part of the vehemence against unbelievers may derive in part from the conviction that, given the obviousness of the truth, those who fail to see do so out of perversity and recalcitrance. As Trediakovskii explained in the prose summary of the second part of his *Feoptiia*, which itself represents a theodicy based on the visual,

Chapter 14. The "Obviousness" of the Truth in Eighteenth-Century Russian Thought

> ...in order...to demonstrate the truth incontestably and clearly,...it is not necessary to use great subtlety of argument, but one simple glance at the world — together with some general reasoning and attentiveness in scrutinizing things — is alone sufficient.[11]

The truth is so clear and unmistakable, all one has to do to be convinced is to open one's eyes. A careful reading of such passages suggests some measure of equivocation; while "great subtlety of argument" may not be not needed, some "general reasoning" is, and despite the "one simple glance" that "alone is sufficient," "attentiveness in scrutinizing things" is also required.[12]

In any case, if seeing means believing, not to see represents a purposeful refusal to accept the truth. Those who do not see are prevented either by ignorance or by their own prideful egos. In this context, reason taken too far or not far enough (either the skepticism of a Hobbes or the deism of a Spinoza), becomes an obstacle to the truth. This denigration of critical reason may help explain the nature of eighteenth-century philosophy in Russia, which was oriented more toward systematization or popularization of truth than on testing its limits. After all, if the truth is obvious, one does not really need philosophy; the problem is simply to get people to open their eyes:

> И не ослепленный грубых заблуждений тьмой,
> Весь в природном свете пребывающий с собой,
> Гнусными ниже страстьми сердца восхищенный,
> Ни пороками, ни злом скотства развращенный,
> Не возможет тотчас Бога жива не познать,... (197)

> (And one who has not been blinded by coarse error, abiding with himself, completely in nature's light, and not enthralled to vile passions of the heart, nor by vices, nor perverted by the evil of bestiality — cannot fail to recognize the living god right away,...)

---

11 V. K. Trediakovskii, *Izbrannye proizvedeniia*. Biblioteka poeta, bol'shaia seriia (Leningrad: Sovetskii pisatel', 1963), 211. Further citations of *Feoptiia* in the text are to this edition. On the *Feoptiia*, see note 6 above, and the study by Wilhelm Breitschuh, *Die Feoptija V. K. Trediakovskijs: Ein Physikotheologisches Lehrgedicht im Russland des 18. Jahrhunderts* (Munich: Sagner, 1979).

12 This passage paraphrases the opening sentence of Fenelon's opening sentence (I quote it in Kantemir's prose translation): "I cannot open my eyes without amazement at the wisdom and art visible in nature; the slightest glance is sufficient (samyi poslednii vid dovol'no) for the all-powerful creator to show his hand" (A. D. Kantemir, *Sochineniia, pis'ma i izbrannye perevody*, ed. P. A. Efremov [St.-Petersburg, 1867], II: 25). The motif of the "simple (or single) glance" and "merely opening up of one's eyes" was a staple of physico-theological writings.

Смотрение его толь ясно зримо есть,
Что не возможет скрыть от нас никая лесть
И что без слепоты извольныя не можно
Не видеть нам везде того, что есть неложно. (251)

(His [God's] surveillance [of us] is so clearly visible, that no kind of flattery can hide it from us, and it is not possible without intentional blindness not to see that which truly exists all around us.)

Мудрости в сем вышни, в мудрованиях нелеп,
Точно кто не видит, и с очами тот есть слеп;
Тот не токмо назван быть может малоумным,
Но бессмысленным совсем и страстями шумным. (272)

(The one who has divine wisdom within, but is made foolish by philosophizing, is like one who doesn't see, one with eyes but still blind. Such a person may be called not only weak of intellect, but completely senseless, disturbed by passions.)

However, the fact that this truth was deemed to be obvious did not obviate the need for repeating it ad nauseum.

The cluster of images associated with Lomonosov's syllogism recur with variations in many eighteenth-century Russian literary works. In the remainder of this article I will center on one: the use of the traditional biblical trope of the "book of nature" that Lomonosov uses to illustrate the notion that God's existence may be proven merely by opening one's eyes. This contrasts sharply with the older Baroque handling of this image. In such poems as Simeon Polotskii's "The World Is a Book," "Book," and "Writing," the meaning to be found in the book of the world is emblematic and allegorical, not empirical, and is not easily accessible to sight.[13] Hence the unlearned and uninitiated may easily misunderstand what they see, and be led astray. Vision alone is insufficient, as illustrated in the poem "Writing." Here written words are compared to a rushing river: one is in jeopardy of seeing only the flickering surface, missing the deeper truth that may elude the untrained eye (prekhodiashcha zrenie neiskusna oka), and drowning. As in Trediakovskii, insufficient or excessive reason can be harmful, even fatal.

---

[13] See P. N. Berkov, P. N., "Kniga v poezii Simeona Polotskogo," *Trudy Otdela drevnerusskoi literatury* 24 (1969): 260–266; A. M. Panchenko, "Slovo i znanie v estetike Simeona Polotskogo," *Trudy Otdela drevnerusskoi literatury* 25 (1970): 232–242, his *Russkaia stikhotvornaia kul'tura XVII veka* (Leningrad, 1973); and L. I. Sazonova, *Poeziia russkogo barokko: vtoraia polovina XVII — nachalo XVIII v.* (Moscow, 1991). These poems may be found in Simeon Polockij, *Vertograd mnogocvetnyj*, ed. A. R. Hippisley and L. I. Sazonova. 3 vols. (Köln: Böhlau, 1996–2001).

Chapter 14. The "Obviousness" of the Truth in Eighteenth-Century Russian Thought

The Classicist, physico-theological interpretation of the image of the book of nature, as in Lomonosov's paraphrase of Cicero, is that the truth to be read there is obvious, transparent, and open to everyone, even without training. As if in response to Polotskii, in his ode entitled "Reading," for example, Kheraskov asserts that

> Всегда у нас перед очами
> Отверзта книга Естества;
> В ней пламенными словами
> Сияет мудрость Божества.[14]

> (The book of Nature is always open before our eyes; the wisdom of Divinity shines from it in flaming words.)

Similarly, in his sermon on Catherine's ascension to the throne, published in 1782, Metropolitan Platon also employs the "world as a book" metaphor to suggest that

> Knowledge of God is of the most accessible (udobneishikh) kind, because it is the most necessary (Ibo ono est' samonuzhnoe). This book is open to the entire universe. It is written in letters which the educated and uneducated can understand, and all of the peoples on earth, who speak different languages, can read them without difficulty and without preparation (bez nauki). It is enough to open ones eyes and see the Creator and Ruler of all things.[15]

The "book of nature" metaphor also served as a key image in Lomonosov's defense of modern science, which he couched as a defense of sight. In an addendum to a 1761 speech concerning astronomy, he used it to assert science's right to explore the visible, physical world:

> The Creator gave the human race two books. In one He showed His greatness, in the other His will. The first — is the visible world, which He created so that a person, looking upon the immensity, beauty and harmonious construction of the edifice, would recognize divine omnipotence, to the extent of the understanding given him. The second book is holy writ. In it is shown the Creator's concern for our salvation. In these divinely-inspired prophetic and

---

[14] *Tvoreniia M. Kherskova, vnov' ispravlennyia i dopolnennyia.* Vol. 7 (Moscow, 1796), 389. For another example of this key image in poetry, see "The Polemic with Rousseau over Gender and Sociability in E. S. Urusova's *Polion* (1774)," chap. 18 in this volume.

[15] "Slovo na den' vozshestviia na prestol eiia imperatorskogo velichestva," *Pouchitel'nye slova i drugie sochineniia*, vol. 10 (Moscow, 1782), 277.

apostolic books the interpreters and elucidators are the great teachers of the church. [In contrast,] astronomers reveal the temple of God's power and magnificence, and seek the means for our temporary welfare, united with reverence and gratitude to the All-High. Both together assure us not only of God's existence but of the untold blessings He gives us. (IV: 375)

Notably, Lomonosov grounds the reading of the first "book of nature" on the authority of the second, the "inspired prophetic and apostolic books" by "the great teachers of the church."[16] One of the main philosophical issues of the century of light was the compatibility between these "two books."[17] For Lomonosov, and for the Russian Enlightenment tradition in general, there was no doubt: they were completely in harmony, and the visible world, the one susceptible to human reason and scientific inquiry, offers an equally valid path to divine truth as that of revelation and faith. Nevertheless, the very terms in which Lomonososv couches this argument suggest a fundamental tension between open-ended scientific inquiry, as something exploring unknown truths and applying critical reason, on the one hand, and its pre-determined purpose of revealing the "temple of God's power and magnificence," on the other. However, what might well seem problematic and even contradictory for the later tradition, for the great majority Russian eighteenth-century thinkers remained — obvious.

---

[16] In particular, Lomonosov cites the authority of St. Basil's *Hexaemeron* (in Russian *Shestodnev*), sermons that examine the "six days" of creation as described in Genesis, and that attempt to accommodate science to scripture. Lomonosov also refers to St. John of Damascus' "Exposition of the Orthodox Faith" (part three of the *Fount of Knowledge*, a kind of *Summa theologica* for the Eastern Orthodox). Notably, "The Exposition" begins with a guarded defense of reason, necessary not only for scientific pursuits but for theological speculation itself. These, together with the works of St. Gregory of Nazianzus (Grigorii Bogoslov), were among the central Eastern Orthodox works that contributed to the physico-theological tradition. Notably, all three of these church fathers were famous both as theologians and as poets or orators, and were well known in the East and West. In the introduction to the *Feoptiia*, Trediakiovsky notes that in discussing these (physico-theological) issues, "it was impossible for me not to use metaphysical arguments... They have long been used in our language, and are if you please to be found everywhere in our ecclesiastic and theological books..." V. K. Trediakovskii, *Psalter 1753*. Ed. Alexander Levitsky (Paderborn, 1989), 465.

[17] See also my discussion of Lomonosov's 1761 passage in "The Rapprochement Between Secular and Religious Culture in Mid-to-Late Eighteenth Century Russia," chap. 13 in this volume.

15

THE THEOLOGICAL CONTEXT OF LOMONOSOV'S "EVENING" AND "MORNING MEDITATIONS ON GOD'S MAJESTY"

While Lomonosov's "Evening Meditation on God's Majesty on the Occasion of the Great Northern Lights" (Vechernee razmyshlenie o Bozhiem Velichestve pri sluchae velikogo severnogo siianiia) and "Morning Meditation on God's Majesty" (Utrennee razmyshleniia o Bozhiem velichestve) have long been rightfully recognized as masterpieces of Russian poetry, the question of their religious content has not only not been studied but not even considered as a valid concern. On the one hand, the theological aspect of Lomonosov's poetry has mostly been ignored, or even denied. As V. Dorovatovskaia wrote in 1911, "Lomonosov's thoughts were not directed at religion and purely religious questions held no interest for him."[1] On the other hand, it was suggested that even if the issue were to be raised (I again cite Dorovatovskaia) Lomonosov "remained an isolated case in the ideological regard."[2] These poems' relation to Russian poetic and religious traditions remains little studied[3] and their correlation with

---

[1] V. Dorovatovskaia, "O zaimstvovaniiakh Lomonosova iz Biblii," in *M. V. Lomonosov, 1711–1911: Sbornik statei*, ed. V. V. Sipovskii (St. Petersburg, 1911), 38.

[2] Dorovatovskaia, "O zaimstvovaniiakh," 65. This neglect of Lomonosov's religious views was shared, understandably, by the great majority of Soviet critics.

[3] L. V. Pumpianskii referred in passing to the poems' serious theological content, which he defined as "a rationalist, Lutheran and Leibnizian-colored theism" and as "a phenomenon of the European bourgeois type" ("Ocherki po literature pervoi poloviny XVIII veka," *XVIII vek*, 1 [M.—L., 1935], 110). The most important works on the religious heritage of Lomonosov's poetry are: Alexander Levitsky, "The Sacred Ode (Oda Dukhovnaja) in Eighteenth-Century Russian Literary Culture," Ph. D. Dissertation, University of Michigan, Ann Arbor, 1977; L. F. Lutsevich, *Psaltyr' v russkoi poezii* (St. Petersburg, 2002). On works concerning the issue of Lomonosov and religion, see: *Khristianstvo i novaia russkaia literatura XVIII–XX vekov: Bibliograficheskii ukazatel'*, ed. V. A. Kotel'nikov, comp. A. P. Dmitriev i L. V. Dmitrieva (St. Petersburg, 2002), 103–106.

European Enlightenment trends unexplored. The goal of this article is twofold: first, to define the philosophical and theological trend to which the "Meditations" belong, and secondly, to offer a reading of the poems in light of this tradition, following in the steps of those critics who have seen in them a well considered argument concerning the existence of God and an attempt to harmonize reason and faith.[4]

The trend I am speaking of is what was described in the eighteenth century as "physicotheology." As is evident from the hybrid term, its primary objective was to reconcile faith and science, or more precisely, to demonstrate God's existence on the basis of evidence from natural science. The concluding lines of the "Morning Meditation" offer a concise statement of this idea:

И на твою взирая тварь,
Хвалить тебя, бессмертный царь.

(And when beholding all Your works, / To give you praise, immortal King.)[5]

See also the following studies that were unfortunately not accessible to me at the time of writing this article: Walter Schamschula, "Zu den Quellen von Lomonosovs 'kosmologicher' Lyrik," *Zeitschrift für Slavische Philologie*, 34: 2 (1969): 225–53; Zhiva Benchich, "Barokko i klassitsizm v *Razmyshleniiakh o bozhiem velichestve* Lomonosova," *Russica Romana*, 3 (1996): 27–50; as well as Kirill Ospovat,"Nekotorye konteksty 'Utrennogo…' i 'Vechernego razmyslenija o bozhiem velichestve'" in *Study Group on Eighteenth-Century Russia Newsletter*, 32 (2004), 39–56, which appeared during the time the original Russian version of this article was at press. Schamschula and Ospovat suggest some sources for Lomonosov's poems, while Benchich focuses on stylistic issues.

[4] For example, I. Z. Serman, who writes that "Disturbed by the orthodox clergy's attacks on science, Lomonosov felt that it was necessary to come forth in its defense. But science had to be shown not as inimical to God or religion but as a way to genuine knowledge of God through the best understanding of His created world. Lomonosov devoted two of his most inspired poetic works [the "meditations"] to such an explanation of the place of science in the cognition of God." (I. Z. Serman, *Mikhail Lomonosov: Life and Poetry* [Jerusalem: Centre of Slavic and Russian Studies, The University of Jerusalem, 1988], 120). Serman writes: "During all his conscious life, Lomonosov conducted a philosophical struggle on two fronts: both against those who censured science for its effort to comprehend everything in the world, and against those who tried to create a world system without the participation of God in it" (115). See also Lutsevich, *Psaltyr'*, chap. 5.

[5] The translations of the "Meditations" are from Harold B. Segel, ed. and trans., *The Literature of Eighteenth-Century Russia: An Anthology*, vol. 1 (New York: Dutton, 1967), 202–208.

Chapter 15. The Theological Context of Lomonosov's "Evening"...

As Thomas Saine has written, "In the first half of the eighteenth century, a flood of physicotheological works, by scientists, divines, and laypeople alike, contrived to see God's hand and his design for the universe in every creature, every rock, and every blade of grass,"[6] that is, they set out to prove God's existence by examining the visible world. In Lomonosov's day there was still no clear division between the natural sciences and "natural" theology, and this was clearly evident in physicotheological works, whose discourse combined secular and religious, classical and Biblical, patristic and contemporary, Orthodox Russian and non-Orthodox Western material. Physicotheological works of the late seventeenth and eighteenth centuries were written in a wide variety of genres, in prose and verse (as well as in combination) and often contained a mixture of generic elements. This was a pan-European, multi-lingual phenomenon, and there was an active exchange of ideas and texts in English, German, French and other languages, including Russian. In eighteenth-century Russia physicotheological ideas were generally accepted by all educated people. They may be found in many scientific and philosophical treatises, in poetry (both religious and secular, especially in so-called nature-philosophical verse) as well as in textbooks, sermons, and theological works.[7] It is thus appropriate to speak

---

[6] Thomas P. Saine, *The Problem of Being Modern, or The German Pursuit of Enlightenment from Leibniz to the French Revolution* (Detroit: Wayne State University Press, 1997), 20.

[7] One of the most extensive expositions of physicotheological ideas in Russia was V. K. Trediakovskii's unpublished poem "Feoptiia ili dokazatel'stvo o bogozrenii po veshcham sozdannogo veshchestva" (1750–1754, published by I. Z. Serman only in 1963 in *Izbrannye proizvedeniia*. Biblioteka poeta. Bol'shaia seriia, 2nd ed. [Leningrad: Sovetskii pisatel', 1963]). In the foreword (not included in the 1963 publication), Trediakovskii offers a long list of physicotheological works, and also includes opponents of this tradition, making up in all "almost the entire circle of philosophy" (V. K. Trediakovskii, *Psalter 1753*, ed. Alexander Levitsky. Russische Psalmenübertragungen; Biblia Slavica, Ser. 3 [Ostslavische Bibeln], Bd. 4 [Paderborn: Ferdinand Schöningh, 1989], 464). "Feoptiia" is an unusual theodicy in verse inspired by Leibniz and Alexander Pope, based on François Fénelon's *Traité de l'existence et des attributs de Dieu* (1712, 1718). See Wilhelm Breitschuh, *Die Feoptija V. K. Trediakovskijs: Ein Physikotheologisches Lehrgedicht im Russland des 18. Jahrhunderts*. Slavistische Beiträge, Bd. 134 (Munich: Sagner, 1979). Fénelon's treatise was one of the most popular physicotheological works in France and was well known in Russia; Kantemir wrote an adaption of this work entitled "Letter on Nature and Man" (1743; published in 1868).
Other physicotheological works that appeared in Russia include: "Razmyshlenie o velichestve bozhiem, po koliku onoe prilezhnym razsmotreniem i ispytaniem estestva

of physicotheological discourse, that is, a particular set of ideas, images and topoi that combine to form a recognizable unity.

Lomonosov's "Meditations" are a prime example of this discourse. As the starting point for our analysis we will consider their titles.[8] This attention might seem exaggerated were it not for the fact that they offer a precise encapsulation of the central themes and topoi of the physicotheological trend. The general formula of the "Meditations'" titles — "meditation on the majesty of God on the occasion of some natural phenomenon" — is very widespread in physicotheological literature. For convenience we may split this up into the following five parts: 1–2) genre and variant of genre (e.g., morning or evening meditation); 3) subject (God); 4) quality

---

otkryvaetsia," *Ezhemesiachnye sochineniia k pol'ze i uveseleniiu sluzhashchie*, November, 1756, 407–438 (a translation from an unattributed German source); D. S. Anchikov, "Slovo...o tom, chto mir sei est' iasnym dokazatel'stvom premudrosti Bozhiei i chto v nem nichego ne byvaet po sluchaiu" [1767] in *Mysli o dushe: Russkaia metafizika XVIII veka*, ed. T. Ar'tem'eva (St. Petersburg, 1996); Iermonah Apollos (Baibakov), *Evgeont, ili sozertsanie v nature Bozhiikh vidimykh del* (M., 1782). Apollos names as his main sources: the works of Fénelon and Roberto Bellarmini (1542–1621) (see: Robert Bellarmin, *Rukovodstvo k Bogopoznaniiu po lestvitse sotvorennykh veshchei* [M., 1783]; also translated as *Lestvitsa umstvennogo voshozhdeniia k Bogu po stepenam sozdannykh veshchei* [St. Petersburg, 1786]); Feodorit Kirskii (see: *Blazhennogo Feodorita episkopa Kira Pouchitel'nye slova o Promysle* [M., 1784], a translation from Greek); George Wolfgang Krafft (see his *Kratkoe rukovodstvo k matematicheskoi i natural'noi geografii...* [St. Petersburg, 1739]), and Leonhard Euler (see L. Eiler, *Pis'ma o raznyh fizicheskikh i filozofskikh materialakh...*, vol. 3 [St. Petersburg, 1768–1774], a translation from the French). There were other translations from unnamed German sources, including two by M. Gromov: *Kartina vsemogushchestva, premudrosti i blagosti Bozhieia, sozertsaemyia v prirode...* (St. Petersburg, 1796; second enlarged edition, 1798) and *Velichestvo Boga vo vsekh tsarstvakh prirody, ili Lestvitsa ot tvarei k tvortsu, ot zemli na nebo...* (St. Petersburg, 1801). One could also include in this list many works of translated belles-lettres such as Pope's "Essay on Man" (1734) and Edward Young's *Night Thoughts* (1742–45; more on this work below). This short survey does not pretend to be complete, and does not include either individual poems or the broad circle of other works which reflect physicotheological ideas and discourse.

[8] V. L. Chekanal, who wrote the commentary on these poems for the main Soviet academic edition of Lomonosov, asserts that "There is no doubt that the words 'on God's Majesty' were included in the official title of both odes primarily out of concern for the censor: the materialistic view of the universe and in particular, about heavenly bodies, provoked significant opposition on the part of church authorities" (M. V. Lomonosov, *Polnoe sobranie sochinenii*, 11 vols. [M.-L.: Akademiia nauk SSSR, 1950–83], VIII: 910). On the formulaic nature of physico-theological titles, which he connects with the poetry of Barthold Heinrich Brockes, see Schamschula, "Zu den Quellen," esp. 242.

Chapter 15. The Theological Context of Lomonosov's "Evening"...

(or qualities) of God (e.g., majesty); and 5) the immediate occasion for the work (e.g., the northern lights).[9]

Before we turn to a closer analysis of these elements, we need to say a few words about the physicotheological tradition and its sources. As noted, physicotheological works made use of materials from various genres and epochs. We may divide this roughly into three main groups — classical works, religious writings, and contemporary Enlightenment material, both by secular and religious authors. In his *Rhetoric* and the "Additions" to the "Appearance of Venus on the Sun" (1761) Lomonosov supplies rich material concerning the broad intellectual and specific textological sources of the "Meditations."[10] The classical sources here include Cicero, whose treatise *The Nature of the Gods* had a powerful influence on Christian theology and Enlightenment thought[11]; and Claudian's long poem "Against Rufinus (In Rufinum)," a fragment of which served as the immediate model for the "Meditations."[12] Of Christian sources, Lomonosov cites

---

[9] In the "Morning Meditation" this last element is absent, although it is quite clear that this is a meditation on the nature of the sun.
Here are three examples of popular physicotheological works that were published and translated many times and that appeared before Lomonosov's poems. The titles all contain comparable elements. 1) John Ray (1627–1705), *The Wisdom of God Manifested in the Works of the Creation: In Two Parts: viz. The Heavenly Bodies, Elements, Meteors, Fossils, Vegetables, Animals, (Beasts, Birds, Fishes, and Insects) More Particularly in the Body of the Earth, its Figure, Motion, and Consistency, and in the Admirable Structure of the Bodies of Man, and other Animals, as also in their Generation...* (1691) (London, 1692). 2) Bernard Nieuwentyt (1654–1718) *Het regt gebruik der werelt eschouwingen: ter overtuiginge van ongodisten en ongelovigen aangetoont...* [Translated into English as: *The Correct Use of Meditation for Understanding the Omnipotence, Wisdom and Goodness of the Creator in the Marvelous Structure of Animals' Bodies...in the Formation of the Elements...[and] in the Structure of the Heavens*] (Amsterdam, 1715). 3) Friedrich Christian Lesser (1692–1754), *Insecto-theologia, oder: Vernunft- und schrifftmässiger Versuch, wie ein Mensch durch aufmerksame Betrachtung derer sonst wenig geachteten Insecten zu lebendiger Erkänntniss und Bewunderung der Allmacht, Weissheit, der Güte und Gerechtigkeit des grossen Gottes gelangen könne* (Frankfurt, Leipzig, 1738). [Translated into English as: *Insecto-theology, or a Demonstration of the Being and Perfections of God, from a Consideration of the Structure and Economy of Insects*].

[10] These are discussed, for example, in Lutsevich, *Psaltyr'*; Iu. V. Stennik, "M. Lomonosov. 'Vechernee razmyshlenie o Bozhiem Velichestve pri sluchae velikogo severnogo siianiia,'" in *Poeticheskii stroi russkoi liriki* (L., 1973), 9–20; and in my article "The 'Obviousness' of the Truth in Eighteenth-Century Russian Thought," included in this collection.

[11] See Levitt, "The 'Obviousness' of the Truth," 297–300.

[12] The passage is from Book I section 3; Lomonosov, *Polnoe sobranie*, IV: 376.

John of Damascus' *Exposition of the Orthodox Faith* and Basil the Great's sermons, works on whose basis he defended himself against his clerical enemies.¹³ The argument that although God is ultimately inconceivable He may be apprehended through the physical world and the senses could be found in the Bible and patristic literature and served as an axiom of the physicotheological trend.

Turning to the first two elements of the title, "Evening" (or "Morning") and "Meditation," the label "meditation" is of primary importance for these poems as it defines their genre and type of philosophical reflection. "Meditation" may refer to both secular philosophical as well as theological thematics. As a philosophical genre, "meditation" suggests the consideration of an already accepted truth, as opposed to, for example, a "treatise" or "proof" whose goal is to logically demonstrate the veracity of a given idea or system. As Iakov Kozel'skii wrote in his *Philosophical Propositions* of 1768, "If we closely examine the parts of some truth, this examination is called meditation (reflexio)."¹⁴ Meditation is a necessary stage in the process of understanding the truth, somewhere between sensual perception and cognition as such. (We may note in passing that in this sense meditation is directly connected with asserting the reliability of vision.)

In the theological context, the function of "meditation" is the same, from the point of view of logic. But as a genre, "meditation" may serve as a synonym for "beseda" (literally, conversation), which in turn may describe a sermon or type of prayer.¹⁵ Lomonosov himself uses the term "meditations" to refer to Basil the Great's *Sermons* (*Besedy*) and to John of Damascus' *Exposition*, asserting for example that "in their books these great luminaries strove to unite (sodruzhit') the understanding of nature with faith, combining this effort with divinely inspired meditations, according to the degree that astronomy was known in their day."¹⁶

---

13   See Lutsevich, *Psaltyr'*, 251–254.

14   Ia. P. Kozel'skii, *Filosoficheskiia predlozheniia* (St. Petersburg: [Senate], 1786), 64.

15   On "meditation" as a type of Orthodox prayer, see for example Prep. Isaak Sirin, Beseda 10 ("O chine razmyshlenii [Sirian, "herga"] i o razlichnykh vidakh ego."), *O Bozhestvennykh tainakh i o dukhovnoi zhizni: Novootkrytye teksty*, trans. Ieromonakh Ilarion (Alfeev) (Moscow, 1998).

16   Lomonosov, *Polnoe sobranie*, IV: 374. In the Russian translation, Basil the Great himself often uses words for "meditation" (razmyshlenie, razmyshliat') to describe his "besedy." See *Besedy sviatogo ottsa nashego Vasiliia Velikogo, arhiepiskopa Kesarii i Kappadokiiskiia, na shestodnev, sirech' na shest' dnei tvoreniia, opisannykh sv. Prorokom Moiseem* (Moscow: Universitetskaia tipografiia u N. Novikova, 1782).

Why "Evening" and "Morning" meditations? This leads directly to the first of the truths on which the poet meditates, that is, the possibility of proving God's existence by the inductive method, based on the evidence of the marvelous organization of the natural world. This is the so-called "argument from design" — "know the Creator by the Creation." In his *Rhetoric* Lomonosov presents this in the form of a syllogism, a condensed paraphrase of Cicero's *The Nature of the Gods:*

> If something consists of parts, of which each one depends on another for its existence, [that means that] it was put together by a rational being. The visible world consists of such parts, of which each one depends on another for its existence. It follows that the visible world was created by a rational being.[17]

But why specifically "Evening" and "Morning" meditations? The issue is that the ontological problem (the problem of the character of being) is connected to the cosmological (how the world came into existence). The alternation of night and day is not only a microcosm of the natural order, the changeless laws of nature, but also of the process of the world's formation ("creation" in both senses). It is no accident that the main Christian works on natural science (cosmologies) took the form of the "Hexaemeron" (in Slavonic "Shestodnev") — commentaries to the first chapter of Genesis, that is, the six days of creation, in the form of sermons or "conversations."[18] Ontology (the essence of the world) becomes known through considering cosmology (the process of creation). Indeed many physicotheological works functioned as cosmologies for the modern era, and many of them specifically centered on the Earth's creation. As in Basil the Great's *Hexaemeron*, in which each "conversation" relates to one day of creation, many physicotheological works employ a similar structural device, alternating days and nights (or evenings).[19]

---

[17] Lomonosov, *Polnoe sobranie*, VII: 319.

[18] On this tradition, see the commentaries to: *Shestodnev Ioanna ekzarkha Bolgarskogo*, ed. G. S. Barankov and V. V. Mil'kov. Pamiatniki drevnerusskoi mysli, vyp. 2. (St. Petersburg: Aleteiia, 2001). See also *Drevnerusskaia kosmografiia*, ed. G. S. Barankov. Pamiatniki drevnerusskoi mysli (St. Petersburg: Aleteiia, 2004), esp. 158–170.

[19] See, for example, Trediakovskii's *Feoptiia* and Apollos's *Evgeont* (see note 5). Edward Young's famous physicotheological poem *The Complaint: or, Night-Thoughts on Life, Death, and Immortality* (1742–1745), which was very popular in Russia, also uses this structural device. This work was "translated" into Russian several times both in prose and in peculiar paraphrases. See P. R. Zaborov, "'Nochnye razmyshleniia' Iunga v rannikh russkikh perevodakh,", *XVIII vek*, 6: *Russkaia literatura XVIII veka: Epokha*

The movement from night to day or darkness to light is not only a microcosm of Creation but also a metaphor for the spiritual process leading a person from meditation to revelation. This process is at the heart of physicotheological works, where, as in Lomonosov's "Meditations," the central action is a change in vision. The archetypal moment of this change of vision occurs when a person raises his eyes to the heavens, sees the glittering stars and planets, and goes into ecstasy over the miraculous structure of the universe. The paradigm or prototype of this moment most likely comes from the passage in *The Nature of the Gods* in which Cicero cites Aristotle's lost treatise *On Philosophy* (the passage that Cicero quotes is the only part that remains). Cicero writes that the Epicureans "talk such nonsense about the universe that it seems to me that they have never gazed upwards at the remarkable embellishment of the heavens lying before their very eyes." He continues, quoting Aristotle:

> Imagine that there were people who had always dwelt below the earth in decent and well-lit accommodation embellished with statues and pictures, and endowed with all the possessions which those reputed to be wealthy have in abundance. These people had never set foot on the earth, but through rumor and hearsay they had heard of the existence of some divine power wielded by gods. A moment came when the jaws of the earth parted, and they were able to emerge from their hidden abodes, and to set foot in this world of ours. They were confronted by the sudden sight of earth, seas, and sky; they beheld towering clouds, and felt the force of winds; they gazed on the sun, and became aware of its power and beauty, and its ability to create daylight by shedding its beams over the whole sky. Then, when night overshadowed the earth, they saw the entire sky dotted and adorned with stars, and the phases of the moon's light as it waxed and waned; they beheld the risings and settings of all those heavenly bodies, and their prescribed, unchangeable courses through all eternity. When they observed all this, they would certainly believe that gods existed, and that these great manifestations were the works of gods.[20]

This moment seems analogous to the liberation of the philosopher in Plato's parable of the cave from the *Republic*, although the liberation here is not from

---

klassitizma (Moscow, Leningrad: Nauka, 1964), 269–279. Aleksandr Andreev's "translation" from French (!), entitled *Dukh ili nravstvennye mysli slavnogo Iunga, izvlechennye iz Noshchnykh ego razmyshlenii...* (St. Petersburg: Gos. Med. Kollegii, 1798), appended thirteen Russian and other poems including Lomonosov's two "Meditations."

[20] Cicero, *The Nature of the Gods*, trans. P. G. Walsh (New York: Oxford University Press, 1997), 81 (Book 2, sec. 94–95).

the physical world into the spiritual realm but occurs within the confines of material reality. It is a process of revelation, a coming to understanding, the acquisition of new, correct vision.[21]

It is precisely here, in the problem of (re)cognition, that one of the central theological issues arises. Meditations on God's existence and on the rational structure of the universe (i.e., ontology) yields to gnoseology and epistemology. *What* we see is defined by *how* "our perishable eye" functions. On the one hand, the epistemological problem is connected to discussion of various natural-scientific theories (in the "Meditations" — about the nature of the northern lights and the character of the sun's surface).[22] On the other, physicotheological works, including the "Meditations," come up against the fact that God is fundamentally unknowable, unproveable, unseeable — beyond the limits of human comprehension. This, one might say, is the basic problem or paradox of monotheism, with which Orthodox theologians have always struggled, from Dionysius the Areopagate to the Hesychasts to the modern followers of Imiaslavie. Physicotheological works resolve the problem in a traditional way, arguing that God may be known if not directly then through His divine manifestations, His signs, qualities, energies, etc. (precisely how, to what degree, and how the process is to be conceived, are all subject to serious debate).

The titles "Evening Meditation on God's Majesty on the Occasion of the Great Northern Lights" and "Morning Meditation on God's Majesty" themselves imply that one may come to knowledge of God through His secondary features in the physical world, first of all, through his majesty or greatness (velichestvo). Lomonosov himself writes about this both in his paraphrase of Cicero's *The Nature of the Gods* in the *Rhetoric* and in the "Additions" to "The Appearance of Venus." Here is the relevant passage from the latter:

> The Creator gave the human race two books. In one He showed His greatness, in the other His will. The first is the visible world, which He created so that a person, looking upon the immensity, beauty and harmonious construction of the edifice, would recognize divine omnipotence, to the extent of the understanding given him. The second book is Holy Writ. In it is shown the

---

21 See Levitt, "The 'Obviousness' of the Truth," 299.
22 As Lomonosov noted in his "Iz"iasneniia" to the "Slovo o iavleniiakh, ot elektricheskoi sily proiskhodiashchikh," "My ode on the northern lights...expresses my long-held opinion that the northern lights might be produced from the movement of ether (efir)." Lomonosov, *Polnoe sobranie*, III: 123.

Creator's concern for our salvation. Of these divinely-inspired prophetic and apostolic books the interpreters and elucidators are the great teachers of the church.[23]

Lomonosov also expressed this idea in his paraphrase of Basil the Great's *Hexaemeron* in words which could serve as a physicotheological slogan and short formulation of the idea of the "Meditations" themselves:

> While the indescribable wisdom of God's deeds is clear (iavstvuet) if only from meditations on the whole of creation (o vsekh tvariakh), to which the study of the physical [world] leads, astronomy more than anything else gives a sense of His majesty and power (velichestva i mogushchestva)...[24]

Majesty is the most outstanding feature of physical reality, combining as it does both power and wisdom.[25] According to physicotheologists, these three traits, together with a fourth — goodness — are the principle attributes of God-the-Creator, and therefore appear in the titles of their works in various combinations (see note 7). Majesty is the mark of God in His role as Creator, cosmic Architect and Artist.

To what extent God's signs are obvious in the material world is a question resolved differently by various physicotheolagal writers. For many, this is not a problem, because the truth is very simply obvious.[26] However, often the degree of obviousness depends on the nature of the one who looks. In Lomonosov's formulation, a person recognizes "divine omnipotence to the degree of understanding given him" (po mere sebe darovannogo poniatiia). For Orthodox theologians, this capacity depends on the moral purity of one's soul; for others, and more secular-minded Enlightenment physicotheologists, it depends rather on one's amount of education (reason). Where for the former the ability to see truly characterizes the saint, for the latter this privilege is given to the geniuses of natural science.[27]

---

[23] Lomonosov, *Polnoe sobranie,* IV: 375. Cf. the image of the "book of the world" (the "kniga vechnykh prav," i.e., nature) in the "Evening Meditation."

[24] Lomonosov, *Polnoe sobranie,* IV: 372.

[25] See this idea in the "Razmyshlenie o velichestve bozhiem, po koliku onoe prilezhnym razsmotreniem i ispytaniem estestva otkryvaetsia," *Ezhemesiachnye sochineniia k pol'ze i uveseleniiu sluzhashchie,* November, 1756, 409.

[26] Levitt, "The 'Obviousness' of the Truth."

[27] This latter opinion was held by the author of the anonymous German translation "Razmyshlenie o velichestve bozhiem" cited above in notes 7 and 25. It is possible that this was the reason the publication was criticized by church authorities. See *Polnoe*

Chapter 15. The Theological Context of Lomonosov's "Evening"...

One of the basic features of Lomonosov's "Meditations" is the depth and seriousness of the epistemological problem they pose concerning the limitations of our "mortal sensations" (brennykh chuvstv). In the "Evening Meditation" this is expressed by the dialogical form of the poem and in the rhetorical power of the repeated questions:

> Но где ж, натура, твой закон?...
> Не солнце ль ставит там свой трон?...
> Скажите, что нас так мятет?...
> Что зыблет ясный ночью луч?
> Что тонкий пламень в твердь разит?
> Как молния без грозных туч
> Стремится от земли в зенит?
> Как может быть, чтоб мерзлый пар
> Среди зимы рождал пожар?

(But where, O Nature, is your law?... / Does not the sun set there its throne?... / What is it so disturbs us, tell?... / At night what vibrates lucid rays? / What subtle flame cuts firmament? / And without stormy thunderclouds / Wherefrom does lightning rush to earth? / How can it be that frozen steam / In midst of winter brings forth fire?)

The poem ends with four more questions, as the poet's doubts seem to remain:

> Сомнений полон ваш ответ
> О том, что окрест ближних мест.
> Скажите ж, коль пространен свет?
> И что малейших дале звезд?
> Несведом тварей вам конец?
> Скажите ж, коль велик творец?

(Your answer is replete with doubts / About the places nearest man. / Pray tell us, how vast is the world [or: light]? / What lies beyond the smallest stars? / Is creatures' end unknown to you? / Pray tell how great is God Himself?)

To some extent, the last question is also an answer, insofar as it is rhetorical, and insofar as defining the majesty of God is equal to defining His nature

---

sobranie postanovlenii i rasporiazhenii po vedomstvu Pravoslavnogo ispovedaniia Rossiiskoi imperii (St. Petersburg, 1912), vol. 4, № 1532, 20 Dec. 1756, 272–273. However, this work's markedly rationalist perspective was not typical of most physicotheological works that appeared in Russia.

in general. Here is the focus of the meditation as "the consideration of an already accepted truth"; God exists, but how can one determine how great He is, and what are the limits to our understanding?

As critics have recognized, the tone of the "Morning Meditation" is far more affirmative that the "Evening" and we may consider the second meditation as offering a direct answer to the questions of the first[28]:

> Чудяся ясным толь лучам,
> Представь, каков зиждитель сам!...
> Велик зиждитель наш господь!

(And marveling at such radiant beams / Just think how God Himself must be!... / Our Lord creator is great!)

But the truth is not so obvious even in the "Morning Meditation." The picture of the sun's surface that makes up the scientific center of the poem's interest, describing Lomonosov's theory in verse (just as in the "Evening Meditation" his theory of the northern lights is proposed[29]), is nevertheless presented not simply as a spontaneous act of sensation but also as an act of imagination:

> *Когда бы* смертным толь высоко
> *Возможно было возлететь,*
> Чтоб к солнцу бренно наше око
> *Могло, приближившись, воззреть,*... (Italics added — M. L.)

(If mortals only had the power / So high above the earth to fly, / So that our perishable eye / Could see the sun, once close to it...)

As Plato and Aristotle and later theologians and philosophers asserted, the act of sight, for all its seeming immediacy (the obviousness of what is seen)

---

[28] From the time of their publication in Lomonosov's *Sochineniia* of 1751, the "Meditations" were published together and under the rubric of "spiritual odes." In eighteenth-century publications the "Morning Meditation" preceded the "Evening," but in many later editions the order was reversed. On the basis of metrical analysis, V. M. Zhirmunskii concluded that the "Evening Meditation" was written first ("Ody Lomonosova 'Vechernee' i 'Utrennee razmyshlenie o Bozhiem velichestve': K voprosu o datirovke," *XVIII vek*, 10: *Russkaia literatura vosemnadtsatogo veka i ee mezhdunarodnye sviazi* [Leningrad: Nauka, 1975], 27–30).

[29] See note 22. A. A. Morozov suggests that the notion of "frozen steam" refers to the theory of Christian Wolff. See M. V. Lomonosov, *Izbrannye proizvedeniia*. Biblioteka poeta. Bol'shaia seriia. 3rd ed. (Leningrad: Sovetskii pisatel', 1986), 510.

nevertheless requires processing, involving memory, thought (meditation), and imagination. Of course the nature of human understanding was also a central issue in Enlightenment thought and also posed the question of the complex interaction of the physical and spiritual.[30]

The solution of the epistemological problem comes in the final stanzas of the "Morning Meditation" which may be taken as the denouement to both poems taken together.[31] First the difference between inner and outer vision is noted and the weakness of sensual sight before God's divine insight:

Светило дневное блистает
Лишь только на поверхность тел;
Но взор твой в бездну проницает,
Не зная никаких предел.

(The light of day casts forth its brightness / But lightens only surfaces. / Your gaze instead much deeper reaches / Not knowing any boundaries.)

Here the secondary role of the sun as simply a pretext for meditation seems particularly clear. The poet's potential crisis of vision is resolved in the final stanza which brings the poem closest to a prayer:

Творец! покрытому мне тьмою
Простри премудрости лучи…

(To me, Creator, steeped in darkness / Extend the rays of [Your] wisdom!)

---

30   See for example our discussion of this issue in "Was Sumarokov a Lockean Sensualist? On Locke's Reception in Eighteenth-Century Russia," chap. 8 in this volume.

31   In this regard it seems significant that in the *Rhetoric*, right after the section that includes the "Evening Meditation" (presented as an example of logical expansion [rasprostranenie], § 270), there follows the "conditional syllogism" in which the arguments proving God's existence from The *Nature of the Gods* are presented. It is clear to all readers of these poems, starting with the titles, that they are closely connected, and one may suggest that they make up a cycle. L. V. Pumpianskii asserted that together with the "Oda, vybrannaia iz Iova, glavy 38, 39, 40 i 41" and several stanzas from the "Oda na pribytie…Elizavety Petrovny iz Moskvy v Sanktpeterburg 1742 goda…" they form a certain unity (Pumpianskii, 108). Notably, the "Job" theme often came up in physicotheological literature that includes many "paraphrases of particular chapters of Job" both in verse and prose. Its connection to the "Meditations" is subject for further investigation. As in Lomonosov's paraphrase, the central problem is the justification of divine justice. In physicotheological writing this issue was linked to Leibniz' book that coined the term "theodicy" (*Essais de Théodicée sur la bonté de Dieu, la liberté de l'homme, et l'origine du mal*, 1710).

"The rays of wisdom" is the culminating image of the entire poem (or cycle), combining metaphorical, spiritual light and real, physical light.[32] For Descartes and the Enlighteners, as for traditional theologians, reason is helpless and vision defective without divine sanction; for Descartes the "light of nature" comes from God, the final guarantor and embodiment of truth.

As Lomonosov himself explained in the passage cited earlier, the proofs of the "majesty and power...of God's works" are everywhere visible in the physical world. But astronomy "more than anything" can supply these proofs, because it demonstrates "the order of heavenly luminaries' movements. We imagine the creator the more distinctly the more precisely our observations accord with our predictions; and the more we achieve new discoveries, the louder we glorify Him."[33] The structure of the heavens was the most obvious example of the divine order for Artistotle, and as is well known became a highly contentious issue for Enlightenment thinkers. The physicotheological movement was precisely an attempt to reconcile the latest achievements of natural science with Holy Writ, and the ancient dispute with the Epicureans over whether or not the universe was purposeful or accidental that had long ago seemed to have been resolved in favor of Aristotle now once again became relevant. The debate over "the plurality of worlds" that commentators have seen raised in the "Evening Meditation" ("Tam raznykh mnozhestvo svetov; / Neschetny solntsa tam goriat" [There are a great number of various worlds; Countless suns there glitter]) and that they attribute to the disagreements over Fontenelle's *Conversations on the Plurality of Worlds* of 1686 might with equal justification be related to the dispute of Cicero and the church fathers against the Epicurean position.[34]

The final segment of the title identifies the immediate pretext for the meditation. We have already noted the significance of the theme of "day and night" on the cosmological and metaphorical level and described the ancient argument, repeated by Lomonosov and the physicotheologists, that observations of the heavens provide the most "distinct" and obvious notion (or proof) of God's existence. Thus focusing on the northern lights and the sun not only reflected the poet's particular scientific interests but

---

[32] The following final lines of the poem also emphasize the parallel between divine and human. Man is characterized in terms of creation, and is himself a creator, i.e., a microcosm or image of God (cf. "Vsegda *tvoriti* nauchi," "*Tvorets!*," "tvoiu *tvar'*").
[33] Lomonosov, *Polnoe sobranie*, IV: 372.
[34] On the parallel with Basil the Great, see Lutsevich, *Psaltyr'*, 252–53; on the connection to Fontenelle, see Stennik, "M. Lomonosov," 16–18. See also the discussion of this parallel in Saine, *The Problem of Being Modern*, chap. 1.

represented a typical subject for physicotheological consideration. Indeed the "astronomical" theme was a popular inspiration for physicotheological works (e.g., William Derham's *Astro-Theology: or a Demonstration of the Being and Attributes of God: From a Survey of the Heavens...* [second edition, London, 1715]) and there were also various physicotheological works concerning meteorological phenomena, including "bronto-theology" (the theology of thunder and lightning) and "helio-theologia" (about the sun), into which category we may perhaps include the "Morning Meditation."[35]

Thus the titles of Lomonosov's poems offer a microcosm of the physicotheological position and clearly indicate their discursive background. Defining this background seems crucial for understanding these works of art, although of course it does not "explain" them. Rather, it presents the basis on which their intellectual and artistic specifics may be better understood.

---

[35] Other quasi-scientific physicotheological treatises included studies of "Testaceo-theologia" (the theology of snails and mollusks); "Hydro-theologia" (the theology of water); "Insecto-theologia" (the theology of insects); "Litho-theologia" (geological theology); "Phyto-theologia" (botanical theology); and so on.

— 16 —

THE ODE AS REVELATION:
On the Orthodox Theological Context of Lomonosov's Odes

The starting point for my analysis are stanzas eleven and twelve from Lomonosov's "Ode on the Arrival from Holstein and on the Birthday of His Imperial Highness Lord and Grand Prince Petr Feodorovich, the 10th day of February, 1742":

> Но спешно толь куда восходит
> Внезапно мой плененный взор?
> Видение мой дух возводит
> Превыше Тессалийских гор!
> Я Деву в солнце зрю стоящу,
> Рукою Отрока держащу
> И все страны полночны с ним.
> Украшенна кругом звездами,
> Разит перуном вниз своим,
> Гоня противности с бедами.
>
> И вечность предстоит пред нею,
> Разгнувши книгу всех веков,
> Клянется небом и землею
> О счастьи будущих родов,
> Что Россам будет непременно
> Петровой кровью утвержденно.
> Отверзлась дверь, не виден край,
> В пространстве заблуждает око,
> Цветет в России красной рай,
> Простерт во все страны широко.
> 			(Lomonosov VIII, 66–67)

(But to where so hurriedly is my captive gaze suddenly raised? My vision raises my spirit much higher than the mountains of Thessaly! I see the Maiden in the sun standing there, holding the Youth in her arms and all midnight countries

Chapter 16. The Ode as Revelation

with him. Adorned with stars all around, she strikes with her thunderbolts, pursuing evils with trouble.

And eternity stands before her, throwing open the book of all ages, and swears by heaven and earth the happiness of future generations that Russians will surely be affirmed by Peter's blood. The door opened, sight is limitless, the eye is lost in the distance, a beautiful paradise blooms in Russia, extended widely in all directions.)

In these lines, as in all of Lomonosov's odes, references to sight are omnipresent (*captive gaze, vision, I see the Maiden, the boundary unseen, the eye is lost*, etc.). Here too, as in the other odes, are also Biblical references.[1] However, the vision of the "Maiden in the sun" is exceptional in that it seems to refer so specifically to the Christian image from Revelations: "A great and wondrous sign appeared in heaven: a woman clothed with the sun, with the moon under her feet and a crown of twelve stars on her head" (Rev 12: 1).

Not all of the details coincide. In Revelations, the woman (or maiden, *deva*) is pregnant; she gives birth and there is a battle over the newborn between angels and a dragon. A recent Orthodox interpreter of the Bible explains that "By the image of this woman commentators unanimously understand spiritual humanity, the Church undefiled by worldly sins, of people truly living in God. The sun in which she is clothed signifies that in this world she is the vessel of heavenly light — the light of revelation, grace, purity (the sun signifies divine powers). The sun under the woman's feet signifies her supremacy over earthly forces and earthly wisdom. The twelve stars of her crown signify the apostles and the twelve tribes of Israel" (NSK 1983, 122–39).[2] At the same time, the image of the "maiden clothed in the sun" is universally seen as an image of the Virgin Mary (Toporkov 2005).

How does this vision relate to the religious content of Lomonosov's odes, and what is the nature of this vision? In general, what role does vision play in the odes, and how does the image of the "maiden in the sun" relate to it?

It is not a simple matter to answer these questions. The ode was not only the leading genre of eighteenth-century Russian literature but also

---

[1] V. M. Zhivov and B. A. Uspenskii (1987, 123) note that for Lomonosov's odes "panegyrical praise of the monarch using sacred imagery is exceptionally characteristic"; see also Dorovatovskaia 1911, 33–65.

[2] M. I. Sukhomlinov (1891, 165) and I. Solosin (1913, 248–49) suggest other possible references to Revelations in this ode. On the apocalyptic motifs in these stanzas, see Pogosian and Smorzhevskikh 2002, which unfortunately was not available to me at the time of writing this article.

perhaps the most complex in terms of its origins and cultural connections. As L. V. Pumpianskii wrote, "Russia received the classical ideal through perhaps the greatest number of refractions; thus Lomonosov's ode derived from the classics, through Malherbe, Boileau, and the Germans…" (Pumpianskii 1983a, 303). The eighteenth-century ode reflected many cultural epochs — ancient Rome, the Renaissance, Baroque, Classicism, as well as specific national traditions. One may speak of the various philosophical, theological, artistic and political tendencies that the ode absorbed. In this context we may cite Stephen Baehr's argument that the ode expressed a "paradise myth," the "master myth" of the Russian eighteenth century (Baehr 1988, 61–79), as well as V. M. Zhivov and B. A. Uspenskii's study "Tsar and God," which traces the development of the Orthodox imperial cult of the monarchy, as also reflected in part in panegyric verse (Zhivov and Uspenskii 1987, 47–152). The significance of this cult expanded significantly with the church's subordination to the secular power in the eighteenth century. Both of these studies demonstrate the complex cultural pedigree of the ode and its new function, expressing a new "political theology." Their authors also in part examine the special status of the ode as carrier of various basic aspects of Orthodoxy, understandably adapted to new conditions. Among other things, they discuss the representation of the tsar-emperor as the earthly image of God as expressed in odes, which they see as a secularization of traditional religious conceptions, including the projection of the Orthodox understanding of the icon onto the political sphere (seen as a new stage of the "Byzantinization" of Russian culture). This approach is fully valid for the image of the "Maiden in the sun," which to some degree may be seen to represent Empress Elizabeth and Tsarevich Petr Fedorovich (Serman 1988, 72–75).[3] We also need to keep in mind the place of the ode in the context of Baroque panegyrics (Sazonova 1987, 103–25) and the influence of German court practice (Alekseeva 2002, 8–27).

In his work on the literary language, V. M. Zhivov describes the way in which odic poetics became the arena that served to reconcile the linguistic purism of Vaugelas with the Church Slavonic literary heritage (Zhivov 1996, ch. 2). The ode thus served as starting point for the "Slaveno-Russian cultural synthesis," in other words, the language of Lomonosov's odes represented a synthesis of Orthodox "church books," on the one hand, and

---

[3] In another ode of the same year Elizabeth appears in the heavens and perhaps also recalls the "Maiden standing in the sun": "*Rukoiu* vyshnego venchannu, / *Stoiashchu* pred ego litsem…" (Lomonosov VIII, 84; my italics).

Chapter 16. The Ode as Revelation

the new demands of Russian culture (secular, national, Enlightenment), on the other. We may suggest in passing that the concept of a "Slaveno-Russian cultural synthesis" better describes eighteenth-century Russian culture than "Classicism" or "Neoclassicism," terms that correspond to a narrower literary and stylistic trend. Here we may also speak of "Orthodox Enlightenment" or "Orthodoxy of the Enlightenment period" (Levitt 1993, 59–74; Tsapina 2004). For Lomonosov and his cohort European Enlightenment ideas were fully compatible with Russian Orthodoxy. The analysis that follows is an attempt to describe one aspect of this compatibility.

Critics have often written about the spiritual and even philosophical aspects of Lomonosov's odes, connecting them with the process of "secularization," that is, arguing that Lomonosov uses religious material pursuant to particularly literary or political aims (for a discussion of problems with the traditional "secularization" paradigm, see Bruce 1992). In the case of the "Maiden in the sun," for example. I. Z. Serman cites several precursors for Lomonosov (Polotskii, Iavorskii, Buslaev) to argue that while they employ the image in a Biblical spirit for Lomonosov it serves other non-religious ends. Here "the apocalyptic image is torn from its context and receives a secular, literary significance." The Maiden (Virgin Mary) functions as stand-in for the "earthly empress," i.e., Elizabeth. According to Serman, it is just a metaphor, a likeness; "mysticism disappears, but poetic ecstasy...remains" (Serman 1988, 75). On the other hand, in his unpublished *Short Guide to Oratory* of the early 1740's Lomonosov classifies the image as an example of "pure invention" (chistyi vymysel) and as a spacial inversion (prostranstvennoe peremeshchenie) (Lomonosov VII, 231); in an earlier, unpublished version the "Maiden in the sun" is also cited as an example of "supernatural invention" (Lomonosov VII, 63). This also seems to contradict the idea that the image merely serves as an allegory for the "earthly empress."

It seems to me that one may also speak of the Lomonosov ode as a religious genre, as a kind of prayer or vision (on elements of prayer in Lomonosov's odes, see Solosin 1913, 247 and 282; on prayer as a "type of religious poetry" see Lustevich 2002, 360–65; on the "genre of prayer lyrics" in Russian poetry see Kotel'nikov 1994, 10; for bibliography on Lomonosov and religion, see Kotel'nikov 2002, 103–106). I will not argue this potion in detail, although some arguments in support will be presented. For the moment I will only note that, as a rule, Lomonosov's odes begin and end with references to God, and regularly include direct address to Him (of the type: "O Bozhe, krepkii vsederzhitel'!" [Oh God, unyielding support or all!] in the ode "Pervye trofei Ego Velichestva Ioanna III…" of 1741; see also the "Oda na den' brachnogo sochetaniia... 1745 goda," "Oda...Elisavete Petrovne... 1759 goda," "Oda...Elisavete Petrovne...1761 goda," all of which begin with direct address to God). In other odes various characters pray to God, as do "Petropol'" and the Russian people (both in the ode of 1754 on the birth of Pavel Petrovich). Lidiia Sazonova (1987, 123) notes that "as a rule, panegyrics and odes culminate with the author's request that [God] bless the addressee and Russia," and she cites Lomonosov's *Rhetoric* that says: "Some conclude panegyrics with the desire and prayer for the well-being of the figure being praised. Others reassure that person of the love and respect that the people have for him. Others offer congratulations that the person has been endowed by God with so many virtues" (Lomonosov VII, 71).

In an ode from 1757 Empress Elizabeth herself offers a prayer to God and He, as if in answer, blesses her. The poet comments on God's words:

> Правители, судьи, внушите,
> Услыши вся словесна плоть,
> Народы с трепетом внемлите:
> Сие глаголет вам господь
> Святым своим в пророках духом;
> Впери всяк ум и вникни слухом:
> Божественный певец Давид
> Священными шумит струнами,
> И Бога полными устами
> Исайя восхищен гремит.
> (Lomonosov VIII, 636)

(Rulers, judges, take heed; listen all flesh who have language; peoples, hear with trepidation; this the Lord says to you; every mind concentrate and consider with your hearing: the divine singer, David, sounds the sacred strings, and Isaiah thunders, ecstatic, with lips full of God's [words])

The poet is God's mouthpiece like the psalmist and prophet. To what extent this trope is "purely literary" is a matter of interpretation.

In this passage images connected with aural perception stand out — *heed, listen, hear, sounds* and *thunders* — and they may be connected with the Old Testament pathos of the lines. Auditory and visual imagery may thus be opposed as two contrasting paradigms of sensual perception that may be correlated to Old and New Testament models (cf. Jay 1993, 33–37) both of which are present in the odes. However, from our point of view one should speak rather about the similarity of the function of hearing and sight, and about the opposition between sensual and spiritual perception. In this regard the many complaints in the odes about the limitations of verbal art are significant. To some extent this is a new version of the medieval topos of "the inexpressibility of feelings in words" that also defines the author's humble attitude toward the divine truths to which he gives expression, thus also emphasizing the sacred nature of the text. In the odes this topos may mark the lyric persona's humility and political subordination, as he defines himself as "all-subservient slave" (vsepoddanneishii rab) in relation to the monarch's greatness (as in the ode "Pervye trofei" [First Trophies]). But "the constant topos of panegyrics and odes — the motif of the inexpressible" (Sazonova 1987, 121) is more than a manifestation of literary etiquette, but emphasizes the problem of the limitations of communicability. The problem is that it is basically impossible for the poet to give adequate expression to his feelings:

> Но ею [Елизаветой] весь пространный свет
> Наполненный страшась чудится:
> Как в стих возможно ей вместиться?
> (Lomonosov VIII, 83)

(But the entire vast world / overflowing with her [i.e., Elizabeth], awestruck, marvels: / How can she be contained in verse?)

The vision of the "Maiden, standing in the sun" is also prefaced by a similar rhetorical confession of the poet's limitation:

> Кому возможно описать
> Твои доброты все подробну?
> Как разве только указать
> В Петре природу в том подобну?
> (Lomonosov VIII, 65)

(Who is able to describe / In detail all of your beneficence? / How, other than just to point / To your nature, similar to Peter's?)

In this regard it is important to note that that which is not amenable to verbalization may be far more effectively expressed in terms of sight.

We will return to this shortly. First it is important to note that this approach to the problem of reproducing or transmitting the truth fully reflects traditional Orthodox views on the problem (cf. Artem'eva 1996, 265–68, on Russian odes as an expression of the Orthodox "apophatic tradition"). Words are insufficient for revelation of divine truths. Orthodox theology often expressed mistrust for "external wisdom," "(false) philosophizing" (mudrovanie) and "wordifying" (razglagol'stvovanie). Similar labels were traditionally applied to classical philosophy and to philosophy in general. As opposed to "empty words," i.e., constructing abstract logical systems, the task of the theologian was sometimes likened to the singer who performs music (often by analogy to the psalmist playing on a many-stringed lyre (cf. Lomonosov's lines cited above: "the divine singer, David, sounds the sacred strings"). The task was not to analyze God's character but to glorify Him. This perspective helps explain why the Psalter was the most popular and well known of the Old Testament books in Russia, and also why the ode that consciously appealed to the example of the Psalms became the leading genre of eighteenth century Russian literature. The genre of the triumphal ode drew upon very powerful sources of Russian cultural memory and its formal characteristics appealed to basic values of the religious tradition, itself defined as "Pravoslavie" — "correct glorfying." The notions of "glorification" (slavoslovie) and "triumph" (torzhestvo), fundamental for Orthodox piety were also primary functions of the ode. Of course, this applies more obviously to "spiritual odes," but the "religious" functions of glorification and celebration were clearly also projected into panegyric genres.

This approach to the tasks of Orthodox theology are very clearly expressed in Gregory Palamas' *Triads in Defense of the Holy Hesychasts* (*Triady v zashchitu sviashchenno-bezmolvstvuiushchikh*), which I will use as the basis for my analysis of the Orthodox view of vision (on Palamas and Russian Hesychasm, see: Maloney 1973; Lossky 1974, Meyendorff 1974, Meyendorff 1974a, Meyendorff 1988; Gromov and Mil'kov 2001, 84–91). Here some words of justification are in order. First of all, Palmas and his treatise were probably not known by Lomonosov, although their ideas undoubtedly were, as they were more or less characteristic of the patristic tradition that had become part of the Russian cultural heritage.[4] The immediate goal of the *Triads* was to defend the Hesychasts against their critics, although at the same time it eloquently summarizes the

---

[4] We may speak here of "supra-personal" cultural memory. In this case (as a recent scholar has written referring to different material and in a different context), "the problem of the autonomous functioning of a text as carrier of memory... shifts the issue from the level of 'the author's [realm of] competence' to the hidden regions of 'the competence of the text'" (Silard 1996, 240), including the realm of cultural memory. (Note: this article was first presented as a paper at the conference "The Memory of Literary Creation" at the Institute of World Literature, Moscow, December 2–4, 2003.)

Chapter 16. The Ode as Revelation

Orthodox view of vision, which in general terms I am suggesting was part of the eighteenth-century Russian cultural memory. The treatise helps to explain what I. A. Esaulov (1998) has recently described as the "visual dominant" of Russian literature.[5] Secondly, Palamas represents the mystical, ascetic, monastic tradition in Orthodoxy which, it would seem, is far from the Enlightenment brand of Orthodoxy. Indeed, in the works in which Lomonosov defended modern science he cited not this tradition but what has been called "theology of a moderate rationalist type" represented by Basil the Great, Gregory Nazianius and John of Damascus (Gromov and Mil'kov 2001, 110–125; Barankova and Mil'kov 2001, 5–294, esp. 29–37 and 111–124; on its connection to Lomonosov, see Lutsevich 2002, chap. 5, and Levitt 2003). However, both trends in Orthodox theology concurred in their defense of icon veneration and also (albeit from different positions) advocated what we may call "optical optimism," a faith in theophany (God's manifestation to men, epiphany [bogoiavlenie]). It is precisely this positive view of the divine potential of physical sight that fully harmonized with that Enlightenment "occularcentrism" (Jay 1993; Levitt 2003) which in our opinion is characteristic of the ode.

For Palamas, striving for truth is not a verbal abstraction, not theology as "bogoslovie" (literally, "words about God") but a question of concrete experience, which his Russian translator gives as "bogovidenie" ("vision of God") (Palamas 2003, 97 and 111).[6] In the odes, as in Orthodoxy and perhaps in Christianity in general there is a basic contrast between inner and outer vision, spiritual and sensual sight — on the one hand, the eyes of physical vision, corporeal eyes, and on the other, "eyes of the soul" or of the mind, vision "with spiritual eyes," mental or spiritual light, light of the soul, etc. Cf. In our stanza:

Но спешно толь куда восходит
Внезапно мой плененный взор?
Видение мой дух возводит
Превыше Тессалийских гор!

(But to where so hurriedly is my captive gaze suddenly raised? My vision raises my spirit much higher than the mountains of Thessaly!)

---

[5] Esaulov, however, bases his argument on Pavel Florevskii, Nikolai Berdiaiev and Lev Shestov and like them rejects (or ignores) its applicability to the eighteenth century.

[6] A partial English translation of the *Triads* is available: Palamas 1983, based on Meyendorff's critical Greek edition (Palamas 1973).

Similar juxtapositions are common in the odes:

> На верьх Парнасских гор прекрасный
> Стремится мысленный мой взор
> (Lomonosov VIII, 137)
>
> (To the beautiful top of the Parnassus mountains strives my mental gaze)

Cf. also such phrases as "Ia dukhom zriu minuvshe vremia" (I see past ages with my spirit), "Pozvol' mne dukha vzor prostert'" (Permit me to extend my spirit's vision), "Bodris'. Moi dukh, smotri, vnimai" (Be Bold, my spirit, look, attend), "Moi dukh krasu liubovi zrit" (My spirit sees love's beauty), "Ia vizhu umnymi ochami" (I see with mental eyes), and so on. In the odes as in Orthodox discourse (and in Palamas in particular), the "mental gaze" (vzor uma) is also equated with "vision of the heart" (for example, in the 1746 ode: "serdtse prosveshchenno / Velichestvom bognini sei / Na budushchie dni vziraet" (the enlightened heart gazes on future days by means of this goddess' greatness) (cf. so-called "cardiology" in Orthodox theology — Gromov and Mil'kov 2001, 92-101). Here both the terminology and basic features of sight virtually coincide. For both Orthodox theology and eighteenth-century writers and poets, the notion of "um" oscillates between "spirit" (cf. the French "esprit") and "(earthly) understanding," "human reason" or "mind."[7]

In the world of Lomonosov's odes, as for Palamas, the ideal of vision — or rather, correct vision — is a balance between inner and outer sight, their interpenetration. In Orthodox theology, three episodes from the Bible are usually cited in this connection: Moses on Mt. Sinai, who experienced the devine darkness and saw God's back (Exodus 33); the prophet Elijah, who stood "in God's presence," also at Sinai (Khoriv [Horeb]; 1 Kings 19 [3 Kings 19 in the Slavonic Bible]); and the miracle of the Transfiguration (Matthew 17: 1-6; Mark 9: 1-8, and Luke 9: 28-36), associated with Mount Thabor (Favor), which in the Orthodox tradition was considered pledge of the second coming. The kingdom of God is not only within us, but around us. In Lomonosov's ode the vision of the "Maiden in the sun" and Russia as

---

[7] In some published versions of the ode, Lomonosov has "Videnie moi *um* vozvodit" in place of "Videnie moi *dukh* vozvodit" (Lomonosov VIII, 66), i.e., "dukh" and "um" are virtually interchangeable. In Enlightenment thought the seeming contradiction or paradox between mind and spirit derives from the way Descartes posed the problem of philosophy, according to which (as for medieval ascetics) the human mind could be cleansed of everything contingent and earthbound and be raised up to the contemplation of God (as pure reason).

Chapter 16. The Ode as Revelation

"beautiful paradise" directly refers to such moments of revelation. On the one hand, this is a miraculous vision of Peter's new Russia, incarnation of paradise on earth. On the other, the vision corresponds to the ecstatic state of the poet and *his* vision. The poet plays the role of the psalmist, a prophet, and the world is presented through his inspired eyes. G. A. Gukovskii described the state of the lyric "I" in words that could easily be interpreted in a religious sense:

> The emotional basis of Lomonosov's entire system is conceived by him as the theme of each of his works as a whole; and this is lyrical ascent, ecstasy, that is the single theme of his poetry, which only receives different coloration in the various odes (and also in his speeches). For Lomonosov the carrier of the ecstasy, that is, the single character of his lyrical theme, is the soul that resides in a state of the strongest affect, ascending to the heavens (voznesennaia k nebesam), to Parnassus; earthly objects do not meet his gaze that is carried off (voskhishchennyi) to the Habitation of the Muses; everything appears amplified to it, raised to the status of the divine. (Gukovskii 2001, 47)

Even such characteristic generic markers of the ode as poetic "ecstasy" (vostorg), "ardor" (zhar) and "rapture" (voskhishchenie) correspond to Orthodox eschatological discourse. The word "rapture" here literally means a physical ascent to God, an involuntary rising up, a kind of spiritual abduction (cf. Paul who "was caught up [voskhishchen] into Paradise and heard inexpressible words, which a person is not permitted [or: which is impossible for a person] to speak," 2 Cor 12: 4. Here, as in the odes, the experience of rapture is inexpressible).[8]

The problem of sight, opinions about which in part define various trends in Orthodox theology, has to do with the correlation between inner and outer vision and the degree of their possible convergence. Some theologians put their main emphasis on the difficulty in overcoming the distance between them. The gap stems from the primal sinfulness of human

---

8   One may see rapture as a special response to the gnoseological problem, as to some extent a natural reaction to the grandeur and boundlessness of the universe. This moment of the sudden revelation of the limits of human existence is also experienced as being "captured" or stupefied. Cf. in Lomonosov such phrases as "Vostorg vnezapnyi um *plenil*" or in our passage "No speshno tol' kuda voskhodit / Vnezapno moi *plenennyi* vzor?" (But to where so hurriedly is my captive gaze suddenly raised?). Cf. also Zhivov's analysis of the Western ascetic and Eastern patristic roots of the notion of "sacred intoxication" (from Boileau's "Ode sur la prise de Namur") that played a crucial role in legitimizing the language and poetics of Lomonosov's odes (Zhivov 1996, 252–54).

life and the deceptiveness of "external" sensations (characteristic of the Protestant position).⁹ For others the main focus is on the final goal and faith that the space between man and God may be overcome; from this point of view both the physical world and the senses themselves take part in the miracle of transfiguration (also: "priobshchenie," union, communion) and man can be "deified" (obozhestvit'sia). This difference of opinion is often encountered in the interpretation of important Biblical texts about vision, for example, the famous verse from 1 Cor 13:12: "For now we see through a glass, darkly." While the image of the "dark glass" is often cited as image of the impossibility of true vision in the sublunary world, the passage as a whole may be interpreted as an assertion of the divine potential of sight, the concrete possibility of seeing God "face to face":

> Charity never faileth: but whether there be prophecies, they shall fail; whether there be tongues, they shall cease; whether there be knowledge, it shall vanish away. For we know in part, and we prophesy in part. But when that which is perfect is come, then that which is in part shall be done away. When I was a child, I spake as a child, I understood as a child, I thought as a child: but when I became a man, I put away childish things. For now we see through a glass, darkly; but then face to face: now I know in part; but then shall I know even as also I am known. (I Cor 13: 8–15, King James Version)

Palamas is among those who believe that the dark glass may become clear, and asserts that divine vision has been proven by the experience of the saints and is thus accessible to human beings. Like all Orthodox theologians, he starts from the assumption that no one can see God's essence ("v sushchnosti"), but only through his manifest "energies" (the three Biblical episodes cited earlier are the exceptions, serving as the promise of total vision at the end of time). Nevertheless, Palamas insists that "in prayer the mind cleared of passions sees itself as if illuminated and lit up with God's light" (Palamas 2003, 67); "in truth a person sees only through the spirit, and not by mind or body; by some kind of supernatural knowledge he knows precisely that he sees the light that is higher than light" (82). For Palamas, epiphany is an ideal, but one which is comprehensible, if not to be fully comprehended. A person who is

---

9 Stefan Iavorskii polemicizes with this view in his anti-Protestant tract *Kamen' very* (Rock of Faith, pub. 1728, 1729, 1730, 1749). Here he cites the "dark glass" passage from 1 Corinthians discussed below in a positive sense (Iavorskii 1999, 201, 212, 215– 16). Like Palamas' *Triads*, *Rock of Faith* is directed against iconoclasts and may serve as another example of the "occularcentric" trend in Orthodox theology.

Chapter 16. The Ode as Revelation

properly prepared, such as a saint whose mind has been "cleared of passions," can attain to correct vision of the surrounding world. He achieves positive knowledge, based on experience rather than abstract theories. The degree of this knowledge depends on a person's inner purity: "the human mind when it becomes like that of angels in its passionlessness...may touch God's light and be worthy of supernatural epiphany, of course without knowing the divine essence, but seeing God in His divine manifestation, commensurate with the human capacity to see" (62). A person "sees not in the full measure of God's beauty but only to that degree that he himself has made himself capable of grasping the power of the Divine Spirit" (77).[10]

We may compare Palamas' ascetic ideal of "the mind cleared of passions" on the part of the saint to Descartes' well-known demand of the true philosopher; for both, a "pure mind" is both goal and source of divine knowledge, although certainly for Palamas this is a far less rational process. While divine transparency is possible via a perfect balance between the inner and outer light, inner light is nevertheless primary, the ontological (gnoseological) foundation for "the human capacity to see." Palamas explains that just as "sensational vision cannot act without light shining from without, so too the mind as possessor of mental feeling could not see and act by itself if Divine light had not illuminated it" (68). Yet such knowledge is the most reliable: "The essence of all this is comprehended by properly mental feeling. I say 'feeling' because of the clarity, obviousness, perfect reliability and the non-fanciful nature of understanding, and besides this because the body also somehow communes with the mental action of grace, reorients itself in accord with it, and itself becomes filled with a kind of sympathy for the innermost secrets of the soul..." (93)

This is more than mere negative (apophatic) knowledge. "Vision is higher than negation"; such knowledge is "inexpressible and inevitable" (63). It is unmediated, based on experience, and derives from "double" vision, on the one hand sensual, physical, and mental (and to some extent even rational), and on the other, spiritual. I write "to some extent" because Palamas specifically rejects the conclusions of pure reason as "fantasy," as empty abstract mentation. Moreover, imagination is included among the features characterizing the earthly mind. The result is a paradoxical "lack

---

[10] Compare in Lomonosov: "The Creator gave humankind two books...The First is this visible world, created by Him, so that a person, gazing upon the immensity, beauty and harmony of its constructions, would recognize divine omnipotence *according to the measure of the understanding given him* (po mere sebe darovannogo poniatiia)" (Lomonosov IV, 375; my italics).

331

of knowledge that is higher than knowledge, and knowledge that is higher than understanding, inner unity with the innermost and an inexpressible vision, a mysterious and unexpressed contemplation and taste of the eternal light" (105).

It is "inexpressible and unexpressed" yet true. It is "higher than understanding" in the sense that "by means of some supernatural knowledge he [a person] knows precisely that he is seeing light that is higher than light, but *how* he sees, he does not know at that time, indeed he cannot penetrate the nature of his vision due to the unanalyzable character of the spirit by which he sees" (82). While a person may prepare him or herself for such an experience, practice ascetic acts, say special prayers, etc., ultimately such vision is an inexplicable miracle, a mystery, an expression of divine grace. Although this miracle may not be amenable to explanation or adequate description, as in the odes it is marked by special signs. "Tasting the eternal light" and the "fusion" of flesh and spirit (cf. 105) is accompanied by a fever, joyousness, ecstasy, rapture, pleasure. Spiritual shock has physical consequences. Thus "in prayer we sense divine pleasure untouched by sorrow by means of mental feeling. ...[I]n this pleasure the body also miraculously transforms, filled with God's love..." (95).

In addition to the ontological and gnoseological functions of light, its aesthetic role is arguably no less important. The issue here is not only its beauty, which as we have already seen, Palamas often mentions, but "aesthetics" in the etymological sense of the word as "sensual perception or sensation" (from the Greek *aisthesis*) (Pelikan 1990, 102; on the importance of beauty in Orthodoxy, see Evdokimov 1990). The exalted state of the body corresponds to the process of "theosis," deification: "God simultaneously and wholly dwells in Himself and wholly lives in us, thus passing on to us not His nature but His glory and radiance. This is divine light, and the saints rightly call it divinity: indeed it deifies; and if this is so, then it is not simply divinity, but deification in and of itself, that is, the basis of the divine" (84–5) (Palamas here cites Pseudo-Dionysius the Areopagite's *Divine Names*; on "deification" in Palamas and in Orthodoxy, see Mantzarides 1984; Williams 1995; Bartos 1999). Notably, this distinction between the divine nature and radiance was a crucial argument for the defenders of icons. Like human beings, icons were attributed with the mystical capacity to reflect divine light: "So when the saints contemplate this divine light in themselves, seeing it by the divinizing communion of the Spirit, through the mysterious visitation of perfecting illuminations — then they behold the garment of their deification, their mind being glorified and filled by the grace of the

Chapter 16. The Ode as Revelation

Word, beautiful beyond measure in His splendor, just as the Divinity of the Word on the mountain glorified with divine light the body conjoined to it" (63; Palamas is citing St. Nilus of Sinai).

The image of "miraculous dressing in light" is connected with various Biblical texts, among the more important being the vision of the "Maiden in the sun" which was also a very widespread Russian folkloric motif (Toporkov 2005). That Palamas resorts to a Biblical, literary trope ("they behold the garment of their deification") in order to describe "communion of the Spirit" returns us to the problem of expressing the inexpressible in words and the strategies used for surmounting it. Although according to Palamas miraculous "double" vision is characterized by "clarity, obviousness, perfect reliability and the non-fanciful nature of understanding" it is still inexpressible. How can this be? On the one hand, for Palamas this is ultimately a question of faith in what "god-seers" have experienced:

> The monks know that the essence of God transcends the fact of being inaccessible to the senses, since God is not only above all created things, but is even beyond Godhead... This hypostatic light, seen spiritually by the saints, they know by experience to exist, as they tell us, and to exist not symbolically only, as do manifestations produced by fortuitous events; but it is an illumination immaterial and divine, a grace invisibly seen and ignorantly known. (Palamas 2003, 197; translation from Palamas 1983, 57)

The saints' vision is perfectly transparent. But on the other hand, how can what is "invisibly seen and ignorantly known" be conveyed to others? The problem here is not so much one of faith (whether or not we take mystical experience seriously) but the limits of communication. What is seen cannot be expressed in words; in the world of dark glass one requires symbols, imagination, and "manifestations produced by fortuitous events." "Not for nothing," writes Palamas, "do they speak of them [God's "inexpressible gifts"], but using examples and metaphorically, not because they also see them in examples and metaphors but because one cannot show what has been seen in any other way" (79).

One may also look at the complex poetics of Lomonosov's odes in this context, and at the "Baroque" means that the poet employs to express rapture that defies description. The problem here is that of the contradiction between the dark glass and transparency, which as we have seen to some extent words themselves confuse. "Examples and metaphors" are inevitable. We can speak here not only of the complex rhetorical arsenal used in panegyric writing but also of the function of classical and pagan imagery.

In the ode of 1742, for example, the vision of the "Maiden in the sun" from Revelations includes the image of the mountains of Thessaly, and the Maiden (Mary) casts "thunderbolts" (razit perunom) down at her enemies. On the one hand, one may speak of the "fundamental metaphorical nature" of Baroque discourse, which as Zhivov and Uspenskii write, conditions the fact that "religious occasions may make reference both to the Christian and to the classical pagan traditions, which are freely combined here [in odes], subordinate to the laws of semantic multidimensionality that is intrinsic to Baroque culture" (Zhivov and Uspenskii 1987, 121). According to these authors, the combination of Christian and classical imagery "neutralizes" or does away with the potential conflict that arose in Orthodox consciousness during the process of sacralizing the monarch. They demonstrate how these elements of the classical (pagan) heritage became part of the new religious consciousness of the later seventeenth century. On the other hand, Palamas himself described the "fundamental metaphorical nature" as an inevitable problem of language itself insofar as any attempt to express the inexpressible cannot help but resort to "examples and metaphors."

If an ode may be seen as a kind of prayer, then perhaps in the unusual sense that Palamas gives to the notion. He describes the special state of the soul when "purity of spiritual mind...allows the light of the Holy Trinity to shine forth at the time of prayer. ... The mind then transcends prayer, and this state should not properly be called prayer, but a fruit of the pure prayer sent by the Holy Spirit. The mind does not pray a definite prayer, but finds itself in ecstasy in the midst of incomprehensible realities. It is indeed an ignorance superior to knowledge." He further describes the "most joyful reality, which ravished St. Paul" and his absolute vision that turned him into "all eye" (Palamas 2003, 83; translation from Palamas 1983, 38) an image that according to Nicholas Gendle comes from Plotinus (Palamas 1983, 122, n. 41).

In this sense, the ode may be seen, like prayer, as not so much a verbal form as a visual experience of theophany. In this regard we may again quote Gukovskii who describes odic poetics in similar terms, using the metaphor of lightning: "Indeed the ecstatic poet is guided in his singing not by reason but rapture; his imagination soars, flying through space in a moment, through time, destroys logical connections like lightning, at once illuminating diverse places" (Gukovskii 2001, 47). Vision (revelation) in the odes transcends the physical bounds of time and space. The corporeal world becomes a metaphor with which the poet describes the indescribable state of his soul, Referring to the unusual use of language in odes, Gukovskii asserts that "The word, limited by its concrete, so to speak earthly meaning, inhibits his upward flight...There results a confusion between thinking about objects and abstractions, the destruction of borders between them" (Gukovskii 2001, 46).

Thus the common motif in the odes of the Russian empire's great size (its "lack of bounds," whose "end can't be seen," etc.), the impossibility of taking it all in, is not simply the registration of a fact but also a characteristic of the poet's spiritual state, just as is his marvelous capacity of his vision to instantaneously take in the entire world in a moment. If he "sees no end" (kontsa ne zrit) it doesn't mean that his sight is weak (analogous to the insufficient power of language) but that Russia's greatness is endless, as is the poet's rapture.[11]

On the one hand, at the center of attention of both Palamas and Gukovskii is the spiritual state of the one who sees the marvelous vision. On the other, the inspired poet, like Gukovskii himself, must resort to oblique references, to symbols, metaphors and similar imaginative means "produced by fortuitous events" in order to make an approximation in words. Among these means are classical as well as Christian images. The odes' vision-revelations thus have but a tenuous connection to the real world and transcend the limits of time and space. The chronotope of the ode is utopian, inspired, and prophetic. The dual light of revelation, in Palamas as in the odes, is "not limited in height, depth, or breadth," and the poet, like the god-seer, "in general does not see the limits of the visible and the light that illuminates him." The very image of the sun that commonly serves as metaphor for God and for divine action in theological tracts plays a major roles in odes, as critics have long recognized. But here, as in the reference to the "Maiden in the sun," in my opinion we are dealing here not with simply the use of a well-known image for certain definite (secular) poetic or political reasons, but also with a manifestation of deeper levels of cultural memory.

---

[11] Cf. in the ode of 1754, there is no end to joymaking:
    Так ныне град Петров священный,
    Толиким счастьем восхищенный,
    Восшед отрад на высоту,
    Вокруг веселия считает
    И края им не обретает;
    Какую зрит он красоту!
              (Lomonosov VIII, 558)
(So today the holy city of Peter / Is enraptured with such happiness, / Having gone, joyous, up to a height / Considers the merrymaking all around / And is unable to find its limit. / What beauty it sees!)

Part Two. Visuality and Orthodoxy in Eighteenth-Century Russian Culture

Works Cited

Alekseeva 2002 — Alekseeva, N. Iu. "Peterburgskii nemetskii poet G. V. Fr. Iunker." *XVIII vek*, 22 (2002): 8–27.

Atrem'eva 1996 — Artem'eva, T. V. *Istoriia metafiziki v Rossii XVIII veka*. St. Petersburg: Aleteiia, 1996.

Barankova, Mil'kov 2001 — Barankova, G. S., V. V. Mil'kov, ed. *Shestodnev Ioanna ékzarkha Bolgarskogo. Pamiatniki drevnerusskoi mysli: Issledovaniia i teksty*, vyp. 2. St. Petersburg: Aleteiia, 2001.

Bartos 1999 — Bartos, Emil. *Deification in Eastern Orthodox Theology: An Evaluation and Critique of the Theology of Dumitru Stăniloae*. Carlisle, Cumbria: Paternoster Press, 1999.

Bruce 1992 — Bruce, Steve, ed., *Religion and Modernization: Historians and Sociologists Debate the Secularization Thesis*. New York: Oxford UP, 1992.

Baehr 1988 — Baehr, Stephen L. "The 'Political Icon' in Seventeenth- and Eighteenth-Century Russia." *Russian Literature Triquarterly*. 21 (1988): 61–79.

Baehr 1991 — Baehr, Stephen L. *The Paradise Myth in Eighteenth-Century Russia: Utopian Patterns in Early Secular Russian Literature and Culture*. Stanford, CA: Stanford UP, 1991.

Dorovatovskaia 1911 — Dorovatovskaia, V. S. "O zaimstvovaniiah Lomonosova iz Biblii." In *M. V. Lomonosov: 1711–1911: Sbornik statei*. Ed. V. V. Sipovskii. St. Petersburg, 1911. Pp. 33–65.

Evdokimov 1970 — Evdokimov, Paul. *L'art de l'icône: Théologie de la beauté*. Paris: Desclée, De Brouwer, 1970.

Esaulov 1998 — Esaulov, I. A. "Problema vizual'noi dominanty russkoi slovesnosti." In *Evangel'skii tekst v russkoi literatury XVIII–XX vekov: Tsitata, reministsentsiia, motiv, siuzhet, zhanr. Sbornik nauchnykh trudov*. Vyp. 5. Petrozavodsk: Petrozavodskskii universitet,1998. Pp. 42–53.

Gromov and Mil'kov 2001 — Mil'kov V. V., M. N. Gromov. *Ideinye techeniia drevnerusskoi mysli*. St. Petersburg: Russkii Khristianskii gumanitarnyi institut, 2001.

Gukovskii 2001 — Gukovskii, G. A. *Rannie raboty po istorii russkoi poezii XVIII veka*. Moscow: Iazyki russkoi kul'tury, 2001.

Iavorskii 1999 — Iavorskii, S. *Skazanie ob Antikhriste, Dogmat o sviatyh ikonah. Bogoslovskoe tvorchestvo russkikh sviatitelei*. Moscow: Palomnik, 1999.

Jay 1993 — Jay, Martin. *Downcast Eyes: The Denigration of Vision in Twentieth-Century French Thought*. Berkeley, CA: University of California, 1993.

Kotel'nikov 1994 — Kotel'nikov, V. A. "Pravoslavie v tvorchestve russkikh pisatelei XIX veka." Avtoreferat diss. na soisk. uch. st. doktora filolog. nauk. St. Petersburg, 1994.

Kotel'nikov 2002 — *Khristianstvo i novaia russkaia literatura XVIII–XX vekov: Bibliograficheskii ukazatel'*. Ed. V. A. Kotel'nikov, comp. A. P. Dmitriev and L. V. Dmitrieva. St. Petersburg: Nauka, 2002.

Chapter 16. The Ode as Revelation

Levitt 1993 — Levitt, M. "Drama Sumarokova 'Pustynnik': k voprosu o zhanrovykh i ideinykh istochnikakh russkogo klassitsizma," *XVIII vek*, 18 (1993): 59–74. (In this volume as "Sumarokov's Drama 'The Hermit': On the Generic and Intellectual Sources of Russian Classicism.")

Levitt 2003 — Levitt, Marcus C. "The "Obviousness" of the Truth in Eighteenth-Century Russian Thought." *Filosofskii vek: Al'manah.* Vyp. 24: *Istoriia filosofii kak filosofiia.*, ch. 1 St. Petersburg, 2003. Pp. 236–45. (See also in this volume.)

Levitsky 1977 — Levitsky, Alexander. "The Sacred Ode (Oda Duxovnaja) in Eighteenth-Century Russian Literary Culture." Diss. University of Michigan. Ann Arbor, 1977.

Lomonosov I–XI — Lomonosov, M. V. *Polnoe sobranie sochinenii.* 11 vols. Moscow: AN SSSR, 1950–83.

Lossky 1974 — Lossky, Vladimir. *In the Image and Likeness of God.* [Crestwood, N.Y.]: St. Vladimir's Seminary Press, 1974.

Lutsevich 2002 — Lutsevich, L. F. *Psaltyr' v russkoi poezii.* St. Petersburg: D. Bulanin, 2002.

Maloney 1973 — Maloney, G. A. *Russian Hesychasm: The Spirituality of Nil Sorskii.* The Hague: Mouton, 1973.

Mantzarides 1984 — Mantzarides, G.I. *The Deification of Man: St. Gregory Palamas and the Orthodox Tradition.* Trans. L. Sherrard. Crestwood, N.Y.: St. Vladimir's Seminary Press, 1984.

Meyendorff 1974 — Meyendorff, J. *Byzantine Hesychasm: Historical, Theological and Social Problems: Collected Studies.* London: Variorum Reprints, 1974.

Meyendorff 1974a — Meyendorff, J. *St. Gregory Palamas and Orthodox Spirituality.* Crestwood, N.Y.: St. Vladimir's Seminary Press, 1974.

Meyendorff 1998 — Meyendorff, J. *A Study of Gregory Palamas.* 1974; Crestwood, N.Y.: St. Vladimir's Seminary Press, 1998.

NSK 1983 — *Nastol'naia kniga sviashchennosluzhitelia.* Vol. 4. Moscow, 1983.

Palamas 1973 — Gregory Palamas. *Défense des saints hésychastes.* John Meyendorff, ed. Spicilegium sacrum Lovaniense; études et documents, fasc. 30–31. 2nd rev. ed. Louvain: Spicilegium sacrum lovaniense, 1973.

Palamas 1983 — Gregory Palamas. *The Triads*, ed. and intro. John Meyendorff, trans. Nicholas Gendle, preface by Jaroslav Pelikan. The Classics of Western Spirituality. New York: Paulist Press, 1983.

Palamas 2003 — Palama, sv. Grigorii. *Triady v zashchtu sviashchenno-bezmolvstvuiushchikh.* Trans. and ed., V. Veniaminov. Moscow: Kanon+, 2003. An earlier edition is available on line at "Biblioteka starootecheskoi literatury," http://www.orthlib.ru/Palamas/triad_cont.html (accessed March 10, 2009).

Pelikan 1990 — Pelikan, Jaroslav. *Imago Dei: The Byzantine Apologia for Icons.* The A. W. Mellon Lectures in the Fine Arts. Princeton, N.J.: Princeton UP, 1990.

Pogosian and Smorzhevskih 2002 — Pogosian E. i Smorzhevskih M. "Ia devu v solntse zriu stoiashchu...": Apokalipitcheskii siuzhet i formy istoricheskoi refleksii." In *Istoriia i istoriosofiia v literaturnom prelomlenii*, ed. A. A. Danilevskii.

Studia russica Helsingiensia et Tartuensia, 8. Tartu: Tartu Ülikooli Kirjastus, 2002. Pp. 2–36.

Pumpianskii 1983a — Pumpianskii, L. V. "K istorii russkogo klassicizma (poetika Lomonosova)." *Kontekst 1982: Literaturno-teoreticheskie issledovaniia.* Moscow, 1983. Pp. 303–331.

Pumpianskii 1983b — Pumpianskii, L. V. "Lomonosov i nemetskaia shkola razuma," *XVIII vek,* 14 (1983): 3–44.

Sazonova 1987 — Sazonova, L. I. "Ot russkogo panegirika XVII v. k ode M. V. Lomonosova." In *Lomonosov i russkaia literatura.* Ed. A. S. Kurilov. Moscow: Nauka, 1987. Pp. 103–126.

Serman 1998 — Serman, I. Z. *Mikhail Lomonosov: Life and Poetry.* Jerusalem: Centre of Slavic and Russian Studies, Hebrew University of Jerusalem, 1988.

Silard 1996 — Silard, Lena. "Blok, Akhmatova i drugie (k dialogu pokolenii)." *Russica Romana,* 3 (1996): 239–64.

Solosin 1913 — Solosin, I. "Otrazhenie iazyka i obrazov Sv. Pisaniia i knig bogosluzhebnykh v stikhotvoreniiakh Lomonosova." *Izvestiia Otdeleniia Russkogo Iazyka i Slovesnosti Akademii Nauk,* 18, kn. 2 (1913), 238–293.

Sukhomlinov 1891 — Lomonosov, M. V. *Sochineniia,* vol. 1: *Stikhotvoreniia.* Ed. M. I. Suhomlinov. St. Petersburg: Akademiia nauk, 1891.

Toporkov 2005 — Toporkov, A. L. "Motiv 'chudesnogo odevaniia,'" *Zagovory v russkoi rukopisnoi traditsii XV–XIX vv.: istoriia, simvolika, poėtika.* Moscow: Indrik, 2005. Pp. 210–71 (In shortened form as "Motiv 'chudesnogo odevaniia' v russkikh zagovorakh XVII–XVIII vv." *Zagovornyi tekst: Genezis i struktura.* Moscow: Indrik, 2002. Pp. 55–62.)

Tsapina 2004 — Tsapina, O. A. "Pravoslavnoe prosveshchenie: Oksiumoron ili istoricheskaia real'nost'?" In *Evropeiskoe prosveshchenie i tsivilizatsiia Rossii.* Ed. S. Ia. Karp and S. A. Mezin. Moscow: Nauka, 2004. Pp. 301–313.

Williams 1995 — Williams, A. N. "Deification in Thomas Aquinas and Gregory Palamas." Diss. Yale University, 1995.

Zhivov 1996 — Zhivov V. M. *Iazyk i kul'tura v Rossii XVIII veka.* Moscow: Iazyki russkoi kul'tury, 1996.

Zhivov and Uspenskii 1987 — Zhivov, V. M. and B. A. Uspenskii. "Tsar' i Bog: Semioticheskie aspekty sakralizatsii monarkha v Rossii." In *Iazyki kul'tury i problemy perevodimosti.* Moscow: Nauka, 1987. Pp. 47–152.

— 17 —

AN ANTIDOTE TO NERVOUS JUICE:
Catherine the Great's Debate with Chappe d'Auteroche over Russian Culture

In the age of Enlightenment, when works of philosophy were often oriented toward analyzing specific political problems, travel notes played a significant part in debates over culture and politics, either providing "proofs" for a given theory or themselves advancing philosophical postulates. At the same time, tendentious histories and travel notes were often written — even commissioned — to serve immediate political goals. Such may well have been the case (I will argue) with the Abbe Chappe d'Auteroche's *Voyage en Sibérie* (1768),[1] which provoked Catherine's *Antidote, ou Examen de mauvais livre superbement imprimé intitulé Voyage en Sibérie* (1770).[2] In the analysis below I will examine two aspects of this exchange: first, I will consider Chappe d'Auteroche's book in the context of France's anti-Russian diplomacy of the time, and locate it more generally within the context of Russia as a problem

---

[1] Abbe Chappe d'Auteroche, *Voyage en Sibérie*, 2 vols. in 3, in folio (Paris: Debure Pere, 1768); 2 vols. (abridged) (Amsterdam: Marc Michel Rey, 1769–70); English version (abridged) as *A Journey Into Siberia* (London: T. Jeffreys, 1770; reprint NY: Arno Press and The NY Times, 1970). Since this article came out there has been a new critical edition of this work: Chappe d'Auteroche, *Voyage en Sibérie: fait par ordre du roi en 1761*, intro. and ed. Michel Mervaud. 2 vols. Studies on Voltaire and the Eighteenth Century, 2004: 03 and 2004: 04 (Oxford: Voltaire Foundation, 2004). Hereafter, and unless otherwise indicated, page citations of Chappe's work given in parentheses refer to the 1770 English translation; the sections cited have not been abridged.

[2] *Antidote, ou Examen de mauvais livre superbement imprimé intitulé Voyage en Sibérie...* (1770, n. p. [St. Petersburg]; 2nd edition, 2 vols. (Amsterdam: Marc-Michel Rey, 1771–72); English version (London: T. Jeffreys, 1772). *Antidote* was published anonymously; on its attribution, see A. N. Pypin, "Kto byl avtorom 'Antidota'?" in *Sochineniia imperatritsy Ekateriny II*, ed. A. N. Pypin, vol. 7 (St. Petersburg: Akademiia nauk, 1901), i-lvi. This is a convincing defense of Catherine's authorship and one of the best critical analyses of *Antidote* in general.

in European Enlightenment thought, with special attention to Chappe's unique attempt to ground political and cultural arguments in physiological terms. Second, I will analyze Catherine's response, both as part of an ongoing defense of her role as Enlightener of Russia, and as a defense of the worth of the Russian state and of modern Russian literature. The state and literature, whose fates were to be so closely intertwined in the later tradition, both intellectually and institutionally, were here explicitly linked, perhaps for the first time in Russian history.

The timing of Chappe's book was peculiar in many respects. Chappe was a French astronomer and geographer who had visited Russia in 1761–62 on behalf of the Parisian Academy of Sciences, in order to observe Venus when it passed across the sun on June 6, 1761.[3] With Russian help he organized an expedition to a superior observation site at Tobol'sk. His *Voyage en Sibérie*, three great folio volumes lavishly published, with copious tables, maps, and beautiful engravings based on illustrations by Jean-Baptiste Le Prince, appeared only six years later, in 1768. A few weeks after the book's approval for publication by the French Academy, Chappe set out to observe the transit of Venus once again, this time from California. On June 3, 1769 he observed the eclipse near San Jose, and soon after caught sick and died on August 1.[4] The *Voyage en Sibérie* was not merely the story of Chappe's expedition, but included an account "Of the MANNERS and CUSTOMS of the RUSSIANS, the Present State of their EMPIRE; with the Natural History, and Geographical Description of their Country, and Level of the Road from Paris to Tobolsky…"[5]

---

[3] For additional information on Chappe's expedition, see A. N. Pypin, "Kto byl avtorom 'Antidota'?" See also the note to "Sobstvennoruchnyi otryvok Ekateriny II s oproverzheniem svedenii Abbata Shappa o Rossii," in *Bumagi Imperitritsy Ekateriny II khraniashchikhsia v gos. arkhive ministerstva vnutrennikh del*, ed. P. Pekarskii (St. Petersburg, 1871), 6, 317–20. This short document, in Catherine's own hand, may be an unused draft foreword to *Antidote*; it requests that the recipient "supplier votre illustre patron de parcourir un ouvrage" refuting Chappe's book and which also "est le juste et eloquent precis des eminentes vertus et des qualites sublimes dont le ciel a decore l'auguste autocratrice" (i.e., Catherine herself) (319). This document helps to confirm both Catherine's authorship of *Antidote* and her interpretation of Chappe's political agenda that I discuss below.

[4] The book was approved on August 31, 1768; Chappe left Paris for California on September 18. See Chappe d'Auteroche, et al., *The 1769 Transit of Venus: The Baja California Observations*, ed. Doyle B. Nunis, Jr. (Los Angeles; Natural History Museum, 1982), 50.

[5] Chappe D'Auteroche, *A Journey into Siberia*, title page. A somewhat abbreviated version of the original French, which also lists "astronomical observations and experiments with natural electricity, and enhanced with geographical maps, plans, and landscapes, and engravings which depict the manners and ways of the Russians, their customs and

Chapter 17. An Antidote to Nervous Juice

(Why the level of the road between Paris and Tobol'sk is important is something to which I will return.) It is possible that the lag in publication was due to the labor involved in compiling the work or to the time needed to execute and prepare Le Prince's illustrations for the magnificent publication.[6] The time lag, however, may also have had a less innocent explanation.

Just at the time when Chappe was making his trip and compiling his book, views of Russia's significance as an ideological problem within French Enlightenment thought was crystallizing into two opposing tendencies.[7] On one side, whose most extreme exponent was Voltaire, stood those who embraced Peter the Great's reforms and looked to Russia as a success story, the embodiment of European Enlightenment values put into practice; as Carolyn Wilberger has written, Voltaire's "optimism about Russia was nothing less than an affirmation of faith in the basic validity of civilization itself and in its benefits for all mankind."[8] The mostly pro-Russia camp included Voltaire's fellow

---

clothing, [an account of?] the divinities of the Calmoucks, and many other bits of natural history" [Les Moeurs, les Usages des Russes, et l'Etat actuel de cette Puissance; la Description geographique & le Nivellement de la route de Paris à Tobolsk; l'Histoire naturelle de la meme route; des Observations astronomiques, et les Experiences sur l'Electricite naturelle; enrichi De Cartes geographiques, de Plans, de Profils du terrain; de Gravures qui representent les usages des Russes, leurs Moeurs, leurs habillements, les Divinites des Calmoucks, & plusieurs morceaux d'histoire naturelle]. Chappe d'Auteroche, *Voyage en Sibérie*, vol. 1 (Paris: Debure Pere, 1768), title page.

6   The drawings from which the engravings for the book were prepared are reproduced in Kimerly Rorschach, *Drawings by Jean-Baptiste Le Prince for the Voyage en Sibérie*. With an Essay by Carol Jones Neuman (Philadelphia: Rosenbach Museum & Library, 1986); see esp. 9–11. On the sexual politics of these images see the works cited in note 26 below.

7   Dimitri S. von Mohrenschildt places the divide at 1760; see his *Russia in the Intellectual Life of Eighteenth-Century France* (1936; rpt. New York: Octagon Books, 1972), 242. On this problem, see also: Albert Lortholary, *Le Mirage Russe en France au XVIIIᵉ siecle* (Paris: Editions contemporaines, n.d.); Francois de Labriolle, "Le Prosveščenie russe et les 'Lumières' en France (1760–1798)," *Revue des études slaves* 45 (1966): 75–91; Nicholas V. Riasanovsky, *A Parting of Ways: Government and the Educated Public in Russia, 1801–1855* (Oxford: Clarendon Press, 1976), chap. 1; Isabel de Madariaga, "Catherine and the *Philosophes*," in *Russia and the West in the Eighteenth Century*, ed. A. G. Cross (Newtonville, MA: Oriental Research Partners, 1983), 30–52; Carolyn Wilberger, *Voltaire's Russia*. Studies on Voltaire and the Eighteenth Century, vol. 164 (Oxford: The Voltaire Foundation, 1976), which argues for a continuum of views rather than two opposing sides (235f); and Larry Wolff, *Inventing Eastern Europe: The Map of Civilization on the Mind of the Enlightenment* (Stanford: Stanford UP, 1994). See also the useful bibliographical essay in *Voltaire and Catherine the Great: Selected Correspondence*, trans. and ed. A. Lentin (Cambridge: Oriental Research Partners, 1974), 178–86.

8   Wilberger, *Voltaire's Russia*, 15–16.

encyclopedists Diderot, D'Alembert, Grimm and Jaucourt, plus La Harpe and Marmontel; into this group also fell the travel writers Ségur, Falconet, Levesque, and De Ligne (although none of these individuals were as committed as Voltaire). Those who criticized Peter as despot and imitator took their cue from Rousseau (especially from the *Social Contract* of 1762) and in part from Montesquieu's *Spirit of the Laws* (1748).[9] The anti-Russia camp saw Russia as oriental (not European), barbarian (not civilized), and despotic (not ruled by law or social sensibility); this group included Mably, Condillac, Raynal, and Mirabeau.

This ideological bifurcation corresponded to the international diplomatic situation of the time, and was in part inspired by fear of Russia as a new major player in European politics and her successes in the Seven Years' War. Political and philosophical positions became intertwined; the defenders of beleaguered Polish independence, for example, decried Russian despotism, and were often sympathetic toward Russia's enemy, Turkey. From the late 1750's and early 60's, despite being allied with Russia, France became extremely alarmed at Russia's military potential as a new continental force, especially after her victory over Frederick's "invincible army" at Kunersdorff in August 1759 and her triumphant occupation of Berlin in 1760. When Catherine came to power by coup in June 1762 she resumed nominal friendly relations with France (briefly interrupted by Peter III's sudden switch of alliances), but Louis XV and his foreign minister the Duc du Choiseul continued to pursue the covert anti-Russian foreign policy begun during Elizabeth's last years, a policy motivated by a combination of fear, jealousy, and miscalculation about Catherine, whose legitimacy and ability to rule they questioned.[10]

It was common practice for governments of the day to promote foreign policy goals by commissioning (more or less openly) the writing of historical

---

[9] Montesquieu's views were greatly influenced by John Perry's travel account, *The State of Russia Under the Present Czar* (1716). On Rousseau and Montesquieu's views of Russia, see the works cited in note 29 and in note 7, esp. Wilberger, *Voltaire's Russia*, chap. 7. On Rousseau in eighteenth-century Russia, see also Iu. M. Lotman, "Russo i russkaia kul'tura XVIII veka," in *Epokha prosvesceniia: Iz istorii mezhdunarodnykh sviazei russkoi literatury*, ed. M. P. Alekseev (Leningrad: Nauka, 1967), 208–281, and Thomas Barran, *Russia Reads Rousseau, 1762–1825* (Evanston, Ill.: Northwestern UP, 2002).

[10] On the political and diplomatic relations between Russia and France during this period, see: Albert Vandal, *Louis XV et Elisabeth de Russie: Étude sur les Rélations de la France et de la Russie* (Paris, 1882), esp. chap. 7; and L. Jay Oliva, *Misalliance: A Study of French Policy in Russia During the Seven Years' War* (New York: New York UP, 1964). For a good recent overview of Russian foreign policy during the eighteenth century and a survey of views on Russian imperialism, see William C. Fuller, Jr., *Strategy and Power in Russia 1600–1914* (New York: The Free Press, 1992), chaps. 3 and 4.

Chapter 17. An Antidote to Nervous Juice

and travel accounts to suit their interests. A famous example is Voltaire's *History of the Russian Empire Under Peter the Great*, which Empress Elizabeth commissioned in 1757 during the Franco-Russian alliance of the Seven Years' War; it was considered by many at the time, and also by later commentators, as (to use Peter Gay's tag) "a collection of gross compliments disguised as history," although that may be unduly harsh.[11] In the *Antidote*, Catherine repeatedly suggests that it was the French government led by Choiseul that was behind the publication of Chappe's *Voyage*, and there is circumstantial evidence to support the contention. Chappe's book seems motivated by the goal of demonstrating that Russia was economically and militarily no true great power.[12] Not long before Chappe's expedition, Rousseau had menacingly predicted in the *Social Contract* (a refutation of Voltaire's idyllic view of Russia in the *History of the Russian Empire Under Peter the Great*[13]) that:

> The Russian empire would like to subjugate Europe, and will itself be subjugated. The Tatars, its subjects or its neighbors, will become its masters and ours. This revolution appears inevitable to me. All the kings of Europe are working together to hasten it.[14]

---

[11] Gay is quoted by Wolff, *Inventing Eastern Europe*, 206; Wilberger surveys the reactions and gives a sympathetic, revisionist view of Voltaire's work (*Voltaire's Russia*, 119–133).

[12] See for example, Chappe's devastating and detailed critique of the Russian military capability, and of the army's size, maintenance, hygiene, morale, and tactics (or lack of these things; 371–395 passim). Cf. Catherine's comment, alluding to France's role in urging Turkey to war against Russia: "Russia blocked the way of the domination of the Goths (Welches); unable to keep this from happening, they take their revenge by speaking as much evil about her as they can. Pretty nation! Is this prettiness? I do not know, but I do know very well that this is all said in the tone of an informer (souffleur) for Mustafa [i.e., Sultan Mustafa III of Turkey]" (9, 230). Catherine repeatedly suggests that Chappe (if he indeed were the true author) was the tool of anti-Russian political forces.

[13] See Wilberger's point by point analysis of the passage of which this is the conclusion, in chap. 7 of *Voltaire's Russia*.

[14] Jean-Jacques Rousseau, *Social Contract*, Book II, chap. 8. See *The Collected Writings of Rousseau*, vol. 4, ed. Roger D. Masters and Christopher Kelly, trans. Judith R. Bush, Roger D. Masters, and Christopher Kelly (Hanover, NH: Dartmouth College, 1994), 158. Rousseau was probably referring to the khanate of the Crimean Tatars, who with its Turkish overlords had been allies of France against Peter I. Captured by Russia during the Russo-Turkish War of 1768–74, the khanate was given independent status, but subsequently taken over by Russia in 1783. On the other hand, as Larry Wolff points out, "in the eighteenth century [for Europeans] the name of Tatary designated a vague and vast geographical space — from the Crimea to Siberia" (*Inventing Eastern Europe*, 39–40).

Part Two. Visuality and Orthodoxy in Eighteenth-Century Russian Culture

Chappe notes near the end of his book that

> While I was in Petersburg, just setting out for Siberia, I received a letter from Paris, desiring me to take an accurate survey of this country, from whence whole nations were in a short time expected to emigrate, and, like the Sythians and the Huns, to over run our little Europe. Instead of such people, I found marshes and deserts. (394)

Thus Chappe concludes that the Russian military threat is not real. This passage also suggests Chappe's role (whether formal or not) as a French agent on a scouting mission and seems to support the contention that this mission was at least in part politically (rather than scientifically) inspired. The title, allegorical frontispiece, preface and first sentence of Chappe's *Voyage* all grandly emphasize that the expedition — and possibly the book as well — was "undertaken by order of the King" (and with the support of the Academy as well as "enlightened Ministers"), and it might not be a mistake to take this literally. Chappe's bold advertisement of Louis XV's support, which could simply be taken in the usual sense as his patronage of the Royal Academy of Sciences, particularly irked Catherine because the expedition had actually been funded by Elizabeth and with the support of the *Russian* Academy of Sciences, which had published Chappe's findings in 1762.[15]

A strong circumstantial case can be made linking Chappe to the clandestine French anti-Russian diplomatic clique called, appropriately, the King's Secret (le Secret du Roi). Unknown even to the French Foreign Ministry, and as the name implies under the King's direct supervision, its main goals in the period after the Seven Year's War were to create a Franco-Prussian alliance in order to protect Poland and the continental balance of power and to support France's traditional allies (and Russia's enemies) Sweden, Turkey and the Crimean Tartars.[16] The group regularly used go-

---

[15] *Memoire du passage de Venus sur le Soleil, contenant aussi quelques autres observations sur l'astronomie et la declinasion de la boussole, faites à Tobolsk en Sibérie l'année 1761* (St. Petersburg: Akademiia nauk, 1762). Chappe's results were delivered orally to the Academy on January 11, 1762. See M. V. Lomonosov, *Polnoe sobranie sochinenii*, vol. 9 (Moscow, Leningrad: Akademiia nauk, 1955), 807–808.

[16] On the history of the King's secret, see L. Jay Oliva, *Misalliance*, 9–10 and passim. See also Alice Chevalier, *Claude-Carloman de Rulhière premier historien de la Pologne: sa vie et son oeuvre historique d'apres des documents inedits* (Paris: Les Editions Domat-Montcrestien, 1939), 10–11.

vernment subsidized publications to further its aims. Specifically, there are numerous threads linking Chappe and Claude-Carloman de Rulhière, an important publicist for the clique, which also included the Comte de Broglie, Jean-Louis Favier, and the French Ambassador to Russia Baron de Breteuil, who had been sent to Russia in 1760 with a secret brief to exert "his utmost ingenuity to prevent a further extension of Russia's power" before becoming ambassador soon after.[17] Upon Chappe's return to St. Petersburg from Siberia on November 1, 1761, Breteuil prevailed upon the astronomer to stay the winter with him in Russia, which he did (he remained until May, thus experiencing most of Peter III's short reign and missing Catherine's coup by only a month). In Petersburg Chappe became close friends with Rulhière, who arrived in Russia in March on Choiseul's orders to serve as Breueuil's secretary. Ruhlière spent three months in close association with Chappe, referred to him as his "premier ami" and even wrote poetry praising the truth of his works and sounding the anti-Russian theme.[18] Rulhière's notorious *Anecdotes of the Revolution in Russia in 1762* was a spicy eyewitness account of Catherine's coup, and helped both confirm and generate hostility toward her on the part of Louis XV's government.[19] The *Anecdotes of the Revolution* reveals in an intentionally lighthearted vein intimate details of Catherine's personal life, and more seriously, the suspicious nature of Peter III's too convenient death. Intervention on the part of Voltaire, Diderot, and other of Catherine's well-wishers prevented publication of the *Anecdotes* during her lifetime (it was published in 1797, the year after she died), but in manuscript the book immediately became a staple of Parisian salons — starting with Choiseul's, and made the rounds of other European capitals for many years.[20] Rulhière's biographer contends that if his views on Russia were demonstrably influenced by Chappe (to the point of suggesting that *Anecdotes of the Revolution* may even even have been a collaboration), it was Rulhière who "provided his friend [Chappe] with

---

[17] von Mohrenschildt, *Russia in the Intellectual Life*, 19–20; before being sent to Russia he was admitted into the King's Secret. Hence he was receiving two sets of secret orders, from Choiseul and from Louis XV. See Oliva, *Misalliance*, 174–175.

[18] Rulhière, *Oeuvres* (Paris, 1819), 2: 346; cited in Chevalier, *Claude-Carloman de Rulhière*, 48 n. 5; see also 226.

[19] Charles Carloman de Rulhière, *Histoire ou anecdotes sur la revolution de Russie, en l'année 1762* (Paris, Desenne, 1797); in English as: *A History or Anecdotes of the Revolution in Russia* (London, 1797; rpt. New York: Arno Press and New York Times, 1970).

[20] For example, Rulhière gave readings in Berlin and Vienna in 1776 (Wolff, *Inventing Eastern Europe*, 273).

his political views."21 In the same year that Chappe's *Voyage* was published, 1768, Choiseul commissioned Rulhière to begin his monumental and anti-Russian *History of the Anarchy in Poland* (1768–1791), and in 1773 he probably collaborated with Favier (on Broglie's orders) on Favier's *Reasoned Conjectures On France's Actual Position In the European Political System*, which may be considered a defense of the clique's position.22 Hence Catherine's assumption — that Chappe's book and its attempt to denigrate Russian power were inspired by external political considerations — seems quite plausible. The fact that the *Voyage's* appearance almost coincided with Turkey's declaration of war on Russia, which France had done much to secretly encourage, made it seem all the more sinister.23

Chappe may also have been inspired by the sentiment Rulhière expressed in his *Anecdotes*: "Scarcely has one spent eight days in Russia than one can already speak reasonably of the Russians: everything leaps to the eye."24 Chappe (like Rulhière) could have been comforted by the fact that he spent whole *months* in Russia (fifteen, seven of which were spent in Petersburg). While Catherine reproved Chappe for taking much of his material from faulty second-hand sources,25 and made fun of the fact that Chappe "saw Russia" primarily from within a totally enclosed, fur-lined Russian sleigh while speeding along the post road in the dead of winter. Chappe made a concerted effort to back up his annihilatingly negative view of Russia with

---

21 Chevalier, *Claude-Carloman de Rulhière*, 227; see also 54, 226, 227 n. 5. Notably, Rulhière was also in profound agreement with the opinions about Russia expressed by his "friend and master" (Chevalier's phrase) Rousseau in the *Social Contract*, which appeared in the same year as Catherine's "revolution." On the sources of Rulhière's book, including Rousseau, see Chevalier, chap. 2. and von Mohrenschildt, *Russia in the Intellectual Life*, 65–68.

22 Chevalier, *Claude-Carloman de Rulhiere*, 10 and 228–229. The history of Poland, Rulhière's masterwork, remained incomplete. For its fascinating history, see Wolff, *Inventing Eastern Europe*, 272–78.

23 Turkey declared war in October; Chappe's *Voyage* appeared some time between September and December. The French Academy of Sciences' recommendation to publish (Chappe d'Auteroche, *Voyage en Sibérie*, vol. 1 [Paris: Debure Pere, 1768], xxxi) is dated August 31, 1768, presumably the book's terminus post quem. Its publication had been announced as early as April 29, 1767, when Chappe had read a prospectus of the book at the Academy, part of which was published (Lortholary, *Le Mirage Russe en France*, 365 n. 123).

24 Rulhière, *Anecdotes of the Revolution*, 52; quoted in Wolff, *Inventing Eastern Europe*, 274.

25 The authorities Chappe cites include: Voltaire, Johann Georg Gmelin, Guillaume Delisle, Philip Strahlenberg, and Laurent Lange.

Chapter 17. An Antidote to Nervous Juice

(what he saw as) objective, scientific data — using a battery of instruments and analytical methods to continually measure almost everything he came across (temperature, size, color, geographical position, elevation, etc.).

For the purposes of this analysis I will center on one such measurement: Russia's alleged lack of "nervous juice." According to Montesquieu's well known thesis, a nation's character directly depended on its climate and geography. Chappe continued this materialist-determinist line of thought, but challenged Montesquieu's view that Russians were essentially European, "a very brave, simple, unreserved, unsuspecting people, without policy or craft, having few vices, and several virtues, a great deal of sincerity and honesty, and whose dispositions are not very amorous" (321).[26] On the contrary, to Chappe these were no *noble* savages, but corrupt, scheming, dishonest, cowardly, sexually promiscuous barbarians riddled with venereal diseases. Chappe based his analysis of the Russians' physiological inferiority on the works of Claude-Nicholas Le Cat, a well known French surgeon and physiologist of the day[27]; it is unclear whether Chappe is being disingenuous when he refers to Le Cat's ideas as "truths and opinions generally admitted" (322). Le Cat followed in the tradition of Descartes, who combined philosophy and physiology in contending that the body and soul have a physical point of interface in the brain at the pineal gland, the place where the "vital" or "animal spirits" within the blood make contact with the soul.[28] According

---

26 Chappe is paraphrasing *Spirit of the Laws*.
George E. Munro analyzes the polemic over Russians' sexuality in "Politics, Sexuality and Servility: The Debate Between Catherine II and the Abbe Chappe d'Auteroche," in *Russia and the West in the Eignteenth Century*, ed. A. G. Cross (Newtonville, MA: Oriental Research Partners, 1983), 124–134. On this, see also Larry Wolff, "Possessing Eastern Europe: Sexuality, Slavery, and Corporal Punishment," chap. 2 in *Inventing Eastern Europe*, and in particular his designation of Chappe's "pornography of barbarism," 76–77.

27 See Theodore Vetter, "Le Cat, Claude-Nicolas," in *Dictionary of Scientific Biography*, ed. Charles C. Gillespie (New York: Charles Scribner's Sons, 1972), 7, 114–16.

28 See: G. A. Lindeboom, *Descartes and Medicine*. Nieuwe Nederlandse Bijdragen tot de Geschiedenis der Geneeskunde, no. 1 (Amsterdam: Rodopi, 1979), esp. 57–85; M. H. Pirenne, "Descartes and the Body-Mind Problem in Physiology," *British Journal of the Philosophy of Science*, 1 (1950): 43–59; David Farrell Krell, "Paradoxes of the Pineal: From Descartes to Georges Bataille," *Philosophy*, 21 (1987), Supplement: 215–228. For a recent sympathetic reading of Descartes' ideas, see Richard B. Carter, *Descartes' Medical Philosophy: The Organic Solution to the Mind-Body Problem* (Baltimore: Johns Hopkins UP, 1983). Descartes' sympathetic readers like Pirenne note that despite the antiquated terminology many of Descartes' fundamental notions about how the nervous system functions are still accepted.

to this doctrine, the animal spirits, starting from the brain, are what act mechanically upon the nerves throughout the body, causing sensation and muscle movement; the mind or soul influences the direction of the nerve impulses as they leave the pineal gland, their point of origin that acts as a kind of switchboard. Chappe contrasts the "human machine" and the "universal spirit" (known by various names including vitriolic acid, phlogiston, electric matter) which he describes as the "primary fluid which gives life to the whole universe" (322). This life force (Descartes' "fire without flame") actuates the human machine; we ingest it with the air we breathe and the food we eat, and it becomes part of our blood via the digestive system and the lungs. In the brain, the blood is purified and the end product — what Le Cat calls "animal fluid" and Chappe (possibly after Montesquieu[29]) "nervous juice" — is formed, "the chief organ [both] of sensation and of the faculties of the soul" (323). The system of nervous juice seems close to that of what we think of as the nervous system, although with the crucial admixture of the spiritual component:

> The nervous juice makes a kind of lake in the brain; the spinal marrow is the principal channel which conveys it from thence, and the nerves are so many rivers or streams which sprinkle and vivify all the parts of the animal. The nerves being tubes, their texture is such, that the sides of the canals are composed of much smaller tubes; which terminate by one extremity in the brain, and by the other in the skin, where they expand and from a net-work of nerves... it forms one continued stream, which becomes the organ of sense. This nervous juice, as subtle as light, transmits instantaneously to the brain, all the impressions it receives. This account of the nerves, and of the nervous juice, establishes the system of our sensations, of our ideas, of the mind, of the genius, and of the faculties of the rational soul. (324)

---

[29] Montesquieu himself refers to "nervous juice" in his discussion of the differences between "northern" and "southern" peoples, in a chapter which Chappe cites repeatedly in criticizing Russia (cf. *Spirit of the Laws*, XIV, 2). However, Montesquieu elsewhere argues that the Russians are not an Asiatic, but a *European* nation, and hence amenable to Peter's civilizing reforms (XIV, 14) — a position that Catherine proclaimed in the famous opening sentence of the *Nakaz* ("Russia is a European nation"). On Montesquieu and Catherine, see the works cited in note 7 above and: F. V. Taranovskii, "Montesk'e o Rossii (K istorii Nakaza imperatritsy Ekateriny II)," in *Trudy russkikh uchenykh za-granitsei: Sbornik akademicheskoi gruppy v Berline*, 1 (Berlin: Slovo, 1922), 178–223; and A. N. Pypin, "Ekaterina II i Montestk'e," *Vestnik evropy*, 5 (1903): 272–300.

Chapter 17. An Antidote to Nervous Juice

Chappe's scientific advance (if we can call it that) is to take Le Cat's theory of the working of the nervous system and apply it "scientifically" to the problem posed by Montesquieu concerning "the influence of the climate on the inhabitants" (325). While "the universal spirit" is "everywhere the same," Chappe argues, its action depends on a host of "secondary causes" (324) — such as the weather, and the elevation and quality of the soil. Bad weather impedes the particles of universal spirit; in a similar way that the quality of the soil determines what sort of plants will grow, "in proportion as we rise, the air will become purer...[and] the universal fluid will become more active" (325). Hence it is essential to know such things as "the level of the road from Paris to Tobolsk." "In any comparison we would make between climates and characters of men, it is necessary to attend to the height of the soil on which they dwell" (326).

On his travels from Petersburg to Tobol'sk Chappe determined "with more accuracy than was necessary for [the] present purpose" that the Russian kingdom is "one vast plain" whose height is "very inconsiderable" (326). As opposed to France, whose "inequalities" "have a remarkable effect on the varieties of soil observable in the French provinces, and on the nature of the atmosphere" (328), Russia is "almost on a level" and is characterized by a "striking uniformity" among its animals, flora and fauna, and people. "Whoever has been through one province knows all the Russians; they are of the same stature, they have similar passions, similar dispositions, and their manners are alike" — and the same goes for their dress, amusements, agriculture, and houses. (How convenient for the traveller on a tight schedule!) More seriously, the moistness of the marshy lowlands and the climate obstruct the flow of nervous juices. In winter, which

> appears to be the only season in which the Russians can enjoy the benefits of a pure atmosphere...the cold is so intense, that all nature seems to be lifeless and totally inactive. All the inhabitants, shut up and confined within their stoves ["poeles," what Chappe calls huts], breathe an air infected by exhalations and vapors proceeding from perspiration. They pass their time in these stoves wholly given up to indolence, sleeping almost all day in a suffocating heat, and hardly taking any exercise. This manner of living, and the climate, produces such a degree of dissolution in the blood of these people, that they are under the necessity of bathing twice a week all the year round, in order to get rid of the watery disposition prevalent in their constitutions, by raising an artificial perspiration. (330)

The conclusion from this is that

> the nervous juice in the Russian is inspissated and sluggish, more adapted to form strong constitutions than men of genius...the floggings they constantly undergo in the baths, and the heat they experience there, blunts the sensibility of the external organs...The want of genius therefore among the Russians, appears to be an effect of the soil and the climate. (330–331)

Chappe cites Montesquieu's dictum that "to make a Russian feel, one must flay him" (331) and echoes Rousseau's cutting praise of the Russians as a people with a "genius" of imitativeness. Beyond the physiological inferiority due to lack of nervous juice, in the tradition of the Montesquieu-Rousseau line on Russia, Chappe also attributes Russia's social inferiority to the effects of despotism, and its concurrent deadening effects on education:

> The love of fame and of our country [France?!] is unknown in Russia; despotism debases the mind, damps the genius, and stifles every kind of sentiment. In Russia no person ventures to think; the soul is so much debased, that its faculties are destroyed. Fear is almost the only passion by which the whole nation is actuated... The fatal effects of despotism are extended over all the arts...these people, though deficient in genius, and deprived of the powers of imagination, would still be a very different nation in many respects, if they enjoyed the blessings of liberty. But the question is, whether they would make any considerable progress, even if they enjoyed this advantage. (332–335)

Following such a pronouncement, Chappe's subsequent statement that "the spirit of the nation seems likely to undergo a total change" under Catherine, and his rhetorically optimistic question "What progress will they not make under this Empress?" hardly seem convincing. They also point to another basic problem with the chronology of Chappe's book. Based on Chappe's experiences in Russia during the reigns of Elizabeth and Peter III, it was published six years into Catherine's, and hence in many respects was wildly out of date[30] (think of trying to explain Russia today on the basis of a visit

---

[30] Or badly edited? Much of Chappe's analysis refers explicitly to Empress Elizabeth. Remarks about Russia as a place of tyranny and terror (275–77) due to its "despotic sovereign" (330), for example, refer to her, and contradict his praise for Catherine as reformer (e.g. 278). Lortholary refers to this as Chappe's "equivoque insupportable" (*Le Mirage Russe en France*, 192). Chappe also gets a lot of mileage out of Russian forms of corporal punishment, esp. the beating of the Countess Lopukhin (see Wolff's comments, *Inventing Eastern Europe*, 76). Although it was not until Catherine's Charter

to Gorbachev's Russia), but could not but cast an extremely unfavorable shadow over Catherine's ambitious program for political and cultural reform then gathering momentum.[31] However, if Chappe was anachronistic, so too was Catherine, challenging Chappe's analysis mostly with examples taken from her own reign, most notably her *Bolshoi Nakaz* (*Grand Instruction*) for the delegates of the Commission to Compose a New Law Code, published in 1767. The *Nakaz* had clearly been aimed as much for a European as for a Russian audience; it appeared in French, English, German, Italian, Greek, Swedish, Dutch, Polish, Latin and Rumanian editions, several sponsored by Catherine herself.[32] After the Commission was ended, Catherine made use of the young literary men who had served as its secretaries and inaugurated the Russian satirical journals, with the publication of her own *Vsiakaia vsiachina* (Odds and Ends) in 1769.[33] During her famous Volga trip the summer before the Commission convened, Catherine organized a group translation of Marmontel's new political novel *Belisaire* (in Russian: *Velizer*), published in Moscow in 1768. In the same year she created the Society for the Translation of Foreign Books into Russian, "probably the leading voice for the French Enlightenment" in Russia,[34] which translated selections of the *Encyclopédie* — which Catherine had even offered to publish in Russia — as well as works by Voltaire, Montesquieu, Mably, and Rousseau; and Russia's open-handed offers of haven to Voltaire, Rousseau, d'Alembert and Diderot were highly publicized.

---

to the Nobility of 1785 that Russian nobles were granted personal bodily inviolability, in the *Instruction* Catherine had followed Beccaria in rejecting torture and corporal punishment, which were largely done away with except in the military.

31 Soviet historians typically condemned Catherine's reform program and denigrated her as a hypocritical promoter of serfdom. Hence sympathy for Chappe's denunciation of "despotic Russia." See, for example, I. M. Kossova, "'Puteshestvie v Sibir'' i 'Antidot'," *Voprosy istorii*, 1 (January, 1984): 185–189.

32 See John T. Alexander, "Catherine II (Ekaterina Alekseevna), 'The Great,' Empress of Russia," in *Dictionary of Literary Biography*, vol. 150, *Early Modern Russian Writers: The Late Seventeenth and Eighteenth Centuries*, ed. Marcus C. Levitt (Detroit: Bruccoli Clark Layman and Gale Research, 1995), 48–49. Strangely enough, the *Nakaz* was also advertised in the 1770 English translation of Chappe's *Voyage*!

33 See my essay on, and translation from, *Vsiakaia vsiachina* (*Odds and Ends*) in *Russian Women Writers*, ed. Christine Tomei (New York: Garland, 1996), 3–27. On Catherine's career as a writer, see John T. Alexander, "Catherine II," 43–54.

34 Gary Marker, *Publishing, Printing, and the Origins of Intellectual Life in Russia, 1700–1800* (Princeton: Princeton UP, 1985), 92. On the translation society, see V. P. Semennikov, *Sobranie, staraiushcheesia o perevode inostrannykh knig, uchrezhdennoe Ekaterinoi II, 1768–1783 gg.: istoriko-literaturnoe izsledovanie* (St. Petersburg, 1913).

Catherine's program of conspicuous political and intellectual toleration seemed calculated in part to highlight the contrast between Russia and France under Louis XV. Indeed, in the *Antidote* Catherine repeatedly juxtaposes her own liberal policies to France's repressive ones — for example, that neither *Belisaire* nor the *Instruction* could be published in France, leading her to ask pointedly which of the two nations was the more "monarchist," and which the more "despotic" (81–82; 289–90).[35] That Catherine took these issues seriously is shown not only by the fact that she took it upon herself to answer Chappe, but by the vehemence with which she did so. Catherine demolished Chappe's book section by section, often sentence by sentence, and even word by word, listing his errors, failings, confusions, lies and biases, mostly in an extremely sarcastic, even abusive, manner. The narrative conceit is that the work is addressed directly to Chappe (it is written primarily in the second person), who at the time of writing was already dead, and several times Catherine spitefully refers to him as "M. Le Defunt"! Such rhetorical improprieties as well as the exhausting catalogue of Chappe's failings lessened the *Antidote*'s impact on European readers. That Catherine could not reveal her authorship (which, indeed, was disputed for a long time, especially in France) and published the work anonymously, also contributed to its obscurity.[36]

Nevertheless, Catherine's *Antidote* is a unique and valuable document, presenting as it does in an extremely direct way the empress' response to what she took as an insult to Russia and as a personal challenge to her entire program of political and cultural transformation. The *Antidote* was composed and published in French and was clearly meant as "a reply to all French detractors of Russia."[37] It shows her to be not only fully conversant with the European debate over Russia's place in the Enlightenment, but

---

[35] Translations from *Antidote* are my own, and are based on the original French text (from vol. 7 of *Sochineniia imperatritsy Ekateriny II na osnovanii podlinnykh rukopisei i s ob'iasnitel'nye primechaniiami*, ed. A. N. Pypin, [St. Petersburg: Akademiia nauk, 1901]) in consultation with the Russian translation ("Antidot [Protivoiadie]: Polemicheskoe sochinenie Ekateriny II-oi ili razbor knigi abbata Shappa d'Oterosha o Rossii," in *Osmnadtsatyi vek*, 4 [1869]: 225–463). Dual citations of *Antidote* given in parentheses refer first to the French and then to the Russian text.

[36] Catherine could not publish the work for many reasons. For one, it would have given Chappe's work greater notoriety. *Antidote*'s outspoken defense and fulsome praise of the empress would also have made the work seem a brazen apologia. On problems of Catherine's authorship, see A. N. Pypin, "Kto byl avtorom 'Antidota'?" On the critical reaction to the *Voyage* and *Antidote*, see Lortholary, *Le Mirage Russe*, 196–197.

[37] Lortholary, *Le Mirage Russe*, 194.

eager to assert her own positive, unique vision of that place. For example, she denied the notion of Russia's total barbarism before Peter the Great, which was shared by Russia's detractors and friends alike (including Voltaire). She defended Russia's "ancient ways" as not only analogous to European historical experience[38] but worthy of interest in their own, indigenous right (thus some historians even consider her a proto-Slavophile). Yet Catherine not only defended the Russian peasant and traditional Russian culture, but also (and unlike the Slavophiles) Russia's contemporary high secular culture, and its achievements in the arts and sciences (a subject on which even Voltaire was notably silent).[39] Catherine's was one of the first in a series of defenses of Russian literature, the most famous of which is Novikov's *Opyt istoricheskogo slovaria o rossiiskikh pisateliakh (Attempt at an Historical Dictionary of Russian Writers)* of 1772, an effort to confirm the modern canon of Russian letters that in a small degree polemicizes with *Antidote*.[40]

---

[38] Cf. Voltaire's comparisons of France before Louis XIV discussed by Wilberger, *Voltaire's Russia*, 72.

[39] Wilberger notes that "the lack of information in this area [Russian culture] is symptomatic of a major weakness in Voltaire's entire concept of Russia" (*Voltaire's Russia*, 106); see also 140–144, 159–160, 275–277, and her article, "Eighteenth-Century Scholarship on Russian Literature," *Eighteenth-Century Studies*, 5 (Summer 1972): 503–526. Wilberger's assertions about Catherine's sense of Russia's cultural inferiority (159), and that she (together with Rulhière!) "summarily dismissed" the notion of a "national character" (259–260 and 270) seem mistaken in light of the *Antidote*, although Catherine's statements certainly were far from a triumphant encomium to Russian letters. It would be interesting to consider the *Antidote* in Wilberger's terms as a further response to Voltaire and his work on Peter.

[40] For a survey of scholarship on the European reception of Russian literature, and a discussion of Novikov's work and his disagreements with Catherine, see I. F. Martynov, "'Opyt istoricheskogo slovaria o rossiiskikh pisateliakh' N. I. Novikova i literaturnaia polemika 60–70-kh godov XVIII veka," *Russkaia literatura*, 3 (1968): 184–191. Novikov's main objection to Catherine's description of Russian letters was her praise of Vasilii Petrov; see my discussion below.
W. Gareth Jones asserts that the anonymous "Nachtricht von einigen russischen Schriftstellern" that appeared anonymously in a Leipzig journal in late 1768 was meant as an answer to Chappe's calumny, but I see no evidence for this view ("The Image of the Eighteenth-Century Russian Author," in *Russia in the Age of Enlightenment: Essays for Isabel de Madariaga*, ed. Roger Bartlett and Janet M. Hartley [London: Macmillan, 1990], 63–64). Jones also asserts that the publication of Antiokh Kantemir's satires in French in the mid 1740's had been "part of what would now be called Russia's cultural foreign policy" (63), but I likewise find no indications that this was the case. Kantemir had supervised the project before his death, and if it was carried out under the auspices of the Ministry of Foreign Affairs, that was because Kantemir had been a diplomat

Catherine begins her defense of Russian letters by noting that Chappe "surveyed the level of our intellectual capabilities and determined that we are fools because there are few mountains in Russia. This reasoning," she added, "inspires us with boundless respect for the Swiss and for Savoyards"; she feigns great distress to think of people of such genius employed as concierges or shoe-shiners (251; 424). She responds to Chappe's physiological excursus in a similar vein:

> He begins by overwhelming us with data from Physics, far more ingenious than trustworthy, in order to prove via composites of solids, spirits and fluids, fibers, vessels and channels; by elemental fire, by the universal spirit, sulphuric acid, phlogiston, electrical matter, etc.; by the digestive system, by chyle, by the circulation of blood, by the way in which it becomes agitated in the lungs and is pushed by the heart through the aorta to the brain, by the nervous juice (suc nerveux), by the conformity of the brain and the spinal marrow, by the skin and the nervous network it forms, by the system of nerves and nervous juice, which, he says, "establishes the system of our sensations, of our ideas, of the mind, of the genius, and of all the faculties of the rational soul"; by the relation of nourishment to the soil and by various secondary causes — from all of this he deduces that the Russians can be nothing more than blockheads (sots)... (263; 434)

> The Abbe is too simple to believe that he has proven, like two and two are four, that all Russians are wanting in genius. Ah well, reader! Will the Abbe's formal declaration, supported by the most beautiful proofs in the world, and appealing to all of the four elements, ever be enough to convince you that I am nothing but a boob (nigaud)? (265; 436)

> Pitiful slander! There is no need to be born in the mountains to see right through it. Even those who are from the plains can judge its merits. (255; 427)

Challenging Chappe more on his own turf, she goes on to dispute (in great detail) his method of using barometers to determine land elevation and hence to deny the validity of the data derived therefrom. She also dissects what she shows to be his preconceived and mistaken conceptions of Russian geography (e.g., that all of Russia is a "vast plain") and of the alleged uniformity of the Russian land and people from region to region. Montesquieu and company

---

in its service; as Helmut Grasshof has shown, Kantemir's European colleagues had their own purposes for publishing the satires. See Kh. Grassgof, "Pervye perevody satir A. D. Kantemir," in *Mezhdunarodnye sviazi russkoi literatury*, ed. M. P. Alekseev (Moscow, Leningrad: AN SSSR, 1963), 101–111, and N. A. Kopanev, "O pervykh izdaniiakh satir A. Kantemira," *XVIII vek*, 15 (Leningrad, 1986), 140–153.

simply "furnish a convenient pretext to say a great many bad things about the inhabitants" of Russia (274; 443).

To Chappe's assertion that despite the efforts of Russia's leaders "not one Russian has appeared in the course of more than sixty years, whose name deserves to be recorded in the history of the Arts and Sciences" (320), Catherine asks: "Is it the Russians' fault that Chappe did not know their language, and had never heard of writers who distinguished themselves before the Dearly Departed (M. le Defunt) had his book approved and printed...?" (255; 428). She "takes up his challenge" and names the following figures: Feofan Prokopovich, "who left many profound and scholarly works"; Antiokh Kantemir, whose satires were "translated into several languages"; Vasilii Tatishchev, and his erudite history; Vasilii Trediakovskii, with his "several good translations"; Mikhail Lomonosov, and his various writings "filled with genius and eloquence"[41]; Alexander Sumarokov, whose many works have brought him "loud fame"; and Stepan Krasheninnikov, whose description of Kamchatka Chappe himself published in French as an appendix to the *Voyage*. While this was no "Pushkin Speech,"[42] and reflects some degree of equivocation (indeed Catherine had helped turn Trediakovskii into a laughingstock for his *Tilemakhida*),[43] this was a clear and straightforward assertion that, yes, Russia does have a literature and a literary life. Catherine adds that

> After the Abbe's departure, and especially in the last years, when literature, the arts and sciences have enjoyed such special encouragement, almost no week passes when several new books, either translations or original, do not leave the presses. (256; 428)[44]

Then Catherine cites Vasilii Petrov as an example of a promising young writer. His poetic gift "approaches that of Lomonosov, and has even more harmony,"

---

[41] Chappe also names Lomonosov as "a man of genius" (apparently in his role as a scientist; 320).

[42] Dostoevsky's famous address at the opening of the monument to the poet in Moscow in 1880, which confirmed Pushkin's canonization as Russia's "national poet." See my *Russian Literary Politics and the Pushkin Celebration of 1880* (Cornell UP, 1989), chapter 4.

[43] On Trediakovskii's reputation, see Irina Reyfman, *Vasilii Trediakovsky: The Fool of the 'New' Russian Literature* (Stanford: Stanford UP, 1991).

[44] According to Gary Marker's figures the annual average of Russian-language books between 1761–1770 was between 150–160 annually, or about 3 books a week. Of these, fifty percent were literary or general interest books. Marker, *Publishing, Printing*, 71–72.

and his uniquely faithful verse translation of the *Aeneid* (pub. 1770), of which none comparable exists in other languages, she asserts, "will make him immortal." Here Catherine may have been playing to the home audience, since Petrov's talent (or lack of it) was a subject of contention on the pages of the satirical journals appearing at this time. Here as elsewhere, defending Russia meant defending her own reign and her own personal actions, down to the poets she patronized.

The immediate political campaign to denigrate Russia, in which we have included Chappe's *Voyage en Sibérie*, clearly backfired. If France had helped push the Turks into war with Russia in October 1768 (which had served as the pretext for disbanding the Commission to Create a New Law Code), by the time of the *Antidote*'s publication in 1770 Russia had scored impressive victories (especially the total destruction of the Turkish fleet at Chesme in June 1770), fully justifying Catherine's defense of Russia's national honor and taste for glory, which Chappe had impugned. As if in answer to such critics, Catherine declared (notably, with stress on Russia's military rather than cultural prowess):

> This war will win Russia a name for herself; people will see that this is a brave and indefatigable people, with men of evident merit and all the qualities that make heroes; they will see that she lacks no resources, that those she has are by no means exhausted, and that she can defend herself and wage war with ease and vigor when she is unjustly attacked.[45]

In a more long-term political perspective, though, Chappe's *Voyage* was one in a series of works that helped prepare and justify subsequent European military aggression against Russia, particularly the Napoleonic invasion of 1812. As Tolstoy dramatized it in *War and Peace*, and as the historian Larry Wolff has recently put it, "one may observe [how] the intellectual formulas of the Enlightenment...[were] deployed in the military maneuvers of the next generation."[46]

The terms in which the debate over the nature (and possibility) of civilization in Russia was posed had perhaps even more lasting repercussions.

---

[45] Quoted in John T. Alexander, *Catherine the Great: Life and Legend* (New York: Oxford University Press, 1989), 134. Alexander's description of the *Antidote*'s tenor as "a bellicose superpatriotism...that brooked no criticism from Europe" (133) seems overstated.

[46] Wolff, *Inventing Eastern Europe*, 363.

Chapter 17. An Antidote to Nervous Juice

In Catherine's debate with Chappe d'Auteroche we may observe the process by which Russian culture (and more narrowly, Russian literature) as an abstract intellectual construct in European debates over Russia came to play such an acute role in the semiotic "Yes" or "No" of later Russian debates over cultural identity.[47] By the time of Petr Chaadaev, the Enlightenment commonality of interests between state and culture presumed by Catherine in the *Antidote* could no longer be envisaged.[48] For the intelligenstsia, the connection between official ideology and Russian culture, whether presumed by Nicholas I in his doctrine of "Official Nationality" or its debunking in the Marquis de Custine's famous travel memoir *Russia in 1839*, could only give rise to despair, and to the long-term cultural crisis whose effects Russia is still experiencing.

---

[47] See, for example, Boris Groys' analysis in "Russia and the West: The Quest for Russian National Identity," *Studies in Soviet Thought*, 43 (1992): 185–98.

[48] See Wilberger's stimulating comments on the connections between Chaadaev's and Rousseau's views, *Voltaire's Russia*, 213–214. The fundamental problem posed by the work of Wilberger, Wolff, Riasanovsky, and others, that the crisis of nineteenth-century Russian identity (most dramatically expressed in Chaadaev's first "Letter on the Philosophy of History" [pub. 1836] and still reverberating) derived from the European Enlightenment debate over Russia's place on the "map of civilization" has yet to be fully explored.

18

THE POLEMIC WITH ROUSSEAU OVER GENDER AND SOCIABILITY IN E. S. URUSOVA'S *POLION* (1774)

One of the basic challenges we face in reading eighteenth-century works of literature is loss of context, the lack of those cultural conventions and points of reference that give meaning, substance, and life to any communicative act. This is particularly the case as regards eighteenth-century Russian women's writing, which has only recently begun to be uncovered and explored. A case in point is Princess Ekaterina Urusova (1747 — after 1816) and her *Polion ili Prosvetivshiisia neliudim, poema* (*Polion or the Misanthrope Enlightened*) (1774), one of the first individual poetic works and the first *poema* published by a Russian woman writer.[1] While many of Urusova's works were published anonymously, there is evidence that she was known and earned significant recognition as an author. In 1772, the year her first individually issued work came out, a verse epistle to P. D. Eropkin, Nikolai Novikov praised the poet's songs, elegies, "and other small poems" for their "pure style, delicacy and pleasant descriptions," even though to that date Urusova had not published any short works — at least, not under her name.[2] A few years later the anonymous reviewer of Urusova's *Heroides Dedicated to the Muses* (1777) noted that *Polion* was by the same unnamed but known woman author, and declared that it had "long since earned the praises and respect of our best Poets."[3] Derzhavin

---

[1] *Polion ili Prosvetivshiisia neliudim, poema* (St. Petersburg, 1774).
[2] N. I. Novikov, *Opyt istoricheskago slovaria o rossiiskikh pisateliakh* (1772; rpt. Moscow: Kniga, 1997), 230.
[3] *Sankt-Peterburgskie Vedomosti* 6: 22 (1777), 174–76; the quoted words are from 175. My thanks to Yuliya Volkonovich for this citation. The prefatory poem in *Iroidy*, "O Muzy! Vy moi dukh ko pesniam vsplamenite," showcases the issue of female authorship. This poem is reprinted in F. Göpfert and M. Fainshtein, eds. *Predstatel'nitsy muz:Rrusskie poetessy XVIII veka* (Welmshorst: F. K. Göpfert, 1998), 160, and also with accompanying English translation in *An Anthology of Russian Women's Writing*,

Chapter 18. The Polemic with Rousseau over Gender

referred to Urusova in his *Memoirs* (*Zapiski*) as a "famous poet (*slavnaia stikhotvoritsa*) of that time" (the 1770's), but noted that he had jokingly declined the suggestion to marry her on the grounds that with two writers in the family "we will both forget, and there will be no one to cook the soup (*shchi*)."[4] Very little, however, is known about Urusova and her works, which have only begun to come under scrutiny in recently years.[5] In a pioneering article, Judith Vowles provocatively suggests that the title *Polion*, the name of the eponymous protagonist, indicates a dialogue over gender (*pol+i+on*–"sex and he"), thus raising fundamental questions about the work that modern readers may ask: what were the precise terms and limits of this dialogue, and how does it clarify the nature of women's early engagement in modern Russian literature?[6]

    1777–1992, ed. and trans. Catriona Kelly (New York: Oxford UP, 1994), 1–2 and 397. *Predstatel'nitsy muz* contains most or all of Urusova's known works, and I cite the text of *Polion* (pp.124–54) from this edition, indicating canto and line in parentheses. A translation of *Polion* and other works by Urusova will be included in Amanda Ewington, ed., *Eighteenth-Century Russian Women Poets* (Chicago, forthcoming).

4   G. R. Derzhavin, *Zapiski*, in his *Sochineniia*, ed. Ia. Grot, vol. 6 (1871; rpt. Cambridge, MA: Oriental Research Partners, 1973), 539. On this and on Russian women writers' association with Derzhavin and his circle, see Sandra Shaw Bennett, "'Parnassian Sisters' of Derzhavin's Acquaintance: Some Observations on Women's Writing in Eighteenth-Century Russia," in *A Window on Russia: Proceedings of the V International Conference of the Study Group on Eighteenth-Century Russia, Gargano, 1994*, ed. Maria Di Salvo and Lindsey Hughes (Rome: La Fenice Edizioni, 1996), 249–56.

5   For useful discussions with some reference to Urusova, see Bennett, "'Parnassian Sisters'"; Judith Vowles, "The 'Feminization' of Russian Literature: Women, Language and Literature in Eighteenth-Century Russia," in Toby W. Clyman and Diana Greene, eds., *Women Writers in Russina Literature* (Westport, CT: Praeger, 1994), 35–60; Wendy Rosslyn, "Making Their Way into Print: Poems by Eighteenth-Century Russian Women," *Slavonic and East European Review*, 78: 3 (2000): 407–38; and Catriona Kelly, "Sappho, Corinna and Niobe: Genres and Personae in Russian Women's Writing, 1760–1820," in Adele Barker and Jehanne Gheith, eds., *A History of Russian Women's Writing* (New York: Cambridge UP, 2002), 37–61; Kelly erroneously refers to *Polion* as a "mock-epic" (44). For a conspectus of earlier sources on Urusova see the entry on Urusova by Mary Zirin in *Dictionary of Russian Women Writers*, ed. Marina Ledkovskaia-Astman et al. (Westport, CT: Greenwood, 1994), 683–84.

6   Vowles, "The 'Feminization,'" 45–7. Detecting an encoded meaning in the title may be overinterpretation. Protagonists of pastoral verse were commonly given exotic names, often foreign or taken from mythology, which, as Joachim Klein notes about Sumarokov's eclogues, was meant to "emphasize the pastoral world's distance from everyday existence" (Joachim Klein, *Die Schäferdichtung des russischen Klassizismus*. Veröffentlichungen der Abteilung für Slavische Sprachen und Literaturen des Osteuropa-Instituts [Slavisches Seminar] an der Freien Universität Berlin; Bd. 67 [Berlin: Otto Harrassowitz, 1988], in Russian in his *Puti kul'turnogo importa: Trudy*

359

Vowles offers a stimulating short reading of *Polion* and suggests an important subtext for this dialogue: Trediakovskii's *Tilemakhida* (1766), his reworking in verse of François Fénélon's popular moralistic novel *Les Aventures de Telemache*. Vowles argues that Urusova inverts the episode in which Telemachus escapes from Circe's island and the clutches of her seductive female minions, preserving his heroic independence as a man. In purposeful contrast, Urusova's protagonist is saved from his false misanthropic education by the love and mentoring of Naida, who may herself be a semi-divine figure ("Наида" clearly suggests "naiad," наяда, water nymph of classical mythology).[7] Vowles situates Urusova's work along the literary axis that begins with the précieux, "feminized" culture of love which Trediakovskii had introduced into Russia with his *Voyage to the Island of Love* in 1730[8] and ends with its implicit repudiation in the high Neoclassicist *Tilemakhida* (1766) that spurns the feminine in favor of male political virtue. This reading is convincing, although Vowles' attempt to extrapolate the poem's male-female dichotomy into linguistic and cultural terms—associating Polion with "with Church Slavonic and ecclesiastical culture" and Naida with "the spoken language of society"—is not.[9] Vowles' reading underscores the challenge *Polion* presents to modern readers: to decode and contextualize the terms in which Urusova's work frames the debate over gender.

---

    po russkoi literature XVIII veka [Moscow: Iazyki slavianskoi kul'tury, 2005]; the quote is on p. 111.) There does exist the name "Polión" in Spanish literary and theatrical works. I know of no other example of a "Polion" in Russian literature, although a similarly exotic "Polidor," meaning "many-gifted," did occur, possibly distantly recalling Greek mythology (Priam had two sons named Polydorus). "Polidor" was the title of Lomonosov's separately published idyll of 1750 (M. V. Lomonosov, *Polnoe sobranie sochinenii* [hereafter: PSS], 11 vols. [Moscow: AN SSSR, 1950–83], 8: 276–81, 963) and the name also occurs in a pastoral context in Kheraskov's philosophical-Anacreontic ode "O razume" (M. M. Kheraskov, *Izbrannye sochineniia*, ed. A. V. Zapadov. Biblioteka poeta, malaia seriia. [Leningrad: Sovetskii pisatel' 1961], 85).

7 *Slovar' russkogo iazyka XVIII veka*, vyp. 14 (St. Petersburg: Nauka, 2004), 115. Alternative spellings listed here include "наяда," "наияда," and "найяда."

8 See Iu. M. Lotman, "'Ezda v ostrov liubvi' Trediakovskogo i funktsiia perevodnoi literatury v russkoi kul'ture pervoi poloviny XVIII veka," *Problemy izucheniia kul'turnogo naslediia* (Moscow, 1985), 222–30, and reprinted in *Izbrannye stat'i*, vol. 2 (Tallinn: Aleksandra, 1992), 22–28.

9 Vowles, "The 'Feminization,'" 47. *Polion* is in the standard middle-range idyllic idiom of "Slaveno-rossiiskii," in the tradition of Sumarokov (see for example his "Epistola o stikhotvorstve"), and I do not detect a contrast between Polion and Naida in terms of language or style. On "Slaveno-rossiiskii" as the eighteenth-century Russian literary language, see Victor Zhivov's fundamental study, *Language and Culture in Eighteenth Century Russia* (Boston: Academic Studies Press, 2009).

Chapter 18. The Polemic with Rousseau over Gender

This paper suggests another important subtext in *Polion* that adds a further piece to this puzzle, as it examines *Polion*'s dialogue with perhaps the most famous Enlightenment-era attack on women's participation in society, Rousseau's "Letter to d'Alembert on the Theater" (1758).[10] Rousseau's "Letter" raised a storm of controversy in its day, marking a major divide in French Enlightenment thought, as it dramatically signaled Rousseau's personal and intellectual parting of ways from the Encyclopedists. (Among other things, the controversy led to Rousseau's rupture with Diderot, d'Alembert's resignation from the *Encyclopédie*, and its loss of permission to publish.[11]) In engaging directly with Rousseau's criticism of the theater and by extension with his critique of women's role in educated society, *Polion* not only offers evidence of how a contemporary Russian responded to his tract (to my knowledge, the only recorded response) but also suggests the terms in which Urusova engaged with European debates over the place of gender in Enlightenment culture.[12] Further, the Rousseau connection may also help to clarify the Russian poetic tradition within which Urusova was writing, as *Polion* may be seen as one in a series of *poemy* that polemicized with Rousseau (particularly with his "Discourse on the Arts and Sciences" and "Discourse on Inequality," precursors to the "Letter to d'Alembert").

Polion's most explicit references to Rousseau come in canto 3, in which the hero receives a letter from a city friend.[13] The following passage depicts Polion's vexation and skepticism as he reads the letter telling of the amusements of the city:

---

[10] Jean-Jacques Rousseau's "Lettre à M. d'Alembert sur les spectacles" is available in English in *The Collected Writings of Rousseau*, vol. 10: *Letter to D'Alembert and Writings for the Theater*, ed. and trans. Allan Bloom, Charles Butterworth, and Christopher Kelly. (Lebanon, NH: Dartmouth College, published by UP of New England, 2004).

[11] James F. Hamilton, "Molière and Rousseau: The Confrontation of Art and Politics," in *Molière and the Commonwealth of Letters: Patrimony and Posterity*, ed. Roger Johnson, Jr., Editha S. Neumann, and Guy T. Trail (Jackson: UP of Mississippi, 1975), 100.

[12] On Rousseau in Russia the most recent and complete discussion is Thomas Barran, *Russia Reads Rousseau, 1762–1825* (Evanston, Ill.: Northwestern UP, 2002), which includes a substantial bibliography. To my knowledge, neither Rousseau nor the "Letter to d'Alembert" are discussed in the secondary literature on Russian women's writing, except for passing mention.

[13] Polion's relationship to this person is tenuous, given that Polion's misanthropy extends even to friendship ("On men'she vsekh ego iz smertnykh nenavidel [He hated him less than all other mortals]," 2.140]). However, it constitutes the only (if minimal) sub-plot of the work — inserted, perhaps, merely as a way of developing the anti-Rousseauean subtext.

Среди веселостей — веселости во граде!
Вскричал он в горести, в смятенье и досаде:
Во граде бедствия единые живут,
И скуку общую там радостью зовут;
Забавой самою сердца обременненны,
Затем, что гордостью они изобретенны.
Читая далее, досады больше зрит.
Там писано: *Театр во граде здесь открыт!*
Мы видели на нем стенящую Заиру,
Плачевный сей пример убийства данный миру,
Когда ревнующий и к теням Орозман,
Сразил ее, любовь приемля за обман:
Со Орозманом мы, с Заирою страдали;
И будто о прямом несчастии рыдали.
Се плод позорищей!¹⁴ — Письма читатель рек,
Иль редко и без них рыдает человек;
И нужно ль выдумкой всеобщу горесть множить,
Дабы встревоженны сердца еще тревожить;
Возможно ль, чтобы я доволен действом был,
Которым бы тоску, удвоил, не забыл!
О! Люди, вам театр, не честь, но поношенье;
Он образ всей земли, лишь только в уменьшенье!
Еще: *мы Талией здесь мысли веселим.*
И вы любуетесь безумием своим!
Смеетесь вы себе, чтоб ввек не исправляться;
Удобно ль слабостью своей увеселяться?
Позволено ли в смех пороки претворять?
Карать их надлежит нам, ими не играть. (3: 217–244)

(*Among the amusements* — amusements in the city! / He cried in sorrow, distress and annoyance. / In the city only dwell misfortunes, / And they call the general boredom joy; / Their hearts are burdened with pleasures themselves, / Because these are born of pride. / Reading further, he is even more vexed. / There is written: *A theater has been opened here in the city!* / We saw there the moaning Zaire, / That lamentable example of murder given to the world, / When Orozman, jealous of phantoms, / Cut her down, taking love as deception. / We suffered along with Orozman and Zaire, / And sobbed as if in actual tribulation. / This is the fruit of spectacle[14]! — the letter's reader spoke, / As if a person weeps so seldom

---

[14] The word *pozorishche* apparently still had the neutral meaning of "spectacle" or "performance," as in Church Slavonic (see this and related words in Grigorii D'iachenko, ed., *Polnyi Tserkovno-Slavianskii slovar'* [1900; rpt. Moscow, 1993], 445),

Chapter 18. The Polemic with Rousseau over Gender

without them; / Does one have to think up ways to multiply the general sorrow, / To upset already upset hearts; / Could I really be satisfied with an action [or play] that doubles my anguish rather than makes me forget it? / Oh, people, the theater does you no honor, just disgrace: / It's the image of life as a whole, given in miniature! / And further: *we cheer our thoughts with Thalia's help.* / You admire your own madness! / You laugh to yourself that you'll never reform; / But is it proper to enjoy one's weakness? / Is it acceptable to make a joke of vices? / We should punish them, not turn them into play.)

There follows Polion's denunciation of love and its amusements as recommended by his unnamed friend (such as evening strolls on the riverbank). The passage refers directly to the substance of Rousseau's letter, as it concerns the opening of a theater, and Polion echoes Rousseau's complaint about its baneful influence, not as a corrective but as an encouragement of weakness and vice.[15] The theater is a microcosm of the world's evil ("the image of life as a whole, given in miniature!"), replicating and redoubling its evils and tears rather than eliminating them.

Urusova introduces *Zaire* as a counter-example in favor of the theater. Voltaire's play is a highly tearful variant of Shakespeare's *Othello*, with Orozman assuming the role of the tragically jealous lover.[16] The play was well known and produced in Russia, and continued to serve as a model of sentiment through Karamzin's generation.[17] Although Rousseau had

---

although the given passage suggests the word's transition toward the later (and contemporary Russian) meaning of "a disgrace or shameful event."

[15] The pretext for Rousseau's letter had been d'Alembert's suggestion in his article on Geneva in the *Encyclopédie* that that city should open a theater.

[16] The play was also held up as a call for religious toleration. For a recent discussion, see Caroline Weber, "Voltaire's *Zaire*: Fantasies of Infidelity, Ideologies of Faith," *South Central Review*, 21: 2 (Summer, 2004): 42–62. Sumarokov defended its Christian message against charges of deism in his posthumously published "Mnenie vo snovidenii o frantsuzskikh tragediiakh," *Polnoe sobranie vsekh sochinenii, v stikhakh i proze*, ed. N. I. Novikov. Vol. 4 (Moscow, 1781), 352–3, declaring that "Zaire will never go out of fashion" (353).

[17] *Zaire* was among Voltaire's most popular and long lasting plays on the Russian stage. Among early instances of its performance were: stagings at court by students from the Kadetskii Korpus in the 1740's and 50's; a production by amateur nobles at court in 1763, and by the French court troupe in 1765; by students of the Smol'nyi institute in 1772; and by an amateur society at court in Petersburg in 1775. See P. R. Zaborov, *Russkaia literatura i Vol'ter: XVIII — pervaia tret' XIX v.* (Leningrad: Nauka, 1978), 37. Zaborov also surveys the play's continuing popularity through the 1820's (45, 86–9, 90–94, 102, 211, 153, 158); on Karamzin, see 90–94. For an example of Karamzin's high praise of the play, see his Sentimentalist manifesto "Chto nuzhno avtoru?" in N. M. Karamzin, *Sochineniia v dvukh tomakh*, vol. 2 (Leningrad: Khudozhestvennaia literatura, 1984), 60.

explicitly exempted *Zaire* from his criticism of theater in the "Letter to d'Alembert," Urusova here cites the play to refute his basic argument. In any case, Polion's friend (and by extension, the authorial voice) offers *Zaire* as an ideal model of that tearful romantic sensibility cultivated by Neoclassical and Sentimental dramaturgy alike. The image of *Zaire* in the friend's letter might also be taken as a partial analogy for Polion's own problem, suggesting the potentially tragic consequences that may come of misinterpreting love as a deception.

More central to Rousseau's critique of the theater in the "Letter to d'Alembert" is his reading of Molière's *The Misanthrope*, a play which *Polion*'s subtitle ("Neliudim") directly calls to mind. The connection between the two works, however, is rather generalized. In *Polion*, as in *The Misanthrope*, the title character's misanthropy runs aground on the shoals of love, although the resolutions are radically different: Alceste's love for the social butterfly Célimène comes to naught, and only serves to discomfit Alceste, who is confirmed in his unhappy misanthropy, whereas Polion is triumphantly converted to Naida's alternative philosophy through her love ("Liubov'! Liubov'! Ty nas mgnovenno prosveshchaesh'" [Love! Love! You enlighten us instantaneously], 5.82). Polion's unnamed friend the letter-writer may be seen to fulfill a similar function as Philinte, Alceste's friend and foil, a well-adjusted man of society. Unlike Molière's pair, Polion and his friend have no direct contact, yet the friend's voice is an important component of the *poema*'s dialogue, as in the passage cited above. Rousseau's defense of Alceste against what he considered Molière's unfair treatment in the "Letter to d'Alembert" caused readers, rightly, to associate Rousseau himself with Alceste, and by extension, Polion with his defense of "misanthropic" views may be seen as a stand-in for Rousseau, as Urusova understood him.[18]

In addition to sparking debate about how the theater functioned, both *Zaire* and *The Misanthrope* became points of reference in an ongoing Enlightenment discussion concerning women's role in society and the relative merits of sociability, a debate that, as in so many other areas, may be seen in terms of a Voltaire — Rousseau dichotomy.[19] Discussion of *Zaire*

---

[18] On Rousseau's association with Alceste, see, for example, Jonas Barish, *The Antitheatrical Prejudice* (Berkeley: University of California Press, 1981), 268–9.

[19] This despite Rousseau's praise of Voltaire in the "Letter to d'Alembert," which may have been calculated to support Voltaire's amateur theatricals held in Geneva (Barish, *The Antitheatrical Prejudice*, 261).

Chapter 18. The Polemic with Rousseau over Gender

had focused in particular on the issue of whether love plots were a necessary and desirable part of tragic drama, and in his 1736 preface to an English translation, Voltaire had connected this feature of his work to the supremacy of French sociability, as founded on the society of women. Even if putting "so much love into our dramatic performances" might be taken as a fault, the French, he asserted,

> have succeeded better in it than all other nations, ancient and modern, put together: love appears on our stage with more decorum, more delicacy, and truth, than we meet with on any other; and the reason is, because of all other nations the French are best acquainted with society: the perpetual commerce and intercourse of the two sexes, carried on with so much vivacity and good breeding, has introduced amongst us a politeness unknown to all the world but ourselves. Society principally depends on the fair sex...[20]

Rousseau's position was essentially the inverse: the theater was corrupted by its very dependence on a society catering to the whims of the fair sex; to Rousseau, the demands of decorum inhibit and destroy rather than further the truth. As Dena Goodman puts it, the "Letter to d'Alembert" signaled Rousseau's rejection of a larger model of enlightenment that she describes as "grounded in a female-centered mixed-gender sociability that gendered French culture, the Enlightenment, and civilization itself as feminine."[21]

Recent critics have challenged the notion of the "anti-feminism" of Rousseau's "Letter to d'Alembert," arguing that such a view disregards the historical and rhetorical context of his writing, among other things, failing

---

[20] *The Works of M. de Voltaire*, trans. and ed. T. Francklin, T. Smollett, and others. 35 vols. (London, 1761–81), 28: 259–60. (Accessed through Eighteenth Century Collections Online [ECCO], http://www.gale.com/EighteenthCentury/.)

[21] Dena Goodman, *The Republic of Letters: A Cultural History of the French Enlightenment* (Ithaca, N.Y.: Cornell UP, 1994), 6. Goodman writes further that "the power of women over men, especially of salonnières over men of letters, became the unstated theme of his response to d'Alembert... The *Lettre à d'Alembert* was Rousseau's philosophical break with the Enlightenment Republic of Letters and his personal break with his friends who constituted it... [Rousseau], who had argued that man was by nature unsociable, rejected the society of the Republic of Letters and began to create his own myth of the solitary seeker of truth, the lone man of virtue in a corrupt world" (39).

In the Russian Enlightenment tradition from Peter the Great through Karamzin, women were allotted a central role in the Europeanization of modern society, at least in theory, but the institutional development of "female-centered mixed-gender sociability" in Russia awaits scholarly exploration.

to account for its appeal to women.²² In the case of *Polion*, the impulse to counter Rousseau's allegedly "anti-feminist" view with an assertion of Urusova's "feminist" response should also be resisted as anachronistic. Urusova's *poema* advocates a Voltairean mainstream Enlightenment "female-centered mixed-gender sociability," as Naida brings Polion onto the true path via her love. The conflict here is not between different, opposing models of sociability, female- or male-centered, but about misanthropy as the negation of *all* human society. Polion's unnamed friend personifies the ideal of moderation and avoidance of extremes as a social skill to be learned, and situates these at the heart of sociability:

> И ведал то, что мы для общества рожденны
> И людям слабости дозволить принужденны;
> Что мы обязаны, чтоб лучшу жизнь иметь,
> И худо иногда спокойно в ней терпеть;
> Такой урок ему был собственно полезен,
> И был он в обществе всем нравен и любезен. (2.143–8)
>
> (And he knew that we are born for society, / And forced to permit people their weaknesses; / That we are obliged, so as to have a better life, / To sometimes calmly tolerate evil; / This lesson was in fact useful to him, / And in society he pleased and was liked by all.)

That this sociability involves the *soobshchestvo* of men and women is clearly implied, but nowhere directly stated.²³ Obviously, conclusions may be

---

[22] On Rousseau as anti-feminist, see for example: Barish, *The Antitheatrical Prejudice*, chap. 9; Victor G. Wexler, "'Made for Man's Delight': Rousseau as Antifeminist," *American Historical Review*, 81: 2 (Apr., 1976): 266–291. Much of recent scholarship, which is substantial, challenges this label. Among the rich literature, see: David Marshall, "Rousseau and the State of Theater," *Representations* 13 (Winter, 1986): 84–114; Joan B. Landes, *Women and the Public Sphere in the Age of the French Revolution* (Ithaca, N.Y.: Cornell UP, 1988), chap. 3; Elizabeth Wingrove, "Sexual Performance as Political Performance in the *Lettre à M. D'Alembert sur les Spectacles*," *Political Theory* 23: 4 (Nov., 1995): 585–616; and her review article, "Interpretive Practices and Political Designs: Reading Authenticity, Integrity, and Reform in Jean-Jacques Rousseau," *Political Theory*, 29: 1 (Feb., 2001): 91–111; Mary Seidman Trouille, *Sexual Politics in the Enlightenment: Women Writers Read Rousseau* (Albany, N.Y.: State University of New York Press, 1997); Helena Rosenblatt, "On the 'Misogyny' of Jean-Jacques Rousseau: The Letter to d'Alembert in Historical Context," *French Historical Studies* 25: 1 (Winter 2002): 91–114; F. Forman-Barzilai, "The Emergence of Contextualism in Rousseau's Political Thought: The Case of Parisian Theatre in the Lettre à D'Alembert," *History of Political Thought* 24: 3 (2003): 435–463.

[23] The word is used in 2.181 (see the passage quoted below), essentially as a synonym for "obshchestvo" (society).

Chapter 18. The Polemic with Rousseau over Gender

drawn from the plot, and by Naida's role as mentor and savior to Polion, that is, the story describes men's need of women and love in order to achieve genuine enlightenment — an eighteenth-century version, perhaps, of Sonia Marmeladova's saving Raskol'nikov.[24] Still, the image of "society" in *Polion* is rather abstract, far from any concrete Russian (or other) reality, although there are a few gestures in that direction, e.g., that Polion is a serf-owner (3.30); that he tries to implement new rational agricultural methods which fail miserably (3.123–140); and that Polion and Naida end up united "in body and soul" (5.332), although whether or not Naida is a flesh and blood woman or a demigod remains ambiguous. For these reasons, it is not possible to say with certainty that Urusova intended *Polion* as an argument in favor of women's writing or female sociability in any but the most general (and traditional male-centered) terms. The criticism of Rousseau refers specifically only to the status of the theater and, by extension, to his alleged misanthropy; and Voltaire enters the picture as an ideal of theatrical sensibility rather than proponent of an explicitly female-gendered sociability. Moreover, there is nothing within the text itself that unambiguously marks *Polion* as the work of a woman author.[25] The one place where the lyric "I" speaks in its own voice, concerning the poet's not having known love, is in the present tense, which is unmarked by gender (2: 41–3). In any case, we should be wary of imposing anachronistic gender constructions, even (or especially?) those that imply a certain inevitability, determining in advance our reactions as readers.

As far as *Polion*'s conception of sociability, it centers on the status of pastoral values, and these are determined by the discourse, poetics, and generic requirements of bucolic verse.[26] The start of canto 3 offers a virtual catalogue of bucolic images, from shepherds weaving wreaths and playing pipes, to the requisite flora, fauna, and pastoral deities:

---

[24] Compare also the role of the Sofiia character in Fonvizin's *Brigadir* and *Nedorosl'*, or the heroine of many other eighteenth-century plays, who embody abstract virtue and provide a mouthpiece for the author and lesson to the other characters. As a prostitute, of course, Sonia Marmeladova is far more of a problem character, although this itself suggests her function as a projection of male moral and psychological dualism.

[25] My thanks to Lada Panova for bringing this point to my attention.

[26] On the Russian pastoral tradition from a literary and cultural perspective, see Stephen L. Baehr, *The Paradise Myth in Eighteenth-Century Russia: Utopian Patterns in Early Secular Russian Literature and Culture* (Stanford: Stanford UP, 1991); and on the poetic tradition, Joachim Klein, *Die Schäferdichtung*.

Part Two. Visuality and Orthodoxy in Eighteenth-Century Russian Culture

В приятных тех местах, где солнце день рождает,
И светом темноту ночную побеждает;
Где все являются природы красоты,
Шумящие ключи, и рощи, и цветы,
Кустарники, луга; натуры все приятства;
Где Флорины сады, Церерины богатства,
Гуляя при стадах венки пастушки вьют
И жизнь свободную, и нежну страсть поют;
В свирели пастухи при хижинах играют
И пышны здания градские презирают;
Там, кажется, еще златые дни текут,
И со свободой мир престол имели тут. (3.1–12)

(In those pleasant days when the sun births the day, / And defeats night's darkness by light, / Where all of nature's beauties appear, / Gurgling springs and groves and flowers, / Shrubs and meadows; all the pleasant things of nature; / Where Flora's gardens, Ceres' riches [are found], / Shepherdesses strolling with their flocks weave wreaths / And sing the free life, and tender passion; / Shepherds play reed-pipes by their huts / And disdain luxurious city buildings. / There, it seems, the golden days are still flowing, / And here peace and freedom maintained their thrones.)

This would seem to be a world before civilization, without art or artifice, and without the sciences, an "image of the golden age":

Художества, труды и хитрости забвенны,
Где нежны таинства природы откровенны;
Не украшалось там ничто искусством рук;
Не видно было тех нигде следов наук,
Которые, свои все силы истощая,
Стремятся нас пленять, природу заглушая;
Везде встречалася приятность и покой;
Нельзя несчастну быть, вкушая век такой!
Там злобу жители и хитрость истребили,
Природы прелести и наготу любили;
Любили; но смутил их счастье Полион. (3.61–71)

Изображение сие златых веков,
Когда был смертных род еще во свете нов
И чужд от хитрости, имел простые нравы,
Не чувствовал сует, но чувствовал забавы... (3. 115–8)

(The arts, labors and crafts are [there] forgot, / And the gentle secrets of nature are revealed; / There nothing is adorned by the skill of hands; / No traces of

Chapter 18. The Polemic with Rousseau over Gender

the sciences [or: scholarly pursuits] are seen there, / Which, exhausting all of their forces, / Strive to capture us, smothering nature; / Everywhere was met peace and congeniality; / One can't be sad experiencing such a life! / There the inhabitants have wiped out malice and calculation, / Loved the charms of nature and nakedness; / They loved them; but Polion disturbed their happiness.

This [was] an image of the golden age, / When the mortal race was still new in the world / And alien to calculation, having simple ways, / [And] did not experience vanities, only pleasures…)

The poem sets up a running contrast between Polion's *grubost'* (coarseness, rudeness, lack of sensibility) and its negative effects on the pastoral world of bucolic *nezhnost'*. Polion sees everything backward, as in an inverted mirror that denies "common sense":

О! Грубость, здравый ум тобою в нем погас,
Ты в мире все ему наоборот являло…. (2.70–1)
В превратном зеркале вселенну представляет (2.87)

(Oh, rudeness, by you his common sense has been stifled, / You made everything in the world seem backwards to him…. The universe appears to him in a mistaken [perverted] mirror.)

He functions as an intruder, an alien element that threatens to turn the idyll into an anti-utopia:

Все мрачно сделалось, превратно и ужасно;
Со грубостью его являлося согласно… (3.105–6)
Преобразилось все как будто бы в хаос (3.135)

(Everything became gloomy, perverse and horrible; / It became consonant with his rudeness… It was as if everything was transformed into chaos)

This polar opposition between ideal nature and evil nurture is characteristic of pastoral and utopian literature, yet there is also a counter-movement in *Polion*, as articulated by Polion's friend in his description of life in society cited above, one which rejects extremism and advocates tolerance in all but cases of radical evil. This counter-movement also undercuts the unconditional exaltation of such concepts as civilization, nature, and perhaps gender roles themselves, as the model of society put forward promotes a neutral or mixed-gender sociability. On one level, these two approaches may be seen as contradictory: while the ideal pre-civilized state is described as lacking in "arts, labors and crafts" and "the skill of hands," the golden age may be regained by those very means. On another level, these two notions accord with eighteenth-century Russians' rejection of the way they understood Rousseau's argument in the "Discourse on the Arts and Sciences" and the "Discourse on Inequality," that — pace Rousseau — the arts and sciences were an unalloyed good, essential tools for attaining (or regaining) an ideal state. Much of the confusion in this case stemmed from defining the precise terms of the "pre-civilized" condition or "state of nature," whether as a Hobbesean nightmare or as a golden age. Part of the problem, as Thomas Barran has pointed out, was due to a simplification of Rousseau's argument and the conflation of his ideal state of nature with the classical scheme of the golden age out of Ovid and Virgil — a confusion perhaps inevitable when the issues were being debated in the medium of pastoral poetry.[27]

In part the problem here has to do with the difficulty of reading Rousseau (whom scholars continue to debate), and also — as Barran argues — with the way Russians interpreted him in terms of their own cultural and philosophical values. The nature/nurture dichotomy and special understanding (arguably, misapprehension) of Rousseau's position is evident in two earlier Russian *poemy* that took issue with him, Mikhail Kheraskov's *Plody nauk, didakticheskaia poema* (*The Fruits of Learning, A Didactic Poem*, 1761), which saw mankind's starting point in a state of primordial violence, and Ippolit Bogdanovich's *Suguboe blazhenstvo* (*A Special Happiness*, 1765, revised as *Blazhenstvo narodov* [*Happiness of the Peoples*]), in which the arts and sciences serve to regain the golden age, but without emphasis on a violent beginning.[28] Both poems rejected what was understood as Rousseau's anti-enlightenment stance of the two discourses, and may be seen as direct predecessors to Urusova's work. All three *poemy* are written in the same meter (alexandrines)

---

[27] Barran, *Russia Reads Rousseau*, via the index, esp. 26 and 99. See also: H. Rothe, "Zur Frage von Einflüssen in der russischen Literatur des 18. Jh.s," *Zeitschrift für Slavische Philologie*, 38 (1966), 21–68; and Iu. M. Lotman, "Russo i russkaia kul'tura," in *Epokha prosveshcheniia: Iz istorii mezhdunarodnykh sviazei russkoi literatury*, ed. M. P. Alekseev (Leningrad, Nauka, 1967), 208–231.

[28] Barran, *Russia Reads Rousseau*, 20–28; and Klein, *Puti kul'turnogo importa*, 65–6. *Plody nauk poema* (Moscow, 1761), reprinted in the *Tvoreniia M. Kheraskova*, vol. 3 (Moscow, 1797), is available for download in a pdf version from the Nekommercheskaia elektronnaia biblioteka "ImWerden," http://imwerden.de/pdf/kheraskov_plody_nauk.pdf (accessed Oct. 9, 2006). *Blazhenstvo narodov* is available in I. F. Bogdanovich, *Stikhotvoreniia i poemy*. Biblioteka poeta, bol'shaia seriia, 2nd ed. (Leningrad: Sovetskii pisatel', 1957), 187–94; this edition is also available in pdf form at http://imwerden.de/pdf/bogdanovich_stixotvorenija.pdf (accessed Oct. 9, 2006).

Chapter 18. The Polemic with Rousseau over Gender

and employ a similar didactic *cum* pastoral poetic discourse, using many of the same specific tropes and devices. As suggested, they also share the paradoxical notion of civilization — on the one hand, as the result of a fall from paradise, and on the other hand, a tool for its re-creation — which is present on several levels in *Polion*. The remainder of this paper will explore this contrast as a way of further analyzing the terms of Urusova's argument.

Naida's position on reaching true enlightenment does not advocate a "return to nature" as the rejection of science and learning — as anti-utopian, corrupting influences — but rather a conversion from false to true teaching. The alternative that she offers Polion is also referred to as "science" (nauka) (e.g., 5.209), and the fact that Polion as misanthrope rejects poetry, including the classics — Homer, Plato, Socrates, Cicero, Pindar, Anacreon, Virgil, and Ovid (1.129–55) — suggests that they are all being claimed for Urusova's brand of enlightened teaching.[29] The single literary source Polion claims for himself is Seneca, a topos in the Russian poetic tradition for severe, puritanical moralism (e.g., Lomonosov's "Conversation with Anacreon"[30]). On the other hand, when Polion asks Naida

> Но где же книги те, — вскричал он вне себя, —
> Которы сделали премудрого тебя? (5: 265-6)
>
> (But where are those books, — he cried, beside himself, — / That made you so very wise?)]

She responds:

> Те книги, — та речет, — которы я читаю,
> Суть вещи зримые, меж коих обитаю;

---

[29] There is a problem here of associating Polion's "male" position with "the learned, written world" and, in consequence, Naida's exclusively with the spoken word and enlightened conversation. As suggested above (note 5), Vowles overstresses this dichotomy. On the status of conversation, see also note 37 below.

[30] In that dialogue, even "Lomonosov," who argues against "Anacreon," says:

> Возмите прочь Сенеку,
> Он правила сложил
> Не в силу человеку,
> И кто по оным жил?
>
> (Take Seneca away, / He composed rules / Beyond people's strength. / Who could live by them?)

(M. V. Lomonosov, "Razgovor s Anakreonom," PSS 8: 763.) The fact that Polion "conversed" (besedoval) with Seneca (4.106) directly recalls this poem.

Печатаны они рукою Божества,
Не в буквах состоят, в глаголах Естества;
Хотя учеными бывают и презренны,
Но каждому они из смертных отворенны.³¹ (5: 267–72)

(The books, she says, which I read, / Are the visible things among which I dwell; / They are printed by the hand of the Divine; / The consist not in letters, but in the language of Nature; / Although they may be despised by the educated, / They are open to every mortal.)

Despite the privileging of nature, the point I think is not a zero-sum contrast between the false books of civilization and those of nature, but rather their ultimate parity: the "book of nature" that is open and available for our reading is fully compatible — one some level equated — with the classics of poetry that themselves reflect true human nature. The paradox here is also reflected in a broader dichotomy present in the poem between two contrasting aspects of "nature" (*priroda, natura, estestvo*), understood both as a perfect, unattainable ideal and also as a principle of immanence, a progressive movement toward enlightenment, working itself out in an imperfect world.³²

---

31   The problem of "misanthropy" and of truth-seeking in general are consistently described in terms of correct / incorrect vision. More specifically, and in contrast to Naida's assertion here of knowledge open to all, Naida's teaching has the marks of a mystery cult. She warns Polion that the secrets (tainstva) of existence "require educated [or: rational, reasoning] eyes" (trebuiut oni razumnykh glaz, 5.235). And when Polion approaches "the light, similar to three spheres" (svet, podobnyi trem sharam, 5.252 — presumably, an image of ultimate truth — his eyes go dark, and Naida warns that he must be "worthy…to see the new light; / Too much knowledge is a burden for infirm souls" (dostoin…uvidet' novyi svet; / Izlishne znanie dlia dush netverdykh bremia) (5.258-9). The enigmatic "three spheres" is not explained, and might refer to a Masonic symbol, although with few exceptions there were no women Freemasons in Russia. There was a Lodge of the Three Globes in Berlin (after 1744 the "Grand Royal Mother Lodge of the Three Globes", whose Grand Master was Frederick II), which according to one source represented "the popular and prevailing rite practiced in Prussia" (Robert Macoy *General History, Cyclopedia and Dictionary of Freemasonry* [1873; rpt. Kila, MT: Kessinger Publishing, 1994], 328). See mentions of this lodge in G. V. Vernadskii, *Russkoe masonstvo v tsarstvovanii Ekateriny II*, 2ⁿᵈ rev. ed. (St. Petersburg: N. I. Novikov, 1999), 33 and 103–4. We may speculate that, even in Masonry, the image suggests the trinity, as in the well-known vision of "three circles" of light in the last canto of Dante's *Paradiso*.
32   Contrast the well-known formulaic description of Socialist Realism, covertly rooted in a comparable idealist framework, as "the truthful, historically concrete representation of reality in its revolutionary development"(*Pervyi Vsesoiuznyi s'ezd sovetskikh pisatelei 1934: Stenograficheskii otchet* [Moscow: Khudozhestvennaia literatura, 1934; reprint: Moscow: Sovetskii pisatel, 1990], 712).

Chapter 18. The Polemic with Rousseau over Gender

In *Polion*, the image of walls both asserts and amends the pastoral opposition between nature and civilization, and may serve as a final example of the poem's resolution of this dichotomy. Polion's friend continues his discussion of sociability by showing him a "picture of the world" in which walls play a significant part. First the special nature of his evidence is described:

Сей друга дикого хотел увещевать
И света стал ему картину открывать;
Смотри, он говорил, сии изображенья,
Хотя уже в них нет натуре подраженья;
Но должно для того почтенье к ним хранить,
Что начертаний сих не можно пременить. (2.149–54)

(He wanted to enlighten his unsociable friend, / And began to reveal to him a picture of the world; / Look, he said, at these images, / Although they no longer are imitations of nature; / One should still respect them, / Because these tracings cannot be changed.)

Notably, the revelation of truth that Polion's friend is about to make — like several others in the work — comes in the form of interpreting "pictures" and "images" (or "depictions"). It is unclear in the given case whether these are visual or verbal; if the former, their explication becomes an exercise in ekphrasis. This procedure of visual-verbal truth seeking may be related to the overall strategy of pastoral verse, especially perhaps in its moralistic "didactic" variant which makes abundant use of allegorical figures. In the lines just cited, the status of the images being offered, as a proof, suggests an authority that both reflects something nonexistent in reality (literally, "in them [the depictions] there are no longer imitations of nature") yet in some sense perfect and true ("these tracings cannot be changed") — corresponding to the two hypostases of "nature" suggested above.

On the one hand, walls symbolize Polion's misanthropy and anti-bucolic position; the walls around Polion's house indicate a suffocating isolation that chokes off "the priceless delicacies of nature":

Труды к расстройности природы положили
И дом высокими стенами окружили; ...
Бесценны нежности природы исчезали (3.93–4 and 97)

(They made efforts to throw nature into confusion / And surrounded the house with high walls. /... The priceless delicacies of nature were disappearing)

On the other, the absence of walls symbolizes freedom, as in the description of Naida's house:

Приятной простотой сиял наружный вид;
И не являлося ни гордых пирамид,
Ни мраморных столбов, огромностию диких,
Ни вида общия неволи, стен великих;
Но сельская везде встречалась красота,
Пред коею скучна мирская суета!
Спокойство, чистота, природе подраженье,
То было лучшее в сем доме украшенье. (3.42–9)

(Its outside view shone with pleasant simplicity; / There did not appear either proud pyramids, / Nor marble columns, savage in size, / Nor great walls, image of general unfreedom; / But everywhere a rural beauty was met, / Before which worldly vanity loses attraction! / Tranquility, cleanliness, the imitation of nature, / These were the home's best ornamentation.)

Similarly, after his rejection of misanthropy, Polion suddenly takes a disliking to walls ("Ogromnost' sten svoikh i mrak voznenavidel" [He came to hate the great size of his walls and the gloom], 4:245).

However, the criticism of walls is in each case qualified: what is criticized are "tall" or "massive" walls — that is, walls are not necessarily evil in and of themselves. The picture Polion's friend describes is of walls that serve not to destroy the pastoral, but to preserve and foster society and sociability:

Здесь видишь градские воздвигнутые стены,
Препона то зверей, соседние измены;
И удержание граждан во тишине;
Спокойство в мирны дни, защита при войне;
Когда усилились в сердцах людских пороки,
То нужны сделались и стены им высоки;
Со безопасностью они хранятся в них,
Извне оружие стрежет от бедства их.
Ты видишь игры здесь, ты видишь здесь забавы,
Утехи разные имеют разны нравы:
Там в поле видишь ты зверей, гонящих псов;[27]
Там глас охотников ты слышишь средь лесов;
Там, уду опустя, пронзают токи водны;
Там пляски, песни там, там зрелища народны;
Огромны здания; убоги шалаши;
Пример мятежныя и тихия души!
Там видишь хоровод между снопов шумящих;
Там слышишь в торжестве орудий звук гремящих;
Там юность скачущу ты видишь во цветах;
Внимаешь пение любви о красотах;

Chapter 18. The Polemic with Rousseau over Gender

Веселости сии и сносны, и безбедны,
Коль обществу они и ближнему невредны.
Для охранения тел наших наконец
Мы стены делаем; законы для сердец!
Но люди не на то стенами разделились,
Чтоб, в оных живучи, ничем не веселились;
Позволили они, сообщество любя,
Беседы, и пиры, и игры для себя;
А знав, что слабости сердца у всех смущают,
С охотою они друг другу их прощают;
И только страшны им пороки таковы,
Которы рвут людей и мучат будто львы;
Кто счастья здесь не зрит, тот всех из нас беднее,
И кто порочит, всех вреднее. (2.155–88)

(Here you see city walls erected, / Protection against wild beasts and neighbor's treachery; / And restraint (to keep) citizens in peace; / Tranquility in peaceful days, defense in time of war; / When vices increased in people's hearts, / High walls became necessary, / [So that people] live within in safety. / And from without arms protect them from misfortune. / You see games here and amusements, / Various dispositions enjoy varied entertainments: / There in the field you see beasts chased by dogs[33] / There you can hear hunters' voices in the forest; / There others pierce the water's currents, lowering a hook; / There are dances, there are songs, and folk spectacles; / Huge buildings; humble shacks; / Example of unruly and placid souls! / There you see a round-dance amid noisy sheaves; / There you hear the sound of thundering arms in triumph [or: in celebration — ML]; / There you see youth capering in the flowers; / You listen to singing about the beauties of love. / These joys are tolerable and without danger / If they are harmless to society and neighbor. / Finally, to protect our bodies / We build walls; laws for the heart! / People did not separate themselves with walls / In order not to enjoy themselves, living within them; / Loving the society of others (soobshchestvo), they allow / Themselves conversations, feasts, games; / And knowing that weaknesses of the heart disturb everyone / They willingly forgive one another. / Only those vices are feared / That rip people and torment them like lions. / The one who does not see happiness here is the poorest of us all, / And the one who defames (porochit) it is the most harmful.)

Walls serve as protection from external enemies as well as from evil inner passions, and create the necessary conditions (restrictions) that allow people

---

[33] The Russian text, "zverei, goniashchikh psov" (beasts chasing dogs), would appear to be a mistake.

to live in peace and harmony.³⁴ The issue becomes, not walls or no walls, complete freedom or captivity, but what size the walls, how commensurate to the evils they would shut out, in accord with moderation and common sense.

The image of happy society spans diverse occupations, people of varying station and temperament ("Huge buildings; humble shacks; / Example of unruly and placid souls!"), as well as a spectrum of amusements — games, entertainments, dances, songs, conversations, hunting, fishing, cavorting in the flowers, as well as the (none too pastoral!) celebration of military successes ("the sound of thundering arms in triumph").³⁵

This image of happy conviviality based on toleration — walls that both separate and unite — reiterates in microcosm *Polion*'s implied argument in favor of women's active participation in social life and, by extension, in literature. The potential contradiction in the bucolic defense of "arts and sciences," and what some have taken to be a mistaken or oversimplified reading of Rousseau, indicate Urusova's optimistic — some would say, naïve — faith in Enlightenment, which was, after all, the source and framework for the establishment of a modern European intellectual life in Russia. Urusova's optimism regarding women reflects the broader optimism of Russian letters concerning the universal efficacy of Enlightenment, and we might note that it was only the demise of this tradition that served as incubator for ideas of independent and exclusive national and gender value. It may also be argued that Urusova's criticism of Rousseau's misanthropy in the name of Voltaire's gender-egalitarian Republic of Letters was fully grounded in the Russian literary tradition, on the side of writers like Sumarokov, Kheraskov and Bogdanovich, who themselves took a positive public stance toward women as writers and at times served as mentors and patrons.³⁶ Urusova frames her argument, as well as her identity as a writer,

---

34 Compare Amphion's founding of Thebes described in very similar terms, including walls surrounding it and the security of a tsar, in Kheraskov's *Plody nauk*, 2.531–82.

35 The image here of a happily functioning society (soobshchestvo liubia), and especially the "people's spectacles" (zrelishcha narodny), may recall the well-known final argument Rousseau makes in his "Letter to d'Alembert" contrasting Geneva's popular rural festivals to the evils of Parisian theater. Despite the larger conflict in perspectives, this parallel may nevertheless suggest the common challenge to both Rousseau and Urusova: in describing the ideal society and imagining its practice, where to draw the line between uncompromising virtue that protects social life, on the one hand, and on the other, the moderating effects of tolerance for other people's pleasures that may leave it at risk of degeneration.

36 For positive statements see, for example, Sumarokov's "Lisitsa i statuia"(1761) and "Oda anakreonticheskaia k Elisavete Vasil'evne Kheras'kovoi"(1762) (*Izbrannye*

fully within an almost entirely male-defined tradition, but one in which the very fact of its being male-defined is not yet raised as a problem.[37]

The terms of the opposition described in *Polion*, as we have seen, offer a choice between misanthropy and sociability, with sociability defined in terms of a necessary and complementary gender equality, and the onus of misogyny assigned to its enemies (and by extension, the enemies of Enlightenment). That *Polion* relies on abstract moralizing and reified allegory rather than on (e.g.) developed plot or psychology to make its argument suggests both the limitations of the "pastoral-didactic" genre as well as the undeveloped state of the social reality to which it might refer. Urusova does not engage in any direct way with the issues facing women writers and intellectuals, nor is any social or institutional basis for women's participation suggested other than the (mostly pastoral) games, dances and interactions of country life described in the passage quoted above.[38] As noted,

---

sochineniia, 103 and 213); and Bogdanovich's guide to versification for women "Pis'mo gozpozhe F-o russkom stikhoslozhenii" (*Priiatnoe i poleznoe preprovozhdenie vremeni*, 1 [1794], cited by Kelly, "Sappho, Corinna and Niobe," 47). As Bennett shows, Derzhavin was also mostly favorably disposed toward women writers ("'Parnassian Sisters'"). Writing was something of a family matter for many early Russian women writers: Sumarokov's daughter Ekaterina Sumarokova was known as a writer, and married to Ia. B. Kniazhnin; and Kheraskov, who was Urusova's cousin and patron, was married to the poet Elizaveta Kheraskova, addressee of Sumarokov's poem just cited. For discussions of both family ties and barriers to women's writing, see also Rosslyn, "Making Their Way into Print"; and Frank Göpfert, "Observations on the Life and Work of Elizaveta Kheraskova (1737–1809)," in *Women and Gender in 18th-century Russia*, ed. Wendy Rosslyn (Burlington, VT: Ashgate, 2003), 163–86.

37   See, for example, Urusova's "O Muzy! Vy moi dukh ko pesniam vsplamenite," the dedicatory poem to her *Iroidy, Muzam posviashennyia* (St. Petersburg, 1777), cited in note 3. Urusova inscribes herself into the accepted scheme of triumphant Russian Enlightenment, and depicts women's writing in terms of the pastoral poetry prescribed by Neoclassical authorities (a prescription for mixing tenderness and virtue that also fits *Polion*). See Kelly, "Sappho, Corinna and Niobe," and Rosslyn, "Making Their Way into Print."

On the other hand, in a recent paper Andrew Kahn argued that Urusova's *Iroidy* offer a more assertive model of specifically women's writing ("Desire and Transgression Urusova's Imitations of Ovid," AAASS National Convention, Washington D.C., Dec. 30, 2007). Bennett argues that, at least in a private correspondence, Urusova expresses "a gendered sense of her poetic identity"("Parnassian Sisters," 251).

38   One aspect of sociability that is not emphasized here is the cult of friendship, notable both for the "Kheraskov school" (see Rothe, "Zur Frage," 63), and for later eighteenth-century women's writing. See also A. P. Murzina's *Raspuskaiushchikhsia roza* (1799), which Amanda Ewington discusses as a response to *Polion*. See her "Aleksandra

Naida's status also remains ambiguous, and may taken as another example of the ambiguity or even contradiction that we have seen resulting from treating social issues within a pastoral frame of reference. On the one hand, numerous pastoral conceits (e.g., Cupid's golden arrow that pierces Polion's breast and comparisons of Naida to Greek goddesses) as well as Polion's love-struck perception suggest the heroine's idealized, more than human status. She emerges more as a figure of male fantasy than a female role model, as such practical issues as the potential gap between "reading from the open book of nature" and the acquisition of the education necessary to have assimilated the classics are not mentioned. On the other hand, Naida herself suggests her mortal nature when she takes Polion to task for seeing people in extreme terms — as either gods or ogres (razvratnykh) (5.108–15).[39] The center of attention and thrust of the argument, however, remain on Polion's drama, and on correcting incorrect (male) attitudes, rather than on ameliorating women's position or encouraging women's writing.[40] Nevertheless, and perhaps for these very reasons, Urusova's *Polion* offers a remarkable — if up till now almost completely forgotten — argument in favor of women's necessary and acknowledged participation in Russian society, and an optimistic if fanciful prognosis for the future.

Murzina's *Raspuskaiushchaiasia roza*: Imagining a Female Readership," abstract for her talk of Dec. 30, 2004, at the AATSEEL National Conference http://aatseel.org/program/aatseel/2004/abstracts/ewington.htm (accessed 8-26-06). Vowles also suggests that Naida stands for what we could call the institution of polite conversation (on which, see, for example, William Mills Todd, III, *Fiction and Society in the Age of Pushkin: Ideology, Institutions, Narrative* [Cambridge: Harvard UP, 1986], 31–3 and passim), yet this does not seem convincing. While Naida certainly conquers Polion with conversation, it is not clear that this is culturally marked, or that for Polion (or for Fenelon's Telemachus for that matter) the temporary loss of speech has any other significance than the emotional-psychological (i.e., falling in love).

[39] She is described among other things as *devitsa*, *krasavitsa*, and *prekrasnaia deva* (4.124), the latter description supplied with a footnote explaining that this is allegorical: "The person of the maid stands for the spirit of understanding" (V litse devy izobrazhaetsia dukh razumeniia).

[40] In contrast, Ewington ("Aleksandra Murzina's *Raspuskaiushchaiasia roza*") demonstrates how Murzina's *Raspuskaiushchikhsia roza* responds to *Polion* by offering an explicitly woman-centered response to the *Tilemakhida* situation, addressing herself primarily to women writers and readers.

— 19 —

VIRTUE MUST ADVERTISE:
Self Presentation in Dashkova's Memoirs

Princess Ekaterina Romanova Dashkova (1743–1810) was one of the most colorful and striking figures of the age of Catherine the Great, itself an epoch of oversize personalities. "Catherine the Little," as Dashkova refers to herself in her memoirs, was, next to the empress Catherine, the most prominent and commented-upon Russian woman of her day. Political activist, author, editor, courtier, first woman head of the Academy of Sciences and founder of the Russian Academy, Dashkova was arguably also Russia's first modern woman celebrity.[1] Much like Benjamin Franklin, she captured the imagination of the educated world as her country's de facto cultural ambassador. While Franklin personified home-grown American democracy, Dashkova was emissary for Russia's special brand of "Enlightened absolutism."[2] Dashkova's main claim to fame was not merely as the extraordinary example of a Russian woman intellectual, but also, and more notoriously, as principle co-conspirator, at the tender age of 19, in the 1762 palace "revolution" that had raised Catherine to the throne and deposed — and dispatched — Peter III.[3]

---

[1] See the new biography by Alexander Woronzoff-Dashkoff, *Dashkova: A Life of Influence and Exile* (Philadelphia: American Philosophical Society, 2008), that appeared subsequent to the writing of this essay.

[2] This essay first appeared in a volume accompanying the exhibit "The Princess and the Patriot: Ekaterina Dashkova, Benjamin Franklin, and the Age of Enlightenment" at the American Philosophical Society, Phildelphia, Feb. 17 — Dec. 31, 2006, part of the celebration of the Benjamin Franklin Tercentenary.

[3] Historians still debate Dashkova's assertion of her key role in Catherine's coup. Catherine herself — to Dashova's dismay — disparaged her role immediately following the coup, which may have been for political reasons, insofar as Dashkova hoped to counter the Orlovs' influence.

Part Two. Visuality and Orthodoxy in Eighteenth-Century Russian Culture

A TRIPLE DEFENSE

In contrast to Franklin's *Autobiography*, a collection of materials begun in mid-career as family history recounted for his son, and fondly recalling a life rich in success and public recognition, Dashkova's memoir was written near the end of her life as an attempt to rescue her public image from oblivion or worse, misrepresentation. Hers is a purposeful *apologia pro vita sua* presented to the court of posterity and public opinion. When Franklin began writing in 1771, his public and literary persona had already become an institution of American life, and the *Autobiography* offered a succinct restatement of his commonsensical philosophy of life, recounted with a calm and lightly self-deprecating irony. In contrast, when Dashkova took up the pen her celebrity was in almost total eclipse, and her memoir had a much more serious and psychologically weighty goal: to defend her life's legacy and that of Catherine the Great's Russia.

That legacy had been called into question almost immediately after Catherine's death in 1796, which Dashkova described in her memoir as "a blow...which for Russia represented the greatest possible disaster." (MPD 248).[4] Catherine's son, the new emperor Paul I, undertook a campaign to rehabilitate the honor of his ignominiously deposed father, stripping Dashkova of her official positions and sending her into exile in northern Russia. Even after her return to court following the accession of Alexander I in 1801, Dashkova was indignant to find "the people surrounding the Emperor...unanimous in disparaging the reign of Catherine II and in instilling in the young monarch that idea that a woman could ever govern an Empire" (MPD 279). This misogynist attitude, which had been codified under Paul in a new law of succession based on male primogeniture, also

---

[4]   E. R. Dashkova, *The Memoirs of Princess Dashkova*, trans. and ed. Kyril Fitzlyon (Durham: Duke UP, 1995), 248. Henceforth references to this edition will be to "MPD," and will be given in parentheses within the essay.
Unfortunately, there still is no fully authoritative version of Dashkova's memoir, which exists in two basic variants. On the history of the problem, see A. Woronzoff-Dashkoff's "Afterword" in Dashkova, *The Memoirs*, 284–89, and his "Additions and Notes in Princess Dashkova's *Mon histoire*," *Study Group on Eighteenth-Century Russia Newsletter* 19 (1991): 15–21. See also the recent composite text that lacks a critical apparatus: *Mon histoire: mémoires d'une femme de lettres russe à l'époque des Lumières*, ed. Alexandre Woronzoff-Dashkoff, Catherine Le Gouis, and Catherine Woronzoff-Dashkoff (Paris: L'Harmattan, 1999).

clearly cast its shadow on Dashkova, "one of the first women in Europe to hold governmental office."⁵

Perhaps just as importantly, Dashkova took up her pen to refute what she referred to as the "flood of pamphlets libeling Catherine II" (MPD 271–72). The eighteenth century had seen the birth of a whole branch of European letters known as "Russica," as Russia's place as a test case for Enlightenment ideas became a major subject of debate. Catherine's detractors, motivated by long-standing political animus, shoveled dirt on the empress' personal life and on her court. Dashkova was outraged by the "cleverly concocted lies and foul fictions" spread by "certain French writers" who "at the same time undertook to blacken and slander her innocent friend" — that is, Dashkova herself.⁶ Any stains on the empress' "spotless reputation" threatened to tarnish Dashkova's own.

Dashkova's memoir is thus a triple defense: it is a vindication of Catherine the Great as a truly "great and enlightened empress"; an affirmation of Russian Enlightenment culture; and, not the least, a justification and clarification of Dashkova's own historical role. The memoir spans Dashova's entire life up through the time of writing (1804–5), focusing on: the story of the "revolution" that brought Catherine to the throne; her two extended European

---

5   A. Woronzoff-Dashkoff, "Disguise and Gender in Princess Dashkova's *Memoirs*," *Canadian Slavonic Papers*, 33: 1 (1991), 62.

6   The quotation is taken from the memoir's dedicatory letter to Martha Wilmot, not included in the Fitzlyon translation or 1999 French edition. I cite it from: E. R. Dashkova, *Zapiski; Pis'ma sester M. i K. Vil'mot iz Rossii*, ed. S. S. Dmitriev, comp. G. A. Veselaia (Moscow: MGU, 1987), 35. See also Dashkova's mention of these libels in MPD, 51, 62, 91, and 279.
    On Dashkova's autobiography in the broader literary context of "Russica," see Kelly Herold, "Russian Autobiographical Literature in French: Recovering a Memoiristic Tradition (1770–1830)," (Diss. University of California, Los Angeles, 1998). On the particular writers Dashkova repudiates, see V. A. Somov, "'Prezident trekh akademii': E. R. Dashkova vo frantsuzskoi 'Rossike' XVIII veka," in *E. R. Dashkova i A. S. Pushkin v istorii Rossii*, ed. L. V. Tychinina (Moscow: MGI im. E. R. Dashkovoi, 2000), 39–53. On Russians' familiarity with Russica, see Somov's "Frantsuzskaia 'Rossika' epokhi prosveshcheniia i russkii chitatel'," in *Frantsuzskaia kniga v Rossii v XVIII v.: Ocherki istorii*, ed. S. P. Luppov (Leningrad: Nauka, 1986), 173–245. On European debates over Russia's status, see Dimitri S. von Mohrenschildt, *Russia in the Intellectual Life of Eighteenth-Century France* (1936; rpt. New York: Octagon Books, 1972); Albert Lortholary, *Le Mirage Russe en France au XVIIIᵉ siècle* (Paris: Boivin, [1951]); Isabel de Madariaga, "Catherine and the *Philosophes*," in *Russia and the West in the Eighteenth Century*, ed. A. G. Cross (Newtonville, MA: Oriental Research Partners, 1983), pp. 30–52; and Larry Wolff, *Inventing Eastern Europe: The Map of Civilization on the Mind of the Enlightenment* (Stanford: Stanford UP, 1994).

trips; her public life in St. Petersburg; her exile under Paul; and, briefly, her last years. The title of the memoir, *Mon histoire*, which may mean both "My Story" and "My History," suggests the merging for Dashkova of the individual and historical narrative. This makes Dashkova's autobiography a valuable record of the cultural ideal of Enlightenment Russia and turns whatever weakness of memory or historical accuracy there may be in it into an all the more eloquent exercise in self-imaging. In the remainder of this essay, I will attempt to come to terms with Dashkova's oversized personality, placing it within the context of the cultural values that she champions in her memoir.

MAKING VIRTUE VISIBLE

We may begin to seek the roots of Dashkova's strikingly powerful sense of self in the circumstances of her early life as she describes them. On the one hand, Dashkova recounts her overwhelming desire for approbation and love, and on the other, her desperate sense of loneliness and being "wounded by indifference," sparked by the loss of her mother at age two. "I became serious-minded and studious...Reading soothed me and made me happy..." (MPD 33) The life of the mind and the satisfactions of superior intellect offered a compensation, as she resolved to become "all I could be by my own efforts,... [in a] presumptuous effort to be self-sufficient" (MPD 34). She was attracted in particular to Enlightenment political and educational theory, an arena in which her "relentless curiosity" could be satisfied. *Mon histoire* offers a sophisticated defense of Enlightened selfhood, as Dashkova constructs and defends a powerful, charismatic, intellectually impressive image of an ideal public self. Struggling to describe the "peculiarities & inextricable varietys" of Dashkova's contradictory character, Catherine Wilmot concluded that

> For my part I think she would most be in her element at the *Helm of the State*, of Generalissimo of the Army, or Farmer General of the Empire. In fact she was born for business on a large scale which is not irreconcilable with the Life of a Woman who at 18 headed a Revolution & who for 12 years afterwards govern'd an Academy of Arts & Sciences...[7]

---

[7] *The Russian Journals of Martha and Catherine Wilmot,...1803–1808*, ed. the Marchioness of Londonderry and H. M. Hyde (London: Macmillan, 1934), 211. By "Farmer General of the Empire" is meant something like a minister of finances, the official in charge of taxes and revenue.

Chapter 19. Virtue Must Advertise

Dashkova fully subscribed to the ideal of her age, defining herself in terms of the "Great Man." As the label indicates, the serious, public, role she chose to emulate was culturally gendered male; indeed the classical Roman heritage that was one of its main sources preserved a direct etymological linkage between the male ("vir") and virtue ("virtus") itself.[8]

At the same time, Dashkova's memoir — by the author's no less eloquent testimony — reveals the dark and unhappy underside of the "Great Man." Dashkova was by her own admission plagued by constant physical ailments, as well as by a "deep dejection" and "bitter disappointments" that haunted her existence — which we might conceptualize as her frustrated "female" shadow self demanding its due. Dashkova herself senses that the protective façade of superior intellect is "presumptuous," and from the very beginning of her conscious life fears that "my sensibility and weak nerves would ruin my life by making it impossible to bear the pain of disappointment and wounded pride...I was beginning to have the foreboding that I would not be happy in this world." (MPD 35) Dashkova's need for approbation, so poignant for a motherless child, was also, and perhaps even more importantly, an especially powerful directive of her age: *the need to be seen and approved.*[9] The need for approval is undoubtedly a universal human necessity, yet self-display — whether in court ceremonial, on the stage, in architecture, urban planning, landscape gardening, clothing, or the fine arts in general — took on special prominence as a cultural imperative during Russia's early modern age. It offered visible proof of Russia's imperial grandeur, demanding recognition of national greatness to vie with that of the West. Beyond its usual function as a simple marker of power and prestige, visual display also played a key role in Russian Enlightenment thought and self-consciousness, according to the conviction that (to put it baldly) virtue must advertise.[10] Visibility, and the visibility of virtue, for example, became an especially important issue in

---

[8] Judith Vowles contrasts Catherine the Great's ability to reconcile "the claims of worldly society and the intellectual life" to Dashkova's rejection of "feminine" social pursuits (e.g, the life of the salon) in favor of serious "male" interests. See "The 'Feminization' of Russian Literature: Women, Language and Literature in Eighteenth-Century Russia," in Toby W. Clyman and Diana Greene, eds., *Women Writers in Russian Literature* (Westport, CT: Praeger, 1994), 40–44.

[9] Arthur O. Lovejoy, *Reflections on Human Nature* (Baltimore: Johns Hopkins Press, 1961).

[10] This is a main thesis of my forthcoming monograph, whose provisional title is *Making Russian Visible: The Visual Dominant in Eighteenth-Century Russian Literature and Culture*. See also the other articles in Part Two of the current collection.

Catherine the Great's political program, especially in the early part of her reign. Catherine justified her assumption of power by means of her superior Enlightenment credentials: she who was self-evidently best qualified to rule, and most virtuous in promoting the public welfare, deserved to rule.[11] Dashkova, having indissolubly linked her fortune with Catherine, fully ascribed to this political and moral program.

VIRTUE UNDER SEIGE

A useful episode for understanding the drama of Dashkova's self-presentation is her description of the crisis that followed Catherine's death. The new emperor Paul ordered her to leave Moscow and retire to her place in the country, where she was instructed to "ponder on the events of the year 1762" and to await his decision on her further fate. Dashkova writes:

> I left Moscow on 6 December. My health was reduced to a struggle against death. Every other day I wrote to my brother and other members of my family, who also wrote very regularly to me. Several of them, including my brother, told me that Paul I's behavior toward me was dictated by what he thought he owed to his father's memory, but that at his coronation he would change our fate. I shall quote my reply to my brother as one of the many prophecies I have made which have come true:
>
> "You tell me, friend, that after his coronation Paul will leave me alone. You do not know him then. Once a tyrant begins to strike he continues to strike until his victim is totally destroyed. I am expecting persecution to continue unabated, and I resign myself to it in the full submission of a creature to its Creator. The conviction of my own innocence and lack of any bitterness or indignation at his treatment of me personally will, I trust, serve me in place of courage. Come what may, and provided he is not actively malevolent to you and those near and dear to me, I shall do or say nothing that will lower me in my own eyes. Goodbye, my friend, my well-beloved brother. All my love." (MPD 251)[12]

---

[11] Her famous Instruction (Nakaz) is the most dramatic expression of this view. See *Documents of Catherine the Great; The Correspondence with Voltaire and the Instruction of 1767 in the English text of 1768*, ed. W. F. Reddaway (1931; New York, Russell & Russell, 1971), and other editions. On Catherine's quest for visibility, see David M. Griffiths, "To Live Forever: Catherine II, Voltaire, and the Pursuit of Immortality," in Roger Bartlett et al., eds., *Russia and the World of the Eighteenth Century* (Columbus, Ohio: Slavica, 1988), 446–468, and Simon Dixon, *Catherine the Great* (New York: Longman, 2001), chap. 3.

[12] Here and below I have changed "Pavel I" to "Paul I."

Dashkova here stands tall on the stage of history. She presents herself like a heroine of tragic drama or a sentimental novel, a "Great Man" displaying the transparency of her virtue for all to appreciate.[13] She describes innocence and virtue pitted against relentless malice, virtue under physical and emotional siege. Her response puts her courage and self-possession into sharp relief. The quoting of the letter both helps Dashkova to establish the documentary nature of the moment — its historical truth — and at the same time reflects her exalted, extremely "literary," self-image. It is as if she were reciting a tragic monologue, or contemplating herself at a remove, as in a mirror.

While Dashkova's dramatic stance might seem appropriate considering the real threat from Paul, similar extreme oppositions — a continual struggle between life and death, salvation and destruction, approbation and opprobrium — operate throughout the text. They characterize Dashkova's understanding of the self as in a constant struggle between absolute virtue and vice whose outcome has highly serious, even metaphysical, consequences. Dashkova presents herself as totally virtuous, and she makes no secret of the pride and self-satisfaction she feels in her virtue. Although her "submission" to God's will may have something in common with the Russian Orthodox notion of "kenosis," the "emptying of the self" in imitation of Christ, Dashkova's language stresses more her adherence to an Enlightenment conviction — strongly echoing classical Stoicism — of righteousness founded on reason and superior self-knowledge. This submission is not humility in the traditional religious sense, born of a sense of sinfulness or guilt, but a defense of pride and self-esteem as an enduring virtue.

THE DENIAL OF THE PERSONAL

What may seem strange, particularly to a modern sensibility, is the extent to which Dashkova and the people of her epoch equated the (good) self with universal and "natural" merit. As in classicist tragedy, the personal or private element, if not in harmony with the demands of family, society, and Nature, is ascribed to the dark side. Conversely, the virtuous self is in perfect accord with

---

[13] Dashkova herself suggests that "my life could serve a subject for a heartrending novel" (*Zapiski*, 35), and the memoir is punctuated with theatrical terms (tragedy, farce, comedy, the stage, etc.). This sort of reference may perhaps be common in autobiographical writing, but my suggestion is that Dashkova shared the special self-image and discourse about virtue and self-display that were reflected in Russian Classicist literary works, whose very function was to offer Russian society a "school for virtue."

the absolute and universal. For Dashkova, to be virtuous is to act unselfishly, "disinterestedly," and conversely, to act in the name of "personal interests" is evil. "Private" merit can only consist of impersonal virtue, and to act in one's self-interest — selfishly — is to act in an evil way. Altruistic self-sacrifice is the measure of goodness. The following passage, in which Dashkova describes the consolations of pride in the face of suffering, is characteristic:

> I never pursued either my personal interests or the criminal elevation of my own family...I...gathered support from the feeling of my own innocence, the purity of my conscience, and a certain moral pride which gave me strength and courage, but which I had never previously suspected in myself and which, after giving the matter much thought, I could only attribute to resignation, a sentiment proper to every rational being. (MPD 263-4)

Dashkova's "resignation" includes a big dose of self-satisfaction, as she elevates herself to the ranks of "rational beings."

Dashkova's English friends Martha and Catherine Wilmot, who convinced Dashkova to write her memoirs, and helped with their actual production, also left several penetrating descriptions of this aspect of her self-image. In speaking of her conspicuous vanity, Martha wrote in a letter to her father that Dashkova's

> establish'd opinion of herself is such that, if I can make you feel what I mean, it is as if she was distinct from herself and look'd at her own acts and deeds and character with a degree of admiration that she never attempts to express the expression of, and that with a sort of artlessness that makes one almost forgive her. Her principles are noble and possess'd of influence which extends to *absolute* dominion over the happiness...[of] some thousands of Subjects. She invariably exerts it for their welfare... As a relation she is everything to her family...[14]

Dashkova presumes "a degree of admiration" for herself that is beyond expression, a conviction so absolute as to suggest her being seen "distinct from herself," as if she were being seen in a mirror or on stage. What, according to Martha, (almost!) keeps this exalted sense of self-worth from being repellent is Dashkova's "artlessness," her presumption that image and reality match, the firm conviction that "her principles are noble" and disinterested. Martha shrewdly associates this attitude with Dashkova's power, both as a landowner (her "*absolute* dominion" over her serfs — Martha's italics) and the great influence she exercises over her extended family. Martha senses

---

[14] *The Russian Journals*, 55-56.

a clear correlation between Dashkova's assertion of political power and its justification as something "invariably" exerted for the "welfare" of those under her dominion.[15]

On the one hand, in an autocratic context, Dashkova's claim on virtue may be seen as staking a claim on political power. As Safonov describes her predicament, "Dashkova had the courage to be a personality...at a time when only one person in this autocratic country had the right to be a personality — Catherine II."[16] This is the Dashkova who heroically challenged tyrants, and who stood up for enlightened ideals. On the other hand, as Martha sensed, Dashkova's uncompromising insistence on her own moral authority itself reflected an uncomfortably authoritarian claim on virtue, which, as we have suggested, stemmed from her exalted altruistic conception of the virtuous self.[17]

DASHKOVA AND FRANKLIN: THE RIGHT TO BE AN ODDITY

Franklin's *Autobiography* offers both some striking points in common with Dashkova's memoir as well as some sharp contrasts that help clarify the

---

[15] Catherine Wilmot likewise commented in a letter to Anna Chetwood that "Three thousand Peasants, 'my subjects' (as she calls them) live most happily under her absolute power; and of all the blessed hearted beings that ever existed on that subject she is the most blessed (excepting your Mother)" (*The Russian Journals*, 199).

[16] M.M. Safonov, "Ekaterina malaia i ee 'Zapiski,'" in *Ekaterina Romanovna Dashkova: issledovaniia i materialy*, ed. A.I. Vorontsov-Dashkov et al. Studiorum Slavicorum monumenta, v. 8 (St. Petersburg: Dmitrii Bulanin, 1996), 21. However, Dashkova did not or would not admit to any contradiction between Catherine's regime and the moral imperative, although as Safonov's argument suggests, it was not too far a distance from Dashkova's "courage to be a personality" to the appearance of revolutionary ferment in subsequent decades.

[17] Compare Richard Wortman's description of Derzhavin's memoirs: "their most striking characteristic for the historian...is Derzhvin's ego, his limitless confidence in himself, the wonderful naïve sense that his personal progress and success are identical to the cause of justice and the national well being. This boundless self-certainty, which would be lacking in memoirs of a later era, provides the central unity and verve of the *Zapiski*." Richard Wortman, "Introduction," *Perepiska (1794–1816) i "Zapiski"* (1871; Cambridge, Eng.: Oriental Research Partners, 1973), 2–3. Writers' insistence on equating personal and universal merit was also a central problem in establishing the norms of literary usage, and made literary critical discourse of mid-century Russia notoriously acrimonious. See my discussion in "Slander, Polemic, Criticism: Trediakovskii's "Letter...Written from a Friend to a Friend" of 1750 and the Problem of Creating Russian Literary Criticism," chap. 4 in this volume.

problem of virtue and making it public. Franklin shared with Dashkova a lifelong preoccupation with living a virtuous life. Both put virtue at the center of their ideal of the good life, and both framed the issue of being virtuous in terms of the good of society. Like Dashkova, Franklin argued that virtue is not of value merely or primarily for is own sake but as the single path to practical well being. As Franklin put it, "vicious actions are not hurtful because they are forbidden, but forbidden because they are hurtful, the nature of man alone considered."[18] No less than Dashkova, Franklin set very high moral standards, as exemplified in the well-known scheme for self-improvement that he laid out in the *Autobiography*. He set forth to train himself in a list of thirteen leading virtues, an undertaking he described as "a bold and arduous project of arriving at moral perfection."[19] He found implementation even more arduous than originally imagined. When it came to the last virtue on his list, humility, Franklin admitted that "no one of our natural passions [is] so hard to subdue as *pride*." He wrote of its stubborn and paradoxical nature:

> Disguise it, struggle with it, beat if down, stifle it, mortify it as much as one pleases, it is still alive, and will every now and then peep out and show itself; you will see it, perhaps, often in this history; for, even if I could conceive that I had compleatly overcome it, I should probably be proud of my humility.[20]

Like Dashkova, and many other thinkers of the day, Franklin recognized the ambiguous status of pride (vanity, ambition, the desire for approbation) as a natural impulse that may be directed either to the good or the bad. Like Dashkova, Franklin argues in defense of what we may call good pride, that which produces "good to the possessor and to others that are within his sphere of action."[21] At the same time — and unlike Dashkova — he gently ridicules his own autobiographical project as not only offering the model of a life "fit to be imitated" but also as the comforting indulgence of an old man's weakness. Dashkova never admits such weakness, nor does she admit the blemish of "bad pride" in herself. Franklin, on the other hand, recognizes both the ideal of the virtuous self and the intractable, all-too-human problems

---

[18] *The Autobiography of Benjamin Franklin*, intro. Lewis Leary (New York: Touchstone, 2004), 74.
[19] *The Autobiography*, 66.
[20] *The Autobiography*, 75.
[21] *The Autobiography*, 2.

of its realization. In coming to grips with his "bold and arduous project of arriving at moral perfection," he notes that

> something that pretended to be reason...was every now and then suggesting to me that such extream nicety as I exacted of myself might be a kind of foppery in morals, which, if it were known, would make me ridiculous; that a perfect character might be attended with the inconvenience of being envied and hated; and that a benevolent man should allow a few faults in himself, to keep his friends in countenance.[22]

While the "something that pretended to be reason" might gainsay the pursuit of moral perfection, Franklin nevertheless recognizes the drawbacks of the kind of militant "virtue on display" of the kind that Dashkova demands of herself. (And indeed she is constantly on guard against those who ridicule, envy, and hate her.) Where Dashkova insists on strict construction of virtue, and on the complete parity of the inner and outer self, Franklin allows for a degree of dissimulation. He either keeps his "extream nicety as I exacted of myself" *to* himself or, as he notes with regard to the attempt at exercising humility, allows himself the *appearance* rather than the reality.[23]

For Franklin, as for Dashkova, virtue and its recognition were an essentially social phenomena, forged in the crucible of sociability — the self as necessarily mirrored and negotiated through one's peers. At the same time, we need to keep in mind the significant differences between the social and political contexts in which this sociability operated. Franklin describes the world of opinion-makers in colonial Philadelphia, a world in which he was a major player. Dashkova, on the other hand, struggled to assert herself within the restricted and highly-stratified setting of the court and European high society, and the "absolutist" context of old regime Russia also left its mark on her thinking. On the level of moral theory, Dashkova was a strict

---

[22] *The Autobiography*, 73.
[23] Franklin describes the efforts he made (and the "some violence" required) to control his "natural inclination" to express his opinions in confident and categorical terms, a moderation that with time he says became habitual. See for example his description of the strategy he used for earning public esteem by means of suppressing the natural inclination to demand immediate satisfaction of his pride (*The Autobiography*, 64). On Franklin's self-control and phenomenally successful pursuit of approbation, see Edmund S. Morgan, *Benjamin Franklin* (New Haven: Yale UP, 2003), especially chap. 1.

constructionist as regards to virtue, and her journalistic writings promote the virtuous life as a necessary goal. For example, she wrote that "Many consider virtue to be harsh and intolerant to human weaknesses (strogoiu i k chelovecheskim slabostiam nesniskhoditelnoiu). True, for people suffering from vice, virtue is insupportable, and they can therefore never be happy; but for those who are able to think and feel, nothing is as pleasant as virtue."[24] In sharp contrast to the Pennsylvania democrat, Dashkova was known for her sharp outspokenness, and she often remarks in her memoir upon her inability to restrain and conceal her emotions:

> Nature had not endowed me with the gift of pretence, so essential when dealing with Sovereigns and even more with the people round them. Disgust, contempt, indignation — there they all were, writ large on my countenance whenever I felt them. (MPD 276)

This was more than simply "natural" lack of self-restraint. Dashkova, like a heroine in a classicist tragedy, finds it almost impossible to dissemble before the great and mighty, as something ignoble and immoral.

Martha Wilmot also remarked upon this impulsiveness that was a hallmark of Dashkova's behavior. She noted in her journal that

> It never enters into her head or heart to disguise any sentiment or impulse…, & therefore you may guess what a privileged sort of Mortal she makes herself! The Truth is sure to come out whether agreeable or disagreeable, & lucky it is she has sensibility & gentleness of Nature, for if she had not she would be a Public Scourge! She is the first by right, rank, sense & habit in every Company; & prerogative becomes such a matter of course that nothing appears extraordinary that she does.[25]

The singularity and idiosyncrasy of Dashkova's behavior — as with the "degree of admiration" she assumes for herself — is defined by the "privileged sort of Mortal she makes herself," that is, her claim to set the norm "by right, rank, sense & habit in every Company" — by right of her greater virtue. Martha also attributes Dashkova's sense of entitlement, of

---

[24] "O istinnom blagopoluchii," *Sobsednik liubitelei rossiiskogo slova*, 3 (1783), 24–34; my citation is from E. R. Dashkova, *O smysle slova "vospitanie": sochineniia, pis'ma, documenty*, ed. G. I. Smagina (St. Petersburg: Dmitrii Bulanin, 2001), 130.
[25] *The Russian Journals*, 196.

expected deference, to her "imperial habits," i.e., she again underscores the connection Dashkova assumes between political privilege and her superior moral virtue. Elsewhere she also comments on the "singularity" of Dashkova's behavior in society:

> ...the compound of contradictions which form Princess D's character exceed belief. There are times when she is perfectly a Woman of fashion & very elegant in her manners, but she has learnt so little of the art of concealing her feelings, whatever they may be, that she often is settling according to her own fancy the dishes on the table at the moment that the guests are all waiting to eat them & a hundred other singularitys which it would be foolish & even wrong to write where they are so thoroughly counteracted by the admirable qualitys of her heart and understanding, by her invariable & comical love of truth (which makes her tell out things that set a large Company staring, twittering, blushing, biting their lips, and betraying a thousand different emotions *not one of which she ever remarks*), by her Celebrity, her rank & age, all which give her a right to be an Oddity, & Nature has stampt her such in the very fullest sense of the word.[26]

Here the "right to be an Oddity" suggests Dashkova's purposeful cultivation of celebrity, her playing upon the notoriety and special privileged status such behavior implicitly bestowed. In any case, the same basic mechanism is at work, as her idiosyncratic behavior is as balanced or justified by "the admirable qualitys of her heart and understanding, by her invariable & comical love of truth." Paradoxically, the most marked *singularity* is founded on the conviction of supra-personal, *universally applicable* virtue. Whether speaking the truth to Sovereigns at court or guests at table she frames her behavior in a way that highlights this special status. At the same time, she asserts both her independence from, and paradoxical reliance on, public approbation. Her silence in the face of the public reaction ("staring, twittering, blushing, biting their lips, and betraying a thousand different emotions"), which in confronting tyrants signals her moral untouchability, here suggests a game in which she can demonstrate her peculiar claim on social superiority. If in one context such self-positioning could make Dashkova "a Public Scourge" who bravely exposes evil, as Franklin had noted, in other contexts "such extream nicety" when perceived as "a kind of foppery in morals" might also easily invite ridicule.[27]

---

26 *The Russian Journals*, 360.
27 Indeed Dashkova is highly sensitive to becoming (as she puts it) "dupe of my own conscientious scruples" (MPD 198), which she feels happening quite often.

THE TRAGIC SIDE: ALLIES AND TRAITORS

Like a heroic "great soul" of classicist tragedy, the protagonist is surrounded by a world that cannot possibly equal or appreciate her. In the confrontation with Emperor Paul Dashkova predicts her imminent maltreatment — "one of the many prophecies I have made which have come true." She thus expresses both her superior understanding of the world, and, perhaps also on some deeper level, a comprehension that she sets the bar of virtue so high as to virtually invite persecution. Dashkova at one point describes herself as "an unhappy princess over whom a wicked wizard had cast an age-long spell" (MPD 242), and this is an apt characterization of the "tragic" self-image that haunts her from childhood. The absolute terms in which Dashkova frames her life tend to turn the world into a huge conspiracy to frustrate her virtuous strivings. Dashkova casts herself in the role of victim, so pure, innocent, and virtuous that the world cannot help but be eternally deficient and ungrateful. Failure, then, is not only inevitable but serves to confirm virtue, and indeed reinforces the conviction of moral superiority. Hers is a Cassandra-like tragic self-consciousness, trapped in frustrated virtue that is both self-defeating and self-justifying.

As in the episode with Paul, Dashkova sees her life as an exalted moral struggle between good and evil, life and death. In this struggle, only a very chosen few are able to live up to her altruistic standards. One such ally is her husband. His early death in 1764, leaving Dashkova with two young children, while one of those "bitter sorrows" that punctuated her existence, also perhaps helped to solidify his ideal image in Dashkova's psychic economy.[28] Dashkova was 21 at the time of his death and never remarried. She describes their love as unconditional and all-encompassing, and tells a remarkable story of how she made a clandestine night visit to him at her mother-in-law's while pregnant (he was sick and trying to conceal this from both wife and mother). This episode strangely prefigures her conspiratorial behavior and dedication to Catherine. Dashkova's relationship with the empress was both the most central and most problematic for defining her self-image. Dashkova's public self image was intimately connected with Catherine, and as we have seen, was predicated on Catherine as an embodiment of political, moral and cultural ideals. Catherine also played a crucial formative role in Dashkova's personal

---

[28] And as Fitzlyon notes, they spent much of their short married life apart (MPD, 305).

development.²⁹ Catherine was an inspiring role model — intellectually brilliant, self-possessed, politically clever and ambitious — and her meteoric career, in which Dashkova took pride in having played a significant part, offered an outlet and powerful vindication of Dashkova's own role in the public, overwhelmingly male, arena. On the other hand, and starting immediately after Catherine's elevation to the throne, Dashkova found many things to be desired in the empress. One constant area of friction was Dashkova's demand for Catherine's greater recognition of her selfless dedication and merit. Another perhaps related issue was Dashkova's disapproval of the empresses' peccadilloes in the private sphere; Dashkova particularly disapproved of Catherine's taking lovers ("favorites"), something magnified by her early opposition to the political influence of the Orlovs and her sympathy for the Panin party.³⁰

DISGUISE, CONCEALMENT, BLINDNESS

With a few exceptions, then, almost none of those people close to Dashkova could fulfill her exalted expectations. Most obviously, and most painfully for Dashkova, were those closest to her — her children. In their adult lives both son and her daughter miserably failed to live up to their mother's expectations. These disappointments, never fully explained, cast the most ominous shadow over her virtuous self-image.³¹ Like the twittering at table, but far more threatening, Dashkova acknowledges, and then purposefully

---

29   Dashkova describes "earning the esteem" of the then Grand Duchess Catherine as a turning point in her young life. Catherine, who shared her intellectual passion — Dashkova asserts (surely a hyperbole) that she was the only other woman of her day "who did any serious reading" — captured her "heart and mind," satisfying the emptiness that her privileged home education had failed to fill (MPD 35–6; cf. 32).

30   Like Panin, Dashkova advocated "limited monarchy" (MPD 60), that is, a limitation of Catherine's autocracy via aristocratic power-sharing, although she did not seem to approve the Swedish model that Panin promoted (see MPD 65 and 67). Dashkova's political disagreements with Catherine, however, remain obscure and should not be overstated. On Panin's program, see David L. Ransel, *The Politics of Catherinian Russia: The Panin Party* (New Haven: Yale UP, 1975). Ransel asserts that Dashkova "suffered from the delusion of having single-handedly organized and carried through the coup d'etat in Catherine's behalf" and notes that she "on occasion served as focal point" for nobles' discontent with the empress (112–13).

31   Worzonoff-Dashkoff's *Dashkova: A Life of Influence and Exil*, which appeared after this essay was written, explores Dashkova's family relationships in depth.

ignores, those episodes that reveal the fragility, not to say immanent collapse, of her façade of unqualified virtue:

> Criticism and malicious gossip, which I could treat with contempt in the perfect confidence that I was acting as a good mother should, were not, unfortunately, the only sorrow that [the] marriage [of my daughter] brought me.
> But I am determined to pass over in silence the most bitter of all the unhappy experiences I have had in my life, and shall continue with my narrative. (MPD 143)

> …if the sorrows which oppressed my heart were such that I should willingly have concealed them from myself, I could not now reveal them to the general public. (MPD 280)

While Dashkova may be credited with discussing her children in the memoir at all — unusual in the mostly male autobiographical writing of the era — and thus to offer what some see as a validation of the female, private sphere, it seems to me that Dashkova's image of motherhood belongs primarily to her virtuous, male, public self.[32] As we have seen, Dashkova denied the autonomous value of "private interest," and she also sees "motherhood" in terms of her disinterested service (to her children and to the public).[33] Dashkova here too asserts her unalloyed virtue in the face of public criticism ("criticism and malicious gossip") that conspires with her children's disloyalty to challenge "the perfect confidence that I was acting as a good mother should." (In later life, the Wilmots — who encouraged her to undertake the memoir — took on the role of surrogate "family," offering Dashkova the security of unconditional veneration.) Characteristically, Dashkova preserves the image of her transparent virtue by an act of intellectual will — by expressing the wish *not to see*.

Dashkova's monolithic ideal of the virtuous self thus constantly threatens to unravel, and, as critics have alleged, there is a basic tension in the memoir between disguise and revelation, a discontinuity among her various "selves"

---

[32] In contrast, Barbara Heldt sees a "blending" of Dashkova's public and private selves, although she argues that a "balance, the classical symmetry she seeks, is almost never realized at any one time" but emerges "over a lifetime." See *Terrible Perfection: Women and Russian Literature* (Bloomington: Indiana UP, 1987), 69–71.

[33] Characteristically, Dashkova has various prominent public figures giving voice to this view, as when the queen of England announces that "I have always known…that there are few mothers like you." (MPD 151)

Chapter 19. Virtue Must Advertise

that Dashkova never quite reconciles.[34] From this perspective, her self-presentation becomes a game of masks, a series of artificial, theatrical poses that do not necessarily cohere into a unified whole. One striking example that also exemplifies her play with gender roles is Dashkova's posture as "a simple old rustic" (MPD 156) whose naïve candor is sharply contrasted to the selfish intrigues of cosmopolitan court life. In contrast to the persona of tragic male virtue, the role of a "Ninette at court" (in reference to Charles Simon Favart's "Ninette à la Cour, ou Le Caprice Amoureux" [1756], a comedy in two acts punctuated with short musical arias) offered a specifically feminine guise, emphasizing virtue not as serious, intellectual and male, but in terms of pastoral values of simplicity and unspoiled "artlessness."[35] If in the tragic role Dashkova was direct and confrontational, this role allowed for comic self-effacement and defensive retreat. At the same time, the role of "Ninette at court" might also be seen as a support for the tragic self, insofar it offered an additional intellectual proof of virtue; here the inability to disguise emotion is motivated not by noble indignation but by innocence and lack of pretense. The fact that in objective terms, Dashkova — a very complex, urban, cosmopolitan woman schooled in high court intrigue, and a princess from one of Russia's best families — hardly fit the role of a simple country innocent, suggests the weight of the psychological burden that the serious self imposed on her, against which this role offered a measure of protection, and as it were, comic relief.

One moment when Dashkova assumes this kind of mask is when Catherine offers her he position as first woman head of the Russian Academy of Sciences. Catherine's appointment triggers a minor crisis for Dashkova, who (somewhat uncharacteristically) fears herself unworthy. The two women engage in a peculiar negotiation of Dashkova's public stature, which hinges

---

[34] This is close to the position of A. Woronzoff-Dashkoff (in "Disguise and Gender," partially repeated in the "Postface" to *Mon histoire*), who foregrounds the concealment and dissimulation in Dashkova's memoirs, arguing that "Dashkova's tragedy was that she could not realize her dreams and desires within the accepted norms of eighteenth-century female behavior" ("Disguise and Gender," 63).

[35] My attention was drawn to this issue by Lyubov Golburt, "Discourses of the Self in the Eighteenth-Century Russia: E. R. Dashkova's *Mon Histoire*," delivered at the AATSEEL National Convention, New York, Dec. 28, 2002 (for the abstract see http://www.aatseel.org/program/aatseel/2002/abstracts/Golburt.html, accessed February 23, 2005). Goubert argues that Dashkova's goal is "to portray herself not as just another court lady, but as a distinct public figure. In addition, pretending to aspire to rustic bliss, Dashkova once again flaunts the conventional, pastoral values for the sake of her autobiographical reliability."

not only on Dashkova's qualifications but on how the nomination will reflect on the empresses' reputation. Catherine concludes on the paradoxical note, typical of a hero narrative, that "your refusal... has only confirmed my opinion that I could not have made a better choice." (MPD 210) Among the arguments Dashkova puts forward against her nomination is that "God himself, by creating me a woman, had exempted me from accepting the employment of a Director of an Academy of Sciences" (MPD 201) — perhaps the only time in the memoir that Dashkova disparages capability purely on grounds of gender. Dashkova expresses amazement at "the extraordinary step you have just taken in making me *Monsieur le Directeur* of an Academy of Sciences" and warns the empress "that you will soon tire of leading the blind, for indeed I shall be an ignoramus at the head of Science" (MPD 204, my italics). She underscores her ignorance and inability by describing herself as blind. However, all this is but prelude to the resounding success of Dashkova's powerful, virtuous, intellectual "male" persona, as Dashkova's presidency takes the Academy to a new level of prosperity and achievement. As one critic has noted, Dashkova "makes protestations of incapacity and modesty, even as she details her capabilities and accomplishments."[36] In the given case Dashkova overcomes her reticence (or the specter of false modesty?) by arranging to be presented to the assembled academicians in her new office by the great mathematician Leonard Euler. Significantly, perhaps, Euler had already by this time become *blind*. Dashkova thus achieves visibility and prominence despite — or perhaps by virtue of — her own evident weakness and "blindness," which paradoxically turns out to signal her own status, comparable to that of Euler, as a "great man." In general, the guise of "Ninette à la cour" fulfills a similar function, offering a way of defensive retreat from the crushing responsibility that falls on the Great Man, but one that also ultimately validates her greatness.

Indeed, Dashkova ultimately emphasizes the complete transparency of her motives. In a key passage in which Dashkova defends her relationship with Catherine she asserts the total openness — the visible virtue — of her writing:

> I want to disguise nothing in this narrative. I shall tell of the little differences that cropped up between Her Majesty and myself, and because I shall hide nothing the reader will see for himself that I never fell into disgrace, as has been claimed by several writers who wanted to harm her interests, and that if the Empress did not do more for me, it was because she had an intimate knowledge of me and was quite aware that every form of self-seeking was entirely alien to my nature.

---

[36] Vowles, "The 'Feminization,'" 44.

Chapter 19. Virtue Must Advertise

> Besides, my heart remained, in the midst of Court life, so artless, so unspoilt, that I forgave even those who showed black ingratitude, egged on as they were by my all-powerful enemies who managed to turn against me those I had done all I could to help. I have waited forty-two years before venturing to reveal the whole of my experience of human ingratitude, which, however, never made me tired of doing all the good of which I was capable, often at the cost of great financial inconvenience, for my means were more than modest. (MPD 96)

This remarkable passage offers a useful summation of the workings of Dashkova's self image. On the one hand, she offers herself as totally virtuous, disguising nothing, someone for whom "every form of self-seeking was entirely alien"; her heart is pure, "artless," "unspoilt" and stoically forgiving. She will tell of the "little differences" she had with the Empress (that is, there were no big ones), and "because I shall hide nothing the reader will see for himself," and all will be revealed. Yet this mask of stoic virtue and all-forgivness is immediately undercut by the fact that the entire reason for writing, it emerges, is precisely *to get back her own*, to set the record straight, to reveal "the whole of my experience of human ingratitude" stored up over the course of forty-two years — that is, from the time of Catherine's ascension to the throne in 1762 to the time she finished writing in 1805. This second, vehemently self-righteous and hyperbolically defensive posture undercuts the pose of artless simplicity, and forces the reader (especially perhaps a modern critical one) to take her pronouncements with a grain of skepticism. From Dashkova's perspective, though, the writing of the text is motivated by the conviction that "virtue must advertise" — if only after holding back for forty-two years. Writing a memoir offered a magnificent opportunity to have the last word.

THE DIALECTIC OF VISION IN RADISHCHEV'S *JOURNEY FROM PETERSBURG TO MOSCOW*

> Но се несчастие смертного на земли: заблуждати среди света и не зрети того, что прямо взорам его предстоит.
> (But this is the misfortune of mortals on earth: to go astray in the full light of day, to fail to see what stands directly before their eyes.)
>
> — Radishchev,
> *Journey from Petersburg to Moscow*

Alexander Radishchev's *Journey from Petersburg to Moscow*, like many works of eighteenth-century Russian literature, is preoccupied with sight and the problem of correct seeing. The *Journey* abounds with language and imagery relating to various aspects of vision, and in it vision is precisely that — a problem. Here the desperate desire to validate the authority of seeing as a path to the truth confronts a major impediment that seemed stubbornly and cruelly embedded in Russian reality: serfdom. When Radishchev held his mirror up to the world (a metaphor for truth-seeking in the *Journey*) he glimpsed the Russia of Catherine the Great not as a utopian paradise (as was ingrained in the imperial discourse of Russian Classicism), but as a veil of tears.[1] Serfdom represented the horrible, shameful, unseen, disregarded underside of the beautiful utopian imperial façade and threatened to eclipse all of the nation's great accomplishments. This was a mirror image of Russia, but in the sense of a total inversion, reversal, and negation.

In his analysis of the origins of human consciousness, Jacques Lacan describes another kind of mirroring — the "mirror-stage," the developmental phase when an infant, still unable to walk or even to hold itself upright,

---

[1] On the former, see Stephen L. Baehr, *The Paradise Myth in Eighteenth-Century Russia: Utopian Patterns in Early Secular Russian Literature and Culture* (Stanford: Stanford UP, 1991).

glimpses its image in a mirror and begins to formulate its relationship to itself as a separate being and to define its relationship to the world around it.[2] During the mirror stage, the child perceives its face in the mirror as a complete image and experiences a feeling of deep satisfaction (*jouissance*). But this is only an "anticipated self," a projection, a potential. Thus according to Lacan together with feelings of jubilation over this anticipated, powerful, integrated self, the infant (of from about six to eighteen months old) also begins to realize that this wholeness is lacking and that the mirror image is a fiction, a delusion. Lacan's self is thus negotiated between two poles of the ego that Elizabeth Grosz describes as "an *affairement jubilatoire* and a *connaissance paranoiaque*, that is between a joyful, affirmative self-recognition (in which the ego anticipates the unity of its image), and a paranoiac knowledge produced by a split, miscognizing subject."[3] The joy of self-discovery is accompanied by anxiety (paranoiac doubt) over whether the promise can be fulfilled and integrated self achieved, although of course the gap between ideal self-image and objective reality can never be fully bridged. In general, for Lacan, unlike Freud, the self is not a static, unchanging entity, but a dynamic ongoing process, whose end can only be death, spiritual or literal.

Lacan himself used the historical formation of modern self-consciousness in the post-medieval world "from the fifteenth century to the imaginary zenith of modem man" as an illustration of his theory.[4] The application of psychoanalytic concepts to history is particularly appropriate to the cultural situation in eighteenth-century Russia, when the country saw itself as being born anew into the post-Renaissance European culture it emulated. Radishchev's *Journey* represents the moment when the problem of vision (or self-image) enters a crisis stage. On the one hand, there was that paradisiacal "Classicist" discourse that conceived of the self in terms of all-powerful sight, a striking case of what Martin Jay has defined as "occularcentrism."[5] This type of vision claims or demands a perfect balance between inner virtue and external appearance, that the outer image reflect inner content. On the other hand, there intruded the *connaissance paranoiaque* questioning whether such a balance is possible, both in the world as a whole but also within oneself.

---

2   Jacques Lacan, *Écrits* (Paris: Éditions de Seuil, 1966), 1–4; in English in *Écrits: A Selection*, trans. A. Sheridan (New York, 1977).

3   E. A. Grosz, *Jacques Lacan: A Feminist Introduction* (London: Routledge, 1990), 40.

4   See Ellie Ragland-Sullivan, *Jacques Lacan and the Philosophy of Psychoanalysis* (Urbana, IL: University of Illinois Press, 1986), 7–12.

5   Martin Jay, *Downcast Eyes: The Denigration of Vision in Twentieth-Century French Thought* (Berkeley: University of California Press, 1993).

Radishchev's *Journey* is permeated with this kind of deep anxiety. It is perhaps not fully fair to refer to this as paranoid, insofar as the threat was immediate and palpable: publishing the *Journey* did in fact threaten the author's freedom and potentially even his life. For Radishchev as for all Classicist authors the problem of the individual and the problem of politics were analogous, in essence practically the same. Exposing the falsehood of the state façade and incorrect vision not only threatened the basic political beliefs of the era but also put the very possibility of self-knowledge in doubt. In the light of Lacan's theory the political problem thus emerges as something more serious and profound. Radishchev exposes something that threatens the cohesion of the self as a psychic whole.[6] While new Sentimentalist trends in the *Journey* are obvious and have been well examined by critics, Radishchev's goal is not knowledge by means of absorption in the self, which may lead to a solipsistic moral and emotional dead end. On the contrary, Radishchev strives to break out of this blind alley and to validate the universal, collective ideal, not only in reference to serfdom but to the Classicist ideal of man as the reflection of eternal laws of nature.

The prefatory dedication that opens the *Journey* may be taken as a key to the work as a whole. Here in a short and pointed way the question is posed as to whether people are able "to look directly on the objects that surround them" (*vzirat' priamo na okruzhaiushshie predmety*) and are outlined all of the basic stages of vision that are played out in the course of the narrative. We may thus take the dedication as a microcosm of the *Journey*'s narrative structure, one of the most thorny and hotly debated problems of the work.[7]

---

[6] This anxiety may be seen as harbinger of the subsequent crisis of Russian self-image in the first half of the next century.

[7] Cf. Andreas Schönle's comment that in Radishchev's book "discourse belongs to no one, except to the truth" and that "the text makes narrator, auxiliary narrator, and author collapse into one" (*Authenticity and Fiction in the Russian Literary Journey, 1790–1840*. Russian Research Center Studies, 92 [Cambridge, Mass: Harvard UP, 2000], 35–6). Andrew Kahn notes that "Radishchev's narrator seems to be at times almost without a self" ("Self and Sensibility in Radishchev's Journey from St. Petersburg to Moscow: Dialogism, Relativism, and the Moral Spectator," in *Self and Story in Russian History*, ed. Laura Engelstein and Stephanie Sandler [Ithaca: Cornell UP, 2000], 284–85; this article also appeared in *Oxford Slavonic Papers*, 30 [1997]: 40–66). Schönle finds Radishchev's search for "authenticity" unfulfilled, insofar as Radishchev "wants us to see humankind both as emanation from and deflection of nature" (22). On the other hand, Kahn, who argues against a politicized, "monological" view of Radishchev, defines the writer's basic position as relativism (Bakhtin's "polyphony"), seen within the context of the Sentimental novel and the theory of sensibility.

Chapter 20. The Dialectic of Vision in Radishchev's *Journey*

The image of Radishchev as implied author is not clearly separable from the other narrative voices which we propose to take as hypostases of a single aggregate authorial consciousness. These voices may be seen to sound in the dedication, which presents in abbreviated form various (even contradictory) models of vision. These various models or stages of vision taken together may be seen to constitute a single collective authorial "I." While few of the individual episodes in the *Journey* contain all of the various stages in the dialectic of vision we will chart, our argument suggests that there is a larger cumulative unity of the *Journey*, a larger drama of selfhood, to which all of the voices taken together (that of Radishchev as implied author as well as the others) contribute. Such a view suggests the unity of the *Journey* as an organic dialectical process.[8]

The dedication presents all of the basic stages of vision represented in the *Journey* except the first, the starting point. It begins in medias res with a moment of crisis: "I looked about me — my soul was stung (uiazvlenna) by the sufferings of humanity." Hence we need to backtrack a little in order to see the nature of the "stinging." The image of the world that is thrown into crisis is that picture of universal happiness, freedom and well being that was long familiar from the rhetorical tradition of the panegyric ode. This was the reigning discourse of enlightened, imperial, Classicist Russia. Here is a dramatic example from the start of the chapter "Khotilov: A Project for the Future":

> We have brought our beloved country step by step to the flourishing condition in which it now stands; we see science, art, and industry carried to the highest degree of perfection which man can achieve; we see that in our realm human reason, spreading wide its wings, freely and unerringly soars everywhere to greatness... With inexpressible joy we can say that our country is an abode pleasing to the Deity because its order is not based on prejudice and superstition, but on our inward perception of the mercy of our common Father... Born in this freedom, we truly regard each other as brothers, belonging to the same family, and having one Father, God.
>
> The torch of learning, enlightening our legislation, now distinguishes it from the legislation of many countries. The balanced separations of powers, the equality of property, destroy the root even of civil discord. Moderation

---

[8] While critics have noted the attention given to imagery of sight in the *Journey* and also tried to define the complex interrelationship of the book's narrative voices, it seems to me that what I am calling the "dialectic of vision" offers a new way to describe the structural unity of the work.

in punishment causes the laws of the supreme power to be respected like the commands of tender parents to their children, and prevents even guileless misdeeds. Clarity in the ordinances concerning the acquisition and protection of property prevents the outbreak of family disputes. The boundary furrow that separates the possessions of one citizen from another is deep and visible to all (vsemi zrima) and sacredly respected by all. Private offenses are rare among us, and are settled amicably. Popular education has taken pains to make us gentle, peace-loving citizens, but above all, to make us human beings (prezhde vsego da budem cheloveki). (66; 142–43)[9]

This image of Enlightened Russia is emphatically visual. It may be taken as a recapitulation of what I would describe as Russian Classicist, occularcentric vision, expressing jubilation in the display of Russia's virtue, greatness, and reason; harmony between inner and outer perception; civil and divine law; on the political level, transparency, equality, and freedom, things that are "visible to all." Taken together these contribute to the supreme goal of being truly human. We hear the familiar high style approbatory discourse that took its direct cue from Lomonosov, and which was also reflected in drama, political and moral writing, and other genres of the day.[10]

Everything, it seems is clear. But what had seemed to be so firm and obvious on second glance turns out to be a lie, a mirage. The second stage of the dialectic of vision is crisis, as the outer world is revealed as a place not of joy and gladness but of pain and suffering: "I looked about me — my soul was stung by the sufferings of humanity." The sentence that follows the passage cited above from "Khotilov" represents an analogous moment of crisis. The sentence starts out like a simple continuation of what went before:

---

[9] Page citations refer to: 1) Aleksandr Nikolaevich Radishchev, *Puteshestvie iz Peterburga v Moskvu; Vol'nost'*, ed. V. A. Zapadov Literaturnye pamiatniki (St. Petersburg: Nauka, 1992); and 2) Aleksandr Radishchev, *A Journey from St. Petersburg to Moscow*, trans. Leo Weiner, ed. R. P. Thaler (Cambridge, Mass: Harvard UP, 1966), from which the translations have been taken with some modification.

[10] In the "Eulogy on Lomonosov," Radishchev makes clear his admiration for Lomonosov's odic vision as an ideal which he shares, even though he fears that Lomonosov has "followed the common custom" of flattery: "If, without offending truth and posterity, it were possible to do so, I would forgive you because you thereby revealed your soul's gratitude for favors received. But the maker of odes who cannot follow in your footsteps will envy you, he will envy you your superb picture of national peace and quiet — that mighty protector of cities and villages and comforter of kingdoms and of kings; he will envy you the countless beauties of your diction, even if someone manages to attain the uninterrupted harmony of your verses, which no one so far has" (121; 233).

Chapter 20. The Dialectic of Vision in Radishchev's *Journey*

> Enjoying inner peace, having no external enemies, and having brought society to the highest state of happiness based on civil association...

but ends up as a cry of despair that totally undercuts everything that preceded:

> ...shall we really be so devoid of humane feeling, devoid of pity, devoid of the tenderness of noble hearts, devoid of brotherly love, that we endure under our eyes an eternal reproach to us, a disgrace (*ponoshenie*) to our remotest descendants [the fact that we are abandoning] — a whole third [sic][11] of our comrades, our equal fellow citizens, our beloved brothers in nature, in the heavy fetters of servitude and slavery? (66; 143)

The jubilant display of Russia's glory gives way to a crescendo of despair and self-censure. This new vision of human misfortune wipes turns the world upside down and negates everything that came before. Serfdom now takes center stage as something that remains "before our eyes as an eternal (*vsegdashniuiu*) reproach." The picture of universal joy and well being gives way to a shameful spectacle:

> The bestial custom of enslaving one's fellow men, which originated in the hot regions of Asia, a custom worthy of savages, a custom that signifies a heart of stone and a total lack of soul, has quickly spread far and wide over the face of the earth. And we Slavs, sons of glory (*slava*), glorified in both name and deed among earth-born generations, benighted by the darkness of ignorance, have adopted this custom, and, to our shame, to the shame of past centuries, to the shame of this age of reason, we have kept it inviolate even to this day. (66–7; 143)

This image of Russia resembles that of its harshest European critics: savage, soulless, ignorant, barbaric. Radishchev here plays upon the popular etymological connection between *Slav* and *slava*, and upon archaic medieval formulas (*imenem i delami slovuty v kolenakh zemnorodnykh*) in order to emphasize the demise of glory and its replacement by shame, shame, and shame. With bitter irony this Russia is geographically grouped not with Enlightened Europe but with "the hot regions of Asia" (as the source of slavery). Serfdom reflects back and taints even the past, as a practice that

---

[11] Elsewhere in the same section ("Khotilov") Radishchev says two-thirds. Thaler clarifies that "According to the census of 1783, about 94.5 per cent of the Russian people were peasants. Of these, about 55 per cent were manorial serfs, 39 per cent crown serfs, and 6 percent free peasants" (Radishchev, *A Journey*, 267–88).

Radishchev caustically notes has been "kept inviolate" (i.e., this is a Russia that Peter's reforms have failed to affect). From this perspective, the previous vision of Russia as "an abode pleasing to the Deity" can only have been a result of self-serving flattery or blindness.

The *Journey*'s dedicatory piece offers a microcosm of the book's intensive scrutiny of this process of miscognition. It begins with an analogous moment of crisis:[12]

> I looked about me — my soul was stung (uiazvlenna) by the sufferings of humanity. I turned my eyes inward — I saw that man's woes arise in man himself, and frequently only because he does not look straight at the objects surrounding him. Is it possible, I said to myself, that nature has been so miserly with her children as to hide the truth forever from him who errs innocently? Is it possible that this stern stepmother has brought us into the world that we may know only misfortunes, but never happiness? My reason trembled at this thought, and my heart thrust it far away. I found a comforter for man in himself: "Remove the veil from the eyes of natural feeling — and I shall be happy!" This voice of nature resounded loudly within me. I arose from the despair into which sensitivity and compassion had plunged me; I felt within me strength enough to withstand delusion, and — unspeakable joy! I felt that it was possible for anyone to be a collaborator in the well-being of others like him. Such is the thought which moved me to sketch out what you are going to read. (6; 40)

We may note again the preoccupation with sight and variety of words for vision (*vzglianul, obratil vzory, uzrel, vziraet, sokryla*, etc.). The passage begins with the moment of crisis, the second glance, looking and being "stung." As in the excerpt from "Khotilov," this passage describes a very unpleasant visual shock, the sight of something heretofore unseen, that now becomes "an eternal (sic) reproach…before our eyes." Compare in "Vyshnii Volochok" when the narrator realizes that "if at first glance my spirit was delighted at the sight of this prosperity, upon second thoughts my joy soon waned." The narrator's shock of miscognition comes while he is enjoying a cup of coffee:

> "Remember," my friend once said, "that the coffee in your cup, and the sugar dissolved in it, have deprived a man like yourself of his rest, that they have been the cause of labors surpassing his strength, the cause of tears, groans, blows, and abuse. Now dare to pamper your gullet, hard-hearted wretch!" The sight of his disgust as he said this shook me to the depths of my soul. My hand trembled, and I spilled the coffee. (75; 157)

---

12 I have left out the opening and closing lines addressed to A. M. Kutuzov.

Notably, in this instance the shock of new vision comes not from looking at some physical evil per se (e.g., seeing slaves suffer, or even imagining the coffee bathed in sweat and tears) but from hearing the truth and seeing the horror and pain reflected in his friend's face. To see the Other as unhappy is painful, a dethroning of the divine signification of the world outside and an inner fall from self-complacency. It is a moment of consciousness in the sense of Dostoevsky's underground man, brought on and defined by pain. The evil that a sensitive person sees in the external world is felt internally.

The horror of being stung by the vision of human suffering leads at first to an extremely negative, even nihilistic, picture of existence. The external world emerges as a place of unrelieved sadness, and the horror of witnessing the pain of others is internalized by the viewer as depression, anxiety, guilt, and despair (three key terms for this in the *Journey* marking this new stage of sight are *skorb'*, *terzanie*, and *otchaianie* [grief, torment, despair]). The external, physical world is a place of sorrow and sin, and sight does not expose a divine world of joy but reveals only falsehood and illusion. Sight is not "the most noble of the senses" (as with Ciciero) but, in the words of Simeon Polotskii,

...зрение начало есть злаго,
раждает в уме помысла сквернаго.
Услаждение из того ся родит,
Та же соизвол мерзостный приходит.[13]

(...the origin of sight is evil / and gives birth to evil designs. / Pleasure comes from the same [source] / and encourages the same vile sanction)

Many passages in the *Journey* expose the falsity of vision in the material world. In particular, fame and glory are repeatedly questioned in the *Journey* as transient and superficial, not only that of individuals but of whole civilizations, whose grandiose constructions, from pyramids to cities, all crumble to dust with time. This "vanitas vanitatis" theme that was characteristic of Baroque poetry, and which continued to be popular in eighteenth century Russian poetry (for example, for Sumarokov and Kheraskov), here extends to the deceptiveness of visual reality. The one who sees the evils of the world most clearly, like the "eye doctor" Priamozvorova

---

[13] Characteristically, for Polotskii the inner moral state of the one who sees is central here — seeing as an extension of human evil — rather than the condition of external reality per se. Simeon Polotskii, *Vertograd mnogotsvetnyi*, ed. A. R. Hippisley and L. I. Sazonova. Vol. 2. Bausteine zur slavischen Philologie und Kulturgeschichte, N.F. Bd.10.2 (Köln: Böhlau Verlag, 1999), 464.

("Direct Vision" or "Clear-of-Eye") from "Spasskaia Polest'," seems a personification of negativity. She is called

> a very dangerous witch who carries venom and poison, and gloats over grief and affliction; she is always frowning, and she scorns and reviles everyone; in her abuse she spares not even thy sacred head [i.e., of the king]. (24; 70)

These words strikingly recall Catherine's description of the author of the *Journey* himself as a man eaten up by jealousy and bile.[14] One may cite many examples of such "nihilistic" vision — pictures of poverty, slavery, the sale of serfs, unequal marriages, prostitution and STDs, etc., with which Radishchev's book is filled. The author "tears the veil" off of Catherinean Russia. But this does not mean, as some scholars suggest, that Radishchev is a materialist and a utilitarian.[15] The negation of false reality and a sharp awareness of the material limits of the visible world are important, but only one stage of an ongoing dialectic. Radishchev's skepsis has definite limits.

The dedication continues: "I turned my eyes inward — I saw that man's woes arise in man himself, and frequently only because he does not look straight at the objects around him..." The crisis that follows opening one's eyes to suffering and experiencing pain leads to a turning inward, and the initial pessimism changes into a new, positive, more critical understanding of correct and incorrect vision. The sensation of pain for Radishchev, in contrast to that of Dostoevsky's underground man, for whom "acute consciousness" becomes more and more painful and tragic, here may play a positive role. The word often used for this pain, a "stinging" (*uiazvlenie*, forms of the verb *iazvit'/uiazvit',* to wound or sting), has several important associations in the *Journey,* and suggests some of the complexity of coming to consciousness. In eighteenth-century usage *iazvit'* could signify physical wounding, as in the case of a soldier wounded in battle. It also (and in modern

---

[14] A. N. Radishchev, *Polnoe sobranie sochinenii*, 3 vols. (Moscow: AN SSSR, 1938–52), 2: 300–308; Radishchev, *A Journey*, 239–49.

[15] This view has been shared by many Soviet-era critics as well as some Western scholars. Of the latter, see, for example, Tanya Page, "Radishchev's Polemic Against Sentimentalism in the Cause of Eighteenth-Century Utilitarianism," in *Russian Literature in the Age of Catherine the Great*, ed. A. G. Cross (Oxford: Willem A. Meeuws, 1976), 141–72; and "Helvetianism as Allegory in the 'Dream' and the 'Peasant Rebellion' in Radishchev's 'Journey from Petersburg to Moscow'," in *Russia and the West in the Eighteenth Century* (Newtonville, MA: Slavica, 1983), 135–43.

usage) signifies a spiritual wounding, a stinging or biting that involves the tongue, most commonly words; forms of this verb are often associated with harsh satire or caustic speech (e.g., *iazvitel'naia rech'*); as in the dedication, it is also possible for one's soul to be "stung" (*dushu uiazvlenna stala*).[16] Seeing, hearing, touch or any other contact with evil — spiritual or physical — is dangerous, and its bites and stings may penetrate and leave a dangerous residue, turning the victim into a callous, indifferent, evil oppressor himself. The logical extension of this image is the cold, stone, or dead heart. Here the process of petrifaction has reached its limit. As for Lacan, the end of spiritual growth (self-reflection) is equal to death. There are several metaphors for this kind of incipient blindness, including "veils" (e.g., the ones that are removed in the dedication) and the "cataracts" (*bel'ma*) Clear-of-Eye removes from the narrator's eyes, which she also describes as "a thick film like a horny substance" (*tolstuiu plenu, podobnu rogovomu rastvoru*) that obscures "natural vision" (*estestvennyi vid*). Truly evil people are the ones whose vision has been obstructed by a "crust" (*kora*), that which is both "impenetrable to light" and invulnerable to all other penetration, a smooth, hard surface that prevents the pricks and stings of conscience. They have become all surface, as the inner self, the heart, turns to stone, and is incapable of being moved by other peoples' suffering or virtue. Radishchev's dreamer in "Spasskaia Polest'" accuses his evil advisors of *okamenelost' zlodeianiia*, the "ossification of evil-doing."

One may also be "stung" with a disease, *iazva* (from the same root as *iazvit'*; in eighteenth-century Russian, this may mean an ulcer, sore, plague or infectious diseases generally, or, figuratively, a curse). "The example of the masters infects the higher ranking servants, these infect the lower, and from these the pestilence (*iazva*) of debauchery spreads to the villages. [Bad] example is the real plague, for everybody does what he sees others do." (63; 137) It is not so much venereal disease itself that infects, but vision of evil behavior. Bad sight — bad example — is infectious, both on the spiritual, moral plane, and on the physical.

The stings of evil may provoke answering blows. In some sense this response to evil is completely logical and represents a "natural" reaction. On

---

[16] See *Slovar' sovremennogo russkogo literaturnogo iazyka* (Moscow: AN SSSR, 1950–65), XVI, col. 1186–87 ("Uiazvliat'") and XVII, col. 2048–49 ("Iazva, Iazvit'"). In the Russian version of the New Testament Jesus' wounds on the cross are also "iazvy" (John 20: 26; cf. Gal 6: 17); my thanks to Irena Reyfman for this reference. On allusions to the Bible in the *Journey*, see E. D. Kukushkina, "Bibleiskie motivy u A. N. Radishcheva," *Russkaia literatura*, 1 (2000): 119–23.

the level of ethics and politics this means resisting evil with "an eye for an eye," and may justify bloody rebellion and a defense of "natural human rights" by means of force.[17] But this is an extreme and undesirable course, because all participants may end up trapped in their shells, blinded. The result of such mutual and escalating "stinging" may be horrendous.[18]

On the other hand, the painful sting of negativity may produce a positive result — a shock that leads to moral awakening and new vision. In "Edrovo," the narrator encounters the peasant girl Aniuta, who acts upon men (like the narrator, cognizant of their own evil and not completely corrupted) with the "beneficent sting of innocent virtue." An arrow or stinger may cause pain, but also may awaken a person from an evil, blind or sleepy disposition.[19] The pain of being stung does not leave Radishchev's narrator stuck in a vicious cycle of sado-masochism, as it does for Dostoevsky's insular underground man. At the same time, and as in Dostoevsky's work, the feminine ideal of divine virtue, innocence, and complete transparency offers a path to self-examination and repentance. In a well-known confessional moment, Radishchev's narrator admits that

> I love women because they embody my ideal of tenderness; but most of all I love village or peasant women, because they are innocent of hypocrisy, do not put on the mask of pretended love, and when they do love, love sincerely and with their whole hearts. (134)

The woman plays the role of Other, a perfectly transparent and virtuous "I." Of course, from the psychological point of view, this is but another fiction, another stage of vision. But in Radishchev's dialectic this is the measure of correct vision, a vision of the heart or of the soul, which is also the counterpart of divine understanding.

Thus for Radishchev's wanderer the righteous sting leads him towards something outside of himself. The initial looking outward and being "stung" by the evil of the world leads to looking inward and new

---

[17] See the works by Tanya Page cited in note 15.
[18] For example, the excesses of the French Revolution which Radishchev decried (V. P. Semennikov, *Radishchev: ocherki i issledovaniia* [Moscow: Gos. izd-vo, 1923], 3–59; see also Kahn, "Self and Sensibility," 280).
[19] Cf. also the many examples of Cupid's love arrows that "sting" in eighteenth-century love poetry. E. D. Kukushkina connects the oppositions of "dream — awakening" and "loss — regaining of vision" to the poetics and imagery of the Bible ("Bibleiskie motivy," 121).

Chapter 20. The Dialectic of Vision in Radishchev's *Journey*

understanding, which in turn allows new outward-directed vision, the ability to look "straight at the objects that surround us." This process of turning inward and outward is not easy or simple, and vision is no longer obvious or automatic. The middle section of the dedicatory piece consists of a series of complex and confusing questions which, it seems, the narrator himself cannot fully answer ("Is it possible...? Is it possible...?" [Uzheli...Uzheli]). The transformation here, the move from inner to outer sight, from reason to feeling (or faith), is on one level that of confession, the realization of error and complicity in evil, and is at times described in traditional terms of sin (*grekh*), "going astray" or "delusion" (*zabluzhdenie* or *bluzhdenie*) and repentance (*raskaianie*), although these are not emphasized, and the specially Christian aspect of confession as a sacrament is absent (see the chapter "Bronnitsy"). Radishchev's religious view, it seems to us, is closest to theism.[20] Although Radishchev sometimes gives voice to the Hobbesean view of humanity in its "natural state," that is, in a constant struggle for existence (which corresponds to the "nihilist" stage of vision), this idea, like the Christian notion of primal sin, is secondary for him. The problem for Radishchev is not so much how to get rid of deeply rooted human evil (although this does concern him) as much as the question whether we, mortals, may physically free ourselves of delusion and "see directly." The impossibility of seeing directly is not only a moral but a practical issue:

> Is it possible, I said to myself, that nature has been so miserly with her children as to hide the truth forever from him who errs innocently? Is it possible that this stern stepmother has brought us into the world that we may know only misfortunes, but never happiness? My reason trembled at this thought, and my heart thrust it far away.

This problem of knowing exists equally for the morally innocent as well as for the guilty and for all other people. If correct vision is impossible, there can be no guilty or innocent, insofar as one can't fault a blind man for

---

20 Radishchev conceives of the divine force not only as omnipresent, but also (and unlike deism) as an active force in the world and in some way functioning on a personal level. More on this below.
Kahn connects the mystical side of the *Journey* to Freemasonry but also sees traces of parody here ("Self and Sensibility," 291–93). On the debated (and perhaps irresolvable) issue of Radishchev's relationship to Freemasonry, see N. D. Kochetkova, "Radishchev i masony," *Russkaia literatura*, 1 (2000): 103–107.

blindness. Is the truth forever hidden from us and our errors then inevitable if unintentional (innocent)? Is true sight possible, or is this just another delusion, simply a fiction? If so, are we then condemned to ignorance and unhappiness? Radishchev questions the nature of "Nature," both the essence (ontology) of the external world and its knowability (epistemology). Morality is a facet of epistemology; how and what we know determines how we act.

Yet as Radishchev's impassioned questions indicate, reason as a mode of knowing does not offer a satisfactory response as the answers which it gives are unacceptable ("My reason trembled at this thought and my heart thrust it far away"). Recall:

> Is it possible, I said to myself, that nature has been so miserly with her children as to hide the truth forever from him who errs innocently? Is it possible that this stern stepmother has brought us into the world that we may know only misfortunes, but never happiness? My reason trembled at this thought, and my heart thrust it far away. I found a comforter for man in himself: "Remove the veil from the eyes of natural feeling — and I shall be happy!" This voice of nature resounded loudly within me. I arose from the despair into which sensitivity and compassion had plunged me; I felt within me strength enough to withstand delusion, and — unspeakable joy! I felt that it was possible for anyone to be a collaborator in the well-being of others like him.

These arguments are difficult and not fully clear. The notion of "nature" assumes at least three different aspects. First, it is as creator — as parent to her children (NB. "priroda" is a feminine noun in Russian) and as "stepmother" who "brought us into the world." Second it is "natural feeling" or sensation (chuvstvovanie) — which may mean either physical, material sensation or some inner spiritual capacity to feel; my suggestion would be that it is the first, the world of external physical existence. The third guise of nature here is the "voice of nature" as the expression of inner spiritual truth which at various moments in the *Journey* is described as conscience or even the voice of God. Thus "Nature" embraces both the physical and metaphysical aspects of human existence. The impassioned language of the dedication (and of the *Journey* as a whole) suggests that for Radishchev the ultimate criterion of truth is the "heart," which we may see as an intuitive, irrational principle — like God. God — or Nature — represents no mere impassive material reality but a parent, implicated (indeed personally interested) in the well-being of her children.

Chapter 20. The Dialectic of Vision in Radishchev's *Journey*

The truth is ultimately validated not by sight but by hearing.[21] The voice of nature "resounds loudly within" and puts an end to doubt and delusion, and gives instruction in how to "remove the veil" so as to "look straight at the objects surrounding" us and be happy. The very "sensitivity and compassion" that had earlier plunged the narrator into despair also make it possible to overcome alienating pain and reach (return to) happiness. He had begun in a state of "inexpressible joy" (neizrechennogo radovaniia, "Khotilov") and finishes in "inexpressible happiness" (veseliia neizrechennogo). But the initial joyful seeing was only apparent (or perhaps the state of blessed innocence of Adam and Eve before the Fall). "Sensitivity and compassion" allow the reconciliation with self and union with others. In some sense, we are returned to the ideal jubilant vision with which we started, or perhaps, that paradisiacal ideal of a balance between inner and outer vision, between individual and communal well-being, has taken on a more conscious character. This new consciousness allows and demands action, both spiritual ("to be a collaborator in the well-being of others") and practical ("Such is the thought which moved me to sketch out what you are going to read").

Thus the very writing of the *Journey from Petersburg to Moscow* in some sense represents the last stage of the dialectic of vision. We should add in conclusion that this does not mean that the dialectic is complete once and for all. For Lacan as for Radishchev, vision remains "dialogical" in Bakhtin's sense, open-ended, never fully realized and unfinalizable. As we have seen, the end of development (spiritual petrifaction and perhaps also the state of perfect bliss) spells death; identity is a process. The self is a site of continued struggle, and the dialectic of vision an unending process. This may be what gives many readers of Radishchev's *Journey* a sense of the text's fragmentary and contradictory character, and allows critics to offer diametrically opposing interpretations. On the one hand, the movement toward a new synthesis, a new validation of sight, has become firmer than that seeming, unconscious vision at the start of the process, as the narrator has gone through a crucible of doubt and philosophical testing. On the other, the new "unspeakable joy" remains fragile, subject to the continuing "stingings" of surrounding reality, including the "eternal reproach" of serfdom and the threat of harsh retribution from Catherine. Both the joy and the reproaches are "eternal" and

---

21 The contrast between visual and aural perception in Radishchev may be related to the ancient Greek and Hebrew (Biblical) models of knowing the world. See Jay, *The Denigration of Vision*, 23–4, 33–6.

continue to assert their pull as long as a person is alive. For this reason the *Journey* continually oscillates between two opposing poles, that of reassuring hope (faith in social justice and universal happiness), and anxiety (a sense of hopelessness and the expectation of inevitable retribution). The narrator perhaps reaches a position closest to a final equilibrium at the end of the chapter "Bronnitsy" when he first paraphrases a verse from Ecclesiastes and then responds to it. The world of sight (and of vanity) gives way to the eternal, inner voice: "And all that we see will pass; everything collapses, everything turns to dust. But some secret voice tells me: something will endure forever alive."[22]

---

[22] If the chapter "Bronnitsy" offers the most optimistic resolution of the dialectic of vision in the religious context. it seems to me that "Spasskaia polest'" comes closest to expressing the *Journey*'s political argument. It is hard to agree with Kahn's suggestion that the verses from Addison's "Cato" that follow the cited words and that conclude "Bronnitsy" throw an ironic light on the chapter's depiction of revelation ("Self and Sensibility," 293–94).

Sources

The articles in this collection first appeared or were presented in the following venues:

Part One

1. "Aleksandr Petrovich Sumarokov," in *Early Modern Russian Writers, Late Seventeenth and Eighteenth Centuries*, ed. Marcus C. Levitt. *Dictionary of Literary Biography*, vol. 150. Detroit, New York, London: Bruccoli Clark Layman, and Gale Research, Inc., 1995, pp. 370–381.

2. "Sumarokov — chitatel' Peterburgskoi biblioteki Akademii nauk," *XVIII vek*, 19. St. Petersburg: Nauka, 1995, pp. 43–59.

3. "K istorii teksta «Dvukh epistol» A. P. Sumarokova," in *Marginalii russkikh pisatelei XVIII veka*, N. D. Kochetkova. Studiorum Slavicorum Monumenta, 6. St. Petersburg: Dmitrii Bulanin, 1994, pp. 16–32.

4. "Paskvil', polemika, kritika: «Pis'mo...pisannoe ot prijatelia k prijateliu» (1750 g.) Trediakovskogo i problema sozdaniia russkoi literaturnoi kritiki," *XVIII vek*, 21. St. Petersburg: Nauka, 1999, pp. 62–72.

5. "Sumarokov's Russianized 'Hamlet': Texts and Contexts," *European Journal*, 38:2 (Summer 1994): 319–341.

6. "Drama Sumarokova «Pustynnik»: k voprosu o zhanrovykh i ideinykh istochnikakh russkogo klassicizma," *XVIII vek*, 18. St. Petersburg: Nauka, 1993, pp. 59–74.

7. "Sumarokov's *Sanctuary of Virtue* (1759) as 'the First Russian Ballet,'" *Experiment / Эксперимент*, 10 (2004): 51–84.

8. "Was Sumarokov a Lockean Sensualist? On Locke's Reception in Eighteenth-Century Russia," in *A Window on Russia: Proceedings of the V International Conference of the Study Group on Eighteenth-Century Russia, Gargano, 1994*, ed. Maria Di Salvo and Lindsey Hughes. Rome: La Fenice Edizioni, 1996, pp. 219–227.

9. "Barkoviana and Russian Classicism," in *Eros i pornografiia v russkoi kul'ture / Eros and Pornography in Russian Culture*, ed. M. Levitt and A. Toporkov. Russkaia potaennaia literatura. Moscow: Ladomir, 1999, pp. 219–36.

10. "The Illegal Staging of Sumarokov's *Sinav i Truvor* in 1770 and the Problem of Authorial Status in Eighteenth-Century Russia," *The Slavic and East European Journal* 43: 2 (Summer 1999): 299–323.

11. "Sumarokov and the Unified Poetry Book: *Ody toržestvennyia* and *Elegii ljiubovnyja* Through the Prism of Tradition," *Russian Literature* (North Holland). Special Issue: Eighteenth Century Russian Literature. LII: I/II/III (1 July — 15 August — 1 October 2002), pp. 111–139.

12. "The Barbarians Among Us, or Sumarokov's Views on Orthography," in *Eighteenth-Century Russia: Society, Culture, Economy, Papers from the VII. International Conference of the Study Group on Eighteenth-Century Russia, Wittenberg 2004*. Edited by Roger Bartlett and Gabriela Lehmann-Carli. Münster: LIT-Verlag, 2007, pp. 53–67.

Part Two

13. "The Rapprochement Between Secular and Religious Culture in Mid-to-Late 18th-Century Russia," Tenth International Congress of the Enlightenment, Dublin, July 28, 1999; revised version delivered at AAATSEEL Conference, Washington, D.C., December 28, 2001.

14. "The 'Obviousness' of the Truth in Eighteenth-Century Russian Thought," *Filosofskii vek*, 24: *Istoriia filosofii kak filosofii*, Chast' 1 (St. Petersburg, 2003): 236–45.

15. "'Vechernee' i 'Utrennee razmyshleniia o Bozhiem velichestve' Lomonosova kak fiziko-teologicheskie proizvedeniia," *XVIII vek*, 24 (St. Petersburg, 2006), pp. 57–70.

16. "Oda kak otkrovenie: O pravoslavnom bogoslovskom kontekste lomonosovskikh od," *Slavianskii almanankh* 2003 (Moscow, 2004), pp. 368–84.

17. "An Antidote to Nervous Juice: Catherine the Great's Debate with Chappe d'Auteroche over Russian Culture," *Eighteenth-Century Studies* 32: 1 (1998): 49–63.

18. "The Polemic with Rousseau over Gender and Sociability in E. S. Urusova's *Polion* (1774)," *Russian Review*, 66 (October 2007): 586–601.

19. "Virtue Must Advertise: Dashkova's 'Mon histoire' and the Problem of Self-Representation," in Sue Ann Prince, ed., *The Princess and the Patriot: Ekaterina Dashkova, Benjamin Franklin, and the Age of Enlightenment*, edited by Sue Ann Prince. (Transactions of the American Philosophical Society, Volume 96, Part 1.) Philadelphia: American Philosophical Society, 2006, pp. 39–56.

20. "Dialektika videniia v *Puteshestvii* Radishcheva," in *A. N. Radshchev: russkoe i evropeiskoe Prosveshchenie: Materialy Mezhdunarodnogo simposiuma, 24 iiulia, 2002 g.* (St. Petersburg: Sankt-Peterburgskiii tsentr Rossiiskoi akademii nauk, 2003), pp. 36–47.

Index

Addison, Joseph — 159, 182
   Cato — 412
Adrianova-Peretts, V. P. — 107
Aeschines — 166, 171
Aeschylus — 39, 166
Afanas'eva, T. A. — 283, 286–288
Aleksei Mikhailovich, Tsar — 7
Alekseev, M. P. — 79, 80, 96, 97, 161, 211, 213, 284, 289
Alekseev, P. A. — 280, 284
Alekseeva, N. Iu. — 223, 230, 235–236, 238, 241, 322
Alexandrian, Sarane — 175, 185, 187
Altshuller, Mark — 290, 291
Amvrosii (Serebrennikov) — 288
Anchikov, D. S. — 308
Anderson, William S. — 226, 227, 232, 237, 239, 241
Angiolini, Gasparo — 123, 125, 131–132, 143, 152
   "Prejudice Defeated" (*Pobezhdennyi predrassudok*) — 125
Anisimov, E. V. — 70, 123, 283
Anna (Empress) — 7, 25, 70, 123
Antoinette, Marie — 146
Antonii (Znamenskii) — 288
Apollos (A. D. Baibakov) — 288, 296–297, 308
Apraksin, M. F. — 193, 196
Aquinas, Thomas — 297
Araia, Francesco — 13, 127, 129–130, 132
Aristophanes — 32
Aristotle — 316, 318
   On Philosophy — 299, 312
Artem'eva, T. A. — 325, 336

Index

Arnaud, Francois	
"Lamentations de Jérémie"	286
Augustine, St.	118, 297
Augustus (Roman Emperor)	175, 209
Avvakum	64
Bacon, Francis	158
Baehr, Stephen L.	138, 205, 213, 236, 237, 241, 322, 336, 367, 398
Baker, Keith	273
Balk, Johanna	7
Barkov, I. S.	5, 173–186, 223
A Maiden's Plaything, or Works of Mister Barkov (*Devich'ia igrushka, ili Sochineniia Gospodina Barkova*)	173, 176–178, 181–183, 185–186
"An Offering to Belinda" (*Prinoshenie Belinde*)	173, 178–179, 181, 183–186
Barran, Thomas	342, 370
Basil the Great	269, 310, 318, 327
Sermons (*Besedy*) / *Hexaemeron* (*Shestodnev*)	304, 310, 311, 314
Beaumarchais, Pierre-Augustin	104, 200
Eugénie	17, 105, 196
Beaumont, Cyril	120, 123, 125
Beccadelli, Antonio	177
Bellarmino, Roberto	286, 297
Belinskii, V. G.	64, 104
Bellarmino, Roberto	286, 297
Belmonti, Giovanni	16, 18, 192, 194, 196–197, 200–203, 210–211
Belogradskaia, Elizaveta	129–131, 136, 144
Belogradskii, Timofei	8, 144
Benchich, Zhiva	306
Bennett, Sandra	359, 377
Berdnikov, L. I.	29, 31, 175, 184, 187, 219, 222, 228, 229, 241
Berkov, P. N.	20, 25, 28, 30, 44, 45, 47–48, 52–53, 57, 64–66, 74, 103, 105, 108, 178–179, 187, 213, 229, 232, 241, 246, 302
Berman, M. H.	48
Bibiena, Carlo Galli	134
Biliarskii, P. S.	50
Blair, Hugh	286

Index

Blok, G. P.	44, 46, 49–50, 56–57
Bobrov, S. S.	279
Bogdanov, Ivan	7
Bogdanovich, Ippolit	159, 173, 228, 289, 376–377
A Special Happiness (*Suguboe blazhenstvo*)	370
Bogdanovich, P. I.	159
Boileau, Nicolas	6, 26, 49, 51, 72, 86, 103, 178, 221, 229, 231, 234–236, 238–239, 322
L'Art poétique	10, 57–59, 155, 233
"Ode de la prise de Namur"	175, 223, 230, 238, 329
Bolotov, A. T.	117, 190, 279
Boquet, Louis-René	131, 144–145
Bourdaloue, Louis	56, 59, 283–284
Bowlt, John	vii–viii, 144
Brehm (Brem), Johann Friedrich	24
Breitkopf, Bernard	198
Breitschuh, William	296, 301, 307
Breteuil, Baron de (Louis Charles Auguste le Tonnelier)	345
Brockes, Barthold Heinrich	308
Broglie, Charles François, Count de	345, 346
Browning, Gary	3
Brumoy, Pierre	
Le Théâtre des Grecs	32, 39
Bukharkin, P. E.	278
Bulich, N. N.	20, 44, 48, 196, 213
Bulwer-Lytton, Edward	201
Buslaev, Petr	323
Butler, Francis	276
Buturlin, A. I.	14
Buzhinskii, Gavriil	273, 288
Camoens (Camões), Luís Vaz de	63
Carestini, Giovanni	129
Carter, Angela	182, 188
Catherine I (Ekaterina Alekseevna)	58
Catherine the Great (Ekaterina Alekseevna)	8–9, 12–19, 27, 96, 117, 125, 136, 143, 146, 182, 191, 194–199, 201–202, 204–209, 211–213, 257, 268, 270, 272, 279, 280–283, 287–288, 290–293, 303, 342, 344–346, 348, 350, 354–355, 379–384, 387, 392–393, 395–396, 397–398, 406, 411

Antidote, ou Examen de mauvais livre superbement imprimé intitulé Voyage en Sibérie	339–340, 343, 352–353, 356–357
Belisaire (Velizer)	281, 351–352
Instruction (Nakaz)	15, 348, 351–352, 384
Odds and Ends (Vsiakaia vsiachina)	17, 249, 351
Russian Primer (Rossiiskaia azbuka)	286
Catullus, Gaius Valerius	31, 36, 226
Chapelain, Jean	58–59
Caesar, Julius	27
Chaadaev, P. Ia.	292, 357
Chaussée, Nivelle de La	104
Chernova, Natalia	144
Chernyshev, I. G.	210, 211
Chernyshev, Z. G.	198
Choiseul, Étienne-François, duc de	342–343, 345–346
Chrysostom, John (Zlatoust)	56, 58, 283–284, 289
Chulkov, M. D.	176, 178, 209
Collection of Various Songs (Sobranie raznykh pesen)	200
Cicero, Marcus Tullius	47, 56, 58, 59, 113, 166, 172, 300, 303, 309, 318, 371
The Nature of the Gods	297–299, 311–313
Cinna, Lucius Cornelius	175
Cinti, Giusseppe	192, 197
Claridge, Laura	182, 188
Claudius Claudian	31, 40–42
"Against Rufinus" (In Rufinum)	309
Colbert, Jean-Baptiste	206
Compan, Charles	
Dictionnaire de dance	147
Condillac, Étienne Bonnot de	342
Congreve, William	
The Old Bachelor	180
Corneille, Pierre	32, 39, 78, 219
"Le Cid"	90
"Polyeucte"	105
Crusius, Christian Gottfried	24
Dacier, André	31–32, 35–36, 232
Dal', V. I.	291
D'Alembert, Jean le Rond	342, 351, 361, 363–365
Damaskin (D. E. Semenov-Rudnev)	280, 282

Index

Dante	221
Paradiso	372
Darvin, M. N.	219, 222–224, 232, 236, 240
Dashkova, Ekaterina Romanova	281–283, 288–290, 379–397
Mon Histoire	380, 382, 395
D'Auteroche, Chappe	268, 341, 345, 347–350, 353–355, 357
Voyage en Sibérie	339–340, 343–344, 346, 351–352, 356
De Coligny, Henriette	227
Poésies de Madame la Comtesse de la Suze; Recueil de pièces galantes en prose et en vers de Madame La Comtesse de la Suze et de Monsieur Pellison	228
De la Motte, Antoine Houdar	
Odes	238
De la Place, Pierre Antoine	11
De la Suze, see: De Coligny, Henriette	
Debreczeny, Paul	4
Defontaine, Pierre	104
De Ligne, Charles-Joseph Lamoral, Prince	342
Demosthenes	56, 58
Derham, William	
Astro-Theology: or a Demonstration of the Being and Attributes of God: From a Survey of the Heavens	319
Derzhavin, Gavriil	4, 17, 169, 173, 196, 211, 271, 277, 279, 282, 290, 299, 358–359, 377, 387
Des Barreaux, Jacques	28, 31
"Grand Dieu! tes jugements sont remplis d'équité"	31, 175, 223
Descartes, René	111, 167, 172, 295, 297, 318, 328, 331, 347–348
Destouches, Philippe Néricault	104
Dettmer, Helena	226–227, 232, 234
D'iakonov, Aleksei	38–39
Didelot, Charles-Louis	125, 128
Diderot, Denis	104, 125, 282, 342, 345, 351, 361
Dionysius the Areopagite	313
Dmitrevskoi, Ivan	137–138
Dmitrevskaia, Agrafena	137
Dobritsyn, A. A.	185, 187
Dolce, Ludovico	32, 39

Index

Dombrovsky, Josef	284–285
Dorat, Jean	234
Dorovatovskaia, V.	305, 321
Dostoevsky, F. M.	355
The Brothers Karamazov	282
Crime and Punishment	367
"Notes from Underground"	405–406, 408
Du Bos, L'Abbé (Jean-Baptiste Dubos)	159
Du Bellay, Joachim	221
Dukes, Paul	199, 214
Duncan, Hugh Dalziel	64
Eagleton, Terry	69
Egorov, B.F.	75
Esaulov, I. A.	327
Eisenstein, Sergei	175
Elagin, I. P.	7, 17, 176, 179–181, 202, 206, 289
"Epistle of Mr. Elagin to Mr. Suma-rokov" (Epistola g. Elagina k g. Sumarokovu)	179–181
Elizabeth (Empress Elizabeth Petrovna)	7, 9, 11, 13, 18, 23, 45, 70, 96, 123, 132, 135, 136, 139, 179, 190, 202, 270, 280, 281–282, 293, 322–325, 342- 344, 350
Emin, Fedor	16, 190, 279
Erasmus, Desiderius	166
Eropkin, P. D.	358
Esaulov, I. A.	326, 327, 336
Etherege, George	
The Man of Mode	180
Euler, Leonhard	297, 308
Ewington, Amanda	4, 250, 253, 255, 260, 359, 377–378
Favart, Charles Simon	
Ninette à la Cour	395
Favier, Jean-Louis	345
Reasoned Conjectures On France's Actual Position In the European Political System	346
Fedor, Tsar	6
Fénélon, François	295, 297, 301, 308
Les Aventures de Telemache	360
Traité de l'existence et des attributs de Dieu	296, 307

Index

Fenoaltea, Doranne	218, 234, 242
Feuillet, Raoul-Auger	152
Filaret (Vasilii Drozdov)	290
Findlen, Paula	178
Fleming, Paul	28–29, 36–37, 222, 228, 235
Florovskii, Georgii	117, 270
Fontenelle, Bernard	27–28, 31
Conversations on the Plurality of Worlds	318
Fonvizin, D. I.	176, 206, 209, 277, 281, 289
Brigadir	19, 367
Fossan	see Rinaldi, Antoinio
Foster, Susan Leigh	148, 150, 152–153
Franklin, Benjamin	379, 388
Autobiography	380, 387–389, 391
Frederick II (King of Prussia)	342, 372
Freeze, Gregory	270, 271, 279–281
Fukui, Y.	228
Gallus, Gaius Cornelius	225
Gassendi, Pierre	158
Gautruche, Pierre	32, 38
The Poetical History (*L'histoire poëtique*)	32, 38
Gavriil (Petrov)	280–281, 289
Collection of Sermons for All Sundays and Holidays (*Sobranie pouchenii na vse voskresnye i prazdnichnye dni*)	283
Gedeon (Krinovskii)	280–283, 288
Collection of Various Sermons (*Sobranie raznykh pouchitel'nykh slov*)	288
Gendle, Nicholas	334
Gessen, Sergei	190, 197, 214
Giustiniano, Orsato	32
Glinka, Sergei	196, 214
Goldblatt, Harvey	267, 271–272
Golitsyn, Aleksei	193
Golovkin, M. G.	7
Goodman, Dena	365
Gottsched, Johann Christian	159
Goulemot, Jean	174
Green, Michael	105, 106, 115
Griffiths, David	199, 208, 211, 214, 271, 272, 384

Grimm, Jacob	125, 195, 342
Correspondance littéraire	212, 214
Grinberg, M. S.	66, 67, 72, 74, 77, 92, 253
Gromov, M.	308
Grosz, Elizabeth	399
Groti, Melchior	201
Grotius, Hugo	297
Gukovskii, G. A.	13, 20, 52, 66, 67, 70–71, 78, 90–91, 93–94, 96, 97, 103, 108, 109, 151, 159, 176, 187, 190–191, 196, 210, 214, 219, 222–223, 225, 227, 236, 238, 242, 243, 277, 329, 334–335, 336
Habermas, Jürgen	68–69
Hammarberg, Gitta	165
Harder, Has-Bernd	90, 97, 103
Harkins, William	108
Heldt, Barbara	394
Hesiod	27
Hilferding, Franz Anton Christophe	13, 123–125, 129, 131–132, 143–144, 147, 151
Hippisley, Anthony R.	190, 214, 236, 243
Hobbes, Thomas	89, 158, 163, 168, 301, 370, 409
Hopkins, William, H.	174, 176, 187
Horace	10, 27, 31, 35–36, 175, 177, 206, 209, 220, 225, 227, 230–232, 234, 239
Hume, David	297
Hunt, Lynn	174, 178, 187
Iavorskii, Stefan	323, 330
Idle Time, Used Well (literary journal) (*Prazdnoe Vremia, v Pol'zu Upotreblennoe*)	12, 28
Iliushin A. A.	174, 187
Ivanova, Elizaveta	192–194, 196
Jacobs, Margaret	183, 187
Jay, Martin	267–268, 295, 324, 327, 399
Jefferson, Thomas	294
Jensen, K. B.	67
John of Damascus (Ioann Damaskin)	327, 279
Exposition of the Orthodox Faith	304, 310
Johnson, Samuel	203

Index

Jones, W. Gareth	70, 198, 215, 353
Joseph II (of Austria)	117
Juncker, G.F.W. (V. F. Iunker)	122, 235
Kahn, Andrew	209, 215, 377, 400, 408–9, 412
Kapnist, V. V.	289
Kantemir, A. D.	51, 57–58, 60, 158, 190, 281, 296, 301, 307, 353–355
Karamzin, N. V.	4, 18, 264, 274–275, 277, 291–292, 363, 365
Moskovskii zhurnal	75
Karlinsky, Simon	78, 90, 97, 106
Kasatkina, E. A.	91–92, 106
Kelly, Catriona	359, 377
Khemnitser, I. I.	289
Kheraskov, M. M.	7, 13–14, 105–106, 111, 178, 228, 238, 279, 289–290, 299, 303, 360, 376, 377, 405
The Fruits of Learning, A Didactic Poem (*Plody nauk, didakticheskaia poema*)	370, 376
"Iulian the Apostate"	115
Novyia ody	223, 232, 238, 240–241
"On Reason" (*O razume*)	360
Poleznoe uveselenie	240
"Reading" (*Chtenie*)	303
"The Venetian Nun" (*Venetsianskaia monakhina*)	105
Kheraskova, Elizzaveta	377
Khmarnoi, Isaakii	
"Drama of Ezikiel, King of Israel" (*Drama o Ezekii, tsare Izrail'skom*)	106
Khvostov, D. I.	289
Klein, Joachim	4, 27, 44, 67, 22, 235, 359, 367
Kniazhnin, Ia. B.	8, 199, 289, 377
Vadim of Novgorod (*Vadim Novgorodskii*)	18
Kochetkova, N. D.	59, 189, 244, 409
Kokorev, V. A.	200, 215
Kollman, Nancy	197
Komarov, Matvei	190
Kotel'nikov, V. A.	278, 323, 336
Kozel'skii, F. Ia.	229
Elegies and Letter (*Elegii i pis'mo*)	228
"Panteia"	228

Kozel'skii, Ia. P.
  Philosophical Propositions   310
    (*Filosoficheskiia predlozheniia*)
Kozitskii, G. V.   195–196, 206, 208, 249, 271
Krafft, George Wolfgang   297, 308
Krasheninnikov, S. P.   281, 355
Krylov, I. A.   173
Kukushkina, E. D.   407, 408
Kurbskii, Andrei   64
Kutuzov, A. M.   404

La Bruyère, Jean   207
Lacan, Jacques   398–400, 407, 411
Lafontaine, Jean   6
La Harpe, Jean François de   342
Landé, Jean-Baptiste   123–124
Lang, David M.   20, 44, 79, 97
LaPlace, P. A.
  Le theatre anglois   26, 78, 98, 101
Leach, Eleanor W.   223, 227, 243
Lecouvreur, Adrienne   130–131
Le Cat, Claude-Nicholas   347–349
Lefevre, Anne   31
Lefloch, Myriam   274, 289, 290
Leibniz, Gottfried Wilhelm   276, 296, 305, 307, 317
Le Picq, Charles   125
Le Prince, Jean-Baptiste   340, 341
Lesser, Friedrich Christian   309
Levesque, Jean   342
Levitt, Marcus   4, 76–77, 92, 98, 175–176, 188, 189, 190, 211, 215, 219, 226, 231–232, 235, 244, 270, 290, 309, 131, 314, 323, 327, 337, 413
Levitsky, Alexander   5, 20, 113, 222, 240, 244, 279, 305, 337
Liberkühn, Philippe Julius   286
Lifar, Serge   123–124
Lillo, George
  The London Merchant, or the History of   104
    George Barnwell
Livanova, T. N.   20, 120, 199, 215
Locatelli, Giovanni-Batista   126, 127, 146
Locke, John   161–172, 276, 297, 317
  An Essay Concerning Human   159–160
    Understanding

Index

Some Thoughts Concerning Education	158
Two Treatises on Government	198
Lomonosov, M. V.	4, 8–9, 11–12, 23, 28, 46, 48–53, 56–57, 67, 75, 122, 136, 170, 176, 179, 186, 190, 206, 212, 233, 235–238, 240, 250, 254–255, 258, 261–262, 268–269, 271, 276–277, 280–282, 289, 291, 298–300, 302–304, 307–308, 310, 312, 314, 319, 321–323, 325–329, 331, 333, 335, 355, 360, 402
"Appearance of Venus on the Sun" (Iavlenie Venery na Solntse)	309, 313
"Ode on the Arrival from Holstein and on the Birthday of His Imperial Highness Lord and Grand Prince Petr Feodorovich, the 10th day of February, 1742" (Oda na pribytie iz Golstiniia in a den' rozhdeniia…velikogo kniazia Petra Fedorovicha 1742 goda fevralia 10 dnia)	320
"Ode on the Arrival from Holstein and on the Birthday of His Imperial Highness Lord and Grand Prince Petr Feodorovich, the 10th day of February, 1742" (Oda na pribytie imperatritsy Elizavety Petrovny iz Moskvy v Sanktpeterburg 1742 goda…)	320
"Ode [based on selections] from Job 38, 39, 40 and 41" (Oda, vybrannaia iz Iova, glavy 38, 39, 40 i 41)	317
"Conversation with Anacreon" (Razgovor s Anakreonom)	371
"Evening Meditation on God's Majesty on the Occasion of the Great Northern Lights" (Vechernee razmyshlenie o Bozhiem Velichestve pri sluchae velikogo severnogo siianiia)	169, 279, 297, 305, 311, 313–318
"Morning Meditation on God's Majesty" (Utrennee razmyshleniia o Bozhiem velichestve)	169, 279, 297, 305–306, 309, 311, 313, 316–317, 319

Index

    Rhetoric / Short Guide to Oratory (Ritorika / Kratkoe rukovodstvo k krasnorechiiu)   57, 178, 284, 297, 309, 311, 313, 324

    Russian Grammar (Rossiiskaia grammatika)   256

    Sobranie raznykh sochinenii (Collection of various works)   231, 316

    Works (Sochineniia)   257

Longinov, M. N.   20, 116, 196, 198, 215
Lortholary, Albert   341, 350, 352, 381
Losenko, A. F.   209
Lossky, Vladimir   326, 337
Lotman, Iu. M.   186, 188, 274, 291, 342, 360, 370
Louis XIV (French King)   146, 150, 152, 206–210, 353
Louis XV (French King)   342, 344, 345, 346, 352
Lovejoy, Arthur O.   383
Lucan, Marcus Annaeus   25, 27, 33, 209
    Pharsalia   27, 34
Lukin, V. I.
    Constancy Rewarded (Nagrazhdennoe postoianstvo)   194
    Prodigal Reformed by Love (Mot liubov'iu ispravlennyi)   194
Lutsevich, Liudmilla   5, 20, 113, 279, 305, 306, 309–310, 318, 323, 327, 337
L'vov, N. A.   289

Mably, Gabriel Bonnot de   342, 351
Magnitskii, Leonid   281
Maikov, Vasilii   13, 173, 194
Makagonenko, G. P.   174, 188
Makeeva, V. N.   56–57
Malherbe, François   51–52, 221, 229, 233–235, 238–239, 322
Maloney, G. A.   326, 337
Mamonov, F.   176
Maria Theresa (Austrian Empress)   124
Marker, Gary   122, 188, 198, 285–287, 351, 355
Marmontel, Jean-François   342
    Belisaire (Velizer)   281, 351
Marsus, Domitis   175
Martial   180
Martsenkevich, Gavriila   135–136
Massimo, Pacifico   177

Index

Maximus of Tyre	166
Menander	63
Meyendorff, John	326, 327, 337
Meynieux, André	190, 216
Miaitskii, Mikhail	295
Michelangelo	221
Miniates, Elias	283
Mirabeau, Comte de, Honoré Gabriel Riqueti	342
Moiseeva, G. N.	103, 178, 188, 285
Molière	6, 52, 92
The Misanthrope	364
Møller, P. U.	67
Montesquieu, Charles-Louis	13, 91, 297, 342, 347–351, 354
Spirit of the Laws	342, 350
Mooser, R.-Aloys	120–121, 130, 132, 136, 192, 216
Morozov, A. A.	111, 232, 240, 316
Mosheim (Mosgeim), Johann Lorenz von	56, 59, 284
Heilege reden	283
Muret, Marc-Antoine	166
Murzina, A. P.	377
Nartov, Andrei	7, 228
Nazianius, Gregory	327
Nebel, Henry M.	88, 159
Nero (Roman emperor)	27
Neustroev, A. N.	28
Newlin, Thomas	215
Nieuwentyt, Bernard	309
Nikolaev, Sergei	4, 21
Nikolev, Nikolai	289
Noverre, Jean-Georges	131–132, 136, 141, 144, 147, 149–154, 156–157
Letters on Dancing and Ballets	125–129, 143, 146, 148
Novikov, Nikolai	17, 19, 22, 26, 44, 48, 65, 196, 198–199, 224, 248–249, 281, 284, 286, 288–289
Attempt at an Historical Dictionary of Russian Writers (Opyt istoricheskogo slovaria o rossiiskikh pisateliakh)	229, 353, 358
Truten' (The Drone)	228
O'Connor, Eugene M.	175, 176, 188
Oksman, Iu.	197, 216

Index

Oldekop, August	197
Olearius, Adam	24, 29, 38
Olsuf'ev, A. V.	176, 289
Opitz, Martin	221, 235
Osipov, I. D.	176
Ospovat, Kirill	4, 306
Ovid	141, 175, 220, 226, 370–371, 377
Amores	227, 232
Epistulae ex Ponto	239
Metamorphoses	130
Oxenstierna, Axel	166
Page, Tanya	406, 408
Palamas, Gregory	327–328, 330–335
Triads in Defense of the Holy Hesychasts	326
Panchenko, A. M.	117, 202, 302
Panin, N. I.	196, 199, 206, 210, 281, 393
Papmehl, K. A.	70, 116, 270, 281
Patouillet, Jean	103
Paul, St.	118, 285, 329, 334
Paul I (Pavel Petrovich)	96, 117, 146, 380, 382, 384–385, 392
Pekarskii, P.	23, 24, 28, 30, 31, 32, 47, 48, 50, 67, 68, 92, 98, 188, 245, 340
Peresinotti, Antonio	132, 134
Perry, John	342
Peter the Great	6, 24, 52, 112, 122, 259, 267, 283, 341, 353, 365
Peter III	13, 70, 198–199, 342, 345, 350, 379
Petrov, Vasilii	17, 196–197, 206, 209, 271, 280–282, 289, 353, 355–356
Philetas	225
Picchio, Riccardo	277
Pindar	27, 31, 38–40, 52, 230–235, 237–239, 371
Piranesi, Giovanni Battista	134
Piron, Alexis	177, 181
"Ode à Priape"	175, 223
Plato	171, 312, 316, 371
The Republic	299, 312
Platon (Levshin)	18, 116–118, 171, 261, 280–283, 288–290, 303
Pliny (the Younger)	27
Plotinus	334

Index

Pobedonostsev, K. P.	290
Pocock, J. G. A.	272–273
Pollak, Ellen	182, 188
Polotskii, Simeon	106, 190, 221, 223, 235–237, 278–279, 323, 405
"Book"	302
"Reading"	303
"The Word is a Book"	302
"Writing"	302
Pompey (Gnaeus Pompeius Magnus)	27
Pope, Alexander	63, 96, 198, 294, 296, 307
"An Essay on Criticism"	294
"Essay on Man"	308
The Rape of the Lock	173, 178–182
Popovskii, Nikolai	158, 178, 271, 281
Poroshin, Sergei	7
Pospelov, G. N.	44
Potemkin, Grigorii	19, 209, 212, 282
Pradon, Nicolas	58–59
Prévost, Abbé (Antoine François Prévost)	79
Prokopovich, Feofan	18, 55, 56–60, 112–113, 118, 158, 168, 235, 261–262, 271, 282, 284, 288, 355
Vladimir	276
Propertius, Sextus	27, 31, 36, 63, 220, 226–227
Proskurin, Oleg	4
Pumpianskii, L. B.	51–52, 175, 223, 229, 235–236, 305, 317, 322
Pushkin, Aleksandr	4, 24, 64, 111, 173, 190, 197, 199, 290, 292, 355
Boris Godunov	18
Eugene Onegin	291
"To Zhukhovskii"	3
Pypin, A. N.	190, 216, 339, 340, 348, 352
Rabener, G. W.	166
Racine, Jean	6, 10, 28, 32, 39, 52, 201, 207, 219
Athalie	105
Brittanicus	90
Esther	105
Radishchev, Alexander	199, 277
Journey from Petersburg to Moscow	398–411
Raeff, Marc	158

Ransel, David	196, 206, 216, 393
Rastrelli, Francesco Bartolomeo	134
Raupach, Hermann Friedrich	13, 131–132
Ray, John	309
Raynal, Guillaume Thomas François	342
Razumovskii, A. G.	7, 11, 39, 45, 70
Razumovskii, K. G.	7, 11, 45, 46, 50, 68, 70
Rezanov, V. I.	44, 51, 60, 61, 62, 92, 98, 105
Reyfman, Irina	52, 355, 407
Richlin, Amy	175, 176, 189
Rinaldi, Antonio	127, 151, 156
Rollin, Charles	
Ancient History	256–257
Ronsard, Pierre	218, 221, 230, 233–235
Rose, Mark	197, 198, 216
Rosslyn, Wendy	359, 377
Rostovskii, Dimitri	
"Dmitrievskaia drama"	106
"On a Repentent Sinner"	106
(O kaiushchemsia greshnike)	
"Rozhdestvenskaia drama"	106
"Uspenskaia drama"	106
Rothe, Hans	278, 370, 377
Rotrou, Jean	32
Rousseau, Jean-Baptiste	117, 158, 238–239, 241
"Ode à la Fortune"	240
"Ode sur un commencement d'année"	240
Rousseau, Jean-Jacques	117, 350–351, 357, 363, 366–367
"Discourse on the Arts and Sciences"	370
"Discourse on Inequality"	370
"Letter to d'Alembert on the Theater"	361, 363–366, 376
The Social Contract	342–343, 346
Ruban, V. G.	271, 279
Rulhière, Claude-Carloman	344, 345, 346, 353
Anecdotes of the Revolution in Russia in 1762	345
History of the Anarchy in Poland	346
Rzhevskii, A. A.	13, 209, 228, 289
Safonov, M. M.	387
Safronova, L. I.	92
Saine, Thomas P.	296–298, 307, 318
Sallé, Marie	124

Index

Saltykov, P. S.	16–17, 191–193, 195–195, 201–205, 207–208, 211, 213
Sanadon, Noël Etienne	31, 35, 232
Sandler, Stephanie	4
Sapov, Nikita	173, 176, 178
Saurin, Bernard-Joseph	283
Sazonova, L. I.	236, 302, 322, 324–325, 405
Scaligeri, Joseph	36, 226
Scarron, Paul	25, 26,
Virgile Travesty	35
Schamschula, Walter	306, 308
Schönle, Andreas	400
Schruba, Manfred	174–176, 178, 180
Schumacher (Shumakher), Johann-Daniel	23–24
Scupoli, Lorenzo	286
Ségur, Louis Philippe, comte de	342
Seneca, Lucius Annaeus	32, 39, 371
Serman, Il'ia Z.	8, 47, 91, 103, 164, 178, 192, 306–307, 322–323
Shakespeare, William	11, 17, 22, 25–27, 33, 63, 76–85, 96, 99, 137, 171, 208, 219, 221–222
Hamlet	26
Othello	363
Shamrai, D. S.	45
Shcherbakova, Mariia	127, 130, 132, 141
Shcherbatov, M. M.	289
Shishkin, A. B.	67
Shishkov, A. S.	291
Shliapkin, I.	196, 197, 209, 216
Shubin, F. I.	209
Shuvalov, I. I.	179, 206, 210, 212, 282, 289
Sidorovskii, Ioann	283–284
Sirin, Isaak (Isaac of Syria)	310
Sivers, K. I.	12
Sloane, David	219, 222, 246
Smith, Douglas	69, 122
Sofronova, L. A.	107
Solosin, I.	321, 323, 338
Sophocles	32
Spinoza, Baruch	89, 158, 301
Sreznevskii, I. I.	291
Staehlin (Shtelin), Jakob von	28, 122–124, 130, 132, 134–135, 143, 147, 235

Index

Stanislav Augustus	14
Starobinski, Jean	268
Starzer, Joseph	132, 146
Statius, Publius Papinius	31, 37, 41–42
Steiner, George	90, 96
Stennik, Iu. V.	21, 90, 98, 103, 106, 109, 309, 318
Stepanov, V. P.	5, 159, 173, 192, 213, 249
Sterne, Laurence	159
Suetonius	27, 36
Sukhomlinov, M. I.	23, 52, 249, 261, 284, 289, 321, 338
Sumarokov, Aleksandr	3–9, 23–24, 32–34, 36, 39, 53, 55, 58, 66, 68–70, 72–73, 75, 88, 97, 110–111, 123, 146–147, 152, 154, 156, 162–164, 166, 172, 176, 179–180, 196–197, 201, 203, 205–207, 209, 211–213, 221–224, 228, 231–236, 240, 250–251, 253–254, 256–257, 259, 263–264, 276, 281, 290, 355, 359–360, 363, 376–377, 405
Alceste (*Al'tsesta*)	13, 120, 131–132, 364
"Answer to Criticism" (*Otvet na kritiku*)	65, 77
The Argumentative One (*Vzdorshchitsa*)	19
Artistona	11
"The Basis of Philosophy" (*Osnovanie liubomudriia*)	168–169
Cepahlus and Procris (*Tsefal i Prokris*)	13, 120, 127, 129–130, 132–133, 136–137, 141
"Chorus to a Perverted World" (*Khor ko prevratnomu svetu*)	14
"Court of Arbitration" (*Treteinoi Sud*)	11
"Cukoo Birds" (*Kukushki*)	195
Dimitrii the Pretender (*Dimitrii Samozvanets*)	16–18
Dimiza	13, 16
Dowry By Deceit (*Pridannoe obmanom*)	16
Eclogues (*Eklogi*)	18, 220
"Epistle on Russian Poetry"	155
"Epistle on the Russian Language"	48, 80, 87, 260, 284
The Extortioner (*Likhoimets*)	16
"Farewell to the Muses" (*Rasstavanie s Muzami*)	12
The First and Main Streltsy Uprising (*Pervyii glavnyi streletskii bunt*)	16

Index

Full Collected Works in Verse and Prose (*Polnoe sobranie vsekh sochinenii, v stikhakh i proze*)	22
Hamlet (*Gamlet*)	10–11, 25–26, 45–46, 49–50, 67, 76–87, 90–96, 101, 137, 167, 170, 219
The Hermit (*Pustynnik*)	13, 59, 91–92, 103–109, 112–113, 115–118, 120, 167–168, 170–171, 270, 278
"On Human Understanding According to Locke" (*O chelovecheskom razumenii, po mneniiu Lokka*)	159–160, 165
Iaropolk and Dimiza	13, 16
The Imaginary Cuckold (*Rogonosets po voobrazheniiu*)	19
The Industrious Bee (*Trudoliubivaia Pchela*)	12, 28, 54, 159, 199, 248
Khorev	10, 16, 25, 45–46, 87, 89, 92, 106
"Letter on the Beauty of Nature"	117
"Letter on Sapphic and Horatian Stanzas"	30
Love Elegies (*Elegii liubovnyia*)	18, 218, 220
"On Meter" (*O stoposlozhenii*)	28
"Minerva Triumphant" (*Torzhestvuiushchaia Minerva*)	14, 143
Monsters (*Chudovishchi*)	11
Mother-Daughter Rivalry (*Mat' sovmestnitsa docheri*)	19
Mstislav	19
Narcissus (*Nartsiss*)	16
New Laurels (*Novye lavry*)	13, 120, 132, 134, 137
"On Nobility" (*O Blagorodstve*)	15
"Notes on Spelling" (*Primechaniia o pravopisanii*)	248–249, 258
"Now my vexation has exceeded all bounds…" (*Vse mery prevoshla teper' moia dosada*)	16
"Oda na Gosudaria Imperatora Petra Velikogo"	229
"Opinion About French Tragedies in a Dream"	106
The Poisonous One (*Iadovityi*)	16
publications in "Monthly Compositions" (*Ezhemesiachnye sochineniia*)	12, 25, 28–31

"On Russian Religious Oratory"	113
The Sanctuary of Virtue (*Pribezhishche dobrodeteli*)	119–121, 124, 126–128, 131–137, 139, 141–144
Satires (*Satiry*)	19, 220
"The Second Streletskii Uprising"	6, 16
Semira	11, 16, 92, 131
"To Senseless Rhymsters" (*K Nesmyslennym Rifmotvortsam*)	9, 248
Sinav and Truvor	11, 16, 131, 143, 146, 191–194, 200, 202, 204, 208, 236
"On Spelling" (*O pravopisanii*)	248–249, 255–256, 262
Three Brother Rivals (*Tri brata sovmestniki*)	16
Tresotinius	11, 56, 67, 73, 77, 92
Triumphal Odes (*Ody torzhestvennyia*)	18, 218, 220, 229, 237–239
Trudoliubivaia Pchela	12, 28, 54, 159–161, 165, 167, 170–171, 190, 199, 237, 248–249
"Two Cooks" (*Dva povara*)	14, 172
Two Epistles (*Dve Epistoly*)	10, 25–27, 29, 35, 44–52, 56–57, 59–60, 67, 77, 178, 226, 284
"To Typographical Typesetters" (*K tipografskim naborshchikam*)	248–249, 252, 262
Various Poems (*Raznyia stikhotvoreniia*)	16, 232
Vysheslav	16
Sumarokov, Anastasiia	14
Sumarokov, Ekaterina	8, 377
Sumarokov, Praskov'ia	8
Sumarokov, Pankratii	6
Sumarokov, Pavel	14
Sumarokov, Peter	6
Svetov, V. P.	
Attempt at a New Russian Spelling (*Opyt novogo rossiiskogo pravopisaniia*)	248–249, 261
Swift, Jonathan	12
Tallement, Paul	
Voyage de l'Ile d'Amour	228, 360
Tasso, Torquato	63, 221
Tatishchev, V. N.	289
Teplov, G. N.	24, 65, 68, 70, 92, 144, 147, 200, 286
After Work, Idleness; or a Collection of Various Songs (*Mezhdu Delom Bezdel'e ili Sobranie Raznykh Pesen*)	8, 143, 199

Terence (Publius Terentius)	63
Thaler, R. P.	402, 403
Theocritus	27
Tibullus, Albius	27, 31, 36, 220, 226–227, 232
Titov, N. S.	192
Tiulichev, D. V.	45
Todd, William Mills III	190
Tolstoi, V. I.	192–193, 203–204
Tolstoy, L. N.	
War and Peace	356
Toomre, Joyce S.	79–81, 98
Toporkov, A. L.	321, 333, 338
Trediakovskii, V. K.	4, 7–9, 11, 18, 23, 26, 28–32, 46–58, 65–75, 77–78, 80, 86–90, 92, 97, 122, 178, 190, 225–231, 238, 240, 250–251, 255–256, 259, 274–277, 279, 281, 284–285, 299, 302, 387
Conversation Between a Foreigner and a Russian About Orthography (*Razgovor mezhdu chuzhestrannym chelovekom i Rossiiskim ob ortografii*)	49, 53, 258
"On Ancient, Modern and Intermediate Russian Poetry"	30
Feoptiia	296, 300–301, 304, 307, 311
"Letter in Which is Contained A Discussion of the Poetry Published Up to Now by the Author of Two Odes, Two Tragedies and Two Epistles, Written from a Friend to a Friend" ("Pis'mo, v kotorom soderzihtsia rassuzhdenie o stikhotvorenii, ponyne na svet izdannom ot avtora dvukh od, dvukh tragedii i dvukh epistol, pisannoe ot priiatelia k priiateliu")	29, 64–75 passim, 85–90, 98
Method for Composing Verse (*Sposob k slozheniiu stikhov*)	30, 31, 223, 225
New and Short Method for Writing Russian Verse (*Novyi i kratkii sposob k slozheniiu rossiiskii stikhov*)	31, 72, 123, 178, 225, 227, 228
"Treatise on Comedy" (*Rassuzhdenie o komedii*)	32
Tilemakhida	355, 360, 378

Index

Voyage to the Island of Love (*Ezda v ostrov liubvi*)	55, 360
Works and Translations (*Sochineniia i perevody*)	30, 178
Tsapina, Olga	273, 279–280, 286, 289, 323, 338
Tumanskii, F. I.	75
Tynianov, Iurii	237–238, 291
Urusov, P. V.	201
Urusova, Ekaterina	360, 366, 371
Heroides Dedicated to the Muses (*Iroidy, muzam posviashennym*)	358, 377
Polion or the Misanthrope Enlightened (*Polion ili Prosvetivshiisia neliudim*)	268, 303, 358–359, 361, 367, 376, 378
Uspenskii, B. A.	49, 52–55, 66, 67, 72, 74, 77, 86, 92, 236, 253, 274, 291, 321, 322, 334
Valeriani, Giuseppe (Iosif)	130, 132, 134, 135, 140, 141
Vanbrugh, John	
The Provok'd Wife	180
Vaugelas, Claude	121, 157, 234, 322
Vega, Lope de	63
Viala, Alain	206–207
Villon, François	221
Virgil	25, 35, 172, 175, 209, 220, 225, 232, 370–371
The Aeneid	27, 209, 356
"Ecologues"	27, 34, 227
"Georgics"	27
Volkov, Fedor	11, 14, 106, 124, 137, 139
Volkov, Grigorii	137
Volkov, Mariia	137
Voltaire (François-Marie Arouet)	4, 6, 12, 16–17, 26, 32, 63, 78, 81–84, 96, 100, 125, 130, 160, 168, 172, 207–208, 210–211, 233, 250, 253, 260, 262–263, 279, 339, 341–342, 345–346, 351, 353, 363–367, 376
Alzire	106
History of Russia Under Peter the Great	288, 343
Lettres philosophiques	11, 79–80, 98, 100, 106, 166–167
Lettres anglaises	see *Lettres Philosophiques*
Micromegas	167
Zaire	362–364
Von Geldern, James	237, 246

Von Mosheim, Johann Lorenz	59
Heilege Reden	283
Vondel, Joost van den	25–26, 63
Treuerspeelen	34
Vorontsov, M. I.	199
Vowles, Judith	359–360, 371, 378, 383, 396
Voznesenskii, Andrei	173
Vroon, Ronald	4, 21, 176, 189, 218, 222–224, 228–229, 236–240, 246
Vsevolodskii-Gerngross, V. N.	3, 103, 107, 120, 124, 126–127, 131, 144, 146
Weaver, John	124
Whittaker, Cynthia H.	69
Wilberger, Carolyn	207, 217, 341, 342, 343, 353, 357
Wilmot, Catherine	382, 386, 387, 394
Wilmot, Martha	381, 386, 390, 394
Winsheim (Vinzgeim), Christian Nicolaus von	24
Wirtschafter, Elise K.	69, 122
Wolff, Christian	276, 295, 316
Wolff, Larry	341, 343, 345–347, 350, 356–357
Woronzoff-Dashkov, Alexander	379, 380, 381, 393, 395
Wortman, Richard	204, 237, 387
Xenophon	166
Young, Edward	
The Complaint: or, Night-Thoughts on Life, Death, and Immortality	308, 311
Zaborov, P. R.	79, 98, 311, 363
Zeikan, I. A.	7
Zhirmunskii, V. M.	316
Zhivov, Victor	4, 52, 54, 72, 86, 121, 122, 175, 192, 221, 223, 230, 233, 235–236, 248, 250–251, 253, 257, 262, 267, 269–71, 274–275, 278, 284–285, 290–293, 321–322, 329, 334, 360
Zhuravlev, A. I.	286
Zorin, Andrei	173, 176, 178, 272
Zybelin, Semen	281

www.ingramcontent.com/pod-product-compliance
Lightning Source LLC
Chambersburg PA
CBHW071355300426
44114CB00016B/2077